Praetorian Kingdom

Praetorian Kingdom

A History of Military Ascendancy in Thailand

PAUL CHAMBERS

ISEAS YUSOF ISHAK INSTITUTE

First published in Singapore in 2024 by
ISEAS Publishing
30 Heng Mui Keng Terrace
Singapore 119614

Email: publish@iseas.edu.sg
Website: bookshop.iseas.edu.sg

The responsibility for facts and opinions in this publication rests exclusively with the author and his interpretations do not necessarily reflect the views or the policy of the publisher or its supporters.

ISEAS Library Cataloguing-in-Publication Data

Name(s): Chambers, Paul, 1966-, author.
Title: Praetorian kingdom : a history of military ascendancy in Thailand / Paul Chambers.
Description: Singapore : ISEAS – Yusof Ishak Institute, 2024. | Includes bibliographical references and index.
Identifiers: ISBN 9789815104240 (paperback) | ISBN 9789815104257 (PDF) | 9789815104264 (epub)
Subjects: LCSH: Thailand—Armed forces—Political activity. | Military government—Thailand. | Thailand—Politics and government. | Civil-military relations—Thailand.
Classification: LCC JQ1743.5 C58C44

Cover photos (Thai military "strongmen", 1932–2023): Field Marshal Plaek Phibun Songkram, Field Marshal Phin Chunhavan, Field Marshal Sarit Thanarat, Field Marshal Thanom Kittikachorn, Field Marshal Phraphas Charusathien, General Krit Sivara, General Prem Tinsulanonda, General Sonthi Boonyaratglin, General Prawit Wongsuwan, General Anupong Paochinda, General Prayut Chanocha and General Apirat Kongsompong. The images of Phibun Songkram, Phin Chunhavan, Sarit Thanarat, Thanom Kittikachorn, Phraphas Charusathien and Krit Sivara are in the public domain. The rest are licensed under the Creative Commons Attribution 2.0 licence. Full attribution and licensing details for these follow. Prem Tinsulanonda: Prem_Tinsulanonda_2010-01-20. jpg: Government of Thailand derivative work: Sodacan (talk) (https://commons.wikimedia.org/wiki/File:Prem_ Tinsulanonda_(Cropped).jpg), "Prem Tinsulanonda (Cropped)", https://creativecommons.org/licenses/by/2.0/ legalcode. Sonthi Boonyaratglin: The Official Site of The Prime Minister of Thailand Photo by Peerapat Wimonrungkarat (https://commons.wikimedia.org/wiki/File:Sonthi_Boonyaratglin_(cropped).png), "Sonthi Boonyaratglin (cropped)", https://creativecommons.org/licenses/by/2.0/legalcode. Prawit Wongsuwan: https://www. flickr.com/people/68842444@N03 (https://commons.wikimedia.org/wiki/File:Prawit_Wongsuwan_(2018)_cropped. jpg), "Prawit Wongsuwan (2018) cropped", https://creativecommons.org/licenses/by/2.0/legalcode. Anupong Paochinda: Kamthorn_Phumhiran_-_Anupong_Paochinda_-_Songkitti_Chakkrabat.jpg: Government of Thailand derivative work: Xiengyod (talk) (https://commons.wikimedia.org/wiki/File:Anupong_Paochinda_(in_1st_Infantry_ Regiment's_royal_guard_uniform).jpg), "Anupong Paochinda (in 1st Infantry Regiment's royal guard uniform)", https://creativecommons.org/licenses/by/2.0/legalcode. Prayut Chanocha: Government of Thailand (https://commons. wikimedia.org/wiki/File:Prayuth_Jan-ocha_2010-06-17_Cropped.jpg), "Prayuth Jan-ocha 2010-06-17 Cropped", https://creativecommons.org/licenses/by/2.0/legalcode. Apirat Kongsompong: Unknown author (https://commons. wikimedia.org/wiki/File:Gen_Apirat_Kongsompong.jpg), https://creativecommons.org/licenses/by-sa/4.0/legalcode.

Cover design by Lee Meng Hui
Copyedited and Typeset by Stephen Logan
Printed in Singapore by Markono Print Media Pte Ltd

To my wife, Napisa,
my late father, Richard, and mother, Peggy,
and to Kit, Rhonda, Callahan, and Ford Chambers

Contents

Figures

Figures

5.1	Kittikachorn Family Tree	204
5.2	Charusathien Family Tree	205
5.3	Total Number of US Troops and Aircraft Stationed in Thailand, 1964–68	207
5.4	Principal US Military Facilities in Thailand	208
5.5	Thailand's Senate, 1968–71	221
6.1	Krit Sivara Family Tree	260
6.2	Thailand's Senate, 1975–76	262
6.3	Known Members of Nawaphon Leadership, 1974–78	267
6.4	ISOC Leadership, 1975–76	278
6.5	Principal Military factions on 1 October 1976	320
6.6	Principal Leaders, Units and Their Roles in the Massacre and Coup of 6 October 1976	330
7.1	Legislative Assemblies, 1976–77	352
8.1	Kriangsak's Family Tree	372
8.2	Thailand's National Legislative Assembly, 1977–79	375
8.3	Thailand's National Legislative Assembly, 1979–81	386
9.1	Thailand's Senate, 1981–85	413
9.2	Arthit Kamlang-ek Family Tree	416
10.1	Thailand's Senate, 1989–91	442
10.2	Sunthorn's Family Tree	445
10.3	National Peace-Keeping Council (NPKC) Leaders	449
10.4	Kraprayoon-Noonpakdi Power Structure	451
10.5	Legislatures Deriving from the 1991 Coup	453
11.1	Thailand's Senate, 1996–2000	477
11.2	Chavalit Yongchaiyudh Family Tree	479

Acknowledgements

I want to acknowledge the help of those people whom I interviewed, taught me various aspects about the Thai military, or assisted me in my research or in making this book come to fruition. Though several of these people remain anonymous, I specifically want to thank Dr Napisa Waitoolkiat, Dr Kullada Kesboonchoo-Mead, Lt. Gen. Nipat Thonglek, Pradab Phibunsongkram, Lt. Gen. Pongskorn Rodchompoo, Dr Puangthong Pawakapan, Ajaan Ukrist Pathmanand, Dr Chaiyan Rajchagool, Dr Srisompob Jitpiromsri, Dr Surachart Bamrungsuk, Dr Katsuyuki Takahashi, Poowin Bunyavejchewin, General Siri Tiwapan, Ambassador Edwin Corr, Dr Michael Montesano, Tom Seale, and Rebecca Weldon. Others have helped me along the way, giving me the key ideas that enabled me to write this book. These persons include my early advisor at Northern Illinois University, Dr Clark Neher; my mentor at Northern Illinois University, the late Dr Ladd Thomas; my dissertation advisor, the late Daniel Unger; and the late Kraisak Chunhavan. I am grateful to everyone at ISEAS for their support, especially that of Stephen Logan and Mr Ng Kok Kiong. I furthermore want to thank the anonymous reviewers of this manuscript for their thought-provoking comments.

Introduction

This study looks at praetorianism in Thailand; specifically, the second most powerful political institution in Thailand in 2023—the armed forces. The study contends that this military, as led by military strongmen, has been able to persevere as a leading political actor principally because it has managed to hold on to its monopoly of violence outside of any oversight by elected civilian actors. This is because the military has continuously ousted those civilian governments that it has perceived to be harmful to its interests, has ensured that laws are in place that have maximized its legal benefits, has possessed an enormous budget, remained beyond the scrutiny of the judiciary, retained its power over the years as junior or senior associate of the monarchy in a partnership of power, and rationalized its clout as essential for protecting that monarchy (thus becoming a "monarchized military") while guaranteeing national security. Persistent interventions by the military in Thai politics across time have led to the socially constructed belief among civilians that the military is either justified in protecting the king or cannot be stopped; soldiers themselves feel that they are privileged as royal protectors to intervene as they please. Thus, the praetorian character of the Thai polity is masked by the apparent need to guard monarchy, and the Thai armed forces have in many respects become a tool of the palace.

To be clear, the focus of this study is on the rapidly changing military strongmen and factions across Thai history. A secondary focus is placed upon the Thai military as an institution. In fact, the book looks at Thai

1

military history within the context of Thai political history, especially with regard to US-Thai relations after World War II, topics that are closely interrelated. Far less scrutiny is given to other aspects of the military—its role in social life, politics, economics, culture, administration, art and technology. While the study's spotlight might seem limited, a thorough analysis of this sort across the period 1932–2023 has been sorely lacking from Thai studies, and this book thus fills an important gap. Other parts of the Thai military deserve research in other studies.

This book sets out to answer three questions: Why did Thailand evolve to become a praetorian kingdom? What is the detailed history of Thai praetorianism? And why has Thai military influences across politics never been curtailed? These questions necessitate an examination of the analytical concept of "praetorianism". Praetorianism has been at the bedrock of Thai politics, especially since the ouster of the absolute monarchy in 1932 (despite the post-1980 upsurge in palace influence). The proclivity for praetorianism in Thailand necessitates an examination of the academic term "praetorianism" in and of itself. In brief, since 1941, scholars have provided different formulations explaining military influence in politics. The earliest term, "garrison state", was vaguely conceived as a "developmental construct" where political/military "elites" led by the "specialist on violence, the soldier",[1] ruled supreme.

Though he never mentioned praetorianism, Huntington emphasized that the responsibilities of the professional soldier and officer involve expertise in the management of violence, responsibility in maintaining the national security of the country, and bureaucratic corporateness. But the participation of military officials in politics undermined their professionalism.[2] The term "praetorianism" became fashionable in the 1960s, with one of the earliest conceptualizations defining it a constitutional form of "government without consent".[3] McAlister further characterized it as "the frequent overthrow of governments by military … coups d'état for nonmilitary purposes".[4] According to Huntington, "typical of the corrupt, *praetorian* [emphasis added], or mass societies is the violent oscillation between extreme democracy and tyranny".[5]

Perlmutter differentiated historical from modern praetorianism. The former referred to the ancient Roman Empire's Praetorian Guard (the military unit tasked with protecting the emperor). The power of this contingent revolved around three factors: "the Guard's monopoly on local military power, the absence of definitive rules of succession, and the prestige of the Roman Senate. But, over time, with the Praetorian Guard being the only military in Rome, it came to impose its preferences on who would be emperor.

On the other hand, Perlmutter's "modern praetorian state" was defined as "one in which the military tends to intervene and potentially could dominate the political system".[6] He also described the factors that contributed to praetorianism (see figure).

Meanwhile, a "praetorian army" is one that is not dictated by ability, expertise or professionalism, but instead by social class, partisanship, personal connections and factionalism.[7] Though he never used the label "praetorian army", Huntington implied its existence when he argued that "subjective civilian control" can exist when civilian groups control the armed forces in "the absence of a professional officer corps".[8]

Perlmutter differentiated arbitrator-type praetorian armies from ruler-type praetorian armies. The former usurps control for a limited amount of time then relinquishes power and becomes a trustee of a civilian government. The latter seeks to maximize military rule, never committing to return a polity to civilian control.[9] To sustain their dominion, however, ruler-type armies often create political parties.[10] This is because some militaries believe that the best method for institutionalizing their rule is through the establishment of political parties that represent them.[11] Nordlinger added a third type of praetorian army: the moderator-type praetorian army, which seeks to dominate politics from behind the scenes.[12] Nordlinger's three types of praetorian army are praetorian guardian, praetorian moderator and praetorian ruler. Though all three exercise veto power over civilian institutions, it is only

FIGURE
Conditions Stimulating Praetorianism

Social conditions	Political conditions
Low degree of social cohesion	Centre-periphery conflict
The existence of fratricidal classes	Low level of political institutionalization and lack of sustained support for political structures
A non-consolidated middle class	Weak, ineffective political parties
Insufficient mobilization of state resources	Frequent civilian influence in the military/frequent civilian endorsement of military intervention

Source: Amos Perlmutter, "The Praetorian State and the Praetorian Army: Toward a Taxonomy of Civil-Military Relations in Developing Polities", *Comparative Politics* 1, no. 3 (1969): 385–91, https://www.jstor.org/stable/421446.

the ruler-type military that seeks a long-term military government. On the other hand, praetorian guardians assume power for only a limited period of time, while praetorian moderators at most engage in displacement coups.

Thailand has experienced all three of these praetorian categories. Some countries, such as Turkey, Pakistan and Guatemala, have been "praetorian republics",[13] whereby secular governments are overshadowed by powerful militaries that regularly involve themselves in politics and sometimes putsch elected leaders from office. Other countries, like Spain, Japan or Nepal, have been "praetorian kingdoms" because the heads of state are monarchs, the heads of government are civilians, and there are militaries of enormous clout that often intervene in politics.

Turning to praetorian-led polities, Janowitz devised five types of polities in "peripheral" areas of the world, of which two involved military dominance over civilians. These were: (1) a military oligarchy, where a cabal of senior military officers control society; and (2) a civil-military coalition, in which the military expands its political activity and becomes a political bloc, with senior officers usually dominant over the civilian leadership.[14] Geddes contended that

> A military regime, in contrast to a personalist dictatorship led by a military officer, is one in which a group of officers determines who will lead the country and has some influence on policy. In an institutionalized military regime (many are not), senior officers have agreed on some formula for sharing or rotating power, and consultation is somewhat routinized. Military hierarchy is respected.[15]

Siddiqa classified praetorian regimes into six types, including (1) civil-military partnership, (2) authoritarian-political-bureaucratic partnership, (3) ruler military domination, (4) arbitrator military domination, (5) parent-guardian military domination and (6) warlord domination.[16]

Most recently, E-Shimy argued that

> The differences ... between a military government and a praetorian state are that the former tends to be short-lived with a small chance of survival.... Praetorian states, conversely, tend to be long lasting.... Also, in praetorian systems, the officers may have a civilian cadre in government, but they will continue to enjoy tremendous power over that government both overtly and covertly. It is safer, therefore, to consider military dictatorships as either a distinct category separate from praetorianism, or that concept could, incidentally, characterize [Perlmutter's] ruling type praetorian military.[17]

Yadav has pointed out that the popularity of praetorianism as a concept seems to have declined since the end of the Cold War. He surmises that this owes to the fact that the apparent necessity to differentiate among authoritarian regime-types and armies amidst socio-economic changes (with threats from communist revolutions) appeared to become irrelevant as liberal democracy and capitalism seemed to have triumphed at the end of the Cold War.[18] Nevertheless, since the 2010s, there has been a rise in military interventions (including coups) in various parts of the world. Such phenomena have rationalized a re-examination of praetorianism in contemporary comparative politics, including in Thailand.

The first post–Cold War study on Thai praetorianism (using the term "praetorian") conceptualized Thailand as a "praetorian kingdom" involving proactive military interventions in the name of the king, with the polity "heavily influenced by monarchical ideology and identity".[19] Since 1932, Thailand has been and remains a praetorian kingdom. According to Puangthong, the concept of praetorianism has been useful in analysing the political power of the Thai military from the 1947 coup to the 2014 putsch: the armed forces have utilized the legal system, administrative clout and internal security authority to intervene in politics through varying methods, with guarding the monarchy becoming the paramount rationale for such intervention.[20] Praetorianism in Thailand might specifically be interpreted in terms of what Croissant et al. see as military influence (formal and informal) over civilians in five decision-making areas of "elite recruitment [sway over who governs]": public policy, internal security, external defence and military organization.[21]

As this study will show, Thailand's armed forces (particularly senior military officers) have played a leading role across the Thai political landscape. Since 1980, that role has remained overwhelming, though junior to the palace. Thailand thus represents a classic case of praetorianism. As such, this book examines the chronology of praetorianism in Thailand—the political history of ubiquitous military influence across the Thai kingdom. The polity is in fact a praetorian kingdom. Originally, security servants either served Siamese monarchs or managed to overthrow them. During the current Chakri dynasty, a twenty-four-hour, seven-days-a-week security force only came into existence in 1852. The purpose of the military was to ensure the monarchy's domestic survival, protect the kingdom from outside threats and spearhead monarch-led development schemes. The military thus became essential in the formation, expansion and consolidation of Siam's absolute monarchy.

Military reforms in the late 1800s served to expand the armed forces to consolidate royal control across the kingdom. But, in 1932, the military (with support from other groups) overthrew monarchical absolutism and effectively became the country's dominant institution, although Siamese kings continued to exist weakly. Between 1947 and 1951, royals exercised some small power. But the period 1951–57 saw the armed forces again completely lord over Thailand. Following a 1957 putsch, the then military coup-maker relied on the monarchy to enhance his own legitimacy. After 1963, a reciprocal relationship intensified between military and monarchy, though a 1976 coup saw the monarchy try to usurp control from military rulers. Though that attempt failed, the subsequent post-1977 military ruler could not lead for long without sufficient royal backing and had to step down in 1980. After 1980, Thailand's military became quite "monarchized" in the sense that it functioned as the junior partner to the palace. A "monarchized military" conceptualizes a military in terms of

> ideological dynamics, symbols, rituals, and processes which enhance its legitimacy [based upon] historical-cultural legacies, whereby soldiers secured a patrimonial monarchy that evolved to oversee a capitalist, centralized state. In this sense, the term should not be understood as turning the military into a monarch but instead reflects the extent to which the armed forces have depended upon a discourse of [monarchism to heighten their clout].[22]

Monarchised military was part of a palace-led "parallel state", akin to such concepts as "network monarchy"[23] and "deep state",[24] which weakened the forces of democratization.

> [A] parallel state is defined as a shadowy network or institutional arrangement that is connected to the state and possesses formal political, social, and economic authority as well as informal clout, prerogatives, and interests outside those of civilian leaders—who must acquiesce to the autonomy of the informal power structure because the parallel state is insulated from and can exert influence over them. The linchpin of a parallel state is the informal structure's influence over "experts in violence"—such as the military—to maximize the informal structure's interests.[25]

The intensifying symbiosis between monarchy and military, with the military as junior partner since 1980, embedded a "khakistocracy" (military plus aristocracy) across the country. This khakistocracy entrenched a sense of entitlement among the military, especially regarding its perceived right to influence decision-making in terms of national security and national development, as a means of serving the monarch.[26]

At the same time, the military's formal and informal monopoly over instruments of violence over time allowed it to accumulate sufficient power to remain the physically strongest institution in the country, with its actions rationalized to support the monarchy. Though the advent of elected prime minister Thaksin Shinawatra created a democratic threat to the dominance of the partnership between monarchy and military, the double coups of 2006 and 2014, followed by post-2019 façade democracy, once again strengthened the status quo ante of khakistocracy.

This book thus chronicles the historical evolution of military power and civil-military relations from before 1932 until 2022 in Thailand. It surveys the history of Thai military clout and the major military personages who have led it, as well as efforts by Thais to achieve democratization. Both internal and external factors facilitating Thailand's powerful military—including factionalism and national emergencies—are discussed. The study is crucial to comprehending how and why Thailand's military acquired enormous political influence, its fluctuations over time, what level it possesses in 2023, and what might be the future of the military's clout across Thailand's political landscape. The book also asks a series of secondary questions. Have security sector reforms ever taken hold? Why does Thailand's military remain such an obstacle to democratization in 2023? What has been the history of military-monarchy relations in Thailand? And how have senior military officials been able to insert themselves into Thai democratization efforts?

In terms of methodology, the work is based upon primary (original) and secondary sources. These include personal interviews, government documents and journalistic as well as academic articles and books in Thai and English. The government documents used include those from Thailand (e.g., the state's *Royal Gazette*), the United States and the United Kingdom. With regard to English-language government documents, the study has sought to use specifically only those directly relevant to the military.

Most books about Thai politics focus on political parties, electoral politics or the monarchy. This work is significant because it focuses upon an institution of perennial political prominence in Thai society—the military—which is only junior to the monarchy. The role of the military as the guardian of the palace has legitimized its power and privileges, with the monarch usually endorsing such clout. As an authoritarian institution, Thailand's military has been reluctant to allow elected civilians to effectively monitor or control them, and has, as such, been the chief impediment to democratization in Thailand.

Generally, the leading studies about the Thai military are written in Thai. One of these, a textbook published by the Thai military itself, is mundanely titled เอกสารประกอบการสอน วิชาประวัติศาสตร์ทหาร (A textbook on military history). The opus offers a formal chronological survey from the forerunners of the Thai army until the 1980s, the Thai military's participation in United Nations Peacekeeping operations, a few other details, but little more.[27] A second important book in Thai is that of acclaimed Thai military specialist Chai-yanan Samudavanija. It illuminates the role of Thailand's "Young Turk" soldiers in politics during the 1970s and early 1980s.[28] He also wrote an English-language version of this book.[29] A useful Thai-language source on Thai military influence in terms of coups is that of Pracha Thepkasetkul.[30] A more recent Thai-language study, that of Surachart Bamrungsuk, argues that in the vortex between Thailand's elections and coups the army has become the core instrument of resolving political problems, and thus it is important to reform the Thai military.[31] There have also been books written in English about the history of Thailand's armed forces. While all of them are excellent, these works generally look at a particular period in time or a specific subject area. For example, Daniel Fineman investigates Thai military power during the period 1947–58.[32] Noranit Setabutr analyses the role of the Thai military during 1958–70.[33] David Elliott, using a Marxist approach, looks at Thai military rule between 1932 and 1976.[34] Suchit Bunbongkarn looks at the political role of the military during the 1980s.[35] Thak Chaloemtiarana focuses upon the regime of Field Marshal Sarit Thanarat.[36] David Murray covers the Thai military during 1991–92.[37] Duncan McCargo and Ukrist Pathmanand investigate Thai civil-military relations under Prime Minister Thaksin Shinawatra.[38] Two useful books on Thailand's 2006 coup and subsequent junta include *A Coup for the Rich*[39] and *Good Coup Gone Bad: Thailand's Political Development since Thaksin's Downfall*.[40] Puangthong Pawakapan offers a fascinating examination of the Thai military through the lens of the Internal Security Operations Command (ISOC).[41] Michael Montesano et al. bring together a collection of articles scrutinizing Thailand's 2014–19 junta.[42]

In addition, several important publications have examined civil-military relations in Southeast Asia. These works examine several countries but do not put special emphasis on the "case" of Thailand. Prominent among them are the following: Alagappa;[43] Hack and Rettig;[44] Beeson and Bellamy;[45] Croissant et al.;[46] Mietzner;[47] Grabowsky and Rettig;[48] and Matei, Halladay and Bruneau.[49]

Within the last decade, a flurry of books about the Thai military have been written—paralleling the resurrection of the influence of armed forces across politics. One recent book by Thamrongsak Phetlertanan in the Thai language focuses on Thai coups.[50] Another study by Wanwichit Boonprong and Thiraphong Bualah, based upon the period 1992–2020, argues that when military leaders became highly popular in society they could maintain and expand the military's role in the political sphere.[51] Yet another book offers an excellent analysis of the relationship between monarchy and military. This study, by Thep Bunthanon, is called ทหารของพระราชา กับการสร้างสำนึกแห่งศรัทธาและภักดี (The king's soldiers and the fostering of faith and loyalty).[52] Three recent English-language books have analysed Thai military history at an expansive and macro level. Gregory Raymond offers an outstanding opus about the evolution of Thailand's military and how it was shaped by a framework of "strategic culture".[53] Supalak Ganjanakhundee magnificently illustrates the evolution of relations between the Thai military and the monarch.[54] One edited book—which includes contributions from Napisa Waitoolkiat, Arisa Ratanapinsiri, Eric Haanstad, Srisompob Jitpiromsri and myself—looks at the history of Thailand's military and police (with one chapter focusing on the counterinsurgency in the Deep South).[55] The work at hand seeks to build upon that 2013 edited volume to produce a much more detailed and updated appraisal of Thai military history.

Beyond books, there have been numerous articles or book chapters written about various aspects of the Thai military, though few recent works focus on its overall history. Some seminal works of this sort include that of Anderson,[56] Morell,[57] Bamrungsuk,[58] Ockey,[59] Pathmanand[60] and Winichakul.[61] More recent relevant work includes that of Chambers and Waitoolkiat, which coined the term "monarchised military" to refer to a regal-led "parallel state".[62] Another recent work, by Sirivunnabood and Ricks, uses interviews with Thai military officers to measure their attitudes toward professionalism.[63] Finally, Kongkirati and Kanchoochat analyse the 2014–19 junta in terms of entrenched power and hierarchical capitalism.[64]

Several excellent works on Thai history and politics in general do look at the Thai military. These include studies by Wright,[65] Chaiyan,[66] Thongchai,[67] Kobkua,[68] Kullada,[69] Handley,[70] Ferrara,[71] Nattapoll,[72] Baker and Phongpaichit,[73] and Marshall.[74] These studies, however, are not focused upon Thailand's armed forces per se. Ultimately, there has never been a book written in English about the detailed history of Thailand's permanent military from its founding in 1852 up until 2023 centred upon strongmen in the Thai military, as well as other features, including yearly military reshuffles, budgets and new insights from new sources such as Wikileaks. In fact, there has been no detailed historical survey of the Thai military written in Thai covering this period. This study is thus relevant in filling this significant gap, making it a valuable addition to the literature on the history of Thailand's military, its relations with the Thai monarchy and how the armed forces have obstructed democratization until 2023. It is to be hoped this book fulfils its purpose. In terms of organization, following this introduction, the book is structured into fifteen chapters, each detailing an evolutionary stage in the political role of Thailand's armed forces until 2023.

Notes

1.   Harold Lasswell, "*The Garrison State*", *American Journal of Sociology* 46, no. 4 (January 1941): 455.

2.   Samuel Huntington, *The Soldier and the State* (Cambridge, MA: The Belknap Press of Harvard University Press, 1957), pp. 10–16, 71.

3.   David C. Rapoport, *Praetorianism: Government without Consensus* (PhD dissertation, University of California, Berkeley, 1960), pp. 14–15.

4.   L. McAlister, "Civil-Military Relations in Latin America", *Journal of Inter-American Studies* 3, no. 3 (1961): 343.

5.   Samuel Huntington, "Political Development and Political Decay", *World Politics* 17, no. 3 (1965): 417, https://www.jstor.org/stable/2009286.

6.   Amos Perlmutter, *Military and Politics in Israel, 1948–1967: Nation Building and Role Expansion* (New York: Cass, 1969), p. 382.

7.   Ibid., pp. 391–92.

8.   Huntington stated that an officer corps could be politically influenced by (1) group affiliations of the officer corps, (2) economic and human resources related to the officer corps, (3) interpenetration of officers in non-military power structures, and (4) the prestige and popularity of the officer corps and its leaders. See Samuel Huntington, *The Soldier and the State* (Cambridge, MA: Belknap, 1957), pp. 80–89.

9.   Perlmutter, *Military and Politics*, p. 392.

10. Amos Perlmutter, *Egypt, the Praetorian State* (New York: Transaction, 1974), p. 132.

11. Samuel Huntington, *Political Order in Changing Societies* (New Haven, CT: Yale University Press, 1968), p. 249.

12. Eric A. Nordlinger, *Soldiers in Politics: Military Coups and Governments* (Hoboken: Prentice-Hall, 1977), pp. 20–27.

13. See Shamsul Khan, "The Military and the Praetorian Regimes in Pakistan Politics: Political Usurpers or Protectors of an Incipient Democracy?" *Journal of International Studies* 5 (January 2009), https://e-journal. uum.edu.my/index.php/jis/article/view/7890; Birikim Yayinlari,

"The Praetorian State and its Owners", https://birikimdergisi.com/articles/7407/the-praetorian-state-and-its-owners.

14. See Morris Janowitz, *The Military in the Political Development of New Nations* (Chicago: University of Chicago Press, 1964).

15. Barbara Geddes, "What Do We Know about Democratization after Twenty Years?", *Annual Review of Political Science* 2, no. 1 (1999): 124, https://www.annualreviews.org/doi/pdf/10.1146/annurev.polisci.2.1.115.

16. Ayesha Siddiqa, *Military Inc: Inside Pakistan's Military Economy* (Oxford: Oxford University Press, 2007), p. 33.

17. Yasser El-Shimy, "A Model of Praetorian States", Working Paper, Middle East Initiative, Belfer Center for Science and International Affairs, Harvard Kennedy School, 2016, https://www.belfercenter.org/sites/default/files/files/publication/2016-01-MEI_RFWP_ElShimy_0.pdf.

18. Vikash Yadav, "Wither the Praetorian State", *The Duck of Minerva*, https://www.duckofminerva.com/2011/06/wither-praetorian-state.html.

19. Paul Chambers, "Assessing the Monarchized Military and Khakistocracy in Postsuccession Thailand". In *Coup, King, Crisis*, edited by Pavin Chachavalpongpun (New Haven: Yale University Press, 2020), p. 171.

20. Puangthong Pawakapan, "The Making of Thailand's Praetorian State from the 1947 Coup to the 2014 Coup", *Journal of Social Sciences* 52, no. 1 (2022): 1, http://www.library.polsci.chula.ac.th/journal2.

21. Aurel Croissant, David Kuehn, Philip Lorenz, and Paul Chambers, *Democratization and Civilian Control in Asia* (Palgrave, 2013).

22. Paul Chambers and Napisa Waitoolkiat, "The Resilience of Monarchised Military in Thailand", *Journal of Contemporary Asia* 46, no. 3 (2016): 4, https://doi.org/10.1080/00472336.2016.1161060. See Supalak Ganjanakhundee, *A Soldier King: Monarchy and Military in the Thailand of Rama X* (Singapore: ISEAS – Yusof Ishak Institute, 2022), pp. 164–65.

23. Duncan McCargo, "Network Monarchy and Legitimacy Crises in Thailand", *Pacific Review* 18, no. 4 (2005): 499–519, http://doi.org/10.1080/09512740500338937.

24. Eugenie Merieau, "Thailand's Deep State, Royal Power, and the Constitutional Court (1997–2015), *Journal of Contemporary Asia* 46, no. 3, http://doi.org/10.1080/00472336.2016.1151917.

25. Paul Chambers, "Democratization Interrupted: The Parallel State and the Demise of Democracy in Thailand". In *Stateness and Democracy in East Asia*, edited by Aurel Croissant and Olli Hellman (Cambridge: Cambridge University, 2020).

26. Chambers, "Assessing the Monarchized".

27. Royal Thai Armed Forces, เอกสารประกอบการสอน [Textbook on Thai military history], 2011.

28. Chai-anan Samudavanija, ยังเติร์กกับทหารประชาธิปไตย การวิเคราะห์บทบาททหารใน การเมืองไทย [Still a Turk with democratic soldiers: An analysis of the role of the military in Thai politics]. Bangkok: Bangit, 1982.

29. Chai-anan Samudavanija, *The Thai Young Turks* (Singapore: Institute of Southeast Asian Studies, 1982).

30. Pracha Thepkasetkul, การแทรกแซงทางการเมืองของทหารไทย: ศึกษาเฉพาะกรณี. การรัฐประหาร เมื่อวันที่ 23 กุมภาพันธ 2534 [Political interference of the Thai military: Case study 1991 coup] (Master's thesis, Thammasat University, 1992).

31. Surachart Bamrungsuk, เสนาธิปไตย: รัฐประหารกับการเมืองไทย [Militocracy: Military coup and Thai politics]. Bangkok: Matichon, 2015.

32. Daniel Fineman, *A Special Relationship: The United States and Military Government in Thailand, 1947–1958* (Honolulu: University of Hawai'i Press, 1997).

33. Noranit Setabutr, *The Role of the Military in Thailand: 1958–1970* (Bangkok: Praepittaya Company, 1971).

34. David Elliott, *Thailand: Origins of Military Rule* (London: Zed Books, 1978).

35. Suchit Bunbongkarn, *The Military in Thai Politics* (Singapore: Institute of Southeast Asian Studies, 1990).

36. Thak Chaloemtiarana, *Thailand: The Politics of Despotic Paternalism* (Bangok: Social Science Association of Thailand, 1979; Ithaca: Cornell Southeast Asia Program, 2007).

37. David Murray, *Angels and Devils* (Bangkok: White Orchid Press, 1996).

38. Duncan McCargo and Ukrist Pathmanand, *The Thaksinization of Thailand* (Copenhagen: NIAS, 2004).

39. Giles Ji Ungpakorn, *A Coup for the Rich* (Bangkok: Workers Democracy Publishing, 2007).

40. Pavin Chachavalpongpun, ed., *Good Coup Gone Bad: Thailand's Political Development since Thaksin's Downfall* (Singapore: Institute of Southeast Asian Studies, 2014).

41. Puangthong Pawakapan, *Infiltrating Society: The Thai Military's Internal Security Affairs* (Singapore: ISEAS – Yusof Ishak Institute, 2021).

42. Michael J. Montesano, Terence Chong, and Mark Shu Xun Heng, eds., *After the Coup: The National Council for Peace and Order Era and the Future of Thailand* (Singapore: ISEAS – Yusof Ishak Institute, 2019).

43. Muthiah Alagappa, ed., *Coercion and Governance: The Declining Political Role of the Military in Asia* (Stanford: Stanford University Press, 2002).

44. Karl Hack and Tobias Rettig, eds., *Colonial Armies in Southeast Asia* (London: Routledge, 2005).

45. Mark Beeson and Mark Bellamy, *Security Southeast Asia: The Politics of Security Sector Reform* (London: Routledge, 2008).

46. Aurel Croissant, David Kuehn, Philip Lorenz, and Paul Chambers, *Democratization and Civilian Control in Asia* (Palgrave, 2013); Aurel Croissant, *Civil-Military Relations in Southeast Asia* (Cambridge: Cambridge University Press, 2018).

47. Marcus Mietzner, ed., *The Political Resurgence of the Military in Southeast Asia: Conflict and Leadership* (London: Routledge, 2013).

48. Volker Grabowsky and Frederick Rettig, eds., *Armies and Societies in Southeast Asia* (Chiang Mai: Silkworm, 2020).

49. Florina Cristiana Matei, Carolyn Halladay, and Thomas Bruneau, eds., *The Routledge Handbook of Civil-Military Relations*, 2nd ed. (2021), https://www.routledge.com/The-Routledge-Handbook-of-Civil-Military-Relations/Matei-Halladay-Bruneau/p/book/9780367540425.

50. Thamrongsak Phetlertanan, ข้ออ้างการปฏิวัติ-รัฐประหาร ในการเมืองไทยสมัยใหม่ [Pretence for the revolution-coup d'état in modern Thai politics] (Bangkok: Social Sciences and Humanities Textbook Project Foundation, 2018).

51. Wanwichit Boonprong, Thiraphong Bualah, การเปลี่ยนแปลงบทบาททางการเมืองของกองทัพไทยตั้งแต่ พ.ศ. 2535–2563 [Changes in political roles of the Royal Thai Army from 1992 to 2020] (Doctor of Philosophy Program, Department of Strategy and Security Burapha University, 2021).

52. Thep Bunthanon, ทหารของพระราชา กับการสร้างสำนึกแห่งศรัทธาและภักดี [The king's soldiers and the fostering of faith and loyalty] (Bangkok: Matichon, 2022).

53. Gregory Raymond, *Thai Military Power: A Culture of Strategic Accommodation* (Copenhagen: NIAS, 2018).

54. Supalak, *A Soldier King*.

55. Paul Chambers, ed., *Knights of the Realm: Thailand's Military and Police, Then and Now* (Bangkok: White Lotus, 2013).

56. Benedict Anderson, "Withdrawal Symptoms: Social and Cultural Aspects of the October 6 Coup", *Bulletin of Concerned Asian Scientists* 9, no. 3 (special supplement, October 1976, the coup in Thailand): 13–30, https://doi.org/10.1080/14672715.1977.10406423.

57. David Morell, "The Political Dynamics of Military Power in Thailand", in *The Armed Forces in Contemporary Asian Societies*, edited by Edward Olsen and Stephen Jurika (London: Routledge, 1986).

58. Surachart Bamrungsuk, "Thailand: Military Professionalism at the Crossroads", in *Military Professionalism in Asia: Conceptual and Empirical Perspectives*, edited by Muthia Alagappa (Lanham, MD: Rowan and Littlefield, 2002).

59. James Ockey, "Thailand's 'Professional Soldiers' and Coup-making: The Coup of 2006", *Crossroads: An Interdisciplinary Journal of Southeast Asian Studies* 19, no. 1 (2007): 95–127, https://www.jstor.org/stable/40860870.

60. Ukrist Pathmanand, "A Different Coup d'Etat", *Journal of Contemporary Asia* 38, no. 1 (February 2008), https://doi.org/10.1080/00472330701651994.

61. Thongchai Winichakul, "Toppling Democracy", *Journal of Contemporary Asia* 38, no. 1 (2008), https://doi.org/10.1080/00472330701651937.

62. Paul Chambers and Napisa Waitoolkiat, "The Resilience of Monarchised Military in Thailand", *Journal of Contemporary Asia* 46, no. 3 (2016), https://doi.org/10.1080/00472336.2016.1161060.

63. Punchada Sirivunnabood and Jacob Ricks, "Professionals and Soldiers: Measuring Professionalism in the Thai Military", *Pacific Affairs* 89, no. 1 (March 2016), https://doi.org/10.5509/20168917.

64. Prajak Kongkirati and Veerayooth Kanchoochat, "The Prayut Regime: Embedded Military and Hierarchical Capitalism in Thailand", *TRANS: Trans-Regional and -National Studies of Southeast Asia* 6, no. 2 (July 2018), https://doi.org/10.1017/trn.2018.4.

65. Joseph Wright, *The Balancing Act: A History of Modern Thailand* (Bangkok: Asia Books, 1991).

66. Chaiyan Rajchagool, *The Rise and Fall of the Thai Absolute Monarchy: Foundations of the Modern Thai State from Feudalism to Peripheral Capitalism* (Bangkok: White Lotus, 1994).

67. Thongchai Winichakul, *Siam Mapped* (Honolulu: University of Hawai'i Press, 1994).

68. Kobkua Suwannathat-Pian, *Kings, Country, and Constitutions: Thailand's Political Development, 1932–2000* (London: Routledge/Curzon, 2003).

69. Kullada Kesboonchoo-Mead, *The Rise and Decline of Thai Absolutism* (London: Routledge/Curzon, 2006).

70. Paul Handley, *The King Never Smiles* (New Haven, CT: Yale University Press, 2006).

71. Federico Ferrara, *The Political Development of Modern Thailand* (Cambridge: Cambridge University, 2015).

72. Nattapoll Chaiching, ขุนศึก ศักดินา และพญาอินทรี [Junta, lords, the eagle] (Bangkok: Fa Diew Kan, 2020).

73. Chris Baker and Pasuk Phongpaichit, *A History of Thailand* (Cambridge: Cambridge University, 2022).

74. Andrew MacGregor Marshall, *A Kingdom in Crisis, Thailand's Struggle for Democracy in the Twenty-first Century* (London: Zed Books, 2014).

Chapter One

Origins

The roots of post-1932 praetorian Thailand necessitate an examination of the military prior to that period. The legacy of a powerful
armed forces was to be expected given that violent disorder in polities
throughout Southeast Asia was only quelled by soldiers using violence.
Indeed, in pre-colonial and/or pre-twentieth-century Southeast Asia,
praetorian traditions flourished, though soldiers were not wage earners
and war was not meant to be a wholesale sanguinary subjugation of
enemy troops (though massive bloodshed did occur). Moreover, the
defence of, or acquisition of, new territories within larger boundaries
was not the objective.[1] The preservation of royalty at that time oscillated
around the preservation of a king vis-à-vis a population of mostly rural
agricultural workers.

In early kingdoms based in present-day Thailand (e.g., Ayutthaya),
ordinary people were required to fulfil manpower needs, but they were
differentiated into a complex hierarchy of labour. Commoners (*phrai*
or *lek*) were a form of bonded labour connected with debt as a result of
economic, social and cultural events.[2] Royal *phrai* or *phrai luang* worked
specifically for the king. Meanwhile, there were private *phrai* (*phrai
sow*) or *khong muang* who worked for local lords (*jao muang*). These
lords acted as tax farmers for kings. Slaves (*tat*) were the socially lowest
form of labour. The latter were bought and sold and could not work off
debt; they were permanent and thus stable fixtures guaranteeing the
economic and infrastructural necessities of kingdoms.[3] *Phrai* and *tat*
were inherited, purchased or granted to lords by the king.[4] Above *phrai*

and *tat* were regular officials (*nai*) and senior officials such as generals and governors (*khun*). At the top of the pyramid were the *jao muang* (local lords), *khunnang* (nobles) and *jao* (princes). The societal value of a person depended on his status within the *sakdina* (power over rice fields) system.[5] People possessing high *sakdina* controlled manpower.

Especially during the Ayutthaya period (1351–1767), manpower needs were crucial for both "civilian" and "military" purposes. Regarding the former, agriculture and hunting were of predominant importance for the subsistence of the people, but also to shore up resources for the kingdom. Regarding the latter, *phrai* were required to provide the manpower for royal armies going to war. Kings would regularly levy corvée obligations upon *phrai* (as a form of unremunerated tax) for a variety of reasons, including construction work, but also the needs of war. To obtain and maintain royal power, it was necessary to control debt peons and slaves.

Moreover, there was no permanent standing army. In general, a small group of royal guards protected the king. When searching for food and manpower or in response to threats from neighbouring kingdoms, the temporary raising of armies from *phrai* for brief wars became necessary. Raiding thus became synonymous with early Southeast Asian warfare. Food and manpower were crucial in obtaining and maintaining military labour power for use in war service.[6] Acquiring slaves (from war captives) to perform civilian work as a result of labour shortages was another related purpose of war.[7]

Yet, ultimately, control over food and manpower was often the rationale behind the establishment, consolidation and sustaining of "state power", with "forced resettlement campaigns" often being "the main rationale for wars" as kingdoms sought either to increase or decrease manpower to obtain necessary labour.[8] Depopulating enemy kingdoms was a useful strategy for weakening temporarily defeated enemy kingdoms. Nevertheless, it was important that the loss of manpower in lives committed to war be kept to a minimum because such manpower—available for working land—was the key to the continuing clout of the nobles who had raised armies for a king. After all, "it was the object of warfare to increase the available manpower, not to waste it in bloody pitched battles".[9] Wars were also fought to ensure internal security so as to consolidate order within the realm.[10] Such post-war order could lead to more labourers through war enslavement. In some cases, the search for fertile land was a primary objective of warfare at the time.[11] Obtaining war booty was another objective, with captured kingdoms plundered before the invading armies returned home. Such booty included the holdings of palace treasuries—gold, silver, jewellery, important religious objects (which could confer perceived rightful entitlement upon rulers), armaments, craftspeople, and kidnapped royals.[12] The plunder of natural and human resources not only enriched the looting victors but also improved the victors' kingdom in terms of trade, further stimulating the kingdom's economy. Thus, war was essential as a type of economy.[13] In addition, kings used war victories to increase their regal legitimacy, by which they expected to cement their stature, esteem and respect among nobles, peasants and (potential) enemies alike. Battye summarizes the motives of war for early Southeast Asian kingdoms (such as Siam) as centred upon (1) plunder (to acquire food, manpower/slaves, treasure, weapons, war animals and tribute), instead of the long-term benefits of controlled trade; (2) prestige (not territory); and (3) preventive security (instead of the expansion of government).[14]

Armies in Southeast Asia were thus always briefly composed affairs, raised temporarily to fight a war and then disbanded. "[A]rmies, now levied now disbanded, had a short life."[15] Armies did not exist during times of peace. Indeed, kings had to oblige nobles of the realm to call up their own men at their own expense to serve in wars, and these peasant-farmer soldiers were thus missed from working the farms that propped up the economic positions of the nobles themselves. The nobles were thus generally reluctant to do without such labour for long.[16] Moreover, such short-term soldiers "traditionally had to fend for and feed themselves even when on duty".[17] The peasant-farmer troops had to live off the land. Sometimes this meant planting, maintaining and harvesting crops themselves; other times it meant extorting food and supplies from those unlucky enough to live where the soldiers were waging war.

Armies of kingdoms such as Sukhothai and Ayutthaya were composed of palace guards, a capital defence corps, and the levies of *phrai*, the latter only being raised just before wartime. The majority of these *phrai* were infantrymen (the bulwark of the army), though some served in the cavalry, artillery, elephant corps and naval corps. In fact, some villages specialized in particular military skills. The main use of war elephants was to charge the enemy, trampling them and breaking their ranks. Although the elephantry units made up only about one per cent of their overall strength, they were a major component of Siamese war strategy throughout the imperial era. The army on the march would bring expert catchers of wild elephants.[18] Wars were sometimes decided by duals between royals mounted upon white elephants.[19]

The weapons used by troops were generally swords, pikes, lances and spears, with archery rarely utilized.[20] A principal task of the Ayutthaya kingdom's military was to secure the centralized power of the king.[21] This was in line with the tradition of Khmer monarchs, which Ayutthaya sought to emulate. Under Ayutthaya king Boromtrilokanat (1431–48), the function of soldiering became separated from civilians, though eighteen-year-old males (mostly *phrai*) began to become required by law to register for military service. Meanwhile, the monarch, as commander, saw to it that members of the royal family and trusted nobles were bestowed with senior military positions. The wars that Ayutthaya waged against its neighbours expanded the kingdom's suzerainty—resulting in Sukhothai, Cambodia, Lan Na (Chiang Mai) and Patani becoming Ayutthaya's tributary kingdoms in 1438, 1594 and 1688, respectively. The Ayutthayan military attempted to guard the Mandala frontiers of the kingdom and withstand attacks or raids made by neighbours, most notably the Burmese, who, in 1569 and 1767, conquered and pillaged Ayutthaya itself.[22] Nevertheless, according to Pasuk and Baker, by about 1600—with the advent of more modern technology such as gunpowder, cannons and guns—the use of elephants in war began to diminish, and in fact the number of wars and violence started to decline, giving way to greater "peace, commerce, and prosperity".[23]

That is not to say that all wars ended. Ayutthaya's successor kingdom, Thonburi, turned Lanna (Chiang Mai) into a tributary in 1776, and Luang Prabang, Vientiane and Champasak (now Laos) into tributaries in 1779. Thonburi's successor, Siam, made Patani (again), Vientiane (again) and Cambodia (again) into tributaries in 1786, 1828 (before incorporating it completely from 1827 to 1893) and 1847, respectively. In 1849–55, Siam attempted to gain control over Kengtung and Chiang Hung, but the Second Anglo-Burmese War—resulting in Burma becoming further colonized by Britain—compelled the Siamese to withdraw their forces. Nevertheless, the Shan state wars led to Siam building for the first time a permanent standing army (in 1852).

Civil wars were another matter. In Ayutthaya, political conflict among elites centred primarily upon succession to the throne. According to Wyatt, such succession struggles occurred predominantly between the Suphanburi and Lopburi houses over several generations.[24] Such nationalist policies were continued by royal successors of Rama V.

As King Rama I's kingdom under the Chakri dynasty emerged (1782–present), Siam's military became a mechanism with the objective

of solidifying the consolidation of central power against other kingdoms, while ensuring that lesser tributaries paid allegiance to her.
Central to the force were the Palace Guard and the Capital Defence
Corps, though the mass of temporarily levied troops was decentralized
and untrained. These existed under the palace's Ministry of Military
Affairs, which had long been overseen by powerful kin groups (e.g.,
the Bunnag family).

Military reform only commenced in 1852. In that year, King
Mongkut (Rama IV), facing both internal and external security issues,
established the Royal Siamese Armed Forces (RSAF) as a small force
trained by Europeans on the European model and tasked with keeping
order. The foreign trainers were two retired members of the British
military, Captain Impey and Lieutenant George Knox,[25] who had arrived in Bangkok in 1851. They educated the soldiers of King Mongkut
and Second King Pinklao in the British military traditions (Knox
later served as Britain's Consul to Siam). Similarly, in 1860, Mongkut
established a small rudimentary police force in Bangkok, which was
designed to keep order and protect Western people in the capital.[26]
There were even Western commanders of the police: Joseph Byrd
Ames (1860–92), A.J. Jardine (1897–1904), Eric Lawson (1904–13)
and Gustave Schau (1913–15).

The RSAF was initially composed of the Royal Siamese Army
(RSA) (which was then divided between infantry and artillery) and
the Royal Siamese Navy (RSN). Mongkut personally commanded the
RSA, and Second King Pinklao commanded the Front Palace Army.
The highly trusted Chuang Bunnag became the first commander of
the RSN (1851–69), while the Front Palace Navy was commanded by
Second King Pinklao (1851–65).

Pressing security issues were behind the creation of the RSAF.
Internal issues centred on challenges of suzerainty, whereby Mongkut
had to ensure local kings would do Bangkok's bidding. At the same
time, he wanted to establish a force that was professional enough not
to bolster any coup against the palace. After all, the new king could
easily remember how his own uncle had usurped power in 1824. As
for external issues, Mongkut wanted to build a powerful army at the
beginning of the Second Siamese invasion of Kengtung (1852–54)
to take that city as a means of successfully prosecuting war against
Chiang Hung, one of the Shan states, over whose people Siam was
attempting to gain control. Krom Luang Wongsathiratsanit, brother of
Rama V, led Siam's military expedition to Keng Tung in 1852. Though
Mongkut's army was trained by European officers, the invasion proved

unsuccessful because of poor weather, unfamiliar geography, and distance from Bangkok.

At the same time, the Anglo-Burmese War had ended successfully for the British in 1853 and Britain was looking for Burmese territory to colonize along the Burmese-Siamese border. As such, Mongkut ordered Siamese soldiers back home. But the failure did not lead to the king disbanding his soldiers. Instead, he kept the forces together, calculating that a European-trained military force would make any potential Western colonizer think twice about taking control over Thailand. By the time Mongkut's son and successor Chulalongkorn (or King Rama V) came to the throne in 1868, Mongkut had brought in Western military trainers to improve Siam's armed forces. Besides Impey and Knox, later ones included an M. Lamache and M. Garnier de Abin from France as well as a George Dupont from the United States.[27]

Nevertheless, the RSAF lacked cohesion, given that the infantry was controlled by the Front Palace, while the artillery was directed by the Grand Palace, and each palace divided control over the navy. Indeed, traditionally, these units operated autonomously from each other, though under the monarch's formal control. The division between two erstwhile united palaces dated back to at least 1590, when King Naresuan the Great had his brother (and future king) Ekathotsarot crowned as *uparaj* (viceroy or vice king). But the bifurcation of the monarchy could not always be trusted, given that the two palaces established their own separate military forces.[28]

Nevertheless, that princes with little military expertise remained in military command postings continued to be a weakness of the Siamese armed forces. Highly trained professional officers were never allowed to hold top commands. By 1887, Rama V trusted only three of his brothers and one of his sons to transform the military administration.[29] Because these princes informally acted as his military modernizers, they each held early key positions. Damrong was grand officer of the army (1887–90), Phanurangsi held the same power as a chief of joint operations (1892–96, 1899–1901) and Narisara was chief of joint operations (1899–1901). Narisara and Phanurangsi were navy commanders (1898–99, 1901–3, 1920–22) and defence ministers (1894–99, 1901–10). Chira was chief of joint operations (1901–10) and minister of war (1910–13).

Under the advice of these royals, on 8 April 1887, the king ordered the combination of Siam's seven army regiments and two navy regiments to create a High Command, or War Office, which became the genesis of the Ministry of Defence.[30] With the archaic Ministry of Military Affairs (suitable for war elephants) fading away, the War Office became the new organizational centre charged with making financial expenditures, military inspections, military law, training and inventories.[31] In 1890 it was renamed the Ministry of War and Marine, a cabinet-level post.

Chulalongkorn continued Mongkut's tradition of hiring Western advisors to oversee these reforms. Indeed, Rama V relied on military instructors who hailed from England, Italy, Denmark, Austria and beyond. In 1887, Saranrom Cadet School was inaugurated (taking its name from the nearby Saranrom Palace) under European tutelage, with Colonel T.N. Walker, a retired British officer who had worked in the British Bengal Staff Corps, becoming the school's first chancellor.[32] In 1888, a non-commissioned officers' school under Danish captain Gustave Schau was created.[33] Separate clubs for army officers and navy officers were established in 1889 based upon the British model. In 1892 a military code was declared, an informal Defence Council was established and Italian Geralomo Emilio Gerini, a captain in the Siamese army, became the head of a new Military Education Department.[34]

The Danish adventurer, naval officer and businessman Andreas du Plessis de Richelieu served as a Siamese admiral, commanding forces at the Phra Chulachomklao Fort (which he designed) during the 1893 Paknam Incident (see below). He was later appointed as commander of the Royal Siamese Navy (1900–1901).[35] In 1897 an Army Chief of Staff's Office was established in the Department of Joint Operations (Army). It was responsible for military schools, strategy, mapping and intelligence.

Military education was meant to be a key reform, though it was primarily geared towards male children of royals and associated elites. The aforementioned Saranrom Cadet School had been created in 1887 from the joining together of the Royal Pages Bodyguard Cadet School and the Front Troops Cadet School—a merger of the two palace's military training facilities. In 1897, Saranrom Cadet School changed its name to the Royal Thai Army Academy because the Royal Thai Navy established its own school in 1898. King Rama V created another military school for secondary education in 1909 (the Royal Military Academy), while reserving Saranrom Cadet School for primary education. These two schools were eventually combined into one in 1925 as Chulachomklao Royal Military Academy, though the Thai state created a short-lived and parallel Army Technical School (1934–46).[36]

As the king's military reform proceeded, in 1901 he appointed his son Prince Chiraprawat Woradej as war minister to see it to fruition. Chira sought to expand the size of the military by initiating a system of universal conscription, though this would not be easy because regional elites did not want to lose their local-level *prai* labour to Bangkok. Chira early on advanced a conscription proposal, and then, in 1904, put forward a National Defence Plan, which would expand the army to ten divisions, including 20,000 foot, and 80,000 reserves. In August 1905, following Chira's recommendations, and under the advice of Western military advisors—but despite opposition from many of Siam's royal elites—Rama V replaced the corvée system (used to require *phrai* to periodically serve as soldiers) with universal conscription.[37] The order affected the army, navy, police, gendarmerie (reorganized in 1915) and the palace attendants. This military draft was extended gradually to each of the *monthon* throughout Siam, applying officially to all men between the ages of eighteen and forty. It entailed two years of active service and fifteen years of reserve duty.[38] The year 1906 saw the implementation of new entry requirements to the military academy whereby only children of well-regarded parents could enter, and they would need to be sponsored by a commissioned government official. By 1909, the three preparatory grades of the military academy became limited "to scions of the royal family … and sons of military officers".[39] But, since the prince at the time was still a minor, an acting commander-in-chief would be chosen from among the older princes on an annual basis.[40] Naturally, these reforms paralleled a skyrocketing of military expenditures.

In 1906, senior military officials became irritated when the minister of finance prevailed in a policy dispute as to whether Siam should pursue a balanced budget in lieu of continually growing military appropriations. Chira's conscription-fuelled military, however, was allowed to continue to grow.[41] By 1909 (one year before Rama V died), there were foreign advisors from countries ranging from Britain, France, Holland, Italy, Japan, the United States and beyond instructing Siam on matters of defence. Indeed, these foreigners were employed across a variety of ministries in the kingdom of Siam, and their entire number in 1909 was estimated to be three hundred.[42] Employing these instructors was a careful strategy of the Siamese crown because it helped to maintain trust and friendship with the countries from which the advisors came—most importantly, Siam's colonial neighbours Britain and France. By 1910 Britain had come to be the principal source of Siam's advisors, and these were spread throughout the bureaucracy.[43]

A further reform was the gradual abolition of slavery. The ban was incremental because King Rama V did not want to outrage the nobility, whose power depended upon their direct control over slaves as a key part of manpower for labour. Thus, reforms inching out the institution developed across 1874, 1884, 1890, 1897, 1900, 1905 and 1908, with the final act criminalizing slavery altogether.[44] The emancipation of slaves increased the tax base, given that former slaves would now have to pay into it. Moreover, the end of slavery created a much larger supply of peasants with corvée obligations.[45] This meant Siam now had a much larger army.

Ultimately, from 1893 until 1932, the armed forces possessed two purposes: (1) ensuring the centralized administration of former tributary states under Bangkok's control (those not already colonized by foreign powers), and (2) physically maintaining the king's control over the Siamese realm. This included a feeling among propertied Thais that it was necessary to militarily safeguard their interests against the growing influence of the Chinese, who seemed to be extending their control across the economy of the country.[46] As such, soldiers came "to regard themselves as the main pillar of governmental power".[47]

Internal and security threats to the kingdom validated Rama V's reforms and indeed were making the creation and maintenance of a professional military crucial.[48] However, in 1893, Siamese forces were ill-prepared to defeat a French naval force that forced its way up the Chao Phraya River to Bangkok and made demands against King Rama V. The final settlement of this Paknam Incident, which became known as R.S. 112 in Thailand, gave France control over territories east of the Mekong River, which form most of what became Laos. Indeed, under kings Rama V, VI and VII (1868–1932), Siam became surrounded on all sides by colonies of Europe: British Burma and Malaya, and French Indochina. Such colonial surroundings brought great power pressure to bear on a small country. Siam concentrated on internal security alone—what Anderson calls "a means for internal royalist consolidation".[49] It became increasingly necessary for Siam to establish a professional army to guard against insurgency and foreign encroachment. A secondary reason to develop the army was to galvanize national prestige.[50] Nevertheless, the army that was created was initially quite ineffective. Yet, despite slackness, sloppiness and continuing organizational inadequacies, the military would improve incrementally and eventually come to challenge the palace.[51] It had moved from being a structure designed to defend the kingdom to a political institution whose senior officers harboured political ambitions.

Indeed, by constructing a large and asymmetrically unified armed forces, "King Chulalongkorn created the conditions of praetorianism and the overthrow of monarchy he raised to an empyrean".[52]

The government of Chulalongkorn's son King Rama VI (Vajiravudh), 1910–25, especially saw the continuation of reforms and an intensifying evolution of the armed forces as a central force in shaping the nation-state. Vajiravudh had himself received military training, having graduated from the Royal Military Academy Sandhurst in 1894. After his ascension to power, the state created the Council of National Defence, which "put military affairs on a governmental footing approximately equal to all civil affairs combined".[53] Indeed, this council, with the king at its head, established national defence policy and coordinated relations between civilian and military ministries. In 1911 the king created the Wild Tiger (Sua Ba) Corps, a paramilitary organization composed of bureaucrats, pages and Vajiravudh's favourites, which was designed to instil notions of nationalism, patriotism and loyalty to the king. The corps soon topped four thousand participants, rivalling the army in size, and it appeared to be a personal force of the king.[54] The corps was specifically tasked with protecting the king as a form of elite royal guard, which seemed to suggest the monarch did not trust the regular army.[55] Military frustrations finally gave way to action. On 13 January 1912, up to as many as three thousand people—led by junior officers of the army who were dissatisfied with the king's absolutism, his creation of the Wild Tiger Corps, and inspired by reforms in Meiji Japan as well as the overthrow of the Manchu dynasty in China that year—began plotting to overthrow Vajiravudh and place the country under a constitution. One of the conspirators, however, confessed the plot before it could be carried out, leading to its entire discovery and eventual punishment for all conspirators (they were, however, pardoned).[56] Moreover, the coup was doomed by the fact that the plotters only had command over small units; they had no plan for how to handle the troops still loyal to the king; and most of the leaders were only obscure junior officers.[57] The 1912 military coup plot perhaps marked the first such attempt against the House of Chakri. But in its aftermath, Rama VI, perhaps realizing that he had gone too far, quietly ensured the fading away of the Wild Tiger Corps (it was officially disbanded in 1925). Still, the corps and its subsidiaries continued until 1925, possibly because the Wild Tiger Corps lotteries were simply too lucrative for the Crown. In fact, in 1925, Phraya Nonthisen, a favourite of Rama VI, even publicly perpetuated a swindle of the lottery, stoking popular indignation, though the king refused to investigate the incident.[58] Another unit that Rama VI established was the Royal Palace Guard. It became the chief unit defending the monarch's residence, composed of regular army members but dominated by the palace.

Army officials objected to the king's direct control over what they saw as the purview of the military.[59] According to Pasuk and Baker, Rama VI's government was shaken by at least two military coup efforts and perhaps "one projected palace revolution".[60] One of these included a 1911 plan by Prince Chumporn (half-brother to Vajiravudh) to place another brother, the Prince of Nakhon Sawan (Paribatra), who had been educated in Germany, on the throne, while Chumporn would take the post of Second King. Nakhon Sawan refused. But, as Chumporn's treasonous activities continued, the palace dismissed him from key positions and soldiers were implored to remain loyal to His Majesty.[61] In 1917 another coup plot was concocted to overthrow the king. This time the source of the plan was Imperial Germany, which, during World War I, did not want a neutral Siam. German diplomats apparently let it be known that if the Central powers won World War I, they would install Rama VI's half-brother, the pro-German Prince of Nakon Sawan (Paribatra), as king. At the time, Paribatra was powerful, commanding the navy (1910–20). But Paribatra had already enraged other princes by introducing telecommunications contracts to Germans over British companies for Siam's navy. Eventually, Rama VI became aware of the German plot. The king later told the British representative (confirmed in a discussion between the Prince of Phitsanulok and the Russian representative) that indeed there had been a coup plot but the Siamese military officers involved in it had been arrested.[62] Perhaps the threat of potential European colonialism had been an underlying reason for Siam deciding to remain neutral during the initial stages of World War I. But Rama VI knew he definitely needed a loyal military to keep him in power. Perhaps to build his support among soldiers and heighten Siam's military clout, Rama VI granted much budgetary funding "to build up a strong war machine", though this came at the expense of allocating funds for "economic reform".[63] In the 1911/12 budget, the Ministry of War and Marines received the most of any ministry, and 23 per cent of the entire state budget. By 1923/24 this had changed little, with the Ministry of War receiving 21 per cent.[64]

Meanwhile, Rama VI continued his father's efforts to modernize the Siamese military. Under the continuing tutelage of foreign advisors, he combined all military command posts under the Ministry of War, though he recreated a separate ministry for the navy. The armed forces were enlarged, more ships were purchased and new weapons bought—all leading to budgetary overruns. The number of annual military exercises increased.[65] Furthermore, Vajiralongkorn had been an avid promoter of air power. In November 1913, he decreed the formation of the Army Aviation Section, under the command of his brother Prince Chakrapongse. On 27 March 1915, this unit was reorganized as the Army Flying Battalion. Additionally, pilots were trained, airplanes purchased and a military airport established at Don Muang, north of Bangkok.[66] Finally, throughout his reign, Rama VI attempted to instil nationalism within the armed forces as a sort of unifying esprit de corps—national pride, fellowship and loyalty to the crown. This he hid through media, speeches, songs, books and poems. In fact, he himself wrote several works about military matters, including a 1916 tract on trench warfare.[67] He also sought to "Thai-ize" the military by diminishing the influence of foreign (including military) advisors. By the last year of Rama VI's reign (1925), one foreign adviser wrote that foreign advisers had been eliminated from positions of actual control of state affairs.[68]

Meanwhile, eight years earlier (in 1917), Vajiravudh had succeeded in proving his mettle militarily in coming to the aid of the Allies. During World War I, though many Siamese princes—led by Prince Paribatra—tilted towards Germany, Rama VI was an anglophile. By early 1917, when it appeared as though Berlin was beginning to lose the war, he informed his ministers that the Allies would be triumphant and dominate the conflict's aftermath. Rama VI supported Siam's entry into the war as a way to bolster military pride and nationalism in support of the king and also to build positive ties with England, France and the United States. Thus, on 22 July 1917, Siam declared war on Germany and Austria-Hungary (formally because of Germany's use of unrestricted submarine warfare). Thereupon, with support from France (though not Britain), Rama VI sent a Siamese Expeditionary Force to participate in the war under the command of Major General Phraya Pichai Charnvarit (Phat Thephatsadin na Ayuthaya). This force landed in France on 30 July 1918, ten weeks before the war's end. It numbered only 1,295 soldiers, including a 370-man aviation corps, which trained but never saw action.[69] The others became a motor transport company during the final year of the war. There were also Siamese medical personnel. Participating in the Champagne and Argonne battles, the expeditionary force suffered nineteen killed,[70] but these casualties were mostly the result of influenza. Post-war, the soldiers participated in July 1919 victory celebrations in Europe and later celebrations in Bangkok organized by Rama VI. Siamese soldiers also served with the Allied

Army of Occupation at Neustade-sur-Arrendt, Germany. Following World War I, Rama VI erected a Volunteer Soldiers' Monument (Anusawari Thaharn Asa) on a traffic island at the northwestern corner of Sanam Luang, near Thammasat University. The four-sided monument is of polished white stone. Because it sided with the Allies, Siam made gains in its relations with European countries, participated in the Versailles Peace Conference and became a founding member of the League of Nations. Indeed, Siam was the only Asian country to voluntarily contribute troops to World War I, and this led to a breakthrough in the renegotiation of unequal treaties with the West by 1925.

At the end of World War I, Rama V sought to build the Aviation Corps into a permanent air force for Siam. In 1919, encouraged by his brother Prince Chakrapongse (who died suddenly in 1920), the king formed the Aeronautical Department of the Army from the Army Flying Battalion and increased the number of pilots to over a hundred.[71]

On 26 November 1925, Rama VI died, succeeded by his brother Rama VII (Prajadhipok 1925–35), who became Siam's final absolute monarch. Like his predecessor and brother Vajiravudh, Prajadhipok had earlier received a military education, graduating from Woolwich Military Academy in 1913, one year before his later-usurping contemporary Plaek Phibun Songkram graduated from the Chulalongkorn Royal Military Academy. The new king's military background seemed to indicate that he, like his elder brother, would champion soldierly causes. In fact, Rama VII did encourage the continuing modernization of the armed forces, a phenomenon that, in the 1920s, witnessed a growing functional division between civilians and soldiers. The three men who Rama VII appointed to direct military/security policy were Prince Paribatra (war minister 1926–28; interior minister 1928–32); Prince Bowaradej (army chief of staff 1926–28; war minister 1928–31) and Vudhijaya Chalermlabha (Prince of Singha) (minister of the navy 1924–32; war minister 1931–32).

By 1932, though political change seemed impending, Siam had already undergone a chaotic trajectory of military institutional evolution (see Figure 1.1). The 1887–1932 period is particularly interesting because it shows the chronology of the military's confusing bureaucratic evolution at this time, with institutions often transforming as a result of bureaucratic disagreements between the army and navy, attempts by the palace to regain control of them, and efforts by the army and navy to extract rent.

Institutional innovation and reform, however, had not changed the structure of command. As in the days of Rama V, under Rama VI and

FIGURE 1.1
Evolution of Military Institutions in Siam, 1590–1932

	Defence	Army	Navy
1.	BIFURCATION	Royal Palace army/ Front Palace army (1590–1885/87)	Royal Palace navy/ Front Palace navy (1590–1885/87)
2.	Ministry of Military Affairs (1782–1894)	(army)	(navy)
3.	War Office (1887–1910)	—	—
4.	Ministry of War (1910–31)	Department of the Army (1890–92)	Department of the Navy (1890–1910)
5.	—	Joint Operations Department (Army) (1892–1921)	Ministry of the Navy (1910–31)
6.	—	Ministry of War (Army) (1921–31)	—
7.	Ministry of Defence 1931/32–present	Royal Thai Army (1931/32–present)	Royal Thai Navy (1931/32–present)

VII, the king exercised overall military command, the heir-apparent was the formal commander-in-chief, and princely relatives held the other topmost armed forces postings, forcing the creation of what appeared to be a glass ceiling that deprived commoner officers of promotions to senior levels.[72]

Notwithstanding the intensification of military reforms under Rama VII, the royal policy of relying on princes to manage security persisted, and this vexed many in the military. Though most of these commoner military officers were royalists, they chafed at the glass ceiling of promotions denied. The issue would turn officers against the monarchy in 1932.[73]

By the late 1920s, urban bureaucrats and merchants, galvanized by political upheavals on the world stage, were anxious for a transition at home. On 5 February 1927, seven men, dubbing themselves "Promoters of Change", came together in Paris, where they had been studying, at the home of Lieutenant Prayoon Phamonmontri on 9 Rue De Sommerard to found Khana Ratsadon (People's Cabal or Party), and they put together a formula for the transformation of Siam's absolute monarchy into a constitutional monarchy. The use of a quick coup to achieve this goal was to be adopted to prevent foreign intervention. The seven Promoters were as follows: Dr Pridi Panomyong (who was elected chair), Lieutenant Prayoon Pamornmontri, Lieutenant Plaek Phibun Songkram, Lieutenant Tasanai Niyomsuk, and civilians Toua Labhanukrom, Nab Bhaholyothin, and an attaché to the Thai embassy in Paris, Siri Raja-Maitri. Months later, navy midshipman Lieutenant Sindhu Songkramchai secretly joined the group as well. Then Lt. Col. Suraridh Prithikrai, Prayoon's commanding officer in the Royal Guards Regiment—who was also the younger brother of deputy inspector-general of artillery Colonel Phraya Phahon—became part of it.[74] Suraridh convinced Phahon that a coup was necessary.[75]

The objective of the Promoters to change Siam was a popular one, and it only needed a match to strike the fuse. The US Wall Street Crash of 1929 and subsequent Great Depression offered that pretext. Already in Siam there had been a sudden downturn in the economy. This recession led to enormous budget cuts, including in the Ministry of Defence at the beginning of the 1930s. Indeed, the minister for war and marines, Prince Boworadej, resigned over the reduction in funding.[76] Amidst the economic crisis, the state increased taxes on civil servants as well as on soldiers.[77]

The idealist Promoters—led by civilian Pridi Panomyong and army Lt. Col. Plaek Phibun Songkram—soon realized that more military muscle would be needed to affect an overthrow of the state. Suraridh convinced his brother Colonel Phraya Phahon, a man known to have misgiving about monarchical absolutism, that a coup was necessary.[78] Nevertheless, aside from the diminished military budget, higher taxes on soldiers and control of senior positions by princes, Phahon was also concerned by possible demotions and retrenchments by the king.[79] Phahon himself formed the head of what was a Young Turks' clique in the military. There were three other leaders: Colonel Phraya Song Suradej, Phraya Ritthi Akkanay and Phra Phrasasphithav. Collectively, they were called the "four musketeers". Like several of Siam's princes, such as Prince Nakorn Phanom (Paribatra), by the 1920s, several non-royal Siamese military officers had studied in Germany (e.g., Song Suradej and Phraya Phahon), and they were members of what was called the "Kaiser" faction. Moreover, they returned home inculcated with notions of greater modernity, professionalization and ideology (e.g., fascism). But these officials remained frustrated that they could never be promoted to command military positions since the topmost postings were reserved for the princes.

At this point, a coup-group-in-waiting was formed, with Phahon as the nominal leader. It comprised four factions. The first was the senior army clique, led by Colonel Phraya Song Suradej, chief instructor of the Army Academy (9 members). This clique included two crucial colonels—Phraya Ritthi Akkanay and Prasas Pittayayudh (in addition to Phahon himself). The second was the junior army officer faction, led by Major (Plaek Khittasangkha) Luang Phibun Songkram (23 members). The third was the navy faction, headed by Lt. Commander Luang Sinthu Songkramchai, director of the Naval Officer School (21 members). Finally, there was a civilian faction led by Pradit Manootham (Pridi Panomyong) (16 members).[80]

Prior to the coup of 24 June 1932, Siam's military leadership was hardly charismatic or even capable. Rather, these officials seemed to have gained their postings because they were related to or were mere fronts for the absolute monarchy. However, the "Young Turk" officer coup-makers seeking reforms in the Thai military were strong in personality and leadership, and they appealed to soldiers in general.

Song Suradej, the man who strategized the coup, specifically planned for a lightning putsch in two stages while King Prajadhipok was away from Bangkok, in Hua Hin, playing golf and viewing target practices.[81] A day earlier, on 23 June, Song had visited several units in central Bangkok and requested the Army Academy commander, the Engineers Battalion commander and two commanders of strategically placed infantry battalions to participate in drills of anti-tank combat in front of the Anantasamakom Throne Hall the following morning at 6 a.m. Because soldiers were highly respectful of Song (he had been an esteemed instructor at the academy), they did not think twice about the matter and duly showed up at the throne hall the next morning.[82]

Meanwhile, earlier on the morning of 24 June, Phahon broke into the arsenal of the Bangkok Cavalry regiment, gathering ammunition, weapons, trucks and tanks. With Lt. Col. Phrasaspittayayuth (Wan Chutin), director of department of the Army Chief of Staff at his side, Phahon then directed the tanks, trucks and infantry to spearhead the coup. They surrounded the Royal Throne Hall, and the soldiers that Song had called together were placed behind iron gates. 1st Artillery Regiment commander Colonel Ritthi and navy Lt. Col. Luang Sinthu (director of the Naval Academy) also brought numerous marines to bolster Phahon's forces. Phahon then read out a brief announcement declaring a change in the political system, though the great majority of soldiers gathered at the throne hall that day "did not know what actually happened".[83] With Phahon's words, Siam's "revolution" was realized. Phrasaspittayayuth then led 111 soldiers in attacking Bang Khun Phrom Palace to capture Prince Paribatra and other royals. Phrasaspittayayuth's deputy, Major Phin Chunhavan, father of future prime minister Chatchai Chunhavan (who had never joined Khana Ratsadon), failed to show up for the coup—though he was a friend and class peer of Phibun Songkram.

What ultimately occurred on 24 June was a coup led by military/ civilian bureaucrats rather than any participatory, popular revolution— and the consequence for the absolute monarchy was a capping of its powers within constitutionalism. Indeed, as a result of the transition to constitutional monarchy, a new bureaucracy-dominant constitution was enacted, the princes lost their top bureaucratic positions, and many—such as Prince Nakorn Sawan (Paribatra)—were arrested. Others immediately resigned their posts and/or fled into exile. Yet 1932 did not mark the beginning of military influence in Thai politics where coups became a prevalent means of changing regimes. Rather, as this chapter has sought to suggest, military coups, coup plots and influence long pre-dated the 1930s, harking back to the country's authoritarian traditions.

Four young military officers who later played roles in overseeing the military's influence across Thailand were present in Bangkok on that fateful day in June. First was Sarit Thanarat, who was the son of Major Luang Ruengdechanan (Thongdee Thanarat), who placed his son Sarit (at age eleven) into Chulachomklao Military Academy in 1919. Following graduation in 1928, Sarit began serving as a sub-lieutenant directly under 1st Company commander and arch-royalist (and later Privy Council chair) Captain Suranurong, who himself served under Lt. Col. Phra Prachonpatchanuk, commander of the 1st Battalion, who served under Colonel Phraya Ramchatarong (Nat Khemayothin), commander of the 2nd Infantry Regiment, King's Guard, next to what is today Thammasat University in Bangkok.[84]

Second, there was Thanom Kittikachorn, who was from a commoner family of Tak province and who early on attended Wat Pkhok Phlu Public School, a temple school in Tak. With help from highly placed family friends, at age nine (1920) he entered Chulachomklao Military Academy class 20. In 1932 he was a probationary officer and instructor studying at the Army Infantry School in Bangkok. Students at the school highly respected the teacher there—Colonel Song Suradej. From studying at Chulachomklao, Thanom had developed close relations with his mentor, Sarit Thanarat, and his military friend Praphas

Charusathien.[85] In 1930 he married Jongkol Jabpraruyuth, the daughter of famed colonel Luang Jabpraruyuth.

Third, there was Praphas Charusathien (Chulachomklao Military Academy class of 1929). Praphas was the son of Amart Ek Phraya Payappiriyakit, a Siamese nobleman who served as governor of Saraburi,[86] Udon Thani and Phadaeng provinces. Praphas was born in Udorn Thani and attended the elite Wat Rachathiwat School in Dusit, Bangkok. By 24 June 1932, he was a fourth-year army cadet and probationary officer soon to be a second lieutenant. He was among the 111 army cadets who followed army chief of staff Lt. Col. Phrasaspittayayuth in charging into Bang Khun Phrom Palace and arresting Prince Paribatra alongside other royals, and he also helped to take over the Ministry of Finance.[87]

Finally, there was Probationary Officer Krit Sivara (another future army commander), son of Chit, who had been a chief of staff in the War Ministry and was the maternal grandson of Colonel Phra Wisetsatthada (Im Thammanon),[88] Siam's first army chief inspector.[89] Krit attended the elite Children's Military School (1921–23), King's Guard School (Wacheeawutwiteealai) (1924) and Thepsirin Temple School (1925–30), an elite boy's secondary school founded by King Rama V. It was at Thepsirin School that he met and befriended other future military officers, including Pramarn Adireksan. He entered Chulachomklao Military Academy in 1931 (class number 33) with his friend Jampen Charusathien (Praphas's older brother) and maintained his ties with probationary officer Pramarn Adireksan (1932's class number 34). Because of Krit's elite family connections, he maintained close ties with important Siamese military figures such as Phra Prasat Prasatpittayayut (Wan Chutin). And because of the trust the coup makers had in the young Krit, on the day of that coup, they placed him in charge of passing information among them during the action.[90]

On the evening of 24 June, a day that had witnessed the putsch oust the absolute monarchy, one of the main "Promoters of Change", Suradej, exclaimed, "It should be settled that this revolution did take place because of the decisive actions of army officers."[91] The reasons for the coup, according to Suradej, were that (1) the king had an "incapacity to use his absolute power ... to work for the ... nation", and (2) "nearly all the senior government officials were intent only on making themselves the king's favorites".[92] Though the victors dubbed 24 June 1932 a การปฏิวัติสยาม (or *ganpatiwat Siam* 2475 [1932 Siamese revolution]), Charnvit Kasetsiri points out that the event was not at all a revolution, because "governing power merely changed hands from the Chakkri princes to a new elite".[93]

> The whole affair was strongly reminiscent of traditional Siamese coups wherein discontent within the Army against the monopoly of power by the ruling family led elements within it to seize the throne and establish a new dynasty. The 1932 coup differed mainly in the fact that it did not abolish the existing royal family.[94]

According to Suradej, the general populace had no inkling about why the putsch had taken place. The princes were certainly unpopular and the economy was in tatters, but the Promoters had thrust a new constitution upon the people from above—they did not participate in writing it. On 27 June, the coup leaders tried to gather people together to explain what had transpired and to explain the new constitution.

> [I]t took a lot of effort to herd the people in to sit in the [Anantasamakom] Throne Hall. But even so, only a handful of them were rounded up and they stood listening blankly to what was being said. If there were to be a *Lakhon* (folk play) with the Chinese selling noodles, more people would certainly turn out.[95]

Also, on 27 June, the king signed a general amnesty for coup makers and also signed the interim constitution. By doing so,[96] he perhaps abetted the putsch in hopes of influencing the "transition". Meanwhile, military generals trusted by Phahon were appointed to exercise administrative power provisionally across the country. Monarchy and monarchization were temporarily downgraded, while military officers became the new elite class.

June 1932 thus proved to be a critical juncture for the military's future. On the night of 23 June, the eve of the coup, Prayoon had suggested that the army be transformed from its highly centralized ten field commands to a form based on structural responsibilities. At the same time, there should be no military rank higher than that of colonel. Meanwhile, Song Suradej recommended that the Army Staff College be dissolved. Another coup plotter vehemently disagreed, however, contending that any shake-up in military organization would produce turmoil. That plotter was Captain Plaek Phibun Songkram.[97] His ability to lord over the post-1932 transformation of the military ensured that it became the singularly dominant institution.

Ultimately, the period up to 1932 represented the culmination of a process whereby a single kingdom (Siam) had become consolidated under the control of one family—the Chakri dynasty. This trajectory saw Siam's armed forces become unified and strengthened, with growing subsidies, especially under the absolutism of kings Rama V (Chulalongkorn) and his son Rama VI (Vajiravudh). Though the palace had created a permanent military and imbued it with an ideology of monarchization, the royals were civilians ruling supreme over soldiers. The king and his princely advisors, who appeared increasingly despotic, could alone decide the future shape of the armed forces, along with the amount of money they would be allocated. During 1929–32, royal subsidies to the military dramatically declined. Several intermediate-level military leaders among the "Young Turks" detested this royalist ultra-control, while others were mere political opportunists. Thus, for different reasons, both supported Pridi Panomyong's plan to overturn the ruling regime, though the soldiers they commanded had little understanding of the reasons for the June 1932 coup. The coup makers of 1932 successfully transformed Siam, not in terms of increasing political space but instead altering the identity of who lorded over the country. Their putsch brought down monarchical absolutism, supplanting it with military oligarchy, initially under the guise of a reformed constitutional monarchy.

Notes

1.   Chris Baker and Pasuk Phongpaichit, *A History of Ayutthaya: Siam in the Early Modern World* (Cambridge: Cambridge University Press, 2017), p. 97.

2.   Oliver Tappe, "Variants of Bonded Labour in Precolonial and Colonial Southeast Asia", in *Bonded Labour: Global and Comparative Perspectives* (18th–21st Century), edited by Sabine Damir-Geilsdorf, Ulrike Lindner, Gesine Müller, Oliver Tappe, and Michael Zeuske (Bielefeld: Transcript, 2016), p. 104.

3.   Neil A. Englehart, *Culture and Power in Traditional Siamese Government* (Ithaca: Cornell University Press, 2018), p. 111. See also Nantiya Swangvudthitham, การควบคุมกำลังคนในสมัยรัตนโกสินทร์ก่อนการจัดการเกณฑ์ทหาร (พ.ศ.2325–2448) [The control of manpower during the Bangkok Period prior to the introduction of modern conscription (BE 2325–2448)] (MA thesis, Chulalongkorn University, 1982); and Anchalee Susayanha, ความเปลี่ยนแปลงของระบบไพร่และผลกระทบต่อสังคมไทย ในรัชสมัยพระบาทสมเด็จพระจุลจอมเกล้าเจ้าอยู่หัว [Changes of the phrai system and their effects on Thai society in the reign of King Chulalongkorn] (MA thesis, Chulalongkorn University, 1981).

4.   Baker and Pasuk, *A History of Ayutthaya*, p. 152. See also Manop Thawarawatsakun, ขุนนางอยุธยา [The Ayutthayan nobility] (Bangkok: Thammasat University Press, 2004).

5.   Baker and Pasuk, *A History of Ayutthaya*, p. 283.

6. Sunet Chutintharanon, สงครามคราวเสียกรุงศรีอยุธยา ครั้งที่ 2. [The Second Ayutthayan War], 9th ed. (Bangkok: Matichon, 2012).

7. Charney contends that where there was a market for slaves, war captives were often auctioned off to cover the cost of raiding expeditions. Indeed, acquiring war captives "seemed to become more important as the scale of the state increased, with large entities such as post-fifteenth century Ayudhya, Burma, and Vietnam pursuing large-scale wars for war-captives". See Michael Charney, *Southeast Asian Warfare, 1300–1900*, *Handbook of Oriental Studies*, Section Three, *Southeast Asia*, edited by V. Lieberman, M.C. Ricklefs, and D.K. Wyatt (Leiden: Brill 2004), p. 18; Chatchai Phanananon, "ทาสอยุธยาในประมวลกฎหมายรัชกาลที่ 1" [Slaves of Ayutthaya in the King Rama I Code of Laws], 10th ed., Silpa-mag.com [Art and culture], no. 10 (August 1989): 96–113; Art and Culture, "ผ่าระบบ ทาสกรุงศรีอยุธยา คนยุคนั้นมีเสรีแค่ไหน? ทำไมปรากฏวลี "เสรีภาพอย่างเจ็บปวด" [Dissecting the slave system of Ayutthaya: How free were people in that era and why does the phrase "painful liberty" appear?], 29 July 2023, https://www.silpa-mag.com/history/article_46652.

8. Volker Grabowsky, "Forced Resettlement Campaigns in Northern Thailand during the Early Bangkok Period, *Journal of the Siam Society* 87, nos. 1–2 (1999): 45–47, https://thesiamsociety.org/wp-content/uploads/1999/03/JSS_087_0g_Grabowsky_ForecedResettlementCampaignsInNThailand.pdf.

9. Anthony Reid, *Southeast Asia in the Age of Commerce: 1450–1680*, vol. 1, *The Lands below the Winds* (Chiang Mai: Silkworm Books, 1988). p. 123.

10. Thak Chaloemtiarana, *Thailand: The Politics of Despotic Paternalism* (Chiang Mai: Silkworm Books, 2007), p. 3; see Horace Geoffrey Wales Quaritch, *Ancient Southeast Asian Warfare* (London: Bernard Quaritch, 1952).

11. Adrian Vickers, "Two Historical Records of the Kingdom of Vientiane", in *Contesting Visions of the Lao Past: Lao Historiography at the Crossroads*, edited by Christopher E. Goscha and Sören Ivarsson (Copenhagen: NIAS, 2003), p. 3.

12. Baker and Pasuk, *A History of Ayutthaya*, p. 97.

13. Silpa-mag.com, จาก "สงคราม" สู่ "การค้า" ความมั่งคั่งร่ำรวยของอยุธยา อีกต้นเหตุการเสีย กรุง!? ["From 'war' to 'trade', the wealth and riches of Ayutthaya: Another cause of the loss of the city!?"], 20 July 2021, https://www.silpa-mag.com/history/article_58708.

14. Noel A. Battye, "The Military, Government and Society in Siam; 1868–1910: Politics and Military Reform during the Reign of King Chulalongkorn" (PhD dissertation, Cornell University, 1974), p. 2.

15. Ibid., pp. 10–11 .

16. Reid, *Southeast Asia in the Age of Commerce*, p. 123.

17. Ibid., p. 71.

18. Elephants were crucial war machines for these early armies, either as vehicles for army officers or for transporting weapons and other supplies. See Silpa-mag.com, "ช้าง-สินค้าส่งออก สมัยกรุงศรีอยุธยา" ["Elephant – export

product, Ayutthaya period"], 3 November 2022, https://www.silpa-mag. com/history/article_95761; Manop Thawarawatsakun, ขุนนางอยุธยา [The Ayutthayan nobility] (Bangkok: Thammasat University Press, 2004).

19. John M. Kistler, *War Elephants* (Westport, CT: Praeger, 2006).

20. Defensive implements centred upon wooden shields; armour was minimal or absent. Given such basic war technology, the relative size of an army was important. Various estimates of the size of Ayutthaya's army around 1550 were given of 20,000, 250,000 and 600,000 men. By the mid-1500s, the arrival of gunpowder technology (especially that used by foreign—mostly Portuguese—mercenaries) had shifted the power balance and character of war. Baker and Pasuk, *A History of Ayutthaya*, pp. 91–92, 99–101.

21. Manop Thawarawatsakun, ขุนนางอยุธยา [The Ayutthayan nobility] (Bangkok: Thammasat University Press, 2004).

22. Paul Chambers, "A Short History of Military Influence in Thailand", in *Knights of the Realm: Thailand's Military and Police, Then and Now*, edited by Paul Chambers (Bangkok: White Lotus, 2013), pp. 110–11.

23. Baker and Pasuk, *A History of Ayutthaya*, pp. 117–18.

24. Inter-elite struggles centred, secondarily, on control over human resources—*phrai* and *tat*. Given that kings traditionally possessed indirect authority over manpower, relying on direct control by nobles of commoners and slaves, such influence over manpower was crucial in and of itself. Thus, tensions occurred among nobles because of elite disputes over the control of manpower. Such conflicts were sometimes soothed through marriage alliances between royals and elites (which at times could help facilitate the incorporation of one principality by another). Other times, these intra-elite conflicts became violent, where they would be fought largely by the personal manpower of the protagonists—their *phrai* and *tat*. In Siam, Rama V (Mongkut) attempted to destroy the dominance of the nobility (in terms of their direct control over human resources) by building direct connections with the people (based around publicly building a Buddhist, monarchical nationalism), therefore "bypassing the control of 'people/manpower' by the nobles in the traditional organization of society". David Wyatt, *Thailand: A Short History* (New Haven, CT: Yale University Press, 1982), p. 56; Andreas Sturm, "The King's Nation: A Study of the Emergence and Development of Nation and Nationalism in Thailand" (PhD thesis, London School of Economics and Political Science, 2006).

25. Battye, "The Military, Government", p. 140.

26. Paul Chambers, "Securing an Alternative Army: The Evolution of the Royal Thai Police", in *Routledge Handbook of Contemporary Thailand* (New York: Routledge, 2020), p. 102.

27. Ibid., pp. 140–41.

28. By the early 1880s, Rama V had gained full control over the army, having reorganized the Palace (ending the Second Palace altogether) and placed trusted princes in positions where only they would manage the army.

More distant blood relatives or trusted nobles who had married into the monarchy could hold more intermediate-level military command postings. This policy shift from the Fourth Reign represented a centralizing of royal control over the armed forces.

29. The brothers were Prince Maha Chakri Sirindhorn Krom Phraya Damrong Rajanupap, Prince Phanurangsi Sawangwong Krom Phraya Phanuphantuwong Woradet and Prince Prince Narisara Nuwattiwong; the son was Field Marshal Prince Chirapravati Voradej, Prince of Nakhon Chaisi. Ibid., p. 279.

30. Kingdom of Thailand, "History of the Ministry of Defense", 2021, https://www.mod.go.th/File/Content/history_mod.aspx.

31. Ibid., p. 283.

32. Ibid., p. 291.

33. Ibid., p. 296.

34. Gerini was tasked with guiding the direction of European-style military education. Though Walker was replaced not long afterwards, his Siamese successor continued to inculcate European military training methods. Also in 1892, the military journal *Yuthakot* began to be published.

35. Kingdom of Siam, "Royal Command Announcing the Appointment of the Commander-in-Chief of the Royal Siamese Navy", 1900, http://www.ratchakitcha.soc.go.th/DATA/PDF/2444/044/842_1.PDF.

36. Napisa Waitoolkiat and Paul Chambers, "Khaki Veto Power: The Organization of Thailand's Armed Forces", in *Knights of the Realm: Thailand's Military and Police, Then and Now*, edited by Paul Chambers (Bangkok: White Lotus, 2013, pp. 86–87.

37. Battye, "The Military, Government", pp. 444–46.

38. David M. Engel, *Law and Kingship in Thailand during the Reign of King Chulalongkorn* (Ann Arbor: University of Michigan Center of South and Southeast Asian Studies, 1978), p. 99.

39. In 1905, the king created the position of armed forces commander. This position was assigned to the crown prince (though the king remained overall commander), thus perhaps reflecting the royal-connected clout of the post. Benedict Anderson, "Studies of the Thai State: The State of Thai Studies", in *The Study of Thailand: Analyses of Knowledge, Approaches, and Prospects in Anthropology, Art History, Economics, History, and Political Science*, edited by Eliezer B. Ayal (Athens: Ohio University Center for International Studies and Cornell University Press, 1978), p. 206.

40. Battye, "The Military, Government", pp. 271–72.

41. Ibid., p. 465.

42. William J. Siffin, *The Thai Bureaucracy: Institutional Change and Development* (East-West Center Press, 1966), pp. 97–98.

43. Stephen Lyon Wakeman Greene, "Thai Government and Administration in the Reign of Rama VI (1910–1925)" (PhD dissertation, University of London, 1971), p. 261, cited in Anderson, "Studies of the Thai State", p. 224n58.

44. See Martin A. Klein, "The Demise of Corvée and Slavery in Thailand", in *Breaking the Chains: Slavery, Bondage, and Emancipation in Modern Africa and Asia* (University of Wisconsin Press, 1993).

45. Fred Riggs, *Thailand: The Modernization of a Bureaucratic Polity* (Honolulu: East-West Center Press, 1966), p. 58, cited in Anderson, "Studies of the Thai State", p. 224.

46. S.R. Sudhamani, "Major Components in Thai Politics, 1958–1963", *International Studies* (April 1978): 279.

47. Judith A. Stowe, *Siam Becomes Thailand: A Story of Intrigue* (London: Hurst, 1991), p. 84.

48. Battye, "The Military, Government", p. 529.

49. Anderson, "Studies of the Thai State", pp. 202–3.

50. Benjamin Batson, "The End of Absolute Monarchy in Siam" (PhD dissertation, Cornell University, 1977), p. 51.

51. Anderson, "Studies of the Thai State", pp. 204–5.

52. Battye, "The Military, Government", p. 557.

53. David Wilson, *Politics in Thailand* (Ithaca: Cornell University Press, 1962), p. 170.

54. Stephen Lyon Wakeman Greene. *Absolute Dreams: Thai Government under Rama VI, 1910–1925* (Bangkok: White Lotus, 1999), pp. 44, 51.

55. Nevertheless, Vajiravudh seemed intent on separating the Sua Ba from the regular army. The army thus became increasingly incensed by the establishment of Sua Ba given that this corps seemed to compete for resources and attention from their own corps and—as a royally managed unit—was not under their direct control. Moreover, they were infuriated when Crown Prince Vajiravudh ordered the public caning of military officers in 1909 following the reluctance of King Chulalongkorn to support it. Finally, some became disenchanted by the situation of Thailand's impoverished peasants, the malaise of Siam's national development, and the inability to move towards democracy. Walter Vella, *Chaiyo! King Vajiravudh and the Development of Thai Nationalism* (Honolulu: University of Hawai'i Press, 1978), pp. 27–52; Greene, *Absolute Dreams*, pp. 51–52.

56. Chris Baker and Pasuk Phongpaichit, *A History of Thailand* (Cambridge: Cambridge University Press, 2005), pp. 111–12; Stowe, *Siam Becomes Thailand*, p. 7; Desmond Ball and David Scott Mathieson, *Militia Redux: Or Sor and the Revival of Paramilitarism in Thailand* (Bangkok: White Lotus, 2007), p. 313.

57. Thawat Makarapong, *History of the Thai Revolution: A Study in Political Behavior* (Bangkok: Chalermnit, 1972), p. 27.

58. Greene, *Absolute Dreams*, p. 164.

59. Ibid., p. 40.

60. Baker and Pasuk, *A History of Thailand*, p. 106.

61. Greene, *Absolute Dreams*, pp. 38–39.

62. Ibid., pp. 103–4

63. W.A. Graham, *Siam* (London: Alexander Moring, Ltd., 1924), pp. 317–18.

64. Greene, *Absolute Dreams*, p. 160.

65. Walter Vella, *Chaiyo! King Vajiravudh and the Development of Thai Nationalism* (Honolulu: University of Hawai'i Press, 1978), p. 88.

66. Edward Young, *Aerial Nationalism: A History of Aviation in Thailand* (Washington, DC: Smithsonian Institution Press, 1995), pp. 1–2, 5–6, 15–16.

67. Vella, *Chaiyo! King Vajiravudh*, p. 89.

68. Ibid., pp. 86–87.

69. See Stefan Hell, *Siam and World War 1: An International History* (Bangkok: River Books, 2017).

70. Keith Hart, "A Note on the Military Participation of Siam in the First World War", *Journal of the Siam Society* (1982): 135, https://thesiamsociety.org/wp-content/uploads/1982/03/JSS_070_0n_Hart_MilitaryParticipationOfSiamInWW1.pdf.

71. Vella, *Chaiyo! King Vajiravudh*, pp. 89.

72. Battye, "The Military, Government", pp. 518–19.

73. Anderson, "Studies of the Thai State", pp. 193–247.

74. Vichitvong na Pombhejara, *Pridi Panomyong and the Making of Thailand's Modern History*, 2nd ed. (Bangkok: Ruankaew Printing House, 2001), pp. 44–49.

75. Ibid., pp. 44–49.

76. Wilson, *Politics in Thailand*, p. 173.

77. Scott Barme, *Luang Wichit Wathakan and the Creation of Thai Identity* (Singapore: Institute of Southeast Asian Studies, 1993), p. 66.

78. Vichitvong, *Pridi Panomyong*, pp. 44–49.

79. Stowe, *Siam Becomes Thailand*, p. 13.

80. Niyom Rathamarit, *Military Governments in Thailand: Their Policies toward Political Parties* (Pittsburgh: University of Pittsburgh, 1984), pp. 20–21.

81. Queen Ramphai, "Queen Ramphai's Memoir", in *Bueng Raek Prachathipathai* [the Beginning of Democracy] (Bangkok: Mitnara, 1973), p. 9; Prayoon Phamonmontri, "The Political Change of 1932", *Bueng Raek Prachathipathai*, in *Thai Politics: 1932–1957*, translated and edited by Thak Chaloermtirana (Social Science Association of Thailand, Thammasat University, 1978), pp. 9, 41.

82. Joseph Wright, *The Balancing Act: A History of Modern Thailand* (Oakland, CA: Pacific Rim; Bangkok: Asia Books, 1991), p. 62.

83. Phraya Song Suradej, "The Revolution of June 24, 1932", in *Bueng Raek Prachathipatai* [the Beginning of Democracy] (Bangkok: Mitnara Press, 1973), in *Thai Politics: 1932–1957*, translated and edited by Thak Chaloermtirana (Social Science Association of Thailand, Thammasat University, 1978), p. 87.

84. "The History and Works of Field Marshal Sarit Thanarat", Bangkok 1964, in *Thai Politics: 1932–1957*, translated and edited by Thak Chaloermtirana (Social Science Association of Thailand, Thammasat University, 1978), p. 690.

85. Thanom Kittikachorn, *A Life over 60 Years* (Bangkok: 1974), p. 9.

86. *Royal Gazette*, 1913, "Announcement Conferring Titles", http://www.ratchakitcha.soc.go.th/DATA/PDF/2456/D/2515.PDF.

87. See *Field Marshal Praphas Charusathien* (cremation volume), 1997; Nong Loi, *Chaofa Prachathipakrachan Phunirat* (Bangkok: self-published, 1987), p. 260.

88. *Life and Works of General Krit Sivara* (cremation volume), 1976, pp. 1, 91.

89. Im became Siam's first army high commissioner or chief inspector. When King Rama V ordered Im to repress the 1902 Shan Rebellion in Phrae, Im ordered a wholesale massacre.

90. *Life and Works of General Krit Sivara* (cremation volume), 1976, pp. 93–94.

91. Phraya Song Suradej, "The Revolution of June 24", p. 73.

92. Ibid.

93. Charnvit Kasetsiri, "The First Phibun Government and its Involvement in World War II", *Journal of the Siam Society* 62 (1974): 26, https://thesiamsociety.org/wp-content/uploads/1974/03/JSS_062_2d_Charnvit Kasetsiri_FirstPhibunGovernmentAndInvolvementInWorldWarII.pdf.

94. Ibid.

95. Phraya Song Suradej, "The Revolution of June 24", p. 73.

96. Wright, *The Balancing Act*, p. 63.

97. Vichitvong, *Pridi Panomyong*, p. 59.

Chapter Two

The Initial "Caesars": Phraya Phahon and Phibun (1932–44)

The 24 June 1932 victory by Khana Ratsadon (People's Party) over King Prachadipok represented the nadir of monarchical power in Siam. But it also marked the unbridling of praetorian ascendancy, no longer blocked by royalty. The armed forces now replaced royalty as the ascendant political institution in Thai society—although the monarchy remained a leading political institution cosmetically. This was because, at least initially, the Thai insurrectionists needed a thin veil of monarchization, in the form of popular support and simple legitimacy, to consolidate their control. Yet, despite appearances of maintaining itself as a monarchized military in terms of ritual and pageantry, the path dependence of military hegemony over society was solid and would generally remain so until 1957.

Dominating Khana Ratsadon in 1932 was Colonel Phraya Phahon Phonphrayuhasena.[1] He was the leader of the "Four Tigers" or "Four Musketeers" and the reader of the revolutionary pronouncement of 24 June 1932. He was born, on 29 March 1887, as Pote Phahonyothin, and was known as Phraya Phahon. He descended from Mon-Chinese heritage. His patron had been his elder half-brother Phraya Phahonyothin Ramnithara Phakdi, a royal military officer. With the help of his brother, Phahon was able to enter the Royal Army Cadet Academy at the age of fourteen (class of 1901), and he graduated near the top of his class. In 1904 Phahon won a scholarship to study in Potsdam, Germany. There he met German student Hermann Goering and Japanese pupil Hideki Tojo.

Phahon became an early member of the "Kaiser" faction: non-royal Siamese military officers studying in Germany. Phahon was also part of the Siamese Artillery; officers in this unit faction also included Song Suradej, Phraya Ritthi Akkanay and Luang Phibun Songkram. Phahon returned to Siam in 1906 and completed his academy training in 1910. He then gained his first commission as second lieutenant. In 1912 Phahon returned to Europe, this time to Denmark, to study engineering at Copenhagen Engineering College. In 1914 Phahon entered the 4th Artillery Regiment, later becoming a captain and the commander of the 9th Artillery Regiment in Chachoengsao Province. He then rose to be the commander of the 2nd Artillery Army. By 1930 Phahon had become the inspector for the artillery, holding the rank of colonel. By 1932 he was the highest-ranking military official who had joined the conspiracy to overthrow the absolute monarchy.[2] Thus, on 24 June, the day of the *patiwat* (revolution), he found himself the leader of the new, military-dominant regime. Phahon was married twice and had seven children, including three sons. One son became an army major, another a major general and the other ascended to the rank of police lieutenant colonel. None became consequential.

One day after the 27 June 1932 promulgation of a provisional constitution, Colonel Phraya Phahon, the post-coup military controller of Siam, presided over the first session of the country's newly appointed seventy-man assembly,[3] fifty-six of whom were military officials.[4] Phahon proposed Phraya Manopakorn Nitithada as president of a new "People's Committee", which would act as the country's executive branch.[5] Mano reluctantly accepted.[6] Mano himself was hardly progressive; he had previously been a senior judge and privy councillor to the king, and his wife had been a lady-in-waiting to Queen Rambhai.[7]

Following the 1932 "revolution", Mano chaired the drafting committee in charge of formulating the 1932 permanent constitution, which was meant to represent a compromise between the monarchy and the People's Party. Indeed, Rama VII initially refused to endorse the 1932 interim charter because it seemed to explicitly diminish the king's powers. In fact, the document did diminish royal powers (e.g., the Privy Council was abolished, while royal writs had to be approved by the government). But King Prajadhipok supported Mano because, with the latter being a moderate royalist holding a high position of power, the king felt he could influence Mano, and this he did when he "pressed Manopakorn to purge ... revolutionists from the government by royal decree".[8]

Mano then chose the other fourteen members of the People's Committee: three senior officials from the previous absolute monarchy and eleven revolutionaries (eight of whom were military). Only in the armed forces did Khana Ratsadon loyalists take all the key positions (see 1932 reshuffle, appendix 4). Most importantly, Phraya Phahon became army commander, while Song Suradej was chosen as his deputy.[9]

Colonel Song was the second "Tiger" or "Musketeer" of the 1932 *patiwat*. Previously known as Thep Panthumsen, he was born on 12 August 1892 in Phra Nakhon province. He was the son of Lieutenant Thai Panthumsen, an artillery officer, and half-brother of Major Luang Naruesarnsamdaeng (Wan Panthumsen). Through the patronage and assistance of his family, Song matriculated into the Royal Army Cadet Academy of 1904. As the valedictorian in his class, Song, like Phraya Phahon before him, was given a scholarship to study engineering in Germany (the Prussian War School). He even served in the German army for a time. In 1913 Song received the rank of second lieutenant of Siam and returned to Siam that year. On 30 April 1915 he received the rank of lieutenant. By 1918 he had been promoted to become a major in charge of the Railway Engineer Battalion at Korat and was assigned the task of overseeing the construction of the Khun Tan to Chiang Mai railroad tunnel. He received the title of Phraya Song Suradej in 1924 and commanded the Ayutthaya Artillery Regiment, before being transferred to be the Headmaster of the Department of Military Studies in the same year (the palace had suspicions about him). In 1930, on an official mission to Paris, Lieutenant Prayoon Pamonmontri apparently convinced him to support the overthrow of the absolute monarchy. He eventually became the overall planner of the *patiwat*.[10]

The third "musketeer" of the *patiwat* was Colonel Phraya Ritthi Akkanay (formerly Sala Emasiri). Born on 14 January 1889, he was the son of Phraya Manusarasat Bancha (Siri Emasiri) and Khunying Leab Emasiri. Because of this noble heritage, he was easily able to enter the Royal Cadet Academy (class of 1899). Like Phraya Phahon and Song Suradej, he entered the artillery, and quickly rose to become a lieutenant colonel by 1915. He was appointed commander of the 5th Artillery Regiment in 1919 and commander of the 10th Artillery Regiment in 1921. As the only commander with infantry under his command, he was instrumental during the 24 June 1932 *patiwat*. After the regime change, Ritthi was appointed to the People's Committee (the first cabinet after the fall of the absolute monarchy), with Phraya Manopakorn Nittithada as prime minister.[11]

The fourth and final "musketeer" was Lt. Col. Prasas Pittayayuthorn. Prasas was previously called Wan Chutin. He was born into a military officer family on 9 June 1894 near Wat Bowonniwet in what is today Bangkok. He entered the Army Cadet Academy in 1908 and graduated in 1911. Since he had excelled at his studies, he was chosen to study at the Army Cadet Academy in Germany. He remained in Europe throughout World War I, though he did travel to Zurich, Switzerland, to study further. When Siam declared war on Germany in 1917, Prasas became a military diplomat under Maj. Gen. Pichai Chanritthi. After returning to Siam in 1921 he became an instructor at the Army Cadet Academy, and then served as the commander of the Army Staff School from 1926 to 1931, holding the rank of lieutenant colonel.[12] He was a close friend of Colonel Song Suradej, who convinced him to join the 1932 *patiwat*. Following this coup, Prasas joined the People's Committee.

Another important officer who was crucial in ensuring the success of the coup was Admiral Luang Sinthusongkramchai (previously Sin Kamolnawin). Born on 23 June 1901 in Samut Sahkon Province, he was the younger brother of the noble Phraya Ratchawangsan. Having studied at the prestigious Suankularb High School as a royal student, graduating in 1914, he was given a scholarship to study naval affairs in Denmark, going there in 1919. But while passing through Paris on a vacation, Thawee Bunyaket, a member of the civilian line of Khana Ratsadon, persuaded Sin to join the plan for the *patiwat*. Sin thereupon convinced other naval officers to join the plot, including Luang Supachalasai and Luang Thamrong Nawasawat. Many of these naval officers supported the civilian Pridi rather than army officers such as Phahon. Sin became the head of the naval line of Khana Ratsadon. By 1932 he had become a lieutenant naval commander and played a key role in the events of 23 June. After 1932, Sin held four cabinet positions, but he simultaneously dominated the navy from 1934 until 1951. Indeed, he was the longest-serving Thai navy commander, holding that post from 1938 until 1951.[13]

On 10 December 1932, the provisional constitution was replaced by a permanent constitution. At this point, the People's Committee resigned, replaced by a state council (cabinet) presided over by Phraya Manopakarn in his new role as prime minister. But Mano brought no consolidation to Siam's governance. Instead, within a few months, factionalism had begun to inundate the Mano coalition. The four cliques of the Mano government included civilian moderates led by Mano himself; senior officers who had participated in the 1932 overthrow of the absolute monarchy (led by Phahon and Song Suradej); royalists seeking a return to absolutism, led by princes Paribatra and Bowaradej; and, finally, a "junior clique", further disaggregated into a civilian faction led by Pridi Panomyong, a junior army faction led by Lt. Col. Plaek Phibun Songkram and a navy group.[14]

In trying to consolidate his position, Mano attempted several strategies. First, he tried to play the various factions off against each other, and even succeeded in dividing the faction of the senior officers. Indeed, Mano created an alliance with the new deputy commander of the army, General Song Suradej, as well as generals Prasas Pittayaudh and Phraya Ritthi, against Phraya Phahon.[15] Second, he accused Pridi of communism in connection with the latter's National Economic Plan, aggravating internal political dissension with the cabinet.[16] In April, Mano implemented an Anti-Communist Act, making it illegal to be a communist in Thailand. Since Pridi had been accused by the state of being a communist, he was forced to leave the country. Third, in mid-April 1933, at the instigation of the king, Mano closed the National Assembly, which prevented any debate on Pridi's plan, and, suspending parts of the 1932 constitution, began to rule by decree—mimicking monarchical and military governance. According to Natapoll, this in effect "amounted to a 'silent coup d'etat'".[17] Fourth, Mano began to re-organize the military, with eighty-two officers considered arch-royalists being promoted, and several junior officers being transferred to inactive positions or sent to further their studies overseas. As such, "Phibun's junior faction was literally being squeezed out of the power picture".[18]

Mano benefited from the fact that deputy army commander Phraya Song Suradej, who was the leader of the senior military faction, detested that members of the military faction led by Phibun were not sufficiently submissive to Song in the manner he expected. Thus, after 1932, Song, seeing Phibun as an ascending threat, sought to transfer him from his post of deputy artillery commander to an inactive position. But army commander Phraya Phahon failed to endorse Song's proposal, so it failed.[19] Meanwhile, Song Suradej sought to unite the Promoters against Pridi's progressive economic reform plan. Eventually, in April 1933, Phahon reluctantly agreed with Mano and Song that Pridi must leave Siam, and so Pridi went into temporary exile.

By June, Phahon, increasingly irritated with Mano's government, sought to send a message to the prime minister. Upon Song Suradej's recommendation that he join Song and two other leading officers in resigning from the government, Phahon responded favourably. Thereupon, Colonel Phraya Phahon, Colonel Phraya Song, Colonel

Phraya Rhitti and Lt. Col. Phra Prasas offered their resignations. In fact, Phahon thought the king would never accept the resignations. But Rama VII and Mano were only too eager to do so—the resignations were to become effective on 24 June 1933. Replacing Phahon and Song were Colonel Phraya Pichai Songkram as (acting) army commander and Colonel Phraya Sri Sitthi Songkram as head of army operations. Lt. Col. Plaek Phibun Songkram took Song's other post as army deputy commander while also continuing in the role of deputy commander-in-chief of the artillery.[20]

Maj. Gen. Phraya Phichaisongkram (Gap Sorayothin) was a highly regarded chief of staff of the Siamese Army during the reign of King Rama VI and King Rama VII. An avid arch-royalist, he had held the post of director general of the Army Strategy Department (responsible for the strategy and tactics of the army) for sixteen years.[21] In addition, he commanded the Army Staff School between 1917 and 1920.

Regarding Sitthi (or Din Tharab), he had been born into a middle-class farming family in Petchaburi province, and he was the valedictorian of his graduating military class. He studied in Germany alongside his friends Phraya Phahon and Phraya Song Suradej, and, like them, was part of the Thai military's so-called "Kaiser's faction" because of his German erudition. Din entered army service as a second lieutenant in 1914, becoming one of the youngest colonels—at the age of thirty-seven—in 1928. By 1930 Din was chief of staff of the army and chief of staff of the 1st Army simultaneously. Din was known to have been unhappy with inequities under the absolute monarchy, but he refused to take part in overthrowing it, though he did not act against the 1932 coup. Nevertheless, Din's lack of clear support for the coup earned him distrust from the post-1932 Khana Ratsadon leaders. Following the 1932 coup, Din had quarrelled endlessly with his old friend Phraya Phahon about which army position the former should be allotted. In the end, Phahon gave him a minor position in the Ministry of Education—clearly a demotion from his pre-1932 post of army chief of staff. Thus, Din was only too happy when Mano promoted him to the state council and the director of military operations (replacing Song Suradej).[22]

Mano's promotion of Plaek Phibun Songkram to one posting while allowing Phibun to continue holding another reflected enormous trust in this young officer. But who was Plaek Phibun Songkram? His original name was Plaek Khittisangka, with *plaek* (Thai for "strange") referring to the perception by his parents that his ears were strangely lower than his eyes. Born on 14 July 1897 close to Wat Paknam Temple in Nonthaburi province, Plaek came from a family that tended durian orchards. His paternal grandfather had migrated to Siam from China. Plaek matriculated into the Army Cadet Academy aged twelve in 1909, after his father begged the permanent secretary of the Royal Thai Army Cadet Academy, Phraya Surasena, to let Plaek and his elder brother, Pakrit, enter. Plaek studied at the academy until graduating as an artilleryman at the end of 1915, aged eighteen. He was initially stationed in the 7th Artillery Division as a second lieutenant in Phitsanulok. There he met Sakul Pankrawee (who became La-iad Phibunsongkram), then a high school student from a noble family. In 1916, aged fourteen, Sakul married Phibun, aged nineteen, in Phitsanulok. They had six children, including three who became military officers. By 1917, Phibun had moved to Bangkok to study at the Artillery School. He then returned to Phitsanulok and was subsequently stationed in the 1st Artillery Regiment, King's Guard, in 1919, becoming a 1st lieutenant in 1920 (under General Prince Pridithephong Thewakul). In 1921 he entered the Army Staff School, moved briefly to the Directorate of Army Operations and, in 1924, went to Fontainebleau, France, on a scholarship to study artillery science, where he remained until 1927.[23] He was promoted to the rank of captain in 1928 and awarded the title of Luang Phibun Songkram. But in Paris he had become influenced by the Promoters to support reform in or the overthrow of the absolute monarchy. Like other young officers, Phibun wanted to end the glass ceiling whereby princes had taken all the top security postings while military commoners' promotions to senior postings had been limited. But after the June 1932 *patiwat*, Phibun had kept his silence in terms of supporting Pridi's Economic Plan. For this reason, King Rama VII and Mano assumed that he was sufficiently royalist and thus allowed him to keep his postings.

With the principals of the 1932 "revolution" replaced, Rama VII pressured Prime Minister Mano to destroy the People's Party and he prepared to order the execution of all its members on 24 June 1933.[24] The king's planned orders, however, never became effective. On 20 June 1933, almost a year after the "revolution", Phahon sanctioned a coup against Mano's government, though it was actually led by junior officers (Phibun and navy deputy commander Bung Supachalasai) and their troops.[25] If the 1932 coup had been seen as a breakthrough event—marking a transition from royalist control of the military to the positioning of soldiers at the pinnacle of authority—the 1933 coup could be seen as the consolidation, once and for all, of the armed forces as the most important element of the power structure in Thai society.[26]

Following the putsch, Mano was ousted from office. Phahon took the prime ministerial position himself a few days later and invited Pridi to return home. As for the earlier resignations of Phahon, Song, Ritthi and Prasas, their military transfer orders had never been formalized; Phahon simply resumed his position as army chief. Likewise, Colonel Ritthi and Colonel Prasas resumed their posts as army artillery commander and army education commander, respectively. Interestingly, Phraya Song Suradej, who had grown increasingly distant from Phahon, refused to return as deputy army commander, leaving Phibun in the slot. Phahon now demoted Mano's army commander, General Pichai Songkram, to army reserve officer. Phraya Sitthi (Din) then found himself again enraged at Phahon as the latter reappointed him to the minor post of minister of education.

Yet, despite Phahon assuming control over Thai politics and administration, in 1933 there remained small enclaves of monarchical resistance, and military leaders were factionalized. In July, Lt. Col. Phibun Songkram, in his new post as acting deputy commander of the army, warned that he had heard rumours that former minister of defence Prince Bowaradej and others were planning an insurrection against the government. Then, at the beginning of October, former prime minister Mano (then retired in Hua Hin, Thailand) warned the "Promoter" Lieutenant Prayoon (who had lately sided with Mano) that a counter-revolution was impending. Such gossip soon proved correct. Almost like clockwork, on 11 October, Prince Bowaradej led an insurrection against Phahon's government, demanding its resignation on the grounds it had "encouraged the people to despise the king".[27] The navy, meanwhile, remained neutral. The counter-revolutionaries—leading army units from Khorat, Saraburi and Ayutthaya—called themselves the National Salvation Group, and their headquarters was centred at King Rama VII's Klai Kangwon palace, three hundred kilometres from Bangkok.

Their palace-endorsed "Blue Army Rebellion" was facilitated by continuing Depression-related economic malaise as well as the fact that many arch-royalist officers remained in sufficient numbers of strategic military positions. The king not only verbally endorsed the uprising but also supported it financially, while Queen Rambhai, her brother and other royals were actively involved in coordinating it. The arch-royalist Nation Party—which the monarch had failed to have accepted by Phahon as a parliamentary competitor with Khana Ratsadon—was tasked with organized support for the rebellion in Bangkok.[28] Bowaradej's motives likely were not simply to protect the royalty, since he had coveted the prime ministerial post that had instead been given to Mano[29] and then went to Phahon. The prince's crucial ally and deputy was none other than Phraya Sitthi Songkram, the half-hearted royalist who remained deeply angry with the Phahon government for depriving him of a senior state posting. But, unlike Bowaradej, Sitthi was a militarily capable leader with the potential to create problems for the government. At the time, the rebel group had captured Don Muang airport (seizing most air force commanders) and was readying to attack Bangkok, the centre of which Phahon had quickly converted into an armed military camp to brace for the attack. To buy time, Phahon at first negotiated with Prince Bowaradej while government troops moved towards Don Muang. Meanwhile, Song Suradej, who could have led security forces against the prince, was then out of the country in Ceylon with Phraya Ritthi. Song cabled Phahon that he could not return to help lead the operation against the rebel troops.[30] Song and Ritthi had, like other Promoters, heard rumours of the impending uprising, but they did not want to protect Phahon from it. Why? Most likely, Song still smarted from his perception that Phahon should have treated him better, that Siam was heading in too progressive a direction, and that, perhaps if the rebels were successful, he might be given a higher post in the army and cabinet.[31]

Phahon ordered Phibun to put together a field force to quickly defeat the rebellion. Phibun was chosen because, first, in actuality Phahon had no other choice as Phibun was the deputy; second, any failures by Phibun could excuse a decision by Phahon to demote him; and third, hunting down the rebels would keep the politically ascendant Phibun busy.

The Bowaradej rebellion was the bloodiest and longest coup attempt in post-1932 Thai history, involving house-to-house fighting and bombings in Bangkok and other cities, though it failed to dislodge Phahon and the People's Party. The rebellion lasted from 11 to 25 October and spread beyond Bangkok to Petchburi, Khorat and Ubon Ratchathani. During the insurrection, top navy officials refused to side with Phibun, contributing to anti-navy feeling among army officials, a phenomenon that would later intensify tensions between the two services.[32]

Working under Colonel Phibun to defeat the rebellion was the 4th Battalion, commanded by Colonel Ronasitthipichai and including platoon leader 2nd Lt. Sarit Thanarat. It was the 4th Battalion that captured Don Muang and then spearheaded the government assault on the retreating rebels back to Ayutthaya. And it was at Ayutthaya on 8 October that government forces, centred upon the 4th Battalion again, ultimately defeated the main rebel forces.[33] Thereupon, the Ubon and Prachiburi garrisons—which had unsteadily supported the rebels—began to waver in their loyalty, while only the Petchburi and Khorat garrisons continued to actively support the insurgents. In the end the rebel forces were pushed back to Khorat. Bowaradej was tasked with defeating the turncoat Ubon's troops, which were nearby, while Sitthi Songkram commanded soldiers to defeat the government troops. On 23 October, after five days of battle, state forces under Major Luang Weerayotha (Weera Weerayotha) defeated the rebel troops. In the aftermath of the battle, scattered rebel forces continued to engage in combat. One group of state forces pursued the rebels to a train station in Khorat, where the two sides engaged in gunfire. It was here that 2nd Lt. Praphas Charusathien, assigned to the 4th battalion in the platoon commanded by Sarit, fired a pistol shot that killed Colonel Phraya Sri Sitthi Songkram, deputy commander of the rebel forces.[34] On 25 October, with Sitthi dead and the rebel forces routed, Prince Bowaradej fled by plane to French Indo-China, where he then lived variously in Hanoi and then Phnom Penh. After a sixteen-year exile and asylum from the government, Bowaradej returned to Thailand in 1948, where he died in 1953.

Casualties from the rebellion included at least fifteen pro-government forces, including Maj. Gen. Luang Amnuay Songkram of the police (Thom Kesakomol), a leading figure of the Khana Ratsadon. In addition, at least fifty-nine soldiers and civilians were wounded, including future major general Luang Kat Katsongkram, then chief of staff of the Bangkok army, who was severely injured—his right ear was severed.[35]

With the defeat of the Blue Army Rebellion, attempts by royalists to force their way back to power evaporated. At this point, direct military rule over the country briefly returned until an indirect rudimentary election took place on 15 November 1933. Only candidates linked to the military-dominated directorate Khana Ratsadon (not the arch-royalist "Nation Party") could compete.[36]

The electoral result was no surprise: Phraya Phahon was elected to a four-year term. The poll validated the military's supremacy over the Siamese polity and Khana Ratsadon—as led by prime minister, defence minister and army commander General Phraya Phahon. Phibun Songkram allegedly viewed the elections of late 1933—and the 1933–37 half-elected parliament—as a direct challenge to his future political ambitions.[37]

The defeat of the uprising led directly to the intensifying influence of Colonel Plaek Phibun Songkram. Compared with the less appealing Prime Minister Phahon, Phibun was already considered by many soldiers to be the quintessential, charismatic, anti-royalist hero, given his success in putting down the Bowaradej rebellion.[38] In fact, a cabinet minister at the time stated that during Phahon's government the "real power rested with Phibun".[39] On 1 April 1934, Phibun was officially appointed to the post of permanent army minister and, simultaneously, that of deputy army commander. In September 1934, Phibun was appointed minister of defence—he was still only in his thirties—succeeding Phahon. Phahon continued on as army commander (concurrent with his position as prime minister) until 1938. But the prime minister needed Phibun because there continued to be dissension within the military establishment.[40] Some soldiers still backed the more conservative Song Suradej, and they were irritated at his ouster from the post of deputy army commander in 1933, as well as his ouster from the army service in 1934—the same year Phibun became defence minister and deputy army commander.

Other officers who had assisted Phibun in defeating the rebels benefited. For example, Luang Sinthu Songkram (who had proven his loyalty by guiding elements of the navy in support of the government) replaced Lt. Col. Phraya Wichit Chonlathi (who had briefly adopted a neutralist position with regard to Prince Bowaradej) as navy commander.

Meanwhile, as a result of his role in the government's victory, Sarit Thanarat was immediately promoted to the rank of first lieutenant. Two years later he was promoted to become an army captain.[41] In 1937, Sarit also became commander of the 4th Infantry Battalion.[42] Three more junior officers associated with Sarit continued to ascend in the army. Second Lieutenant Thanom Kittikachorn continued his training at Army Map School—finishing that coursework in 1934. Praphas Charusathien became first lieutenant in 1935. In addition, the younger Krit Sivara graduated from Chulachomklao as a probationary officer and acting second lieutenant in 1936. That year, he entered the Army Infantry School, Office of the Inspector General, and was in charge of platoon privates there until 1 April 1938. It was at this point that Krit met Captain Sarit, and they immediately became close. Sarit, Krit's mentor, slid into the role as the latter's military patron, propelling Krit up the military hierarchy. At that time, Sarit was the commander of the 4th Army Battalion but attached to the Army Infantry School. In 1938 the Army Infantry School was moved from Bangkok to Lopburi. Sarit and Krit were both transferred there. Krit then became probationary officer heading up platoon corporals at the school until 17 October 1940.[43]

In the aftermath of the 1933 royalist uprising, the Phahon government sought to make changes to the military reform that the state had implemented immediately after the 1932 overthrow of the absolute monarchy. That reform, decreed in July 1932 and originally conceptualized by Phraya Song Suradej, had emphasized reorganization of the structures and chain of command within the army. Because the military leaders of the People's Party who had overthrown the absolute monarchy were intermediate-level officers, they could not simply promote themselves to oversee large military units without factionalism centred on promotion disputes getting in the way. In addition, they were looking for a way to allot more command and sub-command positions to officers within the army. The People's Party therefore formulated a plan to dissolve larger units: cohorts, divisions and regiments. The country's two army regions—1 (Bangkok) and 2 (Ayutthaya)—were disbanded. The principal army unit now became the battalion, containing between 1,000 and 1,200 soldiers, which would encompass companies, then platoons, then squads. "All battalions were put under direct control of the army commander in order to strengthen the chain of command within the army and to prevent members of the army from staging a counter-revolution"[44] or coup. This structural reorganization was repeated in the navy. Thus, though military leaders remained in centralized administrative positions, the military itself became highly decentralized. Geographically, army units were divided across five "Military Provinces", which were (1) Bangkok, (2) Ayutthaya, (3) Prachinburi, (4) Nakon Sawan and (5) Nakorn Ratchasima.

In December 1933, two months after the rebellion, the Phahon government instituted a new military reform (the Act on the Order of Defence of the Kingdom of 1933), which transformed the five army provinces so that they became more hierarchically centralized (across two levels), while retaining the battalion as the principal unit. There were now five large army *monthon*—administrative areas that would cover the country—and within each were fourteen army provinces (see Figure 2.1). Because of the role the Ayutthaya garrison had in the 1933 rebellion, the city was deprived of any military headquarters.[45] A young Phin Chunhavan served as the first deputy commander of Monthon 3.

On 12 January 1934, King Rama VII left Siam for good, having failed to restore power for the monarchy. Though the Phahon government would have preferred that the king become its willing figurehead

FIGURE 2.1
Commanders under the Army Structure Act, 1933

Army Monthon	Monthon Commander	Army Provinces (counties)	Responsible for the Following Provinces
1. Bangkok	Phraya Phahon	Bangkok, Lopburi, Saraburi	Central Siam (14 provinces)
2. Prachinburi	Pra Pinit Senagan	Prachinburi, Chachoengsao	Eastern Siam (7 provinces)
3. Nakon Ratchasima	Pra Rengrugpajamitr; Deputy commander: Luang Chamnan Yutasak (Phin Chunhavan)	Nakon Ratchasima, Ubon, Udon	Northeastern Siam (14 provinces)
4. Nakon Sawan	Pra Graisornsittisarawut	Nakon Sawan, Phitsanulok, Lampang, Chiang Mai	Northern Siam (16 provinces)
5. Ratchaburi	Luang Senanarong (Sak Senanarong)	Ratchburi, Petchburi	Southern Siam (19 provinces)

Source: Based on Pratyakorn Lakhornphon, *The People's Party and Army Modernization in Thailand, 1932–1945* (Master's thesis, Thammasat University, 2018), pp. 100, 102.

within Siam (where it could monitor him), it was content to rule by fiat in the absentee monarch's name without allowing him any real authority whatsoever. At this point, Prajadhipok could only negotiate from weakness. Throughout 1934 he threatened to never return to Siam, and to abdicate, unless the Phahon government granted him more constitutional authority. He threatened to also sell royal properties, including palaces and even the jade Emerald Buddha statuette.[46] When the Siamese government rejected virtually all his demands, the king, on 2 March 1935, abdicated, living the rest of his life in self-imposed exile in Britain (dying in 1941). In his abdication letter, Rama VII condemned the Phahon government's use of military "autocracy" and "absolute power" to sustain itself.[47]

The departure of the angry Rama VII did not mean that Thais supported the post-1932 regime. In fact, Phibun himself clearly had enemies. On 23 February 1935, one week before King Rama VII abdicated, Phibun, in his role as minister of defence, was presiding at a football match in front of the royal palace in Bangkok, with senior officers of the military looking on. After handing out the trophy to the winning team, Phibun walked back to his car, followed by his secretary, Maj. Gen. Luang Sunawin Wiwat, and Captain Tuan Wichaikhatka, a close military officer. At that point, two gun shots rang out. Maj. Gen. Luang Sunawinwiwat then brushed the gun out of the shooter's hand before another shot could be fired. The shooter was Phum Thap Saithong, allegedly a hired gunman.[48] Pridi Panomyong later stated that the father-in-law of the former king, then living in Penang, was behind the attack.[49] Phibun was rushed to hospital. In the treatment room, Lt. Col. Luang Katsongkram directed the placement of guards at every entrance to keep Phibun safe; ultimately, the latter survived.[50]

In August 1935, a coup was attempted against the Phahon government. It was the only putsch ever attempted by non-officers. It became known as the Sergeant Rebellion, being led by sergeants Sawat Mahamad and M.L. Taweewong Watchareewong. The coup leaders were unhappy with the low standard of living of soldiers and the continued apparent neglect by commanders holding key positions. According to Handley, the coup attempt had royalist backing.[51] The coup was planned for 5 August, and preparations were made to kill important state leaders, including Colonel Phibun, minister of defence; Colonel Adul Adul Decharat, director general of the Police Department; and Phra Athit Thiphapha, the regent for King Rama VIII. Phibun, however, learned of the plot before it could take place. From 3 to 7 August he ordered sweeps and raids of military camps, arresting various sergeants and officers. In September, twelve soldiers were convicted. One of these (Sawat Mahamad) was executed.[52] Though the plan failed, leading to arrests and an execution, it reflected the lack of solid military cohesion behind the government.[53] Following this coup attempt, Phibun (supported by Phahon) began to keep a close eye on the leaders of the senior military Promoters faction. Phraya Song Suradej and Prasas Pittayayuthorn (Wan Chutin) were instructed to retire and were closely monitored.[54] Uniformed personnel who were thought to be their supporters were purged.

To buttress support among soldiers and officers for the government, the state vastly increased the military budget—which increased salaries for soldiers—during the mid-1930s. From 1932 until 1937, the military budget expanded from 13.3 million baht (18 per cent of the total state budget) to 32 million baht (27 per cent of that budget).[55] David Wyatt has noted that "the military budget doubled" for the period 1933–37.[56] According to him, the increase came from the leading military faction giving itself financial privileges, with the state expanding conscription and there being growing nationalistic military anticipation of a war looming in Asia.[57] According to Stephen Landon, a US missionary to Siam (1927–37) and later a US State Department expert on Thailand, the doubling of the country's military spending was part of efforts by Siam's defence minister Phibun to expand his political base in the military.[58] As part of his programme to militarize the country—with himself at its centre—Phibun employed the efforts of ideologue and propagandist Wichit Wathakan[59] to socially construct a martial philosophy that would be ubiquitous across the nation. Unlike the ideology of Rama VI (Vajiravudh), who had set in motion the idea that the king was the principal warrior guaranteeing the existence and safety of the Thai people, Wichit developed the notion that the country's saviour was the military alone, and the perfect model of "Thainess" was to be found in the military.[60] Through Wichit's influence, the Defence Ministry underwrote the making of a Thai movie called *Luat Thahan Thai* (The blood of Thai soldiers) to glorify Thai military patriotism. In 1935 the Defence Ministry created maps that disputed territory with neighbouring colonies held by Britain and France. Perhaps Phibun wanted to mimic fascist leaders; he saw Mussolini as exhorting Italy's past in terms of Roman legions, Hitler praising the Teutonic Knights, and Japan with its Bushido samurai warriors.[61]

On the advice of Wichit, in late 1934, in one of his early acts as minister of defence, Phibun began to set up a militaristic youth organization called Yuwachon Thahan (YT) or Soldier Youths. It was implemented more fully in 1935. YT's leader was Phibun's deputy, Prayoon Phamonmontri, who had visited Germany to view Nazi Germany's Hitler Youth Movement. A blatant copy of the Hitler Youth Movement, YT was for young men aged 15–22 years. Membership was voluntary, though encouraged by the state. Members were indoctrinated in irredentist ideology while undergoing three years of military training. A similar organization, Yuwanari, was formed for young women.[62]

In 1936, Song Suradej managed to have himself reinstated in the armed forces, though Phibun, as defence minister, placed him in a non-active and non-threatening post in Chiang Mai, far from Bangkok's politics. Song was already familiar with the Chiang Mai garrison, having overseen the completion of the Khun Tan railway tunnel to Chiang Mai in 1918. Indeed, within Chiang Mai, the Phahon government faced three potential opponents: (1) Song himself; (2) northern Buddhism, as led by forest monk Kruba Siwichai; and (3) Lanna royalty in the form of Lanna's Prince Kaew Nawarat. By 1939, all would be either forced into exile (Song) or dead (Kruba Siwichai and Kaew Nawarat). Their passing created a political vacuum in northern Thailand, which ensured that Phibun loyalists would gain control over the region. Before this, in 1937, Song had been elected to Siam's National Assembly, where he had the potential to create headaches for the government—and even run for prime minister.

As time passed, Phraya Phahon became an increasingly weak premier, with Phibun simply waiting in the wings to succeed him. Phibun, who espoused a proud authoritarianist nationalism for Siam, seemed preferable to many, who saw Phahon as weak since the latter relied on older non-Promoter officers in his cabinets and also gave in to parliamentary approval. The premier had formed six cabinets prior to 1937. Meanwhile, Phibun had managed to place his cronies in top positions of military power. These included General Phraya Sakdadunyut as permanent minister of defence (1934–41) and Colonel Jira Wichitsongkram as head of the Department of Army Operations (1934–39).

In 1937, Phraya Phahon once again announced the resignation of his government, this time amidst a parliamentary investigation into the selling of royal properties by the state (which, in some cases, ended in the hands of senior soldiers such as Phibun).[63] One prominent political leader tarnished by this scandal was a leader of the Promoters' senior army faction, Phraya Ritthi Akhaney.

In the general election of 7 November 1937, Phahon attempted re-election despite the scandal. In this election, the poll was for 91

FIGURE 2.2
Thailand's Legislature, 1932–46

Type of Legislature	Years	Appointed or Elected	Size
Unicameral	1932–33	Appointed	70, of which 56 (78.5%) military reserved domain
Unicameral	1933–37	78 elected by eligible voters; 78 appointed	156, of which 50 (64.1%) military reserved domain
Unicameral	1937–46	91 elected by eligible voters; 91 appointed	182, of which 58 (63.7%) military reserved domain)

Sources: Secretariat of the Senate (2001), pp. 1–3; Chaowana Traimat, *Data on 75 Years of Thai Democracy* (Konrad Adenauer Stiftung, 2007), p. 140; author's calculations.

members of the 182-seat National Assembly, with the other 91 appointed by the king. The 1937 election was remarkable, however, because it was the first poll in which the election was direct (though still no political parties were legally allowed). Once again, voter turnout was low. Following these November elections, Phahon was reappointed to a second term by the members of the assembly. Yet, shortly after the elections, his government encountered an even more hostile parliament. Heading an informal assembly grouping opposed to the government, Colonel Song Suradej was able to create various parliamentary obstacles for the government. Ultimately, in 1938, the assembly succeeded in forcing the government to resign after a vote of no-confidence, and new elections were held. This government censure further demonstrated that the military could suffer restrictions to its capacity from elected representatives—a lesson not lost on Phibun.

The power of the military in Thailand's legislative assembly during the 1930s can be seen in the fact that most parliamentary members were appointed and were from the military (see Figure 2.2).

In November 1938, Phahon, ill and in need of rest, refused to again field himself as a candidate for prime minister in the 12 November poll (once again for 91 members of the 182-member National Assembly). As such, Song, Phibun and Pridi Panomyong competed to fill the prime ministerial slot. The many opponents of Phibun, however, were divided in their support of Song (perceived as more conservative) and

Pridi (seen as more progressive).[64] The Assembly was split, and majority support for Phibun from the appointed parliamentary members catapulted him to the premiership.[65]

But, three days prior to the election, there was a second assassination attempt on Phibun. On the evening of 9 November, around 7 p.m., at the Bang Sue Artillery Regiment, Colonel Phibun stood in front of a glass table in the bedroom. He was preparing to officially send Colonel Mom Sanitwongseni (along with his wife) to be military ambassador to France. At that point, his own gardener, Nai Lee Bunta, attempted to shoot Phibun, but all the shots missed. Captain Phao Sriyanond—secretary to defence minister Phibun—helped snatch the gun from Buntha, who was sent to prison.[66]

The final assassination attempt against Phibun occurred on 9 December 1938. At the time, Colonel Phibun was eating lunch at Bang Sue Artillery Regiment with his wife, Thanpuying Laiad, four other colonels and Captain Phao Sriyanond. In the course of the meal, Phibun suddenly exclaimed that he had been poisoned. At that point he was rushed to the nearby Phrayathai Hospital. Doctors later stated that the lunch had been laced with arsenic.[67]

The state media reliably spread the news for Phibun about the latter's ability to survive three assassination attempts—and this created a popular allure about him that he possessed a special ability to overcome his enemies. Added to this was the fact that Phibun succeeded Phahon as premier in 1938.

Having reached the topmost political office, however, Phibun wasted no time in exacting revenge on any perceived political enemies. In some cases, Phibun ordered mass arrests as a result of his own hysteria, but for the most part the arrests amounted to a political purge of his enemies. He took aim specifically at three of the 1932 "Four Musketeers". Most importantly, Phibun targeted his nemesis Song Suradej (the second "Musketeer"). On 29 January 1939, two weeks after the visit to Siam of King Rama VIII, Song and fifty other soldiers were arrested for allegedly seeking to poison Phibun and plotting to overthrow his government. Phibun had already become extremely perturbed by Song's "War School" in Chiang Mai, which the prime minister felt could become a source of rebellion. Indeed, Phibun had often sent spies to monitor Song's activities in Chiang Mai. Following the graduation of the first cohort from the school in late 1938, Song led the twenty-nine elite graduates on a visit to Ratchaburi. However, Song was thereupon handed a directive to immediately leave government service, with no pension, and was, alongside the others, accused of treason.[68] The charges, regardless of their veracity, led to prison sentences for many plotters, including twenty-five sentenced to life and eighteen executed.[69] Phibun allowed Song to go into exile in French-ruled Cambodia.[70] There he lived with his wife in abject poverty, selling candies on the streets of Phnom Penh. He died in 1944 of sepsis, despite rumours he was poisoned.[71]

Phibun exiled the third musketeer, Phraya Ritthi Akhaney, to British-ruled Malaya, where the latter lived between 1938 and1946. In 1946, Ritthi returned home to serve briefly as a senator until the 1947 coup. Afterwards, he lived quietly in Samut Prakan province, dying aged seventy-seven in 1966.

The fourth of the Four Musketeers, Prasas Pittayayuthorn (Wan Chutin), was, in December 1938, appointed to become Siam's ambassador to Hitler's Third Reich in a sort of diplomatic exile. In fact, Wan was one of the last people to visit Hitler (on 20 April 1945) and survive. Captured by Soviet soldiers in Berlin, Wan spent 225 days in a Soviet concentration camp before being released.[72] After returning to Thailand, he died in 1947 of liver cancer from alcoholism.

Phibun did not exile the first of the Four Musketeers—Phraya Phahon. He saw the ailing man as of little threat and felt he might need him to help instil order across the armed forces. Thus, while Phibun became prime minister, defence minister, interior minister and army commander, Phahon was given the ceremonial posts of armed forces inspector-general and advisor. He largely retired from public life, although he did do some teaching at Thammasat University and in 1942 visited Japan as the head of a Thai-Japanese Celebratory, Diplomatic, Friendship Committee.[73] Phahon reluctantly returned to politics with the fall of Phibun's first government in 1944.

From 1938 until 1944, the period of the Phibun regime, several individuals were rotated through the senior positions in the Defence Ministry and armed forces. Only Phibun retained multiple postings simultaneously during this period in order to forestall coups against him (see 1938–44 reshuffles, Appendix 4). Phibun's official ascendance to power marked Thailand's transformation to a personalist autocracy—reviving a new variant of absolutist rule in the country. Parliamentary processes diminished rapidly, and the new government either executed, imprisoned or exiled anyone thought to be viable political opponents. Even Song Suradej was forced to flee the country.

By mid-1939, Phibun had succeeded in consolidating control. First, senior military commanders of the 1932 coup and royalist-oriented members of the military had been jailed, trotted out of the services or forced out of the country. Second, the influence of civilian leaders—such as Pridi Panomyong—was dramatically eclipsed by that of Phibun's military clique. Third, Phibun assured a major growth in budgeting for the armed forces. Indeed, after he became defence minister under Phahon in 1934, the defence budget increased from 15 million baht to 26 million baht in 1938, the year he became prime minister.[74] Thereafter, during Phibun's years as prime minister (1938–44), military expenditure reached 33 per cent of the national budget—the highest amount ever attained.[75] A disproportionate amount of funding was given to the army to assure its support for him and also to weaken opponents in the navy (the air force was as yet only a fledgling bureaucracy). Moreover, senior officers were allowed to enrich themselves by sitting on the boards of public corporations. Fourth, under Phibun, soldiers were given an increasing number of civilian administrative positions: in the cabinet, the number of military officers holding portfolios rose from 7 out of 15 (46.6 per cent) to 16 out of 26 (61.5 per cent), while the proportion of military officers holding parliamentary seats was high, at 63.7 per cent (see Appendix 2).[76] Fifth, Phibun ensured that allies in his Chulachomklao Military Academy class of 1914 possessed the prime spots among the top army brass. Indeed, he appointed a classmate, Colonel Adul Adul Decharat, to head Thailand's police force.[77] Sixth, besides serving as prime minister, Phibun took for himself the posts of interior minister, foreign minister and army commander. Finally, building upon the efforts of Wichit, Phibun manipulated military ideology towards an anti-French, anti-British and anti-Chinese nationalism in support of an irredentist "Thainess" and the glorification of the military. To this end, with the acquiescence of fascist ally Imperial Japan, he sent troops to fight against the French in Indochina, eventually succeeding in taking "historically Thai" parts of French Laos and Cambodia and northern portions of both British Burma and Malaya.[78] Such military expansionism helped to occupy the energies of soldiers who might plot against him. Ultimately—though Phibun imbued Thai society with nationalistic rhetoric to maintain public support—he relied on backing from the military.[79]

One person who Phibun relied heavily upon to thoroughly securitize his forceful control over the country was Colonel Adul Adul Decharat. Graduating from Thailand's Military Academy in 1916, Adul had already began work as a deputy in the Police Department in 1932. But he began serving as deputy interior minister and director-general of the Police Department in 1936. In the latter role, he proved to be an able enforcer, maintaining order across the state to such a degree

FIGURE 2.3
Phibun Family Tree

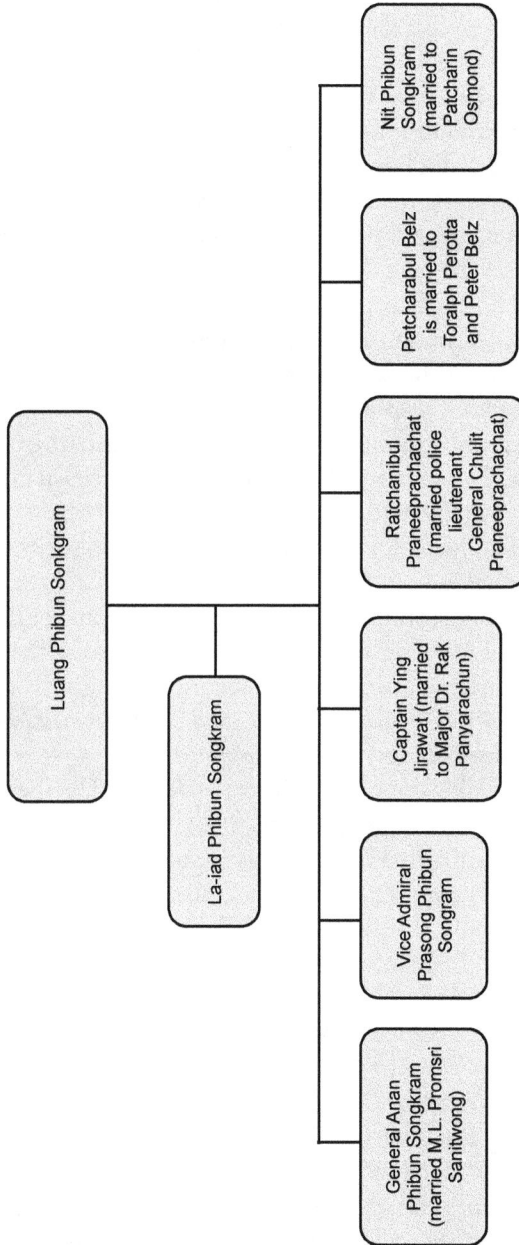

Luang Phibun Sonkgram

La-iad Phibun Songkram

General Anan Phibun Songkram (married M.L. Promsri Sanitwong)

Vice Admiral Prasong Phibun Songram

Captain Ying Jirawat (married to Major Dr. Rak Panyarachun)

Ratchanibul Praneeprachachat (married police lieutenant General Chulit Praneeprachachat)

Patcharabul Belz is married to Toralph Perotta and Peter Belz

Nit Phibun Songkram (married to Patcharin Osmond)

that he was not replaced when Phibun came to office in 1938. Indeed, with Adul not seeking to ascend further, the prime minister felt that he could trust him, and clearly did so—based on the fact he allowed Adul to hold the police commander post until Phibun's fall in 1944. In fact, Adul was fearsome and even ruthless, which is probably another reason Phibun liked him. He welcomed Japanese advisors to train the Thai police based on the Japanese model. In actuality, Adul's image as a tool for Phibun masked that he was willing to betray him—and he did. Indeed, Adul began to work secretly for the anti-Phibun Seri Thai Movement while he remained police chief.[80] But, as later events would prove, Adul was a political opportunist willing to go with the side that offered him the best deal.

By 1939, Phibun quickly began enhancing the leadership cult he had started developing as defence minister back in 1934. This cult was at the centre of the irredentist ultra-nationalism established and managed by Wichit. From June 1939 until January 1942, Phibun decreed twelve cultural mandates ("Ratha Niyom") as part of his new Sammai Sangchat. The first edict changed the country's name from Siam to Thailand—in line with Axis ally's name Deutchland (Germany). Thais were told to henceforth wear Western clothing instead of traditional dress. Indeed, a common expression in the media at the time stated: "Hat Leads Nation to Power."[81] Citizens were to eat meals at set times, and a vocal greeting of "*sawasdi*" was to replace the traditional Thai "*wai*".[82] Finally, patriotic reverence for the military was placed at the centre of society. Phibun also adopted economic nationalism, targeting Chinese participation in the economy.[83]

Despite his enormous political power during the period 1938–44, Phibun did not create any dynastic bastion of political power—which would have mirrored Siam's kings of yore. Instead, his family members, despite possessing senior security postings, lacked any power, given that their clout only reflected that of Phibun (see Figure 2.3).

By 1940, Phibun was seeking to rally Thais around the flag while casting around for alliances on the world stage. His models for a future Thailand were those of the countries and movements he sought to be closest with. Phibun's Thailand thus maintained very cordial relations with Nazi Germany, Mussolini's Italy, Imperial Japan, Franco's Spain and Chiang Kai-shek's New Life Movement (though, at Tokyo's urging, Phibun later called on Chiang to abandon his war against the Japanese occupation of China). Phibun especially took notice when Germany occupied France in June 1940 and Japan invaded French Indochina in September 1940. France had proposed a non-aggression pact with

Thailand in August 1939. France's Third Republic had secretly made a concession in the non-aggression agreement that it signed with Thailand on 12 June 1940. But the successor Vichy government refused to honour this concession. Nor did it agree to any more negotiations on the Indochina-Thai border. Instead, it demanded a non-aggression pact with no border concessions. At that point, with urging from the state, Thai students began to demonstrate across Bangkok. The Thai media painted a picture of France's new "National Humiliation" of Thailand, and Phibun spoke to Thais directly in a radio address explaining the border injustice to them. Among the outside powers, Japan was the only country sympathetic to Thailand. Troops of Thailand and French Indochina now both mobilized. French planes bombed Nakhon Phanom, and Thai troops invaded French Indochina on 5 January 1941. Two weeks later, Thai soldiers occupied Luang Prabang, Sisophon and Siem Reap.[84]

In planning the Indochina War, sometimes called the Franco-Thai War, Phibun wanted to put all the parts of the army to work. He thus established a field navy commanded by Rear Admiral Luang Singsongramchai. In addition, Thailand used its air force, under the command of vice air marshal Luang Athuk-Thewadejas. Phibun also brought back divisions and regiments to oversee battalions for the war effort. The two Thai armies that invaded French Cambodia were the Burapha (Eastern) Army and the Isaan (Northeastern) Army. Burapha, possessing five divisions, was commanded by Colonel Luang Prom Yothee. Yothee later served as Phibun's minister of defence (1941) and minister of the interior (1942–44), while in Phibun's second government he became education minister (1948–49). The Isaan Army—composed of eight divisions plus reserves, an anti-aircraft unit and signals—was commanded by Colonel Luang Kriangsakphichit, who later briefly served as army commander in 1944. Within the Isaan Army, the numerically large Pak Thai Mixed Division was led by Colonel Luang Senanarong, later the deputy army commander. The two armies were tasked with storming across Cambodia and coming together in Phnom Penh before turning around, heading northwards, and destroying French forces along the Mekong River before meeting the Phrayap Army at Vientiane.[85]

Among the Thai military officers involved in the Indochina War, as it came to be known, were several individuals who later gained enormous fame. They included future prime minister Lieutenant Chatchai Chunhavan, alongside his father, Colonel Phin Chunhavan, the commander of Army Monthon 3 (covering northeastern Thailand)

and the deputy commander of the Isaan Army, who arrived at the front lines on 12 December 1940. At the time, Chatchai was a platoon commander, 1st Cavalry Battalion, Royal Guards, and company commander of the King's Guard.[86] Another young cavalry officer was Lieutenant Prem Tinsulanonda, whose force clashed with the French at Poipet, Cambodia.[87]

The Thais fielded 60,000 troops (29 battalions out of a total of 44) against a force of 50,000 for French Indochina (which had 41 battalions). The French troops, however, had been depleted in fighting the Japanese as well as bandits in northern Tonkin. Thus, when the Thai forces first advanced in January 1941, they successfully took most of French Laos and small parts of French Cambodia. They then concentrated the majority of their efforts in Cambodia. But on 17 January 1941, five French naval ships (which were mostly dilapidated) were able to defeat a larger Thai force of two Japanese-built ships, two gunboats, 12 torpedo boats, and four submarines in what became known as the Battle of Koh Chang (Elephant Island).[88] Despite that single French victory, Japanese assistance ensured that Thailand was the victor in the overall Indochina War. With the end of the Indochina War, victory parades were held across Thailand. Phibun promoted himself from major general to field marshal, and also ordered the construction of the Victory Monument in Bangkok. Newspapers compared Phibun to King Taksin, who in the eighteenth century added territory to the kingdom. The territory that Thailand gained from Cambodia as a result of the Indochina War was, with the exception of Battambang province, renamed as Phibun Songkram province.[89] Thailand under Phibun and Vichy France–ruled Indochina now became uneasy Axis allies.

Nevertheless, the Japan-administered Tokyo Peace Accord, which had delivered territory from France to Thailand, left Phibun with a debt he owed to Tokyo—and Tokyo was going to take the quid pro quo. Indeed, in 1940, Phibun had signed a secret deal with Japan whereby he would grant Japanese troops safe passage to cross Thai territory to attack British colonies in exchange for Tokyo's support of Phibun's territorial claims. While he tried to bide his time, remaining neutral in World War II, he could not do it forever. Eventually, on 8 December 1941, Japanese troops entered Thailand at several points along its eastern and southern borders. Though Thai troops resisted fiercely, after a few hours the Phibun government agreed to an armistice. Then, following Japanese military success against the US (Pearl Harbor) and the sinking of two British warships, Phibun became convinced that Japan would be the final victor in the war. Thus, on 21 December 1941, Bangkok signed a military pact with Tokyo. That document formally reconfirmed Thailand's agreement to allow Japanese troops to pass through Thailand. It also ensured that the Thai army—as an ally of Japan—would remain intact.[90] Henceforth, Japanese troops were allowed to reside in or pass through Thailand. To obtain Thai popular support for the agreement, Phibun tried to connect Japan's Pan-Asian rhetoric with Phibun's own irredentist ultra-nationalism, further linking Japan and Thailand as a resistance against Western encroachers. Ultimately, the accord reached its likely conclusion: in January 1942, Thailand declared war on the United States and Britain. However, according to M.R. Seni Pramoj, the Thai ambassador to the United States, he refused to deliver the declaration of war to the Roosevelt administration and also ignored Phibun's recall of him back to Thailand. Nevertheless, "there is nothing in [US Secretary of State Cordell] Hull's office diary or other State Department records to support this story".[91]

Be that as it may, Seni and a large Thai diaspora in the United States and Britain became important opponents of Phibun's alliance with Japan and war against the Allies. Meanwhile, Pridi Panomyong, now serving as privy counsellor to King Rama VIII, was perhaps the most powerful opponent of Phibun still in Thailand. Ultimately, Seni abroad and Pridi in Thailand together formed and served as the leaders of the Seri Thai (Free Thai or Free Siamese) Movement, though they often bickered on how to proceed. In addition, Thailand's military attaché to the United States, Lt. Col. M.L. Khap Khunchon (Kharb Kunchara)—previously a friend and secretary-general to Prime Minister Phibun—became an enthusiastic sub-leader of Seri Thai, though Seni often quarrelled with him. The actual movement within Thailand began operating in early 1943, and it received training and other assistance from the United States' Office of Strategic Services (OSS), the forerunner of the Central Intelligence Agency. OSS head William Donovan was enthusiastic about setting up Seri Thai. His organization began training Thai volunteers on 13 June 1942. That was the same day that President Franklin Roosevelt signed the order that created the OSS.[92] From US planes, Seri Thai volunteers would often parachute into Thailand to conduct surveillance of Japanese or Thai forces. They would also engage in guerrilla operations against them. In the end, Pridi became the leader of Seri Thai in Thailand, with Thai police chief Colonel Adul Adul Decharat secretly acting as Seri Thai deputy leader.

Other Thai military figures who joined Seri Thai, either overtly or covertly, were the following: Lt. Gen. Kat Katsongkram and his son

Colonel Karun Keng, Maj. Gen. Luang Dechatwong Warawat (Mom Luang Kree Dechatiwong), Major (honorary) Khuang Aphaiwong, Lt. Col. Suphasawad Wongsanit Sawatdiwat, Captain Luang Supachalasai (Bung Supachalasai), Air Chief Marshal (ACM) Sitthi Sawetsila, ACM Tawee Chulasub, Captain Krachang Tularak and, from the police, Major Phon Intharathat and Lt. Col. Pangkun.[93] They later played roles on Thailand's political stage.

After the Phibun government's declaration of war on the Allies in January 1942 and establishment of an alliance with the Axis Powers, the prime minister commenced parts two and three of his territorial expansion plan. With prodding from Japan, which was attempting to defeat British forces in Burma, Thailand created a new field army called the Phrayap (Northern) Army, which, in May 1942, entered Burma's Shan States and occupied the area around the old city of Kengtung. The Phrayap Army was a perfect military tool for the Japanese because it was composed of non-Japanese nationals in support of Tokyo's war objectives. The Phrayap army was commanded by Lt. Gen. Charun Ratanakun (Seriroengrit), who was highly skilled in using the railway to transport supplies to the Thai-Burma border to build up the Phrayap force, given that Charun had been the director-general of the Thai state railway from 1936 to 1942.

The Phrayap Army was composed of four divisions. These included the 2nd Infantry Division, which contained nine infantry battalions, three artillery battalions and some supporting units. The division was commanded by Maj. Gen. Luang Phairirayordejd. The 3rd Infantry Division was meanwhile commanded by Maj. Gen. Phin Chunhavan.[94] It included nine infantry battalions, three artillery battalions, a motorcycle reconnaissance squadron and a tank squadron. The 4th Infantry Division, also part of the Phrayap Army, included six infantry battalions and two artillery battalions. It was commanded by Colonel Luang Haansongkhram. Finally, the Cavalry Division, commanded by Lt. Col. Thwuan Wichaikhatkha, contained cavalry and tank battalions.[95]

Future military strongman Captain Sarit Thanarat was appointed as commander of the Phrayap Army's 33rd Battalion (Phitsanulok), which was part of the 2nd Infantry Division. Serving under Sarit was future army chief Lieutenant Krit Sivara as a company commander. Having directly worked for Sarit in the Phrayap Army, Krit became quite close and loyal to the former, perhaps more so than future dictators General Thanom Kittikachorn and General Praphas Charusatien, neither of whom served in Sarit's 33rd Battalion. The 33rd, composed mostly of inexperienced reservists, was ordered to take battle positions only three months after having been formed. Under the command of the 12th Regiment (of the 2nd Division), the 33rd Battalion was first stationed on the Thai-Burma border at Mae Sot, then at Phitsanulok, where the unit was charged with guarding the rail line. Later on it was ordered to march to Chiang Dao and Pai in northern Thailand. In 1942, following intensive Japanese bombing, the Phrayap Army's 3rd Division, commanded by General Phin Chunhavan, succeeded in conquering and occupying Kengtung, Burma. Other units, including the 12th Regiment, reinforced the 3rd Division in Kengtung. Then, at Phin's direction, the 12th Regiment was ordered to take Muang Ma and Muang La in Burma.[96] The attacks, ultimately spearheaded by Sarit's 33rd Battalion, proved successful, with the result that the 33rd and Sarit immediately came to Phin's attention. By the end of Thailand's military involvement in Burma's Shan States in 1944, Sarit and Krit had become close comrades in war, and a younger 2nd Lt. Prem Tinsulanonda (later Thailand's prime minister and Privy Council chair) had served under them.[97] Other Thai soldiers who served in the Phrayap army and later became famous included future army commander Serm na Nakorn and supreme commanders Thanom Kittikachorn, Kriengsak Chomanand and Saiyud Kherdpol.

By 1943, the Phrayap Army had prevailed in the Shan States. By the treaty of 20 August 1943, Japan recognized Thailand's control over the Kengtung area. Be that as it may, Phibun was beginning to have doubts that the Axis Powers would win the war. In January 1943, he ordered the Phrayap Army to open relations with anti-Axis Chinese armies along the Yunnan-Burma border. One such army was the 93rd Division of the Kuomintang at Meng Hai in the Thai Lü district of Sipsongphanna (Xishuangbanna) in Yunnan, China. Both the 93rd and the Phrayap Army were involved in smuggling opium as a means of acquiring badly needed income. The two sides quickly agreed to cease hostilities. Then, in March–April 1944, an OSS-directed Seri Thai team led by Khab Kunchon contacted elements of the 93rd and Phrayap forces, where Khab discovered about the informal ceasefire.[98] Khab sent a letter to a former student in the Phrayap army, discussing the need for Thai troops to switch sides at the appropriate moment as the war wore down and the Allies looked set to win. The letter, which was later seen by Phibun himself, helped to increase cooperation among Seri Thai, the Phrayap Army and the 93rd Division. Khap's American friends stationed in Kunming, China, were Lt. Col. Willis H. Bird and Colonel Paul Helliwell, themselves close to OSS director William Donovan.[99] Nevertheless, many OSS officers in Washington distrusted

Khap because of his close ties to Chinese opium kingpin Tai Li.[100] The structure whereby elements within the Phrayap Army, the 93rd and the OSS built up wartime ties in 1944—which included the profitable distribution of opium—set the stage for such continued collaboration by Thai, Chinese and US CIA officers further down the road.

Having taken control over the Shan States in 1943, Phibun now claimed to the Thai people that he had succeeded in doing what no king in Thai history had ever done—conquered the Shan, a people ethnically similar to the Thai. But Phibun was not finished yet. On 20 August 1943, following diplomatic moves by Tokyo, Phibun was able to obtain control for Thailand over the British-controlled Malay States of Perlis, Kedah, Kelantan and Trengganu (which had once been controlled by Bangkok).[101] Thailand had now grown geographically to the north, south, east and west. Moreover, the prime minister's propaganda machine ensured that all Thais knew that Phibun alone had overseen the expansion. It was Phibun who had recovered territories lost by Thai kings. But Phibun was also a prime minister who had declared martial law in 1938, and, because of the rationale of war, ruled by decree. His ultra-nationalistic authoritarianism seemed to know no bounds. Nevertheless, these were unstable times for the country; perhaps any prime minister would have resorted to martial law given the severe economic and political difficulties of the 1930s.

Imperial Japan worked hard to assist Thailand's economy and military. Indeed, Tokyo sent large amounts of economic and military aid, and even poured money into the local economy, a Keynesian policy that irritated Thailand's conservative elites. Likewise, Thai troops and military officers were trained by the Japanese in Japan's methods of military organization and strategic culture during the period 1942–44.[102] Nevertheless, according to a US government report at the time,

> [Though] the Japanese have succeeded in making Thailand a base for military operations in Burma and for carrying supplies to Malaya … the Japanese have received practically no support from the Thai navy and air force and very little from the army. Thai troops have undertaken to defend the Kengtung border against the Chinese, but they have not done so in the spirit or with the intention of fighting Japan's war.[103]

Yet Phibun's dominance in Thai politics was not to last. His close alliance with the militaristic Japanese, and the fact that the latter looked in 1944 to be losing the war, ultimately contributed to Phibun's fall. In addition, the Thai economy was in tatters and, as such, the government was rapidly losing domestic support. Thus, by the summer of

1944, a majority of the public had become dissatisfied with him. That dissatisfaction had spread to the military and the National Assembly. Members of Phibun's own cabinet, including more top military officers (in addition to police chief Adul Adul Decharat) began to secretly turn to favour the Seri Thai resistance.

In late May 1944, a period during which the National Assembly was not in session, Phibun's government issued two emergency decrees pertaining to the reorganization and improvement of Petchabun city's administration and the construction of a Buddhist centre in Saraburi city. When the assembly began its regular session on 24 June, the government, as required by the constitution, submitted bills requesting the assembly's acceptance of the two decrees. At the time, the National Assembly had largely acted as a rubber stamp for Phibun, especially as he had sometimes declared martial law anyway (e.g., during the Indochina War). But Thailand was not under martial law in 1944. By summer, political opponents of Phibun were becoming more daring. It is in this environment that, on 24 July, parliament denied passage of these two bills. Phibun responded by offering his resignation, apparently expecting this to be refused in parliament, but the assembly accepted it as most in the legislature now supported Pridi Panomyong in his role as royal regent and leader of the increasingly powerful anti-Phibun and pro-US Seri Thai Movement.[104] In any case, the majority of Thai politicians (and soldiers) did not have to be readers of tea leaves to see that the tide had turned against Phibun. Most now turned against him, while the military became disunited. As regent, Pridi accepted Phibun's resignation. However, General Phraya Phahon, tired and ailing, refused to return as prime minister. The position finally went to the civilian Khuang Aphaiwong. Civilians and soldiers now nervously wondered what Phibun would do next.

In conclusion, the period 1932–44 represented the triumph of Thailand's military over the monarchy. Especially after October 1933, armed forces leaders, led by Phraya Phahon, jettisoned royalists from any remaining positions of authority, replacing them with anti-royalist loyalists. There was also a military reform that reorganized the structures and commands of the armed forces as a means of staving off any future royalist uprising, while also decentralizing the military. Finally, the military introduced elections to the country, if only as a means of balancing factions and legitimizing its own political control. Though a few civilians such as Khuang Aphaiwong[105] were allowed to sit on the cabinet, the military never allowed a civilian to become prime minister.

The period 1938–44 represented not just institutional supremacy by the armed forces but, rather, the personalized control over the military and the country by Field Marshal Phibun Songkram. Phibun became the "Caesar" across Thailand, and his word was fiat. As a Caesar, Phibun followed the model of Thailand's pre-1932 kings: he ruled as though the country was under his absolute monarchical control. Ideologically, however, he was an extreme anti-royalist. At the same time, he never created a lineage or dynasty that would keep his family in power. However, Phibun finally connected Thailand closely with the Fascist regimes of the Axis powers such that Thailand ended up on the losing side of World War II. While his alliances with Hitler and Tojo thus contributed to his own demise, it also partly weakened the control over Thailand of the pro-Axis armed forces. As a result, in July 1944, when Phibun resigned as prime minister, supreme commander and armed forces commander, what remained standing was a demoralized and factionalized military. Moreover, as Wright metaphorically stated, "it was [like] 1932 again".[106] The ailing Phraya Phahon again became supreme commander (under a different military title). But Phibun's allies still held leading posts: pro-Phibun General Phichit Kriangsakphichit was defence minister and army chief in August 1944.

Nevertheless, with Phibun gone and the military politically frail, a political vacuum appeared that allowed civilians the chance to construct a pluralist regime that had never existed before in the country. Building such a regime was possible because five factors appeared at the same time in July 1944 to produce a critical juncture: (1) the continuing weakness of the monarchy; (2) the sudden decline of the military; (3) the rise of Pridi Panomyong as Seri Thai leader and champion of a civilian-led Thai democracy; (4) unpopularity of Phibun and intensifying support of urban Thai people for elected civilian rule; and (5) support for civilian rule by the United States. It was this critical juncture that would give Thailand a chance to upend the entrenched authoritarianism which had dominated the country's past. The hope for achieving a form of elected civilian rule that would guarantee control over praetorian forces was certainly real. Whether civilian rule could sustain itself was another question.

Notes

1. *Phonphrayuhasena* is a high honorific for senior Siamese military officers, which Phahon held until 1931.
2. Judith A. Stowe: *Siam Becomes Thailand: A Story of Intrigue* (Hurst: London, 1991), p. 370; Thawan Thamrongnawasawat, พิมพ์ฉักนัยเงิน พระ รัชธาร พระเพลิง สบพนุโท พระยาพหลพลพยุหเสนา (พจน์ พหลโยธิน) นามีน วัดเบญจมบือพิต

วันที [Cremation volume for General Phahonphonphayuhasēnā (Phot Phahonyothin) from Wat Benchamabophit Temple] (Bangkok: Thawan Thamrongnawasawat, 17 April 1947).

3. S. Plainoi. พระยาพหลฯ นายกรัฐมนตรีผู้ซื่อสัตย์ [Phraya Phahon, the honest prime minister] (Bangkok: Matichon, 2012).

4. Calculated by the author from the original list.

5. Thawan, พิมพ์ฉกนัยเงิน พระรัชธาร พระเพลิง.

6. Phahon had originally wanted Prince Bowaradej to take this position. But Pridi Panomyong prevailed on Phahon to nominate Mano instead because Bowaradej was a close relative of King Prajadhipok and could not be trusted, even though Bowaradej had had a cold relationship with other princes about the budget, leading to his 1931 resignation and reports that he would have supported a regime change. The nomination of Mano further angered Bowaradej as he had expected Phahon to appoint him as prime minister. Nakarin Mektrairat, พระยามโนปกรณ์นิติธาดากับการเมืองสยามในปี พ.ศ. 2475: ความคิด ความรู้ และอำนาจในการเมืองในการปฏิวัติสยาม 2475 [Phraya Manopakorn Nithithada and Siamese politics in 1932: Thought, knowledge and power in politics in the Siamese Revolution of 1932], 3rd ed. (Bangkok: Same Sky, 2017); Thawatt Mokarapong, *History of the Thai Revolution: A Study in Political Behavior* (Bangkok: Chalermnit, 1972), pp. 128, 132, 201.

7. Chris Baker and Pasuk Phongpaichit, *A History of Thailand* (Cambridge: Cambridge University Press, 2005), p. 119.

8. Paul Handley, *The King Never Smiles* (New Haven: Yale University Press, 2006), p. 50.

9. The eleven included Phahon, Song Suradej, Phraya Ritthi, Phraya Prasas, Pridi, Luang Plaek Phibun Songkram, Luang Sinthu and Prayoon. Meanwhile, the Promoters allowed many prominent posts to go to individuals who played no role in the 1932 coup. The Promoters realized that they needed the acquiescence of professional bureaucrats to consolidate the country's administration and public policies regardless of partisan tilt. Officers thought to be untrustworthy (14 generals and 22 colonels in the army as well as 5 captains in the navy) were either transferred to unimportant posts or simply dismissed. Thawatt, *History of the Thai Revolution*, p. 133.

10. See Suea Supasophon, *The Life and Struggle of Phraya Song Suradej* (Bangkok: Subcommittee on Publishing the 60th Anniversary Democracy Project, 1992).

11. อนุสรณ์ในงานพระราชทานเพลิงศพ พันเอก พระยาฤทธิอัคเนย์ ป.ม. ณ เมรุหน้าพลับพลาอิศริยาภรณ์ วัดเทพศิรินทราวาส [Memorial at the cremation ceremony of Colonel Phraya Ritthi Akkanay, at the crematorium of the Isariyaphon pavilion Wat Thepsirintrawat], 25 May 1967.

12. อนุสรณ์ในงานพระราชทานเพลิงศพ พระประศาสน์พิทยายุทธ [Memorial album from the cremation ritual for Lt. Col. Prasas Pittayayuthorn], 30 December 1950.

13. อนุสรณ์ในงานพระราชทานเพลิงศพ พลเรือเอก สินธุ์ กมลนาวิน (หลวงสินธุสงครามชัย) [Memorial for the cremation ceremony of Admiral Sinth Kamolnawin

(Luang Sinthusongkramchai)], royal cremation at the crematorium in front of the pavilion Wat Thepsirintrawat, 15 December 1976.

14. Robert Kiener, *An Analysis of the 1981 Unsuccessful Thai Coup* (Hong Kong: University of Hong Kong, 1992), p. 24.

15. Joseph Wright, *The Balancing Act* (Oakland, CA: Pacific Rim; Bangkok: Asiabooks, 1991), pp. 70–71.

16. Ibid., pp. 70–72.

17. Thamrongsak Petchlertanand, cited in Natapoll Chaiching, "The Monarchy and the Royalist Movement in Modern Thai Politics, 1932–1957", in *Saying the Unsayable: Monarchy and Democracy in Thailand*, edited by Soren Ivarsson and Lotte Isager (Copenhagen: NIAS, 2010), p. 156.

18. Kiener, *An Analysis*, p. 27.

19. Thawatt, *History of the Thai Revolution*, pp. 177–78.

20. Ibid., p. 161.

21. Royal Thai Army, "Former Directors of Operations", https://doo.rta.mi.th/DooNew/main_commander_old_1.html.

22. Kulab Saipradist, เบื้องหลังการปฏิวัติ 2475 [Behind the revolution of 1932] (Bangkok: Chamlong Sarn, 1947), p. 160.

23. อนุสรณ์ในการบรรจุอัฐิ ฯพณฯ จอมพล ป. พิบูลสงคราม ณ วัดพระศรีมหาธาตุ [Memorial volume from the cremation ritual of His Excellency Field Marshal P. Phibunsongkhram at Wat Phra Si Mahathat], 30 July 1964.

24. Natapoll, "The Monarchy and the Royalist Movement", p. 156.

25. Kiener, *An Analysis*, p. 26.

26. Samuel Huntington divides all coups into breakthrough, consolidating and anticipatory. See Samuel Huntington, *Political Order in Changing Societies* (New Haven, CT: Yale University Press, 1968), p. 205.

27. Quoted in Wright, *The Balancing Act*, p. 77.

28. Natapoll, "The Monarchy and the Royalist Movement", pp. 157–59.

29. Thawatt, *History of the Thai Revolution*, pp. 128, 132, 201.

30. Wright, *The Balancing Act*, p. 78.

31. Thawatt, *History of the Thai Revolution*, pp. 128, 132, 205.

32. Ibid.

33. "The History and Works of Field Marshal Sarit", Bangkok 1964, translated and edited by Thak Chaloermtirana, in *Thai Politics: 1932-1957* (Social Science Association of Thailand, Thammasat University, 1978), p. 693.

34. General Banchorn Chawansilp, "Mystery Bullet 'Phraya Sisitthisongkram' (Din Tharab) while the Bowondej Rebels Fled", Silpa-mag.com, 3 July 2022, https://www.silpa-mag.com/history/article_48932.

35. TNEWS, "พลิกปูมประวัติศาสตร์!!! «หลวงกาจสงคราม» ผู้เอารัฐธรรมนูญฉบับที่ 4 ไปซ่อนไว้ใต้ «ตุ่ม» ช่วงรัฐประหาร 2490 เหตุใดเขาถึงต้องทำขนาดนั้น?", 4 April 2018, https://www.tnews.co.th/politic/308511.

36. Indeed, with political parties illegal until 1955, only loose political groupings in parliament existed. All candidates thus ran formally as independents, to elect 78 of the 156 members of the National Assembly, with the other 78 appointed by the king. The elections were held on an indirect basis, with voters electing sub-district representatives between 10 October and 15 November, and the representatives then electing members of parliament on 16 November. Turnout was low in this first election in Siam's history.

37. Wright, *The Balancing Act*, p. 96.

38. James Thompson, "The Thai Military: An Analysis of its Role in the Thai Nation" (PhD dissertation, Claremont Graduate School, 1974), p. 40.

39. Thawee Bunaket, cited in Jayanta Ray, *Portraits of Thai Politics* (New Delhi: Orient Longman, 1972), p. 74.

40. David Wilson, *Politics in Thailand* (Ithaca: Cornell University Press, 1962), p. 175.

41. *Kom Chad Leuk*, "Today in the Past, June 16, is the Birthday of Field Marshal Sarit, the Leader of Comprehensive Power", 16 June 2017, https://www.komchadluek.net/today-in-history/282683.

42. "History and Works of Field Marshal Sarit", pp. 692–93.

43. *Krit Sivara Life and Works* (cremation volume), p. 1.

44. Pratyakorn Lakhornphon, "The Army of the People's Party (Khana Ratsadon): The Reform of the Thai Army in the Period of Political Transition (1932–1933)", *Thammasat Journal of History* 7, no. 2 (2020): 65–69.

45. Pratyakorn Lakhornphon, "The People's Party and Army Modernization in Thailand, 1932–1945" (Master's thesis, Thammasat University, 2018), pp. 97–99.

46. Handley, *The King Never Smiles*, p. 53.

47. He ignored, however, that his own government had employed repressive aspects of reactionary, monarchical absolutism to persist in power. Also, on 2 March 1934, Khana Ratsadon's rubber stamp National Assembly appointed Prajadhipok's child nephew Ananda to succeed him. The choice of Ananda derived from the hope that he would be easily manipulated. Wright, *The Balancing Act*, p. 80.

48. Vichit Na Pombhejara, *Pridi Panomyong & the Making of Thailand's Modern History* (Bangkok: Ruankaew, 1983), p. 110.

49. Scot Barme, *Luang Wichit Wathakan and the Creation of a Thai Identity* (Singapore: Institute of Southeast Asian Studies, 1993), p. 171n5.

50. "Assassination Attempts against Field Marshal Phibun Songkram", Silpa-mag.com, 9 July 2022, https://www.silpa-mag.com/history/article_54516.

51. Handley, *The King Never Smiles*, p. 58.

52. KomChadLeuk, "August 3, 1935: 'The Sergeants' Rebellion' Ended but Not Yet Started", 3 August 2018, https://www.komchadluek.net/today-in-history/337387.

53. Supaluck Suvarnajata, *The Thai Military Coup de'Etat: Origins, Withdrawal/Military Control, and Perspectives* (PhD dissertation, Claremont Graduate School, 1994), p. 121.

54. Wright, *The Balancing Act*, p. 87.

55. Pratyakorn, "The People's Party", p. 82.

56. David Wyatt, *Thailand: A Short History* (New Haven, CT: Yale University Press; Chiang Mai: Silkworm Books, 2003), p. 238.

57. Ibid., p. 238.

58. Kenneth P. Landon, *Siam in Transition* (New York: Greenwood, 1968), p. 54

59. Wichit began his career as a junior member of Siam's Foreign Service under King Rama VI in 1918, continuing to work under King Rama VII until the overthrow of Siam's absolute monarchy in 1932. Wichit, serving in Paris in the 1920s, had shown his support for the Khana Ratsadon and had met with Pridi Panomyong and Phibun Songkram prior to 1932. See Baker and Pasuk, *A History of Thailand*, p. 117.

60. Barme, *Luang Wichit Wathakan*, p. 181.

61. E. Bruce Reynolds, "Phibun Songkhram and Thai Nationalism in the Fascist Era", *European Journal of East Asian Studies* 3, no. 1 (2004): 106.

62. Both organizations—as well as another one, Luk Sua (a forerunner of the later Luk Sua Chaobaan in the 1970s)—merged in 1943 to become a National Youth Organization. In 1943 the Japanese state media agency Domei noted approvingly that when the YT movement's objectives are "fully realized ... the people of Thailand will all be soldiers". Reynolds, "Phibun Songkhram", p. 109.

63. Fred Riggs, *Thailand: The Modernization of A Bureaucratic Polity* (Honolulu: East-West Center Press, 1966), p. 230.

64. B.J. Terwiel, *Field Marshall Plaek Phibun Songkram* (University of Queensland Press, 1980), p. 12.

65. Charnvit Kasetsiri and Sothaphum Boonma, eds., จอมพล ป. พิบูลสงคราม และ ท่านผู้หญิงละเอียด กับการเมืองไทยสมัยใหม่ [Field Marshal P. Pibulsongkram and Thanpuying La-iad in modern Thai politics] (Bangkok: Social Sciences and Humanities Textbook, Project Foundation, 2021).

66. "Assassination Attempts", Silpa-mag.com.

67. Ibid.

68. KomChadLeuk, "Retracing the Life of 'Rival' Field Marshal Por: Rebellion, Refuge, and Banana Snacks!", 1 June 2018, https://www.komchadluek.net/today-in-history/328373.

69. Pleng Supa Rieprieng, *The 18 Corpses Coup* (Pailinbooknet, 2010), pp. 76–77.

70. Soonruth Bunyamanee, "A Chronicle of Failed Coups", *Bangkok Post*, 7 September 2008, http://www.bangkokpost.com.

71. The theory that he was poisoned owes to Song's famous good health. Some say that when Phibun was overthrown in 1957, Song was still alive,

aged 65; he then returned to Thailand, lived in Surin, and died on 1 June 1973 at the age of 80. See KomChadLeuk, "Retracing the Life".

72. *225 days in the Russian Prison of Major General Phrasaspittayayuth*, cremation volume of Mrs. Prasat Pittayayuth (Naow Chutin) at the crematorium of Wat Makutkasatrivaram Worawihaan, 1948.

73. General Phraya Phahonpolpayusena, cremation volume, 17 April 1947.

74. Thompson, "The Thai Military", pp. 40–41.

75. Chai-anan Samudavanija, *The Thai Young Turks* (Singapore: Institute of Southeast Asian Studies, 1982), p. 12.

76. Chaowana Traimat, *Data on 75 Years of Thai Democracy* (Konrad Adenauer Stiftung, 2007), p. 140; author's calculations.

77. Wright, *The Balancing Act*, p. 93.

78. John Girling, *Thailand: Society and Politics* (Ithaca: Cornell University Press, 1981), pp. 106–7.

79. David Elliot. *Thailand: Origins of Military Rule* (London: Zed Books, 1978), p. 88.

80. Paul Chambers, "The Partisan History of Police Power in Thailand", *New Mandala*, 2 March 2020, https://www.newmandala.org/the-partisan-history-of-police-power-in-thailand/.

81. Wright, *The Balancing Act*, p. 101.

82. Ibid., p. 103.

83. See William Skinner, *Leadership and Power in the Chinese Community of Thailand* (Ithaca: Cornell University Press, 1958); Riggs, *Thailand: The Modernization*.

84. Shane Strate, *The Lost Territories: Thailand's History of National Humiliation* (Honolulu: University of Hawai'i, 2015), pp. 113, 139.

85. Axis History Forum, "The Franco-Siamese War of 1941", 2014, https://forum.axishistory.com/viewtopic.php?t=103554.

86. Prime Minister (General) Chatchai Chunhavan, cremation volume, Bangkok, 1998, p. 353.

87. *KhaoSod*, "Revealing the Heroism of 'Father' Prem in the Indochina War—World War II", 26 May 2019, https://www.khaosod.co.th/special-stories/news_2553677.

88. A final agreement was reached on 11 March 1941. Charivat Santaputra, *Thai Foreign Policy 1932–1946* (Bangkok: Thai Khadi Research Institute, 1985), p. 240.

89. Strate, *The Lost Territories*, p. 62.

90. Ibid., p. 95.

91. E. Bruce Reynolds, *Thailand's Secret War* (Cambridge: Cambridge University Press, 2004), p. 19.

92. Ibid., p. 29.

93. See John Haseman, *The Thai Resistance Movement during the Second World War* (DeKalb: Northern Illinois University, 1978). See also Sorasak

Ngamkhachonkulkit, ขบวนการเสรีไทยกับความขัดแย้งทางการเมืองภายในประเทศระหว่าง
พ.ศ. *2481–2492* [The Free Thai Movement and domestic political conflict
during 1938–49] (Bangkok: Chulalongkorn University, 1992).

94. Phin's son Chatchai Chunhavan, who was promoted to be a captain,
accompanied his father as part of the Phayap Army. See Prime Minister
(General) Chatchai Chunhavan, cremation volume, Bangkok, 1998,
p. 353.

95. See ประวัติศาสตร์การสงครามของไทยในสงครามมหาเอเชียบูรพา, กรมยุทธศึกษาทหาร กอง
บัญชาการทหารสูงสุด. 2540 [History of the War of Thais in the Great East
Asia War, Division of Strategic Studies, Royal Thai Armed Forces
Headquarters, 1997].

96. See Worapat Aatyukdee, *Life and Works of Field Marshal Phin Chunhavan*
(Bangkok: Amarin, 2009); "History and Works of Field Marshal Sarit",
pp. 694–95.

97. According to Warren, it was during the 1942–45 Thai campaign into
the Shan States that Lieutenant Krit Sivara, who "served as an aid to
the commander there, [became] impressed with the younger officer's
[Prem Tinsulanonda's] dedication". William Warren, *Prem: Soldier and
Statesman* (Bangkok: M.L. Tridosyuth Devakul, 1997), pp. 51–52, 62.

98. Peter Dale Scott, *American War Machine* (Lanham, MD: Rowman &
Littlefield, 2010), p. 70.

99. Richard Michael Gibson, *The Secret Army: Chiang Kai-shek and the Drug
Warlords of the Golden Triangle* (Hoboken: Wiley, 2011), pp. 51–52.

100. See Peter Dale Scott, "Operation Paper: The United States and Drugs
in Thailand and Burma", *Asia-Pacific Journal* 8, issue 44, no. 2 (2010),
https://apjjf.org/-Peter-Dale-Scott/3436/article.html.

101. Charnvit Kasetsiri, "The First Phibun Government and its Involvement in
World War II", *Journal of the Siam Society* 3 (1974), https://thesiamsociety.
org/wp-content/uploads/1974/03/JSS_062_2d_CharnvitKasetsiri_
FirstPhibunGovernmentAndInvolvementInWorldWarII.pdf.

102. See Toshiharu Yoshikawa, 同盟国タイと駐屯日本軍—「大東亜戦争」期の知
られざる国際関係 [The Allies, Thailand, and Japanese troops during the
"Greater East Asia War"] (Tokyo: Tankobon, 2010).

103. United States Army Service Forces Manual, *Civil Affairs Handbook
Japan*, Section 18E, "Japanese Administration over Occupied Areas—
Thailand", December 1944, p. 29, http://www.mansell.com/Resources/
special_files/NDL/M354--18E%20Japanese%20Administration%20
of%20Occupied%20Areas,%20Thailand%2015%20December%20
1944%20Report%20No%2036-a%2827%29%20USSBS%20Index%20S-
ection%206-s.pdf.

104. Another explanation was offered by Laiad Phibunsongkram, Phibun's
wife, who later said that her husband resigned because, since he had
started the war against the Allies, and by 1944 it looked certain the Allies
would win, Thailand would be better off with a new prime minister.

105. Even Khuang received an honorary military post. In World War II,
Phibun made him a major as part of the King's Guard.

106. Wright, *The Balancing Act*, p. 131.

Chapter Three

Establishing Tetrarchy: Phibun, Phin, Phao and Sarit (1944–57)

During the fourteen years of 1944–57, Thailand initially lurched towards growing political space, then back in the direction of authoritarianism and finally towards a form of military-guided democracy loosely dominated by four strongmen: Field Marshal Plaek Phibun Songkram, Field Marshal Phin Chunhavan, General Phao Sriyanond of the police, and Field Marshal Sarit Thanarat.

Initially, hopes by civilians for democratization were bright. But efforts at achieving pluralist rule could not escape the praetorian legacies. In the end, autocratic institutions proved too influential and prevailed across the political landscape. The year 1944 produced a rickety start for civilian rule in Thailand. During this period, Thailand's two institutions of historically durable autocracy—the monarchy and military—were suddenly weak at the same time. It now appeared possible that civilian rule—giving way to elections—could take root. The apparently omnipotent Field Marshal Phibun Songkram had been forced from office on 1 August by a mere vote of no-confidence in the National Assembly. Growing opposition among Thai people to Phibun was reflected in the 182-person National Assembly: it censured Phibun even though 58 of 91 assemblymen were appointed military officers (Figure 3.1).

It remains unclear to this day whether Phibun secretly manipulated his own exit from politics in 1944 so that he could perhaps return in future as prime minister or whether he had been outfoxed by the National Assembly, his cabinet and regent, Pridi Panomyong, to risk censure and put forward his resignation. However, the following morning, soldiers

FIGURE 3.1
Thailand's Legislature, 1937–46

Type of legislature	Years in office	Appointed or elected	Total number of legislators and military contingent
Unicameral	1937–46	91 elected by eligible voters; 91 appointed	182, of which 58 (63.7%) military reserved domain

Sources: Secretariat of the Senate, *Senate of Thailand*, 2001, pp. 1–3; Chaowana Traimat, *Data on 75 Years of Thai Democracy* (Konrad Adenauer Foundation, 2007), p. 140; author's calculations.

were in the streets harassing National Security members suspected of opposing Phibun.[1]

Now, with Phibun gone, there was a clear political vacuum. His prime ministerial predecessor, General Phraya Phahon, refused to again lead the country—though Phahon reluctantly did agree to return as military commander. The National Assembly named Khuang Aphaiwong as prime minister. Khuang was from a lineage of Khmer royalty centred at a principality that is now in Battambang province in Cambodia. Khuang's father had been Battambang's governor.[2] In 1932 Khuang had been a civilian supporter of the end of absolute monarchy in Siam, and by the early 1940s had only lately joined Seri Thai. Moreover, his connections to some royals in the pre-1932 period earned him the distrust of some Promoters. In 1938 he joined the Phibun government as a minister in various postings and was given the military rank of major. He remained in Phibun's government until 1944. That Khuang had been part of Phibun's cabinet while also a civilian made him a suitable compromise premier: Pridi, Phibun and the palace could all tolerate him.

Whilst Phibun was no longer prime minister, however, he continued to serve in the posts of army commander and supreme commander of the armed forces, and refused to vacate them. But, on 6 August, he stepped down reluctantly as army chief, giving the role to his deputy, new acting army commander General Pichit Kriangsakphichit, a friend and colleague.

As a result, on 24 August, three royal proclamations were made. The first abolished the positions of supreme commander (thus jettisoning Phibun from this slot) and deputy supreme commander, while giving General Phraya Phahon—who had to be persuaded to come back—the ambiguous designation of chief field commander and pro–Seri Thai army general Chit Munsil Sinadyotharak the post of deputy chief field commander. The second proclamation appointed Phibun as "general advisor", a meaningless post with no power whatsoever. The third named Phahon as commander-in-chief of the army (and General Chit Sinadyotharak as deputy army chief), thus jettisoning Pichit from the army chief's slot.[3] Phahon then sent a message to all military units directing that only his orders were to be obeyed and that they should have "absolute proof" that any orders received were genuine before acting on them. At that point, naval units loyal to Pridi spirited Phahon to naval headquarters in Thonburi for his protection. Though many expected Phibun to react by directing a violent response, he merely sent a letter to Khuang explaining he had no regrets about being dismissed. Phibun then went into retirement close to Bangkok.[4]

Another of Khuang's early decrees as prime minister was a royal amnesty (countersigned by regent Pridi) to all political prisoners since the 1933 Bowaradej Rebellion. This decree proved, at least initially, to be popular with Thais of many political stripes and with Western countries. The amnesty was especially liked by Thai arch-royalists who had been lobbying the Phibun government for years to release political prisoners sympathetic to palace views. It was thus hoped by the new leadership that the decree would help create reconciliation between the palace and reformers.[5] But the former royalist prisoners—instigated by palace relative M.R. Kukrit Pramoj—united to form a political unit based on revenge. This unit became the "nucleus of Thailand's Democrat Party".[6]

Meanwhile, Khuang's appointment as prime minister did not necessarily mean that Thailand had abandoned its martial friend Japan's side in the war. Indeed, Japan continued to try and appease the Khuang government. But by mid-1944 frictions between Thai and Japanese soldier had grown considerably. Thailand's Phayap Army was working increasingly with the Seri Thai. In 1944 the OSS underwrote a report which declared that Phibun was the only one responsible for declaring war on the Allies.[7]

Thus, though Phibun remained "general advisor" until September 1945, at least beginning in September 1944, Phibun had completely lost his effective power. From August 1944 onwards, leaders of the Seri Thai movement informally dominated Thailand's government: its leader, Pridi Panomyong, was regent; General Adul Adul Decharat was police chief; and Khuang Aphaiwong was prime minister, having been appointed by the National Assembly on 1 August. Riggs refers to the 1944–47 period of Thai politics as the "Second Ruling Circle" following that of Phibun. This "Second Ruling Circle" was much less stable than its predecessor. Though the group met clandestinely, its existence was not unknown. The Circle was led by Pridi (representing the more progressive wing of Seri Thai); Khuang (representing civilian royalists) and Rear Admiral Thawan Thamrong Nawasawat (representing the navy).[8] However, neither Pridi nor Khuang trusted each other; Khuang had been suspicious of Pridi's 1933 economic plan. The navy was more cohesive alone than with Pridi and/or Khuang. Also secretly working with the Second Ruling Circle were Police Chief General Adul; Direk Jayanama, former Thai foreign minister under Phibun; Air Chief Marshal (ACM) Luang Tevaritpanluek, commander of the air force; General Sinad Yutharak, deputy field commander and deputy army commander; Admiral Sangvorn Yuthakit and General Netr Khemayothin (chief of staff of the army).

Despite collaborating with armed forces personnel in Seri Thai, Khuang formed a cabinet that was devoid of army officers who were part of (or had ties to) Phibun's army clique. Khuang's government was frail at best, propped up by the sickly and partly paralysed army chief Phraya Phahon, the often difficult-to-predict police chief General Adul Decharat and the sometimes pro–Seri Thai navy commander Luang Sinthusongkramchai (Sin Kamolnawin), who also became defence minister and agriculture minister on 2 August 1944. With Phahon ill, and with the navy and police being smaller forces, deputy army chief General Sinadyotharak became "the key man".[9] Indeed he was the middleman between the Seri Thai Movement and the Thai armed forces. Sinad put in place a 1944 reshuffle that gave greater concentration to and/or installed anti-Phibun, anti-Axis officers to leading military slots. Assisting Sinad was chief of staff General Luang Chartnakrob.[10] Another important anti-Phibun army official was Luang Chartnakrob's trusted colleague General Prasin Pasattrakom, who was permanent minister of defence. One of the most notable replacements was that of police chief Adul Decharat with the more malleable General Phraram Intara (Duang Julaiyanon), who had little clout within the police corps. Meanwhile, the majority of lower-echelon top officers had been newly promoted (see 1944–46 reshuffles, Appendix 4). Over these lower-echelon officers, however, Field Marshal Phibun still maintained a high degree of influence. Thus, it was critical to ensure that military leaders under Kuang sustained him in office.

Ultimately, Khuang's government remained in office until 31 August 1945—the day that Japan surrendered to the victorious Allies and World War II thus ended. The Allies, especially the United States and the United Kingdom, wanted to ensure that no Axis-leaning government would return to power in Thailand. Khuang's resignation in 1945 stemmed from realization by the Thai government that there should be a prime minister in office who was more acceptable to the victorious Allies—Khuang's earlier participation in Phibun-led governments prevented his continuing as premier.[11] But days before leaving office (16 August 1945), Khuang countersigned a royal decree nullifying the war with the United Kingdom and the United States. Bangkok was mostly worried about the attitude of the United Kingdom, which, in post-war negotiations, was making numerous punitive demands—reaching ultimately to 51—which it seemed would reduce Thailand "to a British protectorate".[12] In fact, Britain in late August 1945 sent an occupying force into Thailand, ostensibly to disarm and arrest Japanese troops; however, these British soldiers could also have been used to enforce London's post-war demands upon Bangkok. Nevertheless, the United States advised the Khuang government not to sign any agreement with the British. The Thai military delegation sent to Kandy, Ceylon, to negotiate with London included some Seri Thai military officials who would later play a role in Thai politics: Lt. Gen. Luang Senanarong (leader of the delegation), Colonel Netr Kemayothin, Wing Commander Thawee Chulasap, Thanat Khoman and Major Puey Umpakorn.

At this point the National Assembly made ready to appoint the highly visible Seri Thai Movement front man M.R. Seni Pramoj as prime minister. Seni was championed especially by the United States, and Thai elites hoped his appointment would ensure Washington's support for Thai interests when and if London attempted to make numerous post-World War II demands against Bangkok. But since Seni had not yet reached Thailand, another Seri Thai official, Thawee Bunyaket, began serving as caretaker prime minister (as well as foreign minister) until Seni arrived in mid-September. Thawee himself had earlier served as secretary-general of Phibun's cabinet. Wright thus refers to Thawee as a man trying to have it two ways: a later critic of Phibun who had been a "collaborator".[13] Thawee was also willing to work with police chief General Adul in 1945 despite earlier calling him Phibun's "Gestapo Chief".[14] Thawee did reassure the United States that he could be counted on to support Washington. In a cable to Washington on 5 September 1945, he said:

> Now more than ever my country needs the precious assistance and support of the United States of America, and now more than ever we feel so much confident that our expectation will meet with favourable response. Please be assured that on my part I will use

every endeavour further to promote the close and cordial relations which happily exist between our two countries.[15]

When Seni reached Bangkok on 16 September, he arrived on a US military aeroplane, to begin presiding over a Seri Thai government, the leaders of which had served with Donovan's OSS. Besides Seni himself as PM and foreign minister, Adul was deputy PM and police chief, Sinad was defence minister and army deputy commander, Thawee was interior minister, and Direk Jayanama became finance minister. All of these cabinet ministers were acceptable to the United States. Though Britain had sought to bully Thailand into signing the penalizing demands, by December 1945 the United States intervened with London to change its policy. Thus, on 14 December, US representative to Thailand Charles Yost informed Prime Minister Seni that Washington had made such an intervention and that Bangkok should refrain from signing all but merely "soft" demands.[16] Nevertheless, many Thais blamed Seni for being unable to keep the territories in Laos, Cambodia and Malaya that Phibun had taken for Thailand during World War II. Meanwhile, though Seni was prime minister, Pridi, in his role as regent to the king, continued to exercise considerable influence within Seni's government. As a result, Seni began to distance himself from Pridi. Eventually, in October 1945, he dissolved the lower house of parliament—Seni remained a caretaker until the 6 January 1946 general election.

To appease the Allies, Seni had introduced (and the National Assembly had passed) a War Criminals Act. As a result, Field Marshal Phibun, General Prayoon Phamonmontri, Vichit Wathakarn and two others were arrested. Later, however, on 23 March 1946, the Supreme Court ruled that the War Criminals Act was unconstitutional, and thus all five of the accused were released. Evidence points to the influencing of the judges' decision by politicians seeking to gain the swing vote of the military officers in the assembly and of the armed forces in general in order to reaffirm the alliance of civilian and military factions of the People's Party.[17] Indeed, the fact that the Seni government introduced the War Criminals Act bill to the National Assembly earned the civilian government undying hatred from those in the military who continued to back the field marshal.

In an attempt to forestall any military coups and control the armed forces, Thailand's civilian prime ministers had sought to gain effective control over the military. The only efficient security organization outside the armed forces was Pridi's security network, composed primarily of former OSS-trained Seri Thai guerrillas. But Pridi was also backed by the police, military police, navy and air force. Nevertheless, these services were not nearly as consequential as the army. As Finer notes, Pridi tried to dominate the army first from within and later from without. As such, he moved to severely reduce the military's budget (particularly that of the army).[18] He also cut short any parades or military glamour that the army had enjoyed under Phibun.[19]

Indeed, Pridi forced the retirement of any officers thought to be pro-Phibun and increased the number of pro-Pridi officers in mid-ranking military positions. Appointees thought to be more manageable included Admiral Sangworn Yuthakit as military police commander in 1945, General Phraram Intara (Duang Julaiyanon) as police chief in 1945, General Adul Decharat as army commander in 1946, the promotion of Rear Admiral Sangworn Suwannachip (a former Seri Thai member) to acting police chief in August 1947 (in addition to his post as army adjutant-general),[20] and General Wirawat Yothin as commanding general of the 1st Infantry Division of the army (Wirawat had served in this post since the fall of Phibun in 1944). However, according to a US report at the time, Wirawat was "prepared to lead the revolt in the crucial Bangkok area".[21] Nevertheless, the pending coup never happened, probably because of the lack of a unified military leadership and insufficient support from Britain and the United States.[22] Another probable reason was because General Phahon was still army commander and he opposed any coups, as did General Sinat, who served as defence minister and deputy army commander for only two years but under the four successive civilian governments of Thawee Bunyaket, M.R. Seni Pramoj, Khuang Aphaiwong and Pridi himself until Sinat retired in March 1946.[23]

January 1946 saw the election of mostly pro-Pridi representatives to half of Thailand's Assembly. The National Assembly favoured Pridi to become prime minister, but, when he declined, the assembly chose, by a close vote, former-PM Khuang Aphaiwong over Pridi's preferred candidate. Khuang, who Pridi had earlier supported as prime minister back in 1944, had now shifted firmly towards the anti-Pridi Seni Pramoj and other royalists. With the help of the appointed military representatives in the assembly, Khuang succeeded in becoming prime minister. This reflected that "the Seni-Khuang group was actively competing [with Pridi] for military support".[24] But by March 1946, amidst increasingly bitter acrimony between this second Khuang government and the Pridi-dominated assembly, Khuang suddenly resigned. With no reliable alternative, and with the Supreme Court having acquitted Phibun of war crimes the previous day, Pridi, on 24 March 1946, reluctantly took the office of prime minister himself—though he agreed to do so only on an interim basis. Pridi's opponents now included not only Phibun and Phibun's military supporters but also royalists suspicious that Pridi would seek to turn the country into a republic, as well as politicians merely jealous of his hold on power. Perhaps Pridi realized the changing balance of power. He is reported to have offered Phibun a position in his cabinet. Partly because of this, military appointees in the new assembly (mostly loyal to Phibun) had swung to Pridi's side (against Khuang) in March, facilitating his rise to the premiership.[25]

Further, it appears that Pridi sought to accommodate royalists—and their military allies—in order to consolidate his government and a stable regime. Indeed, the May 1946 constitution increased the role of the monarchy in Thai politics.[26] At the same time, Pridi apparently negotiated with Prince Suphasawat for the return to Thailand of the ashes of the late king Rama VII, the return to Thailand of former queen Rambhai and the return of many royal properties to the royal family. During the talks, Suphasavat, who was preparing to create a royalist party that would compete with the Democrats, even lodged at Pridi's home.[27]

Yet, once Pridi became prime minister, he was overcome with crises that would ultimately contribute to forcing him from the helm of Thai politics for good. Though the end of war crimes trials and Pridi's apparent accommodation with Phibun brought the former an interlude in which Phibun (who went into temporary retirement) and the armed forces seemed not to challenge him, officers held him responsible for the negative economic climate, especially the post–World War II inflation that diminished soldiers' salaries and the pensions of those officers who he had forcibly retired.[28]

Once prime minister, Pridi made a few significant modifications to the senior military line-up. First, he was forced to appoint a new army commander given that army chief General Phraya Phahon had become physically unfit to continue in the role. On 20 August 1945, Phraya Phahon had suffered a ruptured blood vessel in his brain. He tried for over a year to recover without stepping down as army commander. But as he became increasingly weak he realized he had to retire early. Phahon died on 14 February 1947. In Phahon's place, in March 1946, Prime Minister Pridi (who had given up the regency position in place of that of "senior statesman" in early 1945) appointed former police chief General Adul Decharat to succeed him.[29] Meanwhile, Pridi replaced police chief General Phraram Intara (Duang Julaiyanon), substituting instead Adul-confidant police general Prapijanpolkit (Yousef Dulasampa). Finally, army chief of staff Luang Chartnakrop was also no friend of Pridi, so the latter appointed the pro-Pridi Luang Han Songkram to take Chartnakrop's post.

Soldiers could hardly have liked the replacement of Sinat with Adul. The latter was from the police, and the army and police were known for inter-bureaucratic rivalries. Moreover, by upsetting the normal promotion line by appointing outsiders to top army slots and purging the military of officers considered politically opposed to him, Pridi's internal "stick" approach managed to aggravate many soldiers. Meanwhile, the US legation considered Adul's appointment as "sinister and unpopular" and that it reflected PM Pridi's "anxiety over his own position, and his realization that the army must be held in line" given that "the officer corps is greatly dissatisfied with ... King Ananda's death".[30]

Nevertheless, the March 1946 military reshuffle demonstrated that the Thai armed forces remained quite factionalized among pro-Phibun, pro–Seri Thai and pro-royalist cliques. This factionalism reflected that the military was suffering a deep political vacuum: in 1946 there was no military leader who could have ousted the government. In the end it would take a combination of forcibly retired senior army officers, young intermediate-level military officers, a changing US perspective regarding a military coup, and a highly critical event providing a *raison détre* that led to a putsch the following year.

Pridi put together a cabinet composed mostly of the civilian faction of the Khana Ratsadon, though it also included a few military men. Indeed, since Sinat refused to work with Pridi (and even became active in Thailand's Democrat Party), Pridi appointed General Jira Wichitsongkram (a one-time army chief of staff under Phibun who later joined Seri Thai) as defence minister.[31] For interior minister, Pridi chose another ex-Phibun stalwart, Colonel Chavengsak-Songkram. The most characteristic aspect of this cabinet was that approximately half its members had previously served in Phibun cabinets.[32]

The most substantial accomplishment of Pridi's brief government was the enactment, on 7 May 1946, of a constitution (Thailand's third). This charter—which in 2022 remained perhaps the most progressive constitution in Thailand's history—represented the apex of elected civilian control in Thailand. The military, having sided with the defeated Axis Powers during World War II, was now demoralized and disorganized. Such military frailty provided space for the pluralistic charter (an effort led by Prime Minister Pridi Panomyong). Under the new constitution, only elected civilians could serve as legislative representatives, senators and cabinet ministers[33]—a situation that destroyed

FIGURE 3.2
Thailand's First Senate, 1946–47

Parliamentary Form	Term Length	Form of Selection	Number of Senators and Percentage of Retired Military Senators
Bicameral (First Senate)	1946–47 (terminated by military coup)	Indirectly elected (by the lower house)*	80 (42.5% ex-military of the appointed)

Note: *Article 24, section 2 of the 1946 constitution stated that senators could not be government officials.

Source: Paul Chambers, "Superfluous, Irrelevant or Emancipating: Thailand's Evolving Senate Today", *Journal of Current Southeast Asian Affairs* 28, no. 3 (2009): 9, https://d-nb.info/999559311/34.

the power of the military factions within Khana Ratsadon to directly exercise political power.

Following promulgation of the constitution, Pridi ushered in Thailand's first Senate (See Figure 3.2). This Prudhi Sapha (of 1946–47) was indirectly elected by a committee composed of 178 members of the lower house who had been directly elected by the people. Senate terms were six years, while lower house terms were only four.[34] The 24 May 1946 Senate election proved to be a resounding victory for the alliance of Pridi's Constitutional Front and Sahasip over the new (royalist) Democrat Party of Khuang Aphaiwong and Seni Pramoj. The winners took all eighty Senate seats—over forty per cent of these were ex-military officials.[35]

In the midst of the elections, in early May 1946, Charles Yost informed the State Department that former "strong man" Phibun was saying that he was soon to ordain as a monk.[36] This seemed odd because, on 7 May, Phibun was meeting with thirty military officers.[37]

Days after the Senate election, on the morning of 9 June 1946, the twenty-year-old Ananda Mahidol, heir to the Chakri throne, and soon to be crowned, was found shot dead in his bedroom in the Grand Royal Palace in Bangkok. Amidst inferences by the politically weakened Democrat Party that Pridi was responsible for Ananda's death, it was simple for many soldiers—already alienated from Pridi because of his efforts to legally weaken the military—to become suspicious. There just needed to be a charismatic military leader.

Though it is not the purpose of this book to analyse the death of King Rama VIII, the event is so crucial to Thailand's modern history that it cannot be ignored. Four possible causes have been given for the death of Ananda: accident by Ananda, suicide, murder, or accidental killing by another. A committee investigating the cause of the king's demise was appointed on 18 June 1946, and after four months decided that the death was either caused by murder or suicide. Most Thais and foreign observers remained unconvinced that two royal servants and a friend of Pridi's had committed the murder, even after all three were executed in 1955. One intriguing theory held that Ananda was slain by royalists because he intended to abdicate the throne and become a political reformer.[38] His younger brother was thought to be more malleable. Nine years later, senior prince Subhasvasti invited Rayne Kruger to write a book in English that introduced a new theory of Ananda's death (by suicide),[39] "supposedly to divert the attention away from any allegation that Bhumipol killed his elder brother".[40] There is the possibility that Ananda could have been indirectly murdered by someone who placed a bullet into the chamber of the Colt 45. The weapon (potentially with a bullet inside) had been a gift from Alexander MacDonald, station chief of the US OSS Office in Bangkok,[41] and later the founder of the *Bangkok Post*. But it would be unlikely that MacDonald had intentionally placed a bullet inside a gift weapon. Someone else, such as a military officer with regular access to weapons, could have loaded the pistol unbeknownst to the king. His brother might then have pulled the trigger not knowing the gun was loaded and killed him accidently.

Whatever the truth of the matter (and the mystery will never be resolved), Ananda's death provided the military an enormous dividend: proven or unproven, blaming Pridi for regicide. The killing thus provided military activists a motive for ousting Pridi (and potentially any civilian successor) from office. At this point, the only entity remaining to turn against Pridi was the United States. Anti-Pridi military elements as well as royalists now sought to delegitimize Pridi and legitimize Phibun to Washington.

Delegitimizing Pridi would prove easy. The United States, years earlier, had been wary of Pridi's ideological views. The State Department had eyed his 1934 progressive Economic Reform plan with suspicion and vigorously opposed his (and Phibun's) attempts to regulate and control foreign companies in Thailand. Under Pridi's 1946 government, Washington also took notice of Thailand's expansion of state enterprises in various industries; Pridi's repeal of the Communist Suppression Act of 1933 and resumption of diplomatic relations with the Soviet Union; and the opening of Bangkok-based offices of the Viet Minh, Khmer Serei and the Lao Issara—three independence movement with tinges of progressive communist thought. The US Embassy noted that Pridi's and Thamrong's governments allowed progressive newspapers (e.g., *Mahachon*) to publish scathing criticisms of "American imperialism".[42] Thus, by 1946–47, as the Cold War between the United States and the Soviet Union began to grow, many US diplomats viewed Pridi, if not as a communist himself, then at least as a communist facilitator. Though Thamrong had become prime minister that year, the US Embassy remained concerned that Thailand was becoming a potential hotbed of communism. The CIA noted in October 1947 that

> two hundred Soviet youths are being trained in Moscow in Siamese.... After completion of their courses they will be sent to Bangkok to work in the Soviet propaganda headquarters which will be set up there for the whole Southeast Asian Area.[43]

Back in November 1946, the conservative newspaper *Seri* was already calling for the reinstatement of Phibun as prime minister. The editorial reflected the perception by some Thais that Phibun was a staunch royalist and anti-communist strongman. That same month, Thai PM Thamrong informed the United States that the Thai government had snuffed out a coup plot against him by army and air force officers seen to be close to Phibun, and that Phibun had known of the plot. Meanwhile, the economy was tanking and there was subsequent rising popular discontent. By January 1947, Pridi's political opponents were calling for a "united national government",[44] and then, in March, Phibun himself said he would like to return to politics.[45]

Pridi's lower house opposition leader Khuang thereupon assured Phibun of parliamentary support for his political return—though opposition from US and British representatives in Bangkok, the incumbent government, and the fact that General Adul was firmly in control of the army seemed to be enough at the time "to discourage Phibun's ambitions".[46] At this point the incoming US ambassador to Thailand, Edwin Stanton, approached Pridi and told him that the rumours of a military coup against the government were real and serious. However, a more powerful faction in US State Department circles saw the warnings of a coup as simply a means by which the "Commie" Pridi was seeking to gain US support for placing a more loyal proxy—such as Adul—into the prime minister's chair. Eventually, in August, Pridi made a visit to the United States in an effort to convince policymakers that it was not he but rather Phibun who was Washington's enemy. But the US State Department elite—including Secretary of State Dean Acheson, Ambassador to Thailand Edwin Stanton and the State Department's expert on Thailand, Kenneth Landon—remained distrustful of Pridi, being even of the opinion that Phibun was long retired and that suspicions should be raised only about Pridi's motivations and inclinations in accusing Phibun.[47]

Meanwhile, Thamrong (and Pridi) had another strategy to bolster support from soldiers: the potential for United States military aid. Such assistance would provide the Thai government with direct political benefits, given that it could assuage the discontented officers. Thailand's foreign minister had thus visited Washington in the hopes of establishing an American military training (and assistance) programme for Thailand. Kenneth Landon supported the idea, but it was ultimately killed by higher-ups apparently interested in spending more money on reconstruction projects in Europe. At the same time, there is evidence that the Truman administration, with the advent of the Cold War in 1947, was becoming suspicious of Pridi's ideological inclinations.[48] By October 1947, Prime Minister Thamrong Nawasawat's foreign minister met in Washington with top Truman administration officials to again press for a military training mission, but received only Secretary of State George Marshall's answer that the United States "would consider" the request.[49] The United States never responded.

Back in Thailand, the coalition continued to hit choppy political waters. With Pridi and Thamrong being blamed for regicide amid allegations of corruption and inefficient oversight of the economy, the government continued to sustain blistering attacks in parliament. On 16 July 1947, army commander General Adul averted a coup attempt by junior officers who were also reportedly frustrated with government inefficiency.[50] Clearly, many army officers hated Pridi.

One of these officers was Phin Chunhavan. But who was Phin? Born on 14 October 1891, Phin was only slightly younger than chief Promoter General Phraya Phahon. In fact, Phin was Chinese—born in Samut Songkram province, the son of migrants from China, Mr Khai and Plub Chunhavan, who had been Chinese tax farmers[51] as well as gardeners. One of Phin's brothers was Lt. Gen. Pote Choonhawan (who, in 1952, while his brother Phin was army commander, was appointed as deputy commander of the 3rd Army Region). Phin married Khunying Vibullak Chunhavan and had five children. These included Khunying Udomlak Sriyanon (1913–81), who married police general Phao Sriyanond; Prom Dabbaransi, who married Mr Arun Dabbaransi; Thanpuying Charoen Adireksarn, who married police general Praman Adireksan; General Chatchai Chunhavan, who married Thanpuying Boonruen Chunhavan, the step-sister of King Rama IX; and, finally, Mrs Poonsuk (Phorsom) Chunhavan (1922–present),

FIGURE 3.3
Principal Military Members of the Chunhavan Family

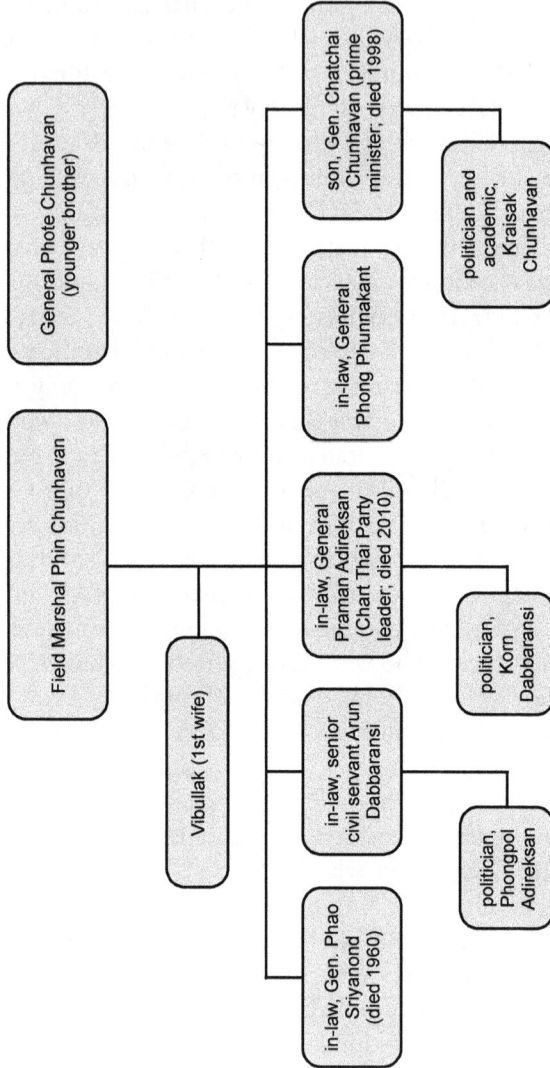

who married Chalerm Chiewsakul. Phin's child by his second wife, Supapa Chunhavan, was Mr Prakromsak Chunhavan, who married Natthinee Chunhavan (former family name Salirataviphak). Phin began his career as a cadet in 1909, graduating from the Army Cadet Academy in 1913, the same class as Plaek Phibun Songkram. After becoming a second lieutenant in 1916, he attended the Staff School, graduating in 1928, and was promoted to the rank of major. After the 1932 "*patiwat*", his promotions continued. In 1933 he was made chief of staff of the Combined Suppression Division and chief of staff of the 3rd Army Battalion. In 1934 he was appointed deputy commander of the 3rd Army Circle. In 1937 he was promoted to become colonel as the deputy commander of Thailand's Northeast Region. In mid-1941 he was promoted to the rank of major general, and in 1943 became lieutenant general. On 1 February 1945 he retired, before re-entering army service in November 1947 following the coup that month.[52] Phin became the head of the important Soi Rajakru family (indicating the address of the household—Phahon Yothin 5 [Soi Ari 1], Phaya Thai, Bangkok 10400), which included significant political personalities, including Phin himself, his son Chatchai (Chatchai's son was the academic and politician Kraisak) and three important sons-in-law: General Phao Sriyanond, General Praman Adireksan (Praman's son was the politician Pongpol) and Arun Thapparansi, a senior civil servant from a high-level noble family whose father had the title "Phraya". Arun's son was the politician Korn Dabbaransi.[53] Two outsiders who were close to the Chunhavan family were Thanpuying Boonruen Chunhavan, the step-sister of King Bhumipol Adulyadej, and Thanpuying Chongkol Kittikachorn, the wife of Field Marshal Thanom Kittikachorn. Nevertheless, by 2023 the political clout of the Chunhavans had mostly disappeared; the new fame of the Chunhavan family was centred upon Prakromsak's daughter Natprapa ("Mink"), a fashion model. The principal military-related members of the Chunhavan family tree are shown in Figure 3.3.[54]

With Phin an up-and-coming military and political figure in Thailand, in August 1947, according to Venkataramani, Phibun had begun to establish and maintain contacts with certain highly placed Americans who themselves had close contacts to the US Embassy in Bangkok.[55] One of these Americans was Willis H. Bird, the OSS lieutenant colonel mentioned in chapter 2. Bird had been based in Kunming, China, during 1944 but had developed deep ties to Thailand's Phayap Army, especially the 3rd Division, which had been commanded by General Phin Chunhavan.[56] Phin had become

well-acquainted with OSS officials, including Willis Bird. When
World War II ended in 1945, Bird went to live in Bangkok. He
had already met Chalermsi Savetsila and married her that year. Bird
opened the Willis Bird Import Export Firm in 1946 (located at
1191 New Road), working with the World Commerce Corporation
(WCC), both of which had offices in Bangkok. According to Scott, in
April 1948 Bird implored (former OSS director) William Donovan:
"Should there be any agency that is trying to take the place of OSS
... please have them get in touch with us as soon as possible."[57]
Washington's fledgling Central Intelligence Agency (CIA) had only
been created in September 1947. Thus, Bird's company, as well as
the WCC, were very informal yet important mechanisms that the
Harry Truman administration used to arm the Thai military—*prior to
Phin Chunhavan's November 1947 coup.* According to Bird's brother-
in-law ACM Sitthi Savetsila, "his [Bird's] import-export company
was designated agent for the importation of equipment destined for
the Thai armed forces as assistance from the US government".[58] The
weapons that Bird provided (alongside the implied message about
Washington's perspective on a potential military coup) amounted
to a form of acquiescence on the part of elements within the US
government to a coup against the Thamrong government. These elements did not officially include US ambassador Stanton or US State
Department official Landon, both of whom, as diplomats, needed
plausible deniability and distance from any military coup.

To build up more support from Thailand's police and some army
elements, Pridi began planning to have Admiral Thamrong stand down,
replacing him with army chief General Adul Decharat. Meanwhile,
three senior navy officials—PM Thamrong, Luang Sangwan Yutthakit
and Luang Singha Sangwangchai—were given senior governmental
slots to help ensure support for the government from navy officials.
As prime minister, Adul would then dissolve the lower house and call
new elections—for which Pridi would be the government candidate.[59]
But this strategy never came to pass. The Thamrong government was
warned about an imminent coup by none other than US ambassador
Stanton (who informed Thamrong it would occur on 8 November)
as well as Phibun (according to Laiad). There is even evidence that
Pridi and Thamrong were preparing to thwart the takeover bid by
installing army commander General Adul as prime minister as early
as 11 November.[60] But 11 November would be three days too late,
and, besides, Adul lacked any real support from the rank and file of
the army, being a police general and having served in the post-war

administrations that had overseen the weakening of the Thai military. In fact, on 8 November, a day before the coup, Prime Minister Thamrong was reassuring US ambassador Stanton that no coup could possibly succeed: "But excellency … the Commander-in-Chief is with me, the Police are with me, and I have the Navy in my pocket."[61]

The instigators of the November 1947 coup were General Phin Chunhavan and Colonel Kat Katsongkram. The two had been army cadet school classmates of 1909 and both were cashiered from the military in 1944. But with Phibun still closely associated with the defeat of the Axis Powers, Phin was the most senior and charismatic military officer of the late 1940s. Having successfully helped lead Thai forces into French Indochina (1940–41) and the British-controlled Shan States (1942–45), Phin was something of a rarity in the Thailand of the late 1940s—an untainted yet popular military leader who had overseen external expansion. Phin felt that the Pridi government had dishonoured Phibun, the military and the nation.

Phin later wrote:

> When I returned to Bangkok, I heard all kinds of criticisms [about the Thai government]….We heard sounds of gunshots almost every day….Worse still, His Majesty King Rama VIII was assassinated…. In food and coffee shops and entertainment places, widespread criticisms of the government were heard. Some said loudly: "Where have all those bloody good patriotic men been sleeping? Why don't they come out to help bring an end to this chaos?"[62]

Intriguingly, Phin had no interest in directly leading Thailand as a political leader should a coup be successful. He recognized instead that his skills were more organizational and logistical, and as such promoted the idea of Phibun's return to power.[63] At the same time he preferred simply not to front the incoming regime.

As the patron and role model of many Thai soldiers at the time, it was not difficult to find support for Phin's coup plans from within the corps. The fact that Pridi had financially downgraded the army relative to the other services helped Phin find tremendous backing from within this, the largest of Thailand's military services. Phin found loyal co-plotters from among those officers who had previously served under him. And there were many: other members of his graduating class, Phibun loyalists, and soldiers disenchanted with the domination of top bureaucratic positions by Seri Thai officers.[64] Chief among those assisting Phin in the takeover were Phin's own son-in-law (and former aide) Colonel Phao Siyanon.

Who was Phao? Born on 1 March 1909 in Bangkok, Phao was the son of Lt. Col. Phra Phlapirak Seni (Plui Sriyanon), who helped Phao commence his military career. Phao's family was Burmese. He married Khunying Udomlak, the daughter of General Phin Chunhavan. Together they had a daughter, Ponglak. Phao entered the Army Cadet Academy in 1926 and subsequently entered government service in 1931 in the rank of second lieutenant. He became an aide to Field Marshal Phibun Songkram and then moved quickly up the ranks: 1st lieutenant in 1934; captain in 1935, major in 1940, director of Thailand's Crown Property Bureau in 1942, adjutant of the minister of defence and the rank of colonel in 1943, and director of the Department of Fuels in 1944. In 1948 he transferred to the Police Department as deputy director general and in the rank of police major general. In 1950 he became police lieutenant general, and in 1951 was appointed as director general of the Police Department.[65]

Other junior coup planners included group captain of the air force Luang Kat Katsongkram, an anti-royalist former Promoter of the 1932 "revolution" who had flirted between both Pridi and Phibun. Meanwhile, army lieutenant colonel Sarit Thanarat—who had served as a field commander under Phin in the Burma campaign, and in 1947 was the commander of the 1st Infantry Regiment—joined the effort out of respect for his patron Phin and the need to restore the dignity of the armed forces. Sarit's loyal following of officers who had served under him when he was part of Phin's Burma campaign also joined the effort. These included Praphas Charusatien, commander of the 1st Battalion of the 1st Infantry Regiment; Krit Sivara, deputy commander of this battalion; and Thanom Kittikachorn, who was now commander of the Cadets Regiment of Chulachomklao Military Academy. Other principals included Lt. Col. Kan Chamnongphumiwet and Colonel Sawat Sawatikiat, director of the Army Commissary.[66]

Meanwhile, Pridi had not been overly ignorant of dissension within the armed forces. Following his 1946 resignation, he left the government under the care not only of new prime minster Admiral Thamrong, but also defence minister General Jira Wichitsongkram, army commander General Adul, navy commander Admiral Sin Songkramchai and marines chief Admiral Thahan Kamhiran. These five men, who had appeared loyal to Pridi during the Phibun years, were deemed capable of protecting the ruling administration and withstanding any pressure from royalists or military opponents. Thamrong, as a former colleague of Pridi in Seri Thai, seemed trustworthy enough. At the same time, given that both Jira and Adul had earlier served under Phibun, it was thought that their presence in the government would mollify the field marshal. But neither Jira nor Adul ever really committed to one or the other side. Further, Thamrong's government was increasingly perceived as corrupt, inefficient, dominated by the navy and former Seri Thai officers, and associated with the burdens that had been placed on the army following World War II.[67] Ultimately—perhaps because these officers were overly hesitant, ambitious or unsure of which side to back—they did little to resist the coup.[68]

In the end the coup of 1947 succeeded because the Thai political balance of power had shifted against Pridi, and he seemed either` ill-prepared for it or failed to do enough to tilt it back in his favour.

With the Thamrong government increasingly unpopular and Washington appearing to offer few if any obstacles to a coup (including, at the least, a letter opposing any putsch against the civilian Thamrong government), on 6 November 1947, the coup leaders General Phin and Colonel Kat finalized their plans. It was discovered, however, that army commander General Adul had learned of the impending putsch and was planning mass arrests in the military. In fact Adul had informed Phin's son Major Chatchai Chunhavan that he would not only comply with the coup promoters but would also convince Thamrong to do the same; he apparently, however, changed his mind. On the night of the coup, Adul's forces rumbled about Bangkok seeking, unsuccessfully, to keep soldiers in their barracks.[69] General Phin recounted his fear at that point of what Adul might do: "But then I thought that we had already cocked the gun, so we had to fire and let future events decide our fate."[70]

Phin thus went ahead and ordered the putsch to proceed. His first order at 5 p.m. on 8 November was to declare the military's seizure of power from the government. The second decree (issued simultaneously with the first) ordered all military units to remain at their posts. Order No. 6 amounted to a wholesale purge as announcements were made across the armed forces leadership, dismissing officials considered untrustworthy and promoting others considered loyal.[71] The first part of the coup, proceeding in the late evening of 8 November, was to detain the senior members of the Damrong government. Thus, Colonel Sarit Thanarat, then commander of the 1st Infantry Regiment and the 1st Military District, personally led 3rd Battalion soldiers to the home of the prime minister to arrest him. Thawan, however, had already escaped.[72] Another group of soldiers failed to apprehend police chief and army adjutant-general Admiral Sangworn, who also escaped. Yet another group, led by Lt. Col. Lamai Uthayanon, failed to arrest Pridi Panomyong—who successfully fled by boat.[73] The coup participants now set up their headquarters at the Ministry of Defence. Students from Chulachomklao Military Academy, led by their commandant Lt. Col. Thanom Kittikachorn, were stationed at the ministry to guard it. But with the coup leaders having failed to arrest any important government leaders, the putschists became worried they lacked a front person to lead a new government. When army chief General Adul Decharat refused to support the coup (instead seeking to halt it), they settled upon Phibun. Phao Sriyanond, a former aide-de-camp to the field marshal, promised he would find him. But after hours had passed and Phibun had failed to appear, an angry Colonel Sarit Thanarat set out in a military vehicle to Phibun's house. There he found Phao, talked with Phibun via telephone, and the field marshal finally was coaxed into returning with them to the Ministry of Defence—where they arrived at 10 a.m. In the end it was Sarit's personal leadership over the troops that was critical to the success of the putsch. As such, Sarit was promoted to become the commander of the strategic 1st Regimental Circle. On 1 January 1948 he became major general, and a month later he became commander of the 1st Infantry Division.[74]

Initial reaction to the coup from the US legation was that

> Phibun appears to be temporarily in complete control of the situation in Bangkok ...[while]... Pridi and Premier Dhamrong [Thamrong] and Generals Adun [Adul] and Wirawat [Yothin] have fled Bangkok and may establish a legitimate government outside Bangkok and rally military forces to their support.[75]

Indeed, the CIA saw a counter-coup by Pridi and Thamrong as a "distinct possibility". Embassy officials added that, "By its forceful method of establishment and by its enhancement of royal power, the new regime represents a reversal of the previous trend toward democratic, elected government."[76]

However, the embassy highlighted one possibility that was a likely reason why the Truman administration ended up supporting the coup: "Phibun's vigorous suppression of communism during his wartime administration may foreshadow new anti-communist measures which will impair Siam's relations with the USSR."[77]

As for the motives for the coup, according to the US Embassy, these included (1) the alleviation of the high cost of living, (2) the elimination of official corruption, (3) the inability of the Thamrong government to hold on to territories taken from France and the United Kingdom in 1941–43, (4) the growth of communism in Thailand, (5) the rise of Chinese influence in Thai affairs, and (6) a military belief that parliamentary methods were inadequate for ousting the government.[78]

The Coup Group itself offered specific reasons for the putsch in the form of seventeen announcements of the "Thai Who Love the Nation Committee", presided over by Field Marshal Plaek Phibun Songkram, Lt. Gen. (and Field Marshal) Phin Chunhavan and seven senior army generals.[79] Announcement No. 9 was especially interesting because it emphasized that Chinese living in Thailand need not worry about their rights and interests in the country following the putsch. This contrasts with the personal view of coup plotter Kat Katsongkram (see below), but it perhaps owed to the Coup Group's desire to gain support from businesspeople, the majority of whom were ethnic Chinese or foreign.[80]

The coup was officially carried out for the following reasons:

1. To uphold the welfare of the nation as a whole
2. To form a government which respected the tenets of Nation, Religion, King and ... constitutionalism
3. To uphold the honor of the Army since the Army had been treated unjustly
4. To restore efficient administration
5. To clarify the assassination plot against King Ananda (Rama VIII)
6. To clean the country of any Communist influences[81]

Lt. Gen. Kat Katsongkram, a principal 1947 coup instigator, later gave thirty-eight reasons why he felt the putsch had been necessary. These are presented below:

Rationales Relating to Parliament:
1. The previous government's improper selling of gold bullion
2. The error-ridden 1946 constitution
3. The registration of all firearms
4. The abolition of the Communist Law
5. Establishing a Savings Bank using children's money
6. Drafting a bill to allow the public to elect a Senate
7. No clarified resolution to the death of King Ananda
8. The previous government allowed too many immigrants into Thailand and is partial to the Chinese [this rationale appears to not correspond to the official reasons for the 1947 coup]
9. Giving away too much to foreign countries
10. Government arrogance toward parliament and newspapers
11. Parliament under the control of vested interests
12. Budgetary incompetence
13. Corruption among members of parliament

Rationales Relating to the Executive:
14. The decline of the Army
15. Rice shortage

16. Negligent import-export policy
17. Cronyism in granting export licenses
18. Growing crime rate
19. Rampant bureaucratic corruption
20. Chinese above Thai law [again this does not correspond to the official coup rationales]
21. Chinese dominance in establishment of schools [again this does not correspond to the official coup rationales]
22. Meat becoming more expensive
23. Aliens do as they please, especially the Chinese [again this does not correspond to the official coup rationales]
24. Politicians practice daring favoritism
25. Cabinet membership a product of partisanship
26. The previous government leaned toward Communism
27. The previous government allowed Thailand to be a base for arms shipments to Communist insurgents in neighboring countries
28. The previous government allowed aliens to have military training in Thailand with their own police
29. Domestic politics has been "childish"
30. The previous government worked with aliens to destroy the economy
31. Though people face hardships, the politically powerful live a lavish life
32. Education, agriculture, communications, and industries remain backward
33. Policy statements have been beautiful but little action has been taken.
34. Control of alien registration circumvented by bribes
35. No control over the selling of contraband
36. Rail transportation costs remain high
37. Thai authorities impotent in negotiations for return of gold bullion from Japan
38. Some Thai criminals backed by the powerful[82]

The November 1947 coup ultimately came about because of realignment in the balance of political forces. From 1941 until 1944, Pridi and his supporters had worked in an alliance of convenience with royalists against Phibun under the aegis of the Seri Thai. But at war's end, royalists feared Pridi's rapidly growing power, including his moves to collaborate with politicians allied with Phibun. The result could have been a Pridi-led reversion to the anti-royalist 1930s. To counter Pridi, royalists thus "joined hands with the military wing of the People's Party".[83] Indeed, shortly after the death of King Ananda in June 1946, royalists requested from then US chargé d'affaires Edwin Stanton in Bangkok that the latter support a coup against the government—an appeal that was declined.[84] Girling furthermore argues that two factors were crucial as rationales for the coup. First, there was a reduction of the army budget. From 1932 to 1956, the army's share of the annual military budget had approximated 43 per cent. But from 1945 to 1947, this share fell to less than 20 per cent. Second, there was the aforementioned provision in the 1946 constitution forbidding active-duty bureaucrats (including soldiers) from serving in parliament or the cabinet.[85] Rong contended that the causes of the putsch were the mystery surrounding the death of King Ananda Mahidol and the plummeting economic conditions leading to a scarcity of rice.[86]

Following his stint as US ambassador to Thailand, Ambassador Stanton wrote a book in 1957 called *Brief Authority*, in which he seemed extremely defensive against any considerations that the United States had not done enough to stop the coup.

> Neither [UK ambassador Geoffrey] Thompson nor I liked this overthrow of the Thamrong government by force; the flouting of the constitutional processes simply set back the hands of the clock.... We deplored the rule of force, the possibility of civil war as well as numerous diplomatic complications which might arise.[87]

But Stanton failed to explain why Washington provided little if any verbal or material support to Pridi and Thamrong against a potential coup; how and why he suggested that Pridi was a communist and may have been involved in King Rama VIII's death; and, finally, why Washington was suspicious of Thailand's 1946 civilian government but willing to support Thailand's post-1947 military-dominated regimes. In fact, Washington's response to the putsch appeared torn between principles of democratic rule of law versus security against communism, and the latter prevailed.

In sum, 1947 saw the United States facilitate the evolution of the Coup Group and its overthrow of the Pridi and Thamrong governments. Washington did not strongly oppose the political comeback of Phibun Songkram in early 1947—and arguably encouraged it. According to Colonel Kat Katsongkram, he sent a secret telegram to King Bhumipol explaining the plans for the coup two months before it happened.[88] Washington refused military assistance to Pridi, instead later offering it to Phibun. Washington's public response to the coup appeared to be more one of annoyance than opposition.[89] The informal standpoint of the United States to the coup—in the form of Willis Bird—was one of complete support. Because of these factors, the putsch was successful, and it allowed Plaek Phibun Songkram and Phin Chunhavan not only to be ushered back into active military service, but to stand at the apex of Thai politics for the next several years.

In the aftermath of the coup, Stanton simply noted that supporters of the democratic government were "rounded up" and the prince regent (who approved the coup for the king)

> was approached to approve what had transpired and to promulgate a new [provisional] constitution drawn up by the military group. It came to be known as the "water-jar" constitution because Colonel Luang Kach [Kach Songkram], the most active figure in these events, had kept it hidden in a large red earthenware water jar.[90]

Nevertheless, the CIA considered that support for the coup was "paper thin".[91] At the same time, it noted that France was "perturbed" by the putsch, given Phibun's role in invading French Indochina earlier, while the British were supportive of the new Phibun-led regime.[92] Though Phibun again stood at the helm of political power, he needed international recognition to sustain it. His only difficulties were that he now led a coup-borne regime and had allied with the Axis powers during World War II. To gain more international recognition, he thus made a bargain with the royalist Democrat Party, appointing Khuang Aphaiwong as prime minister (and M.R. Seni Pramoj as justice minister), though Phibun remained army commander until elections could be held on 29 January 1948.[93]

Nevertheless, Democrat Party (and royalist) consent to the 1947 coup had its cost. This came in the form of slightly rejuvenated royal powers, reflected in the new constitution. Indeed, though the 1947 Coup Group immediately ended the Senate's term since it was packed with Pridi supporters,[94] the 1947 provisional constitution gave the king (and Privy Council) the power to appoint members of Thailand's upper house. Moreover, under the 1947 and 1949 constitutions, the ban on soldiers sitting as senators continued (article 93, section 5 of the 1949 constitution). Article 33 empowered the king to appoint all senators, who were nominated by a five-person Privy Council, an institution then dominated by the army.[95] As a result of the king's enhanced powers, the number of senators with a military background diminished, and these were retired soldiers. Henceforth there were a hundred senators. Of these, thirty-five of them were former military officials aligned with Phin and Phibun (see Figure 3.4). For the next fifty-three years (until 2000), the upper house was strongly influenced by the military.

The charter also fortified the monarch's powers in terms of necessitating his endorsement of any declaration of war or martial law.[96] It further provided for a Supreme Council of State—a five-person privy

FIGURE 3.4
Thailand's Senate, 1947–51

Type of legislature	Years in office	Appointed or elected	Total number of senators and military contingent
Bicameral (Second Senate)	1947–51 (terminated by military coup)	Appointed	100 (35 ex-military)

Source: Paul Chambers, "Superfluous, Irrelevant or Emancipating: Thailand's Evolving Senate Today", *Journal of Current Southeast Asian Affairs* 28, no. 3 (2009): 9, https://d-nb.info/999559311/34.

council that offered advice to the king. On the council sat young King Bhumipol Adulyadej's arch-conservative uncles Prince Rangsit and Prince Dhani. In addition, it included "three men that the military could not object to". Among them was Prince Alongkot Sukhsawat, a former military officer from the seventh reign who had managed to remain clear of suspicion from the People's Party in the 1930s. There was also Phraya Manavarajsevi (Plot Vichien Na Songkhla), who had presided over the People's Party–dominated Assembly on several occasions. Phibun himself had sought to be the fifth councillor in order to maintain greater influence and information regarding the king, but instead former army commander General Adul Decharat was given this seat—though Adul apparently never cared to attend any meeting.[97] Not long after the coup, Rangsit refused to approve all but eight of the Coup Group's nominees for the Senate, instead appointing mostly princes and businesspeople intimate with the palace to the upper house.[98] At the same time, pro-royalist interim prime minister Khuang was clearly a favourite of the Supreme Council. Finally, the minister of justice, Democrat M.R. Seni Pramoj, demanded Phibun's resignation as army commander to hasten international recognition.[99] All of a sudden it appeared that the royalists might gain the upper hand over Phibun, Phin, Pridi, Thamrong and the state.

In the aftermath of the 1947 coup, the legacy and legitimacy of Khana Ratsadon crumbled considerably. Despite the fall of Thamrong, three groups continued to dominate the political scene. These were (1) Phibun and Phin, who, via the army, monopolized the armed forces and, through their Thammatipat Party, could exercise power in parliament; (2) royalists led by Prince Rangsit, who possessed power through the Supreme Council and also in parliament through Khuang's Democrats; and (3) Pridi and Thamrong, who, via former Seri Thai officers and by means of the Sahacheep and Constitutional Front parties, had an influence in parliament. The coup had brought the army (Phibun and Phin) and royalists (Rangsit and Khuang) together. But after November, the former was not so trusting of their ironic ally.

The country was now struck with two levels of power competition. First was the Seri Thai forces of Thamrong and Pridi versus the army of General Phin. Second, within the government itself, were the civilian elements led by Khuang versus Phin's military leadership. According to the CIA at the time, "Abhaiwong reportedly claims to be planning to eliminate Phibun's influence in three months, but military figures believe that Phibun's presence will be 'necessary' for at least a year."[100] By late November 1947, Thamrong was doing all he could to discredit the new regime, and even planned a counter-coup as a means of forestalling international recognition of the Khuang-led government.[101]

By December 1947, Thamrong was still attempting to establish an alternative government while seeking to exploit army-navy divisions to stage a coup against the government. He told the US Naval Attaché that, if he could gain support from the Thai Navy, he would stage a coup on 1 January 1948. He also anticipated exploiting what he called "a serious split which he expected to develop within the army".[102] Pridi, meanwhile, had left Thailand and was temporarily allowed to remain in British colonial Singapore before he again was forced by the United Kingdom to depart. He arrived then in Hong Kong and subsequently went to Shanghai, China. In Shanghai, Pridi obtained a visa for Mexico, but would have to go by way of San Francisco. According to Pridi, while presenting his passport to the Chinese consular officer, a young American named Norman Hannah (then US vice consul in Shanghai) "arrived in a rush, wrenched my passport from the hands of the Chinese official, and canceled the American visa given me by the American embassy in London". This same Norman Hannah was in fact a CIA agent who was later posted to Bangkok.[103] Pridi later stated that the CIA had seen to it that the Thai police imprisoned both his wife and son.[104] Worried that Pridi had become a communist, Washington quickly forgot how he had worked so closely as an ally of the United States during World War II. But there is no evidence that Pridi ever joined a communist party. Nevertheless, according to the biased Edwin Stanton, Pridi, upon leaving Singapore, simply fled to Beijing, where he became "a puppet in the toils of the Chinese Communists".[105]

Two days after the coup, on 11 November 1947, the military leadership (with the exception of General Wirawat Yothin) underwent a wholesale reshuffle. Though Phibun was granted the post of army commander, his new powers were more limited than during his first premiership. True power was vested mostly in Phin and General Kat Katsongkram. As for the police, General Luang Chatrakanson became police director general, with Phin's son-in-law Phao Siyanon, then a colonel, elevated to be a police general and deputy police director. On 25 November and 1 December 1947, further promotions were effected by Sarit, rewarding three minor coup participants (Thanom Kittikachorn, Praphas Charusathien and Krit Sivara) who had served him loyally and who would later play major political roles in Thailand (see 1947 reshuffle, Appendix 4).

A new general election was held in Thailand on 29 January 1948. The polling was for a new 99-member lower house—King Bhumipol's regent, Prince Rangsit, had already appointed the hundred-seat Senate (from nominees of the Coup Group). There was already a growing split, however, between Khuang Aphaiwong and Phibun-led military elements. In January, days before this election, the CIA noted in a cable that if the PM continued his "independent course of action ... the military may discard Aphaiwong even if he is duly returned to office by the elections".[106] Khuang's unofficially formed Progressive Party (which hereafter became the Democrat Party) won a landslide victory. The Democrats and their allied parties gained 65 seats, Phibun's Thammatipat got 5 seats,[107] and Pridi's Cooperative and Constitutional Front obtained 6 seats. But, in an attempt to maximize his electoral power and alliance with royalists, Khuang became involved in a complicated "game" involving Phibun, Pridi and different wings of the royal family.

On 6 February 1948, the CIA station chief in Bangkok cabled Washington that

> The US Embassy, US Military Attaché, and CIA sources in Bangkok report that Field Marshal Phibun intends to form a coalition government, including Elder Statesman Pridi (now in Singapore) and former Premier Thamrong, following a mass rally on 8 February. The basis for such a coalition is believed to be the common opposition of these leaders to Royalist plans for the forced abdication of the present King (now in Switzerland) and the elevation of Prince Chumbot to the throne. The Royalists propose to have the Abhaiwong Government denounce the present King as accidentally responsible for the death of his brother King Ananda, on 9 June 1946... [redacted] (a) [redacted] opposed to the deposition of the present King, are acting as intermediaries for a rapprochement between Thamrong and Phibun; and Pridi may be cleared of charges of complicity in the King's assassination and urged to return to Siam.

(CIA Comment: Phibun's realignment with Pridi, Thamrong, and the navy against the monarchy would represent a repetition of the situation in 1932 when these same army, navy and civilian officials united to overthrow the absolute monarchy.)[108]

If true, the royalist plan demonstrated that relatives within Thailand's royal family were rather divided. On 20 February 1948, the US State Department's specialist on Thailand, Kenneth Landon, then reported that Khuang, with support from Seni and Kukrit Pramoj, was planning on announcing that Bhumipol had killed his brother accidentally, and that the latter would thus abdicate in favour of Chumpot:

> Phibun is antagonized by Khuang's proposal that ... Chumphot become King. It may be true that Bhumiphol killed his brother either intentionally or accidentally. Such a possibility was indicated by an earlier memorandum by me on this subject.... This then becomes a deliberate attempt by Khuang to restore the monarchy to some of its former power and to establish Khuang and the Pramoj brothers firmly as the leaders of a royalist party and of the nation. They apparently hope that they can sustain themselves with Chumphot on the throne because Chumphot is a mature person of considerable wealth who has had long experience with palace politics.... Phibun and Pridi are political opponents within the same political party. They are equally opposed to any return of the monarchy to power. They do not object to the present King because he is immature and without a following. Khuang may be forcing them into each other's arms by the specter of Chumphot as King.[109]

According to Marshall, Phibun thwarted the royalists' plan: Phibun opposed Chumbot's accession, instead seeking to keep Bhumipol on the throne, "believing that the secret of his accidental killing of Ananda could be used to manipulate him".[110] Other possible reasons were that Phibun thought he could handle the monarch and divide the royals.

Whatever the situation, Phibun's forces quickly realized that the royalists might soon garner the legitimacy from the West that Phibun himself lacked. They thus sought to build bridges with none other than Pridi—though there is no evidence that Pridi was receptive. Such an alliance would have been difficult since Khuang and the Phibun-led military had continuously harassed leaders of Pridi-aligned political parties and newspapers. Also, Phibun had for a short time sought the support of Thamrong for a coup against Khuang. Indeed, naval and former Seri Thai forces of the deposed prime minister Admiral Thamrong had continued to attempt a *coup d'etat* against Khuang and Phibun, though this had never played out owing to resistance from the British and US governments.[111] Though no such alliance ever transpired, in early February 1948, thousands of soldiers demonstrated in front of the Supreme Council, demanding that it appoint Phibun as prime minister. In addition, Phibun, Phin and Thamrong insisted that Khuang accept their nominees for the key cabinet positions of defence, finance, foreign affairs and the interior. A coup was finally attempted on 27 February 1948, but the navy—under Admiral Sinthu—successfully resisted it, and Phibun's forces demurred. The failure of the coup and the continuing instability of the Khuang government prompted the United States, Britain, France and other countries at the end of February to finally recognize Khuang as prime minister.[112] Nevertheless, this recognition was too late—the military wanted Khuang ousted.

In 1948, Thailand entered its classic era of military praetorianism—as if the November 1947 coup had let the military genie out of the bottle. But with no international patron willing to regularly supply weapons to the country's military, obtaining arms became an obsession for the Coup Group. For that matter, in 1948, Phin sent his son Chatchai Chunhavan, now a colonel, to Washington DC to act as assistant military attaché, but more importantly to help coordinate any weapons purchases from the United States. According to CIA records, Phin and Kat were purchasing weapons wherever they could get them, including French Algeria, Hong Kong, Bulgaria and the Hainanese China Sea Trading Company, which sounded suspiciously like a CIA front organization. The money for many of the weapons purchases was routed through the commercial arm of the Thai War Veterans Organization, led by Phin himself.[113] Yet another source for arms was the CIA-linked Willis Bird and his Willis Bird Export Import Company. In January 1949, Phibun, Phao and Phin made separate overtures to Bird to help them purchase from the United States (via the Lake Erie Chemical Company) varying amounts of military and police hardware.[114] Within Thailand, Bird's connection to the military was his in-law Flight Lieutenant Sitthi Savetsila, while within the United States Bird maintained ties with Chatchai. Despite being on opposite sides during World War II (Sitthi was a member of Seri Thai), Sitthi and Chatchai were also close. Sitthi later recounted going to the cinema with a young Chatchai in Washington.[115]

By the beginning of April 1948, though Phibun had foiled Khuang's regal manipulation, senior military leaders were becoming restless with the prime minister's continuing independence of their "guidance". Khuang had even threatened to slash military spending. Eventually, four senior officers visited his home on 6 April and accused the prime minister of having a debt of 28 million baht for expenses from his journey from Keng Tung back to Bangkok in 1945. When the PM refused to pay, the officers issued him an ultimatum to, in effect, resign within twenty-four hours given the Coup Group's general perception that Khuang's administration was inefficient. Thereupon, the prime minister requested support from the air force and navy, but they refused to assist. In the end, Khuang complied, but not before writing a letter to King Bhumipol explaining his actions:

> Today at 9am four army officers namely Col. Kan Chamnong-phumiwet, Col. Silapasonchai, Ratanawaraha, Major General Sawat Sawatikiat and Lt. Colonel Lamai Utayanon came to visit me at my house and informed me that the coup group was very dissatisfied with the government and have agreed after a conference to ask the government to resign within twenty-four hours. When the four officers had left, I invited certain ministers who I was able to contact for consultation. After this discussion, we were of the opinion that it would be appropriate to receive further evidence from persons whom the public have accepted as leaders of the Coup Group, for example Field Marshal P. Phibunsongkhram, Lt. Gen. Phin Chunnahawan, or Lt. Gen. Kat Katsongkhram. Therefore, I wrote a personal note to Lt. Col. Kan Chamnongphumivet to ask for the above evidence.... Around 1400 hours of that same day, Lt. Gen. Phin Chunnahawan and Lt. Gen. Kat Katsongkhram came to see me and confirmed that the message delivered by Lt. Col. Kan and associates represented the real intentions of the Coup Group. Subsequently, I called a meeting of the cabinet around 1800 hours and we concluded that because of the quick turning of events, the government must accept the fact that it was in no position to maintain normal conditions as entrusted by Your Majesty. Therefore, we beg your majesty to accept henceforth our resignations.
>
> Your Loyal Subject,
> Khuang Aphaiwong[116]

Known as the *chi nai Khuang* (Khuang's "mugging"), Phin later stated that Khuang's decision to vacate the office of prime minister was the act of "a real sportsman".[117] Privy Council chair and regent Prince Rangsit initially refused, however, to accept the resignation until Khuang reminded him that the Coup Group might simply start another coup in order to get its way. At that point, even Rangsit capitulated. US ambassador Stanton, however, was livid that the military had ignored "constitutional processes", and he encouraged Washington to withhold recognition. But, by 1948, most US State Department officials—following the lead of Kenneth Landon of the Office of Asian

Affairs—preferred a government of anti-communist stability led by Phibun than one dedicated only to "honest civilians".[118]

With Khuang gone, Phibun was immediately elevated to the position of prime minister.[119] The Defence Ministry, however, remained under General Luang Chatnakrop (an older Core Group member close to Phibun), who had served in the position since November 1947 and continued holding it until 1949 (when Phibun took the position himself).

In late April 1948, a letter appeared in a Bangkok newspaper addressed to incoming prime minister Phibun from 1947 coup instigators Phin and Kat. The letter notified Phibun that since the field marshal was now taking up the burden of solving national problems he should henceforth (1) serve only as advisor to the Coup Group; (2) that Phibun's post of army commander should temporarily be left vacant; (3) that the administration of the army be entrusted to army deputy chief Phin and army assistant chief Kat; (4) that all members of the Coup Group would "pledge their support" to Prime Minister Phibun; and (5) that Phin and Kat be allowed to sit with Phibun at every meeting of parliament.[120] A little over a month after the coup, Phin gained the formal power that he already ambiguously held since seizing power—the position of army commander—on 18 May 1948.[121] Kat was promoted to become army deputy chief and 1st Army Region commander. Phin in turn ensured that his son-in-law, Phao, became head of the police in 1951. Sarit Thanarat, then a colonel, became a field marshal and commander of the 1st Army Division (see 1948 reshuffle, Appendix 4). Indeed, power became shared among Phibun, Phin, Phao, Kat and even Sarit.

After April 1948, the top brass proved unwilling to give Phibun the same high powers he had possessed in the late 1930s. With Phibun retired from any active-duty post in the armed forces and serving merely as prime minister, he was weak relative to any military commander or sub-commander. Yet he did manage to at least remain prime minister, given his control over the politicians.[122]

Meanwhile, army commander Field Marshal Phin Chunhavan organized the armed forces with his loyalists in dominant positions. In fact, the military appointments across 1949–54 intensified the power not only of Phin but also of officers connected to Phin's Soi Rajakru faction—especially his son-in-law deputy police commander and then police commander General Phao Sriyanond. At the same time, Phin had to facilitate the growing power of 1st Army chief (and later army deputy chief) General Sarit Thanarat. Prime Minister Phibun

Songkram (who juggled among Phin, Phao and Sarit to maintain influence) also became defence minister in 1949. Another 1947 coup participant, ACM Fuen Ronnaphagrad Ritthakhanee, was elevated to become air force chief in 1949, replacing Air Marshal Luang Tevaritpunluok, and also became influential (see Appendix 4).

Perhaps to mollify royalists into accepting the accession of Phibun, the new government allowed them to dominate the drafting of the 23 January 1949 constitution (promulgated to replace the 1947 temporary charter). The result was one that the Coup Group lived to regret because it produced a document that consolidated royal powers which had been intensified in the 1947 constitution. For example, under the new charter, the king alone could appoint the hundred-person Senate. These appointments (and all laws) were hereafter countersigned by the Privy Council chair rather than the prime minister. Also, the five-person Supreme Council was enlarged to nine and its name was changed to Privy Council (Ongkamontri). Appointments to this council were the sole right of the palace. And the king was given the power of plebiscite, to potentially alter the constitution through a simple majority of Thai voters. Moreover, in terms of succession, it became the Privy Council that would name an heir, not parliament. Furthermore, the monarch was given the decree power to dismiss any military or civilian bureaucrat, and could issue decrees outside of the control of the executive.[123] Finally, the charter banned active-duty civil servants (including soldiers) from serving in parliament or on the Council of Ministers.[124] As such, Phibun was required to again retire from the bureaucracy, while Phin and Phao, as active top brass, did not take any civilian cabinet positions. But the three would eventually jettison the royalists.

Military cohesion remained weak, however. Despite its ousting of Khuang and its apparent control over Thailand, the Phibun-Phin-Phao group suffered six coup attempts within the span of four years (1948–51).

The first military rebellion occurred on 1 October 1948. Officers from the army's general staff connected with Seri Thai (Maj. Gen. Somboon Saranuchit and Maj. Gen. Netr Khemayothin) were accused of plotting to assassinate Coup Group leaders at the wedding of Lt. Gen. Sarit Thanarat, though the plan was foiled before it could be hatched. It is possible, however, that the charges against the alleged coup ringleaders were fabricated to stamp out suspected internal dissent and to further weaken support for Seri Thai within the services.[125] According to Fineman, the purpose of this coup was "primarily aimed at ousting Kat and ending his raid on the Thai treasury and military budget".[126] The abortive putsch had two alternative plans. First, Phibun, Phin, Kat and Phao would be detained and forced to sign orders in support of this countercoup. A new junta under former defence minister (and pro-Democrat) General Sinat would then be formed. The other plan amounted to simply detaining the entire cabinet to compel support for an incoming countercoup government. The countercoup government would have oscillated around General Sinat as prime minister, Democrat Khuang Aphaiwong as deputy prime minister and minister of the interior, Seri Thai former prime minister Thawee Bunyaket as minister of agriculture, and Pridi confidant Direk Jayanama as foreign minister.[127] Ultimately, the coup never got off the ground and all three plotters were arrested. Nevertheless, Phibun, exploiting a general fear of communism, sought to connect the coup with all his political opponents. He thus initiated a purge of military officers and jailed former Seri Thai officials. The coup attempt led to a cabinet reshuffle, a more factionalized military and increasing calls for Kat to resign from the armed forces.

A second coup attempt took place on 26–27 February 1949—another unsuccessful effort, which later became known as the "Palace Rebellion". Led by the exiled Pridi Panomyong, it was meticulously planned and included former Seri Thai elements who were now part of Thailand's marines (within the navy) and the army. According to the CIA, a US sub-chaser ship, the SS *Bluebird*, left Hong Kong on 2 February. Commanding it was US citizen, former air force bombardier and OSS member George Nellis. That evening, the *Bluebird* picked up weapons for the coup from a Chinese merchant ship that had come from Canton. Also boarding the *Bluebird* were eight to nine Thais led by Pridi. The *Bluebird* arrived at an island close to the Thai coast on 7 February and changed its name. From 7 to 24 February, a Japanese junk ferried ashore at intervals the party and the weapons to the outskirts of Bangkok (the *Bluebird* subsequently arrived at Saigon on 2 March and was picked up by French naval vessels).[128] To this day, neither Nellis nor the *Bluebird* has been identified in any further records. Whether Nellis was simply a friend of Pridi, a mercenary or a US agent is unknown.

Phibun became aware of the impending coup days before it happened, and he instituted a state of emergency on 23 February.[129] But Pridi's coup attempt in many respects was initially successful because of a split between senior army and navy officials. It was thus a bloody affair. On 26 February, several marine rebels combined with army elements to usurp power from the Coup Group. These forces, conducting their attempted putsch amidst regularly held military exercises, managed to capture Thammasat University, the state radio station and the Royal Grand Palace. At that point, the radio station broadcast what it claimed to be a royal proclamation, dismissing the Phibun government, appointing a pro-Pridi cabinet and re-establishing the anti-monarchy 1933 constitution. At the last moment, however, other disaffected army and navy officials failed to join the coup forces, and not enough marines were able to cross the Chao Phraya River from Thonburi. At the same time, though Pridi tried to obtain support for the coup from both deputy police chief Phao Sriyanond and 1st Infantry commander General Sarit Thanarat, both declined.[130] Moreover, navy commander Admiral Sinthu apparently decided not to support the coup after obtaining concessions from Phibun in terms of "non-interference from the Army".[131] As such, Lt. Gen. Sarit Thanarat, commander of the army's 1st Division, successfully led government forces in suppressing the coup attempt. Pridi himself managed to escape to Malaya after a few days, and though in April he returned briefly to Satthahip Naval Base for medical care (where navy commander Admiral Sinthu refused to surrender him to Phibun),[132] Pridi thereafter never returned to Thailand.[133] Afterwards, the navy leadership and Phibun began negotiations on fourteen navy demands, including an amnesty for participants in the October 1948 and February 1949 coups, a modification in the proposed 1949 constitution (considered overly royalist by the navy) and the dismissal of the leaders of the November 1947 coup.[134] Only the amnesty (for soldiers) was ever implemented. Following the failed 1949 Palace Rebellion, Phibun used the excuse of the coup attempt to remove General Kat Katsongkram from control over the 1st Army Region. In addition, Phin conducted a massive purge of suspected Seri Thai and Pridi sympathizers from the armed forces—though navy chief Sinthu kept his post. Rear Admiral Thaharn Khamhiran, commander of the Marine Corps, was transferred to an inactive posting in the Naval Staff Department—though he continued to plot against Phibun. The United States was very supportive of the military's crushing of the 1949 coup. This owed to the belief among US policymakers that communist Chinese backed the putsch and that "connections between Russian Communists and Chinese Communists are very strong".[135]

One week after the abortive putsch, deputy police chief General Phao Sriyanond ordered his *asawin* (knights of the diamond ring) police hitmen to eliminate politicians in Thailand considered close to Pridi. Thus, at 2:15 a.m. on 4 March 1949, in a car on the Don Muang Highway near Bangkhen, police "Major Lanthom Chitwimon led the killings of [and] personally shot" four ex-Pridi cabinet ministers—Tieng Sirikhan, Chamlong Daoruang, Tawin Udom and Thong-in Phuriphat (Thai progressives seen as communists by the CIA). "About 100 shots were fired" from the police car that was behind the car carrying the four ministers in the procession of vehicles. "Phibun had prior knowledge of the murders of the four ex-ministers [and] conceived of their deaths as a sop to both royalists and anti-communists".[136]

A third almost-putsch was that of mid-December 1949. Anti-Phibun groups were angered by the government's hoarding of opium smuggling (which prevented illicit profits from going to the former), while the government was worried that navy and air force officials were becoming overly amicable. In addition, the commander of the Territorial Command, Colonel Khun Silsornchai, had been involved in a coup plot against Phibun. Thus, Phibun first forcibly retired air force commander ACM Luang Tevaritpanluek. Phibun then allowed Colonel Silsorchai to retire. The coup attempt plan was thus broken because the Territorial Command was to be the primary source of soldiers to implement it. Meanwhile, former army chief General Adul Adul Decharat was arrested briefly when it was learned he had been privy to the coup. Colonel Prasert Ruchirawong (later police commander) also admitted to being involved in supporting the putsch. There was even a rumour that General Sarit Thanarat participated in the plot. Phibun was "stunned" by this coup and quickly sought to get coup plotters out of Thailand and to military attaché postings abroad. Most interesting, however, was that Phibun was unable to discipline navy commander Admiral Sinthu for his apparent role in the planned putsch. According to the CIA, "The position of the Thai Navy remains influential in the background."[137]

A fourth apparently attempted putsch (which was only a false accusation) occurred on 27 January 1950. In this incident, Phibun, Phin and Phao dealt a decisive blow to the ambitious Luang Kat Katsongkram, who had been a leader of the November 1947 coup that had felled the Thamrong government, but who was increasingly becoming a thorn in the side of the Coup Group leaders. Indeed, Luang Kat, who was becoming increasingly powerful within the army, had demanded (and was granted) promotion all the way from lieutenant colonel to lieutenant general in a single step and was also appointed to army deputy commander. Many officers resented his meteoric rise through the ranks as well as his fiery personality. In addition, he was seen as extremely corrupt. Moreover, Phibun never thoroughly trusted Kat given the latter's defection to Seri Thai in 1941. As early as 1947,

Kat had entered into a rivalry with Phin.[138] In addition, he refused to cooperate with defence minister General Luang Chatnakrap—Kat had wanted the post himself. This is one reason why Phibun took the defence portfolio (in addition to already holding the prime ministerial portfolio) in 1949. Phibun and Phin also suspected that Kat had quietly supported the December 1949 coup attempt. Thus, on 27 January 1950, while working at his desk at Suan Kularb Palace, Kat received a call from Phibun to report to a meeting at Government House. When he arrived, deputy police chief General Phao, leading twenty armed police officers, suddenly moved to detain him. Phao even held a revolver to Kat's head and said, "By order of the government, I will arrest you now." Kat replied, "On what grounds are you arresting me?" Phao replied, "On the grounds of attempted rebellion." Kat then said, "Is there any evidence?" Phao replied in one word, "Yes." Kat then asked, "Can I meet with the Prime Minister?" Phao abruptly replied, "No." Phao then placed Kat in a police car and he was detained on an upper floor at Parukswan Palace. After several hours in detention, Phao again approached Kat and asked, "Where would you like us to send you abroad?" At this point Kat certainly realized that the arrest was a mere pretext to force him out of Thailand. Luang Kat replied, "It depends. I can go to England, Switzerland, France, America, Penang or Singapore."[139] Phao then had an official from the Ministry of Foreign Affairs quickly draw up a passport for Kat. The next day, on 28 January 1950, a convoy of three to four police cars took Kat to Don Muang airport. The procession was led by Phao, and armed police officers sat on either side of Kat. He was ultimately put on a plane bound for Hong Kong. Police informed the military (within which Kat had many supporters in the 1st Army Region) that Kat had fled Thailand. In absentia, Kat was accused of plotting against the Phibun-Phin-Phao triumvirate (on mostly trumped-up charges). He was forced into exile and retirement. The judiciary dropped the charges against Kat when, after returning to Thailand in 1951, he left politics.[140]

A fifth usurpation attempt happened in June 1951. It was by far the most dramatic and also quite bloody, with 1,200 dead and 1,800 wounded, mostly civilians.[141] Known as the *Manhattan* Rebellion, it once again was spearheaded by naval forces who had suffered the most from the anti-Pridi purges of 1949–50. Rather than quashing dissent, these had caused the navy—with its long and bitter rivalry with the army—to more desperately seek the ouster of army career men Phibun and Phin in favour of Pridi. Navy officials originally planned the coup for 22 October 1950. But when the police got wind of it the putsch plan was put on hold.[142] On 6 March 1951, the Thai police arrested

Rear Admiral Thaharn Khamhiran, formerly the head of the Marine Corps, for "planning the overthrow of the government".[143] Thaharn was thought to be heading up a revolt of disgruntled army, navy and police officials, and a number of arrests were made. But, if anything, these arrests merely delayed the coup—which occurred two and a half months later. By that time, army, air force and police groups had become vaguely supportive of a putsch—to get rid of Phao—though they would let the navy take the first steps. Calling it a "coup within a coup", a CIA cable stated:

> In recent weeks there had been a gradual joining of dissident forces with the aim of ousting Phao and his clique. This dissident coalition included Admiral Sind Kammonawin and virtually the entire Navy, the Air Force, the Thai 3 Army under General Wirayot [Wirawat] Yothin at Phitsanulok, Lt. General Sarit Thanarat's units in the Thai 1 Army, and certain pro-Pridi and Seri Thai elements.[144]

Thus, on 29 June 1951, in a Chao Phraya River ceremony—at which the US Navy officially donated the US dredger *Manhattan* to Thailand—Phibun, in his capacity as premier, boarded the ship to officially take charge of it for Thailand. The coup leader recalled:

> When the Prime Minister walked closer, I shouted to him; "I want only the Field Marshal. Those not concerned step back. Please come this way, Field Marshal."[145]

And indeed, armed sailors detained Phibun, holding him hostage aboard the *Manhattan* before transferring him to the naval flagship *Si Ayutthaya*. On land, however, naval forces were only able to take over Fleet Headquarters, and only for a short time. Fierce fighting broke out mostly on land between police and army troops on one side and naval forces on the other. Amidst negotiations carrying over into the following day, planes of the fledgling Royal Thai Air Force (formed in 1947) bombed naval facilities and even the *Si Ayutthaya*, causing the latter to sink. Phibun was forced to swim to shore.

In the aftermath of the failed putsch, US chargé d'affaires William Turner dismissed rumours that it had been borne from communist elements and expressed indignation that an American (Willis Bird) had supported police Commander Phao in quelling it:

> The recent communist coup scare [claims about the causes of the *Manhattan* coup] … is the result of another concoction of the Taipei rumor-mill [w]hereupon an assistant … consult[ed] Mr. Willis Bird in the effort to make the identifications. Mr. Bird, as you may remember, featured somewhat prominently in the June 29th incident as the character who handed over a lot of military

equipment to the Police, without any authorization as far as I can determine, and whose status ... is ambiguous, to say the least. Mr. Bird, again without any authorization, takes the message to Phra Pinit, Acting Police Chief in Phao's absence. Pinit hits the ceiling, rushes over to Pibun, and they decide on a general alarm since the warning emanated from impeccable American intelligence sources! So for several days we had a state of emergency in the city with the Police mobilized and everybody jittery. The story would be funny if it did not have some serious aspects.... Why is this man Bird allowed to deal with the Police Chief in such matters? Why was I not informed[?] Frankly, I don't like it, and unless there is some better effort at discipline, I'm going to take a stronger hand in the matter.[146]

The overall winner of the coup's defeat was Phao, as assisted by his father-in-law Phin, Sarit and Bird. The losers were the navy and Phibun, whose political influence began to diminish.

The leaders of the abortive coup, Commander Manat Charupa and Captain Anon Puntharigapha (as well as several others), succeeded in escaping abroad.[147] As Thak notes, "the Manhattan Rebellion marked the entrance of the Air Force into Thai politics."[148] Meanwhile, after the coup attempt, the navy was re-staffed from top to bottom, its budget was cut considerably and it lost any remaining political power it had. Long-time (thirteen years) navy commander Admiral Sindh Kamalanavin was sacked and tried for involvement in the coup attempt, though he was found not guilty. One of the few original Promoters who still held power, Sindh, now suddenly left politics. He died quietly in 1976. Sindh was ultimately replaced in 1951 by Admiral Luang Yutasat Kosol (Prayun Yutasatkosol), a Phibun loyalist who oversaw the dismantling of the Thai naval forces.

With the defeat of the navy, Pridi lost any lingering military support. Phibun was also weakened. Clearly, the army and air force had been willing to sacrifice the premier's life. Following the attempted coup, top brass demanded changes to his cabinet, which gave them greater control over it.[149] Indeed, with constitutional changes in 1951–52 (see below), active-duty "military men grabbed 19 of the 25 cabinet-level offices". The Phin-Phao clique took five of these, more than any other faction. Phao himself served as deputy interior minister, giving him effective control over the ministry, which directed the police department. Phin acted as deputy prime minister and Sarit became deputy defence minister.[150] The success of Phibun, Phin and Phao in resisting the four coup attempts—with necessary leadership from rising star General Sarit[151]—helped to solidify their control over Thailand's armed forces.

A sixth coup attempt occurred at the end of November 1951 (the second of that year). This putsch proved to be successful because it clinched army control over all political forces in Thailand. The Coup Group had become increasingly annoyed in its dealings with parliament and the palace, including the palace-appointed Senate's censuring of the government for its purge of the navy. Also, Phibun's Sahapap coalition in parliament was becoming increasingly independent of Phibun himself. Some of his MPs refused to continue supporting him unless he made changes to his cabinet. Parliament further voted down bills favoured by the Coup Group. Moreover, students at Thammasat University demonstrated against its being converted into an army barracks. More importantly, however, Phibun, Phin and Phao worried about the impending return of King Bhumipol Adulyadej from Switzerland. They apparently thought that the young monarch would threaten their political power. According to Phibun confidant Sang Phathanothai, the Coup Group abhorred the resurrection of monarchical power enshrined in the 1949 constitution and intended to trash it prior to the king's arrival.[152]

As Bhumipol's ship was approaching on 29 November 1951, several generals arrived at the Privy Council and demanded the abrogation

FIGURE 3.5
Military Hierarchy of the Initial 1951 Junta:
"Temporary Executive Power"

Name	Service
General Phin Chunhavan	Army
Lt. Gen. Dej Dejpradiyuth	Army
Lt. Gen. Sarit Thanarat	Army
Rear Adm. Luang Yudhasastrkosol	Navy
Rear Adm. Chamnan-arthayudh	Navy
Rear Adm. Sunthorn Sunthornnavin	Navy
ACM Fuen Ronnabhakas Ridhakani	Air Force
ACM Luang Cherdvutakas	Air Force
ACM Luang Proongprichakas	Air Force

Source: Communiques nos. 1 and 2, 29 November 1951, translated and edited by Thak Chaloermtirana, *Thai Politics: 1932–1957* (Social Science Association of Thailand, Thammasat University, 1978), pp. 675–78.

of the 1949 constitution, new elections and a new government, with the military in charge. When this was refused, the top brass issued a radio announcement to the same effect anyway. The rationale for the coup centred on the need to "fight communism which is a source of danger to the nation, the Faith and the Throne".[153] The result of the putsch was the voiding of the charter and Prime Minister Phibun's appointment as Privy Council chair in place of the king's uncle Prince Dhani. Real power was placed in a military council: the "Temporary Executive Power" (Figure 3.5).

The "Silent Coup", however, led to two principal consequences. It diminished the power both of elected representatives and of the palace. The objective was clear: the military and the police had monopolized national perks and privileges from 1932 to 1944, had thirsted for this during the years of civilian control until 1947, and now, with authority in their hands, sought to turn the clock back to 1944 once again. The armed forces and police no longer intended to cede any degree of their corporate interests to civilian politicians, and they seemed more than willing to stem the growth of regal power. For elected representatives, the political space that had started to open for them under the 1946 constitution was now severely restricted, with active duty soldiers once again allowed to serve in both the parliament and cabinet. At the same time, the Coup Group dissolved the monarch-appointed Senate. Prior to 1951, the military had relied on the Thammatipat and Sahapap parties in parliament, and soldiers had been hindered by a royalist Senate that worked against their interests. For example, the Senate had vetoed the proposal by Prime Minister Phibun to allow block voting by soldiers. Yet, in one fell swoop, the 1951 Silent Coup ended these annoyances: the armed forces succeeded in "packing" the legislature and Council of Ministers with loyal officers.[154] Meanwhile, in more bad news for the palace, the vehemently anti-monarchist charter of 1932 was restored; the Privy Council lost its enshrined political powers; and the king lost the power to select senators. Ultimately, this recycled 1932 charter effectively transformed the monarch into little more than a figurehead—though the king succeeded in maintaining control over his personal household.[155]

In place of the bicameral parliament, a 103-member unicameral assembly was formed, with all appointees coming from the military or police, and which were not to be nominated by the palace. The "Temporary Executive Power" junta administered the country until military-supervised elections were held on 26 February 1952. This election, however, was a sham: held during a temporary ban on political gatherings of more than five people. The armed forces could easily dominate the poll, especially given that no political parties were allowed to field candidates, and, as such, all candidates ran as independents.[156] Moreover, a few days before the election, the parliamentary opposition, led by Democrat Party bigwigs Khuang Aphaiwong and Seni Pramoj, boycotted the election. The result popularly legitimized Phibun as prime minister for the first time since 1938. Yet elected MPs represented only half of the unicameral assembly—the military appointed the others. During this time, political gatherings were forbidden by law and politicians were not allowed to conduct political activities.[157] Ultimately, the executive exerted tremendous influence.

The people who benefited most from Thailand's post-1951 military monopoly were deputy police chief Phao Sriyanond and his father-in-law, army commander Phin Chunhavan. From 1951 until 1954, the two managed to hold sway over most of the country's security forces, with Phibun possessing diminished power as prime ministerial figurehead.[158] Phao's political and economic power now emanated not only from his role as police chief but also from his promotion in 1953 to the posts of deputy minister of the interior and deputy minister of finance. Phao became minister of the interior in 1957.[159] From these postings he extracted rent.

General Det Deppradityut and General Sarit Thanarat became more powerful after 1951, as did ACM Fuen Ronnabhakas Ridhakani. Det and Sarit became deputy army chief successively in 1951 and 1952, while Fuen—air force chief since 1949—served until 1957.[160]

The power of the armed forces continued to be embedded in the unicameral assembly. As illustrated in Figure 3.6, so many military

FIGURE 3.6
Thailand's Legislature, 1952–57

Type of legislature	Years in office	Appointed or elected	Total number of legislators and military contingent
Unicameral	1951/ 1952–57	123 elected by eligible voters/123 appointed	246, of which 106 (86.1%) military reserved domain of the appointed

Source: Paul Chambers, "Superfluous, Irrelevant or Emancipating: Thailand's Evolving Senate Today", *Journal of Current Southeast Asian Affairs* 28, no. 3 (2009): 9, https://d-nb.info/999559311/34.

officials sat in so many seats of the legislature that it more than ever became a legitimizing rubber stamp of continued armed forces rule.

The military soon became fragmented despite such control, with three factions emerging based around three top leaders. First there was the Phibun Songkram clique, second the Phin-Phao group (Soi Rajakru), and third the Sarit faction (Sisao Thewes). Phibun, despite the fame and respect he possessed in the armed forces, had lost active-duty contact with military officers, first in 1944 and second in 1948. At the same time, the 1947 coup against Thamrong and Pridi had been organized by Phin. Loyalists of Phin (not Phibun) gained key military postings. By 1951, Phibun led the weakest of the three factions. Second, there was the Phin-Phao clique. The faction was colourfully referred to as Soi Rajakru because Phin's home was located on Soi (Alley) Rajakru. By virtue of Phin's role as army commander (and the tremendous respect in which he was held by soldiers given his World War II exploits), Phin managed to unify the army. October 1951 saw the elevation of Phin's son-in-law General Phao Siyanon as head of the police department. Together, Phin and Phao held sway over Thailand's entire security apparatus: leading the army and police, with the air force an army proxy and the navy seriously weakened, their domination seemed assured. The final clique was that of General Sarit Thanarat (Sisao Thewes). In the Phin-led 1947 overthrow of Thamrong and all of the coup attempts against the Coup Group since, Sarit had been instrumental in ensuring the success of Phibun, Phin and Phao. In the aftermath of the suppression of the 1949 "Palace Rebellion", he had been promoted to command the all-important 1st Army Region in Bangkok. In 1951 he had been rewarded for repressing the *Manhattan* Rebellion by being promoted to the position of deputy minister of defence, and, in 1952, concurrently to the positions of army deputy commander, vice admiral and vice air chief marshal. Yet Sarit realized that he only needed to bide his time to succeed Phin. The army commander turned sixty in 1951 and could only extend his term for a few years. Besides, Phin was becoming increasingly distracted by his multiple economic activities outside of the military. Indeed, Phin was often absent from direct responsibilities, giving Sarit the opportunity to position his loyalists (generals Thanom Kittikachorn, Prapas Charusatien and Krit Sivara) in key military positions. Ultimately, with Phibun having lost direct military contact and simply trying to balance the police and army, while Phin was getting older and seemed engrossed in personal interests, Phao and Sarit—roughly the same age—became direct competitors for power. It was inevitable that a clash would take place.[161]

In March 1952, Phao sought to force Phibun from the premiership and take the post for himself. Indeed, Phao accused Phibun of failing to implement a sufficiently strong anti-communist law. Such a broad anti-communist act would have given Phao, in his role as police chief, much more authority to destroy the civilian opposition and strengthen his own political position vis-à-vis Phibun and Sarit. Perhaps knowing that Sarit—as Phao's nemesis—would come to his aid, on 7 March Phibun offered Phao the premiership. The prime minister thereupon publicly announced he would resign and seek to become president of parliament. Though Phao was "elated", Sarit saw that he might soon be out-leveraged by the police commander in terms of holding political and security power. As such, Sarit sought strenuously to convince Phibun to remain as premier.[162] In mid-March, the CIA reported (erroneously) that the Thai Navy had "seized the king on March 14 and that the resignation of the Thai cabinet was imminent".[163] Meanwhile, the Phin-Phao clique was intent on removing "Premier Phibun and assum[ing] control of the administration. General Sarit, commander of the Bangkok garrison, is reportedly attempting to ally himself with Phibun in an effort to block the plans of the PhinPhao group."

By June the CIA was reporting that Phao's plan to depose Phibun in a coup was continuing, and that Sarit had lost control over certain army units. The report continued that

> If Sarit fails to rebuild his position soon, his army supporters may attempt a coup which might result in "general fighting throughout the Kingdom." Press reports of 20 June state that a general alert has been ordered in Thailand.[164]

The chaotic tit-for-tat between Phao and Sarit continued throughout the next several months. In August, Phibun again threatened to resign, implying that he might choose either Phao or Sarit as his successor. Attempting to pre-empt Phibun, Phao and Phin reportedly planned to remove "Phibun from office by engineering the resignation of the cabinet and forming a new one under a figurehead".[165] But the field marshal remained durable because he continued to be favoured in Washington, which helped him to remain in office. Indeed, while the United States saw Phao as corrupt, brutal and an occasional friend to Beijing, Phibun had sent Thai troops to Korea to help fight against communists, had decided to recognize the French-installed Bao Dai government in Vietnam, and had instituted generally pro-US policies for Thailand. Phibun also ordered Phao to arrest members of Thailand's then nascent peace movement, a move that also involved the arrests of junior military officers. The detentions angered other service chiefs, who viewed them as a power grab by Phao.[166] To legitimize the arrests and please Washington, on 13 November 1952 Phibun enacted a new anti-communism law, after which he launched a reign of terror against suspected communists. The CIA gladly saw Phibun as responsible for ordering Phao to engage in anti-communist round-ups "after the latter had 'dragged his feet'".[167] But, possibly to curry favour with the CIA, Phao perhaps implemented the anti-communist law too eagerly: on 12 December 1952, while pro-Pridi progressive politician Tiang Sirikhan attended a special meeting of the Legislative Council, he was summoned by Phao to meet him. Tiang then simply disappeared. It was later revealed that, during the night of 13 December 1952, Tiang and four of his political associates—Chan Bunnag, Lek Bunnag, Phong Khewwichit and Sanga Prajakwong—were brutally murdered. The bodies were then cremated to destroy the evidence.[168] By this action, Phao proved he might be the most fearsome personage in Thailand. But the targeted killings by Phao also showed many US officials that he was a true anti-communist. Indeed, according to Darling, the CIA was privy to Phao's investigations of political dissenters and advised him on how his police should react.[169]

Meanwhile, amidst their quest to dominate politics, Phin and Phao also attempted to dominate the Thai economy. Phin Chunhavan developed an extensive network of business and political contacts, both personal and family connections, who all lived in close proximity to each other on Soi Rajakru. As such, his faction of influence became known as Soi Rajakru. Phin used his son Chatchai to extend his influence in the army: Captain Chatchai was appointed to become company commander, 1st Cavalry Squadron, Royal Guards, following the 1947 putsch. Meanwhile, Phin's four sons-in-law (Phao Sriyanond, Pramarn Adireksan, Siri Siriyothin and Lamai Uthayanon) were also useful. In the army, after 1947, Pramarn, Siri and Lamai served in the Armed Forces Vehicle Department, while Lamai became commander of the 7th Infantry Regiment. Meanwhile, through control over the Veterans' Organization (VO), the Soi Rajakru Group invested in a VO affiliate known as the Thahan Samakkhi Organization (renamed as Saha Samakkhi in 1955) as a means of controlling Thailand's rice trade, including train operations transporting rice to Bangkok. Such control was facilitated with the appointment of Phin's nephew Colonel Pramarn Adireksan to oversee the Railway Authority of Thailand. Phin's Thahan Samakkhi was further strengthened by the fact that it became "the chief recipient of governmental assistance and privileges in commercial fields" from the Phibun government.[170] Soi Rajakru, at the same time, became closely associated with other Chinese-managed groups, including the Bank of Ayudhya. In the mid-1950s, Police General Phao Sriyanond became an important patron for Chin Sophonpanich, the owner of Bangkok Bank. A principal rival to Bangkok Bank was Churin Lamsam's Thai Farmer's Bank, the patron of which was Field Marshal Phibun Songkram.[171] Meanwhile, in the police, Phao Sriyanond and son-in-law Colonel Lamai Uthayanon offered a direct power base for Phin in the security forces. In 1951, sons-in-law Colonel Siri Siriyothin and Colonel Pramarn Adireksan gained the cabinet portfolios of deputy minister of commerce and deputy minister of communications, respectively. In 1954, Siri became minister of economic affairs, while Phao obtained the portfolio of deputy minister of finance. Phin took the slot of minister of agriculture in 1957. According to Thak, Phin and his military in-laws used these positions to facilitate their business dealings.[172]

To some extent, Phin and Phao consolidated their political and economic control by stage-managing close relations with the United States and supporting the Kuomintang (KMT) army beginning in 1950. With the beginning of the Cold War in the late 1940s, the United States had paid increasing attention to Thailand, seeing it as a frontline state against communism that must prepare for an "assault" from Communist China.[173]

In the Thailand of early 1950, the United States was seeking to create an airline that could transport weapons to Bangkok, which would also be ready to move soldiers to war zones. At the time there were no military bilateral agreements. The CIA thus created the Pacific Corporation as a holding company to control various aviation front companies. The latter would ostensibly be private but actually worked in the service of CIA objectives. One of these aviation front companies was Civil Air Transport (CAT), which had actually been the residue of the Kuomintang aircraft created by Captains Claire Chennault and Whiting Willauer in 1946, and Chennault's World War II combat aircraft "the Flying Tigers". The CIA, through the Pacific Corporation, purchased these aircraft in 1950 to start Civil Air Transport. In Bangkok, the agent for CAT and the related Philippine Airlines was William H. Bird, a relative or friend of Willis Bird, both of whom worked indirectly for Washington.[174] Nevertheless, there is much confusion about the identities of Willis H. and William H., given that CAT and Philippine Airlines were sometimes advertised as being under the direction of Willis Bird.[175] Nevertheless, CAT was definitely a US-controlled airline that worked most closely with the Royal Thai

Police and Royal Thai Air Force. The United States funnelled millions of dollars in support of Phao and his police through CAT.

In early 1950, Bird organized a group to lobby for increased US military assistance and devise an anti-communist strategy for Thailand called the Naresuan Committee. It was composed of leading Thai security officials, including Bird's patron Phao, General Phin Chunhavan, General Sarit, air force chief ACM Fuen Ronnapakat and Bird himself. The group's interpreter was Lieutenant Sitthi Savetsila. With Ambassador Stanton and the State Department seemingly slow and unreliable in getting weapons to the army, the Naresuan Committee simply bypassed them, working directly with CIA headquarters in Washington.[176] Moreover, as Sitthi himself later pointed out, "the Naresuan Committee was indispensable because at the time there was no JUSMAG (Joint US Military Advisory Group) [in Thailand] [and] Thailand had no formal military assistance agreement with the United States".[177] A formal US agreement, however, would be soon in coming. Nevertheless, the Naresuan Committee continued to operate as a backchannel between the CIA and Thai military leaders up until the mid-1970s.

Following recommendations of the 1950 Griffin Mission to Thailand, in September 1950, General John Cole arrived in Bangkok to head up a newly created Military Assistance Advisory Group (MAAG) for Thailand, whereby US officers (1) trained Thai officers in conventional warfare, (2) facilitated US military aid to Thailand, and (3) assisted in training Thai soldiers for combat deployment to Korea.[178] The US concluded a Military Assistance Act with Thailand on 17 October 1950 and began sending military assistance into Thailand that year, though such aid started to pour in starting in January 1951. This paralleled Thailand's decision to send troops to fight alongside the United States in Korea. The motives for US military aid were as follows:

> (1) to encourage Thailand to continue on its present political course of alignment with the Free World and to remain a stable force in southeast Asia; (2) to assist the Thai Armed Forces in improving internal security and, by increased defense strength, deterring external aggression; (3) to bolster internal political stability and to help check Communism by strengthening the Thai Government.[179]

Meanwhile, on 30 July 1951, Thailand passed a royal decree concerning military modernization following the influence and advice of Phin and Sarit. The decree jettisoned the decentralized 1933 model of military organization (which itself had been a reaction to palace-centralized control of the armed forces). Such a recentralization had been advocated by foreign (British, Japanese and American) advisors to Thailand. Thus, unit commands were officially brought back under the command and control of the 1st Army Region and its commander.[180] The 1st Army Region was the largest regional command; however, a 2nd Army Command (centred on Thailand's Northeast) and a 3rd Army Command (in Thailand's North) were also created. This 1st Command was most relevant: it was larger than the other military regions in terms of manpower, and its close proximity to the seat of government made it a necessary tool to protect governments or support coups. The purpose of setting up these latter two regions was officially for the protection of borders, both North and South. Unofficially, their establishment enabled the army commander to place potentially troublesome military commanders far away from Bangkok. Indeed, charismatic General Wirawat Yothin,[181] following the 1947 coup, had appeared to side with the deposed government. Though he denied these charges, incoming army commander Phin moved Wirawat to become commander of the 2nd Army Region (1948–50) and later the 3rd Army Region (1951). When Wirawat seemed as though he might support the 1951 *Manhattan* Rebellion, he was demoted to an inactive post. At least with regard to the 3rd Army Region, its creation helped to maintain the military's interests in opium smuggling along the Thai-Burma border.

Another part of Thailand's 1951 military modernization was an attempt to recreate it in the image of the US military, with US advisors and equipment, and a vast enlargement of the available officers and soldiers.[182] Beginning in 1951–52, multiple Thai military officers began regularly to be sent to the United States for military training. Already in 1948, Thailand had moved from the Prussian and French models of military structure and education to that of the West Point model. Indeed, beginning that year, the two Thai military schools were merged into one, which reflected West Point instruction. When Phin retired as army chief in 1954, it was his successor, Sarit, who sustained the "American Model" ever afterwards.

In mid-1951, the US National Security Council directed the CIA to work with Phao's Thai National Police to construct a paramilitary force that could engage in clandestine operations, espionage and surveillance. The project was placed under the regional control of the CIA's Bangkok cover organization, the Overseas Southeast Asia Supply Company (SEA Supply). SEA Supply was headquartered in Miami, Florida. Its CEO was Paul Helliwell, a former OSS official and a friend of Donovan. Its Bangkok branch was helmed by James W. "Bill" Lair, who, like Willis Bird, married a sister of Sitthi Savetsila (Charoensuk

Savetsila). Nevertheless, SEA Supply's office manager in Bangkok was former OSS agent Willis Bird, as directed by another former OSS official, Colonel Sherman B. Joost, who opened SEA Supply's offices at 10 Pra Athit Road, Bangkok, in September 1950. It should come as no surprise that SEA Supply and Willis Bird worked closely together in supplying weapons to the Thai military and police. Through SEA Supply, the CIA provided massive funding for Phao's police units.[183] Indeed, SEA Supply established a camp eighty-five miles north of Bangkok in Lopburi City, where it trained special Thai police, air force personnel and navy SEALs. It later relocated to Hua Hin and trained Royal Guards.[184] Finally, in 1958 it began to train Police Aerial Reinforcement Units (PARU).[185] PARU was part of what was later called the Border Patrol Police (BPP), a paramilitary organization controlled by the Interior Ministry that had been put together from the Territorial Defence Police Corps, the Gendarmerie Patrol Force and the Border Defence Police. Indeed, all of these CIA-created paramilitary units became known as the Border Patrol Police in 1958.[186] One of the trainers working under the BPP was Colonel Vitoon Yasawat, a Thai officer who soon began to play a central role between the CIA and the Thai security apparatus.[187]

Meanwhile, on 22 September 1953, the US Department of Defense and US State Department (through the US Embassy in Bangkok) established JUSMAGTHAI (Joint US Military Advisory Group Thailand), superseding MAAG Thailand. US officials felt that JUSMAG was necessary because

> The present government of Thailand is completely controlled by a group of military officers which … holds all the principal positions within the Army, Navy and Air Force. In order to ensure their retention of control of the civilian government these same military officers have in all cases assumed civilian government responsibilities which include cabinet positions. In addition, these persons have used their position of power to assume many and varied commercial interests to enhance their financial status. The end result of this is that the principal military commanders and their staffs can devote but a small portion of their time and energy solely to the military situation. Further, they are reluctant to delegate any authority for fear the delegation will result in usurpation. This state of affairs constitutes one of the greatest obstacles to creating an efficient military establishment in Thailand.[188]

JUSMAGTHAI, or JUSMAG, was meant to more effectively coordinate US-Thai military matters (especially US military aid to Thailand) as well as improve Thai military effectiveness and strength.

Thus, building on MAAG, the Pentagon began pouring money on a regular basis into training and weapons for the Thai military.

Given the Thai government's close security relationship with Washington, perhaps it was no surprise that, on 4 September 1953, General William Donovan became US ambassador to Thailand. Though the former OSS chief and mentor to the CIA had sought to become the latter's director, becoming the ambassador to a country with a strong CIA influence was an acceptable alternative for him. Once in Bangkok, he spent a great deal of time with his long-time friend and colleague Willis Bird, and immediately began bolstering the Thai police. Indeed, Donovan favoured Phao over Sarit and attempted to increase US aid for Phao's operations.[189] Through Donovan's help and pressure, the Phibun government established both the aforementioned Border Patrol Police and the Police Aerial Reinforcement Units in 1951.[190] These versatile paramilitary units—creations and tools of Washington—received financial support and training from the CIA. But they existed formally under Phao's powerful police department and were outside the line of command of the traditional Thai security establishment. Hyun demonstrates how these units, originally formed by the Thai military at the instigation of the United States as anti-communist fighting forces, became secularized into a "nation-building" apparatus under the Thai monarchy in 1980.[191] Prior to 1980, these units were more directly controlled by the military strongmen who led them.

By the mid-1950s, thanks to Donovan and US aid, Phao's police were coming close to balancing firepower against Sarit's army. When US general Cabell visited Bangkok and met with Phao in August 1953, Phao asked for even more security assistance.[192] Washington obliged. Ultimately, the year 1953 saw few security problems or clashes between Phao and Sarit. Indeed, by beginning to transform Thailand into a dependency, Washington had created, at least temporarily, pro-US stability, equally appeasing Phao, Sarit and Phibun, though Phao was ascendant. Nevertheless, perhaps Sarit was simply awaiting the impending retirement of General Phin from the command of the army in 1954.

In fact, 1954 was an eventful year. With regard to the army, though Phin Chunhavan was officially the commander, his attention continued to be focused on the economic gains of the office rather than military improvements. On the other hand, deputy army commander Sarit Thanarat was actively involved in completing the (aforementioned) formalized recentralizing of the army to the way it had been in 1933. Such centralized control would produce dividends (military, political and financial) for Sarit, especially once he became army chief himself—and it did. In October 1954, Phin, under tremendous pressure from Sarit, retired as army commander at age sixty-three, having reached the mandatory retirement age at sixty, with three annual extensions tacked on. Sarit's popularity had soared three months earlier, following a July 1954 visit to the United States. At that point, the size of the Thai army stood at a little over 40,000 troops.[193] But in Washington, Sarit succeeded in negotiating a three-year and approximately US$400 million deal to increase the number of Thai soldiers to 181,728 troops (army 148,654, navy 10,662, and air force 22,412); finance construction of the Saraburi-Ban Phai Highway; develop three suitable air bases at Korat, Tha-Pli and Songkhla; make improvements in the Thai navy and air force; and CIA-assisted modifications in Thai Intelligence. In actuality, the number of military grants to Thailand grew from US$111.2 million for 1946–54 to US$40.8 million in 1955 and US$43.4 million in 1956.[194] Sarit specifically wanted US money to reorganize existing army units in the 1st Army Region into a single army corps (including three infantry divisions, corps artillery and other corps troops), one separate infantry division and four horse cavalry squadrons.[195] With the agreement in hand, Sarit departed from Washington much-satisfied and possessing more leverage with his rivals back in Bangkok.

When Sarit became army commander on 1 October 1954, he immediately appointed his loyalists to top and/or strategic postings. Most prominently these postings included General Luang Suthi Suthisarn Ronakary as deputy army commander, General Sawai Sawai Saenyakorn as assistant army commander, General Thanom Kittikachorn as 1st Army commander, General Praphas Charusathien as Thanom's deputy (and 1st Division commander) and Colonel Krit Sivara as commander of the 1st Infantry Regiment (see Appendix 4).

Meanwhile, as if to counter Sarit's earlier visit to the United States, in November 1954, Phao also visited Washington. Only three months earlier, on 14 August 1954, Malay-Muslim separatist leader Haji Sulong, seen by the Phibun regime as a threat to the Thai state, had disappeared, along with his son, while in the custody of police. Phao later wrote that he had received an order to kill Sulong.[196] Washington at the time likely saw Sulong's disappearance as enhancing southern stability. Now, in November, Phao, despite the clandestine CIA funding for his police, requested more direct funding from Washington for his National Police and the paramilitaries controlled by it. Specifically, he sought funds to increase the Volunteer Defence Corps—which at the time was controlled by the police—to the level of 120,000 troops. Washington granted Phao US$3 million for this purpose. Following the meeting, US officials stressed the importance of Phao's police, then numbering 42,000 men, given that they were the "first line of defense as they are responsible for the patrol of Thailand's borders and inland waterways".[197] US officials also noted that though army chief Sarit controlled more "guns" than Phao, the "generally superior training and effectiveness of the police and the capacity for rapid action might well outweigh the greater numerical strength of the Army in a coup situation".[198] Finally, the report subsequent to Phao's visit argued that Phao and Sarit, rather than being zero-sum competitors for power, actually worked together to maintain complementary clout, as seen by the fact that they were joint stockholders in several businesses, they often helped seek security funding for each other's bureaucracies, and had "both been raised to their high positions by Prime Minister Phibun Songkram".[199] Such an argument ignored growing frictions between the two men.

In September 1954, Thailand acceded to the Southeast Asia Collective Defence Treaty, or Manila Pact, thus creating the Southeast Asia Treaty Organization, and joined the Manila Pact and the Southeast Asia Treaty Organization (SEATO). Phibun was now more than ever trusted in Washington, quite an irony given his alliance with the Axis Powers during World War II. Nevertheless, many US officials saw Phao as the most likely successor to Phibun as prime minister, especially since Sarit seemed to involve himself less in politics.[200]

Meanwhile, despite the advent of formal US-Thai military relations, CIA cooperation with Thai military forces had expanded. Back in February 1951, the CIA commenced "Operation Paper", a CIA strategy to arm KMT nationalist soldiers who, following the 1949 Communist Revolution in China, had been pushed into northern Burma. By providing weapons for troops of KMT general Li Mi of the 93rd Division and others, the Truman administration sought to facilitate a harassment invasion into southern China.[201] As part of this effort, a special Thai police unit was secretly established inside northern Burma to train KMT forces in jungle combat. Rather than fearing Chinese wrath for their complicity with the KMT, Thai security heads saw the nationalists as a useful buffer between Thailand and China. Besides, the military and police increasingly needed US military assistance: by 1953 it accounted for 70 per cent of all money spent on Thailand's defences that year, making the Coup Group and Thai security forces ever more dependent on US military aid.

From the outset, General Phao was instrumental in the CIA operation. He personally delivered the first arms shipments and used a police operation in northern Thailand as cover for enhanced Thai police involvement in it. Phao worked closely with CIA officials Willis H. Bird (SEA Supply) and William H. Bird (Civil Air Transport) to obtain weapons for anti-Beijing efforts from the United States and to deliver them to the KMT. Still another US official with whom Phao worked was Robert North. North was under cover in the United States Information Agency (whose head in Thailand at the time was American Jorge Orgibet, a friend of Bird's). North was also the president of Far East Films, a CIA front company that produced pro-US films in Southeast Asia in cooperation with Phao's police. With CIA money, North helped to strategize covert operations along Thailand's frontiers. He worked with Li Mi and Phao in planning attacks on Yunnan province.[202] The 1952 arrival of Vern Gresham in Thailand as CIA station chief increased formal US efforts for this mission.

As such, amidst these CIA-directed efforts, Operation Paper expanded rapidly. But the programme produced personal dividends for Phao and perhaps also for Phibun—a fact that US officials (both in the CIA and the US State Department) were only too keenly aware of. But not everyone in the US Embassy was kept abreast of CIA actions. On 28 September 1951, the US Embassy's Chargé d'affaires in Bangkok (Turner) cabled Washington that:

> British Ambassador … said that it was probably unnecessary to mention that he had sufficient information to prevent any illusions about the real source of supply of KMT troops in Burma; he mentioned flights of four-motored planes; crashing of helicopters; American Major Stewart proceeding on same plane with General Phao to north; huge profits made by Phao and probably Prime Minister in opium in return trip of planes from north.[203]

The US Embassy noted "that there was no 'Major Stewart' in Southeast Asia at that time" and that he was probably "a private citizen employed by a foreign aviation company".[204] Clearly, that "foreign aviation company" was none other than Civil Air Transport.

By March 1952, reports had even reached the US Embassy in India about Phao's growing US-supported political power and opium trafficking.

> [R]eports state several Amers [Americans] said to be with troops but definitely states total of six or seven Amer natls [American nationals] now living Nhai Narong Hotel in Chiangmai, northern

Thailand. Under orders from local police said to be exempt from registration.

Reports continue Thai Govt itself does not appear be committed but supplies to KMT escorted regularly by Thai local police under control Gen Phao. Report goes on to say Gen Phao enjoys power out of all proportion his position and since police in Thailand function more or less as independent organization, Gen strong enough challenge Army chief Gen Sirith [Sarit] and even PriMin Field Marshal Pibul [Phibun] himself.

Stated most important reason for police protection given by Gen Phao is his interest in opium traffic in and about area where KMT troops stationed. Stated that through his close ties with KMT Gen Phao able move opium out for sale and export through Thailand, and as long as this arrangement endures Phao not likely put any obstacle in way of supplies going through Thailand to KMT troops.[205]

When the pro-Phao William Donovan retired as US ambassador in August 1954, US policymakers were divided about whether to support Phao, as opposed to Sarit, in terms of a successor to Phibun. Persons connected with the CIA such as Willis Bird also supported Phao. However, according to Fineman, Donovan's successor as ambassador to Thailand, John Peurifoy, was "a Phibun supporter" who soon turned "against Phao".[206] Phibun had initially feared Peurifoy when the latter began as ambassador in August 1954 owing to Peurifoy's role in the CIA ouster of the Arbenz regime in Guatemala earlier that year.[207]

In early 1955, Phibun, supported by Peurifoy, was feeling that he could count on US support and maintain stable control over Thailand. In this environment, the premier decided to make a partial move in foreign policy towards Beijing as a means of diminishing any future military threat from China, and also for domestic political reasons, with a general election only two years away. Thus, Phibun sent his foreign minister, Prince Wan, to the African-Asian Bandung Conference in April 1955. Phibun publicly announced that Wan was going to the meeting because the Thai government intended to collaborate with "all sides" (implicitly including the Chinese and Soviets) in "building world peace".[208] Only one month after Prince Wan's visit to Bandung, Phibun apparently felt that his overtures of "peace" towards Beijing might not sound so harmonious to Washington's ears. Thus, in May 1955, Phibun visited the United States, where he insisted that he was determined to resist communism at all costs. Peurifoy did his best to maximize Phibun's standing with US officials.

Meanwhile, by mid-1955, Peurifoy, like increasing numbers of US officials, had become critical of Phao's exploitation of the KMT operation to bolster his own opium trade profits. But when CIA station chief Justin O'Donnell (a Phao opponent who took over from Gresham in 1954)[209] bluntly castigated Phao for his corruption and opium dealings, the CIA did not want to make an enemy of Phao; instead, they replaced O'Donnell[210] with John Hart as new station chief in 1955. Hart "regenerated the relationship with both Phao and SEA Supply".[211] However, Phao's ability to pressure the CIA to remove O'Donnell worsened Peurifoy's views of Phao.

Nevertheless, though he preferred dealing with Phibun to Phao, Peurifoy realized that Washington had to tolerate the influential police commander. In June 1955, Phao had reportedly attempted but failed to have Sarit dismissed as army commander. In mid-July 1955, Peurifoy met with Phao, who had apparently been drinking alcohol. Phao had just clashed with premier Phibun in an attempt to compel the latter to dismiss army chief Sarit:

> In private conversation with General Phao last night, he asked me abruptly if I would like to have him start a revolution, said coup party was very dissatisfied with Phibun. His only explanation was that Thailand should become a full democracy which he indicated was in line with US objectives. Phao implied that move of some sort to oust Phibun was imminent and that he (Phao) had strong backing to remove or replace Phibun. I told Phao emphatically that my recent advice to him, with reference to the possibility of coup within the Army and its serious implications, held good in this instance. I also said that, as one friend to another, I really doubted that he wanted the burdens of prime ministership and believed he preferred role of king maker to king; that I frankly did not think he was now qualified for job. I emphasized that US Government supported present Thai Government and its recognised head; that, while internal politics a Thai affair, if government reconstituted by force US would have to reconsider its relationship with Thai Government and that US strongly supports goal of democracy but coup would be poor start; moreover, that Thailand probably not yet ready for full democracy which should be developed gradually. Phao obviously had been drinking and was in jovial mood but did not appear to be joking.[212]

Though several officials in Washington (notably, the CIA's Allen Dulles) ordered Peurifoy to acquiesce to any coup by Phao, Peurifoy informed Phao that Washington would not endorse a putsch. Thus, Phao, who realized that Peurifoy was not on his side, did not make a move. Instead, he prepared to go to Washington to lobby for support among his friends in the Eisenhower administration. Phibun feared that the police chief might foment another putsch.

Thus, just before Phao departed for the United Kingdom and the United States in August 1955, Phibun publicly attacked Phao for his opium monopoly and ordered the suppression of opium traffic (on which Phao depended for income), stripped Phao of his positions as deputy minister of finance and press officer, replaced Phao ally Pramarn Adireksan with Sarit confidant Sawai Sawai Saengyakorn as deputy minister of communications, and brought in another Sarit ally, Thanom Kittikachorn, to become deputy minister of cooperatives. Furthermore, Phibun removed Colonel Chatchai Chunhavan from the latter's command of the strategic Bangkok-centred 2nd Cavalry Regiment, a move that fundamentally weakened the Soi Rajakru faction within the army.

When Phao went overseas, Phibun temporarily assumed police veto power over paramilitary activities.[213] But when Phao returned, the latter immediately regained his authority as police chief. Phibun, however, took for himself Phao's position as deputy minister of the interior (presiding over police and civil defence forces). Phibun also dismissed Phin from the portfolio of deputy prime minister, though the latter remained agriculture minister.

While Phao was away in the United States, the anti-Phao Peurifoy suffered a fatal car accident in August, which also killed his son. Though most US officials refused to consider foul play, one CIA document noted a report by David Sentner, chief of Hearst Newspapers' Washington Bureau, that stated that "American military intelligence sources feel there is more than a fifty-fifty chance that the car-truck collision which killed Ambassador Peurifoy and his son was not an accident … mention of CIA".[214]

If there was foul play, Phao certainly had the most to gain since Peurifoy was his enemy. Peurifoy also had his CIA-linked enemies in Thailand; most notably, Willis Bird. The 1955 death of the anti-Phao ambassador Peurifoy, dismissal of the anti-Phao O'Donnell and the appointment of pro-Phao Hart were good news for the police chief.

Phao's August 1955 visit to the United States succeeded in its goal of shoring up US support for the police chief and helping him obtain more US security assistance for Thailand. In a meeting with US State Department officials (and Thai ambassador to the United States Pote Sarasin), Phao noted that

> Thai military expenditures have increased. As a result of the intensified training program, operating costs of the military establishment are mounting. General Phao emphasized that

in these circumstances Thailand is dependent on U.S. assistance and expressed the hope that the level of aid would be maintained and, if possible, expanded. Mr. Hollister asked if the training and mechanization of the Army would make it possible to reduce the number of soldiers. The General said that this would not be possible; that JUSMAG had advised Thailand to maintain 10 regimental combat teams. General Phao described the need for strengthening the Gendarmérie Police Force and commented on this organization's work. Mr. Hollister indicated that he was aware of the accomplishments of the Thai, and of General Phao personally, in this respect.... The General and Ambassador Sarasin expressed their regret at the death of Ambassador Peurifoy.[215]

Three months after Peurifoy's death (and perhaps because Peurifoy was no longer alive to prevent it), the US Embassy in Bangkok became less sure about Phibun's public preferences for a Thai neutralist policy. Reports from the embassy warned of a potential move by the premier towards the communist world. Perhaps surprisingly, given his hard-line stances, CIA director Allen Dulles supported Phibun:

> American embassy ... sources in Bangkok have recently reported several indications that the Thai government may be reassessing its anti-Communist outlook. Prince Wan, the Thai foreign minister, is reported to be increasingly optimistic about the prospects for regularizing relations. There are, in addition, signs of the Thai becoming increasingly attracted to trade with Communist China. There are also indications that the USSR and Communist China are actively encouraging Thai neutrality.... [But] there appears to be little reason to believe that an abrupt or major change in Thailand's pro-Western orientation is imminent. American aid and the Manila Pact are still regarded by the Phibun regime as the chief guarantees of Thailand's security, and Bangkok is actively soliciting the one and promoting the other.[216]

In fact, by November 1955, both Phibun and Phao had begun jointly supporting secret Thai missions to Beijing to discuss the normalization of relations between Beijing and Bangkok. When American officials discovered the identities of some Thai left-wingers who had visited China on the government's behalf, Phibun and Phao denied knowing about it, maintained that they were strictly pro-US, and even briefly jailed the men.[217]

However, when Max Waldo Bishop was appointed to succeed Peurifoy as US ambassador in December 1955, the former demon-strated that he was an ardent anti-communist ideologue in the mould of Senator Joseph McCarthy. Bishop could not abide any Thai accom-modation with China, and thus contacts with China by Phibun and

Phao moved even more underground. At the same time, Bishop proved not to be an advocate for Phao or Sarit; he mostly chose to support Phibun. According to *Time Magazine* at the time, "In his rush to ingratiate himself with Pibul (who smilingly referred to him recently as "my ambassador"), Bishop … ignored or antagonized regular foreign-office channels."[218]

Just prior to Bishop's arrival on 1 December 1955, political strife yet again intensified between Phibun and Phao. Phibun threatened to resign or reshuffle his cabinet to replace Phao and his remaining supporters with pro-Sarit officials. Phibun also threatened to take control of SEA Supply away from Phao. It took extreme pressure on Phibun from acting chief of mission Norbert Anschuetz for the premier to call for an easing of tensions among Phao, Sarit and himself.[219]

Upon his return from the United States in April 1955, Phibun had attempted to appeal to popular legitimacy and gain the support of the public through elections. This was also a way for him to compete with Phao and Sarit, whose clout emanated from their control over security forces. Phibun thus declared that Thailand would henceforth experience "fuller democracy", including regular press conferences by him and his cabinet. Senam Luang (the Pramane Ground, or Royal Cremation Ground), would be turned into a "Hyde Park" for public speeches. In addition, the Press Act was modified and a new election was called, which Phibun insisted would be "clean".[220] Indeed, the prime minister was already preparing for a February 1957 election, given that the four-year parliamentary term would draw to a close in December 1956. He seemed to understand the weapon of public opinion in his attempt to strengthen his political clout through polls.

Moreover, given the growing fissures within the security forces, the centre of power seems to have swung back to parliament. Indeed, it was ironic that Phibun, a military man, contributed (though in a small way) to the enhancement of Thai democratic institutions. In 1955 he facilitated the enactment of a Political Party Law as the Coup Group prepared for new elections. The following year, the military set up its own political party, Seri Manangkhasila (SM), and used government mechanisms and resources to enhance its competitive influence. Phibun was party leader, Sarit was deputy leader and Phao was secretary-general. Sarit was even able to assign Krit Sivara a key role as an SM vote canvasser.[221] Meanwhile, Phibun also continued to hold sway over the Thammatipat Party.

At the beginning of 1956, most US policymakers believed that Thailand, though it needed some improvements, was becoming a useful bulwark in the Cold War. At the same time, Washington's views on the chess game among Phibun, Phao and Sarit had changed little in four years, naively assuming that the balance of power remained static:

> The Thai are controlled by an oligarchy dominated by Prime Minister Phibun, Director General of Police Phao, and Commander-in-Chief of the Army Sarit. Phibun has no further ambition except … to insure [*sic*] a peaceful accession, presumably by Phao…. Phao realizes that he probably will become the next Prime Minister…. Sarit enjoys his command of the Army and his ambition … is limited to preserving the prerogatives of that office.[222]

What Washington did not like, however, was the Thai government's continuing dialogue and relations with Beijing. By early 1956 the United States was becoming wary of the Phibun administration's growing gentle embrace of China. In February, former prime minister Pridi Panomyong (then self-exiled to China) announced he wanted to return to Thailand. Prime Minister Phibun stated publicly that Pridi, as a Thai citizen, had every right to return.[223] Phao had negotiated with Pridi about the latter's potential return since at least February 1956.[224] Phibun and Phao apparently saw Pridi as a useful chip to use in their democratization campaign. Though he never did return, the reports certainly frightened Washington. In March, reports reached Washington that Phao and Phin were in direct contact with Chinese communists. Ambassador Bishop, though he liked Phibun, was becoming especially worried. In July Bishop notified Washington that the Thai government had decided to "normalize" trade with all countries, including "Communist China [as a result of] pressures from opposition political elements castigating [the] government as [a] US puppet", [because of] "people's need for cheap Chinese goods" and "from merchants and influential elements within government seeking quick profit (undoubtedly some bribed by Communist gold)".[225]

In August 1956, Sarit informed US military leaders that he favoured a "forward strategy" to work with the US and the Laotian military against potential communist attacks in Laos by the Pathet Lao guerrillas and North Vietnam's military.[226] In fact, Sarit was favourable to most US military suggestions for Thailand. At the time, in 1956, his military was receiving US$27 million in special Military Defense Assistance Program (MDAP) funding, whilst Phao's police was receiving US$25 million. But in March 1956, Sarit let it be known to US defence officials that he wanted still more US funding for the Thai armed forces. Washington—though it modified the field marshal's "dream proposal" of an undisclosed amount—cautiously agreed to its general outlines.[227]

FIGURE 3.7
Thailand's Legislature, 1957–57

Type of legislature	Years in office	Appointed or elected	Total number of legislators and military contingent
Unicameral	1957–57	160 elected by eligible voters/123 appointed	283, of which 106 (86.1%) military reserved domain of the appointed

Source: Paul Chambers, "Superfluous, Irrelevant or Emancipating: Thailand's Evolving Senate Today", Journal of Current Southeast Asian Affairs 28, no. 3 (2009): 9, https://d-nb.info/999559311/34.

By the end of 1956, Sarit was becoming, little by little, the US favourite, or at least the US military's favourite person in Thailand. Nevertheless, government leaders—Phibun, Phao and even Sarit—were all publicly expressing sentiment in favour of political neutralism, if only to obtain public support as the general election approached.

The anticipated 1957 poll finally came to pass, occurring on 26 February. The poll was for 160 elected seats out of the 283-member legislature. The remaining 123 MPs had been appointed by the Phibun government and would serve until 1962 (see Figure 3.7). A total of 106 (86.1 per cent) of the 123 were military officials.[228]

Phibun's state apparatus—as enforced by Phao's police—oversaw the elections, using the state's financial resources. The result was of little surprise. Seri Manangkhasila won 86 out of the 160 elected seats. In addition to its access to state resources and personnel, the military party reportedly engaged in vote-buying and ballot-box stuffing.[229] Nevertheless, the February 1957 election was likely no more corrupt than any general election in the country before or afterward—though enemies of Phibun cried foul about alleged electoral irregularities.[230] Phao's enemy Sarit fanned the flames of anger, telling protestors that the election winners had "cheated".[231]

The demonstrations led premier Phibun to declare a state of emergency (to be guaranteed by Sarit) on 2 March, alleging that the protests were inspired by communists. Phibun likely hoped that any repression of protestors that army chief Sarit engaged in during this period would make the army commander unpopular. Under the state of emergency, Sarit—as temporary supreme commander—was in command not only of all armed forces but also of the police, a situation that temporarily diminished Phao's power. During this period, though Sarit did not stage a coup, he was able to increase his political bargaining clout. At this point, Khuang Aphaiwong, Democrat Party leader, urged Sarit to step in, oust Phao and support new elections.[232] Six months later, Sarit did exactly as Khuang hoped.

Yet, on 2 Marcy 1957, angry crowds had formed in Bangkok and had begun to move down Ratchadamnoen Road in the direction of Government House. At one point soldiers were dispatched to block the demonstrators, and the former adopted a firing position. To avoid bloodshed, Sarit decided to let the protestors pass, but warned them not to become violent. Sarit allowed students to march across Makkhawan bridge. Much of the media thereupon dubbed Sarit "the Hero of Makkhawan". Then, when the crowd reached Government House, and even broke down a gate into the building, soldiers and police, led by Sarit, were waiting for them. While Prime Minister Phibun prepared to speak, Sarit addressed the protestors first, promising to deliver their complaints to the cabinet. His words subdued them, and he suddenly emerged as a potential leader.[233] 1st Regiment commander Colonel Krit Sivara was impressed by Sarit's actions; sixteen years later, on 14 October 1973, he too refused to order the massacre of protestors, but instead transformed himself into a people's saviour against dictatorship.

Meanwhile, neutralists and leftists took to the streets to protest against the government. Phibun's government released thirty-seven leftist political prisoners, allowed Pridi's wife to visit Thailand, and sponsored a Thammasat University book featuring Marxist articles.[234] These policies created a right-wing uproar. Palace disdain for Phibun and Phao erupted immediately after the February election, with members of the royal community publicly criticizing the two men. Gossip spread that any coup by Sarit had palace support.[235]

Following the election, Phibun reorganized his cabinet. To maintain the balance between and support from Phao and Sarit, on 30 March 1957, Phibun promoted them both. Phao became minister of the interior and Sarit became minister of defence. The prime minister further placated Sarit by placing three of his minions in ministerial posts: Worakan Bancha became finance minister, General Thanom Kittikachorn was appointed as deputy defence minister and General Praphas Charusathien was given the deputy interior minister post. Phao's cabinet allies were also his in-laws: General Phin was appointed agriculture minister, General Pramarn Adireksan was minister of industry and General Siri Siriyothin was minister of cooperatives. But Phibun also gave Sarit the "lion's share of [the] appointed seats in parliament".[236] And Sarit could see that he now held a better hand of cards than either Phibun or Phao. He began to demand that both resign. He also initiated talks with powerful community figures who opposed Phibun and Phao—the palace as well as the Democrat Party.

> On the morning of April 16, 1957, Sarit called a private meeting of "those interested in the future of Thailand." Some eighty attended, including Marshal of the Air Force Fuen, Deputy of the Ministry of the Interior, General Praphas; President of the Privy Council, Prince Dhani; new police-chief designate Luang Chote; Kukrit and Seni Pramoj and a mixture of service personnel and civilians.

> Sarit stated [that] fresh demonstrations were feared; if these occurred, they might not pass off so peacefully as in [the] previous emergency and he might be forced to shoot; this must be prevented at all costs. He then asked the meeting's view about what should be done. It was finally agreed that Sarit should, as soon as possible, tell Pibul that he should take a prolonged holiday abroad; Fuen should similarly tell Phao to go. No dates were fixed but action was to be taken before the assembly reconvenes on June 24. Sarit agreed to do as proposed.[237]

In a heavily redacted memo, on 20 April the CIA reported that "the influence of the king may be used to bring about a new government of 'experts' backed by Defence Minister Sarit and the army".[238] By 30 May the CIA reported that the triumvirate of Phibun, Phao and Sarit was "likely to break up in the near future with Phibun siding with Phao against Sarit, who is supported by elements of the court [meaning the monarchy] and ... Khuang".[239]

Continuing accusations of fraud and electoral irregularities against Phibun and Phao (from the February poll) led to the June 1957 breakaway of the Sarit faction from SM. Led by Chiang Mai tycoon Sukit Nimanhemin and Sarit's half-brother Sanguan Chantarasaka, a new party (Sahaphum) was formed. Sukit preached neutralism in foreign policy, which attracted left-wing support. Sarit's stalwart General Praphas Charusathien, then deputy interior minister, even suggested at one point that JUSMAG had done little to help the army. Two months later, on 20 August, Sarit himself corrected Praphas, proclaiming, "We are pleased to have you [JUSMAG] here because you came to work openly, not like another unit [the CIA] that works underground."[240]

Though Sarit's criticisms of the United States had much to do with domestic political considerations, he had personally been angered by the CIA's long support for his political enemy Phao and for the State

Department's backing of Phibun. Sarit's US allies were mostly fellow military officers in the Pentagon. He had been personally close to and respected the chiefs of MAAG (later JUSMAG), General John Cole and General William Gillmore. Sarit possessed an "effusive ... high regard for General [Richard] Partridge",[241] Gillmore's successor, who was JUSMAG chief in 1957. Finally, Sarit was friendly with Colonel Seth L. Weld, Jr., army attaché at the embassy in Bangkok during the same period.

By August, Sarit was vehemently demanding that Phibun and Phao resign from the government. The climax to the crisis seemed to be near at hand. Then, in a move to try and take control of the situation, Phibun announced in mid-August that all cabinet ministers had to remove themselves from any commercial activities. At this point Sarit tried to gain control of the government by overturning Phibun's cabinet. Such a move was favoured by the palace and the Democrat Party because the royalists would be in a stronger political position if Sarit was to only rule the country as an elected prime minister, not as a military ruler. Indeed, according to the CIA, "the king, with whom Sarit retains close relations, has reportedly counseled against the use of force".[242] Thus, in reaction to Phibun's announcement regarding ministers' business interests, on 20 August, Sarit—along with Thanom and Praphas—resigned his ministerial post. Then, on 9 September, Sarit and forty-five of his loyalist officers resigned from the Seri Manangkhasila party. Sarit demanded that the government resign and a new cabinet be formed. On 10 September, Sarit's military cabal took specific aim at Phao: they signed a petition that he must resign his positions. Phin's son, Brigadier General Chatchai Chunhavan, alone protested that such an act would be an act of revolt. Nevertheless, Colonel Prasert Ruchirawong, commander of the Anti-Aircraft Division, was selected to deliver the message to the government. By 12 September the CIA was reporting that ninety-two Sarit followers in the appointed legislative quota had resigned from the government and the Seri Manangkhasila party; these, combined with enough elected MPs, would be enough for a successful vote of censure against Phibun.[243] The no-confidence vote, however, did not happen. Though Phao and Phin resigned from their posts in the cabinet, Prime Minister Phibun refused to accept their letters of resignation. Negotiations continued between Phibun and Sarit, but on 15 September Sarit learned that Phibun might be seeking his arrest. When a crowd came to Sarit's house that day demanding that he seize power, he now promised to comply.

The next day, 16 September, the army deployed throughout Bangkok, and Phibun and Phao went into exile, never to return. Thailand's King

Bhumipol now appointed Sarit to be the Defender of the Capital.[244] There is some controversy as to whether the monarch had the right to do so, given there was no premier to countersign the appointment.[245] Sarit derived legitimacy from the monarch, popular support and support within the armed forces. The palace, especially, championed the coup. According to the CIA at the time, "the king not only initiated planning of the coup but had to press Sarit to take action".[246]

According to another CIA document,

> The king, who reportedly played an active role in promoting the coup, has publicly endorsed Sarit's takeover and has helped out by ordering the dissolution of the national assembly and new elections within 90 days. He has also approved a new slate of 123 appointed members (nominated by Sarit and mostly military officers) to serve as the legislature in the interim.[247]

Finally, there is this:

> King Phumipon [Bhumipol] evidently played an active role in the events leading to and subsequent to the army coup. In a long talk with Ambassador Bishop after the coup, he virtually admitted as much.[248]

As more information becomes available from Thai and non-Thai sources, it appears increasingly clear that since at least April 1957 Sarit and the palace were planning a coup—and the United States was also likely involved. But Sarit had to camouflage his alliance with right-wing elements behind a somewhat nationalist and sometimes anti-US neutralist stance in order to gain wide popular support.

As the putsch appeared to be moving forward, Phibun visited King Bhumipol twice on 16 September in an effort to get the monarch's approval to fire Sarit as army commander. Bhumipol both times refused.[249] Nevertheless, given the weakness of the monarchy at that time, even had the king supported dismissing Sarit, the latter could probably have ousted Phibun anyway. Nevertheless, the September 1957 alliance between Sarit and the royalists proved effective. Only Washington, where some officials still smarted from the army commander's earlier criticisms, needed to be reassured. They didn't have long to wait.

When the coup finally occurred, on the evening of 16 September 1957, US army attaché Colonel Weld cabled the US secretary of state that Sarit's immediate arrests of suspected communists were conducted for the "purpose [of] gaining US support". The Thai army chief's affinity for the US military establishment was therefore reciprocated by senior American military officers. Of all US bureaucracies, Sarit most preferred JUSMAG (rather than the State Department or the

CIA),[250] and his trusted US contact there was JUSMAG's Colonel Weld. In the end, though all three bureaucracies (State Department, CIA and the Defense Department) ultimately supported Sarit's 1957 coup, US policy towards Sarit could partly be seen through the lens of an inter-bureaucratic struggle, especially between the CIA (which had supported Phao) and the Pentagon (which stood behind Sarit). Indeed, on the very evening of the coup, the arrests began, and these included hundreds of people (communists and suspected communists) such as politician Klaew Norapati and academic Jit Phumisak. Most of the leftists were people with whom Phibun and Phao had associated, though no leftists connected with Sarit himself were included. Those arrested were imprisoned for years under the Anti-Communist Act, pleasing the US Embassy.[251]

Serving under Sarit, the officials who played crucial roles in the coup were as follows: 1st Army commander General Thanom Kittikachorn; 1st Army deputy commander and 1st Division commander General Praphas Charusathien; deputy commander of the 1st Infantry Division and commander of the King's Guard 1st Infantry Regiment, Colonel Krit Sivara; and Colonel Prasert Ruchirawong, commander of the Anti-Aircraft Artillery Division. On the night of 16 September, Thanom and Praphas oversaw the storming of Phao's Naresuan Police Camp at Hua Hin.

Rather than be captured by Sarit's Coup Group, Phibun, his immediate family and some loyalists sped by car to Cambodia on 16 September, where they immediately went into exile. Phibun never returned to Thailand. As for Phao, he surrendered to the Coup Group. Perhaps Sarit's high trust in Colonel Krit propelled the new strongman to give him the task of escorting Phao to the plane that took him into exile to Europe on 17 September.[252] Sarit allowed General Phin Chunhavan to remain in Thailand; though the aging general never again personally engaged in politics, his son Chatchai would become prime minister in 1988. Finally, Sarit's soldiers attempted to occupy the offices of CIA front company SEA Supply, which in 1957 existed at the Grand Hotel, across from the National Stadium, next to the Thai National Police Department. Soldiers were only stopped by CIA station chief John Hart.[253]

Sarit's 1957 coup group was called the Khana Thahan (literally the "Soldiers' Group"), and it was composed of thirty-one individuals, including twenty-four military officers. Of the twenty-four officers, nine senior military officials constituted the core of the group, which itself was dominated by seven senior army officers (including Thanom

Kittikachorn, Praphas Charusathien and Krit Sivara, who became spokesperson for the group).

By the end of 1957, the Phao-leaning CIA station chief John Hart had been replaced by a new one with whom Sarit became fast friends—Robert Jantzen. Ambassador Bishop too was ordered back to Washington—replaced by U. Alexis Johnson, an Asia specialist.

To bestow upon his caretaker government the aura of transparency and neutrality, the entrepreneur and diplomat Pote Sarasin—who also enjoyed close ties to the palace—was chosen to serve as caretaker prime minister until elections were held in December. While Sarit served as both army commander and supreme commander, his two most trusted loyalists, General Thanom Kittikachorn and General Praphas Charusatien, were named defence minister and interior minister, respectively. In all, fifteen out of the twenty-five portfolio slots were filled by active-duty military officers. General Sawai Sawaisanyakorn became police chief, while newly promoted lieutenant general Prasert Ruchirawong was appointed deputy police chief. Thanom's brother Sanga became deputy commander of the Police Crime Suppression Division, but he was already on a fast-track to higher promotions. Sarit loyalist Air Marshal Chalermkiat Wattanankul was named air force chief. Admiral Luang Chamnan became head of the navy. And ACM Thawee Chullasap was appointed deputy chief of staff of the Armed Forces. With this apparently "clean", pro-US government solidly in place, Sarit needed only an election to add popular legitimacy.[254]

In the final analysis, the period 1944–57 represented Thailand's golden age of praetorianism. Initially, the critical juncture of defeat for the country's military forces in World War II suggested that the country had realigned itself on a path dependence of elected civilian control and democratization. But external factors—the advent of the Cold War in 1947 followed by US support for authoritarian right-wing forces—guaranteed that the military would return to power, which it did in 1947, at first in a quasi-alliance with the monarchy. But in late 1952, autocratic strongmen Phibun, Phao and Sarit sidelined the monarchy and dominated Thailand's façade democracy as a triumvirate—supported by their patron, the United States. From 1953 to 1957, the three ruled with an iron hand. The only problems they potentially faced were each other. Eventually, in September 1957, Sarit, possessing the highest amount of firepower, and, of all the three, trusted most by the United States, forced Phibun and Phao into exile. Sarit would thereupon institute the most authoritarian military regime in Thai history, though in a renewed partnership with the monarchy.

Notes

1. Joseph Wright, *The Balancing Act* (Oakland, CA: Pacific Rim; Bangkok: Asiabooks, 1991), p. 129.

2. *KomChadLeuk*, 15 March 2019, สิ้น «ควง อภัยวงศ์» นายกฯ 4 สมัยไม่ครบเทอม [The end of Kuang Aphaiwong: 4 uncompleted terms], https://www.komchadluek.net/today-in-history/365647.

3. Vichitvong Na Pombhejara, *Pridi Panomyong and the Making of Thailand's Modern History* (Bangkok: Ruankaew, 2001), pp. 190–91.

4. Benjamin Batson, "The Fall of the Phibun Government, 1944", *Journal of the Siam Society*, p. 112, https://thesiamsociety.org/wp-content/uploads/1974/03/JSS_062_2e_Batson_FallOfPhibunGovernment1944.pdf.

5. Wright, *The Balancing Act*, p. 146.

6. Central Intelligence Agency (CIA), "The Political Situation", 30 October 1947, https://www.cia.gov/readingroom/docs/CIA-RDP82-00457R001000520003-4.pdf.

7. Shane Strate, *The Lost Territories: Thailand's History of National Humiliation* (Honolulu: University of Hawai'i Press, 2015), p. 127.

8. Fred Riggs, *Thailand: The Modernization of a Bureaucratic Polity* (Honolulu: East-West Center Press, 1966), pp. 233–34.

9. Vichitvong, *Pridi Panomyong*, p. 198.

10. Ibid.

11. Riggs, *Thailand*, p. 234.

12. Vichitvong, *Pridi Panomyong*, p. 218.

13. Wright, *The Balancing Act*, p. 92.

14. Ibid., p. 93.

15. "The Thai Legation to the United States Department of State", 5 September 1945, *Foreign Relations of the United States* (*FRUS*), https://history.state.gov/historicaldocuments/frus1945v06/d961.

16. Vichitvong, *Pridi Panomyong*, p. 221.

17. E. Bruce Reynolds, *Thailand's Secret War: The OSS, SOE and the Free Thai Underground during World War II* (Cambridge University Press, 2005), p. 425n185.

18. Daniel Fineman, *A Special Relationship: The United States and Military Government in Thailand, 1947–1958* (Honolulu: University of Hawai'i Press, 1997), p. 28.

19. M.S. Venkataramani, "Military Coup Pattern in Postwar Thailand: Washington and the First Coup of 1947", *International Studies* 29, no. 3 (1992): 258.

20. Thanet Aphornsuvan, "The United States and the Coming of the 1947 Coup in Siam", *Journal of the Siam Society* 75 (1987): 202, https://thesiamsociety.org/wp-content/uploads/1987/03/JSS_075_0j_ThanetAphornsuvan_USAndCoupOf1947.pdf.

21. Cited in Thanet, "The United States", p. 195.

22. Ibid., p. 195.

23. Fineman, *A Special Relationship*, p. 28.

24. Reynolds, *Thailand's Secret War*, p. 425n185.

25. Ibid., p. 426.

26. For example, though under the 10 December constitution civil servants and soldiers had been forbidden from holding seats in the National Assembly, and members of the royal family could not directly participate in parliamentary politics, the 10 May 1946 constitution reversed the rules such that royals could henceforth participate while soldiers could not. See Wright, *The Balancing Act*, p. 162.

27. Reynolds, *Thailand's Secret War*, p. 426n187.

28. Fineman, *A Special Relationship*, p. 21; Thak Chaloemtiarana, *Thailand: The Politics of Despotic Paternalism* (Chiang Mai: Silkworm Books, 2007), p. 26.

29. อนุสรณ์ในงานพระราชทานเพลิงศพ พลตำรวจเอก อดุล อดุลเดชจรัส ณ เมรุหน้าพลับพลาอิสริยาภรณ์ วัดเทพศิรินทราวาส [Memorial volume from the cremation ceremony of Police General Adul Adul Dejcharat at the crematorium in front of the Royal Pavilion Wat Thepsirintrawat Temple] (Bangkok: Wat Bowonniwet Vihara Temple, 18 April 1970).

30. CIA, "Siam: Premier Moves to Restrain Army", 29 June 1946, https://www.cia.gov/readingroom/docs/Daily%20Summary%20 %23115%5B15493699%5D.pdf.

31. Jira's predecessor, General Sinat, had retired as defence minister in late 1945 under Prime Minister Seni Pramoj officially because of ill health. In January 1946, Sinat had returned as defence minister under royalist prime minister Khuang Aphaiwong (with whom Sinat agreed politically), but he had again retired when the more progressive Pridi became prime minister in March 1946. Though Sinat was an anti-Phibun supporter of the Seri Thai Movement, he was also close to the emerging pro-palace Democrat Party of Khuang Aphaiwong and Seni Pramoj.

32. Vichitvong, *Pridi Panomyong*, p. 228.

33. Kingdom of Thailand, Constitution, 1946, *Government Gazette* 30, no. 63 (10 May 1946), sections 24, 29, 66, 90 (in Thai), Parliament Library, Bangkok, Thailand.

34. Pridi, through his majority control of the lower house, was able to fill the Senate with his supporters. See David Wilson, *Politics in Thailand* (Ithaca: Cornell University Press, 1962), p. 264; "Kiat" [pseudonym], *Political Chronicles* (in Thai) (Bangkok: Kiatthisak Press, 1950), pp. 97–101.

35. Vichitvong, *Pridi Panomyong*, p. 233.

36. Venkataramani, "Military Coup Pattern", p. 258.

37. Ibid., pp. 259.

38. Associated Press, "Was Siam's Boy King Slain Lest He Upset the Apple Cart?" (1950), in *The King of Thailand in World Focus* (Bangkok, Foreign Correspondents Club of Thailand: 2009), http://sutlib2.sut.ac.th/sut_contents/H136464.pdf.

39. Rayne Kruger, *The Devil's Discus* (London: Cassell, 1964).

40. Sebastian Strangio, "Pavin Chachavalpongpun on the Strange Death of King Ananda Mahidol", *The Diplomat*, 11 January 2022, https://thediplomat.com/2022/01/pavin-chachavalpongpun-on-the-strange-death-of-king-ananda-mahidol/.

41. Richard S. Ehrlich, "Buying a Gun in Thailand Can be Expensive", *Free Press*, 27 August 2013, https://freepress.org/article/buying-gun-thailand-can-be-expensive.

42. Thanet, "The United States", p. 197.

43. CIA, "Soviet Propaganda Training for Southeast Asia", 31 October 1947, https://www.cia.gov/readingroom/docs/CIA-RDP82-00457R001000580007-4.pdf.

44. Venkataramani, "Military Coup Pattern", pp. 259–65.

45. See Katsuyuki Takahashi, "How Phibun Returned to the Political Scene: Youth-Led Rallies, Leaflets, and Petitions in 1947, 1948, and 2020, *Asian Affairs: An American Review* (2022), https://doi.org/10.1080/00927678.2022.2128244.

46. CIA, "Replacement of Damrong Cabinet in Siam Expected", Book II … Weekly Summary – 3 January #29 thru 27 June 1947 (#54), https://www.cia.gov/readingroom/docs/CIA-RDP78-01617A001800020001-9.pdf.

47. Venkataramani, "Military Coup Pattern", pp. 260–62

48. Ibid., pp. 265, 274.

49. Fineman, *A Special Relationship*, pp. 29–30

50. CIA, "Siam: Possible Coup Attempt by Junior Army Officers", DAILY SUMMARY #420-445[15507262].pdf, 17 July 1947, https://www.cia.gov/readingroom/docs/DAILY%20SUMMARY%20%23420-445%5B15507262%5D.pdf.

51. Personal interview with Kraisak Chunhavan, Bangkok, Thailand, 3 November 2018.

52. See อนุสรณ์ในงานพระราชทานเพลิงศพ จอมพลผิน ชุณหะวัณ ณ วัดพระศรีมหาธาตุวรมหาวิหาร [Memorial volume from the cremation ceremony of Field Marshal Phin Chunhawan at Wat Phra Si Mahathat Woramahawihan], Bangkok, 7 May 1973.

53. Katja Rangsivek, *Trakun*, "Politics and the Thai State" (PhD dissertation, University of Copenhagen, 2013), p. 145, https://theses.hal.science/tel-00850357v1/file/Ph.d._2013_Rangsivek.pdf.

54. A much more elaborate family tree is offered in Rangsivek, *Trakun*, on page 261, figure 46.

55. Venkataramani, "Military Coup Pattern", p. 265.

56. See Worapat Attayukti, ชีวิตกับเหตุการณ์ของจอมพลผิน ชุณหะวัณ อรรถยุกติ [Life and events of Field Marshal Phin Chunhawan] (Bangkok: Amarin, 2009).

57. Cited in Peter Dale Scott, "Operation Paper: The United States and Drugs in Thailand and Burma", *Asia-Pacific Journal*, 1 November 2010, https://apjjf.org/-Peter-Dale-Scott/3436/article.html.

58. Sitthi Savetsila, *Sitthi's Style of Foreign Policy* (Bangkok: 2015), p. 208.

59. CIA, "Possible Political Developments", 21 October 1947, https://www.cia.gov/readingroom/docs/CIA-RDP82-00457R001000270007-8.pdf.

60. Wright, *The Balancing Act*, pp. 178–79.

61. Edwin Stanton, *Brief Authority: Recollections of China and Thailand* (London: Hillman, 1957), p. 207.

62. "Excerpt from Marshal Phin Chunnahawan's Memories Regarding the Coups of 1947 and 1957", originally published by Prasertsiri Press, 1970, translated and edited by Thak Chaloermtirana, *Thai Politics: 1932–1957* (Social Science Association of Thailand, Thammasat University, 1978), p. 573.

63. Wright, *The Balancing Act*, pp. 172–75.

64. Thak, *Thailand: The Politics*, p. 27.

65. But Buranasompop, ชัยชนะและความพ่ายแพ้ของบุรุษเหล็กแห่งเอเชียม [Victory and defeat of the iron man of Asia] (Bangkok: Unique News Center, 1960).

66. Thak, *Thailand: The Politics*, pp. 28–29.

67. Reynolds, *Thailand's Secret War*, p. 425n185; Thak, *Thailand: The Politics*, p. 26.

68. Fineman, *A Special Relationship*, p. 39.

69. Ibid., p. 39.

70. "Excerpt from Marshal Phin Chunnahawan's Memories", p. 576.

71. Ibid., pp. 576–77.

72. Thak, *Thailand: The Politics*, p. 31.

73. According to Kruger, Pridi and Lieutenant Vacharachai (both of whom would later be tried in absentia of regicide, along with Chit, Butr and Pridi's secretary Chaleo) escaped by ship to Singapore with the assistance of British ambassador Geoffrey Thompson and US ambassador Edwin Stanton, apparently because the latter two recognized Pridi's assistance leading Seri Thai in World War II. See Kruger, *The Devil's Discus*, pp. 117–20.

74. "The Sarit Coup, September 16, 1957: Biography of Sarit Thanarat", originally published by Prasertsiri Press, 1970, translated and edited by Thak Chaloermtirana, *Thai Politics: 1932–1957* (Social Science Association of Thailand, Thammasat University, 1978), p. 702.

75. CIA, Daily Summary #524-546[15507009].pdf, November 1947, https://www.cia.gov/readingroom/docs/DAILY%20SUMMARY%20%23524-546%5B15507009%5D.pdf.

76. CIA, "The Significance of the Siamese Coup detat", Book III – Weekly Summary – 3 July 1947 (#55) Thru 30 Dec 1947 (#79), November 1947, https://www.cia.gov/readingroom/docs/CIA-RDP78-01617A001900020001-8.pdf.

77. Ibid.

78. Ibid.

79. Announcements Nos. 1–17, translated and edited by Thak Chaloermtirana, *Thai Politics: 1932–1957* (Social Science Association of Thailand, Thammasat University, 1978), pp. 541, 546–47.

80. Announcement No. 9, translated and edited by Thak Chaloermtirana, *Thai Politics: 1932–1957* (Social Science Association of Thailand, Thammasat University, 1978), pp. 541, 546–47.

81. Cited from W. Ch. Prasangsit, Phaendit Somdet, pp. 170, 171, in Thak, *Thailand: The Politics*, p. 29.

82. "Letters and Personal Notes of Lt. Gen. Kat Katsongkhram, Army Headquarters, Suan Kularb Palace, January 3, 1950", translated and edited by Thak Chaloermtirana, *Thai Politics: 1932–1957* (Social Science Association of Thailand, Thammasat University, 1978), pp. 551–55.

83. Kobkua Suwannathat-Pian, *Kings, Country and Constitution* (London: Routledge, 2003), p. 137.

84. Ibid., pp. 120–21.

85. John Girling, *Thailand: Society and Politics* (Ithaca: Cornell University Press, 1981), pp. 126–27n5.

86. Rong Syamananda, *A History of Thailand* (Bangkok: Chulalongkorn University. 1988), p. 178.

87. Stanton, *Brief Authority*, p. 209

88. Natapoll Chaiching, "The Monarchy and the Royalist Movement in Modern Thai Politics, 1932–1957", in *Saying the Unsayable*, edited by Soren Ivarrson and Lotte Isager (Copenhagen: NIAS, 2010), p. 166.

89. Fineman, *A Special Relationship*, pp. 62–63.

90. Stanton, *Brief Authority*, p. 209

91. CIA, Daily Summary #524-546.

92. Ibid.

93. Fineman, *A Special Relationship*, p. 39.

94. Wilson, *Politics in Thailand*, 264.

95. See Thak, *The Politics of Despotic Paternalism*, p. 32.

96. Paul Handley, *The King Never Smiles* (New Haven: Yale University Press, 2006), p. 88.

97. Paul Handley, "Princes, Politicians, Bureaucrats, Generals: The Evolution of the Privy Council under the Constitutional Monarchy", paper for the 10th International Conference on Thai Studies, Thammasat University, Bangkok, 9–11 January 2008, pp. 9–10.

98. Handley, *The King Never Smiles*, p. 89.

99. Fineman, *A Special Relationship*, p. 50.

100. CIA, Daily Summary #524-546.

101. Ibid.

102. CIA, "Siam: Opposition to Present Regime", Daily Summary #547-572[15507011].pdf, December 1947, https://www.cia.gov/readingroom/docs/DAILY%20SUMMARY%20%23547-572%5B15507011%5D.pdf.

103. Pridi Panomyong, *Pridi by Pridi: Selected Writings on Life, Politics and Economy*, translated by Chris Baker and Pasuk Phongpaichit (Bangkok: The Pridi Panomyong Foundation; Chiang Mai: Silkworm Books, 2000), p. 265.

104. Ibid.

105. Stanton, *Brief Authority*, p. 210.

106. CIA, "Siam: Current Siamese Politics", Office of Reports and Estimates, CIA Far East/Pacific Branch Intelligence Highlights Week of 20–26 January 1948, https://www.cia.gov/readingroom/docs/CIA-RDP78-01617A004600020003-6.pdf.

107. During this period, parties were not formalized but rather only political clubs. Phibun's Sahapap (or United Parties) Front was formed to provide him with a parliamentary foundation. Sahapap was composed of Phibun's loyalist Thammatipat Party, the Prachachon Party (whose leader instrumentally formed the coalition), the Independent Party, the National Social Democrat Party (led by a military officer, Colonel Banyat Thephasadin), the Agro-Labor Party, the Rasadorn Party and even the Democrat Party! Sahapap served merely as a quid pro quo: it acted to dispense political spoils to participating parties in return for legitimating Phibun's premiership.

108. CIA, "Siam: Possible New Anti-Royalist Coalition Government", Daily Summary 194801-1948[15520827].pdf, 6 February 1948, https://www.cia.gov/readingroom/docs/DAILY%20SUMMARY%20194801-1948%5B15520827%5D.pdf.

109. Kenneth Landon, assistant chief, Southeast Asia Division, United States State Department, 20 February 1948, cited in Andrew MacGregor Marshall, "Thailand's Saddest Secret", 2022, https://www.zenjournalist.com/2013/03/thailands-saddest-secret/.

110. Ibid.

111. Fineman, *A Special Relationship*, p. 46.

112. Ibid., pp. 51–52.

113. CIA, "Offers of Arms and Ammunition to the Siamese Ministry of Defense", 25 January 1949, https://www.cia.gov/readingroom/docs/CIA-RDP82-00457R002300140007-8.pdf.

114 CIA, "Siamese Request for Arms through Willis H. Bird", 4 March 1949, https://www.cia.gov/readingroom/docs/CIA-RDP82-00457R002400490004-2.pdf.

115. Sitthi, *Sitthi's Style*, p. 192.

116. Khuang Aphaiwong, "Khuang's Letter of Resignation", 6 April 1948, translated and edited by Thak Chaloermtirana, *Thai Politics: 1932–1957* (Social Science Association of Thailand, Thammasat University), 1978, p. 592.

117. Thak, *Thailand: The Politics*, p. 34; Wright, *The Balancing Act*, p. 182.

118. Fineman, *A Special Relationship*, pp. 55–56.

119. อนุสรณ์ในการบรรจุอัฐิ ฯพณฯ จอมพล ป. พิบูลสงคราม ณ วัดพระศรีมหาธาตุ [Memorial volume from the cremation ritual of his excellency Field Marshal P. Phibunsongkhram at Wat Phra Sri Mahathat], Bangkok, 30 July 1964.

120. CIA, "Siam: Letter Reveals Objectives of Military Group", Office of Reports and Estimates, CIA Far East/Pacific Branch, Week of April 20–April 26, https://www.cia.gov/readingroom/docs/CIA-RDP79-01090A000400060001-1.pdf.

121. อนุสรณ์ในงานพระราชทานเพลิงศพ จอมพลผิน ชุณหะวัณ ณ วัดพระศรีมหาธาตุวรมหาวิหาร [Memorial volume from the cremation ceremony of Field Marshal Phin Chunhawan, Wat Phra Si Mahathat Woramahawihan], Bangkok, 7 May 1973.

122. Niyom Rathamarit, *Military Governments in Thailand: Their Policies Toward Political Parties* (Pittsburgh: University of Pittsburgh, 1984), p. 80.

123. Handley, *The King Never Smiles*, pp. 91–92.

124. Thak, *Thailand: The Politics*, p. 42.

125. Ibid., pp. 35–36.

126. Fineman, *A Special Relationship*, p. 82.

127. CIA, "Operational Plans of the Abortive Countercoup D'etat Group", 1 December 1948, https://www.cia.gov/readingroom/docs/CIA-RDP82-00457R002100340008-7.pdf.

128. CIA, "Participation of Former United States Navy Ship in the Attempted 26 February Coup", 4 May 1949, https://www.cia.gov/readingroom/docs/CIA-RDP82-00457R002700370010-5.pdf.

129. Katsu Yuki Takahashi, *The Peace Movement during the Early Cold War Years in Asia* (in Japanese) (Waseca University Press, 2014). pp. 40–41.

130. Ibid.

131. CIA, "Siam: Unsuccessful Coup d'état May Bring Government Changes", Intelligence Highlights, No. 41, 24 February – 1 March 1949, https://www.cia.gov/readingroom/docs/CIA-RDP79-01082A000100020020-6.pdf.

132. CIA, "Navy Refusal of Phibun's Demands for Surrender of Pridi, Now Ill at Sattahip", 29 April 1949, https://www.cia.gov/readingroom/docs/CIA-RDP82-00457R002700250004-5.pdf.

133. Wright, *The Balancing Act*, p. 185.

134. CIA, "Siamese Navy Demands in Current Negotiations with the Army", 10 March 1949, https://www.cia.gov/readingroom/docs/CIA-RDP82-00457R002500140009-4.pdf.

135. CIA, "Chinese Communists in Siam", 16 May 1949, https://www.cia.gov/readingroom/docs/CIA-RDP82-00457R002700580007-6.pdf.

136. CIA, "Added Information Concerning the Murders of the Ex-Ministers", 29 April 1949, https://www.cia.gov/readingroom/docs/CIA-RDP82-00457R002600450004-4.pdf.

137. CIA, "Current Political Crisis in Thailand", 27 December 1949, https://www.cia.gov/readingroom/docs/CIA-RDP82-00457R004000600004-1.pdf.

138. Wright, *The Balancing Act*, p. 134.

139. "เมื่อ รอง ผบ.ทบ. ถูกจี้กลางทำเนียบรัฐบาล โดนปืนจ่อแล้วบอก 'ขอจับท่านบัดนี้'" [When the deputy commander-in-chief of the Royal Thai Army was hijacked in the middle of the Government House got a gun pointed and said "I want to arrest you now"], Silpa-mag.com, 5 February 2022, https://www.silpa-mag.com/history/article_26186.

140. Thak, *Thailand: The Politics*, p. 37.

141. Fineman, *A Special Relationship*, p. 148.

142. Manat Charupha, "When I Held up the Field Marshal", *Buang Raek Prachatippatai*, translated and edited by Thak Chaloermtirana, *Thai Politics: 1932–1957* (Social Science Association of Thailand, Thammasat University), 1978, p. 609.

143. CIA, "Possible Attempt at Coup d-etat Reported in Thailand", CURRENT INTELLIGENCE BULL[15587398].tif, 6 March 1951, https://www.cia.gov/readingroom/docs/CURRENT%20INTELLIGENCE%20BULL%5B15587398%5D.pdf.

144. CIA, "Factors behind Attempted Coup D'etat of 29 June", 10 July 1951, https://www.cia.gov/readingroom/docs/CIA-RDP82-00457R008100160008-1.pdf.

145. Manat Charupha, When I Held Up", p. 630.

146. "The Chargé in Thailand (Turner) to Mr. Robert P. Joyce, Policy Planning Staff", 7 November 1951, *FRUS*, https://history.state.gov/historicaldocuments/frus1951v06p2/d91.

147. Pleng Supa Rieprieng, *The Manhattan Coup* (Bangkok: Pailin Booknet, 2001), p. 88.

148. Thak, *Thailand: The Politics*, pp. 40–41.

149. B.J. Terwiel, *Field Marshal Plaek Phibun Songkram* (University of Queensland Press, 1980), p. 26.

150. Fineman, *A Special Relationship*, p. 154.

151. Sarit's role in repressing the coup attempts had meteorically propelled him up the ladder of army leadership. From a colonel and commander of the 1st Infantry Regiment (1945–48), he had ascended to become commander of the strategic 1st Army Region in Bangkok (1950–52). In 1952 he was appointed deputy army commander, second only to Phin. Meanwhile, Sarit's army loyalists followed in his footsteps. Thanom Kittikachorn served as commander of the 1st Army Division (1950–52); Praphas Charusatien subsequently took this post (1952–57), as did Krit Sivara (1957–61). Each seemed positioned to move up the "classic" route of Thai military power: (1) commander, 1st Infantry Regiment; (2) commander, 1st Army Division; (3) commander, 1st Army Region; (4) deputy commander-in-chief of the army; 5) commander-in-chief of

the army. See Chai-anan Samudavanija, *The Thai Young Turks* (Singapore: Institute of Southeast Asian Studies, 1982), pp. 79–80.

152. Kobkua, *Kings, Country*, p. 139.

153. Communiques Nos. 1 and 2, 29 November 1951, translated and edited by Thak Chaloermtirana, *Thai Politics: 1932–1957* (Social Science Association of Thailand, Thammasat University), 1978, pp.675–78.

154. Thak, *Thailand: The Politics*, pp. 51–52.

155. Kobkua, *Kings, Country*, p. 141.

156. D. Nohlen, F. Grotz, and C. Hartmann, *Elections in Asia: A Data Handbook*, vol. 2 (2001), p. 284.

157. Niyom, *Military Governments*, p. 81.

158 Thak, *Thailand: The Politics*, pp. 44–45.

159. Boon, ชัยชนะและความพ่ายแพ้ของบุรุษเหล็กแห่งเอเชีย [Victory and defeat].

160. อนุสรณ์งานพระราชทานเพลิงศพจอมพลอากาศฟื้น รณนภากาศ ฤทธาคนีฉ ฌาปนสถานกองทัพอากาศ วัดพระศรีมหาธาตุวรมหาวิหาร [Royal cremation memorial volume from the cremation ritual of Field Marshal (Royal Thai Air Force air chief marshal) Ronaphakat Rittakanee, Wat Phra Sri Mahathat Woramahawihan Temple], Bangkok, 5 October 1987.

161. Wilson, *Politics in Thailand*, pp. 179–80.

162. Fineman, *A Special Relationship*, pp. 46, 161–62, 296n67.

163. CIA, "Political Upheaval in Thailand Reported Underway", CURRENT INTELLIGENCE BULL[15638427] (1).pdf, https://www.cia.gov/readingroom/docs/CURRENT%20INTELLIGENCE%20BULL%5B15638427%5D.pdf, March 16, 1952,

164. CIA, "Overthrow of Thai Premier Reportedly Planned", CURRENT INTELLIGENCE BULL[15638466].pdf, 21 June 1952, https://www.cia.gov/readingroom/docs/CURRENT%20INTELLIGENCE%20BULL%5B15638466%5D.pdf.

165. CIA, "Thai Military Leaders Reported Planning to Replace Premier Phibun", CURRENT INTELLIGENCE BULL[15653013].pdf, 6 August 1952, https://www.cia.gov/readingroom/docs/CURRENT%20INTELLIGENCE%20BULL%5B15653013%5D.pdf

166. Katsuyuki Takahashi, *The Peace Movement during the Early Cold War Years in Asia* (in Japanese) (Waseda University Press, 2014), p. 17.

167. CIA, "Thai Prime Minister Seen as Responsible for Drive against Communists", 16 November 1952, "Central Intelligence Bulletin", https://www.cia.gov/readingroom/docs/CIA-RDP79T00975A000900310001-7.pdf.

168. "ตำนานนักสู้ "เตียง ศิริขันธ์" จากครูหนุ่มไฟแรง สู่สี่เสืออีสาน ขุนพลหนุ่มแห่งภูพาน" [Legend of the fighter 'Tieng Sirikhan' from the young teacher to the four tigers in the northeast: The young commander of Phu Phan], Silpa-mag.com, 17 January 2022, https://www.silpa-mag.com/history/article_58106.

169. Frank Darling, *Thailand and the United States* (Washington, DC: Public Affairs Press, 1965). p. 115.

170. William Skinner, *Chinese Society in Thailand* (Ithaca: Cornell University Press, 1957), p. 358.

171. Krirkkiat Phipatseritham and Kunio Yoshihara, *Business Groups in Thailand* (Singapore: Institute of Southeast Asian Studies, 1983), p. 23.

172. Thak, *Thailand: The Politics*, p. 64n88.

173. Frank C. Darling, "America and Thailand", *Asian Survey* 7, no. 4 (1967): 217.

174. This William H. Bird established Bird Air in 1960 and it was later integrated into Continental Airlines. Whitney Webb, *One Nation under Blackmail* (Walterville, OR: Trine Day, 2022), chapter 1 ("The Underworld"), note 61.

175. *Commercial Directory for Thailand*, Department of Commercial Intelligence, Ministry of Economic Affairs (Bangkok: 1953–54), p. x.

176. Fineman, *A Special Relationship*, pp. 133–34.

177. Sitthi, *Sitthi's Style*, p. 208.

178. One member of MAAG, Lt. Col. John Stose, later recounted his days in 1950 as part of that outfit: "It was November 1950, at Camp Breckinridge, Kentucky. I was handed ... orders transferring me from Fort Meade to Thailand. On one of my visits to the MAAG compound I noticed a Thai Army Major ... who pointed in my direction. The Major extended his hand and said, 'Johnny. Call me Chow Chow'. He was the liaison officer handling the setup of the local currency account and had a lot of questions about my procedures. I explained that MAAG had no Army Regs. governing the account so I would use my own system. It was 'no problem.' He guffawed when he heard me say that so I used the phrase 'no problem' to lead every answer to his every 'What if?'. His real name was not Chow Chow. It was Chatichai Chunhavan. His father, Phin Chunhavan, was CINC, Royal Thai Army. Chow Chow told me he was a graduate of West Point and of the Armor School.... We had a great relationship and quite a few beers together over the rest of my tour there." See USMAAG 1951, LTC John Stose, Rafino Report, 26, https://rafino. org/Rafino_Report_Past/issue26/issue26_thai.htm.

179. "No. 384. Edwin M. Martin, Special Assistant to the Secretary for Mutual Security Affairs, to John H. Ohly, Assistant Director for Program, Office of the Director of Mutual Security", 7 October 1952, *FRUS*, https:// history.state.gov/historicaldocuments/frus1952-54v12p2/d384.

180. Thak, *Thailand: The Politics*, p. 64.

181. General Wirawat Yothin was a national hero of Thailand. During the Indochina War (1940–41), as a lieutenant colonel he had commanded the Surin Brigade. In the Payap Army (1941–43), he commanded the 8th Battalion under 3rd Division commander Phin Chunhavan (and was a superior to Captain Sarit Thanarat). The 8th Infantry Regiment under his command—and though he was wounded—captured the Shan city of Keng Tung, earning him instant celebrity status. See Cremation volume, Major General Luang Weerawatthanayothin (Weerawat

Weerawatanayothin), Royal Thai Army, Wat Somanat Wihan, 28 January 1969

182. Thak, *Thailand: The Politics*, pp. 63–64.

183. Ibid., p. 58.

184. Timothy Castle states that the purpose of this operation was to build paramilitary units as a means "to halt Chinese inspired insurgent activity along Thailand's long and mostly undefended borders". By 1953, over four thousand Thai security officials graduated from the SEA Supply school. See Timothy Castle, "At War in the Shadow of Vietnam: United States Military Aid to the Royal Lao Government, 1955–75" (PhD dissertation, University of Hawai'i, 1991), p. 92, https://apps.dtic.mil/sti/pdfs/ADA243492.pdf.

185. Ibid.

186. Desmond Ball, *Tor Chor Dor: Thailand's Border Patrol Police* (Bangkok: White Lotus, 2013), pp. 74–75; Sinae Hyun, "Indigenizing the Cold War: Nation-Building by the Border Patrol Police of Thailand, 1945–1980" (PhD dissertation, University of Wisconsin-Madison, 2014), p. 125n104.

187. Sitthi, *Sitthi's Style*, p. 209.

188 "Memorandum by the Chief of the Joint Military Mission to Thailand (Gillmore) to the Joint Chiefs of Staff", 30 September 1953, *FRUS*, https://history.state.gov/historicaldocuments/frus1952-54v12p2/d404.

189. Fineman, *A Special Relationship*, p. 181.

190. Sinae Hyun, "Indigenizing the Cold War", pp. i, 308.

191. Ibid., p. i.

192. CIA, "Conversation with General Phao", 6 August 1953, https://www.cia.gov/readingroom/docs/DOC_0005772606.pdf.

193. Even by 1956–57, the size of the Thai army stood at only 45,000 troops, compared with 48,000 members of the police. Phao used US aid to equip the police force with tanks, boats and modern weapons—literally creating an alternative army. See Ball, *Tor Chor Dor*, p. 65.

194. Thak, *Thailand: The Politics*, p. 58.

195. "Memorandum by the Executive Officer of the Operations Coordinating Board (Staats) to the Executive Secretary of the National Security Council (Lay)", 15 July 1954, *FRUS*, https://history.state.gov/historicaldocuments/frus1952-54v12p2/d432.

196. BBC Thailand, "หะยีสุหลง อับดุลกอเดร์ โต๊ะมีนา: 66 ปี บังคับสูญหายผู้นำทางศาสนาและการเมืองคนสำคัญของปาตานี" [Haji Sulong Abdul Qader Tohmena: 66 years of forced disappearance, important religious and political leader of Patani], 13 August 2020, https://www.bbc.com/thai/thailand-53761549.

197. "Paper by the Operations Coordinating Board Working Group on NSC 5405, 20 December 1954, *FRUS*, https://history.state.gov/historicaldocuments/frus1952-54v12p2/d439.

198. Ibid.

199. Ibid.

200. "Memorandum by the Regional Director for Far East, Foreign Operations Administration (Moyer) to the Director of the Foreign Operations Administration (Stassen)", 1 December 1954, *FRUS*, https://history.state.gov/historicaldocuments/frus1952-54v12p2/d437; Thak, *Thailand: The Politics*, p. 63.

201. Victor S. Kaufman, "Trouble in the Golden Triangle: The United States, Taiwan and the 93rd Nationalist Division", *China Quarterly* 166 (2001): 441.

202. Richard Gibson and Wenhua Chen, *The Secret Army: Chiang Kai-shek and the Drug Warlords of the Golden Triangle* (New York: Wiley, 2011), p. 38.

203. "The Chargé in Thailand (Turner) to the Secretary of State", 28 September 1951, *FRUS*, https://history.state.gov/historicaldocuments/frus1951v06p1/d145.

204. Ibid.

205. "The Ambassador in India (Bowles) to the Department of State", 19 March 1952, *FRUS*, https://history.state.gov/historicaldocuments/frus1952-54v12p2/d17.

206. Fineman, *A Special Relationship*, p. 216.

207. Paul Chambers, *Guatemala's Reactionary Reversal: Castillo Armas and the Liberal Restoration, 1954–1957* (Master's thesis, Ohio University, 1991).

208. Fineman, *A Special Relationship*, p. 213.

209. Ball, *Tor Chor Dor*, p. 70.

210. Fineman, *A Special Relationship*, p. 216.

211. Ball, *Tor Chor Dor*, p. 70.

212. "475. Telegram from the Embassy in Thailand to the Department of State (Ambassador John Peurifoy to US State Department)", 14 July 1975, *FRUS*, https://history.state.gov/historicaldocuments/frus1955-57v22/d475.

213. Surachart Bamrungsuk, *United States Foreign Policy and Thai Military Rule, 1947–1977* (Bangkok: DK, 1985), p. 64.

214. CIA, "Probe Envoy's Death Ride", 15 August 1955, https://www.cia.gov/readingroom/docs/CIA-RDP75-00149R000600300030-3.pdf.

215. "477. Memorandum of a Conversation", Department of State, Washington, 12 August 1955, *FRUS*, https://history.state.gov/historicaldocuments/frus1955-57v22/d477.

216. "482. Memorandum from the Director of Central Intelligence (Dulles) to the Chairman of the Joint Chiefs of Staff (Radford)", 18 November 1955, *FRUS*, https://history.state.gov/historicaldocuments/frus1955-57v22/d482.

217. Fineman, *A Special Relationship*, p. 226.

218. "Thailand: A Time for Skill", *Time Magazine*, 9 July 1956, https://content.time.com/time/subscriber/article/0,33009,893459,00.html.

219. Fineman, *A Special Relationship*, p. 223.

220. Albert Pickerell and Daniel Moore, "Elections in Thailand", *Far Eastern Survey* 26, no. 6 (1957): 92–93.

221. Krit Sivara, ประวัติและผลงาน พลเอก กฤษณ์ สีวะรา [History and achievements of General Krit Sivara] (Bangkok: ผู้แต่ง, 1976), p. 6; King Prajadhipok's Institute, "Krit Sivara", http://wiki.kpi.ac.th/index.php?title=%E0%B8%81%E0%B8%A4%E0%B8%A9%E0%B8%93%E0%B9%8C_%E0%B8%AA%E0%B8%B5%E0%B8%A7%E0%B8%B0%E0%B8%A3%E0%B8%B2#_ftn13.

222. "484. Staff Study Prepared by an Interdepartmental Working Group for the Operations Coordinating Board", *FRUS*, 4 January 1956, https://history.state.gov/historicaldocuments/frus1955-57v22/d484.

223. CIA, "Pridi Reportedly Seeking to Return to Thailand", 21 April 1956, https://www.cia.gov/readingroom/docs/CURRENT%20INTELLIGENCE%20BULL%5B15740189%5D.pdf.

224. "486. Despatch from the Embassy in Thailand to the Department of State", telegram no. 424, 8 February 1956, *FRUS*, https://history.state.gov/historicaldocuments/frus1955-57v22/d486.

225. "499. Telegram from the Embassy in Thailand to the Department of State", 16 June 1956", *FRUS*, https://history.state.gov/historicaldocuments/frus1955-57v22/d499.

226. "375. Memorandum from the Chairman's Staff Group to the Chairman of the Joint Chiefs of Staff (Radford)", 23 August 1956, *FRUS*, https://history.state.gov/historicaldocuments/frus1955-57v21/d375.

227. "491. Memorandum from the Secretary of Defense's Deputy Assistant for Special Operations (Godel) to the Assistant Secretary of Defense for International Security Affairs (Gray)", 21 March 1956, *FRUS*, https://history.state.gov/historicaldocuments/frus1955-57v22/d491.

228. Paul Chambers, ed., *Knights of the Realm: Thailand's Military and Police, Then and Now* (Bangkok: White Lotus, 2013), p. 151.

229. Niyom, *Military Governments*, pp. 83–84.

230. Personal interview with Phibun's grandson, Pradap Phibun Songkram, 12 October 2022.

231. Fineman, *A Special Relationship*, p. 235.

232. CIA, "The Situation in Thailand", 3 March 1957, https://www.cia.gov/readingroom/docs/CIA-RDP79T00975A003000100001-6.pdf.

233. "The Sarit Coup", pp. 707–8.

234. Fineman, *A Special Relationship*, pp. 236–37.

235. Handley, *The King Never Smiles*, p. 136.

236. CIA, "NSC Briefing: Thailand", 12 March 1957, https://www.cia.gov/readingroom/docs/CIA-RDP79R00890A000800050016-7.pdf.

237. Sir S. Gage, "From Bangkok to Foreign Office", telegram no. 220 of 17 April 1957, Ministry of Foreign Affairs, United Kingdom.

238. CIA, "Thai Premier Reportedly in Precarious Situation", 20 April 1957, https://www.cia.gov/readingroom/docs/CURRENT%20 INTELLIGENCE%20BULL%5B15755574%5D.pdf.

239. CIA, "Early Crisis in Thailand Feared", 30 May 1957, https://www. cia.gov/readingroom/docs/CURRENT%20INTELLIGENCE%20 BULL%5B15755598%5D.pdf.

240. Fineman, *A Special Relationship*, pp. 240–41.

241. "494. Telegram From the Embassy in Thailand to the Department of State", 2 July 1958, *FRUS*, https://history.state.gov/historicaldocuments/ frus1958-60v15/d494.

242. CIA, "Possible Consequence of Current Developments in Thailand", 14 September 1957, https://www.cia.gov/readingroom/docs/CIA-RDP79R00904A000400010016-2.pdf.

243. Ibid.

244. Thak, *Thailand: The Politics*, p. 82.

245. Natapoll, "The Monarchy", p. 171.

246. CIA, "National Security Council Briefing", 21 November 1957, https://www.cia.gov/library/readingroom/docs/CIA-RDP79R00890A000900010020-5.pdf.

247. CIA, "Thailand", 21 September 1957, https://www.cia.gov/readingroom/ docs/CIA-RDP79R00890A000900010020-5.pdf.

248. CIA, "Sarit Consolidates Control of Thailand", 21 September 1957, https://www.cia.gov/readingroom/docs/CIA-RDP79-00927A001400080001-9.pdf.

249. Natapoll, "The Monarchy", p. 171.

250. Fineman, *A Special Relationship*, pp. 233, 240.

251. Ibid., p. 254.

252. United States State Department, "General Krit's Future", 26 September 1975, Wikileaks, 1975BANGKO20381_b, https://wikileaks.org/plusd/ cables/1975BANGKO20381_b.html.

253. Fineman, *A Special Relationship*, p. 242.

254. Thak, *Thailand: The Politics*, pp. 84–85.

Chapter Four

Sarit's Stratocracy (1957–63)

This chapter examines the period from 16 September 1957 until 11 December 1963, six years within which one army faction took control of Thailand, attempted to rule it first through a façade democracy, and then instituted complete authoritarian control. It was a period in which Field Marshal Sarit Thanarat completely dominated the country, though he was assisted by King Bhumipol Adulyadej, the United States, supportive leading military officials, and right-wing aristocrats. The putsch of 1957 moved Thailand towards what it achieved in 1958—a "militocracy"[1] or "stratocracy".[2] A stratocracy is a form of government of, by and for military commanders.

Sarit's 16 September 1957 coup took only an hour. Referred to as Rerkdi Thanarat (Good auspices for Sarit Thanarat), it involved merely his declaring of martial law and the securing of all strategic military and police centres in Bangkok by military and police officials, who were wearing white armbands as a coded sign of purity.[3] With Phibun ousted from the premiership, Sarit's chief nemesis, police chief General Phao Sriyanond, as well as the commanders of the navy (Admiral Prayoon Yuthasastrkosol) and air force (Field Marshal Fuen Ronnaphagrad Ritthakhanee), were all dismissed. Thereupon, Sarit established a committee of thirteen senior military officials, with himself as chair, for the purposes of maintaining "peace and security".[4]

In reaction to the putsch, Phibun immediately raced out of Bangkok in his Citroen sportscar (with an entourage of close supporters), heading, via Chanthaburi province in eastern Thailand, to initial exile in Cambodia, where it was thought he might plan a counter-coup. Those traveling with Phibun included his wife, Laiad; Major General Bulsak Wannamas, a military adjutant; Chai Wirotsiri, secretary-general to the prime minister; and security police officer Lt. Col. Chumphon Lohachala. According to Phibun's grandson Pradab Phibunsongram, Phibun set up a decoy for the pursuers at Sattahip base in Chonburi. He then raced towards the border with Cambodia. Only a boy familiar with the boundary marshes and sea areas was able to get Phibun and his company safely through to the neighbouring country.[5]

By November 1957, US officials were of the opinion that it would be

> unlikely that Phibun could, or would, return to the premiership by reaching a compromise with Sarit, since the King and the royalists would undoubtedly resist such a step. [The US officials added that] Phibun's political and administrative abilities [were] highly regarded by many in the military group ... and there is a possibility that at some future date he may be able to re-enter politics as the only man capable of managing the government.[6]

For the next seven years, until his death, suspicions continued that Phibun was plotting to return home and take power. He never did. Later on, Phibun left Cambodia and resided in Shinjuku, Tokyo, for almost a year, in the home of his friend Wada, a wealthy manager of the Marusen Oil Company. In 1960 Phibun then travelled to India to ordain briefly as a monk at a Buddhist temple in Bodhgaya, before going to the United States and staying there for approximately two years. He then returned to Japan, where he died aged sixty-six on 11 June 1964. He had earlier survived three assassination attempts during the years 1934–38 (two by gun, one by poison), but in the end died (presumably) of heart failure in Sagamihara, Kanagawa Prefecture, Japan.

Phao, unlike Phibun, chose not to flee following the 1957 coup, but rather to stay in Bangkok. But, within twelve hours of the putsch, he was escorted to a plane by General Krit Sivara, under orders from Sarit, and flown to exile in Switzerland. While in Switzerland, Phao gave one interview, in 1959, with a Thai journalist. When asked about Field Marshal Plaek Phibun Songkram and his return to Thailand, he said: "As long as Field Marshal Sarit is still alive I will definitely not go [to Thailand]. I will come to Thailand again only if there is a political party and democratic elections, then perhaps I can become Khun Sarit's opposition." He added that, "I admit that I was wrong.... I have also contributed to Field Marshal Phibun's dictatorship." One year after the interview, Phao died (21 November 1960), presumably of a heart attack, just after smoking a cigar and playing table tennis.[7]

The man who had staged the coup—General Sarit Thanarat—was not part of any elite family or connected to royalty. He seemed simply to be a common soldier who had come along at the right time to oust the apparently corrupt and draconian Prime Minister Phibun. But who exactly was Sarit Thanarat? Born in Pahurat, Bangkok, in 1908, he had grown up in the Mukdahan district of Nakhon Panom province. His father, Luang Ruang Detanan (Tongdi Thanarat), an ethnic Khmer from Battambang, eventually became an army major working in northeastern Siam.[8] In 1893, Detanan had been stationed with a Siamese expeditionary force that had engaged in combat against Haw Chinese marauders, where he served as a French interpreter. Not long thereafter, Detanan married the woman who would become Sarit's mother, Chanthip Thipayawong (an ethnic Laotian from Mukdahan). The ceremony was blessed by Thai army commander Prince Prachak Sinlaphakhom. Because her husband was abusive and had many mistresses, Chanthip left him and remarried. Sarit thus grew up in a broken home until he was allowed to leave for Bangkok to continue his education. Sarit's father later worked on helping to demarcate the Siamese–French Indochinese (especially Cambodian) border, translating French texts into Thai. Through Detanan's connections, in 1919, the eleven-year-old Sarit entered Siam's military officers' school (which became Chulachomklao Military Academy). In 1926, now aged eighteen, Sarit became a military officer. Perhaps following the model of his father, Sarit would have many women in his life; he married four times and had at least eighty-one mistresses.[9] He also had several children, at least six of them legitimate. It is thus impossible to construct a family tree for Sarit. In 2023, the senior member of the Thanarat household is Sarit's son, retired general Somchai Thanarat.[10]

Sarit's first posting was in 1929, serving in the 2nd Battalion, 1st Regiment, King's Guard under Colonel Nat Kemayothin. Sarit's mentor and close friend was 1st Lt. Santiyuthakan (later General Sanit Yuthagan Thaiyanon), who became army chief of staff in 1951.[11] Sarit served with distinction during World War II under General Phin Chunhavan, commander of the 3rd (Phayap) Region army. Phin was later the driving force behind the 1947 coup; proved instrumental in repressing coups in 1949, 1950 and 1951; and became army chief in 1954. By 1957, most army officials in senior posts had served under Sarit.

However, the two senior officers who helped Sarit carry out the coup, Field Marshal Thanom Kittikachorn and Field Marshal Praphas Charusathien, who were considered to be the most loyal to Sarit and also at the time the most influential in the army, would now exert tremendous power over Thailand. In 1933 the two had served under Sarit in helping to quell the royalist Boworadej rebellion. Both had supported the 1947 coup led by General Phin Chunhavan (and actuated by Sarit), with Thanom rewarded with command over the 11th Infantry Regiment and Praphas given command over the 1st Infantry Regiment in 1948. Because of their closeness to Sarit, Thanom and Praphas naturally obtained the top positions in Sarit's post-1957 regime.

Sarit did feel closer to Thanom than Sarit. But though Sarit generally trusted Thanom, it had rankled him that the latter had been closely associated with Sarit's predecessor as army chief, General Phin Chunhavan, as well as with Phibun himself. Indeed, Phin had promoted Thanom to be the 1st Army Region commander in 1954 (a post which he held until 1957). Meanwhile, in 1955, Phibun had promoted Thanom to be deputy cooperatives minister, enabling Thanom to extract a substantial amount of rent. Nevertheless, Sarit recognized Thanom's skills as a public orator and politician, and he increasingly used him as a front man. Following Sarit's 1957 coup, he elevated Thanom to the political position of defence minister. And then, on 1 January 1958, he appointed Thanom as prime minister.

One entity destroyed by Sarit shortly after the coup was SEA (Overseas Southeast Asia) Supply, the CIA conduit for weapons to Phao's police and the KMT. SEA Supply CIA officers burned secret documents on the roof of their headquarters in Bangkok's Grand Hotel throughout the night of the 1957 coup, anticipating the mob of civilians, which finally did arrive alongside soldiers on 16 September. Though a wholesale ransacking of its offices was ultimately averted (blocked by CIA Bangkok station chief John Hart), SEA Supply was closed permanently. US ambassador Bishop and Hart, who were no friends of Sarit, were soon to be sent back to Washington. Willis Bird, a close friend of Phao, now temporarily maintained a low profile—though he remained in Bangkok. Sarit only allowed the Phao-dominated paramilitary Border Patrol Police (BPP)—ostensibly under the Royal Thai Police—to continue existing under Royal Thai Army operational control.[12] The CIA's William Lair, who had trained the BPP and had been close to Phao rather than Sarit, was deployed by Washington to Laos in 1960 (though he would return regularly to Bangkok after Sarit's death in 1963). The survival of the BPP partly owed to the fact that its commander, Special Colonel Chan Anguchote, was the husband of Sarit's sister. Meanwhile, within the Royal Guards (under Colonel Pranet Ritileuchai), which had for four years been cultivated by the CIA's William Lair, it was Pranet's friend and classmate Colonel Phytoon Inkatanwat, commander of the nearest RTA garrison, who was charged with disarming the BPP. As a result, this was carried out without incident. Shortly thereafter, an editorial in a local newspaper by someone close to the king praised the Royal Guards. As a result, Sarit did not dismantle the Guards. He compelled them, however, to change their name to the Police Aerial Reinforcement Unit (PARU). And, like the BPP, PARU was placed under the army's operational control.[13] Finally, as SEA Supply appears to have been the institution that earned the ire of Sarit, the CIA and Sarit government agreed on 11 October to commence transferring SEA Supply's activities to the State Department's International Cooperation Agency, a cover of the CIA. Though Civil Air Transport (CAT) remained, on 26 March 1959 it changed its name to Air America.[14]

The initial caretaker cabinet of Sarit was led by pro-US frontman Pote Sarasin, serving as prime minister. Pote had just previously been the Thai ambassador to the United States[15] and also had close ties with the palace. But, of course, the real power in the regime was Sarit and the military. Of the twenty-nine cabinet positions in the new government, fourteen were held by active-duty military officers, not including Sarit. While Sarit initially chose to not be in the cabinet—having the roles only of junta leader, army commander and supreme commander until 1958—his two most trusted loyalists, General Thanom Kittikachorn and General Praphas Charusatien, were named defence minister and interior minister, respectively.[16]

Not surprisingly, the 16 September 1957 military appointments reflected the rise of Sarit and his loyalists. He again named his mentor, General Sanit Yutagan, as permanent minister of defence. ACM Thawee Chullasap was appointed deputy chief of staff of the armed forces. His close friend General Luang Suthi Suthisarn Ronakary remained the deputy army commander. However, he named his loyalist general Thanom Kittikachorn as assistant army commander. Thanom continued as 1st Army commander. Sarit's friend General Sawai Sawai Saenyakorn continued as assistant army commander while also taking over from Sarit's enemy General Phao to direct the Thai police.[17] Lt. Gen. Prasert Ruchirawong was appointed deputy police chief. Thanom's brother Sanga became deputy commander of the Police Crime Suppression Division. Another friend of Sarit's, General Kruan

FIGURE 4.1
The Fourteen Army Officials in General Sarit Thanarat's First Cabinet

General Sarit Thanarat	Junta leader (1957–58)
	Prime Minister (1958–63)
General Thanom Kittikachorn	Prime Minister (December 1957– October 1958)
	Defence Minister (1957–63)
General Prapas Charusatien	Interior Minister (1957–73)
General Chitthi Nawisathien	Deputy Minister of Economy (1957–59)
	Deputy Minister of Defence (1971–72)
ACM Bunchu Chantarubeksa	Deputy Minister of Defence (1957–57)
Maj. Gen. Krit Punnakan	Deputy Minister of Agriculture (1957–57)
	Minister of Industry (1958–58)
Maj. Gen. HRH Prince Krom Muen Naradhip Bongsprabandh	Deputy Prime Minister (1958–69)
	Minister of Foreign Affairs (1957–58)
Maj. Gen. Pongse Punnakanta	Deputy Minister of Transport (1957–57)
	Minister of Transport (1958–69; 1972–73)
	Minister of Industry (1969–71)
Lt. Gen. Jiam Yanothai	Deputy Minister of Finance (1957–58)
Maj. Gen. Pacheun Nimiputra	Deputy Minister of Culture (1957–58)
	Deputy Minister of Education (1957–58)
Lt. Gen. Luang Kampanatsaenyakorn (Kampan Uttarawanich)	Deputy Minister of Interior (1957–58)
Rear Admiral Jaroon Chalermteerana	Deputy Minister of Transport (1957–58)
Vice Admiral Sanong Thanasak	Deputy Minister of Defence (1957–58)
General Luang Sawasdikalayutha (Sawasdi Krairiksh)	Minister of Industry (1957–57)
General Amporn Chintakananda	Deputy Minister of Justice (1957–59)

Note: Ratio of military to civilian ministers: 16/29 (55.1 per cent).

Sutaninot, became army chief of staff. Kruan had royal ties and would later serve as defence minister after 1973.[18] Meanwhile, Sarit gave the posting of 1st Division commander, 1st Army Region, to his confidant General Krit Sivara. Finally, with Sarit having dismissed the air force and navy commanders during the September coup, he replaced them with his friends ACM Chalermkiat Watanakul and Admiral Luang Chamnan, respectively. Though Sarit's class was 1920, the leading class of the 1957 reshuffle was 1922. The two up-and-coming senior officers under Sarit following the 1957 coup were army deputy chief Suthi and General Thanom (see Appendix 4).

Following the coup, Sarit appeared to have three principal challenges: (1) maintaining US support; (2) ensuring enough backing for himself from among Thai senior security officials, the monarch and politicians; and (3) making sure he could remain healthy, given his poor constitution.

Regarding US support, Washington early on seemed generally satisfied with Sarit. Although there is no current evidence from US documents of any detailed US involvement in the 1957 coup, Frank Darling, then a professor at the University of Colorado, in 1962 stated that "the United States was deeply involved in this sudden turn of events."[19] The day after the coup, on 17 September, the CIA stated that:

> There will undoubtedly be strong pressures for the adoption of a more 'independent' policy involving the loosening of ties with the West. Available information suggests, however, that Sarit has acknowledged the importance of American economic and military aid, although he may seek a greater degree of Thai supervision in its administration. He has also publicly endorsed Thailand's membership in SEATO [Southeast Asia Treaty Organization]. Another factor militating against his moving toward an accommodation with the Communists is that much of his present popularity is based on his being identified as the champion of monarchy and of "traditional Thai values."[20]

Four days after the coup, on 20 September, Sarit, in his capacity as military governor of Bangkok, called upon Ambassador Bishop to see him.

> Sarit opened discussion by expressing hope I understood situation. He felt regretful at necessity [in] taking action.... After noting I was returning to US on consultation, assured me Thailand would "strictly observe old foreign policy and adherence to UN and SEATO" and cautioned about listening to newspapers speculation.... He informed me King would shortly make choice of Prime Minister ...

and wished me to know … choice would be pleasing to US and to me personally…. Sarit said he understood US position thoroughly, as did His Majesty. They desired closest cooperation with US and had the same principles.[21]

Three day later, S. Everett Gleason, the deputy executive secretary of the US National Security Council, reflected growing US optimism in Thailand's new government

> The King and Sarit have now installed as Prime Minister in the new government the former Thai Ambassador to the United States and the former Secretary of the SEATO organization. Sarasin, the new Premier, was perhaps not a very strong figure, but he was a good man and very pro-Western in his sympathies. Meanwhile, categorical assurances had been given to Ambassador Bishop by the new government on their devotion to the tie with the West. The new government insisted that it was even more strongly anti-Communist than its predecessor. Despite all these assurances, continued Mr. Dulles, there is still much in the situation in Thailand which will bear careful watching.[22]

The following day, 24 September, CIA director Allen Dulles convened a meeting of top US intelligence officials in Washington, where he "commented that the latest reports were more encouraging and discussed with the members matters such as the political orientation of Thai leaders and the possible role played by the King in recent events".[23]

But, in fact, on 4 October the United States was still having doubts about the extent to which Sarit would tilt towards Washington. CIA director Dulles noted to his aides that the United States had already trained numerous Thai border patrol police, but that Sarit might look upon them as a programme of his enemy Phao and thus stop the programme altogether.[24]

However, on 5 October, Ambassador Bishop cabled Washington:

> As provisional government has given all assurances that could be reasonably expected re continued alignment with SEATO, recognized all international obligations, and issued a fairly satisfactory foreign policy statement, there appears little current justification use aid programs as leverage obtain objectives with present provisional government…. Thus for present consider we should proceed with aid programs on basis good faith discharging our prior commitment in a normal manner under normal procedures.[25]

Still, regarding the new government, CIA director Dulles saw two primary problems.

(a) how encourage suitable political forces join in viable combination satisfactory US objectives Thailand and Southeast Asia and (b) how induce them take measures enhance SEATO and counter Communist subversion and neutralist pressures.

The cable further emphasized "that it was necessary to decide on proper courses of action in the event that an unfriendly or uncooperative government came to power in the impending elections".[26]

A US State Department cable sent on the same day, 22 October, placed "future aid commitments to Thailand on an ad hoc basis pending determination of the political direction of the new government which will emerge after the elections in December 1957".[27]

A final problem with Sarit that Washington noted was his poor health. In fact this was something that had been known about for several years. The issue kept the United States worried that his poor health might cause them to lose a close ally should he die. At the same time, soldiers potentially challenging Sarit might use the rationale of his poor health to contest his hold over Thailand. On 23 September, a US cable pointed out that Sarit "was suffering from cirrhosis of the liver, and probably had no more than six months to two years of life ahead of him".[28] The following week, on 1 October 1957, General Praphas Charusathien publicly announced that the military dictator had cirrhosis of the liver and had been confined to his home. But the CIA wondered in a report whether Praphas had intended his announcement "as the first step in contesting his chief's fitness to be Thailand's de facto ruler".[29] In fact, Praphas (a potential coup maker within the army) was only one of many military officers who might seek to stage a putsch against Sarit. On 17 October, the CIA noted in a report that Sarit was convalescing for a fifteen-day vacation with evidence indicating he was "gravely ill".[30]

Nevertheless, Sarit had many allies, not only in the military but also among the palace, politicians and the people. In the immediate aftermath of Sarit's coup on 16 September, King Bhumipol appeared extremely pleased that Phibun was gone, while politicians seemed placated by the fact that the country's frail democracy would continue to exist. The monarch immediately issued a royal decree dissolving the Phibun-dominated National Assembly and calling for a new general election to take place within ninety days. The king had asked the Sarit junta to act as a caretaker government until the election could occur. The election would be held to replace only the 160 elected members of the outgoing legislature. The remaining 121 appointed members would be reshuffled by Sarit to guarantee that he retained control over the assembly no matter the result of the upcoming election. In the run-up to the election, the country remained mostly under martial law. At the same time, journalists considered to be subversive were arrested. Sarit's purpose in the election was to try to ensure that his proxy military-backed political party Sahaphum was victorious. The Sahaphum (Unionist) Party, formally led by Chiang Mai aristocrat Sukit Nimmanhemin, was informally controlled by Sarit's half-brother Sanguan Chantharasakha.

The December poll produced a victory for Sarit's Sahaphum, a close second by the right-wing Democrats, and a poor showing for left-wing candidates. As a result of the election outcome, US officials, overjoyed, speculated that Sarit would now maintain his pro-US foreign policy, and only worried that with Pote Sarasin having previously said he would retire from politics following the election, that there might not be an adequate replacement unless Sarit took the premiership himself.[31] For his able support of Sahaphum, Sarit rewarded Krit with the post of commander of the 1st Infantry Division, 1st Army Region, on 30 December 1957, and promoted him as a major general two days later.

Six days after the election, Sarit announced the creation of his new National Socialist Party (NSP), to be composed of MPs who were members of Sahaphum, appointed members and any other MPs who wanted to join. NSP's leader was Sarit. Its deputy leaders were Thanom Kittikachorn and civilian MP Sukit Nimanmenin, while its secretary general was Praphas Charusatien. NSP was clearly a military proxy. The Nationalist Socialists formed a government under the premiership of General Thanom Kittikachorn, Sarit's immediate deputy, with most portfolios held by military officials and civilian bureaucrats.

Meanwhile, on 24 December 1957, Sarit suddenly suffered an intense internal haemorrhage and needed immediate surgery. Eventually leaving the Thai government under the care of acting prime minister General Thanom Kittikachorn in early January, Sarit, on 23 January 1958, was taken to Walter Reed Hospital in the United States for surgery—which took place on 14 February 1958. In a cable, Dulles noted that a Thai doctor had placed Sarit's life expectancy to now be about five years—a prophecy that proved to be true.[32]

In one of his first moves in the role of prime minister (on 28 January 1958), Thanom oversaw a new military reshuffle for Sarit in which Praphas (army advisor and interior minister) replaced Thanom as 1st Army Region commander, and thus gained direct control over troops on the ground. At the same time, Praphas remained interior minister.

Meanwhile, the post-coup September 1957 appointments of General Chalor Jarugala and General Prapan Kunpichit to become commanders of the 2nd Army Region and 3rd Army Region, respectively, were formalized in this reshuffle (see Appendix 4).

Meanwhile, the NSP had collected 80 MPs and, with the support of 122 appointed members, was able to form the new government.[33] However, with Sarit going to the United States for medical treatment, and Thanom proving to be an unsuccessful coalition leader, factions of MPs jealous of cabinet allocations wreaked havoc upon the coalition. Worried about Sarit's health and disheartened by the poor showing of the NSP top generals, Thanom became increasingly anxious. Indeed, he told the media he would be willing to resign. The brass was temporarily satiated, however, when the king approved promotions for over fifty generals, including Thanom, who was elevated to the position of full general. Yet economic woes managed to provide new headaches for the prime minister.

By early February 1958, the NSP was still highly factionalized, with some MPs who were Sahaphum party members still refusing to join. In late February, 26 MPs (members of Sahaphum) resigned in opposition to cuts in the education budget while the defence budget continued to soar. By-elections were therefore set to replace the 26.[34] Other by-elections were already necessary before 1962 to replace the appointed component of the lower house with elected members.

Meanwhile, the military pulled out all the stops to help the NSP. On 30 March 1958, the immediate by-election for the 26 seats took place. Sarit's National Socialists fared poorly: the Democrats garnered 13 new seats, while NSP got only 9. The result was a new balance of electoral power of 53 seats for NSP and 52 seats for the Democrats. But Sahaphum had refused to dissolve itself, and some MPs—although in new parties—continued to refer to themselves as members of Phibun's and Phao's Seri Manangkhasila party. Eventually, in June 1958, Democrat Party leader Khuang Aphaiwong submitted a petition to the president of the National Assembly for a general debate. It was signed by 51 members of the Democrat Party and enough independents to ensure that the debate would take place. Nevertheless, in June the police and army warned that there was an ongoing coup attempt against the government.[35] The implication was clear: the lower house should stop grilling the government or potentially face a military coup. In late June 1958, Sarit briefly returned to Thailand following a five-month absence. He convinced enough (13) independent MPs in the lower house not to join a petition to censure his government, and the debate motion collapsed. He then brought together four tank companies to oppose any potential troublemakers within the army or among political parties. Sarit then left the country again.[36]

By July 1958, Sarit's regime had survived lower house opposition, and parliament seemed to be functioning capably. Despite his September 1957 coup, he had allowed the legislature (composed of elected and appointed members) to continue on as a unicameral parliament. This format lasted until the enactment of the 1968 constitution. During this time, between 70 per cent and 80 per cent of the members of the Senate were military officers. The ostensible rationale for the prolonged existence of this assembly was that its members were busy writing a new constitution. From 1959 until 1968, this apparent charter writing continued. But when the junta applied pressure on the legislature, it merely rubber-stamped the decisions of Sarit or his successors Thanom and Praphas.

Amidst the continuing parliamentary strife between July and September 1958, a period during which Sarit remained abroad for recuperation in hospital, he increasingly warned politicians and journalists that he might end Thailand's defective democracy altogether.[37] In addition to this pandemonium, Sarit was worried about a possible coup attempt while he was away from Thailand. Indeed, within the army's 1st Division, "disunity"[38] seemed to be growing. Tensions were growing especially between a group of infantry units led by Praphas and a group of armoured units led by Thanom, with Praphas "the principal troublemaker".[39] At the time, Krit, as 1st Division commander,

FIGURE 4.2
Thailand's Senates, 1957–58 and 1959–68

Type of legislature	Time in office	Appointed or elected	Total number of legislators and military contingent
Unicameral	1957–58 (terminated by military coup)	160 elected by Eligible voters/121 appointed	281, of which 98 (80.9%) military reserved domain of the appointed
Unicameral	1959–68	Appointed	240, of which 175 (72.9%) military reserved domain

Source: Paul Chambers, "Superfluous, Irrelevant or Emancipating: Thailand's Evolving Senate Today", *Journal of Current Southeast Asian Affairs* 28, no. 3 (2009): 9, https://d-nb.info/999559311/34.

remained loyal to Sarit, but there were sub-commanders sympathetic to a possible putsch. In addition, border troubles with Cambodia had grown and there was more dissension in parliament.

Thus, on 19 October 1958, following a request from Thanom, Sarit suddenly returned to Thailand, arriving secretly from London, amidst growing rumours that a military coup against him was being planned. According to former US Air Force official Fletcher Prouty, the CIA "rushed [Sarit] home in a US military plane", and "CIA-trained bodyguards responded with such a bristling display of efficiency that [Praphas's] coup was averted".[40] Critical support from Krit also ensured that army units in Bangkok supported Sarit. Thus, Sarit's 1958 coup served to completely "forestall any plans Deputy Prime Minister and Minister of Interior Praphas Charusathien may have had to seize leadership of the ruling group from Sarit".[41]

At 9:00 p.m. on 20 October, General Thanom resigned as prime minister and Sarit succeeded him. Troops were called into position to vital points such as communications centres to prevent sabotage. Subsequently, at 9:15 p.m., a public announcement was made of the formation of a "Revolutionary Group" consisting of Sarit as chief, General Thanom as his deputy, and Admiral Chamnarn and ACM Chalermkiat as the other two members. The Revolutionary Group issued a declaration of martial law. Thereupon the constitution was abolished, parliament was dissolved, the political party law was abolished and there was an announcement of the formation of a committee to draft a new constitution. The "takeover again ... had full concurrence of the king."[42] A representative of Sarit reassured Washington that the putsch "portended no change in Thailand's foreign policy of alignment with the free world, its obligations under SEATO, et cetera."[43] The coup was thus motivated primarily by the junta's "desire to ... forestall the outbreak of a struggle for power stemming from increased factionalism within the present ruling group [including] any plans Deputy Prime Minister and Minister of Interior Praphas Charusathien may have had to seize leadership of the ruling group from Sarit."[44] Indeed, Sarit had told the king about the proposed move by Praphas when the former had returned to Thailand on 19 October. However, the motivation of diminishing the power of Praphas was cloaked in the "cake icing" of needing to prevent communist subversion through establishing an ironclad, right-wing military dictatorship.

Regarding Praphas, he had become an astute though ambitious senior army official who had, as 1st Division commander (simultaneous to being deputy commander of the 1st Army Region), played an instrumental role in Sarit's 1957 coup. His performance landed him the position of 1st Army Region commander, where he served until 1960. Simultaneously, Sarit had given Praphas the plum position of minister of the interior. Meanwhile, Praphas was connected to General Kriangkrai Attanand (1st Army Infantry Regiment commander [1957–60]) because, though Kriangkrai was a member of Krit's class at Chulachomklao military academy, Attanand had recently married Praphas's third daughter. Praphas was further boosted by the 1958 marriage between his daughter and Thanom's son Narong. There were even two more marriages between daughters of Praphas and key army officials (General Att Sasiprapha and Colonel Uerm Jirapong). The growing power of Praphas worried Sarit; indeed, between 1957 and 1963, Praphas was rumoured to be involved in various coup plots. Praphas began to become "systematically excluded by Sarit" from senior army posts.[45]

As for Thanom, following the 1958 coup, Sarit demoted him to the non-threatening post of deputy prime minister and the ceremonial military position of deputy supreme commander, alongside Thanom's earlier position as assistant army chief. None of the three posts gave Thanom command of any troops. Sarit's October 1958 coup was similar to the November 1951 coup (and the later 1971 coup) in the sense that both were carried out by military officials who already held power. In both cases the purpose was not only to terminate the clout of specific powerful military officials but also to rein in the influence of the legislature. In the case of 1958, Sarit's illness made it impossible for him to actually transfer Praphas until 1960. In addition, both cases sparked revisions in constitutions.[46]

Yet, despite Sarit's ouster of his own government, he made no changes among the topmost military appointments. This perhaps owed to his continuing recovery from surgery abroad—he did not want to anger any senior officers while he was gone by demoting any of them. In the 1st Army Region, however—the centre of power of alleged attempted coup maker Praphas—Sarit now began to rely thoroughly on General Krit Sivara, commander of the 1st Division, thus obviating Praphas's military clout on the ground.

At this point, Sarit sought to create mass-based understanding for his new military despotism. Like Phibun, he tried to cultivate obedience based on national ideology. Just after the 1958 putsch, Phibun's former ideologue Luang (now Major General) Wichit Wichitwathakan worked to socially construct and disseminate the idea of the Sarit-led regime swathed in ideological paternalism, where the dictator referred to himself as a *pho-khun*, or "father-figure", and metaphorically stood over the nation.[47] Indeed, as Sarit stated on 6 September 1960, "I happen to have the responsibility of being the head of the family at this moment. I have extended to all my goodwill, but if any person in this household creates trouble, it is my duty to stop that person."[48] Sarit's regime developed a notion of *patiwat* ("revolution") and *patthana* ("development") in that his 1958 coup had brought political order to Thai society so that development could commence. Within Sarit's "order", there was a "three-tiered segmented socio-political system defined in terms of *lv-t/ratthaban* (state/government), *kharatchakan* (bureaucracy), and *prachachon* (people)", in which Sarit's policies and programmes aimed at

> maintaining the boundaries between hierarchical sectors while the process of phatthana was applied; and that phatthana was meant to reinforce pattiwat. Development and modernization were to be extensions of regime paternalism and great care was to be taken to see that change did not undermine the integrity of traditional boundaries of the political system.[49]

In this 1958 post-coup environment, Sarit was immediately suspicious of senior military brass who may have colluded against him. He reportedly planned to dismiss and perhaps execute ACM Thawee Chulasap for possible participation in the plot. "Sarit [had] accused Dawee [Thawee] of being closely associated with the deposed Pibul Songkhram and had ordered that he be shot. Krit intervened on Dawee's behalf and his life was saved."[50] In addition, with Thawee a long-time associate of the United States dating back to his cooperation with the Office of Strategic Services during World War II, incoming CIA station chief Robert Janzten backed Krit up that the accusations against Thawee were not true, and Sarit exonerated Thawee.[51] Jantzen's defence of Thawee was seconded by General Krit Sivara. Afterward, Thawee, Jantzen and Krit became firm allies.

At this point, Sarit now simultaneously became prime minister, supreme commander of the armed forces and army commander, ruling through the Martial Law Act (1914). The enforcement of martial law was based upon Sarit's control over the armed forces. Sarit controlled the military by balancing factions and rewarding top brass with positions on state corporate boards—as had been practised by the 1947–57 Coup Group of Phibun, Phin and Phao.

Not since 1932 had Thailand witnessed the utter autocracy that the 1958 putsch unleashed. Phraya Phahon and Phibun Songkram had each dominated the country and led coups, but each at least had observed the appearance of highly limited electoralism as a legitimizer. During World War II, of course, Phibun became an autocrat, but his method of entering and leaving the office of prime minister (from 1938 to 1944) owed at least superficially to decisions of parliament. Sarit's *patiwat*, on the other hand, essentially developed into an explicit personalist and direct dictatorship. This use of force was the first factor that enabled Sarit to sustain his regime's clout. The 1959 constitution Sarit enacted was simply a façade for carte blanche rule.

A second factor that contributed greatly to stabilizing Sarit's hold on power was his decision to bolster the political participation of the monarchy. Through his efforts, Sarit and his military became the guardian of the palace, while the monarchy legitimized his rule and the power of the armed forces. Indeed, under Sarit, the armed forces became a "monarchized military". This offered him a useful ally in the palace as well as much-needed legitimacy. Such legitimacy extended from the king's support for Sarit's usurpation of power in 1957/8, ensuring elite acquiesce to Sarit's continued hold on power and assisting in relations with the United States and other foreign powers. The king's credentials as a solid anti-communist were unquestioned, and his support for Sarit's Coup Group thus facilitated international backing for it. According to Thak, the monarchy further served as an intermediary to receive private funds destined for publicly controlled charities, thus increasing the popularity of the sovereign and government alike. Sarit's use of the king to consolidate his own power base paralleled a rise in the presence of the monarch throughout Thailand as well as programmes related to his majesty.[52] Indeed, in 1958, Sarit increased the budget available to the palace by almost 30 billion baht, and he increased this sum substantially every year thereafter. In addition, the dictator restored numerous palaces, restored landholdings of the royal family, and helped to establish the king's Crown Property Bureau. Also, Sarit encouraged the king to make trips abroad and up-country, which allowed more Thais to see their king face-to-face. The travels of the king helped then to bolster the credibility of the Sarit-led government, something that Sarit needed because he was not known to be a charismatic speaker and was bedridden in the last year of his life. The king and royal family, with Sarit's encouragement, embarked on a growing number of royal projects to help "develop" the countryside and to intensify linkages between the *thammaraja* and his subjects. Furthermore, in 1960 Sarit allowed the royal family to establish control over national holidays. Moreover, he moved National Day to coincide with King Bhumipol's birthday, on 5 December.[53]

Regarding the king's relation with the military, in 1959 the role of the king as the ceremonial head of the armed forces intensified, as troops now had to drink holy water annually in front of the king or his picture. In 1959 the royal family gained control over its own military forces: the 21st Infantry Regiment in Chon Buri, and the 2nd Infantry Division (Buraphapayak or Eastern Tigers) in Prachin Buri, under the 1st Army Region in Bangkok. The queen was made honorary commander of the 21st Infantry Regiment, and as such it became known as the Queen's Guard.[54] Commanders of the Queen's Guard possessed a close affinity with the palace. Though the Guard had originally been established in 1908, 1959 marked a departure in that the unit acted now with greater autonomy from the rest of Thailand's military; its priority, first and foremost, was to the king. In this way, it would serve as a model for what the armed forces in 1973 would ultimately become: a servant of royalty. After the stint of Maj. Gen. Chalor Charuklad, who oversaw the Guard from 1951 to 1966, the Queen's Guard leadership became increasingly royalist in nature. The Queen's Guard began recording annual graduating classes in 1992 and began to dominate senior army positions in 2007.

Along with an emphasis on the king as the central figure in the political system, Sarit also imposed a redefinition of democracy onto the nation. This de-consolidated version of democracy, referred to as "Thai-style democracy", had five requirements:

1. It must be practical and relevant to the Thai environment. Elections are not necessary.
2. Contribute to political stability
3. Be accompanied by a liberal economic system that is minimally guided by the government
4. Uphold the monarchy
5. Facilitate national development[55]

Finally, Sarit sustained his power based upon harmonious relations with and support from the United States. In terms of relations with Washington, Sarit early on demonstrated a close affinity for pro-American anti-communism. By appointing former secretary-general of SEATO Pote Sarasin as prime minister in 1957—as well as the Sarit regime's promise not to deviate from the policies of its predecessor and its proven suppression of suspected Thai communists—Thailand was able to garner $58.9 million in total US economic aid, which was more than double the assistance of the previous year.[56] In addition, the number of US firms operating in Thailand jumped from nine in

1954 to eighty-eight by 1961. Moreover, total police aid mushroomed from $0.013 million in 1957 to $19.61 million in 1967. Furthermore, given that Sarit allowed Thailand to become a junior partner to the United States in the war against communists in neighbouring Laos, US military assistance to Thailand began to grow in 1959. Indeed, military assistance to Thailand skyrocketed from $18 million in 1959 to $122.7 million (at its highest) in 1972. Such military aid represented 24.94 per cent (1959) and 47.60 per cent (1972) of the Thai military budget.[57] As such, Thailand's military budget became increasingly tied to US military aid, fastening the Thai military to a growing dependency on the United States. Furthermore, in May 1962, 6,800 US troops were temporarily deployed in Thailand to bolster the right-wing government next door, as well as to facilitate US military supplies to that government. Following the 1962 Geneva Convention, the Sarit government helped the CIA in continuing the supply line covertly. Finally, on 6 March 1962, Thailand and the United States signed the Thanat-Rusk Agreement. The bilateral collective security accord stated that each country would come to the other's defence in case of armed attack against either. It further provided a framework for US assistance to Thailand as an indirect means of meeting aggression. Finally, it gave way to the implementation of a US-designed internal security policy for Thailand.[58]

The United States was of course relieved that Sarit had managed to stabilize Thailand's political situation with the 1958 coup. Nevertheless, Sarit's continued precarious health worried the United States while stirring up generals who might try to be his successor. As early as 5 November 1958, in a telegram to secretary of state John Foster Dulles, US ambassador to Thailand Alexis Johnson "expressed concern about Sarit's health and said that Sarit gave every appearance of drifting without any clear course of action in mind".[59] Dulles responded the next day:

> [I] agree importance maintaining good relations with Sarit while not prejudicing our ability work with other appropriate leadership which may emerge.... Request your estimate re possibility of effective Praphas/Thanom cooperation.[60]

In fact, clearly realizing that Sarit's days were numbered, incoming US ambassador Alexis Johnson went so far as to compare the two in terms of succeeding the strongman:

> Thanom's advantages are reputation honesty and integrity which brings wide-spread loyalty in military group, especially among

more junior officers, and also some general support outside military. Praphas's advantages are evident strong ambition and readiness engage political in-fighting as well as direct command position over key army units.[61]

By 24 January 1959, however, friction between Sarit, on one side, and Thanom and Praphas, on the other, seemed to be growing. Sarit had apparently ignored their advice on matters of state. Both military and civilian elements of the Thai government had increasingly become dissatisfied with Sarit's performance as well as with his delay in forming an interim government. Thanom and Praphas, however, had "submerged their past differences [and] would prefer to avoid trouble since they expect[ed] that Sarit's declining health w[ould] soon force him to give up power."[62]

Finally, on 28 January 1959, a new provisional charter was enacted that clothed Sarit's dictatorship in constitutionalism, calling for the creation of a 240-person appointed unicameral assembly that would act as the legislature until a permanent constitution could be drawn up. This new temporary charter remained in place for the next nine years and was perhaps the most repressive in Thailand's history. For example, Article 17 stated the following:

> Whenever the Prime Minister deems appropriate for the purpose of repressing or suppressing actions whether of internal or external origin which jeopardize the national security of the Throne or threaten law and order, the Prime Minister, by resolution of the Council of Ministers, is empowered to issue orders to take steps accordingly. Such orders or steps shall be deemed legal.[63]

As such, Article 17 legitimized any execution, detention or use of force that the premier saw to be appropriate. Sarit meanwhile established a government, on 5 February, with a cabinet composed of nine civilians and five active-duty top brass officers.

The appointed 240-member assembly, formed on 3 February, served as the national legislature pending promulgation of a permanent constitution. It was appointed by the king but selected by Sarit. Between seventy-three and seventy-five per cent of its members were actively serving military officers.[64] The new junta's cabinet contained fifteen posts, six of which were held by military officers.

Sarit's foreign policy towards Thailand's neighbours was framed in terms of anti-communist national security concerns, especially with regard to Cambodia, Laos and Vietnam. In Cambodia, neutralist prime minister Prince Norodom Sihanouk often conjured up nationalistic anti-Thai and anti-Vietnamese vitriol in his speeches, threatening to turn to Beijing for help. Ngo Dien Diem, president of South Vietnam, and Sarit together worked to overthrow Sihanouk throughout the period 1958–63. They promoted the efforts of anti-Sihanouk dissidents such as Sam Sary and Son Ngoc Thanh as well as former Khmer Issarak leader General Dap Chhuon. Under Sihanouk, Dap was appointed Cambodia's internal security minister and Siem Reap governor. But he soon became openly anti-communist and anti-Beijing (a fact that led to his dismissal from Sihanouk's cabinet in 1957). By 31 July 1958, South Vietnam, Thailand and the United States had begun to worry about Sihanouk's recognition of China and realized that it might be necessary to oust the prince.[65] On 31 December 1958, Dap formally asked the United States to approve a coup led by him against Sihanouk[66]—with the time of the ouster originally set for mid-March 1959. Thailand and South Vietnam would become deeply involved in the plan, while Dap coordinated with Sam Sary, Son Ngoc Thanh and other Cambodian dissidents.[67]

Eight days later, a CIA report revealed the extent of the Sarit regime's involvement. According to the report, Thailand's General Praphas "had assumed full control of Thai and South Vietnamese efforts to overthrow Sihanouk".[68]

> Prapat apparently intends to utilize several disaffected Cambodian political and military leaders including the army chief of staff, in a psychological warfare campaign culminating in a coup. At this point, Prapat plans to send into Cambodia upwards of 2,000 armed dissident Cambodians now in Thailand and South Vietnam who would be joined by other dissatisfied military elements now on the scene. He expects Dap Chhoun, a warlord in western Cambodia, to throw in his lot with the invaders.

In February 1959, Saigon and Bangkok had supported Cambodian dissident Dap Chhuon in a plot against Sihanouk also involving the CIA. As this plot against Sihanouk continued into February 1959, "Thai authorities ... supplied Sam Sary with money and a house ... assured him their policy toward the coup plotting ha[d] not changed ... tolerated the comings and goings of Vietnamese agents, and ... continued to allow the development of Cambodian dissident bands in Thai territory."[69] But Sihanouk's agents got wind of the plot before it could be enacted. On 21 February, a battalion of Cambodian troops was deployed to arrest Chhuon, where he was discovered with CIA radio equipment. Though Chhuon may have died in opaque circumstances while under arrest, the government claimed that Cambodian forces had intercepted Dap on 5 March while he was trying to flee to Thailand, killing him in the process.[70] Whatever the story, Lon Nol, the leader of the soldiers who caught Dap, likely ordered him shot to prevent Dap from revealing Lon Nol's own involvement in the plot—the latter overthrew Sihanouk eleven years later, again with help from the CIA.[71] Thailand and South Vietnam were also likely complicit. Despite Dap's death, Sarit's plots against Sihanouk persisted. In May 1959, Sarit green-lighted Praphas to approve sending a Thai emissary to Saigon during that month to prepare more covert actions against Sihanouk's government. These included the dissemination of anti-Sihanouk tracts and broadcasts as well as continuing to assist anti-Sihanouk dissidents such as Sam Sary and Son Ngoc Thanh.[72]

In June 1959, following enormous pressure from the United States, the Sarit government made the sale of opium illegal in Thailand. Nevertheless, Sarit, Praphas and other members of Thailand's military regime continued to earn money from the opium trade. In a letter to Washington, US ambassador Johnson noted that his staff,

> particularly Bob [CIA station chief Robert 'Red'] Jantzen always take advantage of the opportunities we have in conversations with Praphas and others to give them to understand that we are aware of the opium traffic and regard it with much disfavor.

Janzten, though liked by Johnson, was personally close to Sarit and later Praphas. Johnson continued his message:

> While ... I believe that there is a certain amount of sincerity on Sarit's part in suppressing opium consumption in Thailand, I do not believe that it necessarily follows that there is a corresponding interest in suppressing the very lucrative traffic from and through Thailand to other countries. In fact, I am inclined to believe that with the present reduction of revenue from other sources resulting from his anti-corruption campaign, [Sarit] and the military group are now more dependent than ever on the profits from opium exports. With respect to ... the traffic through Thailand of opium grown elsewhere, I am not sanguine concerning the willingness of the military group to do anything about this problem. As I have mentioned, I believe that the military group is now more dependent than ever on the profits from this trade. Also, the opium is produced in areas beyond the control of Thailand and outside the effective control of Burma and Laos. In this connection ... a knowledgeable source estimates that over 300 tons of opium pass through the KMT area in Burma each year.[73]

By August 1959, dissatisfaction had again intensified in the ruling junta about Sarit's leadership decisions, which involved defence budget cuts and reallocation to civilian agencies, as well as perceived inadequate compensation to "second echelon officers for their support of his regime".[74] At the time, Krit informed the US military attaché that some senior officers were "consulting on ways to curb Sarit". Implying that a coup might be in the offing, Krit continued that "something" would be done in "the foreseeable future" to rid Thailand of "the Sarit-type operation".[75] Rumours of potential coup makers included General Praphas, General Krit Punnakan—as well as his brother General Pong Punnakan—and General Krit Sivara himself.[76] With regard to the latter, Krit told US military officials in Bangkok that the political situation had deteriorated since the beginning of August 1959 to such an extent that certain military officers were in serious discussions about halting Field Marshal Sarit and even bringing back Phibun. At the time, Sarit did not completely trust Krit and considered that the latter might be in communication with the exiled Phao. Thus, even though Krit was his dear friend, Sarit decided in 1960 to move him out of Bangkok to become commander of the 2nd Army Region in the Northeast.[77]

Meanwhile, on 20 October 1959, Ambassador Johnson issued what might be termed a rationale for Washington's continued support for Sarit's military dictatorship:

> We need not ... feel self-conscious about our support of an authoritarian government in Thailand based almost entirely on military strength. [T]he generally conservative nature of Thai military and governmental leaders and of long-established institutions (monarchy, Buddhism) furnish a strong barrier against the spread of Communist influence. Moreover, the Thai military rule does not weigh onerously on the people. It is not my purpose here to whitewash Marshal Sarit, to ascribe to him virtues he does not possess or to make the obviously false claim that graft and corruption have been eliminated in Thailand never to return. I believe, however, that it is fair to say that Sarit's concepts and actions as we perceive them approach the Department's definition of the "happy medium" from the standpoint of US interests as a situation which encompasses "a military regime 'civilianized' to the greatest extent possible and headed by a military leader who saw security and development in perspective and thereby evidenced political leadership of the type required in a developing society. The principal disadvantages we face in Thailand are precisely those which the Department foresees as the possible long-range concomitant of authoritarian government—a stifling of democratic values and parliamentary procedures. Sarit's "revolution" of October 1958 and its aftermath unquestionably constitute a setback for the trend, however faint, toward a more democratic form of government which had its origins in the 1932 coup d'etat. Nevertheless, as the Department's paper in Thailand correctly points out, there is

growing in Thailand a political consciousness among urban Thai
and, I venture to add, elsewhere in the countryside as well. The
various components of this [United States] mission ... as well as
the Embassy proper—have all played a part in the furthering of
this process. As communications and educational facilities continue
to improve in Thailand and as increasing numbers of Thai military
personnel, government and business leaders and technicians
are exposed to the US and to US habits of thinking, political
consciousness in Thailand will continue to develop.[78]

As Johnson points out, "various components" of the US "mission"
furthered a "political consciousness" among "urban" Thais. Ironically,
it was this changing political consciousness that helped to unite Thais
against the dictatorship in 1973.

Thailand's October 1959 annual armed forces reshuffle reflected
stability more than any changed balance of power among the senior
military brass. The only change was that Sarit added the posting of
police commander to the two slots he already held: supreme commander and army commander. As he had also been prime minister
since October 1958, Sarit now ascended to the height of his power.

Despite distrusting Krit to some degree, Sarit trusted him more than
any of his other generals. Indeed, on 1 January 1960, Sarit had named
Krit as deputy commander of the 1st Army Region simultaneous to
retaining Krit as 1st Infantry Division commander. By December 1960,
with Sarit fearing increased communist insurrection and border troubles
with Cambodia and Laos in Thailand's Northeast, he appointed Krit as
commander of the 2nd Army Region, and three months later promoted
him to lieutenant general. Yet Krit also remained commander of the
1st Infantry Division. But as commander of the 2nd Army Region,
Krit was able to build up strategic linkages with multiple northeastern
businesspeople and up-and-coming politicians—connections that were
later important when Krit served as whip of the junta's Saha Pracha
Thai (SPT) political party, especially for the northeastern region.[79] In
fact, the core of Krit's meetings with local politicians were to occur at
Sri Pattana Hotel in Khorat City, Nakorn Ratchasima province. By
moving Krit into these key postings, Sarit demonstrated his trust in
Krit—whose star seemed to be waxing.

Meanwhile, by early January 1960, Sarit was starting to increase his
influence in Laotian politics—working with the United States. One
month earlier, on 30 December 1959, his nephew, Laotian general
Phoumi Nosavan, had sent troops to surround Prime Minister Phoui
Sananikone's house, forcing the latter to resign. The staunch anti-communist Phoumi was supported by the CIA, which backed him in his

ouster of Phoui.[80] In a cable from Alexis Johnson, US ambassador to Thailand, to the US State Department, he stated:

> [W]e were able to let Sarit know that his relations with and support of Phoumi were becoming fairly widely known and matters of common gossip. While he did not admit to such relations, he did not flatly deny them, and I hope that our additional statements to him will have an additional restraining effect.... In dealing with Sarit on this matter, we must recognize that, whatever we may think of it, Sarit will continue to regard himself as not only the actual but also the political Uncle [or older cousin] and patron of Phoumi. There is a long-time close personal relationship there which he is going to maintain regardless of what anyone may think.... As I see the present situation, Phoumi and the Royal Lao Government have, in spite of the success of their "coup" accepted the reimposition of civilian government and it does not appear that they intend to challenge it for the time being. They are also accepting elections.[81]

The State Department acknowledged Johnson's cable, noting that Phoumi, who was now defence minister, was working with "seven Thai advisers", and responded favourably with regard to proposed April elections in Laos, though making any "solution" via Sarit only a second option:

> [F]or the time being it is unnecessary to go further with Sarit.... [E]very effort should be made to find a solution here in Laos and ... only if these fail and as a last resort should any further attempt be made to approach Sarit on this subject.[82]

The 24 April election in Laos ultimately produced dividends for Laotian anti-communists, though preparatory rigging by the CIA had occurred as early as February.[83] In early September 1960, CIA agent Jack Hasey, a friend of Phoumi, arrived in Savannakhet to help the Laotian general put together an army and help set up an airfield for CIA Air America aircraft. These planes arrived from Bangkok with supplies and "C-ration boxes crammed with US dollars... [whereby] Phoumi instantly commanded greater respect from among his fellow officers".[84] On 19 October, the CIA's William Lair, who had helped to establish paramilitary forces in Thailand, flew money in to Phoumi's troops in Savannakhet.[85]

The CIA also began working closely with Sarit to help in Phoumi's efforts. Sarit had created a special military advisory group called the Thai Committee to Support Laos. Thai officers working for this unit included Colonel Wanlop Rachanwisut, head of the Intelligence Operations Center at the Royal Thai Armed Forces Supreme Command.

Dispatched to Savannakhet was Colonel Chamnien Pongpairot, who oversaw the influx of Thai assistance in support of Phoumi's forces there.[86] Chief of staff was Lt. Col. Pranet Ritileuchai, who was also the commanding officer of PARU. The unit cooperated closely with staff belonging to the United US Military Assistance Advisory Panel in Laos (MAAG LAO). The CIA's William Lair coordinated this operation with another agent, Pat Landry, as his deputy. The mission was clear: start from Savannakhet to recapture Vientiane from the forces of Captain Kong Le.

Indeed, though they sometimes squabbled, the Pentagon worked closely with the CIA to achieve this mission in support of Phoumi. On 16 September, US generals advised the US secretary of defense to "[e]ncourage Phoumi with King's blessing promptly to liquidate Kong Le coup group even at cost of some bloodshed" and "[p]ersuade Sarit to arrange discreet transit of FAL [Phoumi's Forces Armées de Laos] troops through Thailand from Savannakhet to Vientiane".[87]

In October, CIA officials took direct control over Phoumi's troops in Savannakhet:

> To ensure that necessary controls are exercised at Savannakhet, high level political and military advice is being assigned to ensure appropriate control. It is essential to this overall plan that Phoumi cooperate and understand the overall plan and concept which will form essential part of Advisors' approach to him. This of course implies Phoumi's being subject to his government if Souvanna meets the conditions. Appointment of advisors will be subject of subsequent message [e.g., Bangkok's CIA station chief Robert "Red" Jantzen]. In addition, it is recognized that PEO personnel will be required to serve in continuing advisory capacity in operations and logistics. In this matter both latitude and discretion required but caution must be observed to ensure US advisory personnel [will] not serve with units in combat.[88]

In addition, US president Eisenhower approved the use of "Thai transport aircraft, and US transport aircraft as well".[89] However,

> Sarit ha[d] stated that if Thai combatant forces [were] used, he would want a firm commitment from the U.S. to come to his support should he be "jumped" by the Chinese or the Russians.... The President said that ... we are committed through the SEATO pact to maintaining the security of the area of Laos, even though Laos is not itself a member.... The President suggested that an immediate check be made of the possibility of giving a bonus to the troops of Phoumi to reward their success and inspire further effort.[90]

With assistance from the CIA and Sarit, Phoumi succeeded in capturing Vientiane, but not without a drawn-out battle that took place during 13–16 December 1960. Indeed, the central part of the city was levelled and there were approximately six hundred civilian casualties.[91]

Moreover, an embarrassing incident gave away Thailand's role in the attack. In the early hours of 15 December, a ferry carrying a 105 mm howitzer emblazoned with Royal Thai Army markings, bound from Nong Khai to Vientiane, ran aground on a sandbar in the middle of the Mekong River, revealing Thailand's involvement in the coup.[92]

Nevertheless, after four days of combat, Captain Kong Le and his forces were forced out of Vientiane. They thereupon moved northward to occupy parts of the Plain of Jars, renamed themselves the Forces Armées Neutralistes (Neutralist Armed Forces), and accepted supplies from both the Soviet Union and North Vietnam. The CIA-advised Thai military base of operations in Laos thereupon moved from Savannakhet to Vientiane, before again relocating to Nongkhai in 1962 and Udorn Thani in 1963. Colonel Juan Wanarat became head of Thai operations in Laos in late 1961, replacing Colonel Chamnien. In November 1963, Colonel Juan was replaced by Colonel Thongchai Nipitsukarn. At this point the unit became known as Army 333.[93]

Meanwhile, 1960 had witnessed the beginning of a state-sponsored counter-insurgency programme—initiated five years before the onset of CPT (Communist Party of Thailand) attacks in August 1965. Indeed, in early 1960, with the promulgation of the Ministry of Defence Administration Act, Thailand's armed forces had undergone a major transformation. This involved the abolition of the position of defence chief of staff and its replacement with the Supreme Command Headquarters. Thereupon, the army, navy and air force were placed under the Office of the Supreme Command rather than being directly under the Ministry of Defence. The modification effectively terminated cabinet-level tinkering, which meant that whatever military budgets and plans were decided at Supreme Command Headquarters would be final. Since most supreme commanders had been army commanders, a tradition was maintained whereby the army received the lion's share of military responsibilities and budgeting. In addition, given that the army commander directly controlled all land forces, the person holding this position was effectively the most powerful Thai soldier. A supreme commander, however, was too far removed from the troops to effectively veto an army commander's word. As such, Praphas, as army chief, exerted more direct control over military affairs than did Thanom in his post as supreme commander.[94]

Under the 1960 Administration Act, the armed forces enshrined two military responsibilities into law: internal security and rural development. Furthermore, the act placed the army, navy and air force under the aegis of the supreme commander instead of the Ministry of Defence. Later, in 1962 the Supreme Command Headquarters set up the Central Security Command (CSC)—the first military agency charged with stemming the communist insurgency. But it was not until December 1965 that the Thai military established (under pressure from the United States) the Communist Suppression Operations Command (CSOC) to coordinate national anti-Communist operations.

In June 1960, there was a renewed spate of coup rumours, reflecting a heightened state of political uneasiness. There was even gossip that the king or Sarit might be kidnapped.[95] By mid-1960, the Sarit government had requested more economic and military assistance from the United States. On 1 July, the US Embassy announced to Sarit that the US government had increased aid to Thailand. On 8 July, Sarit expressed his appreciation for the upsurge in Washington's financial support.[96] By the end of the year, however, Thailand was again dissatisfied. In November, Sarit stated that Thailand was prepared to establish closer economic relations with the Soviet Union and to accept Soviet aid for commercial development, though the announcement probably underscored the Sarit government's complaint that "neutral" countries were receiving more US assistance than those, like Thailand, who had become US allies. In response, the CIA reported that though "there is no current intent in Bangkok to make significant changes in foreign policy ... if the state of restiveness continues, Thailand may move toward a more neutral position".[97]

The October 1960 annual armed forces reshuffle (see Appendix 4) involved five changes at the senior level of appointments. Sarit demoted Thanom, replacing him with his trusted friend army commander General Luang Suthi Suthisarn Ronakary (who remained simultaneously deputy army commander). Sarit also moved the capricious Praphas from the strategic post of 1st Army Region commander to assistant army commander. With General Kruan retiring, Sarit replaced him as army chief of staff with his friend General Chitthi Navisatien (also a friend of General Krit Sivara). Regarding Krit, Sarit promoted him to 2nd Army Region commander, while keeping him on simultaneously in the strategic post of commander of the 1st Division, 1st Army Region. Finally, for the post of 1st Army Region commander, it was important for Sarit to replace the overly ambitious Praphas with a suitably trustworthy general. At first he chose General Wichai

Ponganan. But when it appeared that Wichai might not obey orders as sufficiently as Sarit wished, the latter immediately replaced him with his old friend General Chalor Jarugala. The 1960 reshuffle was meant to consolidate Sarit's power over the top military postings.

With Sarit realizing that his poor health had contributed to potential military coups against him, he decided to firm up his support within the junta. Thus, in December 1960, Sarit named Thanom "premier-designate" and Krit as "military commander" in the event that he died or was incapacitated.[98] Sarit's move, however, effectively ostracized Praphas and any senior army official who felt they had a chance at succeeding Sarit. Thanom and Praphas simply awaited Sarit's impending death. But they would need to bide their time for three more years.

As 1960 drew to a close, Ambassador Johnson summarized his belief that Thailand had become a more stable nation with Sarit at the helm:

> Five years ago, leadership was divided between Phibun, Phao and Sarit with uneasy balance.... Regime was cool toward Monarchy and there appeared be possibility change to republic. Phao was increasingly controversial figure making political use hoodlums, resort to violence and even murder. Phao's election-rigging activities Feb 1957 outraged Thai sense of proprieties.... Sarit skillfully handled popular resentment to force Phao into exile in Sept 1957, bringing about downfall Phibun regime and beginning Sarit-dominated era that still continues.... Thailand enters 1961 with far fewer disturbing elements present.... Conservatives are particularly satisfied with Sarit's deliberate enhancement prestige Monarchy.[99]

In 1961, Sarit remained in solid control of Thailand, and he persisted in involving Thailand in the Cold War. On 1 January, Phoumi informed a US official that he had made an urgent request to Thailand for four armed T-6 aircraft with Thai pilots for immediate combat use. He had also asked for two Thai parachute battalions.[100] They reached Laos nine days later.

On 23 January, US secretary of state Dean Rusk of the incoming John F. Kennedy administration presented the recommendations of a joint task force on Laos by the CIA and Department of Defense . The report proposed:

> to land United States contingency forces in Thailand, on Thai request, in such a way as to give a clear indication that this did not indicate any expectation or acceptance of the loss of Laos.... [Also] the Introduction of Thai and/or other non-U.S. SEATO troops.... Stationing, subject to Thai's request, of U.S. military unit (probably

a battle group and an air squadron) at Ehorat [*sic*; Khorat]....
This unit to fly SEATO flag.... Thailand has assets which could be
committed to Laos.... Thailand has three divisions, one regimental
combat team, one ranger battalion, and 128 aircraft in tactical units
(33 jets).... The United States [could] provide air support from
carriers or from bases in Thailand.[101]

What is sadly interesting is that these 1961 recommendations had
become reality in Thailand by 1965, with multiple US soldiers stationed
in the country and Thai soldiers complementing the latter. Nevertheless,
when US vice president Lyndon Johnson visited Sarit in Bangkok in
May 1961 and "specifically asked [the prime minister] whether he
wanted to have US soldiers stationed in Thailand now … Sarit replied
in the negative".[102] Sarit did promise, however, to substantially increase
Thailand's defence budget.

On 29 August 1961, Kennedy approved a "Plan for Southeast
Asia" under which the exacerbation of communist attacks in Laos
would trigger SEATO Plan 5, which involved using military force to
expel communist forces "from all of Southern Laos and the Mekong
River line, including the Luang Prabang area … conditional upon the
willingness of Thailand … to commit additional forces to Plan 5."[103] If
SEATO Plan 5 were not activated, then there would be a SEATO exercise in Thailand "about October 10 employing ground combat troops,
supported by tactical air units and, on completion of the exercise, leaving behind in Thailand a SEATO command and communications 'shell'
prepared on a contingency basis to expedite the implementation of
SEATO Plan 5, undertaking additional rotational training of SEATO
combat units in Thailand, introducing into Thailand a SEATO River
Patrol along the line of the Mekong, and … seeking Thai agreement to
supplying an equal number of Thais for the same purpose."[104]

By October 1961, US military and economic aid to Thailand
was skyrocketing. The two countries had begun increasingly to plan
together for collaborative military education, exports of US military
hardware into Thailand, and joint military exercises. And the reliance
of each country on the other was becoming more and more reciprocal.
Sarit's Thailand was becoming a US dependency, while the United
States depended upon Thailand as a hub of anti-communist operations. Nevertheless, Thailand's military leaders, given the support from
Washington, had shored up their power, enabling them to sustain it.
According to Johnson, who was then US ambassador to Thailand:

Thailand is now an unofficial and disguised base of operations
for the United States in Southeast Asia. The Thai Government is

allowing us to carry on an increasing number of operations in and out of Thailand which we could not conduct from any other piece of real estate in Asia. If we lose this base of operations, we will have to retreat to the island chain and depend solely on sea and air power. I will not repeat the long list of activities we are carrying on here, some of them of a highly sensitive nature. I just wish to stress that Thailand is a growing asset of great value strategically for United States interests and purposes. We have no treaty, formal agreement or any kind of institutional arrangements sanctioning these activities and operations except indirectly under SEATO. The self-interest of the Thai Government, its desire to cooperate with the United States, the goodwill we have here in Thailand, and the friendliness of the Thai people towards Americans are our guarantees for continuation of this base. But the sine qua non is continued economic and military assistance.[105]

Regarding the October 1961 annual military reshuffle, Luang Chulayongyon was a respected "elder brother" of Sarit, motivating the latter to promote him to become permanent minister of defence upon his predecessor's retirement that year. Meanwhile, General Prayoon Noonpakdi ascended to become commander of the 1st Division, 1st Army Region, filling the shoes of General Krit Sivara, who had the year previously been promoted to become commander of the 2nd Army Region (in addition to 1st Division commander). This reshuffle represented continuing consolidation of power by Sarit.

By November 1961, Sarit was again becoming frustrated because of the absence of an increase in US military and economic assistance he had expected. At the same time, the Kennedy administration was worried about Sarit's health given that he seemed to have "slowed down from fatigue and other factors and [was] resting at seaside for several weeks at his initiative. Besides, Thanom and top military [had] been in Burma."[106] But Sarit was able to carry on, and Washington's anti-communist partnership with him persevered.

By 21 January 1962, the Kennedy administration had for months been backing Prince Souvanna Phouma as a compromise neutralist to lead Laos as prime minister and to also hold two other key ministries. In so doing, Kennedy rejected the tainted General Phoumi Nosavan, who had received more backing from Eisenhower and who was connected to Sarit by blood. Sarit saw Souvanna Phouma as being close to communism and argued that if Souvanna Phouma became prime minister he could not also hold both the defence and interior ministries:

It would be a disaster for lao anti-Communists and for Thailand. Notwithstanding [US] efforts to dissuade them, [right-wing Laotian

Prince] Boun Oum, Phoumi, and Sarit agreed that the [Royal Laotian Government] could not concede … the … Ministries.[107]

It also just so happened that Thai military interests would have been best served by a Laos led by Phoumi instead of Souvanna Phouma. In February, during a visit to Thailand by attorney general Robert Kennedy, Sarit expressed his displeasure with US policy towards Thailand. But he fumed even more, apparently, to CIA station chief in Bangkok Robert Jantzen rather than to Kennedy himself. In discussions with General Suthi Suthisarn Ronakary, deputy commander-in-chief of the army; General Chitthi Nawisathien, minister of defence; Lt. Gen. Wallop Rochanawisut, director of joint intelligence of the army; and Maj. Gen. Chalermchai Charuwat, aide to Sarit and director of tourism, Sarit stated, "We are not threatening to get out of SEATO, we are getting out."[108]

As for Laos, Sarit and his generals criticized the U.S. position in Laos, complained about sporadic aid to Laos, our foolishness for thinking that Souvanna [Phouma] could form a neutral government, our throwing money down the drain in Laos and other places in the area, and having … tight purse string as concerns Thailand.[109]

What Sarit wanted was a formal bilateral treaty with the United States similar to that which existed between the United States and the Philippines rather than the more informal security understanding that existed under the SEATO arrangement. At a meeting on 2 March 1962, US secretary of state Dean Rusk told Thai foreign minister Thanat Khoman that "a bilateral US-Thai treaty would create domestic problems for us. We already have a Senate-approved agreement linking us together, and the Congress would almost certainly question the need for a separate treaty."[110]

Thus, what Thailand and the United States signed was a joint statement, on 6 March 1962, known as the Thanat-Rusk communiqué. The non-binding agreement—which thus required no US Senate ratification—was a mutual defence pact that formed the basis for an upsurge in US military aid to, construction of military bases in, and US counterinsurgency planning for Thailand. As a result, on 15 May 1962, Sarit agreed to allow eight thousand US troops to enter Thailand to assist the country against communist insurgents in neighbouring Laos, potentially also in Thailand, and "to encourage the Thais".[111] The communiqué thus formed the basis in 1964 for Project 22 and, later, Operation Taksin. From 1962 until 1976, thousands of US troops would remain stationed in Thailand.

Regarding the continuing problem of non-recognition by Sarit and Phoumi Nosavan of Souvanna Phouma's government in Laos, eventually, by April 1962, Bangkok came around to reluctantly backing the Laotian Prince. This change in posture was perhaps stimulated by Washington's intensifying aid to Thailand. Phoumi refused, however, to support Souvanna Phouma. Only after Sarit used both "carrots" and "sticks" did Phoumi finally come around. But, Sarit said, Souvanna Phouma would have to offer "assurances against letting Patet Lao–Viet Minh take over Laos [and] Sarit recommend[ed] that [the] US government resume financial payments as soon as possible after [the] agreement between [the] Royal Lao Government and Souvanna Phouma [becomes] firm".[112]

Turning to Thailand's relations with Cambodia, in June 1962 Sarit encountered a thorny new obstacle—the International Court of Justice (ICJ). Previously, the fact that Thailand was simply larger than Cambodia meant that Bangkok tended to trump Phnom Penh whenever they disagreed. Sarit and neutralist Sihanouk had each publicly excoriated the other, leading to a break in diplomatic relations in 1958 (and in 1961). However, in 1959 Phnom Penh had appealed to the ICJ to decide on the sovereignty of a temple straddling the Thai-Cambodian border, which the Cambodians called Preah Vihear. After almost three years, the ICJ, on 15 June 1962, made its judgement, awarding the temple to Cambodia.[113] The decision dealt an emotive blow to the prestige—and self-perceived identity—of Thailand and Sarit. The court refused to rule on a 4.6 square kilometre area of land close by the temple. In reaction, Sarit, referring to the temple by the Thai name, stated, "We speak with tears about Khao Phra Viharn.... At the cabinet meeting where we considered the World Court's judgement, many ministers wept." The deputy PM and defence minister General Thanom Kittikachorn opined: "We should not accept the judgment and we should not give Kao Phra Viharn to Cambodia.... As far as I am concerned, I will fight to keep what is Thai."[114] In fact, "Sarit was ready to refuse to hand it over [but King] Bhumibol said the court's order would be obeyed, and it was."[115] Nevertheless, though Washington formally "welcomed" Thailand's acceptance of the ICJ's decision, Sarit "sent reinforcements into the area and placed the border police on alert. Thailand also initially boycotted SEATO and Geneva Laos Conference meetings."[116] In the end, though Thailand lost the legal dispute over Preah Vihear temple, Sarit gained enormous domestic legitimacy as the champion of Thai territorial nationalism. If anything, Thai-Cambodian relations became even frostier following the court's awarding of the temple to Cambodia. Sarit and Sihanouk would remain hostile to each other until Sarit's death.

Meanwhile, US troops began to be spread out in several military bases throughout Thailand, mostly in the Northeast. While Sarit in May was seemingly content with these soldiers being hosted by his country, by September 1962—especially after having supported, under pressure from Washington, the 23 July 1962 Geneva Accords on peace in Laos—he began "having some second thoughts. There are also indications that some of the Thai military leaders are jockeying for power or at least a redistribution of the spoils of office. In such a situation Sarit may need an issue behind which he can unify squabbling factions."[117] He saw Praphas as hungering for power, but still felt he needed the latter's support among the troops.

In November 1962, Sarit demanded that US ground forces depart from Thailand. According to the US Embassy in Bangkok:

> Sarit would like, however, to retain the 250-man Tactical Air Squadron. On November 5 our Ambassador informed the Thai Foreign Minister that, barring unforeseen developments, we would be prepared to withdraw the Battle Group by December 1. The Fighter Squadron was excluded from this arrangement and the future status of this unit will be reviewed by the US in late November.... Retaining the air unit in Thailand for an additional period beyond December 1 offers several advantages. Presence of this unit in Thailand would indicate our continued interest in developments in Laos. It would also be responsive to Sarit's wishes and would provide a basis for maintaining the presence of Australian and possibly New Zealand units in Thailand....We have also discussed with Prime Minister Sarit the possibility of future rotational training in Thailand by US forces.[118]

Nevertheless, when the United States announced that more military aid would be provided to Thailand, Sarit's qualms about US troops diminished rapidly. Washington quickly learned that Sarit could be easily satiated when more money was provided.

Regarding the October 1962 military reshuffle, Sarit maintained almost the same line-up among the senior brass as had existed in 1961. In fact there were only two changes. First, following an accident that led to General Prayoon Noonpakdi becoming paralysed, General Kriengkrai Attanand, son-in-law of Praphas, succeeded him to become commander of the 1st Division, 1st Army Region. The other appointment was that of Admiral Sawats Puthianands, a friend of Sarit's. Sawat succeeded to become navy commander upon the retirement of Admiral Luang Chamnanarthayutha in 1962.

In early 1963, relations between Sarit and the Kennedy administration appear to have markedly improved. At the same time, Sarit, the ailing field marshal, seemed to have managed to achieve complete control over his senior officers—or, rather, they were simply awaiting his impending death. On 8 April, foreign minister Thanat Khoman, speaking for Sarit, informed US secretary of state Dean Rusk of Sarit's

> appreciation for [President Kennedy's] statement of US support of Thailand through SEATO. This 'very welcome' statement had cleared atmosphere Thai-US relationships. Sarit also wanted him convey Thailand's firm intention continue work closely with US and clarify there no change in Thai position. Secretary [Rusk] responded President would be pleased and heartened to know that our close relationship remains unchanged. Said US position regarding security SEA also remains solid.... In continuing, Thanat 'speaking frankly' said Thailand had practically accepted US military base.[119]

In mid-1963, as Sarit appeared to become sicker and more bedridden, US officials appeared determined to ensure that, in the time he had left alive, Washington would achieve an even closer security relationship with Bangkok. In a September meeting with Sarit, deputy under secretary of state Johnson asked Sarit to consider an increase in the number of US/allied ground and air units to Thailand as a contingency measure in the event of a possible communist military threat from Laos. Though Sarit did not specifically endorse the idea of more US troops deployed to Thailand, he did not reject it. Foreign minister Thanat gave his personal opinion that deploying more US troops to Thailand would be useless unless Washington was willing to send them into Laos if an emergency arose there.

In the October 1963 military reshuffle, Sarit maintained Thanom in the three militarily powerless positions of deputy supreme commander, deputy prime minister and defence minister. Meanwhile, Sarit "promoted" Thanom's brother-in-law Praphas from the equally powerless posting of assistant army commander to the even more impotent post of assistant supreme commander. In that same reshuffle, Sarit appointed Krit to the extremely strategic posting of commander of the 1st Army Region. Among other postings, General Pong Bunsom, a class peer of Thanom, became permanent minister of defence; Krit's ally General Chitthi was promoted to become army deputy commander; Sarit's friends General Chalor and General Prapan were reshuffled to each become assistant army commanders; two other of Sarit's friends, General Sanit and General Jit, became army chief of staff and 2nd Army Region commander, respectively; and Praphas's son-in-law,

General Aat, was promoted to become 3rd Army Region commander, while another of Praphas's sons-in-law, General Kriangkrai Attanand, remained 1st Division commander, 1st Army Region. This reshuffle appeared to be an attempt by Sarit to weaken the influence of Thanom and Praphas while boosting Krit and Chitthi.

By December 1963, with Sarit's health rapidly deteriorating (he had developed cirrhosis of the liver), it appeared that his death or incapacitation was fast approaching. Assuredly, there would soon be a struggle for power among his top generals. According to the CIA, with his death only days away, "Sarit named a leading Thai general, Krit Sriwara, to succeed him in his role as overall military commander".[120] The announcement reconfirmed Sarit's 1960 decision to make Krit supreme commander if the former died. Simultaneously, Sarit named Chitthi Navasatien (then deputy army chief) as acting army commander.[121] Sarit, Chitthi and Krit had all been close. Finally, Sarit promoted the US-favoured Thanom to be acting prime minister on 4 December 1963. With these appointments, Sarit seemed to be signalling that he intended to leave the military under the control of Krit and Chitthi, while Thanom would carry on as the junta's figurehead prime minister. Yet Thanom had other ideas. On 8 December, Sarit died. As a result, "Sarit's wishes [for Krit's appointment] were probably never given more than lip service by the other members of the military oligarchy."[122] With Sarit dead, Thanom became acting prime minister and refused to sign off on Krit's appointment. Thanom would now resurrect the power of his brother-in-law Praphas, and the two would dominate Thailand—while professing obedience to the monarchy—for the next decade.

In the final analysis, the 1957–63 period was marked by three transformations: (1) military-dominated democracy to stratocracy; (2) a balancing of army and police clout to complete army control; and (3) the transition of power from Phao, Phibun and Sarit to the personalization of Sarit's power alone. As a paternalistic despot, he continued to amass power while using the weaker monarchy to legitimize himself as the nation's *pho khun* or father figure. Upon Sarit's death, Thanom's plans resulted in the revival of Praphas to assist in the consolidation of a military-entrenched, informal diarchy and greater Thai economic, political, military and cultural dependency on the United States. Washington, as well as the palace, endorsed Thanom's moves, taking larger roles upon Thailand's political stage.

Notes

1.   Surachart Bamrungsuk, เสนาธิปไตย: รัฐประหารกับการเมืองไทย [Militocracy] (Bangkok: Matichon, 2015).

2.   Samuel Finer, "The Retreat to the Barracks: Notes on the Practice and the Theory of Military Withdrawal from the Seats of Power", *Third World Quarterly* 7, no. 1 (1985): 18-19.

3.   Thak Chaloemtiarana, *Thailand: The Politics of Despotic Paternalism* (Ithaca: Cornell Southeast Asia Program, 2007), p. 80.

4.   CIA, "Current Intelligence Bulletin", 17 September 1957, https://www.cia.gov/readingroom/docs/CIA-RDP79T00975A003300130001-0.pdf.

5.   Interview with Pradab Phibun Songkram, 28 January 2023.

6.   CIA, "Central Intelligence Bulletin", 8 November 1957, https://www.cia.gov/readingroom/docs/CURRENT%20INTELLIGENCE%20BULL%5B15757355%5D.pdf.

7.   "Phao Sriyanon Told Field Marshal Phibun 'He Always Thinks of Going Home' after Sarit Took Power", Silpa-mag.com, 7 January 2022, https://www-silpa--mag-com.translate.goog/quotes-in-history/article_80365?_x_tr_sl=th&_x_tr_tl=en&_x_tr_hl=en&_x_tr_pto=sc.

8.   อนุสรณ์ในงานพระราชทานเพลิงศพ ฯพณฯ จอมพล สฤษดิ์ ธนะรัชต์ นายกรัฐมนตรีและรัฐมนตรีว่าการกระทรวงพัฒนาการแห่งชาติ [Memorial volume from the royal cremation ceremony of His Excellency Field Marshal Sarit Thanarat, premier], 17 March 1964.

9.   Ibid.; "สวย ขนตางอน มีไฝจุดซ่อนเร้น" สเปกคุณหนูๆ 81 คน ของ "จอมพลผ้าขาวม้าแดง" ["Beautiful, curly eyelashes, hidden mole" the spectrum of 81 of the young mistresses of "Marshal Red Loincloth"], *ThaiRath*, 22 April 2019, https://www.thairath.co.th/news/politic/1550413.

10. Retired general Somchai Thanarat possesses little political influence but instead holds economic sway as the chief executive officer of Thipaya Group Holdings Public Company Limited. See Stock Exchange of Thailand fact sheet about Thipaya Group Holdings Public Company Limited, https://www.set.or.th/th/market/product/stock/quote/tiph/factsheet.

11. Khana Ratamontri, "ประวัติและพฤฒิพงศ์ จอมพลสฤษดิ์ ธนะรัชต์" [The history and achievements of the Honorable Sarit Thanarat], *The Sarit Coup, September 16, 1957 (Biography of Sarit Thanarat)* (Bangkok, 1964), in *Thai Politics, 1932–1957: Extracts and Documents*, edited by Thak Chaloemtiarana (Social Science Association of Thailand, 1978), pp. 681–91.

12. Daniel Fineman, *A Special Relationship: The United States and Military Government in Thailand, 1947–1958* (Honolulu: University of Hawai'i Press, 1997), p. 242.

13. Kenneth Conboy (with James Morrison), *Shadow War: The CIA's Secret War in Laos* (Boulder, CO: Paladin, 1995), p. 59.

14. Desmond Ball, *Tor Chor Dor: Thailand's Border Patrol Police*, vol. 1, *History, Organization, Equipment, and Personnel* (Bangkok: White Lotus, 2013), pp. 82–84.

15. อนุสรณ์งานพระราชทานเพลิงศพ ฯพณฯ พจน์ สารสิน [Memorial for the cremation ceremony of His Excellency Pote Sarasin] (Bangkok: Bangkok Printing Company, 2000).

16. Thak, *Thailand: The Politics*, pp. 84–85.

17. อนุสรณ์งานพระราชทานเพลิงศพ พลเอก ไสว ไสวแสนยากร [Memorial volume from the cremation ritual of General Sawai Sawai Saenyakorn], 21 March 1981.

18. อนุสรณ์ งาน พระราชทาน เพลิง ศพ พลเอก ครวญ สุทธานินทร์ [Memorial volume from the cremation ritual of General Kruan Sitaninon] (Bangkok: 1991).

19. Frank C. Darling, "American Policy in Thailand", *Western Political Quarterly* 15, no. 1 (1962): 93, https://doi.org/10.2307/446100.

20. CIA, "Current Intelligence Bulletin", 17 September 1957, https://www.cia.gov/readingroom/docs/CIA-RDP79T00975A003300130001-0.pdf.

21. "524. Telegram from the Embassy in Thailand to the Department of State", 20 September 1957, *Foreign Relations of the United States (FRUS)*, vol. 12, https://history.state.gov/historicaldocuments/frus1955-57v22/d524.

22. "525. Memorandum of Discussion at the 337th Meeting of the National Security Council, Washington, September 23, 1957", *FRUS*, https://history.state.gov/historicaldocuments/frus1955-57v22/d525.

23. CIA, "Minutes of Meeting Held at CIA", 24 September 1957, https://www.cia.gov/readingroom/docs/CIA-RDP61-00549R000300110010-0.pdf.

24. "171. United States Minutes of the ANZUS Council Meeting, Department of State, Washington, October 4, 1957", https://history.state.gov/historicaldocuments/frus1955-57v21/d171.

25. "528. Telegram from the Embassy in Thailand to the Department of State", 5 October 1957, *FRUS*, https://history.state.gov/historicaldocuments/frus1955-57v22/d528.

26. "529. Telegram from the Department of State to the Embassy in Thailand", 22 October 1957, *FRUS*, https://history.state.gov/historicaldocuments/frus1955-57v22/d529.

27. "530. Memorandum from the Officer in Charge of Economic Affairs, Office of Southeast Asian Affairs (Whittington), to the Deputy Assistant Secretary of State for Far Eastern Economic Affairs (Palmer)", 22 October 1957, *FRUS*, https://history.state.gov/historicaldocuments/frus1955-57v22/d530.

28. "525. Memorandum of Discussion at the 337th Meeting of the National Security Council, Washington, September 23, 1957", *FRUS*, https://history.state.gov/historicaldocuments/frus1955-57v22/d525.

29. CIA, "Central Intelligence Bulletin", 6 October 1957, https://www.cia.gov/readingroom/docs/CIA-RDP79T00975A003300300001-1.pdf.

30. CIA, "Current Intelligence Bulletin", 17 October 1957, https://www.cia.gov/readingroom/docs/CURRENT%20INTELLIGENCE%20BULL%5B15757359%5D.pdf.

31. CIA, "Central Intelligence Bulletin", 18 December 1957, https://www.cia.gov/readingroom/docs/CIA-RDP79T00975A003400390001-1.pdf.

32. "464. Telegram from the Department of State to the Embassy in Thailand", 17 February 1958, *FRUS*, vol. 15, https://history.state.gov/historicaldocuments/frus1958-60v15/d464.

33. Niyom Rathamarit, *Military Governments in Thailand: Their Policies toward Political Parties* (Pittsburgh: University of Pittsburgh, 1984), pp. 86–87.

34. Thak, *Thailand: The Politics*, p. 90.

35. David A. Wilson and Herbert P. Phillips, "Elections and Parties in Thailand", *Far Eastern Survey* 27, no. 8 (1958): 116–17.

36. CIA, "Central Intelligence Bulletin", 8 July 1958, https://www.cia.gov/readingroom/docs/CIA-RDP79T00975A003800160001-2.pdf.

37. Ibid., pp. 90–91.

38. Fineman, *A Special Relationship*, p. 255.

39. CIA, "Central Intelligence Bulletin, Daily Brief", 18 October 1958, https://www.cia.gov/library/readingroom/docs/CIA-RDP79T00975A004000320001-1.pdf.

40. Wikileaks, "Anderson Alleges CIA Influence in Palace Guard", 26 February 1975, Wikileaks, 1975STATE043545_b, https://wikileaks.org/plusd/cables/1975STATE043545_b.html.

41. "497. Memorandum from the Director of the Bureau of Intelligence and Research (Cumming) to the Acting Secretary of State", 20 October 1958, *FRUS*, https://history.state.gov/historicaldocuments/frus1958-60v15/d497.

42. "499. Telegram from the Commander in Chief, Pacific's Political Adviser (Steeves) to the Department of State", 11 October 1958, *FRUS*, https://history.state.gov/historicaldocuments/frus1958-60v15/d499.

43. "496. Telegram from the Embassy in Thailand to the Department of State", 20 October 1958, *FRUS*, https://history.state.gov/historicaldocuments/frus1958-60v15/d496.

44. "497. Memorandum from the Director".

45. "273. Memorandum for the Record", Honolulu, 1 June 1964, *FRUS*, https://history.state.gov/historicaldocuments/frus1964-68v27/d273.

46. Ibid.

47. Tak, *Thailand: The Politics*, p. 119.

48. Ibid., p. 107

49. Tak Chaloemtiarana, "Reflections on the Sarit Regime and the Process of Political Change in Thailand: Some Conceptual and Theoretical Reassessment", *South East Asian Studies* 16, no. 3 (1978): 409, https://kyoto-seas.org/pdf/16/3/160303.pdf.

50. Defense Minister: Gen. Krit Sivara", *Bangkok Post*, 20 April 1976, p. 2.

51. Fineman, *A Special Relationship*, p. 250.

52. Thak, *Thailand: The Politics*, pp. 204–6.

53. Paul Handley, *The King Never Smiles* (New Haven: Yale University Press, 2006), pp. 142–44.

54. Ibid., p. 144.

55. Saitip Sukatipan, "Thailand", in *Political Legitimacy in Southeast Asia*, edited by Muthiah Alagappa (Stanford: Stanford University Press, 1995), p. 204.

56. Thak, *Thailand: The Politics*, p. 158.

57. Surachart Bamrungsuk, *United States Foreign Policy and Thai Military Rule, 1947–1977* (Bangkok: DK, 1985), p. 195.

58. Ibid., pp. 84–111.

59. Note 2 (Telegram 1108, November 5) in "500. Telegram from the Department of State to the Embassy in Thailand", 6 November 1958, *FRUS*, https://history.state.gov/historicaldocuments/frus1958-60v15/d500.

60. "500. Telegram from the Department of State", 6 November 1958, *FRUS*, https://history.state.gov/historicaldocuments/frus1958-60v15/d500.

61. 502. Telegram from the Embassy in Thailand to the Department of State", 11 November 1958, *FRUS*, https://history.state.gov/historicaldocuments/frus1958-60v15/d502.

62. CIA, "Central Intelligence Bulletin", 24 January 1959, https://www.cia.gov/readingroom/docs/CIA-RDP79T00975A004300420001-7.pdf.

63. Article 17, 1959 constitution, cited in D. Insor, *Thailand: A Political, Social and Economic Analysis* (London: Allen & Unwin, 1963), p. 99.

64. "514. Memorandum from the Assistant Secretary of State for Far Eastern Affairs (Robertson) to the Acting Secretary of State", 13 February 1959, *FRUS*, https://history.state.gov/historicaldocuments/frus1958-60v15/d514.

65. CIA, "National Security Council Briefing", 31 July 1958, https://www.cia.gov/readingroom/docs/CIA-RDP79R00890A001000030017-5.pdf.

66. CIA, "Central Intelligence Bulletin", 31 December 1958, https://www.cia.gov/readingroom/docs/CENTRAL%20INTELLIGENCE%20BULL%5B15777451%5D.pdf.

67. CIA, "Central Intelligence Bulletin", 13 February 1959, https://www.cia.gov/readingroom/docs/CENTRAL%20INTELLIGENCE%20BULL%5B15787481%5D.pdf.

68. CIA, "Central Intelligence Bulletin", 7 January 1957, https://www.cia.gov/readingroom/docs/CENTRAL%20INTELLIGENCE%20BULL%5B15787440%5D.pdf.

69. CIA, "Central Intelligence Bulletin", 17 February 1959, https://www.cia.gov/readingroom/docs/CENTRAL%20INTELLIGENCE%20BULL%5B15787506%5D.pdf.

70. CIA, "Central Intelligence Bulletin", 5 March 1959, https://www.cia.gov/readingroom/docs/CIA-RDP79-00927A002100090001-1.pdf.

71. Seymour Hersh, *The Price of Power: Kissinger in the White House* (New York: Summit Books, 1983), p. 175

72. CIA, "Central Intelligence Bulletin", 16 May 1959, https://www.cia.gov/readingroom/docs/CIA-RDP79T00975A004500050001-6.pdf.

73. "522. Letter from the Ambassador in Thailand (Johnson) to the Director of the Office of Southeast Asian Affairs (Kocher)", 29 June 1959, *FRUS*, https://history.state.gov/historicaldocuments/frus1958-60v15/d522.

74. CIA, "Central Intelligence Bulletin: Discontent Reported Increasing in Ruling Thai Military Group", 31 August 1959, https://www.cia.gov/library/readingroom/docs/CIA-RDP79T00975A004600530001-2.pdf.

75. Ibid.

76. CIA, "Central Intelligence Bulletin", 28 May 1959, https://www.cia.gov/readingroom/docs/CENTRAL%20INTELLIGENCE%20BULL%5B15787576%5D.pdf.

77. "ข่าวลือ 'รัฐประหาร' และการแบ่งขั้วอำนาจในกองทัพ สมัยรัฐบาล 'จอมพลสฤษดิ์'" [Rumours of '*coup d'etat*' and the polarization of power in the army during the government of 'Marshal Sarit'], Silpa-mag.com, 28 April 2022, https://www.silpa-mag.com/history/article_86284.

78. "534. Despatch from the Embassy in Thailand to the Department of State", 20 October 1959, *FRUS*, https://history.state.gov/historicaldocuments/frus1958-60v15/d534.

79. David Morell, *Power and Parliament in Thailand: The Futile Challenge* (PhD dissertation, Princeton University, 1974), pp. 125–26.

80. Walt Haney, *The Pentagon Papers and the US Involvement in Laos*, vol. 5 of *The Pentagon Papers*, Gravel Edition, p. 257, http://legaciesofwar.org/files/The_Pentagon_Papers_and_the_United_States_Involvement_in_Laos.pdf.

81. "Letter from the Ambassador in Thailand (Johnson) to the Assistant Secretary of State for Far Eastern Affairs (Parsons)", 2 February 1960, *FRUS*, https://history.state.gov/historicaldocuments/frus1958-60v16/d327.

82. "329. Letter from the Ambassador in Laos (Smith) to the Assistant Secretary of State for Far Eastern Affairs (Parsons)", 11 February 1960, *FRUS*, https://history.state.gov/historicaldocuments/frus1958-60v16/d329.

83. See "328. Telegram from the Embassy in Laos to the Department of State", 2 February 1960, *FRUS*, https://history.state.gov/historicaldocuments/frus1958-60v16/d328.

84. Conboy, *Shadow War*, p. 35.

85. Roger Warner, *Backfire* (New York: Simon & Schuster, 1995), pp. 26–29.

86. Ibid.

87. "397. Memorandum from the Joint Chiefs of Staff to the Secretary of Defense", 16 September 1960, *FRUS*, https://history.state.gov/historicaldocuments/frus1958-60v16/d397.

88. "421. Telegram from the Department of State to the Embassy in Laos", 8 October 1960, *FRUS*, https://history.state.gov/historicaldocuments/frus1958-60v16/d421.

89. "487. Memorandum for the Record of a Telephone Conversation between the President and the President's Staff Assistant (Goodpaster), Washington", 14 December 1960, *FRUS*, https://history.state.gov/historicaldocuments/frus1958-60v16/d487.

90. Ibid.

91. Ibid., p. 42.

92. Ibid., p. 41.

93. General Banchorn Chawansilp, "นามนั้น 'เทพ 333' กำเนิด 'บก.ผสม 333'" [That name "Thep 333" originated "Mixed Land 333"], *Matichon Weekend*, 29 April 2021, https://today.line.me/th/v2/article/3v1yPk.

94. Chai-anan Sanudavanija, Kusuma Snitwongse, and Suchit Bunbongkarn, *From Armed Suppression to Political Offensive* (Bangkok: ISIS, 1990), pp. 92–96.

95. CIA, "Current Intelligence Weekly Summary", 30 June 1960, https://www.cia.gov/readingroom/docs/CIA-RDP79-00927A002800030001-0.pdf.

96. "553. Letter from the Chargé in Thailand (Unger) to Prime Minister Sarit Thanarat", 1 July 1960, *FRUS*, https://history.state.gov/historicaldocuments/frus1958-60v15/d553.

97. CIA, "Central Intelligence Bulletin", 8 November 1960, https://www.cia.gov/readingroom/docs/CIA-RDP79T00975A005400070001-4.pdf.

98. CIA, "Central Intelligence Bulletin", 15 March 1962, p. 8, https://www.cia.gov/readingroom/docs/CIA-RDP79T00975A006200470001-1.pdf.

99. "575. Telegram from the Embassy in Thailand to the Department of State", 24 December 1960, *FRUS*, https://history.state.gov/historicaldocuments/frus1958-60v15/d575.

100. CIA, "Central Intelligence Bulletin", 2 January 1961, https://www.cia.gov/readingroom/docs/CENTRAL%20INTELLIGENCE%20BULL%5B15815777%5D.pdf.

101. "13. Memorandum from the Ambassador to Thailand (Young) to the President's Military Representative (Taylor)", 27 October 1961, *FRUS*, https://history.state.gov/historicaldocuments/frus1961-63v23/d13; "10. Memorandum from the Assistant Secretary of Defense for International Security Affairs (Nitze) to Sec. of Def McNamara", 23 January 1961, https://history.state.gov/historicaldocuments/frus1961-63v24/d10.

102. "408. Telegram from the Embassy in Thailand to the Department of State", 19 May 1961, *FRUS*, https://history.state.gov/historicaldocuments/frus1961-63v23/d408.

103. "171. Memorandum from Secretary of State Rusk to President Kennedy", 29 August 1961, *FRUS*, Laos Crisis, https://history.state.gov/historicaldocuments/frus1961-63v24/d171.

104. Ibid.

105. "13. Memorandum from the Ambassador to Thailand (Young) to the President's Military Representative (Taylor)", 27 October 1971, *FRUS*, https://history.state.gov/historicaldocuments/frus1961-63v23/d13.

106. "421. Telegram from the Embassy in Thailand to the Department of State", 7 November 1961, *FRUS*, Southeast Asia, https://history.state.gov/historicaldocuments/frus1961-63v23/d421.

107. "24. Telegram from the Department of State to the Embassy in Thailand", 23 January 1962, *FRUS*, Southeast Asia, https://history.state.gov/historicaldocuments/frus1961-63v23/d424.

108. "432. Memorandum", 26 February 1962, *FRUS*, https://history.state.gov/historicaldocuments/frus1961-63v23/d432.

109. Ibid.

110. "433. Memorandum of Conversation", 2 March 1962, *FRUS*, https://history.state.gov/historicaldocuments/frus1961-63v23/d433.

111. "358. Memorandum of Conversation", 15 May 1962, *FRUS*, https://history.state.gov/historicaldocuments/frus1961-63v24/pg_771, p.771.

112. "337. Telegram from the Embassy in Thailand to the Department of State", 1 May 1962, *FRUS*, https://history.state.gov/historicaldocuments/frus1961-63v24/d337.

113. Former US secretary of state Dean Acheson led the Cambodian team, and Thailand protested to the United States.

114. "A Matter of National Pride", *Bangkok Post*, 15 April 2013, p. 6, https://www.bangkokpost.com/thailand/politics/345427/a-matter-of-national-pride.

115. "Thailand: Holder of the Kingdom, Strength of the Land", *Time Magazine*, 27 May 1966, http://content.time.com/time/subscriber/article/0,33009,835641-1,00.html.

116. "456. Memorandum from the President's Deputy Special Assistant for National Security Affairs (Kaysen) to President Kennedy", 12 June 1962, *FRUS*, https://history.state.gov/historicaldocuments/frus1961-63v23/d456.

117. "464. Memorandum from Michael V. Forrestal of the National Security Council Staff to President Kennedy", 24 September 1962, *FRUS*, https://history.state.gov/historicaldocuments/frus1961-63v23/d464.

118. "471. Paper Prepared in the Bureau of Far Eastern Affairs", 7 November 1962, *FRUS*, https://history.state.gov/historicaldocuments/frus1961-63v23/d471.

119. "477. Telegram from Secretary of State Rusk to the Department of State", 8 April 1963, *FRUS*, https://history.state.gov/historicaldocuments/frus1961-63v23/d477.

120. CIA, "Thailand: Concern over Succession Problem Stirred by Rumors about Sarit's Health", 20 November 1963, p. 5, https://www.cia.gov/library/readingroom/docs/CIA-RDP79T00975A007300440001-2.pdf.

121. CIA, "Weekly Summary: Orderly Change of Leadership in Thailand", 13 December 1963, https://www.cia.gov/library/readingroom/docs/CIA-RDP79-00927A004300030001-3.pdf.

122. Ibid.

Chapter Five

The Diarchy of Thanom and Praphas (1963–73)

This chapter examines the period from 11 December 1963 to 14 October 1973, a solid decade in which the lieutenants of Field Marshal Sarit Thanarat together dominated Thailand in an informal diarchy. It was a period marked by four phenomena: the stifling of political space in a continuing stratocracy, manipulation of party politics by the military, the occupation of Thailand by US military forces, and the beginning of Thai communist insurgency and counter-insurgency.

Sarit's death in December 1963 effectively prevented Krit and Chitti from ascending to the top of Thailand's military leadership. Naturally, their regime opponents—General Thanom and General Praphas—tended to view Krit and Chitti as possible threats to their own hold on power. The United States had favoured Sarit, Krit and Chitti while backing Thanom.

As the prime minister and supreme commander of the armed forces of Thailand, Thanom had reached the apex of his career. A part-Chinese migrant to Bangkok, he had been born into an impoverished family in the Thai border area of Tak on 11 August 1911. At the mere age of nine, well-placed friends of Thanom's family had begged the Army Cadet Academy in Bangkok to enrol him. Thanom was accepted and excelled in school. His "big brother" was Sarit Thanarat, who had entered the academy in 1919. Thanom continued his military studies at the Royal Thai Army Map School, Royal Thai Army Infantry School and National Defence College (class 1), respectively. Thanom's promotions had continued thanks to Sarit's patronage. In 1963, with Sarit dead, Washington became his patron, and his brother-in-law General Praphas Charusathien ensured support from the military.

Praphas was a self-made strongman, having evolved, like Sarit, as a child of the Northeast (in this case, from Udorn Thani province) to become army commander and deputy prime minister. Praphas, however, wanted more—he aspired to be premier, like Phibun, Sarit and Thanom before him. But two obstacles stood in his way: first, Thanom—both a friend and an in-law—was already prime minster; second, was Washington.

Indeed, the United States was less enthusiastic about Praphas, whom it saw as corrupt and undemocratic, though Washington did acknowledge the post-Sarit dominance of the Thai military by Praphas.[1] Thanom was thus forced to move fast to outmanoeuvre Krit and Chitti, while helping out his brother-in-law Praphas. Three days after Sarit's death, in his role as acting prime minister, Thanom refused to sign off on Krit's promotion, instead promoting himself to become supreme commander and army commander, and transferring Chitti to the innocuous post of deputy assistant supreme commander.[2] Thanom then appointed Praphas to be interior minister, deputy prime minister, deputy supreme commander and deputy army commander. Finally, Thanom promoted police general Prasert Ruchirawong to succeed Sarit as director of the police (which was then under the Ministry of the Interior), assuming that Praphas could control Prasert through the latter's power over the ministry. Krit remained 1st Army Region chief.

At the time, the US Embassy predicted that because Thanom was "relatively weak" there would be power manoeuvrability among Chitti, Krit and Praphas. Meanwhile, Thanom perhaps prevailed upon Washington and King Bhumipol to instead back the Thanom-Praphas regime. With specific regard to Thailand's approval for hosting more US troops, the US ambassador to Thailand, Graham Martin, stated:

> I think Thanom would be inclined to agree [to station US troops in Thailand] without much argument over detail but he would be under considerable pressure from Gen Chitti, Marshal Dawee [both military allies of Krit] and Foreign Minister Thanat Khoman to refrain from doing so until and unless there was a clear indication of the necessity for their use.[3]

In the end, Thanom's pliancy towards Washington ensured that the United States would support him in power, but Washington's backing thus became the *sine qua non*, without which a military coup could easily have ousted him as prime minister. Indeed, in early March 1964, rumours swirled that a coup led by the exiled General Phibun

Songkram—supported by Praphas or Chitti and Krit—was then un-folding. Some suggested that there were "grumblings" in the military about Thanom's demotion of Chitti, since Sarit had positioned Chitti and Krit to succeed him.[4]

Roger Hilsman at the US State Department even queried Graham Martin, the US ambassador to Thailand, about the possibilities of a putsch:

> [T]he coup rumors emanating from Thailand recently have us all feeling a bit uneasy. Given the situation in the rest of Southeast Asia, a coup d'etat in Thailand at this time 'is all we need'. Quite seriously, we are concerned about the impact on American public opinion of such an event, which would undermine the present faith in Thailand as the only stable country in the area, thus adding to the growing feeling of pessimism about the future of Southeast Asia and our ability to influence favorably the course of events there. Do you have any suggestions as to things which we might appropriately do to introduce greater stability into the situation?... We are most reluctant to see the United States become identified with any faction in Thailand, much preferring the present happy state in which all serious contenders for power are quite friendly to us.... If he [Thanom] lacks the acumen necessary to political survival in Thailand, we most certainly do not wish to put our prestige behind an effort to maintain him in office. On the other hand, if he has it, presumably our intervention is not required.[5]

In reply, Ambassador Martin, an adamant promoter of Thanom, quickly dismissed Hilsman's worries, saying simply, "shifting allegiances may, of course, trigger a coup at any time. But as we see the situation now, there appears to be none in the offing."[6]

Amidst the putsch gossip, the military prowess of Praphas, which had grown disproportionately since December 1963, proved indispensable in temporarily neutralizing Thanom's military opponents. Yet, unlike their handling of Chitti, Thanom and Praphas took pains not to alienate Krit. Krit was, after all, a formidable and popular commander who was directly in charge of troops in Bangkok. The two thus did not dare try to remove him from his command, but rather they attempted to co-opt him. In April 1964, the CIA noted that Krit appeared to have come to an agreement to support the Thanom-led regime.[7]

By 1 June, Ambassador Martin expressed the following:

> the judgment that the Thanom regime [had] smoothly consolidated its power and [was] operating well ... more as a collegial institution than the personally authoritarian regime of Sarit ever did. There has been considerable decentralization, and delegations to the

Ministries have noticeably speeded up the decision-making process. Contrary to general expectations in December, Thanom seems to be clearly in charge and is publicly deferred to by General Praphas. The personal and family relationships between these two permit an intimate behind-the-scenes which is obviously effective.... Praphas [had] concentrated the major portion of his time and energies on restoring his position and power in the Royal Thai Army from whose councils he had been systematically excluded by Sarit ... with a fair amount of success. Dawee, as deputy Minister of Defense and Chief of Staff Supreme Command, [was] playing an increasingly important and useful role in over-all coordination of military affairs. While coup rumors [were] endemic, the frequency of their circulation [had] been greatly reduced.[8]

Meanwhile, in June 1964, Praphas went to the United States for a much-needed eye operation for cataracts. But on 31 July, Thanom suddenly asked Praphas to return to Bangkok amidst renewed rumours of a possible coup attempt—involving Krit, Chitti and ACM Thawee Chulasap, as well as Sarit loyalists, disaffected junior officers, and officials who had been close to Phibun Songkram. Thanom had earlier ordered a military and police alert on 28 July following reports from soldiers of the planned coup on 27 July. The alert was extended beyond 31 July amid the decision to ask Praphas to return home following the reported abortive plan to kidnap Thanom as he was leaving the US ambassador's residence on 31 July.[9] The very fact that the prime minister was welcomed at the ambassador's home following the coup attempt was likely meant to show all potential coup-makers (including possibly even Praphas) that Washington was backing Thanom. It thus appeared that the prime minister's continuation in office almost singularly depended upon Washington. The rumours of coups and domestic turbulence of 1964 led David Wilson to emphasize that the "most noteworthy outcome" of 1964 was "the survival of Field Marshal Thanom Kittikachorn's leadership".[10] Indeed, by 1964, as Thailand became a US dependency, Washington, which began to rely on Thai bases and soldiers for Cold War purposes, became the only obstacle preventing a coup against Thanom.

Perhaps a more embarrassing discovery of the year was the revelation regarding the wealth of the late dictator Sarit. On 9 July 1964, Prime Minister Thanom disclosed that Sarit had left an estate of well over US$140 million, most of which had been acquired since 1952, when, as an army officer with growing power, he became chairman of the State Lottery Board. It was also revealed that the "hard-drinking" Sarit, who had died aged fifty-five, had held vast numbers of properties.

Thanom then stated that the government would investigate whether any of Sarit's assets derived directly from state sources. The prime minister's statement followed court action by Sarit's first wife (and two sons) in February 1964 seeking to prevent his second wife, Lady Vichitra Thanarat, from taking control of Sarit's estate. In June, a special committee had been appointed, chaired by Phra Manuvej Vimolnath, to investigate Sarit's wealth. Phra Manuvej said that approximately US$600,000 from "Funds for Secret Work" had been given to Sarit's minor wives (these numbered more than twenty, and perhaps as many as fifty-one) in cash or in the form of cars or houses.[11]

In the October 1964 reshuffle, Thanom and Praphas sought to further consolidate their rule. Praphas was appointed as army commander while remaining deputy supreme commander and interior minister, thus overshadowing Krit and other senior military officials. Meanwhile, Krit was kept on as 1st Army Region commander while Praphas and Thanom considered how to deal with him. One faction that they promoted was that of military academy class 29—Praphas's class. Among senior brass, this consisted of the new army commander, the assistant army commander, the 2nd Division commander (within the 1st Army Region) and the 2nd Army Region chief.

Despite the reshuffle, discontent towards Thanom and Praphas within the armed forces because of the duo's domination of the security services continued. Nevertheless, by late 1964, most potential opponents of the pair were dead: Sarit Thanarat, Phao Sriyanond, Chalermkiat Wattanakul and Phibun Songkram (who died in Japan on 11 June 1964). Amidst the power vacuum, General Thanom and General Praphas grew closer.

Their initially unsteady alliance led to one more attempted putsch. On 1 December 1964, police arrested ten members of the air force, navy and police (most of them were air force officers) who were apparently conspiring to hatch a rebellion on 3 December. The accused included the coup group's purported leader, ACM Nakrob Pinsiri, as well as former deputy commander of the Royal Thai Air Force Air Vice Marshal La-ep Pinsuwan, Air Vice Marshal Ekkachai Musikabut, Lt. Col. Bunbotok Jatamra, Lt. Col. Sudjai Awngkomanurak and navy lieutenant Norachai Jatamra. Perhaps to maintain support within the armed forces, the plotters were lightly punished, sentenced to only three years in prison.[12] And perhaps because of this tolerable penalty, their sufficient power over the military, backing by both the king and the United States, and legitimacy as heirs to Sarit, Thanom and Phrapas succeeded in maintaining control.

The Thanom-Praphas alliance ultimately succeeded for six reasons. First, it appears that the partnership between the two was based on the forging of ties between their two families.[13] Second, as during 1950–63, the stability of the Thanom-Praphas regime owed partly to the wholehearted support of the United States, which continued to expand its military and economic assistance after Sarit's death in 1963. At the same time, the United States preferred Thanom to Praphas as the regime front-person, and this guaranteed no coup by Praphas against Thanom. Third, Thanom and Praphas jointly allocated the top military and police positions among themselves. In the case of the latter, this extended to the cabinet. As such, from 1963 to 1973, Thanom, as prime minister and supreme commander,[14] and Praphas, as deputy prime minister, army commander and interior minister, dominated the military, police, politics and parts of the Thai economy. Fourth, Thanom and Praphas sought to appease and balance most military elements, and they did not exact a punishment on the 1964 coup plotters. The only factor distinguishing Thailand's stability of 1949–57 from the rule of Thanom-Praphas, however, was the fifth one; that is, the government of the latter enjoyed the full support of a popular, charismatic king, whose political power was growing by leaps and bounds. Throughout the 1960s, the king's image was emblazoned throughout the kingdom, and he had made hundreds of trips to the provinces.[15] His legitimation provided the necessary publicity for a military regime that seemed otherwise merely to be more of the same of what came in the 1950s.

The family connections between Field Marshal Thanom Kittikachorn and Field Marshal Praphas Charusathien—as well as among their families and other military families—can be seen in Figures 5.1 and 5.2. The first of these focuses on the Kittikachorn family linkages. The second maps out the Charusathien family ties. The two families continued to possess some political clout in 2023. For example, General Somtat Attanand, son-in-law of Praphas, was the army commander under Thaksin Shinawatra from 2022 to 2023. Another of Praphas's sons-in-law, General Yuthasak Sasiprapha, was the minister of defence during part of the Yingluck Shinawatra government (2011–14). Songsuda Yodmani, a daughter of Thanom, was serving as an appointed senator during 2019–24.

The informal pact between Thanom and Praphas and between them and the palace occurred simultaneous to an intensifying communist insurgency in Laos and the beginnings of communist insurgency in Thailand. In response (and in a decision that mollified the United States), on 22 June 1964, Thanom and Praphas agreed to increase the

FIGURE 5.1
Kittikachorn Family Tree

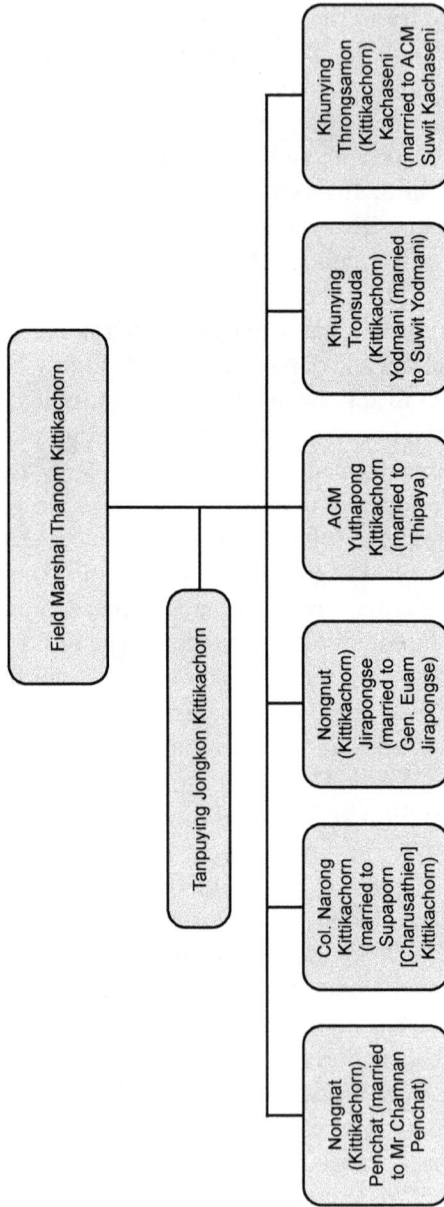

Field Marshal Thanom Kittikachorn

Tanpuying Jongkon Kittikachorn

Nongnat (Kittikachorn) Penchat (married to Mr Chamnan Penchat)

Col. Narong Kittikachorn (married to Supaporn [Charusathien] Kittikachorn)

Nongnut (Kittikachorn) Jirapongse (married to Gen. Euam Jirapongse)

ACM Yuthapong Kittikachorn (married to Thipaya)

Khunying Tronsuda (Kittikachorn) Yodmani (married to Suwit Yodmani)

Khunying Throngsamon (Kittikachorn) Kachaseni (married to ACM Suwit Kachaseni)

Source: Derived from Katja Rangsivek, "Trakun, Politics and the Thai State" (PhD dissertation, University of Copenhagen, 2013), p. 262, figure 47.

FIGURE 5.2
Charusathien Family Tree

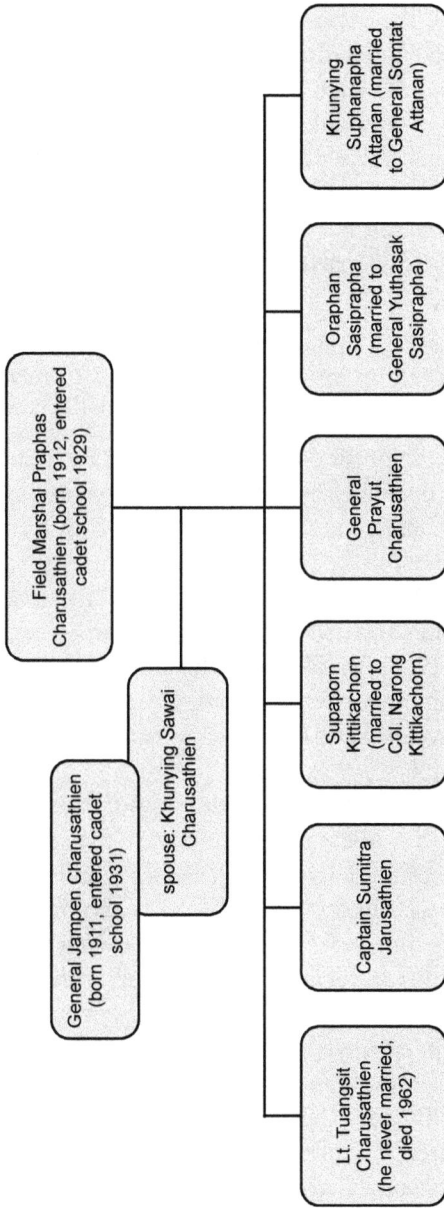

Note: It should be added that General Yuthasak's father was General Aat Sasiprapha. Yuthasak's brother and Aat's son was Akaradej Sasiphrapha, who was married to the daughter of General Jaruai Wongsayan. Such exemplifies the ways in which elite military families interconnect among each other.

Sources: Author's calculations and Paul Handley, *The King Never Smiles* (New Haven: Yale University Press, 2006), p. 145.

number of Thai (military) "volunteers" fighting communist insurgents in Laos from a little over one hundred (earlier established under Sarit) to ten thousand soldiers.[16] Also on 22 June, US president Lyndon Johnson approved Project 22, "the codename for joint US-Thai military planning initiated in June 1964 and authorized by President Johnson on 22 June 1964 (hence its name). Though a small number of US soldiers had been temporarily stationed in Thailand since 1962, this new initiative was much more ambitious. Project 22 was a plan for joint US-Thai military cooperation for the contingency of any North Vietnamese/Pathet Lao attempts to take over the Mekong lowlands.[17] It had originated in a memo from the State Department's Roger Hilsman, who, in 1964, had stated:

> We should consider encouraging further Thai reinforcements along the Mekong backed up by visible preparations to introduce US Marine landing battalions and air elements into Thailand.[18]

As approved by the president, the plan called for Thai and US soldiers to potentially invade Laos without any notification to Congress, as the project was based on SEATO obligations. Only later would Congress find this out.

By late June 1964, Washington was also trying to vastly improve and enlarge Thailand's army so that it could become adept in counter-insurgency. By late 1964, Ambassador Martin had encouraged Thanom and Praphas to implement several counter-insurgency programmes, such as Mobile Development Units, while using the army-controlled Border Patrol Police.[19]

Perhaps the events that galvanized support from Thanom and Praphas for more US soldiers in Thailand were the attacks—allegedly by North Vietnamese—that took place on 2 and 4 August 1964 against US naval vessels in the Gulf of Tonkin and the subsequent US retaliatory strikes against North Vietnam. Following the incidents, on 8 August 1964, Ambassador Martin consulted with Prime Minister Thanom, and the latter responded favourably about increasing the number of US troops deployed in Thailand beyond the eight thousand already there should they be needed for combat across the Mekong.

In November 1964, the Royal Thai Army, working ever closer with the CIA, restructured its anti-communist forces in Laos, establishing the 333rd Combined Army, which included sending an artillery company and an aviation unit to assist the government in Vientiane. On 1 November 1964, Colonel Vitoon Yasawat (known as "Thep") was appointed to be the commander of this mixed unit, and Colonel Tawatchai Nakwanich became Vitoon's deputy.[20] Vitoon continued to

FIGURE 5.3
Total Number of US Troops and Aircraft
Stationed in Thailand, 1964–68

Year	US Military Personnel	US Air Force Aircraft
1964	6,300	75
1965	13,700	200
1966	34,000	400
1967	43,669	527
1968	43,994	589

Source: Surachart Bamrungsuk, *United States Foreign Policy and Thai Military Rule, 1947–1977* (Bangkok: DK, 1985), pp. 84–111, 151.

command this unit until 11 October 1973, when he arrived in Bangkok. Tawatchai's son Thirachai later served as army commander (2015–16).

Ultimately, Thanom and Praphas allowed the US military to station more troops and aircraft in Thailand. The purpose was to both secure Thailand against communist advances in Laos and North Vietnam and to have forces available for use in a possible Project 22 deployment. Figure 5.3 illustrates a growing rise in the number of US troops and aircraft in Thailand from 1964 to 1968, paralleling America's deepening commitment to the Vietnam War.

By 1973, Thailand was housing more than 50,000 US servicemen and 750 US aircraft, which were used to bomb Vietnam and Laos. Meanwhile, "countless" other US soldiers visited Thailand under the rest and recuperation (R&R) programme. Finally, a network of listening posts for the US National Security Agency was developed throughout the country.[21]

Also, by early 1965, Thanom and Praphas permitted the United States to station its troops at eight military bases in Thailand, a policy that would continue to some degree until the mid-1970s. Four bases were located in the northeastern provinces of Udorn Thani, Ubon Ratchathani, Nakon Phanom and Nakorn Rachasima (Khorat); and four others were located at the following locations: Takhli, Don Muang (Bangkok), U-tapao and Nam Phong. There were also several smaller US sites controlled by the US National Intelligence Agency (listening in on China and Indochina),[22] such as the listening posts at Ramasun (Udorn Thani), Chiang Mai and Lampun. Finally, there was JUSMAGTHAI (the Joint United States Military Assistance

FIGURE 5.4
Principal US Military Facilities in Thailand

Base	Years of US Military Use
Don Muang Royal Air Force Base	1961–70
Khorat Air Force Base	1962–75
Nakhon Phanom Navy Base	1962–76
Takhli Royal Air Force Base	1961–74
U-Tapao Royal Navy Airfield	1965–76
Ubon Air Force Base	1965–74
Udorn Air Force Base	1964–76
Nam Phong Air Force Base (Khon Kaen)	1972–73
MACTHAI / JUSMAGTHAI	1953–76 / 1953–present
Ramasun Listening Post	1964–?

Source: R. Sean Randolph, "Thai-American Relations in Perspective", in *United States–Thailand Relations*, edited by Karl Jackson and Wiwat Mungkandi (Berkeley: University of California Press, 1986), p. 29.

Group Thailand), a central office for US military officials in Bangkok. With solid US military investments in Thailand (assistance, troops and infrastructure), the Thanom and Praphas regime, like the Sarit dictatorship before it, obtained support from Washington for its control over Thailand.

Bangkok's cooperation paralleled growing amounts of US military funding for the Thai armed forces through Washington's Military Assistance Program (MAP). By April 1965, the Johnson administration was "strongly" supporting more military assistance for the Thais since

Thailand [had] cooperated with us so totally in the past few months that we tend at times to assume that cooperation as a constant, and to overlook the possibility of its diminution or withdrawal. The readiness of the Thai to allow us to launch air attacks on Communist targets in Viet-Nam and Laos from Thai bases is essential. Thai pilots and artillerymen in Laos and the logistic base Thailand provides for operations there are of critical importance. The clear-cut commitment to us by the most stable country in the area is an asset of immeasurable importance. Of course, the Thai took this commitment for reasons of their own self-interest. They have our assurance that we will hold the enormous Communist land forces at bay. But this alone is not enough. Nor will "political payoffs" do the job. The Thai, and especially the Thai military, must feel that their partnership with the U.S. is of a permanent nature, consonant with the clearly increasing threat. This means greater emphasis on counter-insurgency in face of stepped up Communist activities in the northeast. It means gearing up for possible implementation of the plans drawn up in "Project 22" which envisages possible joint US-Thai action in the Mekong Valley. It means continuing effort to improve Thai capability to carry out their SEATO missions. The goal is maintenance of an atmosphere of growing capability and growing confidence in that capability.[23]

During a meeting on 18 May 1965 in Washington between General Thawee Chulasap of the Supreme Command, US secretary of defense Robert McNamara and US ambassador Graham Martin, among others, Thawee was specifically told about US preferences. First, Washington wanted the Thai government to increase the size of its military. Also, in terms of counter-insurgency, the US was disturbed at the inefficiency of several Thai military units. Thawee responded that "he had established a Joint Operations Center to exert proper control over service actions", in what appeared to be the forerunner of the Communist Suppression Operation Command (CSOC), which army commander General Praphas agreed to establish in December that year. At the same time, Martin commented that he "hoped that ... the delivery of MAP equipment ... would be pointed towards helping the Supreme Command, rather than the individual Thai services" since there had been an "earlier [problem of] MAP deliveries bypassing the Supreme Command". Dawee said he would appreciate help.[24] Unfortunately for Thawee, though US funding of the MAP was officially channelled through the more accountable Supreme Command, the army was institutionally far more powerful in terms of budgeting and manpower.[25]

Still, by 25 May 1965, US officials appeared to be content that, though Thailand's budgeting was not sufficiently prioritizing military purposes, and in fact Thailand's military structure was not as efficient as it could have been, increasing the size of the country's armed forces did not at the time seem to be urgent. Washington accepted the fact that the politics of the Thai army was two-fold, with different power bases supporting Thanom as opposed to Praphas.[26] This appraisal came, however, prior to the August 1965 beginnings of Thai communist party insurrection.

On 6 August 1965, the first violent clash between Communist Party of Thailand (CPT) insurgents and state officials occurred—at Nabua Village, within Sakon Nakon, a province in Thailand's impoverished rural northeast. The attack came following public announcements by Beijing and US intelligence reports that CPT operations against the Thai state would soon commence. Indeed, according to then CIA director Richard Helms,

> There has been, in the past few years, an increasing Communist concentration on agitation and organization within this area with Thailand being singled out by the Chinese Communist Government as the next country in Asia in which a war of national liberation would most likely develop. This statement was made by Vice Premier Chen Yi in January 1965 following the announcement of the Thai Independence Movement and the Thai Patriotic Front. Soon thereafter, two ex-members of the Thai parliament, Phayom Chulanond [father of General Surayud Chulanond] and Mongkhon Na Nakhon, who had earlier left Thailand for Communist China to evade arrest, were installed as spokesmen for these two exile front groups. Since August 1965, several jungle camps have been discovered by Thai Security Services; and concurrently, intelligence reports began to indicate that Thai Communist cadre have received instructions to switch from the defensive to the offensive and since that time several jungle camps have been discovered. During 1965 there were over 30 attacks by subversives against government officials and police informants, with 25 occurring in the last half of the year.[27]

As CPT attacks and skirmishes against security officials intensified, the United States began pressing Thanom and Praphas to establish a larger, more efficient and integrated counter-insurgency security machine. Simultaneously, Washington dangled the carrot of greater US financial aid.

> [W]e have examined Thai military needs carefully and desire to do utmost in FY 66 program to meet them at most rapid rate possible.... we are willing to provide for FY 66 MAP some increase over FY 65 (which FYI was $38.3 million end FYI) provided we have Thai commitments with respect to measures we believe Thai must take to achieve more effective counterinsurgency effort and increased combat effectiveness of their forces. With respect to the counterinsurgency effort, our concern is that a major emphasis must be placed today on speeding up the program of coping with potential insurgency in the northeast and northern areas of Thailand.... From the military side of counterinsurgency, this means such things as increased deployment of forces from headquarters to outlying areas, more effective training exercises and instruction for the military forces for counterinsurgency, increased civic action and the development of systematic analysis of efforts to meet any future insurgency.... As you know, serious maintenance and other deficiencies noted in last two years have given us grave concern

about effectiveness of our assistance and general organization of Thai effort in relation to threat which we believe to be basically subversion but including possible Communist overt moves against Mekong for which Project 22 planning has been designed.[28]

With the United States increasingly pressuring Thailand to establish a more effective counter-insurgency initiative amidst growing amounts of US aid, the moment came when a Thai counter-insurgency mechanism was finally created. Washington's wishes closely matched the desire by army commander General Praphas to move expeditiously towards becoming Thailand's definitive military strongman. He heartily proved his credentials as the right-wing champion for Washington in 1965 by establishing the Washington-suggested Communist Suppression Operations Command (CSOC), which was under the Office of the Supreme Commander. CSOC's beginnings happened like this: On a December morning in 1965, General Praphas called into his office the US-trained army operations director Maj. Gen. Saiyud Kerdphol to establish CSOC, which was specifically aimed at combating insurgency. CSOC merged police, civilian, navy and air force bureaucrats under the army to integrate and improve all counter-subversion efforts. CSOC was also a convenient method for the army to try to rationalize its dominance over security operations. According to Saiyud, Praphas told him, "if we divert enough resources to this effort, we'll crush the communists in six months.... [I]ts not a job for the army alone. [T]here have to be other components—police and civilians."[29] CSOC had emerged from a US blueprint, and its initial headquarters was at Bangkok's Suan Kularb (Rose Garden) Palace, within which, after the 1932 coup, the army had used several buildings. Indeed, Prime Minister Phibun had once lived there. Alongside CSOC, Praphas applied the Martial Law Act (1914) in the north and northeast, proclaiming them counter-insurgency zones to prosecute a scorched earth war against insurgents.

In practice, CSOC simply became an alternative agency sponsoring "more diverse paramilitary organizations".[30] Under its aegis, CSOC established the Village Security Force and its Village Security Teams in 1966–67, supported closely by the US Operations Mission in Bangkok.[31] As such, CSOC organized rural villagers as local militia, intelligence sources and additional military manpower. Washington influenced CSOC's activities through a direct advisory role: The CIA station chief (Robert Jantzen, 1959–66; Peer de Silva, 1966–68), following the request of Ambassador Martin, became CSOC's special assistant/counter-insurgency. In this position, the United States was able to achieve better "coordination on ... more adequate communication with the Thai on counterinsurgency matters".[32] Praphas's acquiescence to the creation of CSOC—coming at the suggestion of US ambassador to Thailand Graham Martin, the CIA and the US "Special Group"—was accompanied by massive US military infusions of money for Praphas's counter-insurgency efforts.[33] Such funding for CSOC enhanced the influence of Praphas across the country.

CSOC was initially under the overall control of the Supreme Command (tasked through army commander Praphas), which was directly responsible to the prime minister (and supreme commander). But intra-CSOC meetings of army, police and civilian bureaucrats began to devolve into inter-service clashes. The army informally took full control of CSOC in 1967 in a bureaucratic "coup".[34] Thus, though it continued to merge other security agencies, CSOC came under the direct control of Praphas in his role as Thailand's army commander, and his powers intensified. Indeed, he directed CSOC until he was overthrown in 1973.[35] Praphas became the point man between the United States and Thailand for US-designed counter-insurgency operations. Directly heading up CSOC were General Saiyud Kerdphol and Chamnan Yuwabool, director of the Department of Local Admin. The two jointly oversaw CSOC civil affairs staff.

Sayud had earlier been the director of the Army Operations Center of the Directorate of Operations of the Royal Thai Army before becoming CSOC director of operations. Saiyud and Chamnan were also trusted associates of Praphas. At the same time, the creation of CSOC and the intensified role of the army in Thailand's counter-insurgency was heartily welcomed by Thanom and Praphas, at least partly because it ensured a general satisfaction among officers (who might otherwise have considered carrying out a coup). But a putsch was now unlikely since Washington guaranteed for Bangkok higher military aid than Thailand had ever previously received.

The October 1965 military reshuffle (see Appendix 4) continued to consolidate the dominance of Thanom and Praphas over the armed forces. The deputy slot and one of the assistant army commander slots were given to aging, uncharismatic senior officers who faced mandatory retirement the following year. The new army chief of staff was General Surakit Mayalarp, who worked well with both Praphas and Krit Sivara. Praphas granted two other top slots to his class of 1929 peers. To appease Krit, in 1965 Thanom and Praphas awarded him the position of assistant army chief in addition to keeping him on as 1st Army Region commander. They also promoted him to the post of "General of the Army". Ultimately "the duo [Thanom and Praphas] bought him [Krit] off—and he stayed bought".[36] Another reason for Krit's durability was his close association with the palace. Indeed, he could be considered an arch-royalist soldier. He had served as a royal aid-de-camp in 1949, 1952, 1955 and 1958. Thus, Thanom and Praphas could not simply demote Krit to oblivion.

By 1965, the United States began to realize it faced a major problem. Though the Thai government had granted almost all US requests above and beyond what the US could have wanted—including stationing US troops on Thai soil, Thai tutelage in counter-insurgency operations and Thai "volunteers" in Laos—the fact remained that Thailand had no permanent constitution, and the Thanom government was a dictatorship. Sustaining Thanom and Praphas in a manner considered politically legitimate by the US Congress meant that the two despots would have to be reinvented as supporters of democracy. Washington felt that the Thai regime's growing lack of popularity was reflected in the country's continuing CPT insurrection (amidst the continuing war in nearby Laos and Vietnam) and allegations of corruption against leading generals such as Praphas. This message was delivered not just to the generals but also to King Bhumipol. After returning from a 1967 visit to the United States, the monarch personally pressured the government to promulgate a new charter.[37] Thus, beginning in 1965, Ambassador Graham Martin already started to make plans for a transition in the regime. The idea to establish a military proxy party began with Ambassador Martin in September 1965.

> Ambassador [Martin] felt that an ideal solution would be to get 303 Committee [the US interdepartmental committee authorizing covert operations] agreement in principle for support of the Thai election. Mr. Bundy [assistant secretary for Far Eastern affairs] said that he felt that it might be worth [less than one line of source text not declassified] dollars to have control of the Thai political scene but that he did not want to see the government's administrative machinery used as a political party. This had always been done in the past and he did not think that it augured well for the future of democracy in Thailand if this practice were to continue.[38]

US officials then had the CIA report on the feasibility of Martin's advice. Eighteen days later, the report was completed and sent to the 303 Committee. It concluded:

> If [Thailand's] Constitution is promulgated it is estimated that by the end of calendar year 1966 general parliamentary elections will be held in Thailand.... Ambassador Martin has proposed ... a program of covert political action to include the financing of a political party, electoral support for this party, and support for selected candidates for parliament from this party.... Such a

program is now in preparation. Traditionally the ruling groups in Thailand have drawn upon the Government controlled Lottery Bureau for funds to finance political activities, but because the present members of the ruling group have been so critical of the late Prime Minister Sarit's misuse of Lottery Bureau funds, they appear reluctant to use this source.

Although some small remnants of former legal political parties still exist, notably former Prime Minister Khuong Aphaiwong's Democratic Party, they represent little more than disorganized and undisciplined political "outs".

Also, in keeping with traditional Thai politics, there will undoubtedly be a proliferation of political parties organized to contest the elections. The Communists can be expected to attempt to influence and penetrate some of these parties.... To date, the ruling group has done little or nothing to develop and organize politically in preparation for the forthcoming elections, except that largely in response to pressures kept on by the Mission over a long period of time, the key members of the ruling group have agreed to compose any differences they might have and join forces within one party. It is felt that it is both consistent and consonant with U.S. policy objectives in Thailand to support the continuity and stability of the present ruling group. To this end the funds requested ... will be used to underwrite some of the costs of organizing and supporting a government party in preparation for the general elections.... A corollary objective is to attempt to ensure that the party created is successful in winning a comfortable and commanding majority in elections.... It is recommended that the 303 Committee approve the proposal to create a political party in Thailand using as a basis the current ruling group and secure the parliamentary election of leaders of this party.[39]

One week later, Ambassador Martin "emphasized the importance of keeping together the leaders who have established some cohesion" in one overarching government-sponsored political party and also stated, regarding knowledge of the US covert role in the party, that he believed "that the number of witting Thai officials could be kept to a figure of six".[40] The identities of these six, though undisclosed, were likely Thanom, Praphas, Krit, Dawee, civilian Pote Sarasin and Lt. Gen. Sawaeng Senanarong, secretary general of Government House.

On 11 November 1965, following 303 Committee approval, higher authority in the US government agreed to authorize covert funding support for a political party led by government leaders. Paralleling the dilatory process of US covert fund approval, Thailand's junta-appointed assembly delayed approving the draft constitution beyond its earlier expected 1966 enactment.

Still, in February 1966, moves towards political change were confronted by powerful opponents. In particular, General Praphas "made no secret of his distaste for a constitution and elections".[41] His resistance likely delayed the charter's promulgation.

By early 1966, though government policies over the last six years had led to unprecedented economic prosperity at the macro level, relative poverty continued, with marginalization felt especially in the rural North and Northeast where communist insurgency had erupted—and was persisting. Thus, US-advised counter-insurgency operations grew. But in May 1966, elements within the Thai armed forces—some leaders and intermediate-level officers—were increasingly feeling that US aid had been "grudging and even inadequate"; they wondered whether Washington was "in fact a dependable ally in a crunch"; they felt that US operations in Thailand had contributed to more insurgency; and they questioned the degree of commitment the Thanom government had given to Washington.[42] US ambassador Martin discovered in June that deputy PM and army chief Praphas had increasingly argued that he could not depend upon US materiel help and did not desire US troop participation in Thailand. Seeking to change Praphas's mind, foreign minister Thanat "took the unusual step of intervening with the king, who used his influence with Praphas to add Army elements to the suppression operation".[43]

> Thanat indicated that if the Thai could be reasonably certain of materiel assistance, they could handle the job without American troops. The Secretary indicated that he would review the situation, (and attempt to insure [*sic*] that the necessary materiel support would be forthcoming).[44]

To demonstrate Washington's complete support for Thanom's government, US president Lyndon Johnson visited Thailand in October 1966. Fiscal year 1966–66 saw US military aid to Thailand grow from US$45 million to US$60 million. Washington also dispatched special US army units to train the Thai army in counter-insurgency methods. Meanwhile US helicopters and crews began providing training for the Thai air force and transport for Thai army and police units on operations against insurgents.[45] Though insurgency had grown in rural Thailand, US-backed Thai military counter-insurgency soared, sustaining militarization of the country.

By the time of Johnson's 1966 visit, Thanom and Praphas had succeeded in monopolizing most political, military and economic postings. The two gave themselves the most lucrative cabinet positions. In comparison, deputy army commander General Krit Sivara, during 1963–69, was not allowed any cabinet posts. In the military, year after year, Thanom remained supreme commander, while Praphas was deputy supreme and army commander. Other senior officers were mostly rotated. Though Praphas greatly exceeded Thanom in terms of corporate board memberships and shares in companies, there were few senior military officers beyond the two who held close to as many. In 1967, internal meetings among US government officials especially stressed the immensity of Praphas's corruption.[46] Morell noted that "Of all the senior military leaders, Praphas was the most heavily involved in financial and commercial activities."[47] Thanom himself was no threat to Praphas given the matrimonial linkages between the two families as well as Thanom's decade of absence away from effective military commands. Krit Sivara, however, was another matter. To control Krit's army clout, in 1966 Praphas "promoted" him to the post of deputy army commander, removing him from his 1st Army Region command post and thus direct command over troops. Praphas replaced Krit in the 1st Army Region commander position with General Aat Sasiprapha. Aat was Praphas's own son-in-law, since Aat had married Praphas's second daughter. As such, with Thanom and Praphas hoarding the top three posts, new deputy commander Krit reached the junta's "glass ceiling" in terms of military promotions. But there were other senior officers who were feeling increasingly frustrated with the lack of available advancement. Thus, by 1966, a loose faction had formed secretly among senior and middle-ranking Thai security officials in opposition to the dominance of Thanom and Praphas. Led by Krit, it included generals Chitti Navasatien, ACM Thawee Chulasap, Surakit Mayalarp, Tawich Seni-wong Na Ayuthaya, Boonchai Bamrungpong, Chote Hiranyotsiti, Sangad Chaloryu, Kamon Dachatungkha, Kriangsak Chomanand, Prasert Ruchirawong and Prachuab Santarangkul. During the Thanom-Praphas regime, few of the clique's members held direct commands over troops. But after 1973, they came to dominate the Thai armed forces.

Regarding the October 1966 military appointments, besides Krit and Aat, the others included several uncharismatic Praphas supporters as well as a couple of ambitious younger officers. The latter two were General Prasert Thammasiri as 1st Division commander and General Pat Urailert as 2nd Division commander. They both had close connections with Krit Sivara.

In January 1967, the Johnson administration entered into a secret agreement with the Thanom regime to send a combat division to South Vietnam and assist the United States in its war against North

Vietnamese–backed guerrillas there in return for US$50 million per year. Even before this accord, beginning in 1964, Thanom and Praphas had assisted Washington in South Vietnam, sending small numbers of mostly air force officials.[48] But from 1967 onwards, the Thai commitment became much more entrenched. On 6 January of that year, PM Thanom publicly proclaimed to the Thai nation that the government was seeking volunteers for a thousand-man expeditionary force to fight in South Vietnam for the "direct defense of Thailand".[49] The Thai commitment that ultimately developed involved the Royal Thai Volunteer Regiment (Queen's Cobras), a unit of some two thousand soldiers, which began military operations in Vietnam in July 1967, serving under the United States 9th Infantry Division. The unit was replaced by the larger Royal Thai Army Expeditionary Division ("Black Panthers") in July 1968.[50] Ultimately, by the time it ended its services in South Vietnam and returned home in early 1972, Thailand had sent 37,644 troops to engage in combat in South Vietnam as part of the Free World Military Assistance Forces.[51] The programme was completely underwritten by the United States and provided lucrative income for the Thai government. In addition to such sponsorship, by 1969, Washington had augmented its military assistance by US$30 million for two years, agreed to supply Thailand with a "battery of Hawk anti-aircraft missiles in return for the 11,000-man Thai unit in Vietnam" and had invested $702 million in construction of military bases in Thailand.

Amidst these income-earning projects for Thailand involving US national security, by mid-1967 revelations of military corruption increasingly emerged. By then it was becoming public knowledge that Deputy Prime Minister Praphas was an unsavoury character who personally participated in corruption while condoning malfeasance by his cronies. Washington held its nose because it needed support from Thailand for US security objectives in Southeast Asia. But the US Embassy in Bangkok as well as the Thai monarch were increasingly appalled. Following a speech by King Bhumipol denouncing malfeasance in the government, the judiciary convicted General Surachit Charusareni, former minister of agriculture, his wife, and the wife of 1st Army Region commander General Aat Sasiprapha of extortion and/ or involvement in corruption.[52] However, Surachit was a close friend of Praphas, while Aat's son Yuthasak had married one of Praphas's daughters. The scandal led to Aat's imprisonment (he died in prison in 1972). Prime Minister Thanom's refusal to cover up this case increased Praphas's anger at Thanom. His fury may have led to the rumours of a Praphas-led coup in September 1967.[53]

In early 1967, the 303 Committee gave a favourable review of the 1965 plan to create a pro-government political party in Thailand, a decision reconfirmed by higher US authorities on 15 September 1967. At that point, second and third readings by the rubber stamp assembly of Thanom and Praphas were continuing to delay the implementation of the constitution. The approval of the charter might have been delayed because of an impending September 1967 coup by Praphas (and perhaps Thawee).[54]

Indeed, by 1967, Praphas appeared clearly to have succeeded in dominating Thailand's military altogether. Praphas reportedly planned "to oust Thanom" in order to establish a "true 'military dictatorship' prior to December 5".[55] Indeed, given that Thanom and Praphas had succeeded in quashing or co-opting other military officers, in 1967, the only factional division that really mattered was that between themselves. By this point, the junta leaders must have thought that other military officers had been successfully sidelined.

> [Secretary of State Dean Rusk began by stating that] 'Praphas is personally corrupt.... Unger will want to talk to the King and it may be possible to head it off. From our point of view, in normal times we could take chances on a coup but we can't have a coup now with Vietnam going on. We must try to keep this in the icebox.... [T]he First Army around Bangkok decides coups. The head of the First Army has been in touch with Praphas.' Unger said 'Praphas is trying to line up support.' [US Secretary of Defense Robert] McNamara said 'General Dawee is one of the keys to this. General McConnell is close to him and we have taken good care of him.... We can have McConnell visit Thailand and he could find out if Dawee is behind this and if so could turn him around.' Rusk pointed out in 1965 we provided [less than one line of source text not declassified] money and this has not been called on yet.[56]

Thawee, who had allegedly "put the bug in Praphas's ear", apparently believed that the latter might oust Thanom but would then realize that he was not a suitable prime minister given his unethical reputation and would thus ask Thawee to become front-man, given Thawee's "clean" image. Also, Thawee "had always claimed that the King liked and trusted him and probably believed that he could count on the King's support".[57] To discourage a coup by Praphas, Washington "proposed that Thanom come to the US on an official visit; this would be a sufficient signal to Praphas that we disapproved of the plotting now going on. [Also, incoming US] Ambassador Unger was going to indicate to Dawee our approval of Thanom."[58]

Despite an attempted coup by Praphas, what remains unclear is whether it was procrastination on the part of the Johnson administration or problems in the Thanom government that held up the promulgation of the constitution. After all, any delay would have forced the government following the Johnson administration to deal with any new government in Thailand.

The October 1967 military reshuffle was significant because there were so few changes in the senior armed forces postings. The only real new face was that of General Samran Paetiyakul, a palace favourite, who became the 1st Army Region commander. Samran's father had worked for King Rama VI (Vajiravudh), and King Bhumipol had long known him.[59] Samran had commanded the 31st Army Infantry Regiment (strategically located in Lopburi, near Bangkok) in 1957–61. One year earlier, the 31st had become part of the 1st Infantry Division, King's Guard. As rural insurrection began to accelerate, Samran was transferred to the 3rd Army Region, where he prosecuted counter-insurgency in the North. He was not a favourite of army chief Praphas, however, and was transferred again in 1964 to the inactive posting of Chulachomklao Military Academy director, serving there until 1967. Royal pressure helped to catapult Samran from this lowly post to command the 1st Army Region in 1967—in place of Praphas's son-in-law Aat Sasiprapha.

The 31 March 1968 announcement by President Johnson that he was going to start diminishing military assistance to South Vietnam in anticipation of peace negotiations created fears for the Thanom government, which was concerned that Washington would likewise diminish aid to Thailand. Nevertheless, with insurgency growing across the country's North, Northeast and Far South, US economic and military aid for Thailand continued at high levels. In May, Thanom visited Washington, where he was assured that Thai fears of a drop in US aid were unjustified.[60]

As of early 1968, US plans under Washington's Project 22 in Thailand had continued apace. It had continued to evolve from the details of the original letter from President Lyndon Johnson on 27 June 1964 to Prime Minister Thanom, in which the former authorized the US ambassador to begin consultations towards "joint Thai-US military planning of measures to be taken in the event of a Communist drive towards the borders of Thailand".[61] Project 22 provided for "the defense of Thailand, military operations to hold the Mekong Valley, its principal cities, and its military facilities (in Laos as well as Thailand)".[62] In November of 1965, a draft plan was submitted to the national authorities, and on 23 December 1966, the final plan was promulgated by Thanom in the presence of US ambassador Martin and General Stilwell. Nevertheless, Praphas and Foreign Minister Thanat Koman increasingly criticized Thanom to the effect that

> recent American construction projects and deployments had no relevance to Thailand's security needs and that America was 'occupying' Thailand. To help the PM fend this off [US ambassador Martin sent out a letter which] linked these construction projects to existing agreements and to both SEATO and Project 22 contingency planning.[63]

Nevertheless, the United States and Thailand had approved further components of the project. However, at the beginning of 1968, according to US ambassador Unger,

> [A] top secret working paper which gave a fairly clear picture of the plan disappeared from the trunk of a car belonging to a Thai member of the Project 22 working group. We do not know whether or not the plan fell into unfriendly hands. Following this the name of the exercise was changed from Project 22 to Project Taksin.[64]

In September 1969, Henry Kissinger, who was then national security advisor, informed President Richard Nixon that "Project Taksin itself originated as a Democratic effort to convince the Thai that we meant business when we said that we would do anything necessary to defend the Mekong, including the re-introduction of American troops." Kissinger continued that the "the plans were developed at our initiative more than that of the Thai".[65]

When senators Fulbright and Symington later opened a Senate investigation into US operations in Thailand in November 1969, their committee viewed Project Taksin, as well as the Rusk-Thanat communiqué upon which it was based, as unauthorized executive commitments under SEATO, especially Taksin, since the latter had been negotiated without even the knowledge of the Senate.[66] Senator Fulbright publicly alleged that the US had concocted a secret agreement with Thailand "much broader than any publicly-known commitment".[67] Despite Senate opposition, Project Taksin survived, resurrected as a plan rather than an agreement. In March 1972, Thanom queried Ambassador Unger as to whether Taksin still existed. Unger replied, "that while it [was] still in existence, Project Taksin [was] a military plan".[68]

Meanwhile, in its final form, Thailand's 1968 constitution, which was finally approved by the junta-appointed unicameral legislature in February 1968, became essentially a resurrection of the 1949 charter, though with enhanced military prerogatives enshrined into law.

Specifically, it helped to legitimize the Thanom-Praphas government, which had overseen the writing of the charter, its promulgation, and general elections under its auspices. Under the new constitution, the legislature reverted to its pre-1951 bicameral form, with the creation of a new rubber-stamp upper house on 4 May 1968, given that the military prime minister nominated—and the king endorsed—the appointment of all senators. Seventy per cent of new senators were active-duty military officers. Thus, from 1968 until 1971, as in the past, the Senate continued to serve as a means through which military-dominated executives could prevail over assemblies containing political parties that might seek to pre-empt the government with legislative challenges. Also, the Senate Speaker automatically became president of parliament. Though senators could simultaneously serve in the prime minister's cabinet, lower house representatives could not. Furthermore, the Senate could delay lower house legislation for up to a year. Finally, in joint sessions with the new 219-member lower house, the military-dominated 164-member Senate could easily unite with pro-government elected MPs to guarantee that the executive would maintain political control. Moreover, most important legislative matters were to be decided in such joint sessions given the enormous leverage of the upper house. Finally, the infamous Article 17 (of the 1959 constitution)—effectively authorizing the prime minister the use of carte blanche powers whenever he saw fit (e.g., the imposition of martial law)—was placed into the charter.[69] Ultimately, the 1968 constitution enshrined a partnership between military officers and royalists.

FIGURE 5.5
Thailand's Senate, 1968–71

Type of legislature	Years in office	Appointed or elected	Total number of senators and military contingent
Bicameral (Third Senate)	1968–1971 (terminated by military coup)	Appointed	1968: 120, of which 93 (78%) military reserved domain 1969: 44 additions (26 military) = 164 total and 72.5% military reserved domain

Source: Paul Chambers, "Superfluous, Irrelevant or Emancipating: Thailand's Evolving Senate Today", *Journal of Current Southeast Asian Affairs* 28, no. 3 (2009): 9, https://d-nb.info/999559311/34.

Meanwhile, by 1968, Praphas had accepted the impending enactment of a constitution and the fact that there would soon be a general election. Indeed, he was eager for this, given his "enviable position to organize grass-roots support for the regime".[70] As minister of the interior, Praphas "commanded an extensive and far-reaching bureaucracy that stretche[d] from provincial capitals to isolated villages. Whatever its weaknesses, it [was] the best apparatus in the country." Praphas's vehicle was the Free People's League of Thailand, a quasi-official anti-communist group set up the previous year by him and his crony Chamnan Yuwabool, director of the Department of Local Affairs. A spin-off from this organization was the Free People's Party (FPP). "Praphas ... assured other government leaders that [FPP] would merge with the government party once the latter [got] off the ground." In fact, Praphas used FPP to further his political ambitions.

Only on 16 August 1968 did the Johnson administration finally give its approval to create a proxy political party for the Thanom-Praphas regime, and it subsequently helped to financially guide that party to an electoral victory. On 20 August, US assistant secretary of state for East Asian and Pacific affairs Bill Bundy informed US secretary of state Dean Rusk that

> [T]he 303 Committee last week reviewed the long-standing commitment we made in 1965 to give covert financial support to [less than one line of source text not declassified] in the Thai elections. This commitment was originally made in 1965 on the express authority of the President.... [A]ll hands have concluded that the essence of the commitment remains valid.[71]

Ten days earlier, US ambassador Leonard Unger (who had succeeded Graham Martin in Thailand in October 1967) gave the Thai political party project the nickname "Lotus".

Six months after the promulgation of the February 1968 constitution—and only two weeks after final approval from Washington (on 31 August 1968)—covert funding for Lotus began to be disbursed. This was completed on 4 February 1969—six days before the 10 February 1969 election.[72] Four months prior to the poll, in October 1968, the regime officially established its proxy Saha Pracha Thai (SPT; United Thai People's) party. A retread of the previous military political parties of Phibun (Seri Manangkhasila party) and Sarit (Sahaphum party), twelve out of seventeen of SPT's party council members simultaneously served as military officials. SPT also represented only the latest attempt by the regime to establish party power for itself.[73] Thus, SPT was a vivid reflection of Thailand's military hierarchy. The

SPT party leader was PM Thanom himself, its two deputies were pro-US aristocrat Pote Sarasin and General Praphas Charusatien, while the secretary general was ACM Thawee Chulasap. Krit served as one of three deputy secretary generals, with the others being Pichai Kullanavich of the police (father of privy councillor General Pichit Kullanavich) and Lt. Gen. Sawaeng Senanarong (who headed party organization). Krit was the senior of the three because he was part of the core of the junta and because Praphas had "delegated ... management decisions to" Krit with regard to "political matters".[74] Krit's position as deputy secretary general provided him a source of economic patronage and political opportunity, given that he was tasked with being a party whip. As a whip, he was responsible for ensuring party discipline among SPT legislators and the factions in which they were grouped. He was also responsible for helping to guarantee votes for SPT—especially soldiers' votes.

In Bangkok, US officials worked with General Sawaeng, the man the junta had placed in charge of registering the party on 24 October and organizing it as well as preparing for the upcoming polls. According to US ambassador Unger, SPT "matters [were] left largely to General Sawaeng".[75] Ambassador Unger was continuously reassured by the junta that it was and would continue to be a conservative and reliable ally, even following the election. In a private conversation between civilian Pote Sarasin and Unger,

> Pote ... commented on his continuing satisfaction with Prime Minister Thanom, above all because of his continuing loyalty to King and religion, the prime cements of the Thai nation. He reminisced about Phibun's alienation from the King and said even Sarit had shown signs of beginning to feel above the monarchy toward the close of his regime. Thanom remains absolutely loyal.[76]

Turning to military appointments, just like the 1967 reshuffle, the 1968 reshuffle saw only one new appointment at the senior level. That is, army assistant commander General Pisit was transferred and replaced by General Tuanchai Kosinanon. Both men were close to Praphas, and each were thus given a chance to occupy the assistant army commander posting.

Under Prime Minister Thanom, the Thai government mobilized some 250,000 rural and urban bureaucrats and spent at least $5,100,000 on the February 1969 general election—the first since 1958, after which political parties had been banned. There were reports of "double voting by military units, bribery, and ballot box stuffing".[77] Besides doing their job in overseeing the election, leaders of the Thanom government (including military and police chiefs) simultaneously rooted for their SPT party in the poll. The SPT platform emphasized:

> 1) the need for strong centralized leadership to ensure continued stability in the Kingdom; 2) the ability of the existing military regime to meet the dangers of Communism; 3) the success of the government's economic development program; and 4) the advantages UTPP [SPT] candidates would have in terms of access to government funds for local development projects.[78]

The three deputy secretary generals, led by General Krit Sivara, attempted to organize and subsidize a structure of political party support for SPT throughout Thailand. Though the opposition Democrats remained strong in Bangkok, rural Thailand, especially the North and Northeast, were fertile grounds for SPT to attract votes or attract independent candidates. Krit had built up a powerful base of economic support in the 2nd Army Region (northeastern Thailand) when he had served as its commander during 1960–63. Similarly, Krit had built up backing in the central plains when he had served as the 1st Army Region commander during 1963–66. Krit's regional bases proved invaluable when SPT established interconnected rural vote canvassing networks in 1968. But Krit was especially influential in the voter-rich Northeast. He personally maintained a hotel in the provincial capital city of Nakorn Ratschasima (Khorat). Called the Sri Pattana Hotel, it opened in 1967[79] and became a centre for politicians and vote-canvassers to come together to receive factional and party funding as well as to strategize for the 1969 election. Similarly, in Khon Kaen, the hotel that Krit (and Thailand's northeastern region army) used for such political activities was the Kosa Hotel. The hotel built and utilized by Thailand's northern region army was the Amarintr Nakhorn Hotel in Phitsanulok.

Given that the poll was an event carried out by and for the junta, it predictably produced a victory for SPT as it had received enormous financial support from the US, the CPT remained illegal and other parties were relatively small and disorganized. The SPT obtained 75 seats in the 219-member lower house. A total of 72 independent candidates (those not in a party) won seats, over half of whom were backed financially by Praphas. The opposition Democrats won 57 seats, and the remaining 15 seats went to various minor groups. According to US officials, the election "enhanced" Praphas's position and was likely to result in "a stronger behind-the-scenes role" for him.[80] But Praphas's FPP garnered only two seats.

Following the triumph of the SPT, autocrat Thanom was predictably selected by the SPT-led coalition as prime minister.[81] For its part, the

CIA felt the results were "embarrassing" because SPT had failed to achieve a majority in the electoral outcome. Praphas and the rest of the military cabal knew that Praphas's sordid reputation precluded him from becoming prime minister. Besides, he was sufficiently satisfied with influencing state affairs on a more indirect level. Meanwhile, it became necessary for SPT to merge several independent MPs into the coalition to stabilize it. Praphas in fact relied on General Krit Sivara "to liais[e] with various elected representatives within and outside the government party".[82] Partly through his manoeuvring, SPT and the government used "special funds and other financial incentives" to expand the party's number of MPs from 75 to 127 (38 per cent to 58 per cent of the overall lower house).[83]

To bolster its support in the military, on 7 March 1969, Thanom and Praphas gave leading members cabinet positions. This necessitated enlarging the cabinet, from nineteen to twenty-eight members, and reshuffling it, bringing seven generals into the Council of Ministers. These included Police General Prasert Ruchirawong as minister of public health, General Chitthi Navisatien as deputy defence minister, Admiral Chalee Sundosupon as deputy transport minister, General Amporn Srijayanta as deputy minister of justice, Police General Pichai Kullayamitr as deputy minister of economy, General Sawaeng Senanarong as minister to the Office of the Prime Minister, and General Krit Sivara as deputy education minister. ACM Thawee Chulasap was promoted from deputy defence minister to become minister of transport, and General Pongse Punnantanta was moved from minister of transport to become minister of industry, both of which were lucrative postings. Of course, Thanom remained premier, while Praphas remained deputy PM and interior minister.

Moreover, according to Sangchai, almost immediately SPT became divided into four factions. These included the faction of Thanom; the clique of Praphas; the faction of Krit and Thawee; and the police faction of Pichai, Sawaeng, Prasert Ruchirawong and Sa-nga Kittikachorn.[84] An analysis by Morell gave a similar picture, except that he divided them into five, led in descending order by faction leaders Thanom, Praphas, Krit, Prasert and Thawee.[85] This small group of strongmen jostled for power within the parameters of parliamentary politics.

Indeed, after the establishment in March of the new cabinet, Krit Sivara decided to continue manipulating parties in the lower house. He assigned Prasit Kanchanawat, an MP from the eastern province of Chachoengsao, to surreptitiously gather approximately thirty non-party MPs to create a secret political group. This ambiguous grouping came to be called "the Ghost Party."[86] The "Ghost Party" later caused turbulence in the lower house. And this is one reason that could have contributed to the decision by Field Marshal Thanom to conduct a *coup d'etat* on 17 November 1971.

In the October 1969 military reshuffle, there were four key changes. First, Praphas stalwart General Tongjim Sanwanit was promoted from 2nd Army Region commander to Royal Thai Army assistant commander. Succeeding Tongjim as 2nd Army Region commander was his (and Praphas's) confidant General Jamlong Singha. Meanwhile, General Kriengkrai Attanand, a son-in-law of Praphas, became the 1st Army Region commander, replacing ultra-royalist General Samran Paetiyakul, who became 3rd Army Region commander, fighting insurgency in the North.

In 1970, Thailand's party politics became even more factionalized. A large clique of SPT members in the lower house strongly objected to PM Thanom's selection of his brother Sanga Kittikachorn as deputy foreign minister. In November, Thanom agreed to another cabinet shakeup as another concession for SPT MP dissidents. But there continued to be other factional demands. Some wanted diminished powers for the Senate; others sought to give the SPT a greater voice in the cabinet. One faction wanted the five oldest cabinet members (including Thanom and Praphas) to resign and be replaced by fresher faces. In addition, a forty-four-member faction that was generally loyal to Praphas demanded more democratization of the constitution. At the time, Praphas, though an SPT faction leader, was also influential in the Liberal Party, which had been created after the 1969 election. The government was only able to persuade the National Assembly to pass the 1970 budget bill by agreeing "to transfer central reserve funds from the Bureau of the Budget to the more easily politically pressured Ministry of Finance". Finally, a tax bill was only passed after Praphas personally pressured the lower house to do so. Predictably enough, SPT party disunity, combined with instability among the other parties in the lower house, diminished the government's ability to administer the country as effectively as it had earlier done under dictatorship.[87]

Thailand's foreign policy also began to undergo some changes in 1970. Thailand's foreign minister, Thanat Khoman, was beginning to show signs of a neutralist sentiment. At the same time, PM Thanom proclaimed that Thai troops would depart from Vietnam by no later than 1972. Nevertheless, Thai CIA-trained paramilitary "volunteers"—under General Vitoon Yasawat—continued to be secretly stationed in Laos.[88] Thailand's Black Panthers regiment was overtly combating insurgents in South Vietnam. But a new development occurred shortly after the CIA-backed overthrow of neutralist Prince Norodom Sihanouk's regime in Cambodia on 18 March 1970; Thanom and Praphas agreed to send Thai "volunteers" to Cambodia to help prop up the new rabidly anti-communist government of Lon Nol. These "Special Guerrilla Units" (SGUs), like many Thai soldiers in Laos, were not clearly under the orders of the new Nixon administration in Washington at a time when US congressional investigators and journalists were expanding their scrutiny of the war in Southeast Asia. Even US foreign service bureaucrats—which included ambassador to Thailand Leonard Unger—seemed unaware in 1970 that Thai soldiers or Thai SGU's were engaged in combat in Cambodia under Nixon administration direction, though official approval from Washington was never granted.[89] Nevertheless, revelations obtained in 2015 indicate that the Thai SGUs had already begun their service in Cambodia at least by 1 June 1970. In a secret memo, national security advisor Henry Kissinger told White House Press secretary Ron Ziegler the following:

> There is a story out of Bangkok where the Thai Prime Minister said we are going to equip Thai volunteers for Cambodia. Ziegler: Yes. Kissinger: You've seen the story? Z: Yes. Kissinger: How are you going to handle it? Ziegler: I'm waiting for the pearls of wisdom. Kissinger: Well, the problem is, it's essentially true, but we don't want to admit it. There's enough truth in it that a flat denial could be damaging.[90]

By mid-June, the Nixon and Thanom administrations seem to have already approved the deal.[91] Thus, in its secret collaboration, the Thanom/Praphas regime merely became part of a grandiose deception about US policies in Cambodia as practised by the president Richard Nixon and his national security advisor Henry Kissinger. The only public mention of Thai soldiers near Cambodia at this time was on 21 April, when PM Thanom announced that Thai troops had been sent to the Thai-Cambodian border as a "security precaution", adding that Thailand would consider providing military help to Lon Nol's newly established regime in Phnom Penh.[92]

In the October 1970 military reshuffle, 2nd Army Region commander General Jamlong Singha retired. He was succeeded by General Payom Pahonrat. Payom remained the commander of the region for three years. Indeed, the 2nd Army Region had by then become the hub of insurrectionary problems for the Thai state. It was under Payom that the army and CSOC massacre in 1970 at Ban Na Sai village in Nong Khai province was later uncovered.

During 1971, insurgency grew in rural Thailand. The Thai military increasingly relied on US military assistance. Meanwhile, the economy soured, forcing Thanom to depend on more US economic assistance.[93] Relative poverty remained entrenched in rural areas. Also in 1971, despite facing mandatory retirement, Thanom extended his term as PM and supreme commander by a year.

By late 1971, the 1969–71 façade democracy of Thanom and Praphas had become less appealing, even to the two co-dictators. Political parties were increasingly demanding more control over public policies, and by 1971 the SPT was feeling pressured "to give two million baht to each [parliamentary] member for projects in the constituencies".[94] Some US policymakers began planning a repeat of "Project Lotus", designing an operation to pump money into the SPT in preparation for the next general election—to be held in 1973 at the latest.[95] Senior military officials were especially piqued by growing civilian criticism of regime corruption, economic morass and continuing communist insurgency alongside the role of civilian politicians in creating parliamentary delays in passing the budget. Ultimately, more and more senior Thai military officials were tiring of electoral politics.[96] Meanwhile, by mid-1971, it had become increasingly difficult for Praphas to harness his SPT associates. Parliamentary dissension caused the government—especially Praphas—to expend numerous efforts to ensure that its favoured bills were passed.[97] Praphas especially felt that electoral governance had helped to strengthen his political enemies (such as Krit and police chief General Prasert Ruchirawong) while diminishing the available economic patronage he could pay to his supporters.[98] By bringing electoral democracy back to Thailand, Thanom and Praphas had metaphorically opened a can of worms. Their creature, SPT, was becoming an uncontrollable dragon. Prime Minister Thanom was quite annoyed, exclaiming: "Never, in my long political career, have MPs caused such trouble to government administration as in recent times."[99]

Meanwhile, the US Nixon administration gradually came to endorse a Praphas-initiated putsch as a way to rid itself of long-time foreign minister Thanat Khoman, whose advice had increasingly veered towards neutralism—making moves towards Beijing[100]—or occasional anti-Americanism.[101] As a result of Thanat's foreign policy changes, Thailand signed a trade agreement with Moscow on 25 December 1970, and also, in early November 1971, signed the ASEAN "Southeast Asia neutralization" declaration in Kuala Lumpur, Malaysia. On 16 November 1971, US undersecretary of state Alexis Johnson met with Thai government officials, as well as the king, bringing funds for anti-narcotics efforts.[102] As Kullada Kesbunchoo-Mead stated, these funds possibly served to subsidize the coup that occurred on the following day.[103] Under pressure from Praphas and with Alexis Johnson's "green light" from the US, Thanom led an auto-coup on 17 November 1971, returning Thailand to direct dictatorship.

On 17 November 1971, four tanks and fewer than fifty troops surrounded parliament amidst a public radio announcement that Thailand was now under the control of the "Revolutionary Party" or National Executive Committee (NEC). The committee was composed of the core leaders of the Thanom-Praphas group: Thanom and Praphas, as well as ACM Thawee Chulasap, deputy army commander General Krit Sivara and General Prasert Ruchirawong of the police. Pote Sarasin was the only civilian included. Martial law was invoked, the 1968 constitution voided, political parties dissolved, the Cabinet was effectively reshuffled, and both houses of parliament were dissolved.[104]

The coup received the tacit support of King Bhumipol, after which Thanat Khoman was dismissed as foreign minister. Washington thus felt assured of "no change in Thai relations with the US",[105] and Nixon and Kissinger were elated that the putsch had "freed" the Thanom regime from "the disruptive actions of Thanat".[106] In the evening of 17 November, Prime Minister Thanom met, at his own request, with US ambassador Unger to discuss the reasons for the coup. With Thanom were Praphas, Pote Sarasin, Thawee Chulasap and General Kriangsak Chomanand. Thanom told Unger that the coup had been necessary for many reasons.

> [C]ollectively and individually Parliament and its members [had] attacked the government for its performance and also made many personal attacks and [had] spread among the people a growing lack of confidence in the government. There [had] been serious budgetary delays [in 1971] as in previous years...; members of Parliament [were] obstructing appropriation of funds for essential government purposes including national security and want[ed] money to be diverted instead to funds which would be spent in their districts for pork barrel purposes.[107]

The coup leaders added that certain members of parliament "were stirring up discontent and unrest and misunderstanding in complete disregard of the stability of the government and the country and had communist leanings".[108]

Despite this public rationale, for Thailand's military the coup represented "power consolidation by the Praphas faction",[109] and especially the elimination of "the influence of Police Chief Prasert [Ruchirawong]."[110] For Prasert, after the coup he became director of civilian affairs for the junta-created "Revolutionary Party" as well as minister of education and minister of public health, although these postings were rather peripheral in the relative power equation. Though Prasert continued on as chief of police (having held that post since 1963), Praphas's post-coup preponderance of power increased the likelihood that Prasert would have to step down when he reached mandatory retirement in October 1972—and not be able to extend beyond retirement. Indeed, in 1972 Praphas succeeded Prasert as police chief, while remaining on also as army commander, interior minister and deputy prime minister. For Krit, the coup was somewhat beneficial because he was now elevated to the post of secretary general of the "Revolutionary Party" in addition to continuing on as deputy army commander. However, Krit likely realized that the continuing extensions on retirement by Thanom might be copied by Praphas, thus depriving Krit of the ability to ever succeed Praphas as army commander.

Morell lists three reasons based upon Thai domestic politics for Thanom and Praphas to carry out the auto-coup. These included (1) legislative interference in the executive's responsibilities; (2) the need to ensure a stable political succession upon premier Thanom's impending retirement from the armed forces; and (3) pressure by the Praphas faction to ensure their clique's growing sway over the government.[111] With regard to the first issue, Thai MPs increasingly were pressing the government to modify the budget. Many politicians were holding up the bill because they each wanted a "development project" allocation of 2 million baht![112] In terms of the second issue, General Thanom had been required to retire at age sixty in 1971 but had been granted an extension so that he could continue on in the largely ceremonial role as supreme commander and maintain the frontispiece for the Thanom-Praphas regime. In 1972 Praphas would have to retire as well, but he too had plans to obtain an extension. Yet junior officers would not tolerate endless extensions of terms. Given the ages of Thanom and Praphas, a succession crisis was becoming increasingly likely. The final issue involved the future of Praphas. He exerted the real muscle in the regime, controlling the army, police and a large faction in parliament. By 1971, Thanom by himself seemed to hold approximately the same amount of power that Phibun had possessed in the 1950s: an aging military man with no direct connection to active troops. But Praphas needed Thanom to ensure his own consolidation of power. As such, both men agreed to promote Thanom's son—and Praphas's son-in-law—Colonel Narong Kittikachorn. This became a crucial by-product of the coup.

Narong was appointed assistant secretary general of the 1971 Coup Group and chair of the Committee to Suppress Those Dangerous to Society (CSTDS), as well as the deputy secretary-general of a newly created anti-corruption agency—the Board of Inspection and Follow-up of Government Operations (BIFGO). CSTDS eventually merged into BIFGO. Through BIFGO, Narong began the systematic destruction of individuals within the patron-client networks of Krit, General Prasert Ruchirawong and ACM Thawee Chulasap—who he considered his chief political competitors.[113] In this way, Narong earned the undying hatred of Krit and Prasert. Following Prasert's 1972 retirement, Krit became the only potential threat to the monopoly on power of Thanom, Praphas and Narong. And it is likely that the end of 1971 marked the beginning of plans by Krit to overthrow the regime.

By 1972, insurgent attacks and counter-insurgent state reactions were intensifying on a grand scale in the Northeast, North and South. The result was a growth in violence across Thailand's rural areas. In the South, specifically Pattalung province, General Sant Chitpattima implemented a harsh military programme to quash insurgency in that region. It culminated in a massacre at Tambon Lam Sai, Phattalung province, in late 1972. Dubbed the "Red Drum Massacre", it involved the mass killings of between two hundred and three thousand civilians suspected of supporting communists. Suspects were placed in two-hundred-litre red drums and burned alive.[114] State agents involved in these torturous killings included army, police and paramilitary officials of CSOC.

Also in 1972, the military government's foreign policy drew closer again to the United States and it endorsed all US activities in Southeast Asia. Washington's air war in the region led to the intensification of US military activities through the air bases in Thailand (e.g., Takhli, Nam Phong and U-Tapao). By mid-year, US troops based in Thailand reached their apex: fifty thousand. Meanwhile, Thai "volunteer" SGUs continued to fight for Washington in Laos and Cambodia. Thai troops in Vietnam returned home in 1972.

Meanwhile, the sudden death in early 1972 of General Kriangkrai Attanand,[115] 1st Army Region commander, upset the apple cart of potential continuing power for Thanom and Praphas—who would soon need to retire—as Kriangkrai was Praphas's son-in-law and had been on the verge of becoming army commander. In October 1973, however, several Thai newspapers alleged that Thanom, Praphas and Narong had "engineered" Kriangkrai's death (with Narong supposedly placing a bomb aboard the helicopter). The apparent motive for the alleged assassination was that Thanom and Praphas "feared [Kriangkrai] was about to launch a coup against them".[116]

However, 1972 also witnessed the diminution of General Prasert Ruchirawong's power. Chief of police since 1963, he had built up enormous bureaucratic clout over nine years in leading the 75,000-man police force. He was thus a police powerbroker in the same vein as General Phao Sriyanond during the 1950s. Prasert had increasingly quarrelled with Praphas—who ostensibly served over Prasert as interior minister. Their struggle was one over village security forces and commercial interests. Prasert was a former army major general and commander of the Anti-Aircraft Artillery Division in Bangkok. But as he was due to reach the mandatory civil service retirement age of sixty in 1972, he sought an extension of his tenure from the NEC, as Thanom had done for himself in the post of supreme commander of the armed forces. Prasert apparently even approached the king about endorsing his extension, but he received no royal backing. Meanwhile, given that Praphas had built up much more bureaucratic leverage against Prasert following the 1971 coup, the former succeeded in standing him down. Prasert was also opposed by Thanom's son (and Praphas's son-in-law) Narong and Narong's mother, Thanphuying Chongkol Kittikachorn.

> Their animosity dates from an incident two years ago when Army troops under Narong's command, apparently drunk, attacked and demolished a police installation in Bangkok. Prasert publicly criticized Narong for this incident, and Narong never forgot the insult.[117]

Ultimately, Prasert was compelled to retire as police chief on 1 October 1972, and he was replaced by Praphas. There were strong rumours of a police coup in the first week of October, but none ever materialized. On 1 December the NEC appointed army lieutenant general Prachuab Suntharangkul, director of the Port Authority, as deputy chief of police. But Prachuab had long held close ties with Prasert, which helped in the downfall of Thanom and Praphas on 14 October 1973.

Perhaps the most interesting phenomenon of 1972 was the meteoric rise of Narong Kittikachorn. With excellent political and family connections, and his career constantly publicized in leading Thai newspapers, Narong was widely known to head an NEC anti-corruption campaign, which was designed to give him a popular public image but also to weaken his political enemies. He also directed a programme to suppress heroin smuggling, promoted land reform, helped girls kidnapped for work in brothels, met with university students, and even discussed problems of pollution. Narong's official positions continued to be assistant to the NEC's director of national security (Praphas) and deputy secretary general of BIFGO. According to Morell, Narong utilized five sources of political power: "(1) his father [Thanom]; (2) his father-in-law [Praphas]; (3) the senior associates and clients of both; (4) his personal clique of young military men; and (5) certain intellectuals and academicians".[118] Key battalions in the 1st Army Region in Bangkok in 1972 were commanded by Narong's military academy class 5 classmates.

Despite the 1971 coup, and notwithstanding their family connections, Thanom and Praphas persisted during 1972 in competing for power. Praphas anticipated Thanom's impending retirement, which would perhaps take place in October 1972. Still, in March, Praphas again contemplated carrying out a coup against his brother-in-law, before deciding against it.[119] By late 1972, Thanom's personal power vis-à-vis Praphas and others had grown stronger.[120] At the same time, Narong and General Krit Sivara (deputy commander of the army, NEC secretary general and minister of industry after December 1972) had become leading political figures. Others, such as ACM Thawee Chulasap and Pote Sarasin, had become much weaker, while General Prasert, Generel Sawaeng and other potential military contenders had all been kicked out of the competition for power.

In the 1972 military reshuffle, the results of the November 1971 coup became evident. The most important reshuffle was that of Colonel Narong Kittikachorn, who became commander of the 2nd Battalion, 11th Infantry Regiment, 1st Army Region Infantry Division.[121] This promotion placed Narong (the son of Thanom and son-in-law of Praphas) in line to eventually become army commander. The second significant reshuffle was that of Praphas Charusatien, who succeeded the retiring General Prasert Ruchirawong to become police commander. With this appointment, Praphas's power was now immense, given that he now commanded the police and army while also being interior minister, deputy supreme commander and deputy prime minister, all simultaneously. Meanwhile, 1972 saw Thanom Kittikachorn again extend his retirement, thus continuing on as supreme commander of Thailand's armed forces. Other appointments included that of General Tawich Seniwong na Ayuthaya (who tried to align with all sides), who became assistant army commander, succeeding the retiring General Tongjim Sanwanit. Also, General Prasert Thammasiri, who often sided with Krit, was appointed to become 1st Army Region commander. Yet another appointment was that of General Uerm Jirapong, a son-in-law of Praphas, who was appointed to command the strategic 1st Army Division in Bangkok. In addition, Admiral Komon Sitakalin, another loyalist of Thanom, was promoted to become navy commander. Komon was disliked by navy officers for his closeness to Thanom and Praphas.

On 15 December, King Bhumipol endorsed Thailand's latest NEC-created constitution, thirteen months after the November 1971 coup. The document, containing twenty-three articles, was a near clone of Sarit's 1959 constitution. Many of the articles were similar to those of previous charters enacted by Thai juntas: (1) the prime minister was empowered to take any steps "appropriate for the purpose of preventing, repressing or suppressing actions which jeopardize the national security, or the Throne, or the economy of the country, or the national administration, or which subvert or threaten law and order or the good public morals or which damage the health of the people;"[122] (2) an all-appointed unicameral National Assembly would be the legislative body; (3) the Cabinet was empowered to draft the kingdom's next constitution; and (4) all decrees issued by the NEC were declared legal. The coup-makers could thus not be tried for carrying out a coup.

On 18 December, a new cabinet was formed in which, in terms of the number of cabinet positions held, the power of Thanom and Praphas expanded dramatically. Also, twelve out of the twenty-eight cabinet ministers were military officials. In addition to cabinet postings and the posts of deputy supreme commander and army commander, Praphas remained head of Communist Suppression Operations Command and officially became head of the Police Department. Sixty-six per cent of the newly appointed members of the unicameral legislature were military officers, and, as usual, these were tilted in favour of the army (the breakdown of military senators was as follows: 134 army, 30 navy, 20 air force and 13 police).[123] In an apparent attempt at greater collaboration with the network of General Phin Chunhavan, Phin's son General Chatchai—an experienced diplomat who also got on well with the United States—was appointed minister of foreign affairs.

The year 1973 proved to be one of living dangerously in Thailand. At the beginning of the year, the government, with its 1972 temporary charter already in place, began plans to enact a permanent constitution. A constitutional drafting committee under the chairmanship of Praphas was set up. Praphas made it quite clear that enacting a new constitution would take no less than three years. The public (spearheaded by the media), however, put pressure on him to speed things up.[124]

Meanwhile, the credibility of the government suffered a major hit on 29 April when a Thai army helicopter crashed at the Thung Yai game preserve. Six senior military and police officers were killed and five injured in the crash. PM Thanom immediately announced that those in the helicopter had been on a "secret mission". But an investigation by students and newspaper reporters revealed that the helicopter, filled with carcasses of protected animals, was returning from an illegal big game hunting expedition. "Thung Yai" suddenly became synonymous with governmental abuse of power.[125]

Already, in February 1973, Thanom was beginning to become unsettled by (1) the growth of communist insurgencies in Thailand and also in neighbouring countries; (2) the fact that Washington seemed to be beginning to reduce its commitments and assistance to the regime in Thailand; and (3) problems within his own governing cabal.

A memo of a discussion between US vice president Spiro Agnew and Richard Nixon on 10 February 1973 had this to say:

> The Vice President said he had never seen Thai Premier Thanom more nervous. He had openly committed himself as a friend of the United States and was afraid that we may leave him. He was also concerned at movements within his government and needed our support. Thanom was concerned about the degree to which we would draw down our forces in Thailand, and about the longer term of what would happen after the Nixon years, – for example, what if the doves get into control.[126]

Meanwhile, as if testing the waters for dissension within the army, Thanom early in the year suggested that all high-level government officials resign from all postings they held in commercial firms, except for banks. Narong actually disagreed with his father's recommendation, but there was speculation that Thanom would use BIFGO to ensure that the resignations occurred. In the end, only Krit complied, disposing of the shares he held in over fifty firms.[127] According to Zimmerman, Krit most probably and surreptitiously transferred his shares to a straw for a temporary period of time.[128]

Meanwhile, in Spring 1973, Thanom—who had already reached mandatory retirement age as a civil servant back in 1971—again sought to extend his active duty. Field Marshal Krit and Thawee voted against the extension, indicating their displeasure.[129] Though the two were in the minority, the writing for Thanom appeared to be on the wall. Indeed, he would have to retire sometime soon. A growing number of senior security officials had become incensed by the monopolization of power by Thanom and Praphas and by Narong's BIFGO prosecutions.

But who could stand up to the trio? If necessary, who would dare lead a coup? There needed to be an appropriate excuse. For the sake of legitimacy, royal sanction was necessary.

In early August 1973, amidst growing student demonstrations and divisions among senior officers—and with the continuing communist insurgency—political turbulence appeared to be descending all across Thailand. At the time, US secretary of state Henry Kissinger informed the prime minister of Singapore, Lee Kuan Yew, who was visiting Washington, "We will have difficulties [in Thailand] but between now and mid-September, we will do some decisive things." When Lee re-marked that Washington should quickly prop up Thanom and Praphas but should not support a coup against them or "look the other way", Kissinger retorted, "We won't support a coup but looking the other way…".[130] Kissinger's statement appeared to indicate that Washington had become tired of dealing with Thanom and Praphas and was in fact willing to look the other way, or even encourage their political overthrow.

With the military becoming increasingly faction ridden, deputy army commander Krit was approached in mid-1973 by several security officials, including retired general Prasert Ruchirawong and the CIA-connected General Vitoon Yasawat to spearhead a coup. Krit declined, however, to lead one.[131] Thanom likely doubted Krit's gumption for coup making and he knew Krit would have only a brief posting as army chief given his age (58 or 59), but he also understood that his own retirement could not be put off much longer. Thus, on 11 September, Thanom announced a military reshuffle, including the appointment of Krit as army commander. This decision proved to be the "straw which broke the camel's back" in creating a chance for a coup.

Narong, who had long opposed Krit, was "quite upset" by Krit's promotion, while Krit saw Narong as ambitiously wanting to ascend too high too quickly.[132] According to the CIA, the decision by Thanom and Praphas was not an easy one:

> Praphas has been reluctant to turn over direct command of the army [which he had held for nine years], especially since he and Krit [had] never been particularly close.… Prime Minister Thanom probably prevailed upon Praphas to change his mind. Thanom and Praphas apparently agreed that Krit has sufficient seasoning to handle the greater responsibilities that go with the army command and that, as a loyal member of the original 1957 coup group, he [was] suited to take over this politically sensitive job.[133]

Besides establishing Krit as army commander, the October 1973 reshuffle reflected the rise of Krit's active-duty friends and followers in the security services. These postings included army chief of staff General Boonchai Bamrungpong and assistant army chief General Chote Hiranyathiti. At the same time, Krit's occasional ally Prasert Thammasiri continued on in his position as 1st Army Region commander. In the navy, senior officials such as deputy navy commander Admiral Sangad Chaloryu—who had a fractious relationship with Thanom and Praphas (and opposed the repression of student protesters in October 1973)—were on the ascendancy. Another sometime ally of Krit, ACM Thawee Chulasap, rose from chief of staff, Supreme Command, to assistant supreme commander (occasional Krit confidant General Surakit Mayalarp thereupon became chief of staff, Supreme Command). Though Thawee's posting in the Supreme Command was a promotion to a weaker post, Thawee possessed close links with the US government, the palace and the Thanom faction. Moreover, like the king, Thawee increasingly looked unfavourably upon Praphas. Thawee thus joined Krit in 1973 to oppose the continued extensions of retirement for Thanom.

The reshuffle of 1 October 1973 saw Praphas's friend General Tuanchai Kosinanon promoted to the desk post of permanent minister of defence. Succeeding Tuanchai as assistant army commander was arch-royalist General Samran Paetiyakul—not a Praphas loyalist. Meanwhile, occasional Praphas ally General Tawich Seniwong na Ayuthaya, assistant army commander, was appointed to the post of deputy army commander. Two newly promoted officials, the army chief of staff General Chote Hiranyatthiti and the assistant army commander General Bunchai Bamrungpong, were part of Krit's faction. New navy commander Admiral Cherdchai Tomya was a loyalist of Thanom's but was unpopular in the navy. Finally, the two new commanders of the 2nd and 3rd Army Regions, though trusted by Thanom and Praphas, were too far away from Bangkok to interrupt any coup by Krit should the latter foment one. The incoming deputy commander of the 2nd Army Region, however, was Krit-ally General Prem Tinsulanonda.

Turning to the police, on 1 October 1973, despite Praphas having reached the mandatory retirement age of sixty in 1973, he chose to continue on as chief of police—a post he had held for a year. But Praphas held only shallow roots of support within the police. Indeed, the deputy police chief since 1972, General Prachuab Suntarangkul, secretly was not a loyalist of Praphas and detested the partisan prosecutions of Narong's BIFGO. Prachuab had begun serving in 1946 as an army company commander of the 3rd Combat Vehicle Regiment under Colonel Prasert Ruchirawong, and it was during this time that Prachuab became a loyalist of Prasert. Since Prasert was part of General Sarit Thanarat's Kiakkai clique, Prachuab's career soared through the influence of his patron Prasert. Thus, Prachuab in 1962 was appointed to the rank of major general as the commander of a military brigade. Serving under Prasert, in 1969 he was appointed to the rank of lieutenant general. In October 1972, even though Prasert retired that year and Praphas promoted Prachuab to become deputy director of the police, Prachuab remained part of Prasert's Kiakkai clique (Prasert was known as "Godfather Kiakkai").[134] Indeed, in 1973, Prasert remained the most influential person across the police, given that he had led the police for eight years (1964–72), making it into his personal fiefdom. At the same time, by 1973, after a decade of lording over political, military and economic posts by Thanom and Praphas, Prasert and Prachuab had become secret allies of Krit and Thawee in support of political change. They and many other officers were increasingly looking for an excuse to oust Thanom, Praphas and Narong.

Following the new appointments, which became effective on 1 October, Krit could conceivably—with help from Prachuab and the retired Prasert—use his new power to overthrow Thanom, Praphas and Narong. He seemed to be biding his time, but he would not have to wait long.

By 1 October 1973, Thanom and Praphas had been pressured to relinquish some of their military powers and to partially retire, though Thanom continued on as the ceremonial supreme commander, while Praphas was the deputy supreme commander and police chief. And as time went on they would come under even more pressure to retire from more junior military officials. The two—especially Praphas—were reluctant to hand over their military postings to younger officers who might be untrustworthy or less efficient. Such younger leaders included General Prasert Thammasiri, who had proven his loyalty to Sarit as commander of the 21st Regiment (Queen's Guard) (1958–60) and commander of the 1st Regiment (1960–64). With the transition to the Thanom-Praphas regime, Prasert seemed to become part of the pro-Praphas clique,[135] and by 1971 he was serving in the important post of 1st Division commander.[136] But Prasert also exhibited a subservient closeness with Krit in terms of shared business interests.[137] In 1972, Thanom appointed Prasert as chief of the 1st Army Region (he served until 1975).

Thanom and Praphas had of course relied upon intermarriages with key army officers to help sustain their power. General Aat Sasiprapha, General Kriangkrai Attanand and General Uerm Jirapong had each married daughters of Praphas and served as commanders of important army units. Though Aat served as 1st Army Region commander only until 1967, from 1969 until 1972, Kriangkrai was appointed to command that unit.[138] Meanwhile, between 1964 and 1969, General Uerm Jirapong, who was married to Thanom's daughter Nongnut, commanded the strategic 1st Army Regiment (1964–69). From 1971 until 1973, he commanded the 9th Division, until Thanom appointed him 1st Division chief in 1973.[139] Working with 1st Army Region commander General Prasert above (if Prasert proved dependable) and Narong below, Uerm would be an important asset to Thanom and Praphas when the latter two became compelled to retire from the military. If Thanom and Praphas had continued to control military promotions after 1973, then they might have ensured their indirect control over the armed forces for years to come.[140]

The only problem with this plan was that Krit Sivara had been appointed army chief in 1973. Thanom and Praphas had been unable to extend their active-duty military posts anymore, and Krit was second to none in seniority among the possible army commander successors. The two strongmen, however, were not close to Krit. There was thus the possibility that he might upset their plans for continued dominance over Thailand. Their only hope was that, since he would have to retire in 1975, Krit would have only two more years of active service. As US ambassador Leonard Unger had noted in a cable to Washington in 1971, "General Krit Sivara is waiting in the wings but age would make his tenure at most a brief one."[141] Moreover, by early 1973, the last time Krit had directly commanded troops on the ground was in 1966, when he had been 1st Army Region commander. He might be out of touch. Finally, if any potential protesters needed to be repressed, Krit would have the responsibility to do it—an onus that would only diminish his popularity. It thus seemed like a wise decision for Thanom and Praphas to appoint Krit as army commander effective 1 October 1973.

At the same time, Thanom and Praphas had, since the late 1960s, sought to co-opt Krit economically. For example, they supported the move by Sura Mahakuna Distillery Company to place Krit on its board of directors, alongside themselves, as well as General Thawee and General Prasert in 1967.[142] With the blessings of Thanom and Praphas, by 1969 Krit personally dominated the greatest number of firms (a total of 52), although his family was associated with 53.

Some of the military allies of Krit who capitalized with him on various economic ventures included ACM Thawee Chulasap, General Prasert Ruchirawong, General Chitti Navisathien, General Chote Hiranyathiti and General Amporn Chintakanond, among other military figures.[143] These individuals would later side with Krit against Thanom and Praphas.

The large number of firms Krit was involved in appeared to place him favourably relative to Praphas (44), police commander General Prasert Ruchirawong (33) and Thanom (1).[144] The few firms noted for Praphas and Thanom of course ignore that one of Praphas's aides was linked to 31 firms, another was connected to 27 firms, his wife was influential across 19 firms, and Thanom's wife was linked to 4 firms. Finally, Thanom's son Narong (Praphas's son-in-law) was influential across 40 firms.[145]

Meanwhile, in another mollifying effort, in 1969 Thanom and Praphas had begun to offer cabinet positions to Krit that represented convenient "cash cows". Indeed, following the 1969 junta-monitored general election (which returned Thanom to the premiership), Krit was appointed deputy minister of education, serving from 1969 until 1970. In 1970 he switched ministerial portfolios, replacing the ailing General Chitti Navusatien as deputy minister of defence, and serving until 1971. Then, from 1971 until 1973, Krit was appointed as minister of industry. Now, as army commander in 1973 (after seven years as deputy army commander), he was the most senior and probably the only senior military officer able to stand up to Thanom and Praphas (in terms of support within the military).

At this point, the events of September to October 1973—friction within the Thanom-Praphas junta and student protests—were coming to a head, and they provided Krit the opportunity to move against Thanom and Praphas. Below, the key events of October 1973 are provided by the days on which they occurred:

6 October: Five days after the military appointments took effect, and with Praphas and Prachuab continuing on as police director and deputy director, respectively, the police arrested Thirayuth Boonmee, formerly the secretary general of the National Student Center of Thailand (NSCT) and ten other activists (who had distributed leaflets demanding a new constitution) for violating Section 17 of the 1972 constitution.

7 October: Police arrested another student, activist Kongkiat Kongka. Demonstrations, led by the NSCT, begin to grow, centred on the Thammasat University campus.

8 October: Praphas announced that the state had uncovered information that those arrested were involved in a Chinese communist plot to take over the government. Demonstrations continued.

9 October: At a cabinet session, the regime invoked Article 17 of the 1972 constitution, giving it total power with regard to national security. The cabinet appointed Praphas to head a Commission to Restore Peace and Order, with new army commander Krit as his deputy. In fact, Praphas's power was only formal, while Krit actually controlled the soldiers on the ground. The new suppression force was headquartered at CSOC. Police arrested former member of parliament Khaisaeng Suksai. Meanwhile, thousands of students began to assemble at Thammasat University for a Hyde Park–style demonstration, and they decided to march to where the detained students were being held. Thousands of students refused to attend class and instead joined the demonstration.

10 October: Demonstrations continued by several thousand student protestors from universities throughout Bangkok, centred at Thammasat University. The students demanded that the detained students be immediately released and that a new constitution be enacted by 10 December (Constitution Day). Rumours spread that a secret riot order had been sent to the Public Disaster Relief and Fire Brigade, that a special commando force was being prepared to confront the students and that the regime was using "communism" as a rationale to suppress protestors.

11 October: A group of ten NSCT students—led by the NSCT's secretary general, Sombat Thamrongthanyawongse—delivered an ultimatum to Praphas that the regime immediately release the students it had arrested; otherwise, they promised to expand protests. Praphas promised a new constitution within twenty months and stated that the state would only prosecute those who use moves for a new constitution to oust the government. Other arrested students would be expeditiously released. Nevertheless, the military continued to be placed on full alert. This day also saw the number of student protestors rise to at least fifty-thousand. It was likely on this day that General Vitoon Yasawat arrived in Bangkok from Udorn Thani province (near Thailand's northeastern border with Laos), where he had been working with the CIA in US anti-communist efforts in Laos. Vitoon said that a "senior chief" had instructed him to proceed to Bangkok to work on getting the thirteen activists released. The "senior chief" Vitoon referred to was likely General Krit Sivara.[146] Vitoon arrived in Bangkok simultaneous to the arrival of incoming CIA station chief Hugh Tovar, who had previously worked with Vitoon in Laos and who in 1965 had overseen the CIA station in Jakarta during the Indonesian military's massacre of as many as a million people.

12 October: A state representative announced that five student activists would be released if investigations showed that they had not been part of a plot to overthrow the regime. Prosecutions of the other detained individuals would begin immediately. At 12 noon, the NSCT issued a deadline of twenty-four hours for the unconditional release of the thirteen detained. Two hours later, security officials held a meeting at the CSOC headquarters. At 8 p.m. it was announced that the thirteen had been granted bail, but at 11:25 p.m. students learned that the thirteen had not been released because they refused to sign a paper accepting only a temporary release. That same night, Praphas announced that there would be a new constitution by October 1974. Though his motive for this announcement remains unclear, it probably came at the instigation of the king.

13 October: NSCT reconfirmed their demand for unconditional release of the thirteen. The twelve students being held at Ban Khen Detention Center (who still demanded their unconditional release) reluctantly left the prison. At 11:30 a.m. approximately 200,000 students began to march from Thammasat University, heading down Ratchadamnern Avenue towards the Democracy Monument and the Equestrian Square. In response, Praphas ordered the deployment of police along the road, and Krit posted soldiers in front of the CSOC headquarters. These soldiers were from the 2nd Battalion, 11th Infantry Regiment—formally commanded by Colonel Narong Kittikachorn. Sometime in the afternoon, Thanom and Praphas, apparently with Krit, had a two-hour audience with the king, in which they restated that they would draw up a new constitution. During the late afternoon, King Bhumipol received a delegation of NSCT students led by Sombat and he reaffirmed the promise by Thanom and Praphas of a new constitution within twelve months. Nevertheless, Thanom and Praphas had often made promises of a new constitution over the past several years. Thus, there was no guarantee they would enact one, and the king knew that. In fact, a confidant of the king, police general Vasit Dejkunchorn, recounted that the king felt that Thanom and Praphas had already been sufficiently generous, providing more than the students had wanted.[147] But the students were apparently mesmerized by the king's words. Feeling reassured that the king would hold the regime to its promises, the NSCT leaders, presided over by Sombat, now believed they had achieved victory and decided to end the protests. They sent messages to this effect both to protestors at the Democracy

Monument as well as to the headquarters of the regime's Commission to Restore Peace and Order. But by 8 p.m., Seksan, leading the protests of his hard-line Federation of Independent Students of Thailand at the Equestrian Square, was still unaware or unsure—or perhaps unable to believe—that a truce between the regime and the NSCT had been reached. Seksan may also have felt disgruntled "at being left out of the decision-making loop".[148] He therefore ordered members of his group to march to Chitralada palace to seek help from the king. Sombat fetched Thirayuth and other released detainees from Ban Khen and headed with them towards Chitralada palace.

14 October: When Sombat and Thirayuth arrived at the palace, there were already rumours among the crowd that the regime had killed the student leaders. The two then argued with Seksan about the need to demonstrate at the palace. At 3 a.m., the king granted nine student representatives an audience, in which he again called for law and order and promised a new constitution. After the meeting ended, at 5:30 a.m. Colonel Vasit of the police read a speech by the king from a sound truck in front of the student demonstrators calling for a return to law and order and reaffirming that the thirteen detainees had been released, that a new constitution would be enacted by the following October and that the protestors should disperse. Sombat also asked the students to disperse.

What happened next remains unclear to this day. What is known is that some students refused to go home and wanted further clarification from the palace. The following is the probable six-part chronology of events that occurred in rapid succession:

1. Police began to attack demonstrators in front of the palace. According to Narong Kittikachorn, deputy police chief Prachuab ordered tear gas to be fired at the demonstrators.[149] At this point, some fleeing students fell into the moat surrounding the palace, while others attempted to enter the southern palace entrance. This route was blocked, however, by police commandos led by acting metropolitan police commissioner General Narong Mahanond, under General Monchai Pankongehuen, and directed by deputy police chief Prachuab. These police fired at the students, most of whom then fled to Ratchadamnern Avenue.

2. Once at Ratchadamnern Avenue, fleeing students were confronted with a mysterious source of gunfire: snipers on tops of buildings facing the road fired upon students and soldiers alike. Police Colonel Kosol Limpichart, commander of the Metropolitan Mobile Patrol Unit tasked with security on Ratchadamnern Avenue, denied that he and ten other policemen had fired at the protestors from the upper floors

of the Revenue Department, claiming that unknown individuals at the top of that building were using submachine guns and dropping grenades on protestors in the street. General Vitoon Yasawad later revealed that these gunmen were members of his 1964–73 Thai-led Elite Ranger Mercenary (or Thai Volunteer) Force, organized into SGUs, which had fought with the CIA against communists in Laos, and that "some of them" fought "alongside the students and some of them volunteer[ed] to fight for Col. Narong".[150] He also stated that these very same "volunteers" were at the time employees of the US government, with Washington's funding for them ending on 30 September 1974.[151] Between 1 July and 17 December 1973, the number of SGU battalions remaining in Laos was reduced from seventeen to ten, meaning that as many as seven battalions had returned to Thailand during that period and could have participated in the violence of 14 October. The remaining ten battalions in Laos had returned to Thailand by July 1974.[152] Interestingly, the US Embassy in Laos viewed funding for the volunteers as "continuing through October 1 ... but if contingency arises during period prior [to] November recruitment could commence to flesh out force to full strength".[153] That many of these fighters in 1974 became members of the Red Gaur right-wing militia in Thailand, a programme paid for by the US government, demonstrates financial evidence of the link between the CIA-funded SGU programme and the Red Gaurs. The year 1974 was when the remaining battalions of SGUs returned from Laos to Thailand, given that US funding for them in Laos dried up that year.[154] Vitoon died in 2011, but prior to his death admitted to acting as the agent of a "third hand" behind the 1973 killings, though he refused to identify who the third hand was, only saying that "the secret will die with me".[155] Thanom Kittkachorn later said that he specifically issued orders to all soldiers not to open fire on students, and that the snipers were definitely members of Vitoon's 333 unit. Thanom's son Narong alleged that Vitoon's snipers sparked the beginning of the 14 October shootings for the benefit of Thailand's leading armed forces personnel who sought to topple Thanom, Praphas and Narong via a "silent coup".[156] Later that day, Thai security officials said that "there was definite proof that these armed 'agent provocateurs' had fired at both the students and the police... [and] a number of these people had been arrested".[157]

3. Meanwhile, at around 9 a.m., army tanks and trucks full of soldiers began entering Ratchadamnern Avenue and facing off against the students. These soldiers belonged to the 1st Army Division,

commanded by General Ueam Jirapongse, specifically from the 2nd Battalion of the 11th Regiment, normally commanded by Colonel Narong Kittikachorn, but who had been temporarily transferred to be under the Supreme Command's Center for Riot Operations on the afternoon of 13 October.[158] The Center for Riot Operations was headed by General Kriangsak Chomanand, deputy chief of staff of the Supreme Command, who was under Supreme Command chief of staff General Surakit Mayalarp, who in turn was under ACM Thawee Chulasap, the latter of whom, according to the British Embassy, definitely played a role in the events of 14 October.[159] Kriangsak, Thawee and Surakit were allies of Krit. It was under orders of the Supreme Command, led by these three officers, that soldiers of the 11th Regiment aimed their weapons at (but mostly above) the protestors. A tank driver later stated that Krit had personally ordered him to move onto Ratchadamnern Avenue.[160] At 11:45 a.m. the demonstrators started to set fire to the Revenue Department. At 1:30 p.m. tear gas canisters were thrown into the crowds from the Public Relations Ministry. At 2:47 p.m. the BIFGO building began to burn. At 3:30 p.m. security forces appeared to have gained control of Thammasat University, though there were still thousands of students fighting police along Ratchadamnern Avenue at the Democracy Monument and especially at the Pan Fa Bridge. Meanwhile, a helicopter appeared high above the student demonstrations; its pilots had allegedly been commanded by Colonel Narong Kittikachorn to shoot the protesters below. These and other alleged orders were later denied by Narong. Indeed, Narong and others have stated that Krit and several co-conspirators were the ones behind the violence and that they put the blame on Thanom, Praphas and Narong.[161]

4. By the late afternoon, Krit appears to have refused to issue orders to assist Praphas's police against the students at this location—effectively double-crossing Thanom and Praphas. A later press report succeeded in boosting Krit's image politically for years to come. It stated that, in the late afternoon of 14 October, Thanom and Praphas had demanded Krit take stronger measures to "wipe out" the demonstrators, but he allegedly retorted: "These young people … they are our children."[162] Krit's reply, which was later spread throughout Thailand's media, made him appear as a loving father for the country. It also demonstrated that he alone now dominated the military and police, and that Thanom, Praphas and Narong should leave Thailand.

5. The official resignation of Thanom's government was announced on the radio at 6 p.m. Interestingly, the announcement of a new regime came only after Krit refused to assist Thanom and Praphas. At 7:15 p.m. the king, who clearly saw that Krit now had the upper hand but did not want the army general to formally take power himself, declared over the airwaves that Thanom's government had resigned and was being succeeded by an appointed civilian caretaker government headed by Professor Sanya Dharmasakdi, though Thanom remained supreme commander of the armed forces and Praphas continued in the post of deputy supreme commander.

6. At this point, Thanom and Praphas attempted to order Ranger troops to Bangkok from nearby Lopburi to quell the uprising. Krit, however, convinced 1st Army Region commander General Prasert Thammasiri, who commanded the Lopburi troops, to deny their request. Sensing that the two dictators remained in the government, some students still refused to go home. These hard-line students attempted to seize the Metropolitan Police Headquarters, entering into pitched battles with police. Police from other districts either did not show up or responded very late in offering to help. It could be surmised that Krit's allies Prachuab and Prasert influenced their late arrivals. At 11:15 p.m., Prime Minister Sanya, speaking over radio and television, proclaimed that a new constitution would definitely be drafted, and that elections would be held within six months. Meanwhile, supreme commander of the armed forces Field Marshal Thanom ordered all forces to do their fullest to "prevent undesirable incidents and to protect state property".[163] The commanders of the army, navy and air force refused to allow their forces to engage in repression.

15 October: During the morning, the hard-line students continued to try to storm the Metropolitan Police Headquarters. The Supreme Command announced at 11:30 a.m. that the continuing riots were organized by communist insurgents working with the students, and that as a result many police had been killed. At 1 p.m., students succeeded in burning part of the police headquarters (Chalerm Thai Theatre was already burning down). In the end, police reinforcements, negotiations with student leaders, royal calls for order and the fact that the army leadership refused to support Praphas in repressing the protestors contributed to a diminishing of tensions. In the evening, following a demand from King Bhumipol, Thanom, Praphas and Narong resigned from their remaining postings and agreed to leave Thailand for a temporary period. At 8:45 p.m., Praphas and Narong departed for Taiwan. Thanom made one more attempt to remain in Thailand, using his confidant air force commander ACM Bunchu Chandrubeksa to appeal to the king. Following the king's refusal, Thanom departed Thailand on the night of 16 October, with Bunchu giving him a send-off at the airport.[164]

Army commander General Krit, 1st Army Region commander General Prasert Thammasiri and 1st Division commander General Ueam Jirapongse, who had refused to assist the army in quelling the demonstrations, endorsed Sanya's new government as well as the departure of the "Three Tyrants" from Thailand.[165] Admiral Sangad Chaloryu, a Krit ally who had clashed with PM Thanom because the latter had not promoted him to be navy commander in 1973, lent his support to the students and then to Krit.[166] General Prasert Ruchirawong and General Prachuab Suntarangkul used their influence over the police to greatly increase division among the force, thus hindering Praphas's ability to use the police to quash the protests.

In directing the army ostensibly in support of an unpopular, heavy-handed regime but in actuality working against it, Krit became a rousingly popular figure. Under his influence, Thanom, Praphas and Narong were forced into exile and King Bhumipol appeared to reluctantly support him. In addition, as Hewison points out, the actions of Krit in 1973 allowed for a "rehabilitation" of the military, which had been tainted through its association with the Thanom/Praphas/Narong regime.[167] All of this showed that Krit had learned well from the example of his mentor Field Marshal Sarit Thanarat about how to stage a popular coup. For Sarit, it also involved his treatment of protestors during March–September 1957. Where Prime Minister Phibun Songkram had ordered him to repress demonstrators, he had instead listened to their grievances of state corruption and had become quite popular in the process. Ultimately, Sarit led a bloodless coup against Phibun, supported by the king. Like Krit with regard to Thanom, Praphas and Narong, Sarit had forced the heads of a deposed regime into exile. This included Phibun and his trusted police chief Phao Sriyanond. Their colleague, the aging Phin Chunhavan, Phao's father-in-law, was allowed to remain in Thailand (perhaps because Sarit found him harmless), while Phin's son Chatchai was forced to become a diplomat abroad.

Ultimately, the 14–15 October massacre resulted in at least 77 deaths and 857 injuries.[168] But these sacrifices did not lead to any lasting progressive political reform. Instead, "the Day of Great Tragedy", as King Bhumipol called it, specifically benefited him as well as Krit Sivara by increasing their political clout behind the scenes. The new political equilibrium appeared to be the result of tacit bargaining between Krit and the king. Thanom, Praphas and Narong left the country believing that the king had made an "agreement" with them to support their later return to power.[169]

From 1963 until 1973, Thailand experienced a decade of military-dominated, diarchic rule, continuing the pattern of governance from the 1950s. The authoritarian stratocracy of 1958–69 had exhausted Thais who hungered for a greater voice. The years 1969–71 gave them some political space, but they wanted more. The regime's attempt to turn back the clock to dictatorial diarchy in 1971 thus proved impossible. At the same time, following Sarit's death in 1963, the Thanom and Praphas regime came to represent a period where the two monopolized senior military posts among themselves, their cronies and their friends, creating deep dissension among military officers. This pent-up anger led to intra-military squabbles that eventually paved the way in October 1973 for the end of the regime altogether. The withdrawal by army commander General Krit Sivara of backing for Thanom and Praphas at the precise moment they needed troop support the most forced the king to withdraw his endorsement of the two. Thanom, Praphas and Narong were forced into exile, leaving Thailand controlled by Krit and the king alone.

Notes

1. In May 2000, former ambassador to Thailand Leonard Unger told this author that his perception—and the perception of the US government—was that Thanom had been an honest and trustworthy leader, whereas Praphas was corrupt and a military Mafioso. Personal Interview with Leonard Unger, DeKalb, Illinois, 2 May 2000.

2. The question remains as to why Krit and Chitti did not attempt to carry out a putsch against Thanom and Praphas. In fact, several generals approached Krit to turn against them, but according to one foreign observer "the duo bought him off—and he stayed bought". See L.B. Smith to P.G. Hood, Foreign Commonwealth Office (UK), cited in Kullada Kesboonchoo Mead, "The Cold War and Thai Democratization", in *Southeast Asia and the Cold War*, edited by Albert Lau (London: Routledge, 2012), p. 229.

3. United States Ambassador to Thailand Graham Martin, "283. Telegram from the Embassy of Thailand to the Department of State", 8 August 1964, *Foreign Relations of the United States* (*FRUS*), https://history.state. gov/historicaldocuments/frus1964-68v27/d283. See also "Memorandum from the Assistant Secretary of State for Far Eastern Affairs (Hilsman) to Secretary of State Rusk", "The Succession Problem in Thailand", 9 December 1963, *FRUS*, https://history.state.gov/historicaldocuments/ frus1961-63v23/d481. As early as 1962, US officials had predicted that,

as Sarit's health increasingly worsened, "he would probably be succeeded by Defense Minister Thanom with Praphas exercising a strong role in the background. Chitti and Krit are potential successors." "469. Summary of Discussions at Honolulu Conference", 11 October 1962, *FRUS*, https://history.state.gov/historicaldocuments/frus1961-63v23/d469.

4. "Rumors of Coups Agitate Bangkok; Thai Regime Guards Power Amid Talk of Upsets", *New York Times*, 8 March 1964, https://www.nytimes.com/1964/03/08/archives/rumors-of-coups-agitate-bangkok-thai-regime-guards-power-amid-talk.html.

5. "266. Letter from the Assistant Secretary of State for Far Eastern Affairs (Hilsman) to the Ambassador to Thailand (Martin)", 2 March 1964, *FRUS*, https://history.state.gov/historicaldocuments/frus1964-68v27/d266.

6. "267. Letter from the Ambassador to Thailand (Martin) to the Assistant Secretary of State for Far Eastern Affairs (Bundy)", 19 March 1964, *FRUS*, https://history.state.gov/historicaldocuments/frus1964-68v27/d267.

7. CIA, "The President's Intelligence Checklist", 30 April 1964, https://www.cia.gov/library/readingroom/docs/DOC_0005959145.pdf.

8. Ambassador Graham Martin, "273. Memorandum for the Record", 1 June 1964, *FRUS*, https://history.state.gov/historicaldocuments/frus1964-68v27/d273.

9. "281. Information Memorandum from the Deputy Assistant Secretary of State for Far Eastern Affairs (Green) to Secretary of State Rusk", 4 August 1964, *FRUS*, https://history.state.gov/historicaldocuments/frus1964-68v27/d281.

10. David A. Wilson, "A Survey of Asia in 1964: Part II, Thailand—Scandal and Progress", *Asian Survey* 5, no. 2 (1965): 108, https://doi.org/10.2307/2642487.

11. "Thai Premier Says Sarit Estate Is Now Figured at $140 Million", *New York Times*, 10 July 1964, https://www.nytimes.com/1964/07/10/archives/thai-premier-says-sarit-estate-is-now-figured-at-140-million.html.

12. "The 1964 Coup-Attempt" (in Thai), *Thai Political Base*, http://politicalbase.in.th/index.php/%E0%B8%81%E0%B8%9A%E0%B8%8E_2507.

13. The family ties between Thanom and Praphas derived from the 1958 marriage of Thanom's son Narong to Praphas's daughter, just as Phao Siyanon had been married to the daughter of Phin Chunhavan. Similarly, one of Praphas's other daughters married Yutthasak Sasiphrapha, son of Praphas loyalist General Att Sasiprapha. Another one married Somthas Attanand, son of General Kriengkrai Attanand, while yet another married General Uerm Jirapong. Interestingly, all three generals, like Praphas, came out of the (Wongthewan) King Guard's 1st Division faction.

14. อนุสรณ์งานพระราชทานเพลิงศพ จอมพลถนอม กิตติขจร [Memorial volume from the cremation ceremony of Field Marshal Thanom Kittikachorn] (Bangkok: Royal Thai Armed Forces, 2005).

15. Paul Handley, *The King Never Smiles* (New Haven: Yale University Press, 2006), p. 145.

16. "278. Memorandum from Director of the Joint Staff (Burchinal) to the Acting Chairman of the Joint Chiefs of Staff (LeMay)", 22 June 1964, *FRUS*, https://history.state.gov/historicaldocuments/frus1964-68v27/d278.

17. "291. Letter from the Assistant Secretary of State for Far Eastern Affairs (Bundy) to the Assistant Secretary of Defense for International Security Affairs (McNaughton)", 24 April 1965, *FRUS*, https://history.state.gov/historicaldocuments/frus1964-68v27/d291.

18. "3. Memorandum from the Assistant Secretary of State for Far Eastern Affairs (Hilsman) to Secretary of State Rusk", 15 February 1964, *FRUS*, https://history.state.gov/historicaldocuments/frus1964-68v28/d3.

19. "286. Memorandum for the Record", 29 January 1965, *FRUS*, https://history.state.gov/historicaldocuments/frus1964-68v27/d286.

20. General Banchorn Chawansilp, "นามนั้น 'เทพ 333' กำเนิด 'บก.ผสม 333' [That name "Thep 333" originated "Mixed Land 333"]", *Matichon Weekend*, 29 April 2021, https://today.line.me/th/v2/article/3v1yPk.

21. R. Sean Randolph, "Thai-American Relations in Perspective", in *United States–Thailand Relations*, edited by Karl Jackson and Wiwat Mungkandi (Berkeley: University of California Press, 1986), p. 29.

22. Ibid.

23. "291. Letter from the Assistant Secretary of State for Far Eastern Affairs (Bundy) to the Assistant Secretary of Defense for International Security Affairs (McNaughton)", 24 April 1965, *FRUS*, https://history.state.gov/historicaldocuments/frus1964-68v27/d291.

24. "293. Memorandum of Conversation", 18 May 1965, *FRUS*, https://history.state.gov/historicaldocuments/frus1964-68v27/d293.

25. 300. "Memorandum from the Assistant Secretary of Defense for International Security Affairs (McNaughton) to Secretary of Defense McNamara", 2 August 1965, *FRUS*, https://history.state.gov/historicaldocuments/frus1964-68v27/d300.

26. "295. Letter from the Assistant Secretary of State for Far Eastern Affairs (Bundy) to the Assistant Secretary of Defense for International Security Affairs (McNaughton)", 25 May 1965, *FRUS*, https://history.state.gov/historicaldocuments/frus1964-68v27/d295.

27. "307. Memorandum from the Deputy Director for Plans of the Central Intelligence Agency (Helms) to Secretary of Defense McNamara", 14 January 1966, *FRUS*, https://history.state.gov/historicaldocuments/frus1964-68v27/d307.

28. "302. Telegram from the Department of State to the Embassy in Thailand", 9 August 1965, *FRUS*, https://history.state.gov/historicaldocuments/frus1964-68v27/d302.

29. Saiyud Kerdphol, *The Struggle for Thailand: Counterinsurgency 1965–1985* (S. Research Center Co., Ltd., 1986), p. 13.

30. Desmond Ball, *Militia Redux: Or Sor and the Revival of Paramilitarism in Thailand* (Bangkok: White Lotus, 2007), p. 35.

31. Ibid.

32. "344. Report of the Thai Working Group to the East Asia and Pacific Interdepartmental Regional Group", 26 April 1967, *FRUS*, https://history.state.gov/historicaldocuments/frus1964-68v27/d344.

33. "308."Telegram from the Embassy in Thailand to the Department of State", 15 February 1966, *FRUS*, https://history.state.gov/historicaldocuments/frus1964-68v27/d308.

34. R. Sean Randolph, "The Limits of Influence: American Aid to Thailand, 1965–70", *Asian Affairs: An American Review* 6, no. 4 (1979): 257 https://www.jstor.org/stable/30172916.

35. Surachart Bamrungsuk, *United States Foreign Policy and Thai Military Rule: 1947–1977* (Bangkok: Duang Kamol, 1988), pp. 146–48.

36. Kullada Kesboonchoo Mead, "The Cold War and Thai Democratization", in *Southeast Asia and the Cold War*, edited by Albert Lau (London: Routledge, 2012), p. 229.

37. Handley, *The King Never Smiles*, p. 194.

38. "304. Memorandum from Richard K. Stuart of the Office of the Deputy Director for Coordination to the Director of the Bureau of Intelligence and Research (Hughes)", 10 September 1965, *FRUS*, https://history.state.gov/historicaldocuments/frus1964-68v27/d304.

39. "305. Memorandum Prepared for the 303 Committee", 28 September 1965, *FRUS*, https://history.state.gov/historicaldocuments/frus1964-68v27/d305.

40. "306. Memorandum for the Record", 8 October 1965, *FRUS*, https://history.state.gov/historicaldocuments/frus1964-68v27/d306.

41. Donald E. Nuechterlein, "Thailand: Another Vietnam?" *Asian Survey* 7, no. 2 (1967), p. 127, https://www.jstor.org/stable/2642524.

42. "313. Information Memorandum from the Assistant Secretary of State for Far Eastern Affairs (Bundy) to Secretary of State Rusk", 16 May 1966, *FRUS*, https://history.state.gov/historicaldocuments/frus1964-68v27/d313.

43. "314. Memorandum of a Conversation", 28 June 1966, *FRUS*, https://history.state.gov/historicaldocuments/frus1964-68v27/d314.

44. Ibid.

45. Nuechterlein, "Thailand: Another Vietnam?", p. 129.

46. "Memorandum from the President's Special Assistant (Rostow) to President Johnson", *FRUS*, https://history.state.gov/historicaldocuments/frus1964-68v27/d353.

47. David Morell, *Power and Parliament in Thailand: The Futile Challenge, 1968–1971* (Princeton, NJ: Princeton University, 1974), p. 121.

48. Stanley Robert Larsen and James Lawton Collins, Jr., *Allied Participation in Vietnam* (Vietnam Studies, Department of the United States Army,

1975), p. 26, https://history.army.mil/html/books/090/90-5-1/CMH_Pub_90-5-1.pdf.

49. Cited in Richard Ruth, *In Buddha's Company: Thai Soldiers in the Vietnam War* (Chiang Mai: Silkworm Books, 2012), p. 31.

50. Larsen and Collins, Jr., *Allied Participation*, pp. 32, 42

51. Ruth, *In Buddha's Company*, p. 1.

52. Frank Darling, "Thailand: Stability and Escalation", *Asian Survey* 8, no. 2 (1968): 121, https://www.jstor.org/stable/2642342.

53. "361. Telegram from the Embassy in Thailand to the Department of State", 27 September 1967, *FRUS*, https://history.state.gov/historicaldocuments/frus1964-68v27/d361.

54. "356. Memorandum from the Assistant Secretary of State for East Asian and Pacific Affairs (Bundy) to Secretary of State Rusk", 15 September 1967, *FRUS*, https://history.state.gov/historicaldocuments/frus1964-68v27/d356.

55. Ibid.

56. "358. Memorandum from the President's Assistant (Jones) to President Johnson", 15 September 1967, *FRUS*, https://history.state.gov/historicaldocuments/frus1964-68v27/d358.

57. "360. Memorandum of Conversation", 21 September 1967, *FRUS*, https://history.state.gov/historicaldocuments/frus1964-68v27/d360.

58. Ibid.

59. Handley, *The King Never Smiles*, p. 227.

60. Frank Darling, "Thailand: De-escalation and Uncertainty", *Asian Survey* 9, no. 2 (1969): 115–17, https://doi.org/2642310.

61. "23. Telegram from the Embassy in Thailand to the Department of State", 9 September 1969, *FRUS*, https://history.state.gov/historicaldocuments/frus1969-76v20/d23.

62. Ibid.

63. Ibid.

64. Ibid.

65. Ibid.

66. "36. Editorial Note, Southeast Asia, 1969–1972", *FRUS*, https://history.state.gov/historicaldocuments/frus1969-76v20/d36.

67. "14. Telegram from the Department of State to the Embassy in Thailand", 9 July 1969, *FRUS*, https://history.state.gov/historicaldocuments/frus1969-76v20/d14.

68. "53. Telegram from the Embassy in Thailand to the Department of State (Eliot) to the President's Assistant for National Security Affairs (Kissinger)", 10 March 1972, *FRUS*, https://history.state.gov/historicaldocuments/frus1969-76v20/d153.

69. Darling, "Thailand: Stability and Escalation", p. 118.

70. "407. Special Report by the Central Intelligence Agency", 18 October 1968, *FRUS*, https://history.state.gov/historicaldocuments/frus1964-68v27/d407.

71. "404. Memorandum from the Assistant Secretary of State for East Asian and Pacific Affairs (Bundy) to Secretary of State Rusk", 20 August 1968, *FRUS*, https://history.state.gov/historicaldocuments/frus1964-68v27/d404.

72. "3. Memorandum Prepared for the 303 Committee", 7 February 1969, *FRUS*, https://history.state.gov/historicaldocuments/frus1969-76v20/d3.

73. In fact, Civilian Minister of National Development Pote Sarasin had originally been chosen (back in 1964) to organize a political party for the regime. But these efforts became stymied by a separate effort by director of local administration Chamnan Yuwabool to create a political party only for General Praphas. See "376. Research Memorandum from the Director of Intelligence and Research (Hughes) to Secretary of State Rusk", 19 January 1968, *FRUS*, https://history.state.gov/historicaldocuments/frus1964-68v27/d376.

74. Morell, *Power and Parliament*, pp. 121–22, 126.

75. "408. Memorandum of Conversation", 16 November 1968, *FRUS*, https://history.state.gov/historicaldocuments/frus1964-68v27/d408.

76. Ibid.

77. Clark Neher, "Thailand: The Politics of Continuity", *Asian Survey* 10, no. 2 (1970): 161, https://www.jstor.org/stable/2642249.

78. Ibid.

79. สุดยอดโรงแรมดังเมืองโคราช "ศรีพัฒนา"ประกาศขาย250ล้านเซ่นพิษโควิด [The most famous hotel in Korat "Sri Phatthana" announces the sale of 250 million due to the toxic effects of Covid-19], *Tan Setakit*, 21 August 2021, https://www.thansettakij.com/economy/492746.

80. "5. Telegram from the Embassy in Thailand to the Department of State", 11 March 1969, *FRUS*, https://history.state.gov/historicaldocuments/frus1969-76v20/d5.

81. Pasin Nuengchompoo, "บทบาททางการเมืองของผู้นำฝ่ายทหารกับฝ่ายพลเรือนในระบบรัฐสภา: ศึกษากรณีนายกรัฐมนตรีจอมพลถนอม กิตติขจร กับพลเอกชาติชาติ ชุณหะวัณ" [Political roles of military and civilian leaders in the parliamentary system: A case study of Prime Minister Thanom Kittikachorn and General Chatchat Chunhavan]. Bangkok: Ramkhamhaeng University, 2001.

82. Morell, *Power and Parliament*, p. 126.

83. Ibid., p. 181.

84. Somporn Sangchai, *Coalition Behaviour in Modern Thai Politics*: A Thai Perspective (Singapore: Institute of Southeast Asian Studies, 1976), p. 9.

85. Morell, *Power and Parliament*, pp. 207–10.

86. *Komchadluek*, ฟื้นสูตรลับ โมเดล "สีวะรา" พรรคทหาร-พรรคผี [Reviving the secret formula, model "Sivara", the military party – the ghost party], 6 November 2017, https://www.komchadluek.net/scoop/301285.

87. Clark Neher, "Thailand: Toward Fundamental Change", *Asian Survey* 11, no. 2 (1971): 131–33, https://www.jstor.org/stable/2642712.

88. ที่ระลึกในงานพระราชทานเพลิงศพ พลตำรวจเอก วิฑูรย์ ยะสวัสดิ์ เมรุวัดตรีทศเทพ [Commemorative volume from the cremation ceremony of Police General

Vitoon Yasawat, Tri Thotsathep Temple Crematorium], Bangkok, 17 February 1993.

89. "66. Backchannel Message from the Ambassador to Thailand (Unger) to the Under Secretary of State for Political Affairs (Johnson)", 21 May 1970, *FRUS*, https://history.state.gov/historicaldocuments/frus1969-76v20/d66; "102. Memorandum of Conversation", 15 December 1970, *FRUS*, https://history.state.gov/historicaldocuments/frus1969-76v20/d102.

90. National Security Advisor Henry Kissinger, "Telephone Conversation with Ron Ziegler", National Security Archive (George Washington University), 1 June 1970, https://nsarchive.gwu.edu/sites/default/files/documents/3474889/01-Telephone-conversation-with-Ron-Ziegler-1.pdf.

91. John Holdridge, United States National Security Council, "Memorandum for Dr. Kissinger", 17 June 1970, https://www.cia.gov/readingroom/docs/LOC-HAK-459-6-1-5.pdf.

92. UPI, "Thai Troops Reported Sent to Border with Cambodia", *New York Times*, 21 April 1970, https://www.nytimes.com/1970/04/22/archives/thai-troops-reported-sent-to-border-with-cambodia.html.

93. David Morell, "Thailand: Military Checkmate", *Asian Survey* 12, no. 2 (1972): 158–61.

94. Iver Peterson, "Thanom Gives His Reasons for Seizing Power by Coup in Thailand", *New York Times*, 20 November 1971, https://www.nytimes.com/1971/11/20/archives/thanom-gives-his-reasons-for-seizing-power-by-coup-in-thailand.html.

95. "120. Letter from the Ambassador to Thailand (Unger) to the Under Secretary of State for Political Affairs (Johnson)", 28 May 1971, *FRUS*, https://history.state.gov/historicaldocuments/frus1969-76v20/d120.

96. John Girling, *Thailand: Society and Politics* (Ithaca: Cornell University Press, 1981), p. 114.

97. Michael Mezey, "The 1971 Coup in Thailand: Understanding Why the Legislature Fails", *Asian Survey* 13, no. 3 (1973): 310–14.

98. Morell, "Thailand: Military Checkmate", p. 163.

99. Chris Baker and Pasuk Phongpaichit, *A History of Thailand* (Cambridge: Cambridge University Press, 2005), p. 186.

100. CIA, "Weekly Summary", 13 August 1971, https://www.cia.gov/readingroom/docs/CIA-RDP79-00927A009000030001-1.pdf.

101. CIA, "Thai Foreign Minister Thanat Criticizes US", White House Memorandum, 1 March 1971, https://www.cia.gov/readingroom/docs/LOC-HAK-12-3-8-6.pdf.

102. "141. Telegram from the Embassy in Thailand to the Department of State", 16 November 1971, *FRUS*, https://history.state.gov/historicaldocuments/frus1969-76v20/d141.

103. Mead, "The Cold War", p. 226.

104. Morell, "Thailand: Military Checkmate", p. 156.

105. "143. Memorandum from the President's Assistant for National Security Affairs (Kissinger) to President Nixon", 17 November 1971, *FRUS*, https://history.state.gov/historicaldocuments/frus1969-76v20/d143.

106. Kullada Kesbunchoo-Mead, "The Cold War", pp. 226–27.

107. "142. Telegram from the Embassy in Thailand to the Department of State", 17 November 1971. *FRUS*, https://history.state.gov/historicaldocuments/frus1969-76v20/d142.

108. Ibid.

109. Morell, "Thailand: Military Checkmate", p. 163.

110. Suchit Bunbongkarn, "Political Institutions and Processes", in *Government and Politics in Thailand*, edited by Somsakdi Xuto (New York: Oxford University Press, 1987), p. 50.

111. Morell, "Thailand: Military Checkmate", p. 163.

112. Ibid., pp. 163–64.

113. David Morell and Chai-anan Samudavanija, *Political Conflict in Thailand: Reform, Reaction, Revolution* (Cambridge, MA: Oelgeschlager, Gunn & Hain, 1981), p. 146.

114. See Tyrell Haberkorn, *Getting Away with Murder in Thailand: State Violence and Impunity in Phattalung* (Lexington: University Press of Kentucky, 2013).

115. อนุสรณ์ในงานพระราชทานเพลิงศพ จอมพล เกรียงไกร อัตตะนันทน์ ณ เมรุวัดเทพศิรินทราวาส [Memorial volume from the cremation ceremony of Field Marshal Kriengkrai Atthanand at Wat Thepsirintrawat Temple], Bangkok, 11 September 1973.

116. Veera Prateepchaikul, "The Praprass-Narong File", *Bangkok Post*, 28 October 1973, p. 3.

117. David Morell, "Thailand", *Asian Survey* 13, no. 2 (1973): 164, https://www.jstor.org/stable/2642733.

118. Ibid., p. 165.

119. CIA, "Central Intelligence Bulletin", no. 533, 25 March 1972, https://www.cia.gov/readingroom/docs/CIA-RDP85T00875R000800020069-3.pdf.

120. Ibid., p. 163.

121. "Ex-Chief of 11th Infantry Reinstated", *Bangkok Post*, 27 October 1973, p. 3.

122. Morell, "Thailand", pp. 176–77.

123. Frank Darling, "Student Protest and Political Change in Thailand", *Pacific Affairs* 47, no. 1 (1974): 10.

124. M. Rajaretnam, "The Thai Situation: Between Freedom and Authority", in *Southeast Asian Affairs 1974* (Singapore: Institute of Southeast Asian Studies, 1974), p. 307, https://www.jstor.org/stable/27908229.

125. Jeffrey Race, "Thailand 1973: 'We Certainly Have Been Ravaged by Something...'", *Asian Survey* 14, no. 2 (1974): 196, https://www.jstor.org/stable/2643093.

126. "1. Memorandum of Conversation, San Clemente", 10:05–11:30 a.m, 10 February 1973, *FRUS*, https://history.state.gov/historicaldocuments/frus1969-76ve12/d1.

127. "US Embassy Bangkok to Department of State", Airgram, 9 November 1973, ref: Bangkok A-243, 6-3-72.

128. Robert F. Zimmerman, "Reflections on the Collapse of Democracy in Thailand", Occasional Papers no. 50 (Singapore: Institute of Southeast Asian Studies, 1978), p. 50.

129. US Embassy Bangkok to Department of State, "Defense Minister Dawee's Comments on Military Command Structure, Students, and Thanom", 2 November 1973, WikiLeaks, 1973BANGKO17153_b, https://wikileaks.org/plusd/cables/1973BANGKO17153_b.html.

130. Cited in Mead, "The Cold War", p. 231.

131. Morell and Chai-anan, *Political Conflict*, p. 148.

132. "Evaluation of New Senior Military Appointments", United States Department of State, 21 September 1973, WikiLeaks, 1973BANGKO14822_b, https://wikileaks.org/plusd/cables/1973BANGKO14822_b.html.

133. "New Army Commander in Chief Named", *CIA Bulletin*, 12 September 1973, p. 9, https://www.cia.gov/library/readingroom/docs/CIA-RDP79T00975A025200090001-2.pdf.

134. *Komchadleuk*, "เรื่องเล่า '14 ตุลา' ฉบับใต้ดิน [The underground story of '14 October']", 3 March 2020, https://www.komchadluek.net/news/scoop/420284.

135. "Document about 6 October: 6. Military Groups or the Governing Bodies of the Land" (in Thai), 2018, https://doct6.com/learn-about/how/chapter-6.

136. Morell, "Thailand", p. 163n3.

137. Zimmerman, *Reflections on the Collapse*, pp. 49–53.

138. Kriangkrai died mysteriously in a helicopter crash in 1972. Though there were rumours that Thanom and Praphas might have assassinated Kriangkrai, such a plan is questionable given the close kinship and financial interests between the Jarusatien and Attanand families, which have lasted until today. See *Isra News*, "46 ปี 14 ต.ค.ส่องธุรกิจทายาท 'กิตติขจร-จารุเสถียร' ที่ยังหลงเหลือ?" [46 years, 14 October shining on the heir business. The remaining 'Kittikachorn-Charusatien'?], 15 October 2019, https://isranews.org/isranews/81516-isranewss-81516.html.

139. Morell, "Thailand", p. 163n3.

140. Assuming that Thanom's son-in-law Uerm was promoted each year, he would have become army chief in 1976, after a brief 1975–76 posting of uncharismatic General Chote Hiranyathiti (assistant army chief in 1973) or General Bunchai Bamrungpong (army chief of staff in 1973) as army commander (the two had to retire in 1976). In 1977, Uerm could have stepped aside to allow Narong Kittikachorn to assume the post as army chief when the latter had likewise been steadily promoted to this senior

level. Another potential proxy for Thanom/Praphas was 1st Army Region commander General Prasert Thammasiri, who could have been posted as army commander in 1975.

141. "Letter from the Ambassador to Thailand (Unger) to the Assistant Secretary of State for East Asian and Pacific Affairs (Green)", 19 April 1971, *FRUS*, https://history.state.gov/historicaldocuments/frus1969-76v20/d115.

142. Akira Suehiro, "Capitalist Development in Postwar Thailand: Commercial Bankers, Industrial Elite, and Agribusiness Groups", in *Southeast Asian Capitalists*, edited by Ruth McVey (Ithaca: Cornell University Press, 1992), p. 50.

143. Data provided by MP Thammanun Thiengngern (Democrat, Bangkok) to David Morell. See Morell, *Power and Parliament*, pp. 1004–30; "โรงแรม ศรีพัฒนา" ปิดกิจการ [Sri Pattana Hotel closes upon the advent of Covid], *Tan Settakij*, เซ่นพิษโควิดอีกราย, 8 October 2020, https://www.thansettakij.com/economy/452027.

144. Sungsidh Piriyangsan, "Thai Bureaucratic Capitalism, 1932–1960" (MA thesis, Thammasat University, 1980), pp. 223–28; Morell, *Power and Parliament*, pp. 1002–3.

145. Morell, *Power and Parliament*, p. 1003.

146. *Thai Post*, 21 October 1999, pp. 28–30, cited in Tanapong Chitsanga, "Political Roles and Challenges of Monarchy and the Royally Appointed Prime Minister Sanya Dharmasakti from 1973 to 1975" (Doctoral thesis, Waseda University, 2020), p. 88n224.

147. Cited in Handley, *The King Never Smiles*, p. 211.

148. Joseph Wright, *The Balancing Act: A History of Modern Thailand* (Oakland, CA: Pacific Rim, 1991), p. 206

149. "ลอกคราบ 14 ตุลา ดักแด้ประวัติศาสตร์ พันเอกณรงค์ กิตติขจร", 9 March 2014, https://www.youtube.com/watch?app=desktop&v=NNZY52rGZgw.

150. Vitoon also revealed that these volunteers were so deeply involved in the covert anti-communist war in Laos that the US government had been secretly sending 2,520 million baht annually to the Thai government. Cable from US Embassy in Bangkok to the secretary of state, "Thai Press on Thai SGUs", 20 November 1973, WikiLeaks, 1973BANGKO18046_b, https://wikileaks.org/plusd/cables/1973BANGKO18046_b.html.

151. US Embassy (Bangkok) to US secretary of state Henry Kissinger, "Gen. Vithoon on Thai Volunteers in Laos", 24 November 1973, WikiLeaks, 1973BANGKO18295_b, https://wikileaks.org/plusd/cables/1973BANGKO18295_b.html.

152. US Embassy (Bangkok) to US secretary of state Henry Kissinger, "Military Capabilities in Laos", 9 January 1974, Wikileaks, 1974VIENTI00186_b, https://wikileaks.org/plusd/cables/1974VIENTI00186_b.html.

153. US Embassy (Vientiane) to US secretary of state Henry Kissinger, "Thai Volunteers", 26 March 1973, WikiLeaks, 1973VIENTI02208_b, https://wikileaks.org/plusd/cables/1973VIENTI02208_b.html.

154. US Embassy (Bangkok) to US secretary of state Henry Kissinger, "Lao Weekly SITREP— March 27", 27 March 1974, WikiLeaks, 1974VIENTI02469_b, http://wikileaks.org/plusd/cables/1974VIENTI02469_b.html.

155. Ajay Singh and Julian Gearing, "The Murky Events of October 1973", *Asiaweek*, 28 January 2000, http://webcache.googleusercontent.com/search?q=cache:fQ9WANJzXyEJ:www.cnn.com/ASIANOW/asiaweek/magazine/2000/0128/as.thai.history1.html+&cd=1&hl=en&ct=clnk&gl=us.

156. Ibid., "I Didn't Order the Shooting", *Asiaweek*, 29 January 2000, http://webcache.googleusercontent.com/search?q=cache:hRwXe2ljhswJ:www.cnn.com/ASIANOW/asiaweek/magazine/2000/0128/as.thai.history2.html+&cd=1&hl=en&ct=clnk&gl=th.

157. L.B. Smith to P.J. Gregory Hood, Foreign Commonwealth Office (UK), "The Drivers Fled the Scene", 26 October 1973, 15/1784, UKNA. Also cited in Mead, "The Cold War", p. 233, notes 103 and 107.

158. C.W. Squire to Youde, "Situation in Thailand", 17 October 1973, Foreign Commonwealth Office (UK), 15/1784.

159. Cited in Mead, "The Cold War", p. 240.

160. Ibid., p. 234.

161. See Thepmontree Limpopayaum, 30 ปี 14 ตุลาฯ-ข้อกล่าวหาที่ไม่สิ้นสุด-พันเอก ณรงค์ กิตติขจร [30 years, 14 October – unending allegations – Colonel Narong Kittikachorn] (Bangkok: Thepmontree Limpopayayaum, 2003).

162. *Far Eastern Economic Review*, 22 October 1973, p. 17, cited in Wright, *The Balancing Act*, p. 209.

163. Ruth-Inge Heinze, "10 Days in October—Students vs. the Military: An Account of the Student Uprising in Thailand", *Asian Survey* 14, no. 6 (1974): 502, http://www.jstor.org/stable/2642679.

164. Tanapong Chitsanga, "Political Roles and Challenges of Monarchy and the Royally Appointed Prime Minister Sanya Dharmasakti from 1973 to 1975" (Doctoral thesis, Waseda University, 2020), pp. 346–47.

165. Heinze, "10 Days in October", p. 504.

166. Suchit Bunbongkarn, *The Military in Thai Politics, 1981–1986* (Singapore: Institute of Southeast Asian Studies, 1987), p. 17.

167. Kevin Hewison, "The 1976 Thai Coup and Reflections on the Analysis of Recent Coups", unpublished manuscript, April 1977, p. 17, https://kevinhewison.files.wordpress.com/2011/02/hewison-1977.pdf.

168. Achara Ashayagachat, "Few Crisis Lessons Learned, *Bangkok Post*, 3 October 2016, https://www.bangkokpost.com/thailand/politics/1100897/few-crisis-lessons-learned.

169. Thongchai Winichakul, "Toppling Democracy", *Journal of Contemporary Asia* 38, no. 1 (2008): 20, https://doi.org/10.1080/00472330701651937.

Chapter Six

Krit Sivara and the 6 October Massacre (1973–76)

From 1973 until 1976, General Krit Sivara was the most powerful person in Thailand—politically, militarily and economically.[1] From entering Cadet School in 1931, he—like Roman emperor Claudius—had, in the background, outlasted all other military strongmen before him: Phraya Phahon, Phibun, Phin, Sarit, Thanom and Praphas. Indeed, Krit was more powerful than Thanom and Praphas because they had depended upon each other. Krit had come from a military family (see Figure 6.1).

In 1973, Krit was also more powerful than the king; though Krit declared his loyalty to King Bhumipol, he controlled the monopoly on state violence and the king's guards, and he was wealthier than the palace. Though the legitimacy of monarchical endorsement was important for Krit, he possessed a competing ideology, given his stature as the saviour of Thai democratization and the king alike. Thus, despite swearing allegiance to the monarchy, early on Krit already appeared to be a potential danger to the king. Other senior military officers at the time had either been tarnished through their association with Thanom, Praphas or Narong (e.g., General Aat Sasiprapha), were junior to Krit (General Bunchai Bamrungpong and General Prasert Thammasiri), had retired (Thanom, Praphas, General Prasert Rujirawong and General Kruan Sutaninot), had not served in the all-important army (e.g., ACM Thawee Chulasap and Admiral Sangad Chaloryu) or were dead (General Kriengkrai Attanand).[2]

FIGURE 6.1
Krit Sivara Family Tree

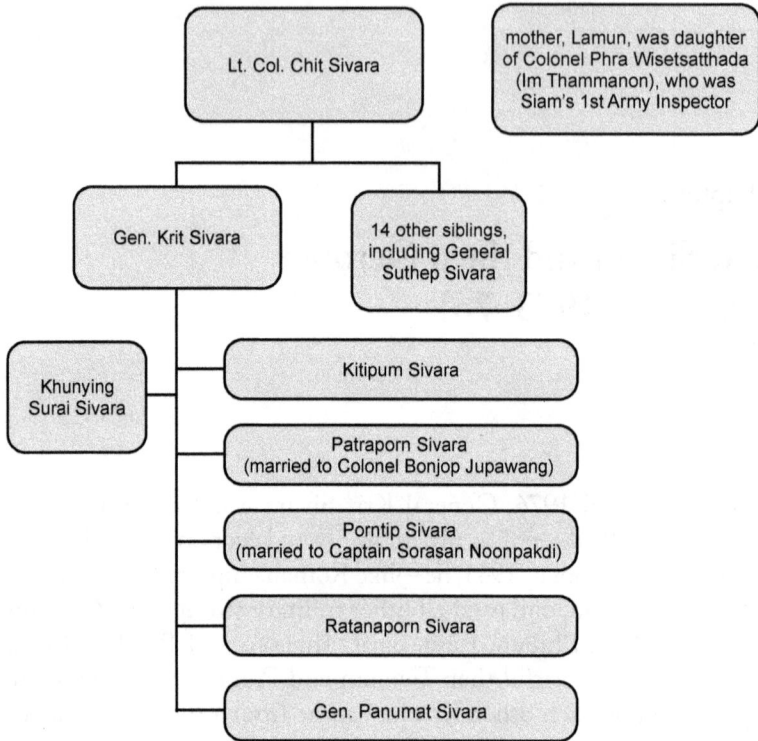

According to some, Krit saw himself merely as the "peace-keeper" successor to Thanom and Praphas, viewing 14 October 1973 "as an opportunity" to be used as an "advantage".[3] In fact, from 1973 until his death in 1976, rumour-mongers constantly speculated that Krit was planning the "reinstatement of dictatorship through a second coup".[4] As post-1973 events transpired, however, Krit turned out to be that rare military strongman who sought to preserve elected governance. With Thanom's departure, Krit immediately proved himself to be an adept military commander. To prevent potential coups from below, he kept his forces under control through a policy of division. As one observer put it, "the army is too divided to think about a coup".[5] Thus, military unity depended upon Krit alone. Nevertheless, with such a policy, should Krit die suddenly, it would exacerbate military division in Thailand, which is precisely what happened in 1976.

Krit also commenced a wholesale leadership purge of the armed forces and police, transferring officials thought to be Thanom/Praphas/Narong loyalists to powerless postings. Thawee was promoted to the position of supreme commander, serving simultaneously as defence minister in Sanya's cabinet. Thereupon, General Surakit Mayalarp became deputy supreme commander, General Prachuab Suntarangkul replaced Praphas as police chief, and General Vitoon Yasawat became deputy police chief.[6] On 19 October, Admiral Sangad Chaloryu was appointed as naval chief. ACM Kamon Dechatungkha had already been appointed air force commander. As such, all of the key security leadership positions were filled with supporters of Krit. Others favourites that Krit promoted included his right-hand man General Bunchai Bamrungpong,[7] General Serm na Nakorn and General Kriangsak Chomanand (in Supreme Command). Indeed, throughout Krit's tenure as army chief, he sought to promote military loyalists while balancing off those factions that rivalled his own.

Sanya was initially quite a popular prime minister. But though sincere, he had little talent or interest in being a premier. He began by making Krit his director in charge of safeguarding peace and order, though Krit refused to accept any cabinet postings, such as the minister of defence (that position was thus allocated to Thawee). Sanya appointed his cabinet on 15 October.[8] Of its 28 members, 9 were military officials (32.1 per cent), a figure not so much smaller than that of Thanom's final cabinet: 13 out of 29 (44.8 per cent). The accomplishments of his government included taking action against malfeasance by Thanom, Praphas and Narong, and Operation "Palace Lightening", which was his order for US troops to begin withdrawing from Thailand. Sanya also oversaw in 1974 the drafting of a new constitution and preparations for a general election, which occurred in 1975. Though there were many variants of constitutions from which the country could choose, the king preferred a charter akin to Thailand's constitution of 1949, which expanded royal power. Krit's preferences for the new constitution were that it should incrementally allow for more democracy: after ten years, the entire legislature would be elected.[9]

Perhaps reflecting the trend of a less powerful, popular military, a new Senate began to function in 1975 devoid of the traditionally tremendous influence of soldiers (see Figure 6.2).

Two weeks after Thanom's departure from Thailand, Krit informed US officials that in fact there had been "no communist influence to any significant degree" in the October protests, but rather that "the fracas" between police and students close to the palace had started because

FIGURE 6.2
Thailand's Senate, 1975–76

Type of legislature	Years in office	Appointed or elected	Total number of senators and military contingent
Bicameral (Fourth Senate)	1975–76 (terminated by military coup)	Appointed	100, of which 17 (17%) retired military reserved domain)

Source: Paul Chambers, "Superfluous, Irrelevant or Emancipating: Thailand's Evolving Senate Today", *Journal of Current Southeast Asian Affairs* 28, no. 3 (2009): 9, https://d-nb.info/999559311/34.

there was "fear for the king's safety since some of the students had been disrespectful toward His Majesty". Krit stressed his allegiance to the monarch and support for Sanya.[10]

Krit also told US officials that he had informed Prime Minister Sanya that there should be no more field marshals and no Supreme Command, given that the king is the only supreme commander.[11] He moreover transformed the Communist Suppression Operations Command (CSOC)—which changed its name to the Internal Security Operations Command (ISOC) in 1974—from being under army control to being under the authority of the prime minister. Krit made this move because he respected General Saiyud Kerdphol's acumen in counter-insurgency, promoting him in 1974 to become chief of staff for the supreme commander (who was Krit himself).[12] But because of long and close ties by CSOC/ISOC to the Supreme Command and to Saiyud himself, the Supreme Command held enormous sway over ISOC.

In November, as Sanya was initiating a series of "Meet the People" television programmes, Krit publicly proclaimed that "soldiers would be the 'tools of the government' no matter who the Prime Minister and Defense Minister might be".[13] By December, however, many top military leaders felt that the Sanya government was hopelessly inept, and that a return to "a more prominent military role" was "inevitable". 1st Army Region commander Prasert Thammasiri, who would soon become a perennial supporter of potential coups, especially pressed his friend Krit to adopt a firmer military position. But Krit apparently restrained Prasert and other generals from ousting the government and publicly reaffirmed his endorsement of Sanya's premiership. Nevertheless, he seemed to have informed the armed forces to be ready to take action if increased labour or student unrest returned.[14] At the same time, he declared that there would be no coup, "advocated a system of 'mild socialism'" for Thailand (which worried Washington) and said he agreed with (Thammasat University rector) Dr Puey Ungphakorn, who had suggested that all military units depart from Bangkok.[15] Krit surely realized that 1973 was not the time for a military putsch; amidst the fall of the unpopular Thanom regime and public anger about action by security forces against student demonstrators, the public image of the military was far too tainted.

At a December 1973 press conference, Krit was questioned as to whether he would allow Thanom, Praphas and Narong to return to Thailand any time soon. He replied that the farther away they were from Thailand, "the better it will be". Should they return, "all three would be arrested.... The amnesty does not include these three persons." A question from another reporter demonstrated that it was becoming necessary for leaders to be careful in their use of language. The reporter asked what Prime Minister Sanya had meant when he said previously that increasing violence might make it necessary to engage in "surgery", and would Sanya utilize the military? Krit responded in the negative, saying that the prime minister, as "surgeon", could use the minister of the interior as an alternative, but would resort to "mild medicines" first, only later perhaps moving on to "stricter measures". Finally, Krit stated that though he would not join any political party and had no interest in politics, he feared that the next general election would be "dangerous".[16]

Also in December 1973, four Thai colonels (known only as Prasong, Prasert, Pachon and Pravieng) visited Montreal, Canada, shopping for military equipment and expertise. One of the colonels opined that following the creation of a civilian government and amidst continuing left-wing student demonstrations in Thailand, "This situation can't go on for too much longer … there may be a coup d'état soon."[17]

Krit's often quiet nature completely puzzled the US Embassy, which urgently sought to learn how he viewed Thai-US relations. In mid-January 1974, Krit told US deputy chief of mission William Kintner that Thailand still wanted and needed US military advisors to continue working with Thai soldiers in insurgency zones at the regimental level. Speaking in English, Krit looked at Kintner and said, "We need democracy and we need your help."[18]

The following week, Kintner held a formal dinner for Krit. Krit indicated to Kintner that the king was unhappy with Sanya's leadership and, following the next election, singled out M.R. Kukrit Pramoj, owner of newspaper *Siam Rath*, as Sanya's most likely successor, followed by Thammasat University rector Puey Ungphakhorn and Democrat Party leader M.R. Seni Pramoj (Kukrit's brother). Krit's selections are interesting because Kukrit, Seni and Puey indeed played major roles in Thailand's politics of 1973 to 1976. Queried on whether General Prasert Ruchirawong would enter politics, Krit stated that he had recently told Prasert not to form a political party. On the question of a potential army coup, Krit "acknowledged that there were hotheads in the army, but he had been telling them to keep cool". While Kintner concluded that Krit supported the king unwaveringly, in retrospect, what was equally fascinating was that Krit said he might enter politics after he retired in October 1975.[19]

On 27 March 1974, Krit told US diplomats privately that though Sanya had been thinking about resigning from the premiership because of the pressures of the job, the latter needed to make the decision by 15 April. Krit stressed, however, that although Sanya was a weak leader, if he resigned there were few alternatives. As for himself, he would not assume the premiership since he needed to concentrate on his job of maintaining law and order. Krit did warn that "a lot of junior officers" were upset at the political pandemonium, but he had told them that the time for any action was "not yet ripe". There would be no coup because the military "would be running things but not occupying the top positions". This reflected Krit's preference to dominate politics from the shadows.[20]

By 15 April, Sanya had still not decided on his political future, and political nervousness was becoming increasingly palpable. During 19–22 April, the drumbeats of coup rumours intensified, propelled by the frustrations of younger officers with Sanya's seeming ineptitude. But perhaps this restlessness was only a smokescreen for Krit: rumour had it that he had "decided to lead them in taking over control of the government [but would only] act with the tacit consent of the king". Krit did jokingly tell journalists in March that if a coup "takes place, he will be the first to inform them".[21] But the continuing chaotic atmosphere forced Krit on 26 April to state "point blank that there … would be no coup".[22]

Despite the absence of coups, instability in the cabinet had been growing since Sanya began governing in October 1973. On 21 May, he finally resigned, alongside his twenty-eight-member cabinet. Following the resignation, Krit issued a nationwide military alert, which he stated was merely a "precautionary measure and not a preparation for a coup".[23] By the end of May, after speaking with both the king and

Krit, Sanya had returned, with a thirty-person cabinet, which contained only one active military officer. In the post of defence minister, retired general Khruan Suthinan was substituted for ACM Thawee. This move appeared to be an attempt to locate someone who was not disliked by student protestors but who was also senior to Thawee. The appointment also weakened Thawee's powerbase. Though Krit and Thawee were friends, the loss of power for Thawee as a potential competitor was undoubtedly something that Krit had "desire[d]".[24] Khruan had previously served under Sarit as army chief of staff and was close to Krit. Meanwhile, to fill the posts of the two deputy ministers of defence, Sanya selected Admiral Thavil Keyanon and ACM Bua Sirithip, who were also close to Krit. With the endorsement of Krit, Khruan immediately nixed Thawee's plan to abolish the post of supreme commander of the armed forces and replace the Supreme Command Headquarters with a Department of Joint Chiefs of Staff headed by a chief of staff who would serve as a mere advisor to the civilian minister of defence.[25] While the May reshuffle enhanced Krit's power in the cabinet, he had also that same month become the official director of ISOC while remaining army chief and director of peace and order. He reported to the king but was the informal patron of Thailand.

Krit did not have to wait long to impose order. During the first week of July 1974, riots erupted on Phlapphla Chai Road in Bangkok's Chinatown and quickly spread to other areas of the city. Following Krit's advice, Sanya declared a state of emergency. Thereupon, Krit sent soldiers and police in to suppress the rioters.[26] Ultimately, the chaos resulted in at least 26 people killed and 120 injured. During that night, Krit informed US ambassador Kintner that he had personally acted in his peacekeeping authority to restore order and was not engaging in a coup. Kintner saw this message as clear evidence of close relations between Krit and Washington.[27]

In September 1974, Krit told the US Embassy that vocational school students—not university students—had borne the brunt of the repression during 14–15 October 1973 and they resented university student leaders claiming to speak for them since most vocational students did not endorse the continuing agitation by these leaders. He added that there are not only more vocational school students, but they are also "tougher" than university students. Moreover, the youth groups had in 1974 become "fragmented". US ambassador Kintner thereupon noted to Washington that "We would not totally rule out the possibility that [Krit] has more than an academic interest in [these vocational students'] activities."[28] The United States, however, already had an interest in right-wing extremist groups—of which vocational students became a part. The major ones—the Red Gaurs, Luksuea Chaobaan and Nawaphon—worked closely with and were organized by CSOC, which had been established in 1965 on advice from the then US ambassador, the CIA and the US "Special Group".[29] The CIA allegedly gave the Red Gaurs and Nawaphon US$12.5 million in start-up money.[30]

Turning to the groups themselves, since mid-1974, under orders from ISOC, Colonel Sudsai Hasdin had already begun training vocational students and dropouts to join the ultra-rightist militia the Red Gaurs.[31] The Red Gaurs was also composed of former or off-duty soldiers and police as well as migrant unemployed people. Sudsai's funding and involvement with the Red Gaurs was so intensive that its members referred to him as "Dad". Metropolitan police permitted the Red Gaurs to use police equipment.[32] Sudsai's son Suebsai Hasdin was also a Red Gaurs leader, as was Praphan Wongkham. Another Red Gaurs group was controlled by General Vitoon Yasawat, while still another was under General Chatchai Chunhavan.[33]

Another right-wing vigilante group was called Luksuea Chaobaan (Village Scouts). It was founded in August 1971 by General Somkhuan Harikul and his deputy General Charoenrit Chamratsomron of Thailand's Border Patrol Police (BPP) as an anti-communist counter-insurgency arm.[34] Under CSOC, it expanded rapidly during the early 1970s under the direction of General Suraphon Chulabrahm (BPP commander, 1971–75). And by 1974, tens of thousands of rural men had been recruited into the Village Scouts.[35]

Still another rightist group that attracted disillusioned vocational students was Nawaphon (Ninth Power). Established by ISOC in August 1974, this group was even more sinister than the Red Gaurs given that though it formally specialized in psychological operations it also conducted political assassinations. Its fifteen-member executive board included senior active-duty and retired military officials, right-wing Buddhist monks and ideologues (Figure 6.3). Its ideological leader, Wattana Kieowvimol, claimed to be connected to US secretary of state Henry Kissinger and the CIA. General Krit never publicly supported or criticized Nawaphon, though most military leaders "tacitly approve[d] of" it.[36] Nevertheless the armed forces leaders were leery of police becoming too influential within the grouping.

Meanwhile, on 2 October 1974, just prior to a royal cremation ceremony honouring the heroes who had died on 14 October 1973, Sanya received a letter from a Thammasat University administrator

FIGURE 6.3
Known Members of Nawaphon Leadership, 1974–78

1.	Chair	General Wanlop Rotchanawisut`	Former director, Armed Forces Intelligence Operations Command (AFIOC), 1961–74
2.	Executive Coordinator	General Chamniam Phongphairot	Director (AFIOC), 1974–?
3.	Member	Sot Kuramarohit	Writer
4.	Member	Colonel Sudsai Hasdin	An army officer under ISOC and founder of the Red Gaurs
5.	Member and chief ideologue	Wattana Kiowvimol`	Civilian employee and advisor of ISOC
6.	Member	Suraphon Chulabrahm	Border Patrol Police chief and founder of Village Scouts
7.	Member	General Samran Pattayakula	Former assistant army commander, privy councillor (1975–86)
8.	Member	Tanin Kravichien	A Supreme Court judge and later prime minister (1976–77)
9.	Member	Phra Kittiwutho	An ultra-right-wing Buddhist monk
10.	Member	General Saiyud Kerdpol	ISOC director (1974–78)

Source: United States Embassy (Bangkok) to US Secretary of State Henry Kissinger, "New Strength (Navaphon)", 2 September 1975, Wikileaks, 1975BANGKO18375_b, https://wikileaks.org/plusd/cables/1975BANGKO18375_b.html.

revealing the reasons for the sudden resignation of Professor Adul Wichiencharoen, interim rector, on 27 September. The letter mentioned that a student at Thammasat University had told Adul that Thammasat University Student Union (TUSU) president Wichit Srisang was phoned by General Krit to alert him that deputy police commander General Vitoon Yasawat and 1st Army Region commander General Prasert Thammasiri had created a group of vocational student "toughs" who would use physical force in opposing TUSU's progressive demonstrations.[37] The "group" established by Vitoon and Prasert likely included the Village Scouts, Red Gaurs, Nawaphon or all three.

Ultimately, the 1974 constitution was approved by the legislature and promulgated on 7 October 1974. On 1 October 1974, Krit Sivara took up another post in addition to that of army commander and ISOC head: supreme commander of the Royal Thai Armed Forces. His deputy supreme commander was his old friend General Surakit Mayalarp. The reshuffle also brought ACM Kamon Dechatungkha to be chief of the Royal Thai Air Force, while Sangad Chaloryu continued on as navy commander. Both were close to Krit. Among the remaining top five army slots (deputy, chief of staff and assistants) and three army regional commands, army officers trusted or mostly trusted by Krit held command postings. These included Bunchai Bamrungpong as deputy commander, Serm na Nakorn as army chief of staff and Chote Hiranyatthiti as army assistant commander. Then there was the king's favourite, Samran Patiyakul, as the other assistant army commander, while the charismatic Prem Tinsulanond (who was rapidly becoming known to the palace for his counter-insurgency skills) as 2nd Army Region commander (Prem was partly a junior member of Krit's faction). Prasert Thammasiri, trusted by Krit, continued on as 1st Army Region commander. Less trusted but an able commander was Yot Thepsadin na Ayuthaya, who became 3rd Army Region chief. This reshuffle of the armed forces once again solidified Krit's military dominance far above any other officer. Given the leftist bent of university students and the instability in Asia at the time, Thailand's rightist-led democracy and the king needed Krit more than he needed them.

Though Krit likely thought that his control over Thai domestic actors was now supreme, two months later, Thanom suddenly returned to Bangkok, ostensibly to visit his ailing father, who was eighty-nine years old, but more likely to test the waters regarding Krit's support among the Thai military. When Thanom initially made the request to return, the king met to discuss the matter with Sanya, Krit, police commander General Prachuab and police deputy General Vitoon. The monarch approved Thanom's request to return but realized that much of Thai civil society (as well as anti-Thanom military elements) were not content. On 28 November, the king was again briefed by his top advisors and decided to support Sanya in forbidding Thanom to return. It appeared, however, as though Thanom might return anyway. On 27 December, the Office of the Prime Minister announced that if Thanom tried to return to Thailand, he would be arrested and put on trial for his role in the events of 14 October 1973. Unexpectedly, Thanom returned home anyway, arriving in the early morning hours. Faced with this fait accompli, the government announced it would apprehend him. The Peace Keeping Committee led by General Krit gave its support to the cabinet resolution. But Krit and the other military service commanders were at the time abroad on a goodwill tour visiting other Southeast Asian countries—a fact that undoubtedly played in the decision by Thanom to return at that time. Nevertheless, university students quickly responded to news of Thanom's return by filing a complaint with local police accusing Thanom of murder and malfeasance. Others began to demonstrate frantically. Even though Krit and King Bhumipol backed the Sanya government, the ISOC-organized Red Gaurs goons, in support of Thanom, attacked the protesting students, throwing "bottle bombs" at them.[38] Sources indicated that Thanom was residing in Thailand at the home of his ally ACM Bunchu Chandrubeksa (air force commander from 1960 to 1974) and was protected by soldiers who supported him. In fact, it appeared that Bunchu (who had served under Thanom in 1971 as deputy defence minister) had been instrumental in receiving Thanom at the airport, arranging for his communications with Sanya and for his personal security.[39] At Bunchu's residence, Thanom talked about entering the monkhood, thus prolonging his stay in Thailand. Thanom's return home even provoked the National Assembly into debate. The cabinet now realized that national pandemonium over Thanom would only dissipate if he left the country. It thus moved to expel him from Thailand immediately. But attempting to do so might provoke disputes with senior army officials such as General Yot Thepsadin na Ayuthaya (3rd Army Region commander) or perhaps General Prasert Thammasiri (then commanding the strategic 1st Army Region), who might support Thanom's remaining in Thailand. Only after Krit finally returned to Thailand on 29 December did Thanom leave the country for Singapore. Following Krit's arrival, his trusted associates deputy army chief General Bunchai Bamrungpong and army chief of staff General Serm na Nakorn hustled Thanom and his wife to Don Muang airport for departure back to the United States. Krit did not accompany them. Krit undoubtedly saw Thanom's presence "as a potential threat to his influence over the military, from which he had been trying to purge Thanom's proteges over the past year".[40] Ultimately, the 1974 Thanom incident demonstrated that Krit's control over the country was not entirely secure.

But Krit's control over Thai counter-insurgency policy was secure. On 23 January 1975, Sanya approved Krit's ISOC-sponsored "Aw Paw Paw" (APP) Plan—"the Village Volunteers and Self-Development Programme (VVSDP)". Although formally under the prime minister and the army commander as national director, the VVSDP called for the consolidation of all paramilitary and pro-government militia organizations under one programme umbrella. General Krit Sivara would be the national VVSDP director, and General Saiyud Kerdpol his deputy. The entire network was to be under army officers.[41] Krit's counter-insurgency policies were thus not only about people's hearts and minds, but also involved repression, as investigators were soon to discover.

By the end of 1974, whilst Krit had talked up the possibilities of his becoming an elected MP, he appeared to prioritize reaching retirement in 1975 before doing so. At a meeting with General Sant Chitpatima, the latter had told US deputy chief of mission Masters that Krit "likes politics" and that Krit "already has [a political party]. Other people are running it for him." Sant stated that Krit had devised a way to constitutionally become prime minister:

> Sant's scenario: January 1975 elections are inconclusive, and eventually a weak coalition regime begins to govern. Problems are too great, however, and regime is unable to take strong stand on inflation, labor unrest, students, etc. Military looks on benignly— 'we intend to play by the rules' (meaning no coups)—but maintains minimal law and order. Mass of political parties begins to coalesce in mid-summer with one faction favoring accession by Krit (most likely ex-government MPs now spread over several parties). By August–September public is dissatisfied by lack of strong leadership and yearns for man on white horse. October 1 sees Krit retire and announce a la De Gaulle that he will be available to run for Prime Minister if nation needs him. New elections called for, which Krit easily wins, and Thai-style fourth republic disappears.[42]

As events were to unfold in 1975, General Sant appeared to be quite prescient. By January 1975, with a general election on the near horizon, party politics were emerging in earnest. Prime Minister Sanya had tried to resign many times, and only the appeals of King Bhumipol and Krit had convinced him to stay on to oversee the January 1975 poll.

Approximately forty-two parties had prepared for the election, but there were really only four groups with any chance: the Democrats, then led by professorial royalist civilian M.R. Seni Pramoj; Social Action, led by Seni's brother, the mercurial and witty M.R. Kukrit Pramoj; the ultra-right-wing Chart Thai (Thai Nation), led by military faction Soi Rajakru (through its new leaders, retired general Pramarn Adireksan[43] and retired general Chatchai Chunhavan[44]); and a group of parties organized under General Krit Sivara. Chart Thai was associated with active-duty generals Chalard Hiranyasiri and Saiyud Kerdphol.

Krit's political parties were connected with ACM Thawee Chulasap, deputy army commander Bunchai Bamrungpong and retired police chief General Prasert Rujirawong, who had worked together since their days leading the 1969–71 United Thai People's Party (UTPP). The cliques of Pramarn and Krit competed against each other to dominate both parliament and the military—if need be through a putsch.[45]

Krit's faction was thus an ambiguous "right wing clique which competed with [Chart Thai]", which, claiming to be a "new breed" of apolitical professional officers, sponsored multiple MP candidates.[46] Indeed, Krit, who had remained in contact with former UTTP MPs since his days as the whip of the UTTP party, reportedly financed approximately a hundred candidates for election who were members of various parties, including Free Nation, Social Justice, Social Nationalists, Social Agrarian and even the Socialist Party (three members).[47] Another party that he financed was the small Thai Party. Given that Krit had served in the 1969 election as deputy secretary-general, whip and a chief manager of finance for UTTP, he held sway over these four parties when they had been factions within the UTTP. In fact, he maintained close personal ties with Social Justice Party leader Tawich Klinpratum,[48] Social Nationalists Party leader Prasit Kanchanawat,[49] Social Agrarian Party leader Sawet Piempongsarn,[50] and Chart Thai's Pramarn Adireksan, Chatchai Chunhavan and Siri Siriyothin.[51] Through Prasit, Krit was also close to Sino-Thai industrialist Boonchu Rojanasatien and Chin Soponpanich, president of Bangkok Bank. Finally, Krit was close with Pong Sarasin, who had co-founded the Social Action Party along with M.R. Kukrit Pramoj. Krit's association with Boonchu, Chin and Pong gave him "a bridge" to Kukrit.[52]

In the end, the 26 January 1975 election led to 108 MPs (out of the 269 National Assembly seats) being controlled by pro-military parties, with 80 of that number having been financed by Krit: Social Justice (45), Social Agrarian (18) and Social Nationalists (16). The remaining 28 were from Chart Thai. Krit also financed three Socialist Party MPs and four Thai Party MPs.[53]

The election failed to result in a solid victory for any single party. The Democrats, with 72 seats, could claim a plurality but would have to build a coalition of other parties to achieve a majority of at least 135 out of 269 seats to obtain a stable government. Though Krit's Social Justice Party claimed the second-highest number of winning seats (45), he could not count on all the parties he had financed to ally with Social Justice. On 13 February, the National Assembly initially selected Democrat Party leader Seni Pramoj as prime minister and formally asked him to form a government, even though the pro-military parties tried to buy MP supporters away from Seni. Nevertheless, Krit managed to ensure the selection of Prasit Kanchanawat as Speaker of the National Assembly (the price for the Social Nationalists to later do Krit's bidding). Krit was worried that the Democrats might weaken the military budget or other military interests. Though his parties had not been victorious in the election, he realized that the Democrats would similarly find it difficult to form a government. Thus, Krit sponsored Chart Thai's Chatchai Chunhavan as Seni's coalition opponent.[54] In the end, Seni put together a minority coalition with only the Democrats and Sawet's Social Agrarian Party, together 91 MPs. He did try to mollify Krit by choosing Krit's preference as defence minister—General Thawit Seniwong na Ayutthaya. This was not enough, however, especially since the coalition was not welcomed by either the king or the ultra-rights.[55] On 1 March, Krit visited the king in Chiangmai to discover that the latter was appalled at Seni's centre-liberal coalition. On 6 March, the Democrats lost in a confidence vote of 152 to 111 against the government. Voting was by secret ballot, "a maneuver engineered by the conservatives to ensure the buying of votes".[56]

Among the alternatives to Seni, "several key army generals, including ... Krit" came to support Kukrit Pramoj of the Social Action Party.[57] This owed to several reasons. First, though the next smallest party after the Democrats with the next right to form a coalition was Krit's Social Justice Party, the party's leader, Tawich Klinpratum, was not an elected MP so he did not have the legal right to become prime minister. Though Chart Thai was third in line to form a coalition, Krit preferred a more controllable government than one led by Pramarn Adireksan or Chatchai Chunhavan. Thus, as an alternative, "Krit ... intervened to exercise a commanding role in designating the next Prime Minister.... Krit's reported choice was Khukrit Pramot."[58] The reasons for Krit supporting Kukrit was purely arithmetical: he had to. The conservative coalition led by Social Justice, Social Nationalists and Chart Thai, alongside Krit's 3 Socialist Party MPs, could command only 89 seats. It would also be necessary to buy the votes of MPs in ten minor parties (30 MPs). But compared to Seni, King Bhumipol found Kukrit's "far-right underpinnings ... more reassuring".[59] At the same time, Kukrit's Social Action, with only 18 MPs, and fourth in priority to attempt to form a coalition, would hardly threaten Krit. Moreover, though Kukrit succeeded in forming his coalition with 140 MPs on 19 March, the unwieldy fourteen-party coalition appeared destined to be short-lived. This might have been good riddance for Krit, since

Kukrit chose as his defence minister Krit's occasional nemesis Pramarn Adireksan. In the end, Kukrit's government lasted for ten months before new elections were called in January 1976, longer than anyone predicted. Krit himself had believed the coalition would only last as long as the budget debate in September, though it could fall sooner.[60] A weak Kukrit would ensure Krit's dominance behind the scenes.

On 10 February 1975, with the election over, Krit's allies in the police decided that the time had come for a change in their careers. General Prachuab Suntarangkul was transferred back to Royal Thai Army headquarters and was succeeded briefly in the position of police chief by placeholder General Phote Pekkanan. Meanwhile, deputy police chief General Vitoon Yasawat also returned to the army, where he was made a special advisor, but, given his help to Krit and the king, looked forward to being rapidly promoted to leading army power positions. Vitoon was succeeded in the post of deputy police chief by General Monchai Pankonchuen (the policeman who directly ordered violence against students on 14 October 1973).

In March, Krit visited Nakorn Ratchasima (Khorat) province to start building support for a potential run for parliament following his October 1975 mandatory retirement from the armed forces. In fact, he was seeking to cultivate Thailand's Northeast (which possessed 93 MP seats in 1975) as his "political base", from which Khorat would be his "take-off point".[61] His Sri Pattana Hotel in Khorat increasingly became the hub of his political meetings with local northeastern politicians.

Despite Krit's conditional support for a civilian-led regime after 1973 and backing of elected governments in 1975–76, he proved to be rather conservative and did not support a more leftward turn in Thai civil society. Indeed, in January 1974, following the burning of Ban Na Sai village (in Nong Khai province), Krit stated that "if it comes out that the burning of the village was done by the officials in order to suppress the Communists, then this is not at all a grave issue".[62] In addition, when a group of activist monks rallied in support of farmers' rights in November 1974, Krit opined that the Buddhist activities were in some way subversive and amounted to "the end of everything ... there is nothing more serious than this".[63] In April 1975, amidst university student investigations into the ISOC-associated "red drum" massacre in Patthalung Province, Krit responded in anger and frustration, threatening to pull the army out of counter-insurgency work (he had in February signed an order pulling the army out of such operations in Patthalung) and hand it all over to the Ministry of the Interior and the police. But Krit's responses in Patthalung derived not from his shock at human rights violations but rather because he had political ambitions and did not want a massacre to destroy his future as a politician, as a similar incident had destroyed the political future of Narong Kittikachorn.[64] In these examples, Krit appeared quite different than the media's portrayal of him on 14 October 1973 as a champion of political openness.

Meanwhile, throughout 1973–76, Krit generally proved himself to be a close ally of Washington in Thailand. For example, he generally backed the continued presence of US troops, especially given the continuing communist revolutionary advances both in Thailand and in the countries of Indochina. Nevertheless, Krit realized that to appease students and progressive politicians it was necessary to publicly urge that a certain proportion of US soldiers start to withdraw.

In another example, in July 1974, the Thai government, led by officials from the Ministry of Foreign Affairs, decided to halt US Navy P-3 reconnaissance patrol flights from Utapao (Thailand) across the Indian Ocean. Supporters of the move included Anand Panyarachun and other Foreign Ministry nationalists who saw the policy modification as a "Declaration of Independence from the United States" and a statement that would be popular with Thai civilian progressives. The US Embassy later learned that Krit was "extremely irritated" that he had not been consulted about the decision, though he claimed he could not change it.[65] In fact, he might have supported the move if only to boost his public standing when, if ever, he entered politics.

Following the rise of Kukrit's disjointed coalition government, Krit's political-economic-military influence across Thailand simply persevered. Moreover, it was generally only Krit who stood in the way of military officials planning coups against the government. A US Embassy cable at the time detailed his power:

> Krit has ... bankrolled many members of the current [Kukrit's] cabinet [and] remains the primary person in Thailand who can effect government changes by indirect influence or outright force. He nevertheless does not run the Royal Thai Government in an operational sense, and does not have the cabinet at his feet. He is the most influential man in the Royal Thai Government to have on our side, but he is not omnipotent in the sense that Sarit Thanarat was.[66]

Because of Krit's clout, he was able to promise the US Embassy that an airlift from Cambodia (then seeking to beat back the eventual Khmer Rouge revolution) to Thailand would continue despite defence minister Pramarn declaring that the airlift would cease. Krit added that the United States should contact him if the government issued an ultimatum that the flights must end. In fact, Krit's stance strengthened the US standpoint that it was not necessary to check with the prime minister or his cabinet about national security issues with which the US was involved.[67] When the US deputy chief of mission Masters queried Krit about the Kukrit government's stated one-year deadline for the total withdrawal of US troops from Thailand, Krit immediately replied with the question: "Do you really think that Kukrit's government will last 12 months?"[68] In fact, it was becoming increasingly clear not only that Krit anticipated the impending fall of Kukrit's coalition in September, but perhaps, give his own political ambitions, he portended the opportunity to become Kukrit's elected successor.

In late April, with the United States seeking to evacuate local dependents out of Vietnam, the US Embassy approached generals Krit and Kriangsak to inform them of the outline of Option IV of the proposed "Operation Frequent Wind", involving helicoptering some Vietnamese nationals through bases in Thailand. Krit and Kriangsak stressed that Thailand's "Supreme Command alone would handle matters on [the] Thai side" and that matters "should not be taken up with civilian departments of the Royal Thai Government". The embassy thereupon followed Krit's advice, deciding not to hold any discussions with Kukrit's elected government about Operation "Frequent Wind".[69]

Despite Krit's reliable pro-US stance, as Washington was increasingly pulling out from South Vietnam, Cambodia and Laos, he did make some impassioned public statements, perhaps playing to Thai public opinion, which was shifting against Washington. On 23 April, Krit stated that "If America deserts friends, as it has, it is a cause for worry and concern also."[70] Perhaps this rhetoric was not entirely empty, however. After all, during the month of April, Thailand increasingly saw itself becoming surrounded by eastern bloc countries following revolutions in Cambodia and Laos, and North Vietnam's impending takeover of South Vietnam. In April, Krit "reluctantly concluded that Thailand must seek closer ties with the Soviet Union ... to balance Chinese and North Vietnamese influence in the area", though Krit's stance was not the same as that of officials in Thailand's Foreign Ministry, who supported more of a neutralist Thai policy.[71]

Nevertheless, in May 1975, Krit proved to Washington that in fact he was solidly in the US camp. Following the April 1975 Cambodian revolution, some Khmer Rouge cadres seized the US container ship *Mayaguez*, owned by Sea-land Service, Inc., a US company also linked to Krit. To rescue the *Mayaguez*, US president Ford airlifted from

Okinawa to U Tapao Airbase in Thailand a battalion-sized US marine landing team. The US had not, however, received formal permission from the Thai government. The result was a public protest from Kukrit, though Krit privately told the US Embassy that he was "extremely pleased that Washington was acting in a decisive manner".[72] Krit's attitude was similar to that of most senior Thai military officials at the time. Krit's response corresponded with what US secretary of state Henry Kissinger had told US journalists on 30 May. When asked about the Thai government's complaints over the way in which the United States had violated its sovereignty regarding the *Mayaguez* incident, Kissinger told reporters that when it comes to Thailand, they should not pay attention to Thai politicians, but rather to the Thai military. "The military were happy enough for us to use Utapao [base] and that was what mattered", he said privately.[73] Kissinger later denied saying this.

Meanwhile, the Kukrit government seemed to be increasingly weak. In June:

> The Thai military are grumbling about the incompetent and relatively leftward direction of the government, but do not appear ready to engage in an overt move. They will bide their time, and probably hope that the situation will deteriorate to an extent that will permit the military to take over. The Supreme Commander, Krit Sivara, is the only candidate at this stage, and he is clearly thinking of moving up within the constitutional process, i.e. via election.[74]

In August, conservative groups were outraged when Kukrit, responding to student demonstrations, released nine detainees who had been arrested for occupying a mine in Thailand's North, among other things. Upwards of a thousand angry ultra-rightist policemen in civilian clothes mutinied against the government, marching across Bangkok to the home of the prime minister, whereupon approximately a hundred of them looted and wrecked the building. The incident opened up concerns that Thailand's increasing chaos might lead to the return of military rule.[75] In fact, the following day, police, alongside Red Gaurs, Nawaphon and Village Scouts militiamen, used police equipment in anti-Kukrit protests. Krit chose to react to ensure that there would not be a coup.[76] Yet the problems of security brought up Krit's mandatory retirement, which was just around the corner (1 October 1973). Indeed, Krit had not sought an extension of service, nor had King Bhumipol offered him one. One week after the police mutiny, rumours of a possible military coup began to resurface. Army elements were unhappy with "the decline in investment" and felt that Kukrit was "too soft" towards the Left.[77] Krit again denied that any putsch would be possible given that he opposed coups in principle. He also revealed that he had told officers under his command time and again that they should support the elected government.[78]

By September the two issues of Krit's impending retirement and the budget bill were coming to the fore. At the time, Kukrit's Social Action Party, deputy prime minister and defence minister Pramarn Adireksan's Chart Thai Party and Krit were increasingly jockeying for power. A cabinet reshuffle was inevitable. The different scenarios that a reshuffle would result in were (1) a Pramarn-dominated cabinet with Kukrit and Krit out, (2) a Kukrit-run cabinet with Krit and Pramarn out, or (3) a Kukrit-led cabinet with Pramarn in and Krit out. The ministerial post of greatest competition was the defence portfolio. With Krit losing military influence upon his 1 October retirement, taking control over the position of defence minister would allow him to protect his active-duty military followers and also help to preserve his numerous political and economic assets. If Pramarn could hold onto defence, he could weaken Krit and perhaps further build up his family's Phin-Phao (Soi Rajakru) faction in the military. To triumph over Pramarn, Krit would rely on the numerous financial debts that MPs owed him from the 1975 election. Besides the MPs from Social Justice, Social Nationalists and smaller parties, that included as many as half of the MPs in Pramarn's own Chart Thai Party. Nevertheless, Pramarn possessed numerous funds to pay MPs for their votes. Kukrit relied on both men to come to office. The premier's big problem was how to mediate the jousting between Krit and Pramarn while sustaining his government and Thailand's nascent democracy.[79]

Meanwhile, Krit-loyalist, Social Justice Party leader and agriculture minister Tawich Klinpratum threatened to pull Social Justice's 45 MPs out of the Kukrit-led coalition by 2 October if Pramarn did not resign from the defence minister position by that date and hand over the position to Krit. Tawich accused Pramarn of trying to dominate the armed forces and reassigning names of military personnel for partisan gain. Tawich further urged as a compromise that Kukrit himself take the defence minister's post. Pramarn replied that if he were forced from the defence position, he would take Chart Thai out of the government, forcing the coalition to fall. In his castigating of Pramarn, Tawich was acting as the attack dog for Krit, while Krit and Pramarn remained on courteous terms. Finally, Tawich was sanctioned by his Social Action party and he stopped making demands of Pramarn.[80]

Tawich's efforts were useless anyway. By 29 September, Pramarn had trumped Krit in keeping hold of defence. Although Kukrit offered Krit the posts of deputy prime minister, member of the Privy Council and advisor to the prime minister, he turned them all down, saying he would only accept the defence portfolio. Ultimately, Krit agreed to remain as advisor to ISOC. Nevertheless, there was talk in some circles that Kukrit's denying of Krit the defence portfolio could force him to oust Kukrit's government—though Krit assured the government he would never resort to a coup.[81] Krit did succeed in maintaining almost his entire preferred list of military appointees for 1975–76, though a few changes were made to satisfy Pramarn (see 1975 reshuffle, Appendix 4). Of the 1975 new appointments, eight key ones were filled by Krit's faction. The senior military officials close to Pramarn Adireksan and his Soi Rajakru faction (Chart Thai Party) were new assistant army commander General Chalard Hiransiri and new 1st Army Region commander (pro-Praphas) General Yot Thepsadin na

FIGURE 6.4
ISOC Leadership, 1975–76

Post	Holder
Director	Army commander General Bunchai Bamrungpong
Ddvisor	General Krit Sivara, retired
Deputy Director	Armed forces deputy chief of staff General Saiyud Kerdphol
Deputy Director	Army deputy commander General Chote Hiranyatthiti
Deputy Director	Police director General Sisuk Mahintorntep
Assistant Director	General Prachuab Suntharangkul
Chief of Staff	Armed forces chief of staff General Pralong Wirapriya
Deputy Chief of Staff	Army assistant chief of staff for personnel General Vitoon Yasawat
Deputy Chief of Staff	Army assistant chief of staff for logistics General Chalerm Suttirak
Deputy Chief of Staff Director of Operations	General Phinyo Watchararathet

Ayuthaya. One newcomer was a favourite of the king: 1st Division King's Guard commander General Aroon Twatsin (see Appendix 4).

Given that Kukrit had not selected Krit as defence minister, but had instead appointed him as ISOC advisor, Krit was able to retain ISOC as his personal fiefdom (figure 6.4).

Previously, when army commander General Krit had been ISOC director, he had shown little interest in the organization, allowing General Saiyud Kerdphol, ISOC brainchild and chief of staff, to effectively take full responsibility for its day-to-day management, generally continuing the policy of General Praphas Charusatien. As such, Saiyud would be allowed to run ISOC on Krit's and Bunchai's behalf.[82] The ISOC assignments of former police commanders Generals Prachuab and Vitoon (members of Krit's faction) were meant to ensure Krit's influence within the structure given that Saiyud was associated with Chart Thai. Also, whilst Prachuab ostensibly served under Saiyud, Prachuab outranked him. Thus, Saiyud's ISOC staff became troubled by the potential for Krit's partisan takeover of it. His influence over ISOC ensured that Krit would maintain the posting until the end of Kukrit's government. He could even be defence minister and ISOC advisor concurrently.

On 30 September, Krit formally resigned as army commander and supreme commander, going into retirement. At the Ministry of Defence farewell ceremony, in response to a reporter's question as to whether he would run for election to parliament, Krit responded that he would. Pramarn, who was arm and arm with Krit, jokingly responded that Krit would run as a member of Pramarn's Chart Thai. The jovial appearance of the two men together suggested that antipathy between them had receded.[83] But a clash would reappear.

In early October, Kukrit managed to have the legislature ratify the budget bill, something that Krit had not initially expected, although Kukrit received help from Krit in ensuring sufficient votes to ensure its passage. Kukrit also delayed a no-confidence vote as long as possible. Krit was temporarily forced to remain on the political sidelines rather than throw his hat into the ring as a potential prime minister. Over the next two months, Kukrit's government hung on partly because of the prime minister's charisma, his negotiating abilities, by not putting pressure on political parties or the military, and by leaving well enough alone.

The 2 December witnessed the fall of Laos to the communist Pathet Lao guerrillas and the end of monarchy in that country. Many wondered whether Thailand would be next. Amid a growing fear by the elite that Thailand's CPT guerrillas might achieve victory, and with Krit (the guarantor of Thai democracy) having retired, support for the armed forces as the antidote to the intensifying instability intensified. Such a belief in a right-wing military solution gained further legitimacy when, following the birthday of King Bhumipol Adulyadej, he made a speech in December that appeared to call for domestic military intervention. Extracts of this speech are below:

> There have been various forms of sabotage against our Kingdom. This has developed to such a serious stage that it is direct aggression against our country.... Let all you soldiers decide on your own whether to continue protecting our country. If you think it's important to continue protecting this country, then beware of the danger which is coming close.... Our country has been able to preserve its sovereignty and freedom until this year because the Thais understand joint national interest and have united to perform their individual duties to fulfill the goal.... This has created an immense force which enables us to defend ourselves against various forms of danger which have threatened us.[84]

In fact, that Krit was no longer an active-duty military officer, the growing threats of communism both internal and external to Thailand, and that the United States was going to completely withdraw from Southeast Asia were most likely the principal factors influencing the king towards supporting a coup. But given the continuing power of civil society in the country at the time, any putsch would be unpopular and involve bloodshed. A successful coup would need to involve adequate preparations.

Also in December, there was growing speculation that Kukrit's government would not last much longer. Deputy Democrat Party leader Pichai Rattakul opined that Krit would make an ideal premier and that the Democrats should woo Krit over to their party. Krit, at the time, seemed to be keeping his options open, maintaining close links with politicians and businesspeople. Some also believed that Krit would soon be forming his own party, though he could be tempted to join an existing party. His conservative background seemed to make him acceptable to the military and aristocracy.[85]

Meanwhile, by January 1976, there were new demonstrations, leading to calls from ultra-rightists to repress them. The protestors—composed of farmers, labourers and students—were not persuaded that the fledgling democracy led by Kukrit was ably representing their interests. At the same time, rightist forces were frustrated that Kukrit's government was appearing to be surrendering to the Left. To please demonstrators, Kukrit had announced in December that all US troops would be out of Thailand by 15 March. Ultra-right-wing Buddhist monk Kittiwutho led a crowd of several thousand Nawaphon activists demanding that Kukrit turn over power to a military regime. Though Krit had retired, his influence in the military was still immense. He gave his support to Kukrit, and the ultra-rightists backed off. But when public employees demonstrating for higher wages were rewarded by Kukrit with a labour contract, Kukrit's opponents spread the word that this once again proved the prime minister's sympathy for communism. In addition, the military had become incensed with Kukrit because the prime minister (1) seemed to have lost interest in supporting the general concerns of the military, and (2) he had tried vigorously to control the military's secret slush funds. Added to this was that right-wing newspapers had been spreading stories since 1975 of foreign communist intrusions into Thailand.[86]

But Krit clearly washed his hands of Kukrit when the latter publicly stated that all US forces would depart Thailand by 20 March 1976. At this point, some political parties in Kukrit's ruling coalition announced they likely would be withdrawing support. Anticipating that Kukrit's end was near, the Democrats scheduled a no-confidence vote for 14 January 1976. Alongside their 72 MPs, the Democrats were allied with three other parties: the Socialists (12 MPs), New Force (12 MPs) and Socialist Front (10 MPs).[87] Though this amounted to less than half the members of the lower house (106/269 seats), it was expected that there would be multiple defections among MPs in Krit's coalition. In fact, it is intriguing that two parties that Krit himself had bankrolled supported this censure motion. Indeed, Prasit Karnchanawat's Social Nationalists secretly agreed to vote for the no-confidence motion against Kukrit in exchange for cabinet seats, while some members of the Social Justice Party also apparently supported the motion.[88]

Perceiving that Kukrit's government was on the ropes, and seizing the political opportunity, on 11 January, Krit and army commander General Bunchai, leading close to a hundred intermediate and top-ranking officers, visited Kukrit at his residence, in a similar version of what had befallen Prime Minister Kuang Apaiwong on 6 April 1948. The two generals personally delivered an ultimatum to the prime minister: either he dissolve the lower house and call new elections, or permit the military under Krit and Bunchai to seize power. Kukrit did not need to think too long. He chose the first option.[89] In a memorandum seemingly critical of Krit Sivara's move, the CIA reported that Krit "was instrumental in stimulating the present crisis".[90] After all, Krit could have merely staged the coup clear and simple. Likewise, dissolving the lower house was a choice that King Bhumipol endorsed since he too likely preferred a simple putsch. Indeed, the palace during 1975 had grown weary of electoral governance and seemed to prefer a reversion to autocracy.[91] In the end, following Kukrit's formal advice on 12 January, on 13 January the king signed a royal decree dissolving parliament and setting a general election for 4 April 1976. Kukrit would remain as caretaker prime minister until then, while simultaneously competing in the election. But the move towards elections would effectively push Thailand in the direction of ever more political pandemonium—unless Krit could help the country weather the storm. By February, that storm was to loom ever larger.

At the time of Kukrit's January announcement of an 4 April election, Seni's Democrat's appeared to have the edge over other parties, especially since Kukrit was identified as a weak leader and sometime-puppet of America, while Seni had in January boldly made that progressive deal with left-wing parties. If the Democrats won the election, that same deal would probably hold, leading to a Democrat-led coalition governing a centre-left Thailand. Meanwhile, since becoming prime minister in 1975, Kukrit himself appeared to be moving leftward. His agreements with protesting students and striking workers, as well as his March ultimatum on US forces withdrawing from Thailand, seemed to be proof of this. At the same time, it seemed that the intermediate- to large-sized parties of the right—Chart Thai (Pramarn Adireksan and Chatchai Chunhavan) and the Krit-financed Social Justice (of Thawee Chulasap and Tawich Klinpratum)—were less popular than the Democrats and Social Action, and would thus fare worse in the upcoming general election. But the military leadership was much more united when it came to the issue of US troops in Thailand; most senior Thai military officials wanted them to remain. This was an issue that, interestingly, united pro–Soi Rajakru and pro-Krit officers. The increasing chaos in Thai politics—with leftists gaining influence—was anathema to the country's military, monarchy and associated right-wing elites. These elites saw Thailand increasingly surrounded by external communist forces, menaced by communist insurgency and threatened with a growing number of urban and rural activists who could potentially use their vote to install a government willing to cow to communism.

To more effectively oppose the Left, it was rumoured that Seni's Democrats and Pramarn's Chart Thai might, after elections, form a coalition together. In addition, Krit became central to an effort to defeat progressives at the polls. He gave most of his financial, networking and organizational support to the Democrats and "'bought' many of the ones who had joined Kukrit's [1975] coalition".[92] In addition, according to the *Far Eastern Economic Review*, the US Embassy (Bangkok) had "channeled a large sum of money to [Thailand's] Democrat party".[93] Given that Krit and the United States were both willing to donate enormous sums of money to the Democrats in the election, it goes without saying that they probably helped each other—just as they had previously collaborated in the 1969 and 1975 elections. It was the "Lotus Project" all over again.

In fact, Krit was fed up with Kukrit but personally despised both Pramarn and Chatchai. By mid-January, the only civilian who was electable as prime minister and possessed the outstanding charisma necessary to unite the country was Krit Sivara—though, as a retired general, Krit was certainly no true civilian. Most Thai centrists (including US officials) were confidently speculating that Krit would run as the "De Gaulle" or "Man on a White Horse" for Thailand in the election, given that, according to the 1974 constitution, any person becoming a prime minister must already be an elected MP.

It was thus quite unexpected when, on 18 January, he suddenly called a news conference at his home and stated that he would not run (as an MP) and that he would not form a political party for the 4 April general election. Krit added: "When I said in the past that I would stand for election next time I meant I believed that it would be held in another three years. Now that parliament has been dissolved unexpectedly, I am not ready to enter the political arena yet."[94]

What we will never know is why Krit suddenly decided not to run for office, since he would have clearly been chosen as prime minister. The announcement was even more astounding given that Krit had, on earlier occasions, announced his interest in a post-military political career and had even established Thailand's Northeast, centred upon Nakorn Ratchasima, as a political base. Between 11 January—the day Krit had appeared at Kukrit's door—and 18 January, he appeared to have made a 180 degree turn away from politics. Kukrit later stated that Krit had not run because he "had nothing to gain from the elections, being confident of riding the emerging center-left coalition".[95] Still, reviewing Krit's background, he does not appear as any sort of centre-left politician. Perhaps he simply wanted to take a cabinet posting with no MP obligations, or was expecting Thai people to try to push him towards the premiership, which would have necessitated either a constitutional amendment allowing him to become premier without being elected or his running in a later by-election? Clearly, he knew many people wanted him to become prime minister, but he wanted to take the job on his own terms. He might agree to be a post-election, nonpartisan, drafted premier or a non-political caretaker in the mould of Sanya Thammasak, though an ex-military variant.

Nevertheless, though Thailand appeared to be in crisis, King Bhumipol did not ask Krit to participate in the 1976 election or become a stabilizing caretaker. Except perhaps for the Chart Thai Party and Samak Sundaravej's right-wing Democrat Party faction, the king appeared to have completely lost hope in democracy for Thailand, as evidenced by his formal backing of groups supportive of a military coup (e.g., the Village Scouts, Nawaphon and Red Gaurs). With Krit as prime minister, the palace would be confined to continue backing a democratic narrative but revert to the pre-1973 equilibrium of competing against military strongmen (though in this case a retired "democratic" one) for influence—a situation that might give the preponderance of power to Krit. Since Thanom had served as prime minister for ten years, would the popular Krit ultimately do the same? Would Krit's popularity overshadow that of the king? With these questions in mind, it is possible that between 11 and 18 January, Krit was told by the king—the only person who had the stature to tell Krit—not to compete in the April election, ostensibly to keep the military out of politics. After all, it would have been the king's very own request.

Meanwhile, aside from Thailand's right-wing forces, Washington was also becoming worried about Thailand's seemingly leftward tilt. The United States feared that Thais might elect a Socialist-leaning government, become neutralist and force the remaining US troops out of the country. With South Vietnam, Cambodia and Laos having already fallen, Thailand's move to the Left would further upset the balance of power in Asia in favour of the Soviet Union.

Powerful forces external and internal to Thailand were rapidly moving to shape the country's future. In these circumstances, events came to a head in February 1976. By February 1976, according to Admiral Sangad Chaloryu in a later interview, rumours were spreading that a military coup might soon be occurring because the Left had been overly active and disturbing the peace everywhere.[96]

On 2 February 1976, caretaker premier Kukrit met with the US ambassador and told him that he had just been informed by the Thai National Security Council of a possible Krit-led putsch against Kukrit that was being planned. According to Kukrit:

> Retired General Krit Sivara, with the help of Army Assistant Commander in Chief Chalat Hiranyasiri, might attempt to seize

power through a military coup before February 15. Khukrit ... discussed this possibility with the current army commander in chief, General Bunchai, and ... Bunchai had assured him that he would make a preemptive move if there were indications that Krit actually planned action. Khukrit said he was clearly not interested in either of these coup possibilities. In the case of the first, he assumed he would be entirely out of a job and in the case of a coup by Bunchai would almost certainly be relegated to figurehead status.[97]

What was interesting in this case is that Krit had generally opposed overt military coups, while apparent fellow coup-maker Chalard tended to side with Krit's nemesis Pramarn Adireksan. Which begs the question, why were they together? The effort could have indicated that Krit and Pramarn had surreptitiously come to an agreement to push Kukrit out of office prior to the latter's deadline for US troops to withdraw from Thailand. There might also have been another reason. In his discussion with the US ambassador, Kukrit added that if the Democrat Party won the April election and cobbled together a coalition with left-leaning parties, it "would pave the way for a communist takeover", and that Thailand had run out of time for "further experimentation".[98]

On 4 February, only two days after the Thai embassy dispatched this cable to the US State Department, CIA director George Bush sent a memorandum[99] to national security advisor Brent Scowcroft, a confidant of Henry Kissinger, in which Bush warned that:

> Thailand is experiencing a growing sense of malaise concerning the country's experiment with parliamentary democracy. This sentiment is expressed by King Phumiphon [Bhumipol], the military and many prominent civilian figures. In these circumstances, there is a strong possibility that the military might decide to assume control. For the moment, the King appears to be against such a course, and many military leaders would be loathe to act against the King's wishes. The situation is fragile, however, and subject to quick change.
>
> Some younger officers are maneuvering to force their superiors to take a stand on the question of the military takeover. [This could refer to the alleged Krit-Chalard coup effort on 2 February 1976.]
>
> Given the rivalries within the military, it is also possible that one or another military leader might attempt a preemptive coup. [This is in fact what happened on 6 October 1976.]
>
> Other developments which would increase the likelihood of a coup are:
> – a sharp deterioration of the security situation
> – A breakdown in public order caused by widespread strikes or anti-government disorders

– the prospect of a left-of-center coalition coming to power which would threaten the vested interests of the military and conservative elements in Thailand.

In the event of a military takeover [underlined], the resultant government would be sympathetic to US interests.... A military government might call for a substantial increase in US assistance if faced with a greatly expanded insurgency or a breakdown of civil order in the country. Short of a coup, there is also a possibility that the elections might be postponed, leaving Khukrit the present caretaker prime minister, to rule through emergency decree.... The election campaign probably will complicate Thai-US relations.... A government in which the Socialists had a strong voice ... could prompt the military either to force the government to resign or to overthrow it.

We ... believe there is a threshold for military action against the political system. Any one or a combination of the [three aforementioned] circumstances would likely galvanize the military into action against the civilian government.[100]

Bush believed that the two-month period before the 1976 Thai elections appeared to "weight the odds against a blatant military move to scrap the parliamentary system" since there still seemed to be "considerable support" for democracy "among the Thai power elite".[101] He ventured that the military, seconded by the king, might delay the election, or that Kukrit would be pressured to "move his government toward a more authoritarian and stable footing".[102] Bush noted that "there is also growing sentiment within the armed forces for the post-ponement of the elections and the replacement of the present unwieldy coalition cabinet with a new civilian team that would rule through the emergency powers of the present constitution".[103] Regarding the palace's position, Bush stated that "We believe the King would probably go along with an agreement between Khukrit and the military leader-ship to postpone the elections and rule through emergency decree."[104] Nevertheless, Bush mentioned the "political ambition of former army strongman Krit Sivara" as "a complicating factor", but noted that "he [Krit] may also fear that charges of corruption will be aired against him in the campaign [though] if he does remain out of the race, he will almost certainly provide financial support to various parties and candidates on the political right, and he will be a factor in the nego-tiations to form the next government".[105] Bush then presented three scenario outcomes of the April 1976 election: a centrist-conservative coalition, a centrist-socialist coalition, or a rightist coalition, with the centrist conservative coalition the most likely. Any of the three would, however, be unstable, with the result that a military coup beneficial to US interests would probably occur:

> If Praman, Krit or some other rightist figure comes to power through a military backed overthrow of the parliamentary government, their inclination to cooperate closely with the US would probably prevail ... over any attempts by the Foreign Ministry to steer a more neutral foreign policy course.[106]

On 5 February, Thomas Barnes of the US National Security Council staff also sent a memorandum (413) to Scowcroft, reaffirming Bush's concerns about Thailand.[107] Then, on 20 February, Barnes sent out memorandum (414) to Scowcroft, which is a summary of Bush's 4 February document. Also titled "Thai Elections and its Implications for the US", it was initialled by Scowcroft, and included the attached 4 February memorandum from Bush. Barnes's entire memorandum is reproduced below):

> The Intelligence Community has prepared an inter-agency memorandum assessing the current Thai election campaign and its implications for the United States. We have already briefed the key points of this assessment to you and the President. Because the memorandum indicates that there is a strong possibility that the Thai military may assume control of the government at some point before the elections or sometime soon thereafter, we are sending it to you again to ensure that you are familiar with it.
>
> In his covering memo transmitting the study to you, George Bush states that ... the situation in Thailand is fluid, and subject to quick and dramatic changes.
>
> Coup plotting has continued since the Intelligence Community issued the memo. Two Americans have approached our Embassy on behalf of groups allegedly ready to attempt a military takeover of the government. [text not declassified] several military officers have been actively discussing this possibility. Ambassador Whitehouse's most recent judgment on this subject is that, while several groups are actively considering a coup, there is nothing to indicate an imminent attempt.
>
> The key points of the intelligence study are:
> - Thailand is experiencing a growing sense of malaise concerning the country's experiment with parliamentary democracy.
> - In this circumstance, there is a strong possibility that the military might decide to assume control.
> - A sharp deterioration of security, a breakdown in public order, or the prospect of a left-of-center coalition government coming to power after the election would increase the likelihood of a coup.

- The election campaign will probably complicate Thai-U.S. relations. The U.S. presence is likely to become an issue in the campaign, and some pressures may force candidates to insist on a total U.S. military withdrawal.
- The U.S. will probably be able to complete the negotiations now in train with the Khukrit government regarding the residual U.S. military presence.
- But there is no assurance that a new government will honor what Khukrit agrees to.
- If the election goes ahead as scheduled, another centrist-conservative government would likely come into power.
- Such a government would probably keep Thai policy toward the U.S. more or less along present lines.
- A less likely possibility is either a coalition based exclusively on rightist elements, or one which included the Socialists.
- A government in which the Socialists had a strong voice would make it difficult, if not impossible, for the U.S. to maintain any military presence in Thailand. Such a government could prompt the military either to force the government to resign or to overthrow it.
- In the event of a military takeover, the resultant government would be sympathetic to U.S. interests.[108]

On 5 February 1976, only hours after the Bush/Barnes memorandums, the State Department sent a cable to the US Embassy (Bangkok) ostensibly outlining the Gerald Ford administration's "opposition to any military coup attempt in Thailand". The denial can perhaps be read in two ways. The US reaction to the impending April 1976 election shared similarities with how Washington had responded to other elections in the world where fear of overly progressive political parties winning the elections caused enormous fear among US policymakers. Indeed, such could be seen in the Chilean general election of September 1970.[109] In Chile, as in Thailand, Washington wished to play a "double game": (1) potentially manipulating the election outcome so that it would be favourable to US interests; and (2) secretly maintaining support for a coup as a second option if the election results later appeared to harm US interests. But, publicly at least, the denial of US support for a coup seemed to be more of an attempt to prove to the world that Washington opposed any military adventurism. The CIA document from which I gleaned this information is Top Secret and all save the part in which the US stressed its opposition remains classified.[110]

Weeks later, on 24–25 February, army chief General Bunchai Bamrungpong hurriedly called together all military commanders for what he called a twenty-four-hour "military alert", which he later said was simply an "exercise" apparently "to test preparedness with no intention [of] staging [a] coup".[111] The incident provoked governmental suspicions that the army commander was carrying out a coup, and Kukrit immediately cancelled a proposed trip to Singapore. US ambassador Whitehouse opined that Bunchai was well-known for opposing the withdrawal of US forces from Thailand, which the Kukrit government had publicly promised to accomplish in some fashion by 20 March. Bunchai had stated that a "miracle" before 20 March might keep US forces in Thailand, but, barring such a "miracle", Bunchai might have used the "alert to pressure the government toward such a decision but keep to democratic principles at the same time".[112]

Bunchai's motive for the military "alert" might in fact have verged closer to preparation for a coup. On 25 February, US Embassy officials met with Phongpol Adireksan, son and personal secretary to Chart Thai Party leader (and deputy PM/defence minister) Pramarn Adireksan. Phongpol asserted that Bunchai's military alert was "practice for a real coup" and that "army leaders [were] definitely planning to stage a coup before the April 4 elections". Phongpol added that, in addition to the army, the navy had also been put on alert. Nevertheless, the ultimate decision to proceed with the coup had "not yet been made". Phongpol said that his father, Pramarn, in the latter's role as defence minister, had been asked to sign the alert order but had refused to do so, fearing that he would be accused of planning a coup (according to Phongpol, Pramarn was not involved in any putsch). Rather, Phongpol said any coup order had to come from Bunchai orally. Phongpol further stated that the army leadership was divided as to who should lead a coup. On one side there were the "professionals" led by Bunchai, chief of staff General Serm na Nakorn and assistant army chief General Prasert Thammasiri, who wanted a civilian-led government. On the other side was a faction led by assistant army commander General Chalard Hiranyasiri and assistant chief of staff for the armed forces General Vitoon Yasawat, who favoured returning Thailand to being under the control of a military regime as it was prior to October 1973. Phongpol said that if his father had to choose, he would support Bunchai's group—Vitoon's cabal would not offer a leadership role for Pramarn. Phongpol finished the conversation by stating "that if the army does move, they will round up large numbers of people" and "any coup will be bloody".[113]

Not everyone at the US Embassy was surprised at the news of military coup-plotting against Kukrit. In fact, rumours of coups had been common since the 1973 fall of Thanom and Praphas. Perhaps

US ambassador Whitehouse, a political appointee, had no knowledge of any US interest regarding a putsch in Thailand. But deputy chief of mission Edward Masters (concurrently CIA), Bangkok's 1973–76 CIA station chief Hugh Tovar and his deputy Daniel Arnold (who became Tovar's successor) were well aware of the February 1974 memorandum from CIA director George Bush, which had concluded that a coup could perhaps suit US interests. Tovar and Arnold may have already begun encouraging Bunchai to stage a coup against Kukrit via Bunchai's professionals or Chalard/Vitoon.

Indeed, even before Bunchai's 24–25 February coup preparations, supreme commander Admiral Sangad Chaloryu had visited the king's Phuping Palace on Doi Suthep mountain in Chiang Mai following a royal invitation on 20 February. Sangad was accompanied by Bunchai; ACM Kamol Dechatungka, then commander of the Royal Thai Air Force; and General Kriangsak Chomanan, then assistant supreme commander. Admiral Sangad informed the king that the situation in Thailand was dire and that if nothing was done it might disintegrate in the same fashion as post-1975 Cambodia and Laos. Admiral Sangad thus proposed that a military coup should be carried out against Kukrit, that his "professionals" faction should lead it, and that he wanted to receive blessings from His Majesty for a putsch. Sangad stressed that the coup plotters were searching for an appropriate person to be premier following the coup. Sangad looked for the monarch to suggest a name. But the king did not give a direct answer. Like General Bunchu and General Serm, Sangad was a loyalist of the retired, popular Krit Sivara—and indeed the king knew this. So, by implication, Sangad could have been assuming that the king would back Krit's candidacy. But, instead, the king replied: "If the military seized power and ruled, it should not wish to remain in power. Therefore, I would like a civilian to run the country. So, following a coup, who should be the Prime Minister after that?"[114] Admiral Sangad said that he suggested fifteen names, including Prakob Hutasing, Luang Atthasitthisoonthon, Khun Praphas Aoychai and Khun Chao Na Silawan. But the king did not seem to be impressed with any of these choices. Thereupon, Admiral Sangad prepared to depart, but before doing so the King said that "whatever you do, consult with Thanin Kraivichien".[115]

Thanin was a little-known judge of the Supreme Court who was rabidly anti-communist and ultra-monarchist (and also a Nawaphon leader). Thanin had apparently gained the king's attention because the former had made several anti-communist broadcasts on radio and television that were eventually suspended by the Kukrit government.

In January 1976, however, the army allowed Thanin to make renewed broadcasts on its Royal Thai Army TV Channel 5. Though Sangad did not know Thanin, when he returned to Bangkok, he met with him and afterwards began to use Thanin to write up various statements and documents.

The events of February 1976 were significant because they appear to show that (1) Thailand's monarch was taking the lead in pushing for a military coup against an elected government; and (2) with Krit retired, the king seemed to be increasingly interested in reconstituting military leadership positions in order to shape his personalized control over the armed forces. In fact, since February of that year, the king asked the then military leadership alongside Thanin to establish an arch-royalist "Master Plan" whereby, following the planned overthrow of Thailand's elected government, the country would temporarily exist under civilian-led dictatorship followed by an incremental transition to a guided democratic regime with the king as head of state. Nevertheless, it was unclear to what extent Krit Sivara himself would support such a master plan and whether, following an eventual coup, the military would agree to arch-royalist civilian control and even the return to democracy.

Of course, if Sangad's group had not proved forthcoming, Bhumipol could have backed Vitoon's coup plans given the king's close support for him over the years. Vitoon had married into the royal family—his spouse was Mom Rachawong Jitrapha Nuanrat, a close relative of the king. Indeed, during the CIA war against the Pathet Lao guerrillas and Vietnamese army in Laos, King Bhumipol had sponsored Vitoon's Task Force 333 unit (Taharn Sua Pran [Tiger Ranger Soldiers]), telling them to take the US song "Dream the Impossible Dream" as their anthem. Vitoon, who had served in Laos since 1964, was also close to the CIA's Pat Landry, the head of the CIA war in Laos following the departure of William Lair in 1971. In fact, under orders from Vitoon, the Royal Thai Army's entire 13th Regiment had fought against communists in Laos in 1970.[116] The events of 1973, in which Krit had obtained help from Vitoon, were also supported by the palace. Thus, to some extent, the king clearly liked Vitoon, trusted his aversion to communism, and might have supported a Vitoon-initiated coup in 1976.

On 28 February, Whitehouse cabled Kissinger and Scowcroft, stating that he "now believe[d] that a "military takeover … will occur sometime before the April 4 elections". Whitehouse added that:

> He does not expect a traditional style coup involving military seizure of the radio station and other key installations by force. Rather, his judgment is that some military, in alliance with like-minded

civilians, will carry out a 'quiet takeover' with the King's blessing to 'protect the nation.' Whitehouse warns that no matter how quiet the takeover is, students and other groups will not accept a return to military rule, and that serious clashes will erupt in Bangkok when the coup occurs.[117]

Whitehouse's perceptions of turmoil in Thailand were not farfetched. In the early morning (1 a.m.) prior to his cable (28 February), unknown gunmen assassinated Dr Boonsanong Punyodyana, secretary-general of the Socialist Party of Thailand (but only a mild leftist) as he was returning to his home from a dinner party at the Australian Embassy. He was shot in the head at point-blank range in what was clearly a professional hit. His enemies were only political, and police never found the perpetrators. Next to Boonsanong's body were found two .45 calibre cartridges, the kind used by the Thai military. His assassination represented a vivid warning to progressives not to even dare try to compete in the election.[118]

But the incident involving Boonsanong was only part of the anti-communist campaign of violence prior to the April 1976 election. Indeed, during the nine weeks from early February until the election, over thirty people were killed: grenades were thrown into crowds listening to political speeches, a firebomb exploded at the New Force party headquarters in Bangkok, and political party canvassers were killed.[119]

The month of March 1976 proved to be of vital importance to US-Thai relations. This was because Washington was seeking to keep as many US forces and as much military equipment as possible in Thailand despite Kukrit's earlier pronouncement that they must all be withdrawn from the country by 20 March. Already, the last US combat aircraft had officially left Thailand on 18 December 1975, while the final US airbase to be closed (in Nakorn Ratchasima) had officially been turned over to Thailand on 29 February 1976. At that point, discussions persisted between the Ford administration and the caretaker Kukrit government on the remaining US "residual presence" in Thailand. According to one anonymous source, senior US officials informed a US journalist as follows:

> We'll have some 3,000 American soldiers left after March 20, and the Thai government has already agreed on this point. But of course this is a period of a general election. The verbal agreement may be changed. However, until today we still would like to believe that it will continue to be in effect even after the April 4 election.[120]

In fact, while the US was willing to withdraw most of its forces from the country, it insisted upon retaining some three thousand troops in Thailand, including personnel belonging to the US Air Force, the CIA and army personnel described only as "advisors". These three thousand officials were to be divided among the Ramasun Central Intelligence Base, Chiang Mai listening post, the JUSMAG headquarters in Bangkok, and elsewhere in the country. Most senior Thai military officials enjoyed the continuing high levels of US military aid to Thailand and they were also supportive of allowing the three thousand US soldiers to remain. Nevertheless, the negotiations became more difficult given that the Kukrit government demanding direct jurisdiction over all US forces. When this issue was not resolved by the 20 March deadline, the Kukrit government announced that all US forces would have to depart Thailand by 20 July 1976.[121] At that point Washington appeared to try to delay the negotiations to take its chances with the next Thai government, given that Thailand's general election was to take place on 4 April and the Democrat Party was likely to win. Washington knew that Krit Sivara, who continued to support a US troop presence in Thailand, backed Thailand's Democrats and that he (and his military faction) would likely have a powerful voice in a Democrat-led government

Meanwhile, during March, the pre-election violence continued. On 3 March, Red Gaurs terrorists detonated bombs at the Rama VI Engineering School, killing three students (the school was owned by Dilokchai Sunatwanitkul, who was suspected by ISOC of being a Soviet agent).[122] Seni Pramoj stressed that the situation was becoming so unstable that anything could happen, including a military coup. The US Embassy noted that the killings of progressives had made "'left wingers' … fear for their lives", and others suspected that "these incidents may have [been] planned or, at the very least, would be used by 'right wingers' as an excuse to stage a coup or to postpone the April 4 elections".[123] This "fear" harks back to the Bush memorandum of 4 February 1976 in which the then CIA director seemed to express hope for either a coup or a delayed election.

As March proceeded, NSCT and affiliated groups increased their demonstrations. On 17 March, right-wing Nawaphon demonstrators led by Watthana Kieowimon delivered flowers to the gate of the US Embassy in Bangkok, where they were received by a US counsellor.[124] On 21 March 1976, in anticipation of that day's governmental announcement of the end of the US military force deployment in Thailand (and expecting that the Kukrit government might allow US forces to remain longer), a large demonstration took place, with the leaders demanding the withdrawal of all US troops from Thailand. The rally, organized by the NSCT and the Federation of Labor Unions of Thailand (FLUT), was met by Red Gaurs militia toughs who assaulted demonstrators and even hurled grenades into the crowds, wounding and killing people.[125] According to a reliable source, Krit maintained enormous influence over six of the twenty-odd members of FLUT's executive committee, and he secretly encouraged them to protest to destabilize the Kukrit government.[126] The Red Gaurs' actions were ignored by nearby police. In fact, police allegedly transported Red Gaurs members, who possessed police radios.[127] Many of these Red Gaurs were linked to General Vitoon Yasawat, who was often an ally of Krit.

Amidst the pandemonium of 21 March, and with combat troops in Bangkok on full alert, defence minister Pramarn attempted to convince Kukrit to declare martial law, establish temporary military rule and delay the election. But Kukrit refused.[128] He simply did not want to rule by extra-constitutional means. At the same time, the king, Krit and Bunchai did not support a coup at that time. Thus, Pramarn's hopes for a pre-poll coup were dashed. The anti-communist objectives of Nixon and Kissinger were also put on hold. All three would have to await the 4 April results or later military intervention. Nevertheless, several right-wing soldiers might have supported a coup. According to the CIA at the time, the government's announcement of US troop withdrawals

> probably angered the military, most of whom desired a continued US presence, but the retention of the assistance group could mollify them somewhat. There are no indications that the military plans any overt action to protest the withdrawal, unless provided an excuse by violent demonstrators. They will, however, view the government's action as another example of its inability to resist the demands of the left.[129]

The March violence effectively helped military-coup fomenters because it increasingly destabilized the country, softening it up for a potential putsch. At the same time, the violence of February–March 1976, perpetrated by right-wing groups against progressives, combined with the unwillingness of leftist forces to respond in kind prevented a pretext for a military coup.

The CIA used its own finances during the nine-week election for three purposes: (1) to promote centrist-conservative candidates in the Social Justice, Social Nationalists and Chart Thai parties; (2) arm ultra-right-wing groups to disrupt rallies by progressive demonstrators and sow the fear of instability in the hearts of Thais; and (3) help pay for the dissemination of propaganda such as placards of Chart Thai Party that read "Right kill Left".

An 1 April 1976, CIA assessment of the upcoming election argued that it would produce a weak coalition, perhaps as fragile as the previous one. "Many Thais believe that if [the election] does not result in a stable government, the military will resume power." The assessment noted that Kukrit might again be prime minister unless he was defeated at the polls (at the time, only an elected MP could constitutionally become premier) and it was emphasized that Krit Sivara was working towards Kukrit's electoral demise:

> Some key military officers, as well as former army strongman Krit Sivara, hold Khukrit responsible for the failure of negotiations on a continued US military presence in Thailand, and have vowed to block his re-election. Khukrit is running in a district heavily populated by military families.[130]

The assessment concluded that, if Kukrit lost his seat, then his non-charismatic brother Seni (as Democrat Party leader), ultra-rightist Pramarn Adireksan (as Chart Thai Party leader) or Krit-associate Thawee Chulasap (as Social Justice Party leader) would become the next prime minister. There did not seem to be any fear in the report that left-wing politicians would win a majority at the polls.

As the election approached in Thailand, a State Department internal analysis correctly predicted that the next prime minister in Thailand would be either Kukrit or Seni Pramoj, leading a centre-right coalition of four parties. The report stated that "the Democrat Party is also rumoured to be interested in having retired General Krit Sivara as its minister of defence (Krit had close connections with the Social Justice Party and Thawee [Chulasap] as well)". The report favoured a coalition led by Seni rather than Kukrit because Kukrit's side possessed more corrupt politicians, which would inhibit US aid to Thailand. It also stressed that any one of the possible coalitions would be a weak government that would not remain in office longer than "a few more months and would be effectively overturned by a military coup or its personnel and policies drastically changed by a civil-military takeover in some form". But, it continued, any coup would encounter "substantial resistance from the students and the political parties" as well as "many casualties ... [leading to] significant bloodshed [which would] increase ... the communist insurgency".[131]

On the same day, at another meeting at the US State Department, participants' moods, rather than fearful, appeared instead as deprecating and gleeful. On 2 April, at a staff meeting, the secretary of state Henry Kissinger seemed to favour a return of Sarit, Thanom or Praphas to power:

ASSIST SECRETARY OF STATE PHILIP HABIB: The election there [in Thailand] takes place on the 4th, but it's quite likely that it — well, nobody knows how it will turn out.... Whether the military will be fed zip with the thing and take a move, I think is just due for a period of uncertainty; and it could, according to Embassy estimates, run as long as three or four weeks before you know what kind of government you have in Thailand.

SECRETARY KISSINGER: Well, we're staying out of it, I trust?

HABIB: Oh, yes, sir. We're staying so far out of it we probably don't know what the hell is going on. (Laughter.)

SECRETARY KISSINGER: Certainly, on this item this Embassy would have played around.

HABIB: No. I say the military and the CIA instinctively tried to put a general in charge and it would have caused us immeasurable difficulty.

SECRETARY KISSINGER: That's the platitude I always here [sic]. Why exactly would a general in Thailand cause us immeasurable difficulty?

HABIB: Because he cannot rule the government unless he did with absolute force of arms, and even then, he couldn't get away with it—let's say a combination of what Kittikachorn did or Sarit did in the old days. This is the bunch that they have now that are venal and corrupt, a recognizably incapable group.

SECRETARY KISSINGER: Well, the other ones were venal and corrupt.

HABIB: Well, they were venal, but they weren't incapable.

EXECUTIVE SEC. TO THE SECRETARY OF STATE LAWRENCE EAGLEBURGER: Corrupt. (Laughter)

HABIB: Prapas was very capable, and also Tanot [Thanom]. And the King in this case has been holding back. And I think, in fact, his attitude has influenced me very much. He is not in favor of the military coup. I think he knows his people better than we do.

SECRETARY KISSINGER: I'm not saying we should favor a military coup. I'm just saying we shouldn't use the usual platitudes about what the effect of a military coup would be or what democracy in Thailand means.

HABIB: I don't think they're going to have democracy in Thailand, but I think we can avoid a situation where you have complete disarray. It's either some measure of orderliness, using the stability of the Crown and the religion and the national identity as a point of cohesion—as an element of cohesion—or creating—having a situation of complete disarray.[132]

During the 4 April 1976 election, about 29 per cent of the population in Bangkok and 40 per cent in provincial Thailand voted, which was far fewer than in the 1975 election. This owed partly to the pre-election right-wing terrorism, which was likely intended to scare progressive voters to stay away from the polls. Nevertheless, with 39 parties participating in this election, the results saw the Democrats garnering the greatest number of seats: 114 out of 279. Most of the rest of the seats went to Chart Thai (56), Social Action (45) and Social Justice (28). But, as the CIA had earlier forecast, Kukrit lost his seat. This occurred allegedly because Krit ordered soldiers in Kukrit's constituency—the Dusit area of Bangkok (the city's principal military area)—not to vote for him.[133] Since he had not been elected, Kukrit could not legally become premier. The CIA may also have had a hand in the inability of Kukrit to win a seat. Whatever the case, Seni, as the leader of the party with the most seats, was given the first opportunity to try to put together a coalition. In this effort he was backed by Krit, who now, thanks to his financing of the Democrats during the election, exerted enormous influence over the party.[134] Krit was able to quickly bond the Democrats into a coalition with Social Justice and the Social Nationalists, the two parties over which Krit already exercised overriding sway. The three parties together accounted for 150 seats out of the total 297. But the Social Justice Party had been known for problems with party discipline—its MPs were rumoured to be "easily bought" despite efforts by Krit and Thawee to control them.[135] Neither did the Democrats thoroughly trust the Social Nationalists, given the latter's willingness in January 1976 to betray Kukrit with their proposed censure motion. Thus, in a move that Krit probably opposed since he was no friend of Pramarn Adireksan, Seni opted to bring in Chart Thai's 56 MPs to further stabilize the new ruling coalition. The government now included the Democrats, Social Justice, Social Nationalists and Chart Thai for a total of 206 MPs out of 279. This grand, centre-right coalition was exactly what Kukrit's government was not: durable and lasting at a time of enormous crisis and including military backing given that Krit and Pramarn both become ministers in the cabinet.

But even before Seni took office (following weeks of coalition negotiations), trouble was already brewing. Days after the election, on 9 April 1976, unsure whether he would return to the cabinet, defence minister Pramarn Adireksan attempted to preserve his personal influence across the armed forces despite being within days of stepping down as defence minister. Pramarn made a plan with his brother-in-law foreign minister General Chatchai Chunhavan at their Soi Rajakru faction's headquarters, aware that the incoming Democrat-led coalition would choose Krit Sivara as the new defence minister and that Krit had accepted. Pramarn and Chatchai thus mapped out a strategy with

General Chalerm Kamropwongse, military classmate of Chatchai and assistant army commander General Chalard Hiransiri. Following the meeting, Pramarn, using his power as defence minister—and not informing Krit or army commander Bunchai, who were themselves strategizing at their own Suen Ruen faction headquarters—made a strategic transfer of six army positions involving three officials. The key part of the reshuffle was that deputy army commander Chote Hiranyatthiti, who was retiring in September 1976, was "kicked upstairs" to the opaque, powerless post of armed forces inspector general. As a result, when army commander Bunchai, who was Krit's man, retired during that same month, the next-in-line, who was another of Krit's men, General Serm na Nakorn (army chief of staff), would be blocked from becoming army chief by Chalard. In fact, Chalard could then serve as army commander until his 1982 retirement (the same year that Serm was set to retire). As another part of Pramarn's reshuffle, General Paitoon Ingkatanuwat, a Soi Rajakru stalwart, was moved to an inactive post in the Office of the Supreme Commander, replacing General Prasan Amartayakul, who took Paitoon's own job at the Supreme Command Headquarters. This allowed Paitoon to attain a full general's rank. The transfers were thereupon agreed to by Kukrit, who passed it on to the king for endorsement—who quickly did so.[136]

A large question mark loomed over these transfers, however. Why did Pramarn make the transfers when the next in-coming defence minister could quickly reverse them? One theory was that Pramarn simply wanted to show other political parties that his Chart Thai still had enormous clout within the military. Another theory was that Pramarn wanted to specifically teach the Democrats a lesson about trying to influence the army. Third, if Krit's Social Justice Party thought it might ease Chart Thai out of the coalition, Pramarn wanted to prove that Chart Thai retained influence among soldiers.[137] Yet another possible motive was that if Pramarn's reshuffle was cancelled by the next defence minister, Chalard might use that decision to stage a coup and appoint Pramarn as prime minister. Finally, a new defence minister might feel pressured not to want to upset the new reshuffle equilibrium that Pramarn had created.

Regardless of the motive for the transfer, Chalard's immediate response was jubilant. He reportedly said: "If the color of the sky doesn't change, I'll be Deputy Army Commander-in-Chief." The move was clearly motivated by Pramarn's efforts to ensure that Chalard would be in line to become army commander upon the retirement of Krit's man Bunchai on 1 October 1976. Krit was furious, allegedly saying that he was not even given the honour of being consulted about the decision beforehand (even though Krit had already retired). Neither did Pramarn inform the Defence Council.[138]

Chalard did receive support from one unexpected quarter. This was the "Young Turks" faction within the army. Formed in the early 1970s among younger and intermediate level officers, this ideological clique sought to jettison Thailand's corrupt parliamentary system, initiate fundamental social, political and social reforms and then incrementally re-establish a more participatory Thai democracy. In early April, the Young Turks distributed leaflets around Bangkok accusing Krit of attempting to eventually promote former police chief Prachuab Suntarangkul (then at a post in the Supreme Command) to control the army, while also being likely to advance the army career of General Vitoon Yasawat (then an army assistant chief of staff). The leaflets supported the rise of General Chalard to the post of deputy army commander and accused General Serm na Nakorn of wanting to be army chief of staff because that position had "full control of the secret [army] fund". Finally, the leaflet threatened that if Krit, as defence minister, tried to promote his friend, assistant army chief General Prasert Thammasiri, "there would be resistance".[139] Also in April, five members of the Young Turks visited incoming prime minister M.R. Seni Pramoj and urged him not to appoint Krit as defence minister but rather to take on the defence minister portfolio himself. The Young Turk representatives opined that Krit was unsuitable to be defence minister because he had been an unprofessional army leader.[140] In the end, regardless of the "advice", Seni appointed Krit as defence minister anyway. Some military officers agreed with the Young Turks that Krit should remain out of politics but for different reasons. These soldiers believed that Krit should stay out of politics as a fatherly stabilizer for the government and the military. As a moderating voice in the background of Thailand's fledgling democracy, Krit would thus be a "barrier" to any coup attempt upon it. In this way, these individuals saw Krit's role as partially comparable to that of the king.[141]

By early April 1976, Thailand's military was increasingly divided between the "professionals" and the "politicals", cohering around one of two retired generals: Krit or Pramarn. The most senior active-duty officers in Krit's group at that time included General Bunchai Bamrunpong, army commander (though he was soon to retire, on 30 September); supreme and navy commander Admiral Sangad; air force commander ACM Kamol Dechatungka; deputy supreme and air force commander General Kriangsak Chomanand; assistant supreme commander General Serm na Nakorn; army chief of staff General Prasert Thammasiri (1st Army Region commander); and General Prem Tinsulanonda (2nd Army Region commander). As for Pramarn's clique, they were bolstered by support from Thanom, Praphas and Narong, though they commanded fewer soldiers. This more hard-line faction included General Chalard Hiranyasiri, deputy army commander (temporarily), and Gen Yot Thephasadin na Ayuthaya, 1st Army Region commander.

Clearly, by April 1976, though he had retired from the military six months previously, Krit retained outstanding political clout, perhaps only behind that of the king. But as to economic clout, Krit's power was unrivalled. He was economically linked with fifty-two companies and held common interests with thirty-two of Thailand's leading Sino-Thai families, including the wealthiest seven.[142] By 1975, according to the CIA, Krit was on the board of directors of at least six Chinese-controlled private firms, notwithstanding his claims that he had severed all such economic connections, which it appears were made for "public relations" purposes.[143]

Among his economic accomplishments, Krit was crucial in building up the Royal Turf Club of Thailand (RTCT; also known as Nang Loeng Racecourse). Founded in 1916 as an alternative to the ultra-royalist Royal Bangkok Sports Club (though on land leased by the Crown Property Bureau), it became a centre of legalized gambling and socializing among Thai military leaders. As commander of the 1st Army Region, Krit developed a string of successful racehorses that competed under the name of K.S. (Krit Sivara) Stable. As such, Krit became a leading successful gambler until his interest finally declined and he sold his stable in 1976.[144] The Crown Property Bureau ended its land lease for RTCT in 2018.

Another example of Krit's 1973–76 economic prowess could be seen in Thailand's sugar market. It was revealed in April 1974 that the Ministry of Interior was requiring all sugar exports to pass through the Thailand Sugar Corporation, whose board chairman was Krit Sivara. No other export agent could legally export sugar from Thai sugar mills outside of Thailand. Moreover, the Ministry of Industry had agreed to the Thailand Sugar Corporation's export of white sugar at a "markedly less than obtainable world market price".[145] The Minister of Industry at the time was Osot Kosin, known to be close to Krit.

Yet another major interest of Krit's was Air Siam. The third-largest domestic carrier in Thailand, it had been started in 1965 by Prince

Varananda, Princess Galyani's consort, as a competitor against Thai Airways International, which was controlled by the Thai Air Force.[146] Air Siam gained its air licence in 1970 through pressure from Premier Thanom. It was reorganized in 1972 by a group of Thai businessmen associated with Krit Sivara, who reportedly obtained 55 per cent of the company's shares. But the company had several cash flow problems and came close to bankruptcy. It began looking for money from military sources, such as Narong Kittikachorn and Krit Sivara. In early 1975, amidst a sagging global economy, the Sanya government proposed a deal to merge Thai Airways and Siam Air. By that time, Krit Sivara's brother was on Air Siam's board of directors. Moreover, Krit had become a major stockholder in Air Siam through a "frontman", and Krit had "made it known" to the Ministry of Communications that all Thai governmental agencies should "help Air Siam".[147] Air Siam's business problems were alleviated by its powerful connections. In addition to the royal linkage, other supporters included then foreign minister Chatchai Chunhavan, then finance minister Bunchu Rotchanasthian and then minister of communications Thawit Klinprathum, who was a close associate of Krit Sivara. Thawit had appointed former senior official for Air Siam Kan Nakhamadi as permanent secretary for communications.[148] The two airlines were eventually merged as Thai Airways International in March 1977, though the royal family apparently lost money in the process.

Krit's most important partner was Yang Hsi Kun, known as "Krit's Banker". Indeed, Krit had been board chairperson on at least five of Yang's enterprises and had collaborated with Yang in manipulating stocks in three oil-related companies. As Zimmerman points out, Krit was so connected in a vast array of businesses that no coup was likely given that coups cost money and as long as Krit remained army commander (or could indirectly influence army commanders). Once retired, Krit had ample amounts of financial resources to continue influencing active-duty military officers and also to ensure his ascent as a politician and prime minister.[149]

On 20 April, new prime minister Seni Pramoj moved to set up his cabinet. Realizing that a military strongman would have to anchor his government, Seni, on 21 April, appointed Krit as defence minister. But in order to appease Krit's chief opponent, Seni also appointed Pramarn as deputy prime minister and agriculture minister. At the same time, Seni appointed General Thawit Seniwong na Ayuthaya, a Democrat MP representing a district in Bangkok (but who had once served under generals Praphas and Krit), as deputy defence minister. In the cabinet,

Thawit had earlier served briefly as defence minister under Seni in 1975. Compared to Krit, Thawit was meek and lacking in charisma.

But, on 23 April, only two days after his appointment as defence minister, Krit suddenly and mysteriously died. His specific value to Seni had been his ability to guarantee the support of numerous conservative groups and military factions, and his sudden absence ensured a vacuum in the military, in parliamentary politics and on the economic landscape. His death occurred even before Seni's government had achieved the necessary parliamentary vote of confidence.

According to the US Embassy, Krit died at 7:30 a.m. from complications of a heart attack he had suffered on 16 April. He had been admitted to Phra Mongkut Klao Hospital in central Bangkok on the afternoon of that day complaining of chest pains. He had recently got over an illness seen as "not serious", but which had temporarily laid him up at home. Now, having been admitted to hospital, he was immediately treated at the Coronary Care Unit (CCU). On doctors' orders, he was permitted only a limited number of visitors. Those who saw him were General Bunchai, General Chote, prime minister Kukrit Pramoj's aide-de-camp MG Fuangchaloei Aniruttwea, General Pramarn Adireksan, and a representative of the king and queen. According to Fuangchaloei, Krit told him that he was sick because he "ate too much sticky rice and mango and played too much golf". Indeed, on 14 April he had played golf at Navatanee golf course with military friends but showed no signs of exhaustion. There was also a rumour that on 15 April he had met with a mistress at Chavalit Hotel.[150] On 15 April he had indeed lunched on sticky rice and mango at the Erawan Hotel and had come down with a terrible pain. On 18 April, the hospital director announced that Krit had recovered and would soon be discharged. The embassy stressed that Krit's sickness was "not serious". In fact, the embassy speculated that because of the timing of Krit's illness its cause was likely "in part 'political'". The reasoning was that Krit took advantage of a case of indigestion and a slight heart problem to avoid commenting on defence minister Pramarn Adireksan's non-endorsed promotion of General Chalard to become deputy army commander.[151]

It was later revealed that Krit would be staying on in the CCU because of an irregular heartbeat resulting from the two left cells in his heart having partially ceased to work. The hospital thereupon announced that Krit would likely remain warded for close to a month. A patient in this condition would usually require an operation. But a committee of physicians and heart specialists ruled out this option. No reason was given. Within a day, Krit's condition improved and he was able to speak. But he was still in an oxygen tent and fed intravenously.[152] From this point his condition continued to improve. Then, on Wednesday, 21 April, the day he was officially appointed defence minister, he was reported as being almost back to normal. But on 22 April he experienced a reoccurrence of heart trouble, which doctors then described as "not improving". On that day, his visitors included deputy prime minister ACM Thawee and deputy defence minister General Thawit. In the evening he ate soup and jelly for dinner, and at 11 p.m. ordered a glass of iced coffee before resting. At 4 a.m., amidst his increasingly palpitating and irregular heartbeat, Krit whispered something to his aide-de-camp, Lt. Col. Sommai Poonsap, which Sommai could not catch. Krit then fell asleep. He was pronounced dead early the next morning.[153]

Though it could well be that Krit died from a heart attack, it seemed unlikely. His death after all was quite sudden and clearly rather odd. The timing and the individual involved was almost too strange to be believable. Indeed, with the king having become amenable to supporting a coup, Krit was the only person who seemed able and willing to preserve Thai democracy—and he conveniently died only hours after being named defence minister. Moreover, he was only sixty-two and his family members had mostly lived long lives. One could ask why the doctors chose not to perform surgery on Krit to address the heart ailment. At the same time, without trying to sound conspiratorial, there were rumours that Krit had been murdered, perhaps via poison.[154] Such rumours have stood the test of time until today, especially given that Krit's body was never autopsied. As such a powerful figure in Thai society, Krit certainly had numerous enemies. Generally speaking, if he did not die from something related to a heart ailment, it would have involved quite a large conspiracy (including doctors and family members), so the question becomes whether someone either helped to bring about a heart attack or later killed him after he was already in the hospital. Nevertheless, decades later, guessing whether Krit was killed and who might have killed him has become a useless parlour game. Ultimately, Krit might indeed have been the victim of foul play. If so, he most probably entered the hospital himself, feigning ill health because he did not want to address the issue of Pramarn's appointment of Chalard at that time. It remains possible that someone poisoned him in the few hours prior to his death in the hospital.

The years 1973 to 1976 marked the surprising ascent to power of Krit Sivara. Dislodging Thanom, Praphas and Narong from their military domination over Thailand, Krit became the senior associate in a power partnership with the king. Without a doubt, Krit was the leading political and economic actor. He also shaped ISOC to suit his political interests. But, perhaps most importantly, he built his power base simultaneous to supporting and sustaining Thai democracy, although it was weakly institutionalized. Perhaps, if he had lived, it would have become stronger.

In the final analysis, these pivotal three years, though being the final years of Krit's life, represented the rise and fall of civilian-led, yet frail, electoral democracy. The period was marked by several agential and structural factors that initially enhanced political space but eventually doomed it. In terms of agency, in 1973 Krit was the vehicle facilitating Thailand's transformation from dictatorship to democracy, through support from the king and pressure for reform by Thailand's organized youth. By 1976, however, Krit was dead and the king was pushing for the resurrection of autocracy. As for structure, domestic and international events of 1973 favoured a move away from military dictatorship and economic malaise towards a new beginning. Also by 1976, the fall of Thailand's neighbours to communism, a growing domestic communist insurgency, and US preferences for a return to autocracy in Thailand made it more difficult for Thailand to sustain democracy during this time.

Krit's death left a huge political vacuum in Thailand at a time when the country was experiencing the most instability it had felt since World War II. Seni's coalition government was weakened, while generals, politicians and the king increasingly competed for power. The military realized that Krit's death opened the gates to a possible military coup since Krit's hostility towards one was gone. His absence allowed for the growing cohesion of the Young Turks faction and the potential revitalization of the trio of Thanom, Praphas and Narong. At the same time, politicians such as Pramarn Adireksan viewed Krit's demise as an opportunity to take the defence portfolio. Finally, with Krit gone, King Bhumipol could now more easily build a military faction with no single individual—such as Krit—possessing greater strength than the crown. The turbulence of 1976, however, would prove to be stronger than any of these groups could handle for long.

Initially, Seni's government was able to deal with potential military mischief. Deputy defence minister General Thawit Seniwong na Ayuthaya, the unassuming and newly elected Democrat MP who had previously served in 1975 as minister of defence, assumed Krit's position as defence minister on 27 April. Thawit was also a Krit loyalist. Within days of forming his coalition, Seni, through Thawit, pushed aside the generals loyal to Pramarn Adireksan. Most importantly, General Chalard Hiranyasiri was transferred from the post of deputy army commander that Pramarn had promoted him to to an inactive post in the Supreme Command. Pramarn, having already accepted the slots of deputy prime minister and minister of agriculture, could not also suddenly seek the defence portfolio—not with Tawich already possessing it. Chalard's transfer re-established control over the military by Krit's faction, which the government assumed was supportive of continued democracy.[155] Krit's man General Serm na Nakorn was now once more destined to become army commander upon General Bunchai's impending 30 September 1976 retirement—and he did.[156] But with Krit now dead, his faction began to lose coherence, especially since Bunchai was soon to retire and Serm was considered relatively weak. At this point, other military personalities who had been close to Krit began to gain increasing importance, including supreme commander Admiral Sangad, deputy supreme comander ACM Kamon and General Kriangsak. Sangad, however, was also set to retire on 30 September.

The Krit faction feared there could be coup attempts by other factions seeking to usurp control over the armed forces. These could realistically come from one or all of the following groups: the trio of Thanom, Praphas and Narong, with help from 1st Army Region commander General Yot Thepsadin na Ayuthaya; Pramarn Adireksan through General Chalard, General Vitoon and perhaps assistant army commander General Prasert Thammasiri; or even the Young Turks. In fact, these groups might work together. The coup cliques might also want to gain support from King Bhumipol. Back in February, the king had already signalled to Admiral Sangad his conditions for supporting a coup: an arch-royalist civilian prime minister who would institute a new constitution that would enhance monarchical powers over Thailand. Indeed, what the king was proposing was similar in some ways to a deal with senior soldiers that the Privy Council had brokered with coup makers in exchange for palace endorsement back in 1947, 1957 and 1973. If the Krit faction wanted to maintain supremacy in the military, it might need to retain the king's support—and carrying out the coup was the way to obtain it. But obtaining royal support would thus mean moving away from Krit's prior support for preserving democracy and establishing an authoritarian regime that itself would require a massacre of those opposed to tyranny. Rationalizing a coup would also require more pandemonium, both in parliament and in civil society.

For its part, the Ford administration completed a review of US policy towards Thailand on 20 April, the date of commencement of the Seni government. The embassy believed that any US attempts to try and keep its soldiers on bases in Thailand would spark violent anti-US demonstrations in Bangkok. The embassy further surmised the following:

> Should the new coalition government prove weak and unable to provide firm leadership, it is probable that the Thai military, after a decent interval, will take control of the government by force.... [A] military takeover, let alone an RTG decision to permit U.S. forces to stay in Thailand, could cause political violence in Bangkok.[157]

Parliamentary politics under Seni's 1976 government were predictably unstable, but they at first seemed to be more durable than under Kukrit. Seni made a good start by strengthening his position within the military, which reflected a strength in parliament, especially toward Pramarn. In foreign policy, Seni's foreign minister, Pichai Rattakul, signalled his intention to continue Kukrit's strategy of omnidirectionality—looking towards greater balancing among the great powers—as well as nationalism. In addition, getting the US troops out of Thailand was generally a popular domestic political issue. As such, Seni persisted with Kukrit's earlier deadline of almost all troops out of Thailand by 20 July 1976. With the handover drawing near, the Thai government formally asked for control over remaining electronic intelligence equipment at the former US Ramasun base, sixteen communications sites, and US bombs still in Thailand. As a concession, the United States was granted refuelling and emergency landing rights in Thailand. On 15 July, the deep-water port at Sattahip was turned over to the Thai government. Then, on 19 July, Seni appeared on a television talk show in which he reassured Thais that his government could protect them from both external and internal enemies. In the programme, foreign minister Pichai Rattakul and supreme commander Sangad (who was then involved in coup planning) stood alongside Seni. The appearance was supposed to stamp out any rumours there might be uncontrollable violent clashes between rightists and leftists on 20 July.[158] In fact, the 20 July handover did pass smoothly. On that day, the radio research facility at Ramasun was formally closed and the US MACTHAI headquarters in Bangkok was shuttered. Thus, the United States met the Thai government's four-month withdrawal deadline. From that date on, there were only 270 military advisers affiliated with the Joint US Military Advisory Group Thailand (JUSMAG). This was a huge drop from the previous 50,000 US troops earlier stationed in Thailand.

Nevertheless, Thailand's defence minister and most senior military officials were reportedly quite opposed to Seni's decision to compel US troops to leave Thailand, and they had lobbed unsuccessfully against it.[159]

Meanwhile, in an interview with a US diplomat, the king disapproved of Seni's forced evacuation of US troops since he "felt that Thailand was cutting itself off from its friends, particularly the US, to too great an extent".[160] The king also expressed concerns with the growing split between the Left and the Right in Thailand. Former prime minister Kukrit likewise stated that:

> Thais were becoming more disenchanted with the parliament. Lawlessness was growing. This increased lawlessness could create a situation in which the military could return to power. But Khukrit also said that Thailand may be saved by the fact that there is no charismatic leader within the military.[161]

But though the Thai military no longer had a charismatic leader such as Krit, what Kukrit perhaps did not realize was that in the absence of such a leader the king might himself be willing to ambiguously fill the void and thus champion a coup against democracy. Already he was vigorously fast-tracking his arch-royalist standard-bearer, Army 1st Division commander General Aroon Twatsin, towards the post of army commander.

One of the core themes that Seni had campaigned on during the 1976 election was reducing police corruption. In July 1976, Seni's trusted secretary-general (of the Office of the Prime Minister), Nithipat Chalichan, stated that the government was already prosecuting one police general for corruption and had ensured the arrest of the Forestry Department director (both cases were meant to reflect Seni's control over bureaucratic corruption).[162] As part of Seni's police reforms, he approved the creation of a Police Narcotics Division. He also approved the appointment of three new police deputy directors (General Suraphon Chunlaphram, General Chumpon Lohachala and General Montchai Phankhongchun) and a new assistant police director general (General Narong Mahanon). These police officials had all played a major role during the events of 14 October 1973, their careers had been supported by Krit Sivara, and they would play major roles in the events of 6 October 1976.

Seni's government also told the US ambassador that Thailand could not continue to "assume steadily increasing defense costs", and that the best method to counter communist insurgency was to improve local administration and provide more economic and social development.[163]

In fact, members of the government coalition in the lower house sought to reduce budgeting for the military and state enterprises, instead seeking more state spending on local-level "pork barrel" projects.[164] Some of these same MPs proposed reining in the power of ISOC and embarking on an even more neutralist foreign policy for Thailand. At the same time, senior military officials were piqued by Seni's apparent turning over of foreign policy to officials at Thailand's foreign ministry (such as foreign minister Pichai Rattakul and Anand Panyarachun), who were pushing a more non-aligned foreign policy and disregarding the military's advice on national security issues. Besides their frustration about the government's heavy reduction in US forces in Thailand, the generals were disappointed that Seni had ordered the withdrawal of a security unit along the Thai-Malaysian border while telling the Malaysian PM that Thailand would limit its "hot pursuit" of insurgents across the border; had dismissed General Sant Chitpattima from his 4th Army Region command in the South; and saw the prime minister as backtracking on promises they thought he had made on not trying to turn Thailand into a neutralist nation. They saw this as being confirmed when foreign minister Pichai visited Vietnam in early August (followed by the establishment of diplomatic relations between Vietnam and Thailand) and made ready to travel to the Lao PDR.[165]

But amidst the government's attempts at building bridges with neighbouring countries, Seni's coalition, besides being divided among the Chart Thai, Social Justice and Social Nationalists parties, was also deeply divided into different cliques, which were partly based on patronage and ideology. These included the progressive faction of Democrat Party secretary general Damrong Lathipiphat, a large southern faction (including Surin Masdit and Chuan Leekpai), a northeastern faction (which had been heavily dependent on financing from Krit Sivara) and a Bangkok faction led by ultra-rightists Thammanun Thiengngern and Samak Sundaravej. Samak in particular was closely connected to the ultra-right-wing generals and Queen Sirikit.[166] By August 1976, the Bangkok faction was at the point of defecting from the party altogether, potentially creating fertile grounds for a coup. Though it would have been quite a challenge for any party leader to instil discipline in this motley bunch of disparate groupings, Seni Pramoj proved especially ill-suited to the task. That the government lasted as long as it did—six months—and was ultimately felled by a military coup most likely testifies to the preference of its coalition participants for "feeding at the trough" of rent extraction while in office.

On 29 July, Seni's government, mired in this internal factional bickering and indecisive leadership, experienced its first legislative defeat when the House of Representatives voted down the cabinet-approved nominations for the proposed anti-corruption committee. The embarrassing loss highlighted the Democrats' penchant for internal squabbling and factionalism, the dilatory pace of their promised reforms, and Seni's image as a disorganized prime minister. Though the Democrats could have dissolved parliament based upon this embarrassing loss, they chose not to, realizing that MP defectors could then easily move to another party, that there might have to be another expensive election, or soldiers could even use the occasion as a pretext for a military coup. In fact, coalition parties pledged to support the upcoming August 1976 budget bill.[167]

Given the continuing instability within the ruling coalition, it was extremely fortunate for Seni that on 4 August the budget sailed to approval in the lower house. This budget looked set to give the Democrats enhanced popularity among voters given that it allocated over US$60 million for local community development programmes. Following the disbursal of the new budget on 1 October, the Democrats would enjoy much more popular support, and any planned military coup would become politically unacceptable. At the same time, since the Democrats already controlled the defence portfolio (through defence minister General Tawich Seniwong Na Ayuthaya), they held some influence over senior appointments within the armed forces—appointments that would occur on 1 October.

On 28 July, secretary of state Henry Kissinger sent a cable to the US Embassy in Bangkok, highlighting the fact that the *Washington Post* had on 24 July published an article by columnist Lewis Simons headlined "Thais Fear a Return to Military Control". According to the article, "Western observers" believe that the Thai army and its allies had decided to stage a coup given that they perceived the Seni government as moving too rapidly to "mend fences" with Thailand's new communist neighbours Laos, Vietnam and Cambodia. Kissinger stated that the article had "aroused [his] interest … about the degree of Thai military dissatisfaction with the Seni government". In all capital letters, he specifically wanted the embassy to comment regarding the following points:

(A) WHERE HAS POWER GRAVITATED IN THE MILITARY SINCE THE DEATH OF GENERAL KRIT AND THE REASSIGNMENT OF PRAMAN? (B) IS THERE SUBSTANCE TO REPORTS THAT THE THAI MILITARY

HAVE TAKEN SPECIFIC ACTION DESIGNED TO SABOTAGE THE MINISTRY OF FOREIGN AFFAIRS' EFFORTS TO REACH A RAPPROCHEMENT WITH THE INDOCHINA COUNTRIES? (C) TO WHAT EXTENT HAS THE COMPLETION OF THE US MILITARY WITHDRAWAL AND RECENT INSURGENT ATTACKS TENDED TO UNITE THE THAI MILITARY IN OPPOSITION TO THE POLICIES OF THE CIVILIAN GOVERNMENT? (D) TO WHAT EXTENT ARE THE THAI MILITARY OR ELEMENTS WITHIN THE THAI MILITARY CAPABLE OF MOUNTING A COUP? KISSINGER[168]

Kissinger's cable could have had one of three meanings. First, and least likely, having been made aware of coup plotting by the Simons article, he simply wanted to know if there was any veracity to it. Second, and more likely, he was pleasantly surprised by the article and was hoping that the embassy could confirm that a coup against Seni could be possible. Third, and most likely, already aware of and supporting an effort by Thai generals and the king to stage a coup, he was hoping the embassy could find its own evidence in support of the Simons article—or was hoping that the US ambassador, not the CIA, was unaware. Though Kissinger could have been assured that events in Thailand were pushing the military towards greater cohesion in support of a coup, the armed forces were still factionalized and in need of a unifying leader to carry it out. Nevertheless, it had rapidly cohered against the policies of the Seni government. Indeed, the military was seeking to sabotage Seni's foreign policy efforts at any turn that it could.

On 5 August, US ambassador Whitehouse cabled Kissinger back regarding the possibility of a coup. Surprisingly, given the growing military opposition to Seni's government, Whitehouse said that he was "unaware of any coup rumor significant enough to report ... [and was] surprised at department's reaction to the Lewis Simons article ... [since] rumors of coup plotting occur constantly in Thailand.... The embassy's view ... [is that] the Thai military continue to be somewhat factionalized and without a charismatic leader." In answer to Kissinger's questions, Whitehouse stated in capitals:

POWER HAS NOT GRAVITATED TO ONE PERSON OR ONE GROUP SINCE THE DEATH OF GENERAL KRIT AND THE REASSIGNMENT OF PRAMAN. THE ARMY REMAINS THE BASE OF POWER WITHIN THE MILITARY. NEITHER THE NAVY NOR THE AIR FORCE ALONE OR IN TANDEM COULD STAGE A COUP WITHOUT ARMY SUPPORT. THOSE WHO OWED

THEIR ALLEGIANCE TO KRIT ARE REASSESSING
THE SITUATION.... ROYAL THAI ARMY OFFICERS
HAVE TURNED TO "CLASSMATE" ASSOCIATIONS
TO FILL THIS LEADERSHIP VACUUM CAUSED
BY KRIT'S DEATH. ACCORDING TO THE ARMY
ATTACHE THE LEADING CONTENDERS OUTSIDE
THE RTA ARE PRAMAN, GEN. THAWIT SENIWONG,
MINISTER OF DEFENSE, AND POSSIBLY ADMIRAL
SA-NGAD CHALOYU. THOSE WITHIN THE RTA ARE
GEN. CHALAT HIRANYASIRI, SPECIAL ASSISTANT
TO THE MINISTER OF DEFENSE; GEN. PRASOET
[Prasert] THAMMASIRI, ASSISTANT COMMANDER IN
CHIEF, RTA; AND LTG WITHUN [Vitoon] YASAWAT,
ASSISTANT CHIEF OF STAFF FOR PERSONNEL, RTA.
NONE HOWEVER, HAS THE NECESSARY TROOP
SUPPORT OR HAS HAD THE TIME TO FILL THE
VACUUM AT THIS TIME. B. THE EMBASSY HAS
NO SOLID EVIDENCE THAT THE MILITARY HAVE
TAKEN ANY CONCERTED ACTIONS TO SABOTAGE
THE FOREIGN MINISTRY'S EFFORTS TO REACH
RAPPROACHEMENT WITH ITS NEIGHBORS.... THE
U.S. MILITARY WITHDRAWAL AND THE RECENT
INSURGENT ATTACKS HAVE GIVEN SOME MILITARY
OFFICERS THE OPPORTUNITY TO CRITICIZE THE
GOVERNMENT'S FOREIGN POLICY MORE ACTIVELY
BUT THERE IS NO EVIDENCE THAT THESE TWO
OCCURRENCES HAVE TENDED TO UNITE THE
MILITARY IN OPPOSING THE POLICIES OF THE
CIVILIAN GOVERNMENT. THE THAI MILITARY OR
ELEMENTS WITHIN THE THAI MILITARY ARE AS
CAPABLE OF MOUNTING A COUP, AS ANY MILITARY
IN THE WORLD. HOWEVER, THE EMBASSY DOES
NOT EXPECT A COUP, ESPECIALLY A SUCCESSFUL
COUP, TO TAKE PLACE IN THE IMMEDIATE FUTURE.
IF THE GOVERNMENT WERE TO FALL SUDDENLY,
SERIOUS CIVIL DISTURBANCES BREAK OUT, AND A
PROLONGED PARLIAMENTARY CRISIS PARALYZE
THE GOVERNMENT, THE COMMANDERS IN CHIEF
OF THE ARMED FORCES, ADMIRAL SA-NGAT
[Sangad] CHALOYU, AIR CHIEF MARSHAL KAMON
DECHATUNGKHA AND GENERAL BUNCHAI
BAMRUNGPHONG COULD, ACTING IN CONCERT,
AND WITH THE TACIT APPROVAL OF THE KING,
LEAD A MILITARY TAKEOVER IN RESPONSE TO
THE NATIONAL EMERGENCY. THE ARMED FORCES
WOULD, UNDER THESE CIRCUMSTANCES, FOLLOW
THEIR COMMANDER. WHITEHOUSE[169]

The problem with Whitehouse's statement was his assumption that any coup would come before the 1 October 1976 military reshuffle (when the more democratic General Bunchai would have to retire), that the coup would be led by mid-ranking or deputy commanders rather than from the top, and that the king would not give the coup his tacit approval. Moreover, Whitehouse was not privy to all CIA (and Kissinger's) activities in Thailand. Moreover, the fact that "power [had] not gravitated to one" military man meant that it was increasingly gravitating to the monarch, who back in February had already told supreme commander Admiral Sangad that he would support a coup—just not at that moment. But regal endorsement for a putsch was fast approaching.

It was at this point that a test for governmental stability entered the picture. Indeed, only two weeks after the Kissinger letter, General Praphas Charusatien suddenly returned to Bangkok's Don Muang airport on 15 August 1976. Many Thai army elements were aware in advance that he would be returning to Bangkok and they even arranged for it. Indeed, he was immediately received at Don Muang by 1st Army Region commander General Yot Thepasadin na Ayuthaya, a Praphas stalwart, and spirited away by Yot's military faction to 1st Army Region headquarters and then to a luxurious safehouse in the city, where he initially remained in hiding. Arriving separately by plane into Bangkok were other members of Praphas's family. Apparently, according to former US ambassador to Thailand Leonard Unger, Praphas's return was coordinated in some way by the Republic of China (Taiwan). Indeed, his air flight from Taiwan to Thailand coincided with the arrivals of General Lai Ming-Tang, chief of staff of Taiwan's Ministry of National Defence; General Wang Yung-Shu, director of Taiwan's National Security Bureau; and Han Lih-Wu, who had been Taiwan's ambassador to Thailand during 1956–64. All of these were close to Praphas, but he also expected to meet with deputy prime minister ACM Thawee Chulasap and General Kriangsak Chomanand.[170] If, indeed, leading Chinese (Taiwan) security personnel were involved in Praphas's visit to Thailand, it raises an interesting question: to what extent might Taiwan have been involved in helping to potentially foment a coup in Thailand?

Two days after Praphas's rumoured return, the NSCT organized a ten-thousand-person rally at Sanam Luang on 17 August, setting a forty-eight-hour deadline for Seni's government to arrest Praphas. At the same time, Thailand's Labour Council beseeched the military allies of Praphas not to exploit the instability to stage a coup, and warned that if there was a coup, labour unions would vehemently oppose it.[171]

On 18 August, the Special Branch Police "located" Praphas at the home of his nephew, Major Chanchai Thiannpraphas. Thereupon, Seni set up a five-person committee designed to pressure Praphas to leave Thailand. Praphas refused, saying that he preferred to answer charges against him in court. He was then placed in the protective custody of his factional follower General Yot (1st Army Region commander). Seni's cabinet then unanimously voted on 19 August to have Praphas sent out of Thailand.

Praphas continued to stall, telling Seni's government that he needed medical treatment. He was then granted an audience with the king. Publicly, Praphas said that he would not leave Thailand. Army commander General Bunchai demanded that Praphas return to Taiwan, while deputy PM ACM Tawee Chulasap advised Seni that Praphas should be allowed to stay to consult physicians.[172]

A CIA report stated that Praphas and his military supporters in Thailand were seeking to bring down the Seni government. His supporters consisted of not only General Yot, but also several other associated generals (e.g., General Thep Kranlert) and the leaders of the Chart Thai Party: Pramarn Adireksan and Chatchai Chunhavan.[173] Seni found it close to impossible to extract Praphas from the country, and apparently the government took three days to even locate him. To the public, Seni meekly stated that "he was not sure that Prapas was in Bangkok", and he was "too busy to follow up on this" case. Later, Seni further vacillated by claiming he could negotiate with Praphas. He later said he would give Praphas another week to go home. When Seni's cabinet demanded that General Yot hand Praphas over to the police, Yot replied that "The military will try to comply ... but I must first ... consult with the commander-in-chief of the armed forces".[174] By this statement, Yot could have been referring not only to supreme commander Admiral Sangad but also to the monarch. The cabinet then reportedly called upon the king to use His Majesty's influence to urge Praphas to leave Thailand. At this point, the pressure was on King Bhumipol. If he ignored or turned down the government request, Yot might be able to use the Praphas issue to stage a coup. In preparation for such a scenario, army chief General Bunchai placed all Thai army units on full alert.[175]

Seni finally succeeded in forcing the departure from Thailand of Praphas because the prime minister was able to exploit the factional rivalries within the military. In addition, he kept Pramarn in line by appointing him to the committee tasked with getting Praphas out of Thailand. That Praphas's return contributed to violence leading to the

death of four demonstrators and the wounding of eighty others following attacks by right-wing vigilante groups (Red Gaurs and Nawaphon)
helped the government bring pressure to bear on Praphas to leave the
country. Alternatively, Handley argues that Praphas left Thailand not
because of the stealthy moves of Seni, but because of the king. The
latter, upon seeing right-wing violence against students and having
been asked to intercede by the cabinet, decided that the moment was
not right for Praphas to return to Thailand (after initially having okayed
it). He thus asked Praphas to depart from the country again.[176] Finally,
deputy PM ACM Thawee Chulasap offered a third explanation for
the ex-strongman leaving Thailand: "Praphas' departure was his own
decision, following conversations with the king and with Praphas' own
friends [e.g., Generals Yot and Thep]".[177]

On 22 August, Praphas returned to Taiwan aboard a special plane,
accompanied by minister of industries General Chatchai Chunhavan,
defence minister General Thawit, 1st Army Region commander
General Yot and deputy commander of police General Chumpon.
Though he had finally been able to galvanize powerful pressure upon
Praphas to leave Thailand, the Praphas "visit" demonstrated that Seni
had little control over events and it increasingly united the progressive
student movement. Praphas and the king both seemed to have used
the former's visit to "test the waters" of progressives' reactions to an
authoritarian resurrection.

A second effect of Praphas's visit was that it led to the resignation of defence minister General Thawit Seniwong na Ayuttaya on
24 August. He did so in the immediate aftermath of the severe criticism he received from the Democrats' progressive faction that he had
been unable to control the armed forces and was in fact an acolyte of
Praphas since he had seemingly sided with Praphas during the latter's
visit to Bangkok. Though a member of the Democrat Party, Thawit was
certainly conservative. In actuality, Thawit could not have ordered Yot
to hand over Praphas since any order that a defence minister makes to
active-duty soldiers must first come through the supreme commander.
Thawit's replacement as defence minister was PM Seni himself, the
first time in Thai history a true civilian (never having previously served
in the military) had assumed the defence minister's post. But there
was speculation that Seni was only keeping the seat warm for apparent
pro-democracy army commander General Bunchai, who was set to
retire in a little over a month.[178] With Bunchai as defence minister, any
coup might not be successful. Indeed, by rewarding senior members of
the military who had stood by him, Seni hoped that it would help to

keep the military under control. But with the armed forces increasingly factionalized, the elevation of Bunchai might also alienate other senior officers.[179]

The systemic necessities of a coup were all in place. But there still needed to be some sort of efficient or proximate factor that would help set it off. Thanom would be it. Already during the week of Kissinger's cable, Thanom had apparently requested from the Seni government that he be allowed to return. By 6 August, the US Embassy was aware of his effort. Korn Dabbaronsi, nephew of Pramarn and Chatchai, told US ambassador Whitehouse that he had been informed of Thanom's request and he hoped it would take place. In the words of Whitehouse, the gist of what Korn said was that if Thanom is permitted to return ... there will be violence, which may lead to a cabinet reshuffle and perhaps even the removal of the Prime Minister ... legally through the electoral process or in the aftermath of a coup".[180] In fact, Thanom's return was to eventually lead to both happening. But Thanom's trip to Thailand was delayed by that of Praphas's.

Only seven days after Praphas's departure from Thailand, Thanom's daughters formally met with Seni to request that their father, soon to be ordained as a Buddhist monk, be allowed to return to Thailand. At the time, Thanom's six children were all variously involved with trying to get him back to Bangkok. In order of age, these included Nongnat Penchat, daughter (married to Chamnan Penchat of Union Bank); Narong Kittikachorn, son, then in exile in West Germany; Nongnut Jirapongse, daughter (married to General Ueam Jirapongse, who had risen from 1st Division commander to become army territorial defence commander); Lt. Commander Yuthapong Kittikachorn (son; Royal Thai Air Force); Songsuda Yodmanee (married to Suwit Yodmanee, an academic businessman with linkages to the military and Chart Thai Party); and Songsamon Kotchasenee (married to Vice Admiral Supha Kotchasenee)

Following government pressure against Thanom's immediate visit, he agreed not to return to Thailand for the time being given the violence that his visit might produce. Seni apparently wanted any visit by Thanom to be limited by a period agreed to in advance between the government and the former prime minister. In the meantime, on 17 September, the full military annual reshuffle for 1 October 1976 was announced. Containing 164 appointments, it represented a near triumph for Krit's faction, though this time minus Krit. In fact, it reflected the growing rise of royal influence within the military, Praphas's persistent sway, and the distant beginnings of influence by General Prem Tinsulanond.

Eventually, Thanom returned to Thailand—doing so despite government advice not to—on 19 September. Unlike Praphas, he did not return secretly. He was accompanied by his son ACM Wing Commander Yuttaphong as well as his son-in-law Chaman Penchat. From Don Muang airport, Thanom was whisked directly to arch-royalist Wat Bowonniwet Temple for an ordination ceremony that would make him a Buddhist monk. At the ceremony were General Yot, deputy police chief General Chumpon Lohachala, commissioner of the metropolitan police General Wichian Saengkaeo, and assistant police chief General Narong Mahanon. Thanom, however, had never been close to Krit, was not a peer of the Krit faction and thus did not find expected backing from the senior military leaders (e.g., supreme commander Admiral Sangad, deputy supreme commander ACM Kamon or army commander General Bunchai). But Thanom did enjoy close ties with the palace. In fact, with Thanom facing pressure to leave the temple and depart Thailand, the king and queen raced back to Bangkok on 23 September from their vacation in Thailand's South and publicly visited Thanom at Wat Bowonniwet. The king wore a military uniform and stood at the head of a group of Nawaphon leaders. It was this obvious expression of support for Thanom and Nawaphon that, according to Handley, "stunned Seni" and caused him to resign as prime minister.[181] The US Embassy suggested that alternatively the resignation owed to Seni's personal pique that both right-wing and left-wing cabinet ministers in his party had constantly been criticizing his handling of Thanom. Indeed, following a lower house resolution to expel Thanom from Thailand, Seni resigned as premier on 23 September, which automatically triggered a cabinet dissolution but not the dissolution of parliament (though Seni could have done so).[182] Amidst wrangling within his party over how to proceed, Seni was finally convinced to return to the premiership, and the king formally reappointed him on 25 September.

According to a Top Secret CIA document, Chart Thai's Pramarn Adireksarn "was financing both right- and left-wing protest groups, hoping the ensuing unrest would force a cabinet reorganization that would strengthen his position" since he wanted Seni to make him defence minister, which would increase his power over the military.[183] Faced with intimidation and pressure from Pramarn, Seni decided to exclude Chart Thai from the coalition and form a two-party government between the Democrats and Kukrit's Social Action, which together would have amounted to 159 members.

Meanwhile, on 24 September, a new crisis developed. Two anti-Thanom student activists, while pasting up anti-Thanom posters in Nakhorn Pathom province, were set upon by local police, who beat them up, strangled them to death, and hanged them at an entrance gate to a home. Police chief General Sisuk Mahinthorathep admitted that the police had killed the two activists—likely for political reasons—and announced that there would be an investigation (which never proceeded). In reaction to the killings, 30 September witnessed the beginning of a new demonstration of approximately ten thousand peaceful protestors, led by the NSCT and labour groups, centred upon Thammasat University. By 4 October, the protestors had occupied the Thammasat University grounds, settling in at about 8 p.m. in preparation for the staging of a prolonged sit-in for the next few days.

University officials closed the institution as a way to guarantee the safety of students, and university rectors across Thailand called for Thanom to leave the country. Mid-term exams were boycotted by many Thammasat University students. NSCT secretary general Sutham Saengprathum announced that the protest would continue "indefinitely". Also on 4 October, students at the Fine Arts College at Thammasat University put together a "street theatre, the plot of which was the murder of the two student activists". Two different students volunteered to act as the activists in a mock hanging. On that day, several military officials told the US Embassy candidly about their

> uneasiness that violence could occur between now and October 14. They were concerned in particular about extreme right-wingers … tossing bombs into the midst of anti-Thanom demonstrators killing some. This could cause a confrontation which could lead to further violence.[184]

But such "concern" involved ad hoc violence among security officials rather than what was already a long-prepared plan to seize power.

The following day, 5 October, several newspapers, including the *Bangkok Post*, carried photos of the mock hanging without providing any commentary. But during that morning, an unidentified woman filed a charge of *lèse-majesté* against the NSCT based upon the hanging since she perceived that one of the "hanged" students coincidentally might have resembled Thailand's crown prince.[185] That afternoon, the ultra-ring-wing newspaper *Dao Siam* republished a photo of this "hanged" student, headlining the story on page 1 with the caption "Hanging a Body that Resembles the Crown Prince: Monarchy be

Warned!"[186] Meanwhile, Armoured Radio (run by Queen Sirikit's cousin Colonel Uthan Sanitwongs and linked with Chart Thai), which had for the last two years continuously transmitted fearmongering against progressives it considered communists, including that Seni and Kukrit were communist sympathizers, added to the fire. Thus, following *Dao Siam*'s 5 October "revelation" about the mock hanging, Armoured Radio announcers, accessing most radio stations across Thailand, accused NSCT of *lèse-majesté*, demanding that the Village Scouts and Nawaphon attack and kill the student demonstrators.[187]

Simultaneously, on 5 October, to Seni's utter surprise, the king refused to endorse this coalition. Thereupon, Seni brought the four parties back into the government, and the king endorsed the coalition. But there were some clear changes among cabinet ministers. The troublesome ultra-right-wing Samak Sundaravej and Sombun Sirithon had been ejected from their posts as deputy interior ministers. In addition, Seni gave up his seat as defence minister in exchange for now-retired supreme commander Admiral Sangad Chaloryu taking up that post. Seni's loyal disciple Nithipat Chalichan became minister attached to the PM's Office and deputy defence minister. In response, Samak and Sombun took to the streets. Pramarn's Chart Thai Party and the Democrats' conservative faction (as led by Samak) encouraged organized demonstrations by Village Scouts hooligans in front of Government House, branding the NSCT as communist and demanding that Democrat MPs Damrong, Surin Masdit and Chuan Leekpai resign immediately.

In fact, right-wing violence had been building since 1974 when a new more progressive constitution had been enacted, and when former members of Vitoon's Thai Volunteers had become a core of the Red Gaurs movement. Right-wing organizations had continued to wreak havoc, attacking not only NSCT student demonstrators but also engaging in assassinations of noted progressives, and finally disrupting the elections of 1975 and 1976. They had attacked progressive activists who had demonstrated against Thamom's 1974 visit to Thailand, Praphas's own stopover and Thanom's second 1976 visit. On 4 October, amidst the intensifying student protests, members of Nawaphon, the Village Scouts, the Red Gaurs and other rightist groups began to mass across the street from Sanam Luang as if making ready to attack the protesting students within Thammasat University. Following publication of the photo of the mock hanging by newspapers, with *Dao Siam* citing it as symbolic regicide and army radio continuously broadcasting anti-Left invective, angry mobs rushed towards

Thammasat University. If anything, the palace, angered by the mock hanging, only encouraged the right-wing hysteria. Seni immediately ordered the arrest of the students who had committed the *lèse-majesté*. By the night of 5 October, responding to the calls on Armoured Radio and likely organized by ISOC, thousands of militia, including members of the Red Gaurs, Village Scouts and Nawaphon, streamed into the Sanam Luang. Their numbers roughly equalled the number of protesting students at Thammasat across the street. Metropolitan police had also surrounded Thammasat. They seemed to be awaiting an order.

What happened to the protestors next has been covered extensively by multiple authors and from different points of view.[188] The most recent narrative is that of Thongchai (in 2020), especially given his personal role as a student leader during 6 October.[189] Looking only at the interworkings of the security forces during the massacre and subsequent coup, 6 October 1976 was certainly quite unlike previous Thai coups and could only have happened in Thailand. First, with Krit having died, no successor army strongman had arisen to take his place. The army had become heavily factionalized into six cliques, though there were crossovers among them. These are detailed in Figure 6.5.

Of these factions, the palace did not necessarily favour any. In the past, the king had generally balanced military cliques against each other (e.g., Phin versus Sarit 1947–57) or bandwagoned with one military faction after another (e.g., Sarit, 1957–63; Thanom/Praphas, 1963–73; and Krit, 1973–76). In February 1976, the king began to give his support to the three leading figures of Thailand's Supreme Command (Admiral Sangad, ACM Kamon and General Kriangsak). All three were part of Krit's faction but because they were not from the army they were more dependent upon the palace then army generals would normally have been. Indeed, by 1976 the monarch's stature among the military had grown given his own post-1973 enhanced stature and amidst increasing disunity in the armed forces. Within the army, the king began to shower praise upon his favourites, including General Aroon Twatsin (1st Army Division commander, 1975–77) and General Prem Tinsulanond (2nd Army Region commander (1975–77).

By September 1976, this lack of a unifying military strongman (giving way to intra-military fission), the apparent royal opposition to a coup and the unwillingness by many military officers to engage in a bloody crackdown of the protestors—because they did not want to taint their image—had led to a slow response by the army to the protestors. The new army commander, General Serm, was weak, not well-respected and perceived by the Young Turks as simply another

FIGURE 6.5
Principal Military Factions on 1 October 1976

Faction name	Faction details
Krit Sivara followers (second generation of Sisao Thewes faction), including Supreme Command sub-faction	Included army commander General Bunchai Bamrungphong (1976–77); the deputy commander, General Choti Hiranyatthiti (1976–77); and the chief of staff, General Serm na Nakhon (1975–76), who later served as army commander (1976–78) and supreme commander (1978–81). Admiral Sangad Chaloryu, navy commander (1973–76) and later supreme commander (1975–76), was another member of this clique, as was ACM Kamon Dachatungkha, air force commander (1974–77) and supreme commander (1976–77). The faction also initially included General Prem Tinsulanond, 2nd Army Region commander (1975–77). In the absence of Krit, the glue holding this faction together was General Kriangsak Chomanand, a wheeler-dealer consensus builder with an army background who had been assigned to the armed forces Supreme Command Headquarters and served as supreme commander in 1977–78.
Soi Rajakru group	The Soi Rajakru group was led by retired military relatives of the late General Phin Chunhavan (died 1973), including General Pramarn Adireksarn and General Chatichai Chunhavan. The two ex-military officers led the Chart Thai political party while maintaining extensive connections among active-duty soldiers. Influential in the Village Scouts.
Praphas Charusatien followers	The followers of General Praphas Charusathien included General Yot Thephasadin na Ayuthaya, assistant commander-in-chief (1976–77); General Thep Kranlert, head of the 1st Army Region (1978–79); and General Amnart Damrikarn, head of the 1st Army Region (1976–78).

FIGURE 6.5 (cont.)
Principal Military Factions on 1 October 1976

Faction name	Faction details
Chalard Hiransiri	General Chalard Hiransiri was former commander of Thai forces in Vietnam (which became the "Black Panthers" army faction), assistant army commander-in-chief (1975–76), deputy army commander (1976), and was attached to the Defence Ministry (1976).
Vitoon Yasawat	Vitoon was former commander of Thai forces in Laos, assistant chief of staff (1975–76) and deputy chief of staff (1976–77). He was linked to militants of the Red Gaurs and Village Scouts, General Sak Shinawatra from Chiang Mai and Seni's Democrat Party. Vitoon had been part of the Krit faction prior to Krit's death.
Junior officers known as the Young Military Officers' Group (Khana Thahan Num) or "Young Turks".	The Young Turks were graduates of Chulachomklao Royal Military Academy class 7. The group, which included about ninety mid-level officers, was extremely anti-communist, but they also castigated the exploitative capitalism of corrupt businesspeople and politicians, which they claimed was destroying the nation and making communism more attractive to the peasantry. They thus believed that honest, clean social reforms that would bring order and unity to the country could only be instituted under military tutelage.

commercial officer. In terms of commanders with soldiers at their immediate disposal, Serm's 1st Army Region commander, General Amnart, was not necessarily going to support Serm, given that Amnart was a member of Praphas's faction, as was Amnart's predecessor, army assistant commander General Yot (1976–77). General Prem, 2nd Army Regional commander, supported General Serm, but he was far away from Bangkok at 2nd Army Regional headquarters in Khorat.

The commanders of the 3rd and 4th armies were also too far away from Bangkok to offer Serm any backup.

With the army so divided, other security forces were used to repress the NSCT and enable a coup. Of the alternative forces, the strongest and easiest to manipulate was the BPP. Though at the time formally a part of the Ministry of the Interior through the Thai Police Department, the BPP was under royal patronage (especially that of the Queen Mother). Like ISOC, it was also de facto under the army. But the BPP was also under the operational control of ISOC and the Supreme Command. The unofficial director of ISOC was still General Saiyud Kherdpol, who had originally built ISOC's earlier incarnation, CSOC, and had continued to dominate ISOC. ISOC exerted control not only over the BPP (which dominated the Village Scouts) but also the Red Gaurs and Nawaphon. The most senior officers in the Supreme Command—the now retired Sangad, supreme commander ACM Kamon and deputy commander General Kriangsak—staunchly supported ISOC's efforts to galvanize the BPP and rightist hooligans to attack the students, not because they were hardliners but because that is what the king wanted given that he was infuriated and deluded that peaceful demonstrators might threaten his throne. Some sources say the army leadership allowed the Supreme Command to take the lead during the events of 6 October because the army did not want to be tarnished as a result of any bloodshed perpetrated by the BPP.[190] After all, the BPP would act towards the peacefully protesting students as if they were killing CPT insurgents in upcountry Thailand—which is what they did. Nevertheless, the massacre and coup appeared more as a long-conceived plan: if there were a putsch, then the army would have had nothing to worry about. More likely, the putsch-planners had all along considered using the BPP for the coup while keeping the Krit-influenced army out of it, especially considering the timing—army chief Bunchai had retired on 30 September and incoming army chief Serm was too "green" to offer any resistance.

With the Supreme Command, ISOC and the palace working together, events were readied to affect a regime change in the name of regal and national salvation. On the night of 5 October 1976, everything had been carefully choreographed for the impending coup that was to occur the next day. There would need to be a clash between the students, supposedly led by communists and Vietnamese. These enemies would have to be imprisoned or worse—with radio and television playing testament. Thais would see a frail, whimpering Seni Pramoj unable to do anything to protect the country, and they would welcome a coup if only to protect the palace from communism. Thus, by 2:40 a.m. on 6 October, units of the Metropolitan police and Border Patrol Police had already surrounded Thammasat University. Several units of BPP left Hua Hin at 2 a.m. and arrived in front of Thammasat at 6 a.m. One contingent of the Police Aerial Reinforcement Unit (PARU) arrived at 7:30 a.m., and another at 8:20 a.m. It is likely that Chart Thai's Pramarn Adireksan and Chatchai Chunhavan, influential with the right-wing militants, were also involved. And General Vitoon Yasawat was a likely planner of this coup from its inception. The PARU commander at the time, Lt. Col. Prasert Kwangkaew, had served under General Vitoon in Laos. Two Supreme Command officers connected with Vitoon were Colonel Chamlong Srimuang (who had served in Laos under Vitoon) and General Saiyud Kerdphol (who had co-founded Thai Unit 333 with Vitoon in Laos).[191] During the night, BPP deputy commander and Village Scouts head Charoenrit Chamratsomron called on Village Scouts to come to Bangkok, and the BPP even provided trucks for this purpose.[192] Village Scouts and BPP, if they were not already in Bangkok, were transported from Petchaburi, Hua Hin, Nakhon Pathom, Singburi and Lopburi provinces to attack the students in a clearly pre-planned operation.

Meanwhile, PM Seni had convened his cabinet all night to look for a solution to the crisis. Little did he know that, at 3 a.m., police chief Sisuk had arrived at Thammasat University and announced, on his authority alone, that at dawn his police forces would clear the university of all protestors and arrest those responsible for the *lèse-majesté* incident. Nor that at 4 a.m. the first shots would be fired—from outside the university grounds. At 5 a.m., the Red Gaurs, with police assistance, broke into the university, using grenades and explosives. At 5:40 a.m., police began to fire a rocket launcher directly into the university grounds. At 5:50 a.m., Red Gaurs and Village Scouts tried to ram a bus they had stolen through the university gate, and some were successful in getting in. Other hijacked buses were more successful. By 6:20 a.m., multiple heavily armed BPP personnel, having arrived from their regional bases, joined with the police and militia members in attacking the students. Ten minutes later, a "free fire" order was given. At 7 a.m., the BPP closed all exits to the university while continuing relentlessly to fire upon students inside. From 6 a.m. until 6:30 a.m., NSCT leaders tried to arrange for a surrender with the prime minister's secretary. Though the latter agreed, the police refused to listen to NSCT appeals and arrested NSCT leader Sutham Saengprathum and five student representatives when they departed in an ambulance to visit the prime minister. At around 8 a.m., the attackers, led by the BPP and followed by the militia, invaded the university. The carnage continued until after 11 a.m.

At 9 a.m. on 6 October, Seni had convened his cabinet to consider whether to declare a state of emergency. Minister of industry Chatchai Chunhavan, alongside Pramarn Adireksan and their Chart Thai Party, were strenuously opposed to declaring a state of emergency because the right-wing Village Scouts, who were gathering at the Equestrian Monument, would then legally be unable to assemble against the student demonstrators. However, Chatchai suddenly brought into the cabinet room Maj. Gen. Charoenrit Chamratsomron of the police, a BPP deputy commander (and the Village Scouts leader). Charoenrit yelled at Seni, vociferously opposing a declaration of a state of emergency saying that the Village Scouts were best prepared to defeat the students since they were more disciplined than the police. Seni objected, saying it was the responsibility of the police to restore order. Minister of agriculture General Pramarn then intervened, contending that now was the best time to suppress the NSCT—Seni should not wait. The arguing continued past noon, with deputy police chief Chumpon Lohachala stating that the students were armed with heavy weapons, that many students and police were dead, and that the police had asked the BPP for assistance. Later, the prime minister asked police commander Sisuk how many police had died, and Sisuk, opposing the account of Chumpon, replied that only a few were injured. The police also told Seni that only three pistols had been confiscated from the students. By the afternoon, a state of emergency had yet to be declared. In fact, Seni never did declare a state of emergency. Many right-wing agitators were now demanding that progressive MPs in the government be arrested. MPs Damrong, Surin Masdit and Chuan Leekpai resigned and later went into hiding. Both Seni and deputy prime minister Prasit Kanchawat stated that since the government had been invested by order of the king, the only way to affect a change was via a vote of no-confidence, and indeed the vote of policy statement had been set for 8 October. Thereupon, Chatchai Chunhavan left the meeting and met with fellow rightists Samak Sundaravej, Thammanoon Thien-ngern and Songsuk Pakkasem, who were leading a growing entourage of Village Scouts in a procession of cars at the Equestrian Monument. It was also at the Equestrian Monument where Colonel Chamlong Srimuang, who was then with ISOC, was trying to incite anti-communist mobs. The cabinet meeting ended at 3 p.m.[193]

As the afternoon wore on, BPP officials and associated militiamen appeared to be everywhere. At 4 p.m., close to fifty thousand BPP troopers, Village Scouts and Red Gaurs demonstrated against the government in front of Government House, demanding its immediate resignation. With police and army officials unwilling to take any action, Seni resigned and the government toppled. Afterwards, BPP commander Lt. Gen. Angoon Tatanon; his deputy, Maj. Gen. Somkhuan Harikul; and Crown Prince Vajiralongkorn celebrated. Vajiralongkorn thanked the BPP and the members of the militias and told them to go home.[194] At 6 p.m., Seni was taken into "protective custody" at Supreme Command Headquarters. His arrest coincided with a coup: at 6 p.m., the leading Thai military commanders—grouped together as the National Administrative Reform Council (NARC), consisting of eighteen four-star generals—seized power. The announcement came simultaneous to the abolition of the 1974 constitution and the dissolution of both cabinet and parliament. At 7 p.m., defence minister and retired supreme commander Admiral Sangad, the NARC chair, declared that military leaders only wanted to lead Thailand towards "a form of democracy under the king" and that the coup had been necessary because the demonstrating students had insulted the monarchy, resisted arrest and were collaborating with "Vietnamese Communist terrorists."[195] More than that, however, the coup announcement added this rationale:

> When it was clear that some cabinet ministers, some political groups, and several mass media strongly and openly supported these [NSCT] activities, it became impossible for the government to regain control of the country through constitutional means. If the situation were allowed to deteriorate further, the nation and the people would encounter greater dangers and [*sic*] solution would be difficult. The Council therefore found it necessary to seize power.[196]

The army did not directly participate in any of the violence at Thammasat University. The commanders of the army—General Serm na Nakorn, 1st Army Region commander General Amnart Damrikarn and 1st Division commander General Aroon Twatsin—did not allow troops to participate in the killings or putsch. On the other hand, the regular police did not participate in the subsequent coup that evening. In fact, after 6 October, police chief General Sisuk was publicly blamed for the abuses by the security forces and fired. The BPP and Supreme Command participated in both massacre and coup. As for the Young Turks faction, there is only evidence today that three of them could have been involved in the events of 6 October. Young Turk Colonel Chamlong Srimuang was working as an intelligence operative at the Supreme Command under orders from General Saiyud Kerdphol. He had a leadership and propaganda role during the events of 6 October. According to another Young Turk, Colonel Prajark Sawanjkit, "Chamlong volunteered to incite military-backed civilian mobs to pressure the government of MR Seni Pramoj to resign before coup plotters mobilized soldiers to seize power in the evening of October 6, 1976."[197]

According to Chamlong, Prajark brought five hundred of his troops from the far northern province of Chiang Rai (where he held a command) to Dusit to assist in general security, arriving on the evening of 5 October. Nevertheless, as has been noted elsewhere, that is a long distance to go "just to help prevent disorder".[198] Nevertheless, Prajark could have contributed troops in support of the coup on the evening of 6 October. The only other Young Turk in Bangkok at the time with command over troops was Major Manoon Rupekachorn. Since 1974, he had been commander of the 4th Armoured Cavalry Battalion in Dusit, not far from Thammasat University and Government House. Given his control over tanks close to Government House and the Supreme Command, Manoon could easily have played a role in the 6 October coup. But, according to Chai-anan, based on an interview with Chamlong, during the 6 October massacre and coup, the Young Turks did not participate at all:

> The army's major combat units in Bangkok, most of which were under the command of members of the Young Military Officers Group [Young Turks] were mobilized but their troops did not participate in the killing of university students. Chamlong revealed that the 6 October 1976 coup was made possible because of his friends' troops. The military leaders who announced the seizure of power from the Seni government did not order the members of the Young Military Officers Group to stage the coup but the presence of [the Young Turks'] troops ... made the coup a *fait accompli.*[199]

One of the Young Turks, however, Lt. Col. Ronnachai Srisuvoranond, disagrees with this account. He says that tanks under Manoon and troops under Prajark were a crucial part of the coup. In a December 1976 interview, Samak Sundaravej stated that only three tanks had been used to effect the 6 October 1976 coup.[200] Manoon's tank battalion was the closest to Government House. Ronnachai also mentions the role of "military headquarters, including its radio and television stations".[201] In fact, by "headquarters", Ronnachai could have meant Supreme Command or ISOC Headquarters. As for Ronnachai's reference to radio and television stations, at the time, ISOC, the Uthan Sanitvong–run Armoured Radio and Army TV Channel 5 were working together under ISOC coordination to broadcast anti-communist hysteria. Even after the coup, on 13 October, ISOC spread a rumour in Bangkok, which Armoured Radio initially denied, that "leftist students intended to kidnap children".[202]

The police were not a party to the 6 October coup. But the police participated during the initial stages of the 6 October massacre. Moreover, following the putsch, the police began cooperating under the control of the NARC. According to one police major interviewed days after the coup happened, "There are military committees in each police precinct headquarters to monitor the activities of the police."[203]

In the end, the only organizations/units that were parties to the coup—which could have provided personnel to support it because of proximity to Government House (where the government was ousted) and the Supreme Command (which took power)—were the BPP, Manoon's 4th Armoured Cavalry Battalion, the 1st Artillery Regiment and Prajark's five hundred troops. The only conclusion is that the coup of 6 October 1976 was a very uncommon putsch. It was one actively pushed by the monarchy, formally led by the Supreme Command, and organized by ISOC. It saw a massacre spearheaded by the BPP, the forced resignation of Seni, and perhaps just three small army units backing the coup announcement.

In the moments leading up to the NARC coup, Krit Sivara's nemesis, Pramarn Adireksan, had been involved in a "concurrent conspiracy" to seize power. The Pramarn plan had not been attached to 6 October in terms of timing, and it had not really envisaged a military coup; it was an underhand political plot to bring about the total collapse of the Seni government and its then replacement under the then existing constitution by a government led by General Pramarn.[204] If Krit had lived, retained his position as defence minister and shared Pramarn's hard-line right-wing views, he probably would have followed this constitutional "Pramarn Plan", given Krit's nature as a supporter of elected governance. Krit's charisma would likely have been sufficient to prevent the events of 6 October taking place at all. Only one day after the putsch, according to Pramarn's son Phongpol:

> The Thai Nation [Chart Thai] party leaders are very unhappy about the military takeover. Phongpon said there was no reason for the coup but pure opportunism on the part of the military. He said that the Village Scouts and the Police already had the situation under control on October 6, and that Surin Mtasadit, Damrong Latthaphiphipat and Chuan Likphai had agreed to resign by 1800 hours October 6 as demanded by rightists. He also said that his

father did not think there would be any place in the new government for Thai Nation leaders.[205]

That statement supports allegations that Chart Thai had been sponsoring rightist militia to attack students and force Seni's resignation on 6 October. Chart Thai had not, however, supported the subsequent military coup. Meanwhile, Kriangsak later implied that Pramarn had been involved with General Chalard in planning an alternative coup and that Vitoon was a potential troublemaker for the new junta. Indeed, there had been an unexplained deployment towards Bangkok of the 9th Division on 11 October, which was later countermanded.[206] This deployment could have been related to the transfer of Chalard Hiransiri's associate General Yutthasak Klongtruatrok from 9th Division commander to 5th Division commander. The 5th Division is farther away from Bangkok. According to US ambassador Whitehouse's account of what Kriangsak said:

> EACH OF THESE OFFICERS HAD BEEN INVOLVED WITH CERTAIN POLITICAL MANEUVERS WHICH COULD HAVE DE-STABLIZED THE GOVERNMENT. HE [Kriangsak] LINKED GENERAL CHALAT DIRECTLY WITH FORMER DEPUTY PRIME MINISTER PRAMAN ADIREKSAN (WHOM HE DESCRIBED AS A "POLITICAL" GENERAL) AND SAID THERE WAS NO CHOICE BUT TO SEPARATE HIM FROM THE SERVICE. WITHUN [Vitoon] HAD, IN KRIANGSAK'S VIEW, A POSSIBLE CONTINUING USEFULNESS, SO HE HAD BEEN PACKED OFF TEMPORARILY TO A POST ABROAD.[207]

In fact, given the abundance of coup plots on 6 October, Whitehouse postulated that:

> IF THE COUP OF OCTOBER 6 HAD BEEN DELAYED ANOTHER COUPLE OF DAYS, THERE WOULD HAVE BEEN A DIFFERENT COUP, WITH A DIFFERENT SET OF LEADERS, AMONG WHOM THE THAI ARMY WOULD HAVE PREDOMINATED.[208]

Partly because the Sangad-led coup was successful and the army leadership itself was so factionalized, the army was temporarily pushed to the backseat of the military hierarchy, behind the king and the Supreme Command. Five years would pass before the army succeeded in restoring its domination over the armed forces.

Ultimately, there was a veritable who's who of persons and units involved in the events of the massacre and Sangad-led putsch on

6 October 1976. Figure 6.6 provides a list of people in power at the time who directly or indirectly contributed to the violence and/or coup.

In summary, as former prime minister Kukrit Pramoj told UK ambassador David Cole shortly after the putsch, "It was the coup they planned against me last February; they just took it out of the cupboard again."[209] Previous army-led practices or attempts at a coup had occurred in late February and late March 1976. But those attempts had been led by army officers, while the coup of 6 October was not. Moreover, only with Krit's death in April and Bunchai's retirement on 30 September were strong military leaders who supported a continuation of Thai democracy removed from power. The army commander after Bunchai, General Serm, was generally too weak to resist a putsch demanded by the monarch. Besides, it was members of Krit's own faction, which included the Supreme Command's Admiral Sangad, ACM Kamon, General Kriangsak and General Charoen, who would be leading the coup. But since nobody in the military wanted to engage in the massacre of the students, that work was left at first to the normal police and later to the Border Patrol Police and the BPP's militias, as directed by ISOC. The BPP also became the coup maker in the sense that it forced PM Seni Pramoj to resign. Given that the CIA was deeply involved with the BPP, ISOC and the Supreme Command, it is impossible that the then CIA station chief Hugh Tovar could not have been aware of the upcoming massacre and putsch. The hurried nature of the putsch (coming only an hour after Seni's resignation) owes to the fact that there were at least two other coup attempts in the works: one by Pramarn, one by Chalard and perhaps even one by General Vitoon. In the end, following the establishment of NARC on 6 October, Chalard was demoted to an inactive posting as a reserve officer attached to the Office of the Undersecretary, Ministry of Defence, while Vitoon himself was put on a plane to Japan to become "superintendent" of Thai students there. Krit's nemesis Pramarn, together with Chatchai and their Chart Thai Party, ironically tried to seize power, though constitutionally.

Why had the coup been planned for 6 October? First, astrologically based numerology was likely a factor. In addition, it had been almost three years since the overthrow of Thanom, Praphas and Narong, and the military apparently wanted to repress the demonstrators before the anniversary of that date. Third, the excuse of the mock hanging had just inflamed public opinion. Fourth, the coup makers were ready. Fifth, with a US election approaching in which human rights was an issue, a bloody Thai coup—broadcast across global media—was clearly the last thing that Washington wanted since it might throw negative light

FIGURE 6.6
Principal Leaders, Units and Their Roles in the Massacre and Coup of 6 October 1976

Leader	Position	Unit	Role
King Bhumipol Adulyadej	King	Palace	Endorse
Queen Sirikit	Queen	Palace	Endorse
General Samran Paeteeyakul	Privy Councillor/ ISOC advisor	King's Privy Council	Link from Crown to ISOC
M.R. Seni Pramoj	Prime Minister	Government	Formal responsibility
Admiral Sangad Chaloryu	Supreme CC, retired	Supreme Command	Coup leader
ACM Kamon Dechatungka	Supreme and RTAF CC	Supreme Command and RTAF	Coup leader
General Kriangsak Chomanand	Deputy Supreme CC	Supreme Command	Deputy coup leader
General Charoen Phongpanit	Chief of Staff	Supreme Command	Assistant coup leader
General Serm na Nakorn	Army CC	Royal Thai Army	Did not resist coup
General Amnart Damrikarn	1st Region CC, RTA	Royal Thai Army	Did not resist coup
General Aroon Twatsin	1st Division CC, RTA	Royal Thai Army	Lent soldiers in Dusit area to coup
Colonel Uthan Sanitvongs	Chief	Army (Armoured) Radio	Propaganda
Admiral Amorn Sirikaya	Navy CC	Royal Thai Navy	Did not resist coup
General Vitoon Yasawat	Deputy Chief of Staff	Royal Thai Army	He could have coordinated massacre and coup

FIGURE 6.6 (cont.)
Principal Leaders, Units and Their Roles in the Massacre and Coup of 6 October 1976

Leader	Position	Unit	Role
General Saiyud Kerdphol	Chief of Staff to Supreme Commander and Chief of Staff, ISOC	Supreme Command, ISOC	He could have coordinated massacre and coup
Lt. Gen. Angoon Tatanon	Commander	Border Patrol Police	Led massacre and forced resignation of PM
Maj. Gen. Charoenrit Chamratsomron	Deputy Commander	Border Patrol Police	Led massacre and forced resignation of PM
Lt. Col. Prasert Kwankaew	Commander	PARU	Led massacre and forced resignation of PM
General Srisuk Mahintarathep	Director-General	Police Department	Led initial massacre
Pol. Lt. Gen. Chumphon Lohachala	Deputy Director-General	Police Department	Led initial massacre
Pol. Lt. Gen. Monchai Phankongchuen	Deputy Director-General	Police Department	Led initial massacre
Pol. Lt. Gen. Narong Mahanon	Deputy Director-General	Police Department	Led initial massacre
Pol. Maj. Gen. Sanae Sittiphan	Assistant Director-General	Police Department	Led initial massacre
Pol. Maj. Gen. Yuttana Wannakowit.	Assistant Director-General	Police Department	Led initial massacre
Maj. Gen. Suwit Sothitat	Commander, Crime Suppression Division	Police Department	Led initial massacre

FIGURE 6.6 (cont.)
Principal Leaders, Units and Their Roles in the Massacre and Coup of 6 October 1976

Leader	Position	Unit	Role
Pol. Lt. Col. Salang Bunnag	Deputy Superintendent of the Crime Suppression Division 2	Police Department	Led initial massacre
Maj. Gen. Charoenrit Chamratsomron	Commander	Village Scouts	Involved in BPP-led massacre and forced resignation of PM
Maj. Gen. Sudsai Hasadin na Ayuthaya	Commander	Red Gaurs	Involved in BPP-led massacre and forced resignation of PM
Wattana Khiaowimon	Leader	Nawaphon	Contributed to massacre
Kittiwutthophikku	Leader	"Buddhist" clergy	Provided ideological rationale for massacre
Hugh Tovar	CIA Station Chief	United States CIA station, Bangkok	Likely assisted in logistics of BPP attack and subsequent coup

on the United States as Thailand's patron and make Thai communist insurgents more popular. A coup before the 1976 US election might be preferable. Nevertheless, Thai military leaders were indifferent to what Washington thought since they realized they were likely to become less reliant on US military aid anyway given that the US Congress had, since at least the end of the United States' Vietnam War, become less than enthusiastic about approving large quantities of military aid to countries abroad.[210] Such a standpoint was supported by former foreign minister Thanat Khoman, who, at the time an advisor for the post-Seni 1976 NARC regime, opined to the US ambassador that though human rights groups might abhor the violence and coup in Thailand on 6 October, it did not matter because "Thailand could expect little in the way of future military or economic assistance [because US] programs were being phased out".[211] Nevertheless, following the "brutality" of

6 October, it was Thailand's king, rather than the military, who "hoped that there was some way by which the US could explain that Thailand's 1976 "change of government had been brought about as a result of the weakness [of] ... Seni ... and ... provocative actions of communist inspired students".[212] Clearly, Thailand's head of state was in fact sensitive to global perceptions of its political appearance.

Before ending this chapter, I would like to address a final matter relating to 6 October 1976 that concerns Thailand's economy. A principal issue that kept raising its head during the summer of 1976 was that of TEMCO/BILLITON. Back in early 1975, the NSCT demanded that US mineral company Thailand Exploration and Mining Co. (TEMCO) withdraw from Thailand. To appease the protestors, in one of its last acts, the 1975 Seni government cancelled TEMCO's mining concession, a decision that turned US investors against Seni. The Offshore Mining Organization (OMO), an organization run solely by the Thai government, took over TEMCO's leases. TEMCO threatened to sue the Thai government. Thereupon, the incoming Kukrit government granted a management contract to Billiton, while the other foreign stockholder in TEMCO, Union Carbide, sold out its interest to Billiton, a subsidiary of Royal Dutch Shell. During the 1976 Seni government, Billiton attempted to get the government's approval for a management contract so that its mining operations could begin again, but its efforts were unsuccessful. Only after the 1976 coup was Billiton able to continue its mining.

Then, on 9 September 1976, exactly one month before the putsch, James Rooney, the president of the US Chamber of Commerce in Thailand, in a widely read article, severely criticized the Seni government for insufficient decisiveness and for not using enough economic tools to improve the investment climate.[213] For Rooney and Thai conservatives, time seemed to be rapidly running out for Seni's government—at least in terms of US business support.

The events of 6 October 1976 marked the termination of Thailand's 1973–76 experiment with civilian rule and limited democracy. That three-year period had been made possible by Krit Sivara's pluralist preferences. In 1973 or 1974, Krit could have installed himself as another military dictator for Thailand, but he did not. Instead, he remained behind the scenes of first appointed then elected civilian rule, keeping military adventurism at bay while maintaining royal support. In fact, during 1973–76, Krit was slightly more powerful—militarily, economically and even politically—than the palace. He was no angel: he promoted corrupt politicians and, like any Thai army commander, was responsible for ISOC human rights violations against rural people. But he did not end the democratic experiment. Krit's death in April 1976 effectively beheaded his military faction, leaving Thailand with no effective military leader and increasing friction throughout the army. Such army factionalism was a political vacuum that the palace exploited. It was at this point that the king began to co-opt members of that faction from the Supreme Command—Sangad, Kamon and Kriangsak—to lead to the 6 October 1976 coup as the culmination of those regal efforts.

Notes

1. Robert Zimmerman, "Reflections on the Collapse of Democracy in Thailand", Occasional Papers Series no. 50 (Singapore: Institute of Southeast Asian Studies, 1978), p. 49.

2. อนุสรณ์ในงานพระราชทานเพลิงศพ จอมพล เกรียงไกร อัตตะนันทน์ ณ เมรุวัดเทพศิรินทราวาส [Memorial volume from the cremation ceremony of Field Marshal Kriengkrai Atthanand at Wat Thepsirintrawat Temple], Bangkok, 11 September 1973.

3. Marion Mallet, "Causes and Consequences of the October '76 Coup", *Journal of Contemporary Asia* 8, no. 1 (1978): 83, https://doi.org/10.1080/00472337885390051.

4. Ibid.

5. Kevin Hewison, "The 1976 Thai Coup and Reflections on the Analysis of Recent Coups", unpublished manuscript, April 1977, p. 18, https://kevinhewison.files.wordpress.com/2011/02/hewison-1977.pdf.

6. ทีระลึกในงานพระราชทาเพลิงศพ พลตำรวจเอก วิฑูรย์ ยะสวัสดี เมรุวัดตรีทศเทพ [Commemorative volume from the cremation ceremony of Police General Vitoon Yasawat, Tri Thotsathep Temple Crematorium], Bangkok, 17 February 1993.

7. An examination of Bunchai's career indicates that he was continuously promoted, generally as a result of remaining within General Krit Sivara's orbit. See อนุสรณ์ งาน พระราชทาน เพลิง ศพ พล เอก บุญชัย บำรุงพงศ์ [Memorial volume from the cremation ritual of General Bunchai Bamrungpong], Bangkok, 1995.

8. Chantana Chainaken, การเมืองในสมัยนายกรัฐมนตรีพระราชทาน สัญญา ธรรมศักดิ์ (พ.ศ.2516–2518) [Politics during the royally appointed prime minister Sanya Dharmasakti (1973–1975 AD)] Bangkok: Dissertation, Thammasat University, 2011.

9. US Embassy Bangkok to Department of State, "The Thai Draft Constitution", 21 November 1973, Wikileaks, 1973BANGKO18192_b, https://wikileaks.org/plusd/cables/1973BANGKO18192_b.html.

10. US ambassador Leonard Unger to secretary of state Henry Kissinger, "Views of Krit Sivara", 25 October 1973, Wikileaks, 1973BANGKO16622_b, https://wikileaks.org/plusd/cables/1973BANGKO16622_b.html.

11. Ibid.

12. Saiyud had emphasized that CSOC/ISOC should be removed from the army chain of command and combined with the National Security command structure directly under the prime minister (the prime minister only became the chief of ISOC in 1987, with the army commander as deputy chief but ex-officio head). US Embassy (Bangkok) to US secretary of state Henry Kissinger, "LTG Saiyud's Comments on the Present Situation Leadership Deficiencies", 10 December 1973, 1973BANGKO19052_b, https://wikileaks.org/plusd/cables//1973BANGKO19052_b.html.

13. US Embassy Bangkok to Department of State, "Prime Minister Sanya's 'Meet the People' Telegram Programs", 16 November 1973, Wikileaks, 1973BANGKO17945_b, https://wikileaks.org/plusd/cables/1973BANGKO17945_b.html.

14. US Embassy Bangkok to secretary of state, "The Internal Political Situation in Thailand after Eight Weeks of the Sanya Government", 13 December 1973, 1973BANGKO19228_b, https://wikileaks.org/plusd/cables/1973BANGKO19228_b.html.

15. US Embassy Bangkok to Department of State, "Readings of the Bangkok Political Barometer through Confidential", 14 December 1973, Wikileaks, 1973BANGKO19397_b, https://wikileaks.org/plusd/cables/1973BANGKO19397_b.html.

16. US Embassy (Bangkok) to US secretary of state Henry Kissinger, "General Krit Sivara's December 3 News Conference", 6 December 1973, Wikileaks, 1973BANGKO18862_b, https://wikileaks.org/plusd/cables/1973BANGKO18862_b.html.

17. Irwin Block, "Arms Sales: 'Bicycles' for Thailand", *The Last Post* 3, no. 8 (March 1974): 6–7. Acknowledgements to Calvin McLeod for providing me with this information.

18. US Embassy (Bangkok) to US secretary of state Henry Kissinger, "Ambassador's Meeting with General Krit Sivara", 18 January 1974, Wikileaks, 1974BANGKO01030_b, https://wikileaks.org/plusd/cables/1974BANGKO01030_b.html.

19. US Embassy (Bangkok) to US secretary of state Henry Kissinger, "Krit Sivara on the Current Political Situation", 23 January 1974, Wikileaks, 1974BANGKO01279_b, https://wikileaks.org/plusd/cables/1974BANGKO01279_b.html.

20. US Embassy (Bangkok) to US secretary of state Henry Kissinger, "General Krit Sivara on the Possibility of Prime Minister Sanya Thammasak's Resignation", 27 March 1974, Wikileaks, 1974BANGKO05022_b, https://wikileaks.org/plusd/cables/1974BANGKO05022_b.html.

21. US Embassy (Bangkok) to US secretary of state Henry Kissinger, "Status of Coup Rumors", 24 April 1974, Wikileaks, 1974BANGKO01279_b, https://wikileaks.org/plusd/cables/1974BANGKO06674_b.html.

22. US Embassy (Bangkok) to US secretary of state Henry Kissinger, "Dispelling Coup Rumors", 26 April 1974, Wikileaks, 1974BANGKO06855_b, https://wikileaks.org/plusd/cables/1974BANGKO06855_b.html.

23. "Thailand on Military Alert as Cabinet Resigns", *New York Times*, 22 May 1974, https://www.nytimes.com/1974/05/22/archives/thailand-on-military-alert-as-cabinet-resigns-no-major-change-in.html.

24. US Embassy (Bangkok) to US secretary of state Henry Kissinger, "Characterization of the Second Sanya Cabinet", 31 May 1974, Wikileaks, 1974BANGKO08909_b, https://wikileaks.org/plusd/cables/1974BANGKO08909_b.html.

25. M. Rajaretnam, "Courts, Camps and Constitutions: The Game of Politics in Thailand", in *Southeast Asian Affairs 1975* (Singapore: Institute of Southeast Asian Studies, 1975), p. 175.

26. According to one source, the right-wing Students' and People's Front (SPF), originally established in 1963 by Sarit, had played a role in instigating the riots. See Boonsanong Punyodyana, "The Revolutionary Situation in Thailand", in *Southeast Asian Affairs 1975* (Singapore: Institute of Southeast Asian Studies, 1975), p. 195.

27. US Embassy (Bangkok) to secretary of state Henry Kissinger, "US-RTG Crisis Consultation", 5 July 1974, Wikileaks, 1974STATE145057_b, https://wikileaks.org/plusd/cables/1974STATE145057_b.html.

28. US Embassy (Bangkok) to US secretary of state Henry Kissinger, "General Krit on Constitutional Crisis", 24 September 1974, Wikileaks, 1974BANGKO15357_b, https://wikileaks.org/plusd/cables/1974BANGKO15357_b.html.

29. "308. Telegram from the Embassy in Thailand to the Department of State", 15 February 1966, *Foreign Relations of the United States* (*FRUS*), https://history.state.gov/historicaldocuments/frus1964-68v27/d308.

30. US Embassy (Bangkok) to US secretary of state Henry Kissinger, "Forgery Alleges CIA Support of Right Wing in Thailand", 19 August 1975, Wikileaks, https://wikileaks.org/plusd/cables/1975BANGKO17101_b.html.

31. Puey Umphakorn, "Violence and the Coup d'Etat, 6 October 1976", in *A Siamese for All Seasons: Collected Articles by and about Puey Umphakorn* (Bangkok: Komol Keemthong Foundation; Suksit Siam, 1981), p. 70.

32. US Embassy (Bangkok) to US secretary of state Henry Kissinger, "The Impact of the Thanom Visit", 14 January 1975, Wikileaks, 1975BANGKO18375_b, https://wikileaks.org/plusd/cables/1975BANGKO00651_b.html.

33. Benedict Anderson, "Withdrawal Symptoms: Social and Cultural Aspects of the October 6 Coup, *Bulletin of Concerned Asian Scholars* 9, no. 3 (1977): 28n57, https://doi.org/10.1080/14672715.1977.10406423.

34. Marjorie Mueke, "The Village Scouts of Thailand", *Asian Survey* 20, no. 4 (April 1980): 408–9, https://www.doi.org/10.2307/2643866.

35. Paul Handley, *The King Never Smiles* (New Haven, CT: Yale University Press, 2005), p. 224.

36. US Embassy (Bangkok) to US secretary of state Henry Kissinger, "New Strength (Nawaphon)", 2 September 1975,

Wikileaks, 1975BANGKO18375_b, https://wikileaks.org/plusd/cables/1975BANGKO18375_b.html.

37. Tanapong Chitsanga, "Political Roles and Challenges of Monarchy and the Royally Appointed Prime Minister Sanya Dharmasakti from 1973 to 1975" (PhD thesis, Waseda University, 2020), p. 323.

38. Zimmerman, "Reflections on the Collapse", p. 62.

39. Tanapong, "Political Roles and Challenges", p. 346.

40. CIA, "Thailand: Thanom's Return Could Spark Public Outbursts", *National Intelligence Bulletin*, 28 December 1974, https://www.cia.gov/readingroom/docs/CIA-RDP79T00975A027300010018-9.pdf.

41. US Embassy to secretary of state Henry Kissinger, "Status of the ISOC-Developed Aw Paw Paw Program", 10 February 1975, Wikileaks, 1975BANGKO02298_b, https://wikileaks.org/plusd/cables/1975BANGKO02298_b.html.

42. US Embassy (Bangkok) to US secretary of state Henry Kissinger, "General Krit as De Gaulle", 11 December 1974, Wikileaks, 1974BANGKO19326_b, https://wikileaks.org/plusd/cables/1974BANGKO19326_b.html.

43. In 1975, the US Embassy in Bangkok referred to Pramarn as "the richest of the Thai rich … leader of the Thai Nation Party (Chart Thai)". The son-in-law of army commander General Phin Chunhavan (1948–54), Pramarn was a member of the 1948–57 Phin-Phao clique (e.g., Soi Rajakru faction), which dominated politics at that time. During this time, Pramarn held several ministerial posts. Sarit's 1957 coup, which Krit supported, forced Pramarn's faction from power. At this point, he retired from the military. Nevertheless, Pramarn continued on in business, even serving alongside Sarit supporters on the boards of directors in several firms. The fall of Thanom/Praphas gave Pramarn the opportunity to reinvent the power of Soi Rajakru. He was closely associated with the Sino-Thai business interests of Sukri Bodiratnangkun, Uthane Techaphaibun, Kiat Sifuangfung and the Sophonphanit family. These interests contributed vast sums to Pramarn's Chart Thai Party. Pramarn's familial connections were vast. His wife, Charoen Chunhavan, was Phin's daughter. From her, Phin was connected to the Kittikachorns because "Phin had adopted Thanom's sick wife … in 1947 and helped nurse her back to good health [and] she remain[ed] grateful to the Chunhawan family." Meanwhile, Charoen's sister Prom was married to Arun Dabbarongsi, whose son was married to the daughter of ACM Bunchu Chantarubeksa, a close friend of Thanom. Another sister of Charoen's was married to Chalerm Chiaosakun, deputy director of the King's Crown Property Bureau. Charoen's third sister was married to General Phao Sriyanond. By the early 1970s, Pramarn was serving on the board and held shares in at least ten leading firms in Thailand and was also the president of the Association of Thai Industries and the Thai Textiles Manufacturers Association. In 1957, Krit had clearly been opposed to the Soi Rajakru faction, since he was a member of Sarit's Sisao Thewes clique. Nevertheless, Krit informed the US Embassy in June 1974 that he thought Pramarn would make "a good

Prime Minister". In fact, Krit and Pramarn had been childhood friends at Thepsirin School, and Krit was only one year older than Pramarn when they each attended Chulachomklao Military Academy. But by the 1970s, Krit likely saw Pramarn as a potential rival. After all, Krit would soon retire, after which he and Pramarn would compete against each other in politics. It would be easier to support other politicians. See US Embassy (Bangkok) to United States secretary of state Henry Kissinger, "Thai Nation Party Leader Praman Adireksan", 23 January 1975, Wikileaks, 1975BANGKO01303_b, https://wikileaks.org/plusd/cables/1975BANGKO01303_b.html.

44. Chatchai was the only son of army commander General Phin Chunhavan. Chatchai married Bunruan, who was close to King Bhumipol's mother, who informally adopted Bunruan. Following the 1957 coup that felled Phibun, Phao and Phin, Chatchai effectively became exiled to serving abroad in Thailand's diplomatic service. He served successively as Thai ambassador to Argentina, Austria, Switzerland, Turkey, Yugoslavia, the Vatican and the United Nations. In 1972 he served as deputy foreign minister in the Thanom government, a position he continued under the Sanya government. In 1974, when his brothers-in-law Praman and Siri founded the Chart Thai Party with him, he served as its first secretary general. He became its party leader in 1986 and served as prime minister of Thailand in 1988–91 before being ousted in a military coup. In 1975, the cooling of relations between Krit and Pramarn had a negative effect on the relations between Krit and Chatchai.

45. Mallet, "Causes and Consequences", p. 84.

46. Ibid.

47. David Morell and Chai-anan Samudavanija, *Political Conflict in Thailand: Reform, Reaction, Revolution* (Cambridge, MA: Oelgeschlager, Gunn & Hain, 1981), p. 149.

48. In January 1975, the US Embassy in Bangkok described Tawich as a "wealthy trucking tycoon ... intellectual lightweight who shifted loyalties from ACM Thawee Chulasap to Krit ... and Krit would have little trouble manipulating him from behind the scenes." In November 1973, Tawich, who had previously led a faction within the UTTP, established the Seri Rath (Free Thai) Party, comprising former members of a faction within the UTTP loyal to Thawee. Thereupon, Tawich combined Seri Rath with three smaller factions to form the Social Justice (Thamma Sangkhom) Party, of which he became the leader. Krit pushed Thawee away from a patron role over the party, resulting in Tawich associating himself with Krit as well as Prasert Ruchirawong—who became the party's patrons. But Tawich also received backing from police chief Prachuab and deputy police chief Vitoon. Back in the days when Prachuab served as director of Thailand's Port Authority, he helped Tawich to jump-start his Trailer Transport Company. See US Embassy (Bangkok) to US secretary of state Henry Kissinger, "Social Justice Party Leader Thawit Klinpratum", 24 January 1975, Wikileaks, 1975BANGKO01432_b, https://wikileaks.org/plusd/cables/1975BANGKO01432_b.html.

49. Prasit worked as an executive at Bangkok Bank from 1953 until 1976. He was a close confidant of Chin Sophonpanich, founder of Bangkok Bank. At the same time, starting in 1952, he was a member of parliament, and later became a cabinet minister. In 1975 he was Speaker of the National Assembly. He was the leader of the Social Nationalists Party, partly sponsored by Krit.

50. Sawet was a faction leader and businessman from Rayong province. He served for eight terms in the National Assembly and worked with Krit in the 1957 and 1969 elections. Under Sarit, he had served in the Finance Ministry. By the 1970s he had become close to Sawat Kamprakob, faction leader of Nakorn Sawan province, and a heavyweight within the Social Agrarian Party.

51. Siri Siriyothin was a son-in-law of Phin Chunhavan and later the Speaker of Thailand's 1969–71 National Assembly. When Chart Thai Party was founded in 1974, he became its deputy leader. He held various ministerial postings under prime ministers Phibun and Seni Pramoj. He reportedly had cordial relations with Krit.

52. Zimmerman, "Reflections on the Collapse", p. 49.

53. Clark Neher, "Stability and Instability in Contemporary Thailand, *Asian Survey* 15, no. 12 (December 1975), p. 1105.

54. US Embassy (Bangkok) to US secretary of state Henry Kissinger, "Seni's Victory", 14 February 1975, Wikileaks, 1975BANGKO02697_b, https:// wikileaks.org/plusd/cables/1975BANGKO02697_b.html.

55. Handley, *The King Never Smiles*, p. 219.

56. CIA, *National Intelligence Bulletin*, no. 638, 7 March 1975, https://www. cia.gov/readingroom/docs/CIA-RDP79T00975A027500010012-3.pdf.

57. Ibid.

58. US Embassy (Bangkok) to US secretary of state Henry Kissinger, "Status of Government Formation", 12 February 1975, Wikileaks, 1975BANGKO02507_b, https://wikileaks.org/plusd/ cables/1975BANGKO02507_b.html.

59. Handley, *The King Never Smiles*, p. 219.

60. US Embassy (Bangkok) to US secretary of state Henry Kissinger, "General Krit Siwara on the Future of the Khukrit Government", 24 March 1975, Wikileaks, 1975BANGKO04887_b, https://wikileaks. org/plusd/cables/1975BANGKO04887_b.html.

61. Ibid.

62. Cited by Tyrell Haberkorn, *In Plain Sight: Impunity and Human Rights in Thailand* (Madison: University of Wisconsin Press, 2018), p. 89.

63. Cited by Eugene Ford, *Cold War Monks: Buddhism and America's Secret Strategy in Southeast Asia* (New Haven, CT: Yale University Press, 2017).

64. US Embassy (Bangkok) to US secretary of state Henry Kissinger, "Counterinsurgency Policy of the Khukrit Administration", 23 April 1975, Wikileaks, 1975BANGKO07111_b, https://wikileaks.org/plusd/ cables/1975BANGKO07111_b.html.

65. US Embassy (Bangkok) to US secretary of state Henry Kissinger, "USN Indian Ocean Patrols from Utapao", 23 July 1974, Wikileaks, 1974BANGKO11938_b, https://wikileaks.org/plusd/cables/1974BANGKO11938_b.html.

66. US Embassy (Bangkok) to US secretary of state Henry Kissinger, "General Krit Siwara's Stance on US Support for Cambodian Assistance from Thailand", 23 March 1975, Wikileaks, 1975BANGKO04798_b, https://wikileaks.org/plusd/cables/1975BANGKO04798_b.html.

67. Ibid.

68. US Embassy (Bangkok) to US secretary of state Henry Kissinger, "General Krit Siwara on US Troop Withdrawals", 24 March 1975, Wikileaks, 1975BANGKO04894_b, https://wikileaks.org/plusd/cables/1975BANGKO04894_b.html.

69. US Embassy (Bangkok) to US secretary of state Henry Kissinger, "Frequent Wind", 28 April 1975, Wikileaks, 1975BANGKO07499_b, https://wikileaks.org/plusd/cables/1975BANGKO07499_b.html.

70. US Embassy (Bangkok) to US secretary of state Henry Kissinger, "RTG Leaders on US Credibility and Dependability", 23 April 1975, Wikileaks, 1975BANGKO07178_b, https://wikileaks.org/plusd/cables/1975BANGKO07178_b.html.

71. CIA, "Thailand-USSR", *The President's Daily Brief*, 12 April 1975, https://www.cia.gov/readingroom/docs/DOC_0006014770.pdf.

72. US Embassy (Bangkok) to US secretary of state Henry Kissinger, "298. Minutes of National Security Council Meeting", Washington DC, 14 May 1975, *FRUS*, https://history.state.gov/historicaldocuments/frus1969-76v10/d298.

73. US Embassy (Bangkok) to US secretary of state Henry Kissinger, "Prime Minister Kukrit Pramot Press Statement May 29", 29 May 1975, Wikileaks, 1975STATE124914_b, https://wikileaks.org/plusd/cables/1975STATE124914_b.html.

74. US Embassy (Bangkok) to US secretary of state Henry Kissinger, "Visit to Thailand", 5 June 1975, Wikileaks, 1975BANGKO10384_b, https://wikileaks.org/plusd/cables/1975BANGKO10384_b.html.

75. "Angry Thai Policemen Attack Home of Premier", *New York Times*, 20 August 1975, https://www.nytimes.com/1975/08/20/archives/angry-thailand-policemen-attack-home-of-premier.html.

76. Handley, *The King Never Smiles*, p. 227.

77. Mallet, "Causes and Consequences", p. 87.

78. US Embassy (Bangkok) to US secretary of state Henry Kissinger, "Army Commander Krit Quashes Coup Rumors", 25 August 1975, Wikileaks, 1975BANGKO17770_b, https://wikileaks.org/plusd/cables/1975BANGKO17770_b.html.

79. US Embassy (Bangkok) to US secretary of state Henry Kissinger, "Khukrit's Grip II", 24 September 1975, Wikileaks, 1975BANGKO20148_b, https://wikileaks.org/plusd/cables/1975BANGKO20148_b.html.

80. Somporn Sangchai, "Coalition Behavior in Modern Thai Politics", Occasional Paper no. 41 (Singapore: Institute of Southeast Asian Studies, 1976), pp. 22–23.

81. US Embassy (Bangkok) to US secretary of state Henry Kissinger, "Thai Political Crisis Eases", 29 September 1975, Wikileaks, 1975BANGKO20539_b, https://wikileaks.org/plusd/cables/1975BANGKO20539_b.html.

82. US Embassy (Bangkok) to US secretary of state Henry Kissinger, "Personnel Changes in the Internal Security Operations Command (ISOC)", 22 October 1975, Wikileaks, 1975BANGKO22313_b, https://wikileaks.org/plusd/cables/1975BANGKO22313_b.html.

83. US Embassy (Bangkok) to US secretary of state Henry Kissinger, "Political Atmospherics; Kukrit Ill", 1 October 1976, Wikileaks, 1975BANGKO20716_b, https://wikileaks.org/plusd/cables/1975BANGKO20716_b.html.

84. Cited in the *Bangkok Post*, 15 December 1975, p. 1. Later cited in Hewison, "The 1976 Thai Coup", p. 11.

85. US Embassy (Bangkok) to US secretary of state Henry Kissinger, "Speculation on New Elections", 24 December 1975, Wikileaks, 1975BANGKO26801_b, https://wikileaks.org/plusd/cables/1975BANGKO26801_b.html.

86. Somporn Sangchai, "Some Observations on the Elections and Coalition Building in Thailand, 1976", in *Modern Thai Politics*, edited by Clark Neher (Cambridge, MA: Schenkman, 1979), p. 382.

87. The conditions demanded of the left-wing parties to join the Democrats was more state control over the economy, abolition of the Anti-Communist Act, all US soldiers out of Thailand by March 1976, and the adoption of a neutralist foreign policy for Thailand.

88. Somporn, "Some Observations", p. 376.

89. Morell and Chai-anan, *Political Conflict*, pp. 261–62.

90. CIA, "Thailand", *National Intelligence Bulletin*, 13 January 1976, https://www.cia.gov/readingroom/docs/CIA-RDP79T00975A028500010020-3.pdf.

91. Handley, *The King Never Smiles*, p. 251.

92. Mallet, "Causes and Consequences", p. 88.

93. *Far Eastern Economic Review*, 30 April 1976, pp. 30–31, cited in Somporn, "Some Observations", p. 395.

94. US Embassy (Bangkok) to US secretary of state Henry Kissinger, "Krit Siwara", 16 January 1976, Wikileaks, 1976BANGKO01022_b, https://wikileaks.org/plusd/cables/1976BANGKO01022_b.html.

95. Roger Kershaw, "The Remarkable Premiership of M.R. Kukrit Pramoj", *Round Table: The Commonwealth Journal of Internationl Affairs* 70, no. 279 (1980): 333, https://doi.org/10.1080/00358538008453470.

96. Somsak Jeamteerasakul, "ใครเป็นใครในกรณี 6 ตุลา ภาค 1" [Who was who on 6 October 1976], 21 February 2008, https://mynoz.wordpress.com/2008/02/21/6-octotor-1976-%E0%B9%83%E0%B8%84%E0%

B8%A3%E0%B9%80%E0%B8%9B%E0%B9%87%E0%B8%99%E0
%B9%83%E0%B8%84%E0%B8%A3%E0%B9%83%E0%B8%99%E0
%B8%81%E0%B8%A3%E0%B8%93%E0%B8%B5-6-%E0%B8%95%
E0%B8%B8%E0%B8%A5%E0%B8%B2/.

97. US Embassy (Bangkok) to US secretary of state Henry Kissinger, "Prime Minister Khukrit's Comments on Domestic Affairs", 2 February 1976, Wikileaks, 1976BANGKO02189_b, https://wikileaks.org/plusd/cables/1976BANGKO02189_b.html.

98. Ibid.

99. The memorandum was prepared jointly by the CIA, the Defense Intelligence Agency, and the Bureau of Intelligence and Research of the Department of State.

100. CIA, memorandum from director of central intelligence George Bush to assistant to the president for national security Brent Scowcroft, "The Thai Election and its Implications for the US", control number 403, 4 February 1976, https://www.cia.gov/readingroom/docs/DOC_0005379420.pdf.

101. Ibid.

102. Ibid.

103. Ibid.

104. Ibid.

105. Ibid.

106. Ibid.

107. "413. Memorandum from Thomas J. Barnes of the National Security Council Staff to the President's Assistant for National Security Affairs (Scowcroft), Washington, February 5, 1976", *FRUS*, https://history.state.gov/historicaldocuments/frus1969-76ve12/d413.

108. "414. Memorandum from Thomas J. Barnes of the National Security Council Staff to the President's Assistant for National Security Affairs (Scowcroft), Washington, February 20, 1976", *FRUS*, https://history.state.gov/historicaldocuments/frus1969-76ve12/d414.

109. In March 1970, Washington's 40 Committee approved the use of moneys for "anti-Marxist" media as well as to financially prop up the rightist-moderate Democratic Radical Party against the Popular Unity candidate Salvador Allende for Chile's 5 September 1970 election. See "29. Memorandum for the 40 Committee", 5 March 1970, *FRUS*, http://history.state.gov/historicaldocuments/frus1969-76v21/29. When Allende won the election in a plurality and was on the verge of taking office, General Rene Schneider, commander of the Chilean Army, declared on 6 September that he would enforce the constitution and ensure that Allende was inaugurated. The CIA thereupon, on 8 September, decided to either manipulate the Chilean legislature or use military action to prevent Allende from coming to office. The Nixon administration quickly decided upon a military coup, code-named Track II. The CIA station in Santiago, Chile, plotted to kidnap General Schneider, paying right-wing Chilean military officials to do the job. In fact, the CIA funnelled weapons and money through the US defence attaché to Chile's Colonel Paul Wimert,

who then passed it on to the kidnappers. After two failed attempts, on 22 October 1970 a hit team surrounded Schneider's chauffeured car. But the third attempt was botched: Schneider was shot at close range and died of his wounds three days later. See "151. Editorial Note", *FRUS*, https://history.state.gov/historicaldocudents/frus1969-76v21/d151; "Cold War: Interview with Paul Wimert", episode 18, "Backyard", CNN. com, 21 February 1999, https://nsarchive2.gwu.edu/coldwar/interviews/episode-18/wimert1.html.

110. Memorandum from national security advisor Brent Scowcroft to President Gerald Ford, "Information Items", 7 February 1976, https://www.cia.gov/readingroom/docs/LOC-HAK-551-6-38-2.pdf.

111. "February 26 EA Press Summary", 26 February 1976, Wikileaks, 1976STATE046767_b, https://wikileaks.org/plusd/cables/1976STATE046767_b.html.

112. US Embassy (Bangkok) to US secretary of state Henry Kissinger, "General Bunchai Comments on Military Alert February 24–25", 25 February 1976, Wikileaks, 1976STATE045426_b, https://wikileaks.org/plusd/cables/1976STATE045426_b.html.

113. US Embassy (Bangkok) to US secretary of state Henry Kissinger, "Pramarn Adireksan and Coup Plotting", 25 February 1976, Wikileaks, 1976BANGKO04299_b, https://wikileaks.org/plusd/cables/1976BANGKO04299_b.html.

114. In the book *Revolutionary Notes 1–3 April 1981*, Boonchana Atthakorn published an appendix containing a memoir written on 20 February 1977 about a conversation he had with Admiral Sangad Chaloryu during the funeral of General Sawaeng Senanarong, which had been held the night before (pp. 186–87). Somsak Jeamteerasakul, "ใครเป็นใครในกรณี 6 ตุลา ภาค 1" [Who was who on 6 October 1976], 21 February 2008, https://mynoz. wordpress.com/2008/02/21/6-octotor-1976-%E0%B9%83%E0%B8%8 4%E0%B8%A3%E0%B9%80%E0%B8%9B%E0%B9%87%E0%B8%99 %E0%B9%83%E0%B8%84%E0%B8%A3%E0%B9%83%E0%B8%99% E0%B8%81%E0%B8%A3%E0%B8%93%E0%B8%B5-6-%E0%B8%95 %E0%B8%B8%E0%B8%A5%E0%B8%B2/.

115. Bunchana Atthakor, บันทึกการปฏิวัติ April 1–3, 1981 กับข้าพเจ้า [Record of the 1–3 April 1981 revolution with me] (Bangkok: Law Professor Dr. Bunchana Attakor Foundation for Study and Research), 1982, pp. 185–87, cited in Thongchai Winichakul, *Moments of Silence: The Unforgetting of the October 6, 1976, Massacre in Bangkok* (Honolulu: University of Hawai'i Press, 2020), p. 37.

116. James Parker, *Battle for Skyline Ridge: The CIA Secret War in Laos* (Philadelphia, PA: Casemate, 2019), pp. 102–9.

117. Memorandum for the president from national security advisor Brent Scowcroft, "Information Items—Embassy Bangkok Predicts a Coup in Thailand", 28 February 1976, https://www.fordlibrarymuseum.gov/library/document/0332/4527399.pdf.

118. Mallet, "Causes and Consequences", p. 89.

119. Morell and Chai-anan, *Political Conflict*, p. 263.

120. US Embassy (Bangkok) to US secretary of state Henry Kissinger, "Press Report: US Military Reductions in Thailand", 21 February 1976, Wikileaks, 1976BANGKO03917_b, https://wikileaks.org/plusd/cables/1976BANGKO03917_b.html.

121. "422. Memorandum from the President's Assistant for National Security Affairs (Scowcroft) to President Ford", 3 May 1976, *FRUS*, https://history.state.gov/historicaldocuments/frus1969-76ve12/d422.

122. US Embassy (Bangkok) to US secretary of state Henry Kissinger, "Bombing of Vocational School", 3 March 1976, Wikileaks, 1976BANGKO04878_b, https://wikileaks.org/plusd/cables/1976BANGKO04878_b.html.

123. US Embassy (Bangkok) to US secretary of state Henry Kissinger, "Violence Casts Shadow on Elections", 5 March 1976, Wikileaks, 1976BANGKO05136_b, https://wikileaks.org/plusd/cables/1976BANGKO05136_b.html.

124. US Embassy (Bangkok) to US secretary of state Henry Kissinger, "Continuing Activities Concerning March 20", 17 March 1976, Wikileaks, 1976BANGKO6157_b, https://wikileaks.org/plusd/cables/1976BANGKO06157_b.html.

125. Mallet, "Causes and Consequences", p. 88.

126. Ibid., p. 100n29.

127. Joseph Wright, *The Balancing Act: A History of Modern Thailand* (Bangkok: Asia Books, 1991), p. 248.

128. Ibid.

129. CIA, *National Intelligence Bulletin*, 22 March 1976, https://www.cia.gov/readingroom/docs/CIA-RDP79T00975A028700010038-2.pdf.

130. CIA, *National Intelligence Bulletin*, 1 April 1976, https://www.cia.gov/readingroom/docs/CIA-RDP79T00975A028800010002-0.pdf.

131. US Embassy (Bangkok) to US secretary of state Henry Kissinger, "Thai Election Prospects and Implications for US Policy", 2 April 1976, https://aad.archives.gov/aad/createpdf?rid=13820&dt=2082&dl=1345.

132. "418. Minutes of the Secretary of State's Staff Meeting, Washington, D.C., April 2, 1976", *FRUS*, https://history.state.gov/historicaldocuments/frus1969-76ve12/d418.

133. Morell and Chai-anan, *Political Conflict*, p. 149.

134. CIA, *The President's Daily Brief*, 5 April 1976, https://www.cia.gov/readingroom/docs/DOC_0006015073.pdf.

135. Somporn, "Some Observations", p. 389.

136. Sutichai Yoon, "Strategy and Hopes behind Pramarn's Miscalculation", *Voice of the Nation*, 17 April 1976, p. 2.

137. Ibid.

138. Ibid.

139. "Leaflets Reveal Signs of Cracks in Army", *Voice of the Nation*, 26 April 1976.

140. Interview with Colonel Chamlong Srimuang, cited in Chai-anan Samudavanija, *The Thai Young Turks* (Singapore: Institute of Southeast Asian Studies, 1982), p. 33.

141. Somporn, "Some Observations", p. 394.

142. Zimmerman, "Reflections on the Collapse", p. 50.

143. CIA, "The Overseas Chinese in Thailand", 24 March 1975, https://www.cia.gov/readingroom/docs/CIA-RDP79T00865A000600160001-9.pdf.

144. "Last of Thai Military Strongmen Passes Away", *Voice of the Nation*, 24 April 1976, p. 1.

145. US Embassy (Bangkok) to US secretary of state Henry Kissinger, "Thai Sugar Export to Khmer Republic", 10 April 1974, Wikileaks, 1974BANGKO05849_b, https://wikileaks.org/plusd/cables/1974BANGKO05849_b.html.

146. Handley, *The King Never Smiles*, p. 246.

147. US Embassy (Bangkok) to US secretary of state Henry Kissinger, "Civ-Air Consultations", 18 April 1975, Wikileaks, 1975BANGKO06717_b, https://wikileaks.org/plusd/cables/1975BANGKO06717_b.html.

148. US Embassy (Bangkok) to US secretary of state Henry Kissinger, "Summary of the Thai International-Air Siam Dispute", 4 August 1976, Wikileaks, 1976BANGKO21994_b, https://wikileaks.org/plusd/cables/1976BANGKO21994_b.html.

149. Zimmerman, "Reflections on the Collapse", p. 50.

150. Personal interview with anonymous individual with close knowledge about Krit Sivara, Bangkok, 4 September 2018.

151. US Embassy (Bangkok) to US secretary of state Kissinger, "Chalat's Promotion and Krit's Illness", 19 April 1976, Wikileaks, 1976BANGKO10547_b, https://wikileaks.org/plusd/cables/1976BANGKO10547_b.html.

152. "Gen Krit One Week in Hospital", *Bangkok Post*, 24 April 1976, pp. 1, 13.

153. "4AM Alert for the Final Battle", *Voice of the Nation*, 24 April 1976, p. 1.

154. Handley, *The King Never Smiles*, p. 231.

155. Kobkua Suwannthat-Pian, "Thailand in 1976", in *Southeast Asian Affairs 1977* (Singapore: Institute of Southeast Asian Studies, 1977), p. 244, https//: doi.org/10.1355/9789812306678-021.

156. งานพระราชทานเพลิงศพ พลเอก เสริม ณ นคร [Memorial volume from the cremation ritual of General Serm na Nakorn], Bangkok, 2010.

157. "420. Memorandum from the President's Assistant for National Security Affairs (Scowcroft) to President Ford, Washington, April 20, 1976", https://history.state.gov/historicaldocuments/frus1969-76ve12/d420.

158. US Embassy (Bangkok) to US secretary of state Henry Kissinger, "Television Appearance by Prime Minister Seni", 19 July 1976, Wikileaks, 1976BANGKO20406_b, https://wikileaks.org/plusd/cables/1976BANGKO20406_b.html.

159. "US Military Units Quietly shut Last Two Major Bases in Thailand", *New York Times*, 21 July 1976, https://www.nytimes.com/1976/06/21/archives/us-military-units-quietly-shut-last-2-major-bases-in-thailand.html; "US Pull-Out from Thailand Will Be Completed On-Time", *New York Times*, 17 July 1976, https://www.nytimes.com/1976/07/17/archives/us-pullout-from-thailand-will-be-completed-on-time.html.

160. US Embassy (Bangkok) to US secretary of state Henry Kissinger, "Views of King and Pramot Brothers", 23 July 1976, Wikileaks, 1976BANGKO20780_b, https://wikileaks.org/plusd/cables/1976BANGKO20780_b.html.

161. Ibid.

162. US Embassy (Bangkok) to US secretary of state Henry Kissinger, "Conversations with Secretary-General to the Prime Minister", 7 July 1976, Wikileaks, 1976BANGKO19432_b, https://wikileaks.org/plusd/cables/1976BANGKO19432_b.html.

163. Ibid.

164 US Embassy (Bangkok) to US secretary of state Henry Kissinger, "The Finance Minister's Leadership on Economic Issues", 3 August 1976, Wikileaks, 1976BANGKO21813_b, https://wikileaks.org/plusd/cables/1976BANGKO21813_b.html.

165. "A Short History of Military Influence in Thailand", *Knights of the Realm: Thailand's Military and Police, Then and Now* (Bangkok: White Lotus Press, 2013), pp. 185–87; US Embassy (Bangkok) to US secretary of state Henry Kissinger, "Thai Visit to Hanoi Concludes with Agreement on Diplomatic Ties", 6 August 1976, Wikileaks, 1976BANGKO22255_b, https://wikileaks.org/plusd/cables/1976BANGKO22255_b.html.

166. Handley, *The King Never Smiles*, p. 231.

167. US Embassy (Bangkok) to US secretary of state Henry Kissinger, "Democrats Suffer First Major Defeat", 4 August 1976, Wikileaks, 1976BANGKO21995_b, https://wikileaks.org/plusd/cables/1976BANGKO21995_b.html.

168. US secretary of state Henry Kissinger to US Embassy (Bangkok), "Coup Rumors", 28 July 1976, Wikileaks, 1976STATE186592_b, https://wikileaks.org/plusd/cables/1976STATE186592_b.html.

169. US Embassy (Bangkok) to US secretary of state Henry Kissinger, "Coup Rumors", 5 August 1976, Wikileaks, 1976BANGKO22032_b, https://wikileaks.org/plusd/cables/1976BANGKO22032_b.html.

170. Former ambassador Leonard Unger to US secretary of state Henry Kissinger, "General Praphas's Return to Thailand", 17 August 1976, Wikileaks, 1976TAIPEI05590_b, https://wikileaks.org/plusd/cables/1976TAIPEI05590_b.html.

171. US Embassy (Bangkok) to US secretary of state Henry Kissinger, "Field Marshal Praphas' Return", 18 August 1976, Wikileaks, 1976BANGKO23241_b, https://wikileaks.org/plusd/cables/1976BANGKO23241_b.html.

172. Wright, *The Balancing Act*, p. 251.

173. CIA, "Weekly Summary", WS 70035, no. 035, 27 August 1976, https://www.cia.gov/readingroom/docs/CIA-RDP79-00927A011400100001-6.pdf/.

174. Mallet, "Causes and Consequences", p. 89.

175. US Embassy (Bangkok) to US secretary of state Henry Kissinger, "Field Marshal Praphas's Return", 19 August 1976, Wikileaks, 1976BANGKO23370_b, https://wikileaks.org/plusd/cables/1976BANGKO23370_b.html.

176. Handley, *The King Never Smiles*, p. 234.

177. US Embassy (Bangkok) to US secretary of state Henry Kissinger, "Political Significance of Praphas's Attempted Return to Thailand", 25 August 1976, Wikileaks, 1976BANGKO23913_b, https://wikileaks.org/plusd/cables/1976BANGKO23913_b.html.

178. US Embassy (Bangkok) to US secretary of state Henry Kissinger, "Defense Minister Resigns", 26 August 1976, Wikileaks, 1976BANGKO23990_b, https://wikileaks.org/plusd/cables/1976BANGKO23990_b.html.

179. CIA, "National Intelligence Cable", 26 August 1976, https://www.cia.gov/readingroom/docs/CIA-RDP79T00975A029200010044-9.pdf.

180. US Embassy to US secretary of state Henry Kissinger, "Thanom's Request to Return", 6 August 1976, Wikileaks, 1976BANGKO22252_b, http://www.wikileaks.org/plusd/cables//1976BANGKO22252_b.html.

181. Handley, *The King Never Smiles*, p. 234.

182. US Embassy (Bangkok) to US secretary of state Henry Kissinger, "Prime Minister Resigns", 23 September 1976, Wikileaks, 1976BANGKO26599_b, http://wikileaks.org/plusd/cables//1976BANGKO26599_b.html.

183. CIA, "Thailand: Back to Square One", 5 November 1976, WS 76-045, no. 0045/76, https://www.cia.gov/readingroom/docs/CIA-RDP79-00927A011400200001-5.pdf.

184. US Embassy (Bangkok) to US secretary of state Henry Kissinger, "Anti-Thanom Rally; Police Involved in Killing of Anti-Thanom Activists", 5 October 1976, Wikileaks, 1976BANGKO27566_b, https://wikileaks.org/plusd/cables/1976BANGKO27566_b.html.

185. Thongchai Winichakul, *Moments of Silence: The Unforgetting of the October 6, 1976, Massacre in Bangkok* (Honolulu: University of Hawai'i Press, 2020), p. 45.

186. *Dao Siam* newspaper, 5 October 1976, https://prachatai.com/English/node/8826.

187. Handley, *The King Never Smiles*, pp. 29, 35.

188. See, for example, Puey Ungphakorn, "Violence and the Military Coup in Thailand", *Bulletin of Concerned Asian Scholars* 9, no. 3 (1977): 4–12, https://doi.org/10.1080/14672715.1977.10406422; Morell and Chai-anan, *Political Conflict*, pp. 273–77; Handley, *The King Never Smiles*, pp. 214–37.

189. See Thongchai, *Moments of Silence*.

190. Duncan McCargo, *Chamlong Srimuang and the New Thai Politics* (London: Hurst, 1997), p. 36.

191. King Prajadhipok's Institute, "Saiyud Kerdphol", 2016, http://wiki.kpi.ac.th/index.php?title=%E0%B8%AA%E0%B8%B2%E0%B8%A2%E0%B8%AB%E0%B8%A2%E0%B8%B8%E0%B8%94_%E0%B9%80%E0%B8%81%E0%B8%B4%E0%B8%94%E0%B8%9C%E0%B8%A5.

192. Desmond Ball, *Tor Chor Dor: Thailand's Border Patrol Police* (Bangkok: White Lotus, 2o13), p. 161.

193. Surin Masdit, เปิดจดหมาย พระสุรินทร์ มาศดิตถ์ 24 ต.ค. 2520 และใครเป็นใครบ้างใน 6 ตุลา 19 [Opening the letter Pra Surin Masdit, 24 October 1977 and who is who on 6 October 1976], 15 February 2008, https://prachatai.com/journal/2008/02/15838.

194. Ball, *Tor Chor Dor*, p. 162.

195. "Brutal Thai Coup, *The Guardian*, 7 October 1976, https://www.theguardian.com/theguardian/1976/oct/07/fromthearchive.

196. "The Takeover Announcement", *Voice of the Nation*, 7 October 1976, p. 1.

197. "Prachak Says Chamlong Offered to Incite Mobs", *Bangkok Post*, 23 July 1987, p. 1.

198. McCargo, *Chamlong Srimuang*, p. 38.

199. Most interestingly, one of the Young Turks leaders, Major Manoon Rupekachorn, was close to General Chalard Hiranyarsiri and had been close to General Krit Sivara. See "Manoon Rupekachorn", King Prajadhipok's Institute, http://wiki.kpi.ac.th/index.php?title=%E0%B8%A1%E0%B8%99%E0%B8%B9%E0%B8%8D%E0 %B8%81%E0%B8%A4%E0%B8%95_%E0%B8%A3%E0%B8%B9%E0%B8%9B%E0%B8%82%E0%B8%88%E0%B8%A3; Chai-anan Samudavanija, *The Thai Young Turks* (Singapore: Institute of Southeast Asian Studies, 1982), p. 33.

200. US Embassy (Bangkok) to US secretary of state Henry Kissinger, "Courtesy Call on Minister Samak", 3 December 1976, Wikileaks, 1976BANGKO32860_b, https://wikileaks.org/plusd/cables/1976BANGKO32860_b.html.

201. Cited in McCargo, *Chamlong Srimuang*, p. 38.

202. US Embassy (Bangkok) to US secretary of state Henry Kissinger, "NARC Developments in Thailand", 13 October 1976, 1976BANGKO28366_b, http://wikileaks.org/plusd/cables/1976BANGKO28366_b.html.

203. US Embassy (Bangkok) to US secretary of state Henry Kissinger, "MILITARY TAKEOVER, SITREP II, 7 October 1976, https://nsarchive.files.wordpress.com/2014/10/19761007-military-takeover-sitrep-ii.pdf.

204. UK Embassy (Ambassador David Cole, Bangkok) to London, "Situation in Thailand", 5 November 1976, https://doct6.com/archives/14481.

205. US Embassy (Bangkok) to US secretary of state Henry Kissinger, "MILITARY TAKEOVER, SITREP II, 7 October 1976, https://nsarchive.files.wordpress.com/2014/10/19761007-military-takeover-sitrep-ii.pdf.

206. US Embassy (Bangkok) to US secretary of state Henry Kissinger, "US Actions in Thailand", 14 October 1976, Wikileaks, 1976BANGKO28514_b, https://wikileaks.org/plusd/cables/1976BANGKO28514_b.html.

207. US Embassy (Bangkok) to US secretary of state Henry Kissinger, "US-Thai Relations", 19 October 1976, Wikileaks, 1976BANGKO28937_b, https://wikileaks.org/plusd/cables/1976BANGKO28937_b.html.

208. US Embassy (Bangkok) to US secretary of state Henry Kissinger, "The End of the Democratic Experiment in Thailand", 14 October 1976, Wikileaks, 1976BANGKO28513_b, https://wikileaks.org/plusd/cables/1976BANGKO28513_b.html.

209. UK Embassy (Ambassador David Cole, Bangkok) to London, "The Military Coup in Thailand", 13 October 1976, https://doct6.com/archives/14481.

210. US Embassy (Bangkok) to US secretary of state Henry Kissinger, "Department's Comments on Embassy's Annual Policy Report", 13 September 1976, Wikileaks, 1976BANGKO25505_b, https://wikileaks.org/plusd/cables/1976BANGKO25505_b.html.

211. US Embassy (Bangkok) to US secretary of state Henry Kissinger, "Conversation with Former Foreign Minister Thanat Khoman Regarding Military Takeover", 14 October 1976, Wikileaks, 1976BANGKO28495_b, https://wikileaks.org/plusd/cables/1976BANGKO28495_b.html.

212. US Embassy (Bangkok) to US secretary of state Henry Kissinger, "Talk with King's Private Secretary", 18 October 1976, http://nsarchive.files.wordpress.com/2014/1019761019-talk-wit-the-kings-private-secretary.pdf.

213. US Embassy (Bangkok) to US secretary of state Henry Kissinger, "American Chamber of Commerce President Criticizes Thai Government for Indecisiveness, Poor Investment Climate", 9 September 1976, Wikileaks, 1976BANGKO25158_b, https://wikileaks.org/plusd/cables/1976BANGKO25158_b.html

Chapter Seven

The Palace's Attempted Coup (1976–77)

The 6 October 1976 coup appeared to have brought Thailand's military back to dominate the country—as a resurgence to the Thanom/Praphas period. But in fact, given that the weak Supreme Command was leading the junta while the army itself was extremely factionalized, King Bhumipol was able to hold overwhelming sway across the new administration. To some extent, he allowed the military to hold the reins of power.

With his endorsement, the military usurpers, self-styled as the "NARC", initially agreed that ACM Kamon, in his role as supreme commander of the armed forces, would "head an internal security force" tasked with administering the country for approximately one month through the guidance of a military council chaired by retired admiral Sangad.[1] A reform government, to be led by an arch-royalist civilian, would then assume power, after which a new constitution would be drafted.[2] Though Sangad formally led the NARC, the pro-Praphas assistant army commander General Yot Thepsadin na Ayuthaya maneuvered to compete for power against him.[3] The NARC was expanded to include more military council members to appease disgruntled army officers who had felt excluded.

Meanwhile, seeking to rapidly put his imprimatur on the new government, King Bhumipol, on 8 October, appointed the obscure, rabidly anti-communist judge Thanin Kraivixien as prime minister, with cabinet formation set for two weeks later. Sangad was quick to support the king's move[4] so as to frustrate the machinations of General

Yot. The military's post-Krit faction and the palace seemed to have allied against hard-line military officers.

Bhumipol appeared to be content that a civilian government under his direct control had ascended to power, and he naively assumed it enjoyed the stable backing of the armed forces. According to US ambassador Whitehouse:

THE MOOD IN THE PALACE IS ONE OF SATISFACTION THAT A NEW CIVILIAN GOVERNMENT IS ABOUT TO BE FORMED, WHICH HAS THE FULL SUPPORT OF THE THAI MILITARY ESTABLISHMENT AND THAT THE KING IS RELATIVELY OPTIMISTIC THAT THAILAND WILL SURMOUNT ITS PRESENT DIFFICULTIES.[5]

Under Thanin, the Martial Law Act, implemented when the coup had been announced, remained in place, bolstered by armed forces support. But any power that Thanin had over the military, of course, owed only to that which the king had given him. But who exactly was Thanin? Born in 1927, Thanin had been a judge since 1955, became chief judge of Chiang Mai province during 1964–67, then later a Supreme Court judge. After 1961, Thanin began to become a specialist on psychological warfare in terms of defending against communism. He had also begun to give special lectures about the dangers of communism at various Thai universities, the Internal Security Operations Center and at the National Defence College. Thanin had been appointed as a representative in the 1973–75 National Legislative Assembly, but he caught the attention of the king in late 1975 and 1976 when his anti-communist shows appeared on Thai television.[6] Importantly, Thanin was a favourite of Queen Sirikit.[7]

Fourteen days after Thanin's appointment, on 22 October, NARC officially turned power over to Thanin's newly organized cabinet. As prime minister, Thanin seemed to revile the more pragmatic NARC generals, placing only five retired military officials in his seventeen-member cabinet, the rest of the ministers being ultra-right-wing civilian confidants. Many of these were Thanin cronies and/or members of "Dusit 99", a conservative political activist clique formed during the National Legislative Assembly (1973–75). Among the cabinet ministers were such reactionaries as Samak Sundaravej (another of the queen's favourites) as minister of the interior and Dusit Siriwan (Thanin's anti-communist media announcer associate) as minister to the Office of the Prime Minister. In his new role, Samak eagerly used his ministry's control over the police to make mass arrests. The apparent distrust between Thanin's clique and that of the NARC officers placed

FIGURE 7.1
Legislative Assemblies, 1976–77

Type of legislature	Years in office	Appointed or elected	Total number of senators and military contingent
Unicameral	1976–77	Appointed	340, of which 155 (45.5%) military reserved domain

Source: Chaowana Traimat, *Data on 75 Years of Thai Democracy* (Konrad Adenauer Foundation, 2007), p. 140; author's calculations.

difficulties on his government's performance from the very beginning. Just under the cabinet was the Prime Minister's Advisory Council (PMAC), comprising Thailand's active-duty military leadership, which was formally led by supreme commander Khamon but effectively dominated by its secretary-general, deputy supreme commander General Kriangsak Chomanand. Meanwhile, a new National Administrative Reform Assembly (NARA) was appointed, in which 155 members were military officers and 35 members were police officials out of a total of 340 members.

Following the formation of his cabinet, Thanin proclaimed: "The Government is like an oyster and the military the shell protecting the oyster."[8] By this, the new prime minister sought to emphasize the primacy of civilians in running day-to-day activities, while the military supported the government in ensuring the survival of the government and guaranteeing national security. But from the outset, the problem for Thanin's oyster was that it was dependent on the shell.

Once in office, Thanin explained to the press that democracy would return to Thailand but only gradually after twelve years. Under a new Democratic Development Plan (placed into the preamble of the 1977 constitution), there was to be a twelve-year plan of eventual democratic development, to be completed in 1988. This three-stage design, also described in detail in the 1976 charter, was designed to move the country incrementally towards an electoral democracy under monarchy.[9] During phase one of the plan (1976–80), Thailand would have an appointed government in which "the people should be encouraged to be interested in and to be aware of their duties". During phase two (1980–84), the government would allow the formation of political parties and an elected lower house alongside an appointed premier and Senate. During phase three (1984–88), the powers of the lower house would be increased, while those of the Senate would continue. During stage four (after 1988), representative democracy would be completely restored. Throughout the life of his brief regime, Thanin led training sessions of Thailand's leading bureaucrats, inculcating them in this strategy.[10] Interestingly, despite the overthrow of Thanin in 1977, Thailand did generally follow the plan. But, perhaps intentionally, the strategy delayed the resurrection of limited democracy.

As prime minister, Thanin immediately gave his executive branch extra powers to imprison suspected communists, putting his ideology of repressive, authoritarian anti-communism into action. These powers were based on a new draconian constitution of 22 October 1976, which Thanin had personally helped to promulgate as a means to facilitate his autocratic, anti-communist crusade. Article 21 (as with Article 17 under Sarit) decreed that the prime minister, "with the consent of the cabinet and his Advisory Council,… shall be authorized to make any order or take any action", which "shall be considered lawful". Order no. 22 stated that anyone arrested under martial law could be held for six months without trial, that all cases would be tried by a military court (with no chance of appeal), that large geographical areas could be designated a "communist-infested zone", and that within these zones searches could be conducted without a warrant and civil liberties would be suspended. Moreover, strikes were banned, the media suffered from intensive state censorship, and universities could be shuttered if they were considered by the state to be a threat to national security. The zealous use of these draconian provisions and the application of martial law by the Thanin government led to thousands of arrests and an un-countable number of young people fleeing to escape Thanin's grotesque perception of communist inroads throughout the country.

Early on, though Thanin publicly trumpeted his administration's drive to make Thailand's armed forces completely self-sufficient, he quickly had his rubber stamp legislature pass the Defence Act of 1976, which authorized the Ministry of Defence to borrow up to US$1 billion from external sources over a five-year period to be used only for defence items. One rationale for passage of the law was to placate Thai military officials who wanted more funding for military appropriations.[11]

In terms of Thai-US economic relations, in the aftermath of Thailand's bloody 6 October coup, Thanin's dictatorship implemented new policies that produced rosier returns for US businesses. Indeed, in December 1976, US ambassador Whitehouse spoke with admira-tion of the economic accomplishments of Thailand's newly installed dictatorship, pointing to how these coup-induced achievements were helping US commercial interests. In all capitals he lavished praise on the regime:

AS THE YEAR DRAWS TO A CLOSE, WE WISH TO DRAW ATTENTION TO THE CONSIDERABLE AND SIGNIFICANT STEPS TAKEN BY THE RTG, AND IN PARTICULAR THE MINISTRY OF INDUSTRY, IN THE APPROXIMATELY TWO MONTHS THIS GOVERNMENT HAS BEEN IN POWER. IN OUR VIEW THIS TRACK RECORD, MADE BY A GOVERNMENT WHICH HAS DONE MORE IN 60 DAYS IN REACHING DECISIONS ON DEVELOPMENT PROJECTS THAN PREVIOUS GOVERNMENTS ACCOMPLISHED IN NEARLY THREE YEARS, AUGURS WELL FOR U.S. COMMERCIAL INTERESTS FOR THE LIMITED FUTURE.[12]

Perhaps most importantly, the new government signed a contract with Billiton, a subsidiary of Royal Dutch Shell, to permit Billiton to resume its tin dredging operations off the coast of Phang-nga province as well as in the area near Phuket province formerly held by the Thailand Exploration and Mining Company (TEMCO). Among other "achievements", Whitehouse boasted of a US$200 million offshore natural gas pipeline, Union Oil Company of California's proposals to drill oil wells in Thai territorial waters, more investment by Thai Zinc (whose parent company is New Jersey Zinc), and Thai governmental approval of US investors' efforts to exploit several soda ash and rock salt deposits in Thailand's Northeast.[13]

In December 1976, Thanin delivered good news for the 1976 military coup-leaders as well as for Thanom, Praphas and Narong. The armed forces leaders received a state amnesty for their actions and, following a police investigation, state prosecutors ruled that there was insufficient evidence to bring any of the three to trial for their actions on 14 October 1973.[14] The three did not, however, get back the assets the Sanya government had taken from them.[15]

By 17 January 1977, the CIA was reporting that "Thai military dissatisfaction with Thanin may be reaching a critical point."[16] Members of the military PMAC were already considering a coup against Thanin for his inability to deal with the country's political and economic problems, but they decided to give him another sixty days. They had in mind replacing him with ACM Thawee Chulasap. Indeed, military leaders had been "uncomfortable with Thanin almost immediately after his selection as prime minister" following the October 1976 coup. This owed to several reasons. First, "the extremism of his right-wing views [was] disquieting [and] some members of the military council, largely from the army, [wanted] the military to take a more direct role in running the government".[17] Second, Thanin's anti-communism seemed to be overly obsessive. Third, Thanin's government began to vigorously pursue corruption allegations against bureaucrats, including those in the military. Fourth, the split between civilian administrators such as Samak (and his oversight of the Interior Ministry) and soldiers such as Sangad (in terms of his control over the Defence Ministry) only seemed to be widening. Fifth, Thanin's anti-communism expanded to include relations with Thailand's communist neighbours Vietnam, the Lao PDR and Cambodia. The government reversed the earlier diplomatic thaw favoured by Kukrit and Seni, replacing it with open enmity, which could enhance regional tensions. Sixth, there was economic deterioration.

Regardless of any opposition from bureaucrats and soldiers, Thanin continued his headstrong anti-communism and anti-corruption campaigns. He worked towards little else. He also increasingly "stepped on the toes of … ranking military officers who … profited from Thailand's flourishing narcotics traffic, prostitution and other illicit activities."[18]

Almost exactly sixty days after senior military leaders had said they would back Thanin, a coup against him was attempted. On 26 March 1977, the ambitious General Chalard Haransiri, now a mere official attached to the Defence Ministry, made the first attempt. Chalard retained close ties to the ambitious assistant army chief Yot, Yot's powerful brother-in-law General Thep Kranlert (who had been demoted from deputy commander of the 1st Army Region to chief of the Army Education Department), former 9th Army Division commander General Yutthasak Klongtruatrok (transferred to southern Thailand to head the 5th Division)[19] and politician General Pramarn Adireksan.

Under Chalard, other 1977 coup leaders were Chalard's son and son-in-law, who were intermediate-level officers leading three hundred soldiers from the strategic 9th Army Division, not far from Bangkok. They secretly entered Bangkok in the early morning and seized several key positions: the Supreme Command headquarters, the Internal Security Operations Command, 1st Army Headquarters, and the public relations department.[20] Thereupon, several senior officers were held at gunpoint, including army chief of staff General Pralong Virapli, army deputy commander General Prasert Thammasiri and 1st Army Division commander Maj. Gen. Aroon Thawatashilp, King Bhumipol's favourite soldier. Prasert was named as the leader of the coup in early broadcasts by the rebel-held radio, but later the government said he had been forced at gunpoint to side with the rebels. Even though he was a hostage, Aroon attempted to grab a weapon, but then Chalard shot Aroon, killing him. Aroon's death turned 1st Army Division soldiers away from supporting the coup. General Amnart Damrikarn, 1st Army Region commander (who swayed between the Praphas faction and Kriangsak's "professionals" faction) did not support the putsch. Other key officers began to back away from it, and there were desertions among the initial three hundred soldiers.

By the evening of 27 March, the coup attempt fizzled altogether. Apparently, Chalard had earlier believed that support was awaiting him among some officers in the 1st Army Division. Ultimately, the coup failed because Chalard had not succeeded in attracting any 1st Army Division support; the king refused to endorse the coup; the lack of a general positive consensus towards a coup from the military leadership; and an insufficiently receptive public mood.[21] Negotiations eventually led to the coup leaders' conditional surrender. Initially, a deal was reached whereby Chalard and the four other coup instigators would be allowed to leave Thailand for exile in Taiwan in return for releasing hostages General Pralong and General Prasert. When the five reached Don Muang airport, however, they were not allowed to board the plane and were instead arrested on charges of treason. The failure of the coup and death of Aroon were not treated lightly by Thanin. Chalard became the first coup plotter with the rank of general to be executed.[22] In addition, several of Chalard's supporters, including Sanan and Veera, were imprisoned on 21 April.

Senior military sources said that one reason Kriangsak supported Chalard's speedy execution in secret without a trial was because he was afraid Chalard might name senior Thai government and military officials as accomplices. These same sources alleged that Kriangsak had also supported the state's speedy execution of a drug lord because that person was "about to name Gen. Kriangsak … as a key conspirator in the Thai drug traffic".[23] General Kriangsak and Prime Minister Thanin Kraivichien signed off on Chalard's execution, while King Bhumipol removed all of Chalard's military ranks but did not sign the execution papers.

The other coup conspirators were sentenced to life in prison. They included General Chalard's son Major Aswin, Lt. Col. Sanan Khachornprasart, Major Boonlert Kaewprasart and Major Visit Kongprasit. Ultimately, there were twenty-two co-conspirators who were either sent to prison or tried and sentenced in absentia. Some civilians were also involved. One who was privy to and supported Chalard's forces was Democrat Veera Musikapong. Sanan later became the Democrat Party secretary-general, and in 1997 he bitterly lamented that "[Chalard] finally agreed to give up the fight when Kriangsak

Chomanan gave him a personal assurance he would be allowed safe passage to Taiwan".[24] This promise was not kept, however. According to the US Embassy, in terms of defusing Chalard's coup, "[Kriangsak] was the person whom the Thai leadership depended on to restore the status quo."[25]

The king pardoned all the March coup participants in December 1977 following the coup that year against Thanin. In 1978, an investigation implicated Chart Thai leader Pramarn Adireksan for indirect participation in the coup attempt.[26] Then, Thailand's monarch publicly opined that, henceforth, the only political changes to be allowed would be constitutional.[27]

Chalard's death did little to quell military dissent against Thanin. The Young Turks faction had been bristling for political change since shortly after Thanin's own accession to power. In May they started planning a coup. But, perhaps responding to the king's abhorrence for putsches, the Young Turks attempted in early June 1977 to remove Thanin from office constitutionally by censuring him in the unicameral National Assembly on charges of corruption. But the motion did not carry. Also, on 3 June 1977, using a more traditional strategy, Colonel Prajark Sawangjit and Lt. Col. Manoonkrit Rupkachorn led sixteen other battalion commanders who were part of the Young Turks to the office of army commander General Serm na Nakorn. They demanded that Serm lead a coup against Thanin. Serm, however, a rather weak and apolitical army leader at a time when the armed forces were greatly fragmented, decided to get the opinion first of General Yot Thepsadin na Ayuthaya, for who a military committee at the time was putting the finishing touches on elevating to become deputy army commander. When the well-respected Yot arrived at Serm's house to discuss the matter, the Young Turks quickly departed and dispersed their troops.[28] Serm's apparent reluctance irritated the Young Turks, and they decided to talk to other generals who might willingly oust Thanin. Indeed, they next approached deputy supreme commander General Kriangsak, but he too seemed to baulk. In fact, Kriangsak likely played a determining role in preventing a coup because, though the Young Turks demanded that Kriangsak authorize a coup and become prime minister, he successfully argued to them that a coup would be bad for Thailand's image and would discourage foreign investment.[29] At the time, Serm, Kriangsak and other military officers clearly wanted to oust Thanin, but they perceived correctly that the appointed prime minister still received support from the palace. In June 1977, Kriangsak, who had shown more obedience to Thanin than other members of the PMAC since the inception of the October 1976 government, began to be-come much more outspoken against the prime minister. He lambasted Thanin as inflexible and narrow-minded and too ready to apply the draconian Article 21 against alleged rapists and smugglers. To the US Embassy, this change in Kriangsak's attitude smacked of rising political ambition. It came after his medical check-up at Walter Reed Hospital in Maryland in April 1977.[30]

In fact, it was during Kriangsak's US visit in May that the Carter administration began to take positive notice of him. While there, deputy secretary of state Richard Holbrooke made it known to him that the United States was worried about the policies of the Thanin government. Kriangsak reassured Washington that, as long as he continued to influence state policy, Thailand would persist in cracking down on narcotics and accepting more regional refugees, while remain-ing an able ally in Southeast Asia. In this respect, the United States began to view him as much more capable than Thanin. In particular, US policymakers appreciated Kriangsak's expression of "deep regret for various undesirable incidents that occurred in Thailand during the past two years, before October 6, 1976 [and that he] hoped that a new start would be made".[31] In late May, US State Department official Robert Oakley visited Thailand, met with Kriangsak, among others, and discussed future Thai-US relations.

By early June, Kriangsak was seriously looking to oust Thanin. With the overly rigid Thanin becoming increasingly unpopular, Kriangsak found growing support from the administration of US president Jimmy Carter. On 5 June 1977, Robert Zimmerman of the US Agency for International Development (USAID) Jakarta, whose brother was then a military attaché at the US Embassy in Bangkok and who was a friend of generals Serm and Saiyud, met with Saiyud at the latter's residence. Saiyud stated that Thanin and the members of PMAC were of the opinion that the then "tightly controlled political process was precisely what the United States wanted to see in Thailand".[32] Saiyud thought that Zimmerman should talk to Kriangsak, so a meeting was arranged for 8 p.m. on 6 June at the La Viendomme Restaurant in Bangkok. Saiyud told Zimmerman to come alone and not to men-tion the meeting to anyone. Kriangsak later asked Zimmerman if he would not prepare notes from the meeting since he wanted nothing on the record. In fact, Kriangsak said that he was willing to meet with Zimmerman because Saiyud had told him "I was a friend who wanted to help". Zimmerman thereupon told Kriangsak that he would later prepare a report on Thailand to be forwarded to assistant secretary of state Richard Holbrooke. Zimmerman was thus "sure Kriangsak saw an opportunity to use me as a direct conduit to at least pass some of his thoughts to Washington".[33] The gist of the three-hour meeting was how Thailand's political situation might be altered so that it would become more responsive "and create a wider base of support".[34] Kriangsak stated that he himself could make no changes, downplaying any impression that he had power behind the scenes. Nevertheless, Kriangsak admitted he might succeed in convincing other PMAC members "to do certain things".[35] They discussed, first, an amnesty for the students arrested on 6 October 1976. Kriangsak said he supported a blanket amnesty for them, though it would be ideal if the palace offered it. With regard to this, Kriangsak stated that the king was still very "disillusioned with the students". Regarding the students, Saiyud later told Zimmerman that the United States should approach the king's aide Colonel Vasit about convincing the king to support an amnesty for students as well as other proposed political changes. A second topic of conversation that Kriangsak supported was the formation of pressure/interest groups to be given weekly access to the prime minister and cabinet instead of engaging in street demonstrations. Third, Zimmerman advised Kriangsak to lift press censorship and political teachings/discussions within universities. Kriangsak seemed partly supportive of this suggestion. As for a fixed term for prime ministers, Kriangsak disagreed with even having a parliamentary system, which he considered too destabilizing. As for parliamentary elections, Kriangsak said that he supported polls within two years and that Thanin's twelve-year programme could be adjusted. Kriangsak asked Zimmerman to put his ideas on paper and deliver them to assistant secretary Holbrooke before leaving Thailand. Kriangsak then said that he wanted to meet with Holbrooke "as soon as possible—the sooner the better". Kriangsak stressed that when he had earlier met Holbrooke in Washington DC, he had come away with a greater appreciation of US president Jimmy Carter's human rights policy. Kriangsak proposed that Holbrooke visit Bangkok to continue talks that the former had had with Zimmerman, though Kriangsak wanted the talks to be kept secret from the US Embassy (Kriangsak feared leaks).[36]

While Kriangsak talked to Zimmerman at the restaurant, the former gestured to General Saiyud, saying, "He will be the next [armed forces] Chief of Staff". It was clear that Kriangsak and Saiyud were friends. Zimmerman posited that Saiyud was a definite liberal general who "saw little hope of any changes unless Thanin was removed [because] he was too narrow and uncompromising". As a counterinsurgency specialist, Saiyud felt that Thanin could not cope with insurgency over the long run since he did not understand political war. Saiyud felt that the PMAC should quickly call new elections and allow the electoral winners to take office, under the condition that if the elected government again made mistakes that created disorder, the military would be back. Zimmerman's conclusion following his talks with Kriangsak and Saiyud were that Kriangsak desired to dominate Thai politics behind the scenes in a manner similar to Krit Sivara, though Kriangsak had few of the sources of power that Krit had. "I believe, however, that he is prepared to try to encourage a freer political process if he can get significant US support."[37]

Kriangsak's discussions with US officials continued through June and July. What the deputy supreme commander wanted and would receive by September was US acquiescence for his quest to overthrow Thanin, albeit in a peaceable and near-constitutional manner. In return, Kriangsak was supposed to follow through on accelerating improvements in the Thai state's respect for human rights, enhanced anti-narcotics policies, continuing receptivity for refugee "boat people" into Thailand, and no changes with regard to Thanin's free market policies. On 7 July, Kriangsak publicly proclaimed that the human rights issue was a "courageous policy declared by President Carter".[38] Nevertheless, a 20 July CIA report poured cold water on Kriangsak's chances of succeeding Thanin as premier, contrasting him with Krit Sivara:

> Kriangsak would have difficulty gaining the premiership or even a role in Thai politics similar to Krit's. First, he does not have the broad military support essential to a successful bid for power, nor does he have any troops under his direct control. Military coup leaders have traditionally come out of the Army's First Division—the Bangkok garrison. A coup attempt without the support of the Bangkok commanders is not likely to succeed—as General Chalat discovered. In order to organize a coup attempt, Kriangsak would have to form an alliance with one or more of the Bangkok area commanders. Second, he is not as popular as Krit was within the military. Kriangsak would have to overcome the distaste of many important army officers, whose animosity would probably grow as his power increased. Finally, the king, whose backing is now virtually essential for anyone making a bid for power, is reportedly not inclined to support an abrogation of the current Thai political system and a return to direct military rule.[39]

Perhaps recognizing Kriangsak's weaknesses, Washington did give Thanin further chances to retain their support. In late July deputy secretary of state Warren Christopher visited Thanin, expressing appreciation for the Thai prime minister's hard-line anti-narcotics policy as well as his willingness to accept Indochinese refugees into Thailand. Christopher emphasized, however, that the Carter administration wanted countries to show more respect for human rights, and he encouraged Thanin to do the same in Thailand. Thanin admitted that some Thai laws infringed on human rights but said there were generally sufficient preventative safeguards to protect against human rights violations.[40] Nevertheless, Christopher came away from the meeting unimpressed by Thanin's commitment to the issue.

By August, the Thanin government was appearing increasingly embattled. First, because of its dismal human rights record; second, as a result of Thanin's harsh and unpopular governance; and, third, on account of growing coup rumours against it. Under Thanin, Thailand averaged over a thousand detainees a month, and there had been ten executions. In early August 1977, Thanin obsessively set the stage for the military trials of eighteen "October 6, 1976" students charged with over ten crimes (including treason, revolt, killing policemen and communist activities). The detained had already languished in prison for almost a year. Because of Thanin's eagerness to engage in repressive policies, global opinion became increasingly negative towards his regime. Meanwhile, the prime minister became more isolated from his top generals. Nevertheless, though they generally despised Thanin, senior military officials seemed in August to be more preoccupied with the upcoming military reshuffle.[41]

By mid-August, Thanin's obsessively anti-labour union and anti-communist foreign policy seemed to be creating more enemies than friends.[42] He seemed to understand the necessary rhetoric for balancing linkages between communist and non-communist countries, but his doctrinaire ultra-conservatism prevented him from engaging in such realism. With regard to Cambodia, Thanin's rigidity was matched by Khmer Rouge bellicosity towards Thailand. On 28 January 1977, Cambodian armed forces made an incursion across the Thai border at Aranyaprathet district, where they massacred thirty Thai villagers. Though this incident was especially deadly, Khmer Rouge troops continued brief crossovers until August. At this point, Thanin's administration began covertly supporting insurgent organizations in Cambodia. The Royal Thai Army's Tactical Operations Center (TOC) 315—the policymaking body that answered directly to the Royal Thai Army's chief of staff—was at the fore of this effort. In early February 1977, TOC 315's new director, Special Colonel Chavalit Yongchaiyudh, met with Tea Banh, a Khmer Rouge defector who had lived in Thailand since 1975. They talked in Aranyaprathet on the Thai-Cambodian border, with Chavalit initiating a discussion of provisioning Tea's group with weapons in an insurrection against the Khmer Rouge.[43] By August, Thanin was increasingly deploring Khmer Rouge cross-border incursions, emphasizing Thailand's desire to be friendly and peaceful with its neighbour. But Thai military support for Cambodian insurgents continued.

On 30 August, US officials met with Thanin to discuss his policy towards the upcoming trial of the eighteen 6 October student detainees, Thanin's restrictive refugee policy and labour unions. The prime minister was "unyielding" with regard to the students and said they would be put before a military court with no access to lawyers. As for unions, he said that they needed to be controlled because of communist influences within them.[44] Washington was becoming appalled by Thanin's unwillingness to (at least cosmetically) moderate his points of view. Though his virulently anti-communist views were reassuring to Washington, as was his support for a continuing US military presence in Asia, Thanin was ridiculed by foreign leaders as naive and too obsessed with communism to ably conduct foreign relations.

On 26 September 1977, the new annual military appointments list was formally adopted (see Appendix 4). Finally ascending to the top was General Kriangsak as supreme commander of the armed forces. His friend Admiral Kawi Singha was named as deputy supreme commander. ACM Kamron Leelasiri was appointed as assistant supreme commander. General Charoen Ponpanit remained the Supreme Command's chief of staff. General Serm na Nakorn, the apolitical army commander who deferred to Kriangsak, continued on as army commander. General Yot, the pro-Praphas assistant army commander, was promoted to become deputy army commander, and 1977–78 would be Yot's final year as an active-duty officer before his mandatory retirement. With support from the king, the up-and-coming and charismatic Prem Tinsulanond moved from commanding the 2nd Army Region to be assistant army commander. Prem was succeeded in the 2nd Army Region command post by General Sawaeng Chamonchand. But Prem and Sawaeng were part of the Cavalry Division faction. Perhaps because General Amnart Damrikarn was instrumental in thwarting the March 1977 coup, he was rewarded by continuing on as 1st Army Region commander. Amnart was becoming ever close to army commander General Serm. The new Royal Air Force commander was ACM Phaniang Kantarat, while Admiral Amon Sirikaya remained

Royal Thai Navy commander. The new 1st Army Division commander replacing the slain General Aroon was General Pat Urailert, who had also demonstrated opposition against the March 1977 coup attempt in commanding the 2nd Infantry Division "Eastern Tigers".

Already, during mid-September, however, there was a flurry of coup rumours. These stemmed from fears by military faction leaders generals Kriangsak and Yot—the two strongest and most senior personalities in the PMAC—that they might be dropped from active roles in the 1 October military reshuffle, given that the prime minister could at the last minute modify the reshuffle list before sending it to the king for endorsement.[45] Though neither of them held commands directly over troops, 1st Army Region commander General Amnart, who controlled troops in Bangkok, could be counted on to move forces against the prime minister if needed.

Meanwhile, Kriangsak seemed to be shortening the timeframe for when he would try to oust Thanin. On 29 September, he told US ambassador Whitehouse that it was no longer a question of "whether to bring about the downfall of the Thanin government but how and when to do it".[46] According to Kriangsak, Thanin was a:

"RIP VAN WINKLE" WHOSE STUBBORNESS AND UNWILLINGNESS TO TAKE ADVICE WERE EXCEEDINGLY DETRIMENTRAL TO THAILAND … WAS A FAILURE BOTH AT HOME AND ABROAD … [was] NARROWMINDED, BIGOTED AND UNWILLING TO TAKE ADVICE. KRIANGSAK SAID THERE WERE THREE COURSES OF ACTION WHICH MIGHT BE PURSUED. THE FIRST WAS WHAT HE DESCRIBED AS A "DRASTIC" MILITARY ACTION. THIS, HE SAID, HE SINCERELY WISHED TO AVOID. HE NOTED IN PASSING THAT MANY YOUNGER OFFICERS WERE CLAMORING FOR HIM TO ASSUME POLITICAL POWER. SECOND, A GOVERNMENT RESHUFFLE MIGHT BE PROPOSED. THIS WOULD PROVOKE A POLITICAL CRISIS OWING TO THE WELL-KNOWN UNWILLINGNESS OF THE PRIME MINISTER TO CHANGE ANY MEMBER OF THE CABINET. A THIRD POSSIBILITY WOULD BE A REPETITION OF OCTOBER 1976 [with] MANY ELEMENTS IN SOCIETY, AND PARTICULARLY ORGANIZED LABOR … EXPECTED TO MOVE DECISIVELY AGAINST THE GOVERNMENT.[47]

October seemed to be a make-or-break month for Thanin. He might be toppled, given the intensifying military opposition against him, or he might survive because the king was reluctant to abandon him. According to the CIA, "The King's continuing support of Thanin … is a major obstacle to any effort to remove him."[48] On 8 October, when reporters asked General Kriangsak whether the armed forces would protect Thanin from a possible putsch, Kriangsak reportedly replied that the "military" would act as an "oyster shell", but "the 'shell' is to protect the three institutions of Nation, Religion, and Monarchy, and the Thai people" rather than any particular group, meaning Thanin.[49]

Later that day, Kriangsak was playing golf with US ambassador Whitehouse. During the course of the game, Kriangsak said that he agreed with the US "position" and "point of view" that "any change of government should be brought about in a way which did minimum damage to Thailand's image abroad". In other words, Kriangsak was ruling out his third option for changing the government—repeating the method of 6 October 1976. Kriangsak stressed that Thanin was at that moment extremely unpopular and that the Young Turks were not appropriate coup-fomenters because they "had no program, no policy and no popular following".[50] Thus, they could not succeed. Kriangsak clearly wanted US support for his planned coup against Thanin. According to Whitehouse, "Kriangsak fully understands our position and I am convinced that neither he nor any other political leaders in this country believe that we [the United States] are involving ourselves in the Thai political scene".[51] But in fact the Carter administration was involving itself in Thailand's affairs by encouraging and pressuring Kriangsak to lead a coup against Thanin. Thanin, tainted by a continuing dedication to practising domestic repression, had become "damaged goods" in Washington's eyes as a result of Carter's human rights foreign policy. Two days later, Whitehouse shot a cable off to Washington in which he said that "US interests in Thailand would not be adversely affected by a peaceful cabinet change". In fact, "a Thai cabinet under a more flexible Prime Minister than Thanin [which is] more liberal … would be met with sighs of relief from a broad segment of the Thai body politic".[52]

Meanwhile, the Young Turks continued to plot ways to oust Thanin via constitutional means or a putsch. By August, this Young Officers Group had found a possible mentor in General Prem Tinsulanond, the charismatic 2nd Army Region commander who was situated in the frontline against Thailand's rural communist insurgency. Like Manoon and other Young Turks, Prem was a cavalry man, and thus they felt an affinity for him, referring to him as *Pa* (Father) Prem. With Prem supporting them, the Young Turks bided their time, awaiting the excuse to either seize power or censure the government. They did not have to wait long.

On 22 September, a bomb exploded near the motorcade of the king and queen when they were touring the deep South. Though the members of the royal court were unhurt, over forty people were injured. Six days later, representatives from five rightist militia groups met at the Royal Hotel in Bangkok to express concern over royal security and to demand that state officials responsible for security resign, including interior minister Samak Sundaravej. The five groups, inactive since 6 October 1976, included the National Vocational Student Centre of Thailand, the National Collegiate Vocational Students' Centre, the Student Teachers Federation, the Red Gaurs and the Throne Protection Group. Deputy army chief General Yot supported the rightist groups, calling their statement "an expression of loyalty to the king".[53]

In early October, using the bomb attack on the royals as their pretext, and with Prem on their side, the Young Turks again attempted a no-confidence vote in the National Assembly. This time the demand was that interior minister Samak Sundaravej be dismissed to take responsibility for failing to provide adequate security for the king and queen. In addition, the Young Turks sought the resignation of eight other ministers, including Dusit Siriwan, Pinyo Sathorn and Lersak Sombatsiri. Prem himself inquired from Thanin whether the prime minister might be willing to compromise with the Young Turks. When the prime minister refused, Prem explained that he and the Young Turks had the backing of army commander Serm as well as supreme commander Kriangsak, and that if Thanin refused to reshuffle the cabinet or simply resign, the top brass would not be averse to staging a coup. In a bid to keep control, Thanin requested an audience with the king, but the monarch refused to see him, illustrating perhaps that the palace's patience with Thanin was finally at an end.[54] Thus, according to Wright, Thanin had perhaps lost favour with the king, a sign that gave the Young Turks the green light to overthrow him on 20 October 1977.[55] Handley, contrarily, argues that the coup had not been backed by the palace, and was seen by the king as an affront to the monarch's "political primacy".[56]

As the Red Gaurs and other militants agitated against Samak, a rationale for forcing Thanin from power was becoming apparent—security for the king. In the end, the Young Turks provided troops to support the formally Sangad-led coup in return for the promise that a military man would be placed at the helm of government and elections would be called within two years.[57] Actually, the senior officers had little choice but to go along with the Young Turks since the latter held direct control over soldiers in the vicinity of Government House.[58] Ultimately, the military clearly removed Thanin from power because they thought he was overly dogmatic, too autonomous from military control, and too aggressive in pursuing policies that could harm military objectives (including Thanin's prosecution of an anti-narcotics campaign that could threaten the drug-smuggling interests of some of the military leaders themselves). In addition, senior military leaders such as Admiral Sangad and General Kriangsak wanted to try their own hands at leading a government.[59]

On 20 October, Prime Minister Thanin and his cabinet were officially ousted by the PMAC. The semi-dramatic transition began with a PMAC meeting in the morning. By noon, the armed forces were placed on full alert. At 4:30 p.m., the police force was also put on full alert. During mid-afternoon, Thanin convened a cabinet meeting attended by most ministers. Samak did not attend. At around 5 p.m., three truckloads of infantry and one tank took positions in front of Government House. At this point, retired admiral Sangad, heading up the reformed NARC, notified Prime Minister Thanin and the cabinet ministers that they had been dismissed and would not be allowed to leave the country. At 6 p.m., Radio Thailand and other media broadcast the official announcement that the Thai armed forces, under the leadership of Admiral Sangad, had again taken control of the government. During the evening, the Thai media carried five announcements and seven orders issued by the resurrected National Administrative Reform Council, now reduced from twenty-four to twenty-three military officers, given the death the previous year of General Aroon (though he was replaced by police director-general Monchai). Its members changed NARC's name to "the Revolutionary Party (RP)", a name similar to that of previous coup groups, including that of Sarit (1957) and Thanom (1971). Six leaders of this RP, including supreme commander Kriangsak, police director-general Monchai and the commanders of the army, navy and air force came on television at 10 p.m. to inform the nation that they had been granted an audience with the king and assuring all Thais that they would uphold the nation, religion and monarchy. To illustrate its sincerity, the new regime lifted press restrictions and announced new elections.

Ultimately, the experience of 1976–77 proved to be a boon for Thailand's military. The king's agent, Thanin, initiated policies that were extremely unpopular among the Thai people, and the king had seemed complicit for endorsing him. By doing so, the monarch had overreached what the Thai people were willing to tolerate. Thus, in the space of only twelve months, Thanin and the palace succeeded in erasing the tarnished image that the military had acquired under the Thanom/ Praphas regime. The October 1977 coup was welcomed not only by most Thais but also by Washington—given the Carter administration's pro-human rights policy—as well as by senior Thai military officials, who no longer had to contend with an obstinate civilian prime minister. The putsch thus provided the military with the chance to commence administering the country on its own, heading up a national security state.

Notes

1. อนุสรณ์งานพระราชทานเพลิงศพ พลเอก พลเรือเอก พลอากาศเอก กมล เดชะตุงคะม [Memorial cremation volume from the cremation ritual of General, Admiral and Air Chief Marshal Polkasek Kamol Dechatungkham], กองบัญชาการฝึกศึกษาทหาร อากาศ [Air Force Education Training Headquarters], Bangkok, 2002.

2. CIA, "National Intelligence Daily Cable: Thailand: Situation Report", NIDC 76-236c, 7 October 1976, https://www.cia.gov/readingroom/docs/DOC_0006466865.pdf.

3. CIA, NIDC 76-248c, 22 October 1976, https://www.cia.gov/readingroom/docs/CIA-RDP79T00975A029400010036-6.pdf.

4. อนุสรณ์ในงานพระราชทานฝังศพ พลเรือเอก สงัด ชลออยู่, จังหวัดระยอง [Memorial at the royal burial of Admiral Sangad Chaloryu, Rayong Province], Bangkok, 7 March 1981.

5. "Briefing Memorandum: Thai Situation Report Update", 19 October 1976, Wikileaks, 1976STATE259151_b, https://wikileaks.org/plusd/cables/1976STATE259151_b.html.

6. Somsak Jeamteerasakul, ใครเป็นใครในกรณี 6 ตุลา ภาค 1 [Who was who on 6 October 1976, part 1], https://mynoz.wordpress.com/2008/02/21/6-octotor-1976-ใครเป็นใครในกรณี-6-ตุลา/.

7. John Girling, *Thailand: Politics and Society* (Ithaca: Cornell University Press, 1981), p. 217.

8. Kamol Somvichian, "The Oyster and the Shell: Thai Bureaucrats in Politics", *Asian Survey* 18, no. 8 (August 1978): 829, 832.

9. Ibid.

10. US Embassy (Bangkok) to US secretary of state Cyrus Vance, "Thanin Outlines Plan to Establish Democracy Training Sessions", 26 July 1977, Wikileaks, 1977BANGKO16365, https://wikileaks.org/plusd/cables/1977BANGKO16365_c.html.

11. US Embassy (Bangkok) to US secretary of state Cyrus Vance, "Thai Defense Spending", 5 September 1979, Wikileaks, 1979BANGKO34349_b, https://wikileaks.org/plusd/cables/1979BANGKO34349_e.html.

12. US Embassy (Bangkok) to US secretary of state Henry Kissinger, "Industrial Development: Progress at Last", 20 December 1976,

Wikileaks, 1976BANGKO34098_b, http://wikileaks.org/plusd/cables/1976BANGKO34098_b.html.

13. Ibid.

14. Office of the Prime Minister, สำนักนายกรัฐมนตรี. คำแถลงนโยบายของคณะรัฐมนตรีซึ่งนายธานินทร์ กรัยวิเชียรเป็นนายกรัฐมนตรี พร้อมทั้งคำปราศรัยของนายกรัฐมนตรี [Cabinet policy statement from Mr Thanin Kraiwichian as prime minister along with the prime minister's speech] (Bangkok: Press Office of the Secretariat of the Cabinet, 1978).

15. US Embassy (Bangkok) to US secretary of state Cyrus, "Another Committee to Investigate Oct 14 Uprising", 15 December 1976, Wikileaks, 1976BANGO34349_b, https://wikileaks.org/plusd/cables/1976BANGKO33786_b.html.

16. CIA, "National Intelligence Bulletin: Thailand: Dissatisfaction with Thanin", NIDC 77-013c, 17 March 1977, https://www.cia.gov/readingroom/docs/CIA-RDP79T00975A029700010027-3.pdf.

17. Ibid.

18. Lewis Simons, "Coup Attempt in Thailand Collapses from Ineptitude", *Washington Post*, 27 March 1977, https://www.washingtonpost.com/archive/politics/1977/03/27/coup-attempt-in-thailand-collapses-from-ineptitude/794783d8-bbae-45e9-a21b-3a5e55227460/.

19. Thomas Marks, "October 1976 and the Role of the Military in Thai Politics", *Modern Asian Studies* 14, no. 4 (1980): 613, https://doi.org/10.1017/S0026749X00006648.

20. David A. Andelman, "Thai Coup, Mostly Just a War of Words, is Foiled", *New York Times*, 27 March 1977, https://www.nytimes.com/1977/03/27/archives/thai-coup-attempt-mostly-just-a-war-of-words-is-foiled-thai-coup.html.

21. CIA, "National Intelligence Daily Cable—Thailand: Situation Report", NIDC 77-071c, 28 March 1977, https://www.cia.gov/readingroom/docs/CIA-RDP79T00975A029900010048-8.pdf.

22. Somboon Khonchalard, Prakob Choprakarn, and Prayut Sittiphan. ปฏิวัติสามสมัย [Three revolutions], 3rd ed. (Bangkok: Ruam Pim, 1981).

23. David A. Andelman, "Thai General is Shot without Trial for Leading Coup", *New York Times*, 22 April 1977, https://www.nytimes.com/1977/04/22/archives/thai-general-is-shot-without-trial-for-leading-coup.html.

24. Sermsak Kasittipradit, "Sanan Divides, Sanan Conquers", *Bangkok Post*, 17 November 1997.

25. US Embassy (Bangkok) to US secretary of state Cyrus Vance, "Political Role of General Kriangsak Chamanand", 22 June 1977, Wikileaks, 1977BANGKO13656_b, https://wikileaks.org/plusd/cables/1977BANGKO13656_c.html.

26. US Embassy (Bangkok) to US secretary of state Cyrus Vance, "Background on Din 92-1A\'Thailand\':Coup Investigation Implicates Former Thai

Nation Party", 30 March 1978, Wikileaks, P850159-0303_d, https://wikileaks.org/plusd/cables/P850159-0303_d.html.

27. Joseph Wright, *The Balancing Act* (Bangkok: Asia Books, 1991), p. 276.

28. Chai-anan Samudavanija, *The Thai Young Turks* (Singapore: Institute of Southeast Asian Studies, 1982), p. 34.

29. US Embassy (Bangkok) to US secretary of state Cyrus Vance, "Political Role of General Kriangsak Chamanand", 22 June 1977, Wikileaks, 1977BANGKO13656_b, https://wikileaks.org/plusd/cables/1977BANGKO13656_c.html.

30. Ibid.

31. US Embassy (Bangkok) to US secretary of state Cyrus Vance, "Transcript of Press Conference by Thai Deputy Supreme", 19 May 1977, Wikileaks, 1977BANGKO10864_c, https://wikileaks.org/plusd/cables/1977BANGKO10864_c.html.

32. US Embassy (Jakarta) to US secretary of state Cyrus Vance, "Memcom by Robert Zimmerman, USAID of Indonesia, of Conversation", 14 June 1977, Wikileaks, 1977JAKARTA07842_b, https://wikileaks.org/plusd/cables/1977JAKART07842_c.html.

33. Ibid.

34. Ibid.

35. Ibid.

36. Ibid.

37. Ibid.

38 US Embassy (Bangkok) to US secretary of state Cyrus Vance, "Kriangsak on Human Rights", 8 July 1977, Wikileaks, 1977BANGKO14951_c, https://wikileaks.org/plusd/cables/1977BANGKO14951_c.html.

39. CIA, "International Narcotics Developments", PS SNIN 77-015, 20 July 1977, https://www.cia.gov/readingroom/docs/CIA-RDP79T00912A001800010016-3.pdf.

40. US Embassy (Bangkok) to US secretary of state Cyrus Vance, "Deputy Christopher's Call on Prime Minister Thanin", 26 July 1976, Wikileaks, 1977WELLIN03050_c, https://wikileaks.org/plusd/cables/1977WELLIN03050_c.html.

41. US Embassy (Bangkok) to US secretary of state Cyrus Vance, "Thanin Government and Human Rights", 24 August 1977, Wikileaks, 1977BANGKO18798_C, https://wikileaks.org/plusd/cables/1977BANGKO18798_c.html.

42. US Embassy (Bangkok) to US secretary of state Cyrus Vance, "Phichai Criticizes Thai Foreign Policy under Thanin", 16 May 1977, Wikileaks, 1977BANGKO10508_c, https://wikileaks.org/plusd/cables/1977BANGKO10508_c.html.

43. Kenneth Conboy, *The Cambodian Wars: Clashing Armies and CIA Covert Operations* (Lawrence: University Press of Kansas, 2013), pp. 110–12.

44. US Embassy (Bangkok) to US secretary of state Cyrus Vance, "Meeting with Primin Thanin", 30 August 1977, Wikileaks, 1977BANGKO19269_c, https://wikileaks.org/plusd/cables/1977BANGKO19269_c.html.

45. "158. Memorandum from Michael Armacost of the National Security Council Staff to the President's Deputy Assistant for National Security Affairs (Aaron)", 21 September 1977, *Foreign Relations of the United States* (*FRUS*), https://history.state.gov/historicaldocuments/frus1977-80v22/d158.

46. US Embassy (Bangkok) to US secretary of state Cyrus Vance, "Conversation with General Kriangsak: Political Developments, 29 September 1977, Wikileaks, 1977STATE234469_b, https://wikileaks.org/plusd/cables/1977STATE234469_c.html.

47. Ibid.

48. CIA, "International Narcotics Developments", PS SNIN 77-015, 20 July 1977, https://www.cia.gov/readingroom/docs/CIA-RDP79T00912A001800010016-3.pdf.

49. Kamol, "The Oyster and the Shell", p. 837.

50. "159. Telegram from the Embassy in Thailand to the Department of State", 10 October 1977, *FRUS*, https://history.state.gov/historicaldocuments/frus1977-80v22/d159.

51. Ibid.

52. US Embassy (Bangkok) to US secretary of state Cyrus Vance, "Prospects for Political Change in Thailand", 10 October 1977, Wikileaks, 1977BANGKO23181_c, https://wikileaks.org/plusd/cables/1977BANGKO23181_c.html.

53. US Embassy (Bangkok) to US secretary of state Cyrus Vance, "Rightist Groups Voice Concern", 3 October 1977, Wikileaks, 1977BANGKO22486Bc, https://wikileaks.org/plusd/cables/1977BANGKO22486_c.html.

54. Wright, *The Balancing Act*, pp. 277–78.

55. Ibid., p. 278.

56. Paul Handley, *The King Never Smiles* (New Haven, CT: Yale University Press, 2006), p. 267.

57. Chai-anan Samudavanija, ยังเติร์กกับทหารประชาธิปไตย การวิเคราะห์บทบาททหารใน การเมืองไทย [Still a Turk with democratic soldiers: An analysis of the role of the military in Thai politics] (Bangkok: Bangit, 1982).

58. Niyom Rathamarit, *Military Governments in Thailand: Their Policies toward Political Parties* (Pittsburgh: University of Pittsburgh, 1984), p. 130.

59. Frank Darling, "Thailand in 1977: The Search for Stability and Progress", *Asian Survey* 18, no. 2 (February 1978): 157.

Chapter Eight

Consensual Kriangsak (1977–80)

The coup of 20 October 1977 saw the resurgence of a military-led regime in Thailand. The new junta was led mostly by the Supreme Command, the weakest of all the services in the Thai armed forces, which was quite a surprise. The army, however, traditionally the most powerful security service, was at the time so extremely factionalized that other security services possessed more leverage. Nevertheless, because of the Supreme Command's frailty, supreme commander General Kriangsak Chomanand, the new political leader of Thailand, was forced to be quite consensual with other security service leaders to control the country.

Kriangsak (previously known as Somjit Chomanan) was born on 17 December 1917 into a prosperous entrepreneurial family (although his father worked previously at the Ministry of the Interior), near Mahachai market in Samut Sakhon (close to Bangkok). Kriangsak obtained a good education, even attending the prestigious Amnuay Silpa School. He graduated at the top of his class.

Given his generally affluent family credentials and proven academic abilities, Kriangsak was permitted to matriculate into the Chulachomklao Royal Military Academy in 1937. Because that period was a time of military urgency amidst the ongoing Phibun-led nationalism, Kriangsak was quickly graduated in 1940. (He later continued his military studies, enrolling at the Army Staff School and the National Defence College, of which he was a member of class 5.) Nevertheless, Kriangsak served in the infantry in Thailand's 1941 Indochina War

FIGURE 8.1
Kriangsak's Family Tree

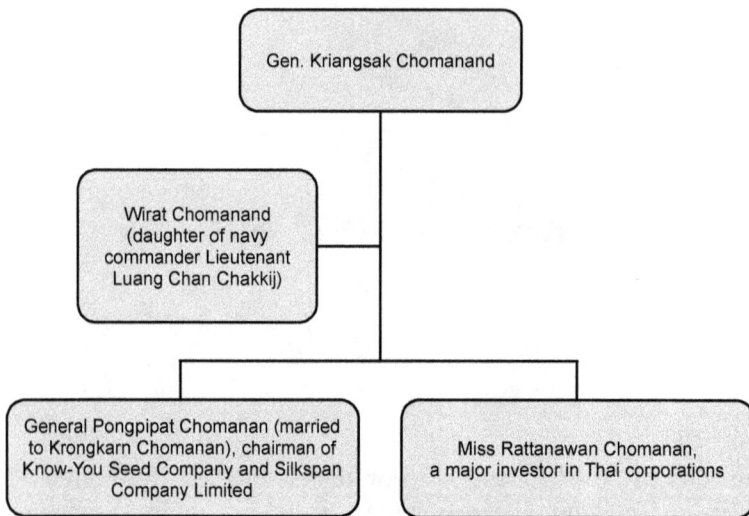

against France. He was a platoon leader and a company commander, reaching the rank of captain. In 1943, Kriangsak was placed in the northern 3rd Army Region, where he became chief of staff, holding the post of infantry battalion commander. In 1952 he went overseas to fight in Thailand's army contingent in the Korean Civil War. His unit was called "the Little Tiger Battalion". After returning to Thailand, he became department head of operations at the Army Staff School and was promoted to the rank of colonel. In 1956 he moved to Thailand's military office for the joint defence treaty of SEATO (Southeast Asia Treaty Organization). Following Sarit's 1957 coup, however, Kriangsak was moved out of the army to the Supreme Command, where he was given a deputy chief of staff of central administration slot. As such, he went abroad to study at the United States Army Staff School.[1] Back in Thailand, Kriangsak married the daughter of a deputy naval commander in 1961 in a ceremony presided over by former 3rd Army Region commander (1951–52) General Luang Sawat Sorayut.[2]

In the mid-1960s, Kriangsak grew closer to General Thawee Chullasap and General Krit Sivara, two individuals who, like him, had been kept from further senior promotions that might deny the over-whelming power of General Thanom (prime minister, defence minister, supreme commander and army commander) and General Praphas (deputy prime minister, interior minister and army commander). But, by 1976, these strongmen had either died or retired. Kriangsak felt closest to the late Krit.

The ghost of this last army strongman—in terms of his surviving faction—continued to lord over the military. The continuing clout of Krit's clique owed to the resurrection of the 1976 NARC (National Administrative Council), revitalized by the 1977 coup against Thanin. The personalities atop the clique, behind the coup and leading NARC remained the same as in 1976: Admiral Sangad Chaloryu, ACM Kamon, General Kriangsak and General Serm. But Sangad and Kamon were not from the army and were retired. Kriangsak was an army man who had transferred into the less respectable Supreme Command, was disdained by the monarch and had but one more year of active duty remaining. Nevertheless, he was charismatic, possessed excellent political skills and was a master at balancing cliques within the military. In fact, Kriangsak appeared to be a younger version of Krit in terms of reformist military views—though again, he was a Supreme Command man rather than an army one. As army commander, Serm would not reach mandatory retirement until 1981. He could therefore presumably stabilize the army while Kriangsak remained prime minister until that year. Unfortunately, the military had become ever more factionalized, and Serm was not as charismatic as Krit. The October 1977 military takeover demonstrated that the "Young Turks" had become the newest strong faction within Thailand's armed forces—since their acquiescence to and participation in the putsch had been critical. Under pressure from the Young Turks, the junta had pledged to be more progressive than Thanin's regime, promising a new constitution and an election by 1979. Almost immediately, NARC renamed itself as the Revolutionary Party and established a twenty-three-member National Policy Council (NPC) of the Revolutionary Party to administer the country, with a civilian-based Advisory Council tasked with offering policy recommendations. As NPC chair, former NARC head Admiral Sangad Chaloryu was again powerful, but his clout was offset by secretary-general General Kriangsak. Their two personalities had been behind the 20 October putsch. Indeed, the two were struggling for power. But while Kriangsak was supreme commander and thus had a built-in bureaucratic advantage, Sangad had already retired. Moreover, it was unlikely that Kriangsak would offer Sangad a cabinet post since they were political competitors. Hence, Sangad needed the NPC chair posting.[3] But because the Young Turks perceived Kriangsak as more willing to implement reforms than Sangad, they favoured him to become leader of the government.[4] After three weeks of haggling, on 10 November a new temporary constitution was enacted, and Kriangsak was to be appointed as prime minister the following day.

King Bhumipol was not amused by the 1977 coup. In fact, he was furious. The putschists had ousted his own handpicked civilian prime minister from appointed office without even requesting permission from him. Indeed, the king signalled his displeasure with the putsch by immediately appointing the ousted Thanin to the Privy Council.[5] Bhumipol had previously supported every one of the previous seven coups during the time he had been king (except for the 1951 putsch). The United States did not see eye-to-eye with Bhumipol on the 1977 coup. Washington was content to see the demise of Thanin since he had, if anything, given Thailand (and hence the United States) an image problem. But Bhumipol disassociated himself from the coup and subsequent junta, angrily accusing Kriangsak of making Thailand appear as a "banana republic" of the ilk of then coup-prone Latin America, except that Thailand should be dubbed a "banana monarchy".[6] Rather than appointing Kriangsak as prime minister at the royal palace in Bangkok, as had traditionally been done, the king endorsed him at Phuphan Palace near Sakhon Nakhon in Thailand's rural Northeast.[7]

Despite the consternation of the palace, on 12 November, Kriangsak's thirty-three-member cabinet took office.[8] It contained nine active-duty or retired military men. These included retired general Bunchai Bamrungpong as deputy prime minister, new defence minister General Lek Laeomali (former deputy defence minister), Admiral Thavil Rajananda (a Sangad confidant) as deputy defence minister, ACM Prasong Gunatilala (a Khamon confidant) as deputy defence minister, General Surakit Mayalarp (Kriangsak's friend in the Supreme Command) as transport minister, Rear Admiral Sanong Nissalak as deputy transport minister, General Kriangsak Chomanand himself as interior minister (ensuring the prime minister's control over the police), General Prem Tinsulanond (assistant army commander) as deputy interior minister, and Lieutenant Yongyoot Sajjavanich as deputy health minister. Kriangsak's appointment of Prem was a foregone conclusion. Besides being a younger member of the Krit Sivara clique and on good terms with Kriangsak, Prem was respected by the Young Turks and they insisted upon giving him a ministerial appointment. He was also a hero of the army's anti-communist counterinsurgency in the northeast and was the king's military favourite. Meanwhile, Sangad became chair of the National Policy Council, as the military

FIGURE 8.2
Thailand's National Legislative Assembly, 1977–79

Type of legislature	Years in office	Appointed or elected	Total number of members and military contingent
Unicameral	1977–79	Appointed	360, of which 217 (60.2%) military reserved domain

Sources: Chaowana Traimat, *Data on 75 Years of Thai Democracy* (Konrad Adenauer Foundation, 2007), p. 140; author's calculations.

cabal now called itself. A newly appointed unicameral National Legislative Assembly (Figure 8.2) was set up on 16 November, with 208 of 360 members being former members of the previous National Administrative Reform Assembly. A total of 217 were from the military or police.

Kriangsak immediately initiated a "charm offensive" towards Thai society, deliberately courting academics, labour unions, journalists, students and intellectuals. He sought to build popular support in regard to democratization and constitutional reform—as led by himself—in preparation for an election that he promised to hold.

Within days of becoming prime minister in November 1977, he was already working towards passage of a new constitution, promising its implementation as early as 1978. Indeed, he urgently needed the charter to be enacted as soon as possible because, as his retirement would occur in 1978, it would be necessary to become an elected prime minister by 1979 to maintain political power. He promised elections in either late 1978 or early 1979. In this sense, Kriangsak sought to borrow a page from Phibun Songkram back in 1957: Phibun, too, had enacted a constitution to obtain popular legitimacy through an election to counterbalance the power of Sarit in the armed forces. By 1979, Kriangsak was trying to do the same—but with a military strongman of the late 1970s.

As such, he sold himself as a unifier for Thailand and also a military man who could vanquish Thailand's communist insurgents. He pushed hard for a pardon of the detained "October 6" students and initiated a policy of amnesty for anyone who defected from the Thai communist insurgency. He promised a new permanent constitution and told Thais to make ready for an election either in 1978 or early 1979. Meanwhile, with regard to external relations, Kriangsak immediately jettisoned Thanin's rigid anti-communism in favour of policy that retained a pro-Washington component (but not overdependence) while also welcoming Beijing and even Moscow. At the same time, with no solid support from troops on the ground, he practised a foreign policy that would play well in terms of domestic politics. The result was the formal resurrection of the pragmatic, moderate "omnidirectionality" (all directions) of Kukrit Pramoj and Seni Pramoj.

Though cordial relations were maintained with Vietnam, Hanoi remained Thailand's most prominent threat since it possessed a battle-hardened army close to Thai territory that had been hostile to Bangkok. But Hanoi was fast becoming open to a rapprochement with Kriangsak, given the worsening of Vietnam's own relations with China and Cambodia. Kriangsak began to open talks with Hanoi, but he also visited Beijing. An agreement enhancing Thai-China trade ties was completed in 1978; Chinese leader Deng Xiaoping promised Kriangsak that the Khmer Rouge would desist from attacking Thailand.[9] Thai-Soviet Union ties improved, and Japanese trade, investment and assistance grew in 1978.

Kriangsak's swing towards at least the appearance of a more balanced foreign policy between Washington and communist countries initially led to a cooling of Thai-US relations. In Bangkok, the US Embassy sent the following cable to Washington:

WE ARE ON NOTICE FROM SENIOR FIGURES OF THE THAI SUPREME COMMAND THAT THAILAND INTENDS TO PURCHASE SUBSTANTIAL QUANTITIES OF MILITARY EQUIPMENT FROM THE US. IF THAILAND IS UNABLE TO MAKE SUCH PURCHASES, BECAUSE OF US LIMITATIONS ON EXPORTS OF MILITARY EQUIPMENT, THAILAND WILL TURN ELSEWHERE, AND US RELATIONS WITH THAILAND WILL BECOME MORE DISTANT.[10]

Kriangsak's ties with Washington were strengthened, however, in May 1978 when vice president Walter Mondale visited Thailand. Mondale reiterated US defence commitments to Thailand under the 1962 Thanat-Rusk Agreement. He promised more US military aid and committed to financially support tens of thousands of Indochinese refugees in camps in Thailand.

The most notable challenge for Kriangsak's foreign policy was in regard to Thai-Cambodian relations. On 15 December 1977, Khmer Rouge soldiers crossed the border and attacked two Thai villages south of Aranyaprathet district. Thai forces based in Ubon Ratchatani province retaliated covertly. Following orders from Colonel Chavalit

Yongchaiyudh, they entered and destroyed a bridge in Cambodia, followed by tit-for-tat attacks by Cambodian and Thai forces continuing into January 1978.[11] A rapprochement began when Kriangsak announced a plan to reopen the Thai-Cambodian border, at the same time sending a letter to Khmer Rouge leader Pol Pot promising Thai friendship.[12]

By late 1978, although Kriangsak seemed to be achieving foreign policy successes, his government survived only because disparate military personalities and factions allowed it to persist in power. Given Kriangsak's background in the largely weak Supreme Command, some army leaders felt that they deserved a larger leadership role than he did. As such, Kriangsak had to juggle the support of army factions to remain atop. Sorely needed backing came from his old friend in the Supreme Command, ACM Thawee Chulasap, who still maintained close connections with key active-duty military officials. The Sangad-led National Policy Council, which included military leaders who had led the 1976 and 1977 coups, was empowered by the 1977 interim constitution to formulate policy guidelines for the state and advise the cabinet. The king could only dismiss the prime minister on the advice of the National Policy Council chair. The overwhelming power of Sangad in this council, alongside the continuing close ties with active-duty troops of assistant army commander General Yot Thepsadin na Ayuthaya, meant that the prime minister would need to rely on the Young Turks (and their mentor, General Prem). At the same time, by announcing that elections would take place soon, Kriangsak was borrowing from the 1955–57 strategy of General Phibun Songkram of using electoral legitimacy to increase popular support in his favour. Nevertheless, the promise of elections did arouse popular expectations that could prove difficult to disappoint. Thus, according to the US Embassy,

> KRIANGSAK IS NOT AS POWERFUL A MILITARY FIGURE AS MANY OF HIS PREDECESSORS AND PROBABLY DOES NOT AT THIS POINT HAVE AS FIRM A GRIP ON POWER AS THEY DID. HE WILL SEEK TO MAINTAIN HIS POSITION BY SKILLFUL MANEUVERING.[13]

Many army factions supported Kriangsak precisely because he had no strong support base with any other faction. In other words, he was a good second choice, and the military had generally been united in supporting Kriangsak's ejection of Thanin from office. At the same time, Kriangsak vastly increased the defence budget in a move to placate security forces. Finally, as junta leader in the position of supreme commander, Kriangsak would be serving only one final year (1977–78). Thereafter he would be forced by age to retire from the military (he had turned sixty), but he would continue on as head of government. This was another reason army factions agreed to support Kriangsak—a retired military man could garner little personal control over troops. His hold on the PM's chair was thus tenuous.

In fact, Kriangsak was propped up initially (1977–78) by four military factions. These included, first, the "professionals" faction, which included retired army commander (deputy prime minister) General Bunchai Bamrungphong, retired Supreme Command deputy chief of staff General Lek Naeomalee (defence minister), army commander General Serm na Nakorn, assistant army commander General Prem Tinsulanond (a mentor of the Young Turks), and 1st Army Region commander General Amnart Damrikarn. Second, there was the Supreme Command faction, which included retired admiral Sangad Chaloryu; retired ACM Khamon Dachatungka; and chief of staff, Supreme Command, General Charoen Phongpanit. Third, there was the faction of General Praphas Charusatien, which included deputy army commander General Yot Thepasadin na Ayuthaya and former deputy 1st Army Region commander General Thep Kranlert. Praphas was reportedly a financial patron of Yot.[14] Yot and Thep were connected through family because Yot's son had married Thep's daughter. Fourth and finally, Kriangsak was supported by the Young Turks army faction, especially Colonel Manoon Rupkachorn and Colonel Prajark Sawangjit, who had since 1977 been promoted to become 4th Cavalry Regiment commander and then 2nd Infantry Regiment commander.[15] The members of the first two factions had been in the earlier clique of General Krit Sivara. During 1977–78, Kriangsak appeased all four factions so as to retain power.

On 1 December 1977, the Kriangsak government delivered its basic policy statement to the appointed National Legislative Assembly, which approved it without objection. For a military-led government, the statement was surprisingly liberal in tone and was appealing even to some progressive Thai politicians. Taking a leaf from Krit Sivara, the statement called for national reconciliation—a stance the palace should have taken. It pledged a return to democracy, an independent foreign policy, and more equitable health services.[16] Though most of these promises might not be quickly achievable, they pointed Thailand back in the direction of progressive change. A new constitution was promulgated in December 1978.

Washington reacted favourably to Kriangsak's accession to power. This owed to his promise to continue working closely with the US Drug Enforcement Administration in anti-narcotics operations. In addition, Kriangsak agreed to accept more refugees into Thailand from Indochina. Finally, the new prime minister pledged to ensure that the Thai state respected human rights.[17] Shortly after his ascension to power, press censorship was loosened, the state became more relaxed towards political opposition among parties, and the government seemed intent on incremental democratic reform.

Kriangsak sought to obtain an amnesty for the eighteen students still imprisoned for their role in leading the demonstrations of 6 October 1976. But King Bhumipol, still sore at the 1977 Kriangsak-led coup and unwilling to pardon the students, snubbed the prime minister by delaying the amnesty until September 1978.[18] Kriangsak's reason for releasing the students appears to relate to his desire to build national reconciliation and his own political future as a unifying leader. The king ultimately agreed to the amnesty because the longer defendants were in prison the more they would be seen as martyrs. With the Red Gaurs threatening attacks on them, Kriangsak banned any celebration of the students' release.[19]

Turning to narcotics, though Kriangsak made appealing promises to Washington to implement a harsh crackdown, he had a long history of working with opium traffickers along the Thai-Burma border. As a Thai officer during the 1960s, he had worked with the anti-communist Chinese KMT (Kuomintang) CIF (Chinese Independent Forces) along the Thai-Burma border. These forces—remnants of the 3rd and 5th Regiments of the 93rd Division of the KMT army defeated by the Chinese Communists in 1949—had regrouped in northeastern Burma's Shan States. Following assistance from the CIA, they gained control over the regional opium trade to help finance attacks they made into China. The opium they produced was marketed by the CIA-assisted Thai police general Phao Sriyanond. Following General Sarit Thanarat's 1957 coup, the latter had replaced Phao as the KMT's opium partner until Sarit's own death in 1963. General Praphas Charusatien replaced Sarit until Krit's 1973 coup.[20]

Praphas had even told a visiting US congressman in 1973: "WE KNOW THEY TRAFFIC IN OPIUM; WE HAVE WORKED WITH THEM FOR 20 YEARS."[21] The account of the congressman continued:

HE SAID THAT THE KMT ARE LARGELY IN THE JUNGLE AND ARE SPREAD ALL OVER THE NORTH

NEAR THE BORDER. THE ROYAL THAI GOVERNMENT DID NOT HAVE THE POWER TO FORCE THEM COMPLETELY OUT OF BUSINESS. WITH REFERENCE TO THE SEPARATE PROBLEM OF THE HILLTRIBE OPIUM GROWERS, PRAPHAS POINTED UP THE DIFFICULTY OF FINDING A SUBSTITUTE CROP FOR OPIUM THAT WOULD OFFER THE SAME MONETARY RETURN.[22]

In 1961, Sarit's government had permitted CIF forces to resettle just inside Thailand on the Thai-Myanmar and Thai-Lao borders. They were officially tasked with helping the Thai army fight communism. But they continued to traffic opium even though Thailand had outlawed opium in 1959. In 1967, the KMT were granted official status as paramilitary forces under the direct command of the Communist Suppression Operations Command (CSOC). At the time, General Kriangsak Chomanand, in his role at Thailand's Supreme Command, helped to direct ISOC policy.[23] By 1969 he was deputy chief of staff at the Supreme Command. In that capacity, he acted in 1970 as the point man for Thailand's offer to resettle CIF forces and their families to Doi Mae Salong district of Chiang Rai province, several kilometres from the Thai-Burma border. In return they would have to fight Thai communists, but they could have land and, eventually, Thai citizenship. In 1971, Kriangsak also oversaw a highly publicized event whereby the CIF turned over twenty-six tons of opium to the Thai government for destruction, but CIF trafficking resumed almost immediately and was able to meet competition.[24] In 1973, Kriangsak negotiated heroin warlord Khun Sa's release from a Myanmar prison and by 1974 he was back in business.[25]

There had been allegations at least as far back as 1973 that Kriangsak had been involved in Thailand's illegal opium trade. In May 1973, Kriangsak offered

> numerous reasons why trafficking into northern Thailand cannot be stopped in defense against our charges of continuing CIF involvement. In spite of General Kriangsak's earlier assurances, it is clear that the Royal Thai Government ... is not keeping up its end of the bargain with us to get them [CIF] out of the guns-for opium network.[26]

In October 1973 there were assertions that the Thai army was protecting the CIF in Thailand not only because the CIF acted as a buffer against communist insurgents but precisely because they handled narcotics caravans. Kriangsak at the time was "rumored to be protecting CIF in return for kickbacks".[27] In November, with the Supreme Command using security laws to prevent police from entering the northern Thai-Burma border area, a top Border Patrol Police general told the *Bangkok Post* editor that Kriangsak "was using his connections with [CIF generals] Li and Tuan to engage in opium trade himself".[28] Indeed, according to a journalist with access to US Drug Enforcement Administration files, Kriangsak, who "had served as a key link in CIA coverts ops during the Vietnam War ... was named in classified intel reports as the direct recipient of payoffs from armed groups [KMT rebel armies] controlling the opium traffic in Thailand and Burma".[29] As deputy supreme commander, on 19 April 1976, he had proclaimed the principal crux of the Thai army's problem: "There appears to be a conflict between our campaign against narcotics and our campaign against communists."[30] Though then prime minister Thanin had sought to prosecute both campaigns simultaneously, when Kriangsak became prime minister, he continued to appear to practice some narcotics suppression efforts while allowing CIF to mostly continue their drug enterprises. Indeed, shortly after coming to power in 1977, Kriangsak had allegedly agreed to allow the Shan State Army (SUA), directed by Khun Sa, to enjoy unrestricted rights to traffic heroin into Thailand in recognition for SUA's help in fighting communist insurgents, though some alleged that Kriangsak was personally profiting from the narcotics trade. In 1977, with Thai military support, Khun Sa's force of 3,500 militiamen provided security for twelve caravans carrying seventy tons of raw opium.[31]

By February 1978, CIF general Li (patron of the Shan United Revolutionary Army, or SURA) and the SUA were entrenched just inside Thailand along the Thai-Burma border combating communists and trafficking opium to heroin refineries. The Royal Thai Army under Kriangsak (as well as the Republic of China on Taiwan) were supplying these forces with increasing amounts of weaponry. According to the CIA, these arms "provide[d] them [CIF] some cover for their smuggling activities along the border ...[and] there were reports that SUA leader Chang Chi-Fu [aka the notorious drug-lord Khun Sa] travels freely in Thailand on Kriangsak's ... authorization".[32] A month earlier, with CIA agents, Kriangsak admitted that

> irregular armed elements in Burma that are involved in narcotics trafficking, have clandestine bases in Thailand and have been getting some logistic support from Thai sources of supply. He has stated quite candidly that his government [and] the Thai armed forces have "some equity" in these "irregular armies in northern Thailand."[33]

In mid-February, Kriangsak publicly committed to drive Khun Sa out of Thailand. But in March it was determined that Khun Sa's SUA and other CIF were now locating their heroin refineries just across the frontier in Burma. Kriangsak's government did not want to antagonize these groups because it might drive them into an alliance with the Burmese Communist Party.[34] By April 1978, although the US Embassy was impressed that Kriangsak had publicly committed Thailand to oppose illicit narcotics trafficking on the same level as Thanin, using police to suppress the drug trade, it faulted the prime minister for failing to appoint a permanent secretary general for the Thanin-created Narcotics Control Board.[35] Back in January, Kriangsak had tried to appoint General Vitoon Yasawat to that position, but the nomination was torpedoed by the combined opposition of two powerful enemies of Vitoon: army commander General Serm and army deputy commander General Yot.[36] The embassy also appeared disappointed that Kriangsak reduced the number of traffickers summarily executed—a more distinctive practice under Thanin. Unlike the US Embassy, Kriangsak was said to be "very close" to the CIA's Bangkok station, especially station chief (1977–79) Daniel C. Arnold.[37] Arnold had been a principal associate of the CIA-influenced Nugan Hand Bank (1973–80) through which, allegedly, Khun Sa's heroin was sold in return for weapons.[38] With embassy and CIA advice, Kriangsak's government began writing a tough new Narcotics Act. It became law on 22 April 1979, mandating stiffer penalties, including death, for traffickers. On 31 January 1979, the government publicly burned an extremely large amount of heroin and other drugs.[39] Meanwhile, the executions of some small-time drug lords continued. However, although Kriangsak claimed plans had been made to capture or force Khun Sa and other major drug traffickers out of Thailand, by the time he left power in 1980, no such plans had come to fruition. Stories about Kriangsak's cosiness with heroin dealers never went away. Rumour had it that Khun Sa's illicit narcotics profits financed Kriangsak's 1979 election.[40]

By the time he retired as supreme commander in October 1978, Kriangsak was forced to rely on his civilian authority via the Office of the Prime Minister and the Ministry of Interior—which he directly controlled. Earlier, in August 1978, in preparation for the annual military reshuffles, Kriangsak took the defence portfolio, switching posts with his friend, General Lek (who now became minister of the interior). With Lek heading the Interior Ministry, Kriangsak could directly supervise the 1979 election. Meanwhile, Kriangsak's loyal associate Admiral Amon Sirikaya became deputy defence minister, while another deputy defence slot was taken by retiring deputy army commander General Yot.[41] This move placated the ambitious Yot, though the inclusion of Amon helped to balance Yot's promotion (and the Praphas faction) with one of Kriangsak's key loyalists.[42] These promotions also helped to maintain military factionalism. With the military still factionalized and lacking a strong leader to oppose him, Kriangsak could remain aloof from the palace—which reluctantly tolerated him until a strongman more to its liking could be found. But, as defence minister, he retained influence over the armed forces.

In this civilian role, on 1 October 1978, Kriangsak set in motion his first annual military reshuffle as prime minister (see Appendix 4). The 1978 set of appointments emphasized offsetting the power of the post-Krit "Professionals" faction (army commander Serm and 1st Army Region commander Amnart) by slightly enhancing the clout of both the Praphas faction and the Young Turks clique. As such, as stated above, General Yot, who retired in September 1978, was promoted to the post of deputy defence minister in August (serving until May of 1979, when he was transferred to be minister at the Office of the Prime Minister from May of that year until 3 March 1980). Also, Yot's brother-in-law General Thep Kranlert succeeded General Amnart (who was promoted to the non-strategic post of deputy chief of staff) to become 1st Army Region commander. The prime minister honoured Serm's preference for his loyal chief of staff, General Sitthi Jirarochana, to become deputy army commander. Serm himself, however, was removed from his position as army commander and "kicked upstairs" to the largely ceremonial position of supreme commander. He was replaced by assistant commander General Prem, who also continued as deputy minister of the interior. Immediately thereafter, a large gathering of pro-Serm loyalists protested in front of Kriangsak's office, but they did not attempt a coup. Their clout was effectively offset by that of the Praphas faction and the Young Turks. This was the first time in Thai history that an army commander had been demoted to supreme commander. Kriangsak told US ambassador Abramowitz that "he [Kriangsak] made a tough decision [in promoting Prem] and he would make it stick. He was not a particularly close friend of … Prem [and] had only gotten to know him in the past few years, but believe[d] that he was very qualified for the job."[43]

To this day, the reason behind Serm's transfer has not been resolved. There are five competing theories. First, Prem was seen as more proactive than Serm in implementing Kriangsak's policies. Second, having directly commanded the counterinsurgency in Thailand's Northeast for five years, Prem was more adept than Serm at leading the army against Thailand's communist insurrection. Third, Kriangsak needed the support of the Young Turks faction, and they demanded that Serm be replaced by Prem.[44] Fourth, after 1977, Kriangsak had been finding Serm increasingly to be a rival for power because Serm held the powerful army post. So Kriangsak replaced Serm with Prem, who appeared much less threatening, while Serm succeeded Kriangsak as supreme commander.[45] Fifth, Serm was appointed supreme commander against the wishes of Kriangsak. According to this argument (which Kriangsak denied five days after the reshuffle[46]), Kriangsak desperately wanted to remain as prime minister after his October 1978 retirement from the military.[47] Thus, in August, he maneuvered to promote Serm (his long-time friend) as supreme commander simultaneous to Serm retaining the army chief post. Since Serm's mandatory retirement would not occur until 1981, he could help Kriangsak maintain control over the armed forces while the latter continued to hold the post of prime minister. But the king indirectly forced Kriangsak to appoint Prem instead,[48] seeing Serm (like Krit Sivara) as too "politically moderate". And, besides, the Serm na Nakorn family was descended from King Taksin, who had been killed by King Bhumipol's relative King Rama I, and thus Serm could not be trusted.[49] In all likelihood, all five of these reasons could have influenced Kriangsak. Thus, Serm's transfer owed to pressure from the palace and the Young Turks, as well as Kriangsak's fear that Serm might oust him in the future.

Prem's appointment as army commander in 1978 brought with it the rise of Prem's own faction—including men who would later serve in high positions of power on their own. The group included General Sant Chitpatima,[50] who became army chief of staff; General Prayut Charumanee, who became the army's deputy chief of staff; General Vasin Isangkul na Ayuthaya as assistant chief of staff for intelligence; and General Laksana Saligupta as 2nd Army Region commander. Colonel Suthep Sivara, younger half-brother of General Krit Sivara (who Prem deeply respected), became commander of the 1st Infantry Regiment, 1st Army Region, King's Guard, a posting in which he served for two years. Young Major Surayud Chulanond became Prem's aide.

Meanwhile, throughout 1978, Kriangsak's efforts at transitioning himself into the leader of a limited Thai democracy persisted. On 25 November 1978, Kriangsak announced he would neither form his own political party nor join any current political party, insisting that he would play politics his own way. He added that he favoured a post-election "grand coalition" government, commenting that he could likely obtain support from the appointed Senate and at least seventy elected MPs (the number necessary to block a censure motion).[51] Eschewing the idea of running for office, he made use of the temporary clauses in the 1978 constitution permitting the appointment of a non-elected prime minister for the charter's first four years of existence.

There would be a bicameral legislature, with the lower house popularly elected and the upper house appointed—following the 1968 and 1974 constitutions. The lower house would have 301 members. Members of parliament, under the temporary constitutional clauses, need not be members of a party to serve in this lower house. The 1978 constitution also stated that cabinet ministers did not need to be elected MPs.

Meanwhile, a new upper house was to be composed of only appointed members—225 in total. Of the 225 seats, allocations would go to military officers, cabinet ministers (chosen by Kriangsak), members of the appointed National Policy Council (which was to be dissolved upon the inception of the elected government), as well as to "Kriangsak's personal choices".[52] Such a rubber stamp Senate guaranteed that the military would keep Thai democracy on a short leash, keeping a lid on any legislation deriving from the lower house. Moreover, these appointed senators—along with members of the lower house—were given the right to select the prime minister as well as to vote on crucial issues such as those affecting national security, the economy and the budget, and to even participate in or launch no-confidence motions against sitting governments.[53] In this way, Kriangsak sought to appease both the military and royalist institutions. Ultimately, with parties weakened and the Senate a loyal crutch, there was really no way that he could lose the election of 1979. One month later, on 22 December, the new constitution was promulgated. In January 1979, the Election Bill passed, and pre-poll campaigning commenced. During the months before the election, the three largest parties—Prachatipat, Kit Sangkom and Chart Thai—emphasized their opposition to Kriangsak. On the other hand, the smaller parties—Palang Mai, Seritham and Kaset Sangkom—backed the prime minister, while most candidates running without a party (allowed under the 1978 constitution) also supported Kriangsak.

With electoral lawmaking complete, polls were set for and held on 22 April 1979—the first since 1976. Although diluted, these elections seemed to move the country back in the trajectory of democratization. The results were not surprising—extreme fission among parliamentary

FIGURE 8.3
Thailand's National Legislative Assembly, 1979–81

Type of legislature	Years in office	Appointed or elected	Total number of members and military contingent
Bicameral	1979–81	Appointed	225, of which 193 (85.7%) military reserved domain

Source: Paul Chambers, "A Short History of Military Influence in Thailand", in *Knights of the Realm: Thailand's Military and Police, Then and Now* (Bangkok: White Lotus, 2013), p. 206.

groupings: fifteen parties, and even multiple factions outside of parties. Party switching was also an easy affair. In this way, Kriangsak succeeded in weakening the power of parties and thus enhancing his own personal influence amongst them, assuring his continuation as prime minister. At the same time, post-election party chaos contributed to the long period of time that it took the prime minister to form a coalition and cabinet.

Meanwhile, the new Senate (Figure 8.3) was appointed by Kriangsak on 26 April. Not surprisingly, most of the new senators were military officials (even more than in the previous legislature). Many were members of military factions, including from the "Professionals" and the cliques of Praphas or the Young Turks. These new Senators were from all arms of the military and included

SENIOR, INFLUENTIAL OFFICERS AND YOUNGER, RELATIVELY UNKNOWN OFFICERS, AT COLONEL AND LT. COLONEL LEVEL, WHO COMMAND KEY UNITS. FOR EXAMPLE, AMONG THE ACTIVE RTA OFFICERS WHO ACCOUNT FOR THE BULK OF THE SENATE'S MILITARY MEMBERSHIP, KRIANGSAK HAS SELECTED, IN ADDITION TO ALL PRINCIPAL STAFF OFFICERS AT RTA HEADQUARTERS, COMMANDERS OF EVERY COMBAT ARMS (I.E. INFANTRY, ARMS, ARTILLERY AND AIR DEFENSE) DIVISION AND REGIMENT WITHIN RTA AND ALL COMBAT ARMS BATTALION COMMANDERS IN BANGKOK AREA. OF THE TOTAL MILITARY APPOINTEES, MORE THAN HALF OCCUPY IMPORTANT COMMANDS THAT HOLD KEY TO CONTROL OF THE THAI ARMED SERVICES.[54]

When the new coalition was appointed in late May 1979, the larger parties—Kit Sangkom, Prachadipat and Chart Thai—refused to be part of it. Thus, Kriangsak included only minor parties in his government. These included Seritham, New Force, Social Agrarian, Nation and People, Democratic Action, Ruam Thai Party, and the Siam Democratic Party. Four of these parties were led by politicians who had previously served with or were connected with Kriangsak in some way, including Krit Sivara loyalist Thawee Chulasap and Sanga Kittikachorn, brother of Thanom. Moreover, the MPs within these parties only added up to 70 out of the entire 301 in the lower house.[55] Furthermore, of the original 44 members in Kriangsak's cabinet (excluding the PM himself) appointed on 24 May 1979, only 8 were elected MPs, and after the 11 February 1980 cabinet reshuffle, this number was reduced to 2.[56] Ultimately, "Kriangsak relied basically upon the appointed senate and ignored the major political parties."[57] The existence of a substantial number of post-election independents and the ability of MPs and factions to switch parties at will prevented the formation of cohesive opposition in parliament. Indeed, it heightened Kriangsak's power at the expense of the political parties.

In effect, Kriangsak sought to turn the clock back to the election of 1969—when elections brought the party of General Thanom to office alongside an appointed Senate—except that Kriangsak refused to have a political party of his own. Also, like Thanom, Kriangsak lost control over the parliamentary process shortly after the general election. This occurred for three reasons. First, by bringing mostly unelected individuals into his cabinet, Kriangsak received only weak support from elected members of parliament. Second, his administration began to suffer from economic difficulties owing to an intensifying global economic crisis. Third, he became dependent upon his army commander to survive in power. Thanom's Krit was now Kriangsak's Prem; if Prem became dissatisfied, Kriangsak would likely fall.

Nevertheless, the election ended the power of Admiral Sangad Chaloryu, who had become a sometimes-opponent of Kriangsak. Since late 1977, the two had led organizations that tended to overlap each other: Kriangsak's cabinet versus Sangad's National Policy Council. During early 1978, there were rumours that Sangad was even planning a coup against Kriangsak because the prime minister had blocked First Trust Company, of which Sangad was an advisor, from moving into commercial banking (nor did Kriangsak consent to returning the frozen assets of Thanom, Praphas and Narong or green light Praphas's opening of a new commercial bank).[58] Throughout the writing of the constitution, the Kriangsak-Sangad duel continued, with each seeking to obtain the power to nominate appointed senators who would be appointed by the king. By December 1978, Kriangsak triumphed. Following the April 1979 election, Kriangsak's appointed cabinet and Sangad's National Policy Council were both terminated. Upon Kriangsak's recommendation, Sangad was to have then become the president of the appointed Senate. But the admiral suddenly suffered a severe heart attack, which ended his political career (he died the following year).

Thailand's transition to a semi-democracy paralleled growing turbulence in mainland Southeast Asia. The heretofore improving relationship with Vietnam was discontinued when the latter invaded Cambodia on 25 December 1978, capturing Phnom Penh on 7 January 1979 and installing its own puppet regime. A CIA report had predicted what eventually unfolded in Thai-Cambodian relations across the next decade:

> Hanoi could find itself involved in an indefinite occupation of Kampuchea in support of a puppet government encircled by anti-Vietnamese guerrillas possibly still supported by China through Thailand.... Thailand, alarmed by the prospect of Vietnamese troops on its border, has contingency plans to back Khmer resistance activity against a pro-Vietnamese government and is probably prepared to cooperate with China in the process.[59]

Following Hanoi's takeover, the Kriangsak government formally declared that Thailand would remain neutral with regard to Cambodia and Vietnam. But the Royal Thai Army, seeking to establish "a robust irritant" against Vietnam's occupation force in Cambodia, clandestinely helped Khmer Rouge leaders along the Thai-Cambodian border (especially in Poipet) escape to safety inside Thailand, though with help from China. Indeed, on 11 January 1979, Thai military officers helicoptered Khmer Rouge deputy prime minister Ieng Sary from Poipet to Don Muang Airport in Bangkok (and then on to Hong Kong). This RTA operation was under the Tactical Operations Center (TOC) 305, as headed by Special Colonel Chavalit Yongchaiyudh. Chavalit also created a subordinate unit called Task Force 838, mandated to handle covert RTA operations in Cambodia, headed by Colonel Kasem Thammakul.[60] Thailand was now directly supporting a Khmer Rouge–led insurgency against the Vietnamese occupiers in Cambodia.

While Hanoi was occupying Cambodia, the revolutionary government in Laos permitted large numbers of Vietnamese soldiers to be barracked on its soil under the aegis of its Lao-Vietnam Treaty of Amity and Cooperation. The result was that hundreds of thousands of

Vietnam's troops were stationed on Thailand's border with Cambodia and Laos. Thus, the regional balance of power substantially shifted. Thailand was now the frontline state in Southeast Asia against communism—Vietnam's communism. It was in these circumstances that Kriangsak sought to increase Thailand's defensive firepower while raising the international chorus seeking to pressure Hanoi to withdraw from Cambodia. Moreover, by agreeing to Thailand's hosting of over a hundred thousand refugees from Cambodia and tacitly allowing the Khmer Rouge to launch attacks against Vietnamese forces in Cambodia, he supported China's policy of restoring the Democratic Kampuchea government.

Meanwhile, Beijing, incensed by Vietnam's occupation of Cambodia, in February 1979 launched a brief invasion into Vietnam itself, allegedly to teach Hanoi a lesson—though it was quickly repulsed. Also in February, Kriangsak travelled to Washington, where he was feted and given guarantees of US military backing.[61] Nevertheless, the Carter administration was not as receptive as other countries (e.g., China) in backing Kriangsak's call for the restoration of Pol Pot to power. It took three more years until Washington joined Thailand and China in covertly supporting insurgency in Cambodia. Indeed, during mid-1982, the US Ronald Reagan administration (1981–89), through the CIA, began to pump money into non-communist, non-Khmer Rouge insurgent groups in Cambodia.[62]

In April 1979, Kriangsak became the first Thai prime minister to visit Moscow. There, he tried to reassure the Soviets that his opposition to Hanoi's occupation of Cambodia did not make him anti-Soviet nor anti-Vietnamese (but rather simply wanting to ensure Thailand's security). His protestations, however, likely fell on deaf ears. Moscow no doubt realized that Thailand's close ties to China had started when Kriangsak took power in 1977. Moreover, since February 1978 there had been numerous reports that China's government had been sending supplies through Thailand, with Kriangsak's approval, to Khmer Rouge insurgents.[63] Ultimately, according to a Thai diplomat accompanying Kriangsak to Moscow, the trip "did not accomplish anything significant and fell more in the category of a 'pleasure trip'".[64]

Civil war increasingly engulfed Cambodia, with fighting occurring mostly along the Thai-Cambodian border. By March, Vietnamese soldiers had begun engaging in limited pursuit of guerrillas just over the border into Thailand. Such intrusions became frequent. In June, the rapidly growing tensions forced Kriangsak to shoot off a letter to US president Jimmy Carter, in which he said:

THERE ARE INDICATIONS THAT VIETNAM MAY LAUNCH AN ARMED INCURSION INTO THAILAND FROM ACROSS THE THAI-KAMPUCHEAN BORDER, ALTHOUGH INITIALLY IT MAY BE LIMITED IN SCOPE AND COME UNDER THE PRETEXT OF A 'HOT PURSUIT' ... SHOULD SUCH AN INCURSION BY VIETNAM OCCUR, ARMED CLASHES WITH THAI FORCES WOULD BE INEVITABLE AND COULD LEAD TO UNCONTROLLABLE ESCALATION.... YOU WILL SEE, MR. PRESIDENT, THAT THE PREVAILING HIGHLY FLUID SITUATION MAKES IT IMPERATIVE THAT THAILAND'S DEFENCE BE BOLSTERED AS QUICKLY AND AS EFFECTIVELY AS POSSIBLE. I SHOULD BE VERY GRATEFUL, THEREFORE, FOR WHATEVER HELP YOU COULD GIVE TO EXPEDITE THE DELIVERY OF ARMS, AMMUNITION AND OTHER MILITARY HARDWARE ALREADY PURCHASED OR COMMITTED TO THAILAND.[65]

By mid-June, Thailand had moved military reinforcements to Cambodia's border to discourage Vietnamese troops from intruding across the Thai-Cambodian border. At this point, Thailand was on the verge of invoking the Manila Pact—the mutual security arrangement between Washington and Bangkok.[66]

Yet, though Washington was willing to aid Thailand because of security commitments through the Manila Pact, the Carter administration did not want to be seen as supporting the Khmer Rouge, with its reviled human rights record. US diplomats thus attempted to persuade Kriangsak to back non-communist insurgent leaders such as Norodom Sihanouk. In August, Kriangsak and Thai interior minister General Lek Naeowmali vehemently opposed even the suggestion that Sihanouk could be an alternative leader for Cambodia. National Security Council secretary-general ACM Sitthi Sawetsila thereupon secretly told US ambassador Abramowitz that Thai opposition to Sihanouk was "not immutable" and that "circumstances could evolve which could change the Thai attitude". Sitthi told Abramowitz that he saw Sihanouk as the only alternative to either Pol Pot or the Vietnamese puppet government, and he would try to convince the prime minister. The reasons for Kriangsak's opposition to Sihanouk owed to (1) Thailand's long-held disgust for his nationalist manner; (2) a preference for keeping options open regarding Cambodia; (3) a preference for supporting the only insurgent group (the Khmer Rouge) with proven military capacities; and (4) not wanting to jeopardize Thailand's positive relationship with China.[67] But the United States now understood that if Kriangsak

insisted only on supporting the Khmer Rouge, other senior Thai officials such as Sitthi could be more flexible.

In a September meeting between Kriangsak and US senior diplomat
Richard Holbrooke, the Thai prime minister again adamantly reiterated
that he would not support Sihanouk. Holbrooke emphasized that
Thailand was the United States' close friend and ally, and that, regarding a potential Vietnamese invasion of Thailand, Washington would
stand by its obligations to Bangkok under the Manila Pact. President
Carter reinforced Holbrook's promise in a personal letter to Kriangsak
in November. By that time, Vietnam's cross-border incursions into
Thailand had increased

On 7 November, Secretary Vance delivered an internal memorandum in which he said:

> WE RECOGNIZE THAT WE COULD BE CALLED UPON
> BY THE THAIS TO INTERVENE IN A MAJOR FASHION…
> AS THE DISPATCH OF U.S. AIRCRAFT OR ADVISORS
> TO THAILAND IN DIRECT RESPONSE TO A MAJOR
> VIETNAMESE CHALLENGE. THE INTRODUCTION
> OF U.S. FORCES WOULD REQUIRE CAREFUL LEGAL
> CONSIDERATION.[68]

Vance much preferred to use diplomacy or symbolic naval visits
to Thailand as a show of strength to Vietnam rather than utilizing
naked force against Hanoi. What if Vietnam invaded Thailand anyway?
Moreover, the Carter administration began to increasingly wonder
whether Kriangsak's support for Pol Pot was worth a US military
commitment.

By December 1979, Kriangsak was becoming ever more disturbed
about what appeared to be an impending Vietnamese invasion across
the Thai frontier into Thailand to eliminate once and for all the Khmer
Rouge insurrectionary forces. CIA officials worried that Kriangsak
would more than likely turn to Washington's alliance under the Manila
Pact and to Beijing to keep the Vietnamese from pursuing Pol Pot's
forces across the border. Indeed, Kriangsak specifically planned to ask
Washington to clarify and publicize its commitment to defend Thailand.
A 7 December CIA memorandum noted that Kriangsak feared that
Hanoi's perception of a lack of US resolve to defend Thailand could
only encourage a Vietnamese invasion.[69] According to then CIA director Stansfield Turner, "if, in the Thai view, US and Chinese support is
insufficient, [Kriangsak] may feel impelled to seek an accommodation
with Vietnam."[70] Also, if Vietnamese forces defeated Thai forces in
battle,

Kriangsak's domestic opponents might try to topple the government by exploiting such issues as the alleged Thai support for Kampuchean resistance forces.... Faced with political downfall, Kriangsak might be prompted to call upon the United States and China to provide military assistance against an external threat and to preserve his government. *Likely principals in a new Thai government would probably not alter internal policies significantly, but a successor to the current Prime Minister would be freer to begin seeking an accommodation with Vietnam.* (emphasis added)[71]

Turner's memorandum suggested that a Thai prime minister other than Kriangsak might be less pro-Beijing, making any eventual settlement with Hanoi more likely. Chinese officials could sense the impending change in government. On 19 December 1979, Chinese military attaché Mao Xianqui told US diplomats that

THE CHINESE ARE VERY CONCERNED ABOUT RUMORS THAT PRIME MINISTER KRIANGSAK IS IN INCREASING POLITICAL DIFFICULTY EVEN FROM WITHIN HIS OWN GOVERNMENT. THE CHIENESE [*sic*] HAVE HEARD THAT GENERAL SOEM [Serm] IS ANGLING TO REPLACE KRIANGSAK AND THAT SUPPORTERS OF FORMER DEPUTY PRIME MINISTER PRAPHAS ARE ALSO PLOTTING TO REMOVE THE PRIME MINISTER.... CHINA'S FORTUNES IN THE REGION ARE CLOSELY LINKED TO KRIANGSAK'S POLITICAL SURVIVAL. THE CHINESE SEE PREM AS KRIANGSAK'S EVENTUAL SUCCESSOR BUT ARE NOT HOPEFUL THAT PREM WILL CONTINUE THE PRIME MINISTER'S SPECIAL RELATIONSHIP WITH THE CHINESE.... CHINESE CONCERN ABOUT A CHANGE OF GOVERNMENT IN THAILAND IS UNDERSTANDABLE SINCE PRIME MINISTER KRIANGSAK HAS BEEN THE ARCHITECT OF CLOSE THAI-CHINESE COOPERATION.[72]

In April 1980, one month after Kriangsak resigned from office, the CIA issued a highly favourable assessment of the foreign policy of Kriangsak's successor in power, General Prem Tinsulanonda:

Under Prem, Thailand may be more receptive to a dialogue with Hanoi in an effort to reduce tensions. Vietnamese Foreign Minister Nguyen Co Thach is expected to visit Bangkok in April or May in response to an invitation from the Prem government.... Unlike Kriangsak, Prem seems more receptive to a possible political role for former Kampuchean leader Prince Sihanouk. [Prem's] Foreign

Minister Sitthi [ACM Sitthi Savetsila] in particular reportedly favors a role for Sihanouk in any future united front.... It is possible that over time the Prem government may shift its support away from the Pol Pot forces to some non-Communist group.[73]

Ultimately, foreign policy played an important role in Kriangsak's political demise. His close alliance with China, unwillingness to work towards a settlement with Vietnam, and preference for clandestinely supporting the genocidal Pol Pot–led Khmer Rouge rather than US-preferred non-communist Cambodian insurgents (while identifying Thailand as neutral) contributed to Washington consenting to his ejection from the premiership on 29 February 1979.

Nevertheless, since April 1979, Kriangsak had managed to linger on as an elected prime minister, though without a party—quite a feat in a period of external and domestic pandemonium. Indeed, after his 1979 election victory, he only enjoyed a three-month post-election honeymoon in office. One could argue that his lack of popularity and the difficult issues he faced were simply too challenging. Kriangsak's elected government clearly had an image problem, as the economy deteriorated amid allegations of growing capital flight abroad. The economic deterioration owed partly to continuing pandemonium in neighbouring Cambodia, enhanced by Vietnam's intervention there, which had made investment in the region uncertain. Many MPs continuously lambasted Kriangsak for poor performance, inaction and incompetence, especially in the areas of economics, foreign affairs and refugee policy. On 26 July, the lower house voted 155-0 to censure him for failure to appear at a house session to answer MPs' interpellation on government assistance programmes for farmers. In August, the prime minister was still in place. With no civilian politician exhibiting sufficient popularity, and army commander General Prem disinterested in politics (while guaranteeing that no military coup would occur), Kriangsak benefited from a factionalized opposition and no credible alternative.[74] In October he survived a lower house vote of no-confidence against his ministers and garnered growing popularity ratings.

From late October 1979 onwards, inflation skyrocketed and the standard of living plummeted. With the economy in a shambles, opposition to the government began to grow. Meanwhile, continuing bureaucratic lethargy and revelations of corruption by local officials weakened the trust that villagers had built with the Kriangsak government. On 1 November, Kriangsak suddenly raised utility rates, responding to the economic downturn. Almost immediately, protests erupted from parliamentarians, student groups and labour groups, with the result that the prime minister cancelled the utility price increase. This flip-flop, though helping him bounce back temporarily, demonstrated the weakness of his coalition and the continuing economic problems the country was facing.[75]

Although the prime minister continued to confront civilian critics, General Prem persisted in standing by Kriangsak. Prem's backing of him and control over the military had grown following Kriangsak's formation of his government in May 1979. The prime minister, under pressure from the Young Turks, moved Prem from deputy interior minister to minister of defence (concurrent with Prem's army commander posting). The latter's growing ascendance over the armed forces temporarily diminished the intense factiousness that the army had experienced since the death of Krit in 1976. But, at the same time, Kriangsak had to rely even more on Prem to stay in power.

By the time of the October 1979 annual military reshuffle, Prem had become so popular with many aristocrats and military officers that he was able to promote almost all of his choices—the "Prem list"—to top armed forces positions.[76] Prem's friend General Sant Chittpatima became deputy army commander, while his loyal associate General Prayut Charumanee became army chief of staff. Another friend, General Pin Thammasri, became commander of the 1st Army Region.[77] General Laksana remained 2nd Army Region commander. Kriangsak had wanted his own trusted friend General Tuangthong Suwannathat to take the post of army chief of staff, but Prem blocked the appointment, instead assigning Tuangthong to the desk job of permanent minister of defence. Other less-trusted officers were similarly placed in posts where they would continue to not hold direct control over troops. This included generals Amnart Damrikarn and Thep Kranlert, leading members of opposing factions (the "Professionals" and the Praphas group, respectively), who each became assistant army commanders.[78] Finally, Prem supporters General Arthit Kamlang-ek became 1st Division commander and General Chavalit Yongchaiyudh became director of operations. With only one year left before his mandatory retirement in 1980, Prem was clearly the most admired and politically powerful person in Thailand other than the king. According to the US Embassy at the time, "[Prem] probably could take over as Prime Minister any time he wants, by coup or even by election.... The king considers him the number one man in Thailand in all ways."[79] But, at least in 1979, Prem was still not interested in taking over political power. First, he owed his job to Kriangsak's appointment of him, and was not suddenly going to backstab him (as Krit had done to Thanom and Praphas). Second, Prem's military was busy during 1978–80 repelling the growing number of Vietnamese, Cambodian and Lao border incursions. Third, Prem was seeking to increasingly professionalize the Thai army—a coup would make a folly of such attempts. Finally, Prem had never shown a habit for power grabbing.

On 12 December, vague coup rumours arose because elements of the military were reportedly unhappy about Kriangsak's policy along the Thai-Cambodian border, his open-door policy to refugees, and government responses in general.[80] By late December 1979, the grumblings of military factions had intensified. This dissension came from the Serm-Amnat faction, the Praphas-Yot-Thep faction and the Young Turks. The first two cliques were frustrated at the way Kriangsak and Prem had distributed power, given that Prem had placed his loyal field-grade officers in strategic 1st Army postings. Praphas was incensed that he had still not recovered the properties that Prime Minister Sanya had frozen previously. The Young Turks were annoyed with Kriangsak's unsuccessful economic policies and the slow movement of democratic reforms.[81]

Given the political and economic turbulence in Thailand at the time, these factions, working with the palace and groups in parliament, could easily threaten Kriangsak's survival as prime minister. Issues such as a potential Vietnamese invasion, a sudden major refugee influx, poor handling of the economy, and serious administrative bungling could easily lead to a no-confidence vote in parliament that Kriangsak might not survive. But it was clear that two people would have to acquiesce to the premier's departure: King Bhumipol and Prem. Since becoming prime minister in 1977, Kriangsak had adeptly used his bargaining skills, his close relationship with Prem and the absence of any suitable successor to retain his position. But now, with opposition to Kriangsak skyrocketing and Prem becoming ever more popular, Kriangsak's days appeared numbered.

The government's austerity measures provoked large and angry—yet peaceful—rallies from MPs, workers and students protesting the policies.[82] By now, Kriangsak's enemies extended from disgruntled military factions and the three main parties in the lower house to the palace. Though King Bhumipol disliked Kriangsak for overthrowing Thanin, Queen Sirikit's feelings towards the prime minister by this juncture had also become extremely "frayed".[83] At this point, Prem's support for Kriangsak was also wavering. It is likely that palace confidant ACM Sitthi Savetsila, then Kriangsak's National Security Council secretary-general, let it be known to both Prem and the United States that the king could no longer tolerate Kriangsak as premier.

With opposition to Kriangsak intensifying, the Young Turks faction started to level harsh criticisms at the prime minister. Their hero, defence minister General Prem, also condemned him. At this point, right-wing demonstrations against Kriangsak led by the Red Gaurs began to grow in Bangkok. Also, former prime minister M.R. Kukrit Pramoj, in his role as Social Action Party leader and leader of the parliamentary opposition, launched a censure motion against Kriangsak. Technically, Kriangsak could have dissolved the lower house, making way for new elections and perhaps a chance to become an elected prime minister. Instead, on 28 February, the king called Kriangsak and Prem to visit him in Chiang Mai, purportedly to discuss the growing chaos in the kingdom. Upon their return, on 29 February, Kriangsak suddenly resigned from the premiership (though he did not dissolve parliament), ostensibly because of parliamentary pressure regarding the threat of mob violence over growing oil prices. Then, with no one else stepping forward to be nominated as prime minister, Kukrit suddenly nominated Prem for the post. Parliament unanimously agreed to Prem's nomination as prime minster on 3 March, and the king endorsed it immediately—an event Handley refers to as "a royal coup".[84] The United States was also quick to support Prem. Upon his resignation, Kriangsak reportedly felt that Washington's lack of support had played a major part in the legislature's ouster of him from office.[85] If so, the reasons for the United States abandoning him were twofold: (1) revelations about Kriangsak's alleged profits from the drug trade; and (2) Prem seeming more pro-US than Kriangsak, given the latter's closeness with China and preference for supporting the Khmer Rouge rather than other Cambodian resistance groups. Though the State Department admitted there were several theories for Kriangsak's resignation:

> we find most credible explanation [less than one line not declassified] that [Kriangsak's resignation] appears to have been precipitated by General Prem's withdrawal of ... support within the last 24 hours ... in order to prevent civilian disturbances [based upon] unwillingness to confront right-wing military activists supporting demonstrations against Kriangsak and decision ... that he [Prem] himself should shape country's fate.[86]

The less than one line declassified was most likely a reference to King Bhumipol. Though Prem and Washington undoubtedly knew beforehand something about the king's intention of stripping Kriangsak of his elected post, the powerplay was clearly made in the palace. Thus, it was a monarch's coup against an elected military coup-maker using a now-stronger military man to guarantee success. In the aftermath of 1980's silent coup, the ascension of Prem brought the 1976–77 royal-ist-cum-military partnership back to the fore. This time, however, there would be no civilian go-between prime minister. Instead, what occurred was the beginning of a monarchy-military partnership between King Bhumipol and General Prem with the latter as junior partner. In that moment, Prem, the once-junior faction member of progressive General Krit Sivara, moved to the right—becoming an unapologetic guardian for the preservation of an overriding and ubiquitous Thai monarchy.

Notes

1. อนุสรณ์งานออกเมรุพระราชทานเพลิงศพ ฯพณฯ พลเอก เกรียงศักดิ์ ชมะนันทน์ ณ เมรุหลวงหน้า พลับพลาอิศริยาภรณ์ วัดเทพศิรินทราวาส [Memorial volume from the cremation ritual of His Excellency General Kriangsak Chomanan at the royal crematorium in front of Issriyaphon Pavilion, Wat Thepsirintrawat], 12 November 2006.

2. Ibid.

3. Kramol Tongdhamachart, "Thailand's 1978 Constitution and its Implications", *Contemporary Southeast Asia* 1, no. 2 (September 1979): 132.

4. Thomas Marks, "October 1976 and the Role of the Military in Thai Politics", *Modern Asian Studies* 14, no. 4 (1980): 640, https://doi.org/10.1017/S0026749X00006648.

5. Kobkua Suwannathat-Pian, *Kings, Country and Constitutions: Thailand's Political Development, 1932–2000* (London: RoutledgeCurzon, 2003), p. 175.

6. Cited in Paul Handley, *The King Never Smiles* (New Haven, CT: Yale University Press, 2006), p. 267.

7. US Embassy (Bangkok) to US secretary of state Cyrus Vance, "King Appoints Kriangsak as Prime Minister", 13 November 1977, Wikileaks, 1977BANGKO28897_c, https://wikileaks.org/plusd/cables/1977BANGKO28896_c.html.

8. อนุสรณ์งานออกเมรุพระราชทานเพลิงศพ ฯพณฯ พลเอก เกรียงศักดิ์ ชมะนันทน์ ณ เมรุหลวงหน้า พลับพลาอิศริยาภรณ์ วัดเทพศิรินทราวาส [Memorial volume from the cremation ritual of His Excellency General Kriangsak Chomanan at the royal crematorium in front of Issriyaphon Pavilion, Wat Thepsirintrawat], 12 November 2006.

9. Kenneth Conboy, *The Cambodian Wars: Clashing Armies and CIA Covert Operations* (Lawrence: University of Kansas, 2013), p. 130.

10. US Embassy (Bangkok) to US secretary of state Cyrus Vance, "Change of Government in Thailand: Development and Prospects", 21 November 1977, Wikileaks, 1977BANGKO30499_c, https://wikileaks.org/plusd/cables/1977BANGKO30499_c.html.

11. Conboy, *The Cambodian Wars*, pp. 115–18.

12. Puangthong Rungswasdisab, "Thailand's Response to the Cambodian Genocide", Genocide Studies Program, Yale University, 2021, https://gsp.yale.edu/thailands-response-cambodian-genocide.

13. Ibid.

14. US Embassy (Bangkok) to US secretary of state Cyrus Vance, "Kriangsak Government Rounds Out First Six Months in Office", 19 April 1978, Wikileaks, https://wikileaks.org/plusd/cables/1978BANGKO11275_d.html.

15. John Girling, *Thailand: Society and Politics* (Ithaca: Cornell University Press, 1981), pp. 228–29.

16. US Embassy (Bangkok) to US secretary of state Cyrus Vance, "Kriangsak Policy Statement Presented to National", 1 December 1977, Wikileaks, 1977BANGKO32273_c, https://wikileaks.org/plusd/cables/1977BANGKO32273_c.html.

17. US Embassy (Bangkok) to US secretary of state Cyrus Vance, "Pending US-Thai Issues", 5 November 1977, Wikileaks, 1977STATE264931_c, https://wikileaks.org/plusd/cables/1977STATE264931_c.html.

18. Handley, *The King Never Smiles*, pp. 266–68.

19. US Embassy (Bangkok) to US secretary of state, "Reaction to Bangkok 18 and Analysis", 21 September 1978, Wikileaks, https://wikileaks.org/plusd/cables/1978BANGKO27368_d.html.

20. *Burma Alert*, no. 7 (July 1990), Harn Yawgwe, Quebec, https://www.burmalibrary.org/docsBA/BA1990-V01-N07.pdf.

21. US Embassy (Bangkok) to US secretary of state Henry Kissinger, "Codel Wolff's Call on Deputy Prime Minister Praphas", 17 August 1973, Wikileaks, 1973BANGKO12888_b, https://wikileaks.org/plusd/cables/1973BANGKO12888_b.html.

22. Ibid.

23. *Burma Alert*, no. 7 (July 1990), Harn Yawgwe, Quebec, https://www.burmalibrary.org/docsBA/BA1990-V01-N07.pdf.

24. CIA, "CIF Involvement in Narcotics Trafficking", n.d., release date 10 April 2012, CIA-RDP86T01017R000808060002-7, https://www.cia.gov/readingroom/document/cia-rdp86t01017r000808060002-7.

25. *Burma Alert*, no. 7 (July 1990), Harn Yawgwe, Quebec, https://www.burmalibrary.org/docsBA/BA1990-V01-N07.pdf.

26. US Embassy (Bangkok) to US secretary of state Henry Kissinger, "Narcotics: Updated Control Action Plan for Thailand", 17 May 1973, Wikileaks, 1973STATE092081_b, https://wikileaks.org/plusd/cables/1973STATE092081_b.html.

27. US Embassy (Bangkok) to US secretary of state Henry Kissinger, "Meeting with French Author on Narcotics Trafficking", 26 October 1973, Wikileaks, 1973STATE212081_b, https://wikileaks.org/plusd/cables/1973STATE212081_b.html.

28. "Coversation with Editor-in-Chief Bangkok Post", 27 November 1973, Wikileaks, 1973BANGKO17448_b, https://wikileaks.org/plusd/cables/1973BANGKO17448_b.html.

29. Github, Ralph McGehee's CIABASE /ABC/DRA, 29 January 2019, https://github.com/ourhiddenhistory/CIABASE/blob/master/ABC/DRA.

30. United States House of Representatives, Select Committee on Narcotics Abuse and Control, "Opium Production, Narcotics Financing and Trafficking in Southeast Asia", vols. 963–968, p. 39.

31. Alfred McCoy, "Searching for Significance among Drug Lords and Death Squads: The Covert Netherworld as Invisible Incubator for Illicit Commerce", *Journal of Illicit Economies and Development* 1, no. 1 (2019), http://doi.org/10.31389/jied.8

32. CIA, "East Asia Biweekly Review", ABR 78-004, 7 February 1978, https://www.cia.gov/readingroom/docs/CIA-RDP79T00912A002200010004-1.pdf.

33. CIA, "International Narcotics Biweekly Review", INBR 78-002, 19 January 1978, https://www.cia.gov/readingroom/docs/CIA-RDP79T00912A001900010002-6.pdf.

34. US Embassy (Bangkok) to US secretary of state Cyrus Vance, "Far Eastern Economic Review Article on Narcotics", 14 March 1978, Wikileaks, 1978BANGKO07589_d, https://wikileaks.org/plusd/cables/1978BANGKO07589_d.html.

35. US Embassy (Bangkok) to US secretary of state Cyrus Vance, "Kriangsak Six Month Roundup", 28 April 1978, Wikileaks, 1978BANGKO12309_d, https://wikileaks.org/plusd/cables/1978BANGKO12309_d.html.

36. US Embassy (Bangkok) to US secretary of state Cyrus Vance, "Narcotics Control Board Leadership Situation", 26 January 1978, Wikileaks, 1978BANGKO02731_d, https://wikileaks.org/plusd/cables/1978BANGKO02731_d.html.

37. Don Oberdorfer, "Diplomat's Enemies Play Role", *Washington Post*, 21 May 1982, https://www.washingtonpost.com/archive/politics/1982/05/21/diplomats-enemies-play-role/cfb642d9-df8c-48ee-92f8-4adab5d63b3e/.

38. See Rodney Stich, *America's Corrupt War on Drugs and the People* (Alamo, CA: Silverpeak, 2013).

39. US Embassy (Bangkok) to secretary of state (Cyrus Vance), "(Lou) Destruction of Seized Drugs in Thailand Ref A. Bkk 03276 (P301041Z Jan 79)", 1 February 1979, Wikileaks, 1979BANGKO03488_e, https://wikileaks.org/plusd/cables/1979BANGKO03488_e.html.

40. McCoy, "Searching for Significance".

41. อนุสรณ์งานพระราชทานเพลิงศพ พลเอก ยศ เทพหัสดิน ณ อยุธยา ณ เมรุวัดพระศรีมหาธาตุ วรมหาวิหาร [Memorial for the cremation ceremony of General Yot Thephusdin Na Ayutthaya at the crematorium of Wat Phra Si Mahathat Woramahawihan], 7 February 2002.

42. Ansil Ramsey, "Thailand 1978: Kriangsak—The Thai Who Binds", *Asian Survey* 19, no. 2, "A Survey of Asia in 1978: Part II" (February 1979), p. 105.

43. US Embassy (Bangkok) to secretary of state Cyrus Vance, "Meeting with Kriangsak: Thai Domestic Developments and Indochina", 5 October 1978, Wikileaks, 1978BANGKO29160_d, https://wikileaks.org/plusd/cables/1978BANGKO29160_d.html.

44. Ramsey, "Thailand 1978", p. 106.

45. Joseph Wright, *The Balancing Act* (Bangkok: Asia Books, 1991), p. 279.

46. US Embassy (Bangkok) to secretary of state Cyrus Vance, "Meeting with Kriangsak: Thai Domestic Developments and Indochina", 5 October 1978, Wikileaks, 1978BANGKO29160_d, https://wikileaks.org/plusd/cables/1978BANGKO29160_d.html.

47. Though they did not attempt a coup following their transfers, Amnat and Serm felt "considerable resentment" against Kriangsak for them. Serm felt betrayed because he believed Kriangsak had led him to believe he would be permitted to occupy both positions at the same time. US Embassy (Bangkok) to US secretary of state Cyrus Vance, "Controversy over RTARF Promotion/Transfer List Appears to be Settling", US National Archives, 10 October 1978, 1978BANGKO29503, https://aad.archives.gov/aad/createpdf?rid=248264&dt=2694&dl=2009.

48. Kriangsak especially favoured Prem's strong palace connections. When palace-connected ex-PM M.R. Kukrit Pramoj had, on 25 September 1979, written in a local newspaper that if Kriangsak named General Serm as supreme commander (which was generally expected), Serm should vacate the post of army chief and let Prem replace him, some observers read into Kukrit's proposal an oblique royal directive. US Embassy (Bangkok) to US secretary of state Cyrus Vance, "Observations Regarding RTARF Promotion List Summary: Annual October 1 RTARF Military Promotion List Has Been Subject of Considerable Speculation in PR", 27 September 1979, US National Archives, 1978BANGKO28130, https://aad.archives.gov/aad/createpdf?rid=240600&dt=2694&dl=2009.

49. Handley, *The King Never Smiles*, pp. 277, 466n1.

50. General Sant Chitpatima, ชีวิตและผลงาน พลเอก สัณห์ จิตรปฏิมา [Life and works of General Sant Chitpatima] (Bangkok: Namagsorn, 2005).

51. US Embassy (Bangkok) to US secretary of state Cyrus Vance, "Kriangsak Decides to Play Politics", 6 December 1978, Wikileaks, 1978STATE307823_d, https://wikileaks.org/plusd/cables/1978STATE307823_d.html.

52. US Embassy (Bangkok) to US secretary of state Cyrus Vance, "Election Campaign Opens", 9 March 1979, Wikileaks, 1979BANGKO08025_e, https://wikileaks.org/plusd/cables/1979BANGKO08025_e.html.

53. Niyom Rathamarit, "Military Governments in Thailand: Their Policies toward Political Parties, 1977–83" (PhD dissertation, University of Pittsburgh, 1984), p. 168.

54. US Embassy (Bangkok) to US secretary of state Cyrus Vance, "Initial Reactions to Senate Appointments", 26 April 1979,

Wikileaks, 1979BANGK13701_e, https://wikileaks.org/plusd/cables/1979BANGKO13701_e.html.

55. See Richard Nations, "Parliament's First Bill", *Far Eastern Economic Review*, 18 May 1979, p. 15; Richard Nations, "A Time for Generalship", *Far Eastern Economic Review*, 1 June 1979, pp. 12–14.

56. Niyom, "Military Governments", p. 190.

57. Ibid., p. 193.

58. Ramsey, "Thailand 1978", p. 106.

59. CIA, "34. Intelligence Memorandum Prepared in the Central Intelligence Agency: Another Cambodian War", RPM 78–10490, 15 December 1978, *Foreign Relations of the United States (FRUS)*, https://history.state.gov/historicaldocuments/frus1977-80v22/d34.

60. Conboy, *The Cambodian Wars*, p. 130.

61. "171. Memorandum of Conversation", 6 February 1979, *FRUS*, https://history.state.gov/historicaldocuments/frus1977-80v22/d171.

62. Conboy, *The Cambodian Wars*, p. 170.

63. US Embassy (Bangkok) to US secretary of state Cyrus Vance, "Press Reports of Chinese Aid to Pol Pot through Thailand", 13 February 1978, Wikileaks, 1979BANGKO04893_e, https://wikileaks.org/plusd/cables/1979BANGKO04893_e.html.

64. US Embassy (Bangkok) to US secretary of state Cyrus Vance, "Kriangsak Visit to USSR", 10 April 1979, Wikileaks, 1979MOSCOW08847_e, https://wikileaks.org/plusd/cables/1979MOSCOW08847_e.html.

65. US Embassy (Bangkok) to US secretary of state Cyrus Vance, "Message for the President", 12 June 1979, Wikileaks, 1979BANGKO20061_e, https://wikileaks.org/plusd/cables/1979BANGKO20061_e.html.

66. US Embassy (Bangkok) to US secretary of state Cyrus Vance, "NE 27 Press Summary", 28 June 1979, Wikileaks, 1979STATE166595_e, https://wikileaks.org/plusd/cables/1979STATE166595_e.html.

67. US Embassy (Thailand) to US secretary of state Cyrus Vance, "Thai Comments on Sihanouk", 11 August 1979, Wikileaks, https://wikileaks.org/plusd/cables/1979BANGKO29180_e.html.

68. United States secretary of state Cyrus Vance to US, Department of State, "SRV Forces in Thailand", 7 November 1979, Wikileaks, 1979STATE291336_e, https://wikileaks.org/plusd/cables/1979STATE291336_e.html.

69. CIA, "Approval of Personal Services Expenses", 7 December 1979, https://www.cia.gov/readingroom/docs/CIA-RDP83B00100R000200180001-5.pdf.

70. CIA director Stansfield Turner to National Security Council, "Thai-Kampuchean Border", 6 December 1979, https://www.cia.gov/readingroom/docs/CIA-RDP83B00100R000300020005-7.pdf.

71. Ibid.

72. US Embassy (Bangkok) to US secretary of state Cyrus Vance, "PRC Military Attache on DK Leadership Changes, Status of DK and

PAVN Forces, and Recent Visit of PLA Delegation", 21 December 1979, US National Archives, https://aad.archives.gov/aad/createpdf?rid=71418&dt=2776&dl=2169.

73. CIA, "183. Intelligence Assessment Prepared in the Central Intelligence Agency", PA 80-10195, April 1980, https://history.state.gov/historicaldocuments/frus1977-80v22/d183.

74. US Embassy (Bangkok) to US secretary of state Cyrus Vance, "The Kriangsak Government: Muddling Through", 13 August 1979, US National Archives, 1979BANGKO29455, https://aad.archives.gov/aad/createpdf?rid=27972&dt=2776&dl=2169.

75. US Embassy (Bangkok) to US secretary of state Cyrus Vance, "Kriangsak Government: Economic and Political Pressures Rise", 14 November 1979, US National Archives, 1979BANGKO46672, https://aad.archives.gov/aad/createpdf?rid=249624&dt=2776&dl=2169.

76. "Thai Military under Prem's Control Continues to Support Kriangsak", 7 December 1979, Wikileaks, 1979BANGKO50365_e, https://wikileaks.org/plusd/cables/1979BANGKO50365_e.html.

77. Girling, *Thailand: Society and Politics*, p. 225.

78. See งานพระราชทานเพลิงศพ พลเอก เทพ กรานเลิศ เมรุวัดพระศรีมหาธาตุวรมหาวิหาร เขต บางเขน [Memorial volume from the cremation ceremony of General Thep Kranlert, Crematorium of Wat Phrasorn Mahathat Woramahawihan, Bang Khen District], Bangkok, 22 October 1988; อนุสรณ์ พลเอกอำนาจ ดำริกาญ จน์ [Memorial volume of General Amnart Damrikarn], Bangkok, 1981.

79. "Thai Military under Prem's Control Continues to Support Kriangsak", 7 December 1979, Wikileaks, 1979BANGKO50365_e,https://wikileaks.org/plusd/cables/1979BANGKO50365_e.html.

80. US Embassy (Bangkok) to US secretary of state Cyrus Vance, "Coup Rumors Strike Bangkok", 13 December 1979, US National Archives, 1979BANGKO51159, https://aad.archives.gov/aad/createpdf?rid=63227&dt=2776&dl=2169.

81. US Embassy (Bangkok) to US secretary of state Cyrus Vance, "Kriangsak Government Stability: The Current State of Play", 29 December 1979, US National Archives, 1979BANGKO53241, https://aad.archives.gov/aad/createpdf?rid=63922&dt=2776&dl=2169.

82. CIA, "Thailand: Political Crisis", 23 February 1980, https://www.cia.gov/readingroom/docs/CIA-RDP83B00100R000200160001-7.pdf.

83. US Embassy (Bangkok) to US secretary of state Cyrus Vance, "The Kriangsak Government: Muddling Through", 13 August 1979, 1979BANGKO29455_e, https://wikileaks.org/plusd/cables/1979BANGKO29455_e.html.

84. Handley, *The King Never Smiles*, pp. 277–78.

85. Oberdorfer, "Diplomat's Enemies".

86. "182. Telegram from the Embassy in Thailand to the Department of State", 29 February 1980, *FRUS*, https://history.state.gov/historicaldocuments/frus1977-80v22/d182.

Chapter Nine

Arch-Royalist Prem (1980–88)

Prem Tinsulanonda played a highly significant role in modern Thai history. From 1978 until his death in 2019, he exerted 40.5 years of enormous sway over the Thai military and Thai politics, including a stint as unelected prime minister from 1980 to 1988, and afterwards becoming the dominant force on the king's Privy Council. Moreover, officers close to Prem or who earned his trust ascended to leading military positions. His endorsement was necessary for the appointment of seventeen out of the eighteen army commanders who followed him after 1981—with the exception of Thaksin Shinawatra's cousin Chaisit Shinawatra (2003–4).

Prem was a follower and admirer of Krit Sivara. But Prem's devotion to Krit owed not to the former's support for Krit's coming out against the dictatorship of Thanom/Praphas. Rather, it was to Krit's ability to develop a structure for the preparation and management of counterinsurgency when the latter was commander of the 2nd Army Region (1960–63), 1st Army Region (1963–66), deputy army commander (1966–73) and army commander/supreme commander (1973–75). Following Prem's 1978 appointment as army commander, in February 1979 the Royal Thai Army camp in Sakon Nakhon was named after Krit to commemorate his successful prosecution of counterinsurgency in the Northeast. In March 2014, Prem christened a monument to Krit within the camp out of respect for his leadership against the insurgents. But despite Prem's allegiance to Krit, he led Thailand's military away from the democratic reformism that Krit had supported.

Indeed, Prem owed to Krit his early rapid rise in the military. Six years Krit's junior, Prem was not a product of Bangkok's elite military families. He was born on 26 August 1920 in the southern province of Songkhla. His father, Bueng, was a moderately high-level bureaucrat who served as the warden of Songkhla prison and eventually rose to be a deputy chief of staff in the Interior Ministry. Following in the tradition of all mid-ranking to senior civil servants at the time, Bueng was bestowed a surname by then king Rama VI. That surname was Tinsulanonda, meaning "contentment in sharp grass". The king gave the title "Luang Winijtham" to Bueng in 1919. Luang Winijthakam (Bueng Tinsulanonda) and his wife Od had eight children together: six boys and two girls (with Prem as the second-to-the-youngest son). Naturally, Prem did not grow up poor.

Two childhood friends with whom Prem would later work when he became prime minister were Charn Manutham and Siddhi Savetsila. In their younger days, Prem became a loyal cavalryman for the state, while Siddhi became an air force officer and joined the anti-government Seri Thai during World War II. In the mid-1930s, Prem decided to go to Bangkok to become a soldier. At the time, there were two curriculums: the traditional Chulachomklao Royal Military Academy and the Army Technical School, which had a French military curriculum. Prem matriculated into the latter institution, studying in class 5 between 1938 and 1941. Two close class peers were Hiran Siriwat and Somsak Panjamanond. His friends in other classes were Sant Chitpattima (class 6, 1939), Prayut Charumanee (class 7, 1940), Vitoon Yasawat (class 9, 1942) and Han Leelanond (class 10, 1943). Two of his mentors were Prasert Wongsuwan (class 2, 1935), father of Prawit Wongsuwan; and Somsak (Siri) Wongwanich (class 3, 1936), father of Wimol Wongwanich.

Though he graduated in 1941 to become a cavalry officer, many of Prem's student friends from the other military school (Chulachomklao Royal Military Academy) later became powerful soldiers or politicians. These included future prime ministers Kriangsak Chomanand (military class of 1937; hereafter, only the class year is given) and Chatichai Chunhavan (1939); Saiyud Kerdpol (1939) (godfather of the Internal Security Operations Command, or ISOC); Sanga Kittikachorn (1939), brother of Thanom (1921); as well as future army commander and supreme commander Serm na Nakorn (1935). Whilst Prem's education was supposed to last for five years, he graduated in just three because of Thailand's need for army officers at the time. Prem fought as cavalry officer in the 1941 Indochina War against France and the 1942–45 northern Burma campaign against Britain, where he earned foreign battle experience under the commands of Lt. Gen. Charoon Ratanakul and Lt. Gen. Phin Chunhavan (1909), but more directly under Colonel Sarit Thanarat (1920) in the service of Field Marshal Phibun Songkram (1909). It was in the army under Phin that Prem met Krit, then an aide to the Phayap Army chief.[1]

It was not until Sarit's own 1957 putsch against Phibun Songkram and Phao Siyanon, however, that Prem's star began to ascend. Sarit boosted him to the post of colonel in 1959 and placed him on a military-controlled constitutional drafting committee. Propelled by the recommendations of Krit, field marshals Thanom Kittikachorn and Praphas Charusatien raised him to major-general in 1971. Most importantly, he served as royal aide-de-camp for the palace in 1968 and 1975, reflecting a growing bond with the monarchy. In 1973, Krit appointed him as deputy commander of the 2nd Army Region, the forefront of the anti-communist counterinsurgency. The following year, Prem became the region's commander, serving until 1977. By that time, his military successes and popularity in the army earned him support in the palace and among the Young Turks faction. He was therefore appointed to assistant army commander. Then, in 1978, the king reportedly helped to raise him to the position of army commander, a move that bypassed more senior officers.

Prem promoted the growth of five different military factions. These included his own unit, the Cavalry faction, the 2nd Army Region faction (where he had served), the class 7 Young Turks faction (as an initial honorary mentor), the informal "Professional Soldiers" faction, and the Eastern Tigers (Buraphapayak) faction of the 2nd Infantry Division, which included the sub-faction of the 21st Infantry Regiment, the Queen's Tiger Guard, whose honorary commandant was Queen Sirikit. The latter unit had originated in 1908, though it was severely downgraded with the fall of the absolute monarchy in 1932. The year 1959 marked its re-ascendance thanks to help from pro-monarchist General Sarit. The unit now acted with greater autonomy from the rest of Thailand's military; its priority, first and foremost, was to the king rather than the direct chain of command. In this way, it would serve as a model for what the armed forces would ultimately become in 1973—a servant of royalty. Development of this unit paralleled the creation of a sixty-man elite palace guard trained by the CIA (and headed by Lt. Gen. Vitoon Yasawad) to guard the royal family.[2] Like the Queen's Guard, it represented a wellspring of staunchly pro-royalist military sentiment. The "Professional Soldiers" faction had developed in 1978 when Prem became army commander. Though an informal grouping, it shared with the "Democratic Soldiers" clique support for democratization (as a method of counterinsurgency), though a version that was controlled and under the kingship. Prem's "Professional Soldiers" eventually trumped the Young Turks, but also the Democratic Soldiers (which fizzled) and class 5, the power of which faded away in 1992.[3] But more than any supporter of traditional army factions, Prem was—and became increasingly so—an agent of deep monarchical influence across the military.

Prem became prime minister on 4 March 1980 with an unblemished, tough soldier image. His immediate challenge was to instil order in a highly factious armed forces and unify the military under his government. This proved to be no easy task. The Young Turks faction had its own agenda, while retired general Kriangsak Chomanand was looking to make a comeback. Meanwhile, Prem's military peers (some of whom did not feel close to the cavalryman from the South) were vying for power. Finally, Prem's own subordinates were building their own power bases. Other problems included insurgency (communism and Deep South separatism), challenges from Vietnam, economic recession, and corruption.

Nevertheless, like Kriangsak before him, Prem did have legislative support on account of his influence within the Senate given that a large majority of sitting senators were military officials. But the new prime minister could not be assured that all such officers would support him. At the same time, Prem enjoyed support from the palace. Also, Prime Minister Kriangsak's decision to resign—rather than being "putsched" or constitutionally forced from office—ensured that recalcitrant military factions would not immediately attempt a military coup. In addition, Prem initially enjoyed popular goodwill because it had been Kriangsak, not Prem, who had implemented the much needed yet highly unpopular economic reforms to restore economic solvency. At the same time, the pledge of cooperation with Prem from M.R. Kukrit Pramoj, leader of the largest party in the legislature (Social Action), guaranteed that any parliamentary opposition to Prem would be stifled.[4]

Prem's first cabinet, appointed on 12 March 1980, seemed to be designed to satisfy the palace, right-wing Thai militarists and economic conservatives. Other than Prem himself, it was composed of thirty-seven members. Thirteen cabinet seats went to non-parliamentary military-associated appointees who were close to Prem. Alongside his long-time friend, newly appointed foreign minister Siddhi Savetsila, Prem sought to build a new policy towards Vietnam and Cambodia.

But with the Carter administration pressuring Prem to support a non-communist Cambodian resistance, Thailand began to build up support for Son Sann's Khmer People's National Liberation Front.[5]

At the same time, through the efforts of deputy chief of staff General Han Leelanond and the director of the Army Operations Directorate, General Chavalit Yongchaiyudh, Prem worked towards establishing a new policy aimed at defeating communist insurgency in Thailand. Building on Kriangsak's earlier efforts, he signed Order 66/2523 on 23 April 1980, which initiated a more moderate counterinsurgency approach, applying a policy of "politics leading the military". The order prioritized an end to social injustice, advocated democracy and included an amnesty for any communist insurgents that surrendered, leading to a decline in insurrection. In the mid-1980, Prem's government also began to reform the administration of the Deep South, where a secessionist insurgency existed. In January 1981, it set up two agencies to promote development and security, working side by side with the Internal Security Operations Command (ISOC). These were the SBPAC (Southern Border Provinces Administrative Center) and Task Force 43, both answerable to the prime minister.

Military factionalism remained disturbingly endemic. The prime minister realized that military factions opposed to him in the appointed Senate could ally with his adversaries in the elected lower house to jettison him from office in a vote of no confidence. At the same time, military rivals might use the opportunity of Prem's weakness to stage a coup. Prem and his supporters hit upon the idea that the king's approval of an extension of Prem's term as army commander might stabilize the country, or at least send a signal to politicians and soldiers alike that the palace did not want Prem thrown out of office. At the time, Prem was simultaneously prime minister, defence minister and army commander. In August, "Prem-ite" General Arthit Kamlang-ek, a fast-rising senior officer who was a member of Chulachomklao School's class 44 and sometime supporter of the Democratic Soldiers faction, petitioned the palace to extend Prem's term as army commander by one year. Despite opposition from parliamentarians such as Chuan Leekpai, the king apparently approved the plan—though he never visibly came out to do so. Arthit likely supported an extension as a means of getting other older officers out of the way of his own promotion.[6] Finally, the palace probably saw the extension as aiding Prem-led arch-royalist sway over the military.

The 1980 military reshuffle itself (see Appendix 4) represented an attempt by Prem to place personal loyalists in leading positions of power.

He appointed his friend Sant as deputy army commander, given that Prem had extended his retirement by one year and he needed someone loyal to have his back. The decision proved to be big mistake, as the 1981 coup later showed. Another loyalist was Prayut Charumanee, who was appointed as army chief of staff. Amnart Damrikarn, a member of Serm's faction, remained assistant army chief, balanced against the incoming Pin Thammasiri, close to Praphas, who was given the other assistant slot. Vasin Israngkul na Ayuthaya, a member of the 1942 faction, seemed to have no core of power himself, and was thus deemed harmless. Two of the four regional commanders were trusted Prem loyalists.[7]

The Young Turks military faction, though it had helped to place Prem in power, was furious at Prem's extension as army commander. It echoed too closely the attempted extension of Praphas Charusathien back in 1973, an event that had helped to trigger Thailand's 1973 student demonstrations. The Young Turks, of course, could have been expected to oppose the extension given that their nemesis, the Democratic Soldiers faction, had proposed it. They did manage to pressure Prem to demote Arthit, who at the time was 1st Army Division commander, to the more remote post of Deputy Chief of the 2nd Army Region.[8]

Meanwhile, Prem had been experiencing difficulties keeping his cabinet and coalition together as it continuously suffered from splits and bickering. As a result of factional divisions in the Social Action Party and squabbling between Chart Thai and (especially the Bunchu faction of) the SAP, Prem initiated a third cabinet shuffle on 11 March 1981. The new coalition line-up—a move by Prem to the ideological right—was made up of the Chart Thai Party, the Democrat Party, the Ruam Thai Party, the Mass Line Party, and the United Parties. The Mass Line Party was led by ultra-right-winger and Prem confidant Maj. Gen. Sudsai Hasdin. The United Parties was led by Prem stalwart and former police chief Senator Prachuab Suntharangkul. Following Prem's extension of his tenure, for the Young Turks, his ignoring of the group's recommendations for cabinet members and their dislike for the right-wing character of the new cabinet left their relationship close to breaking point. Finally, in March 1981, it looked as though Prem would seek yet another extension from the palace as army commander (Prem had reached the mandatory retirement age of 60 in 1980 and had been given a one-year extension by the palace, which expired in 1981).[9] The clique believed that former deputy army commander Sant Chitpatima (who was moving to become permanent defence minister) should replace Prem as army commander.

On the evening of 31 March 1981, leaders of the Young Officers Group dominated by members of class 7 (notably, Colonel Prachak Sawangchit and Colonel Manoon Roopkachorn, the coup group's secretary-general) went to Prem's residence in the Theves District of Bangkok and asked him to lead a coup against his own government. But Prem refused. One story goes that the prime minister simply believed that, although reforms were needed, a coup was simply not the answer—and he would not be a part of one.[10] Another account argues that Prem had supported a coup against his own government similar to the 1958 coup by Sarit and the 1971 coup by Thanom. He apparently did so because political parties were creating obstacles to his government's success in efficiently governing the country. Thus, he backed a coup as a means to lead the country more effectively. But when he discovered that the Young Turks were seeking to replace him if the coup succeeded, he backed away from supporting the putsch.[11] Forty years after the event, members of the Young Turks told a senior Thai military officer interviewed by this author that the linchpin for the coup to begin was a "green light" issued by a young member of the royal family who supported it.[12] Thus, on the following day, the April Fool's Day coup, as it came to be known, commenced.

Prem was supported by his own loyalists, including General Yuthasak Krongtraujroke, then commander of Chulachomklao Military Academy; Prayut Charumanee, then army chief of staff; assistant chief of staff for operations General Han Leenanond; General Chavalit Yongchaiyudh, then head of the Directorate of Joint Operations; Colonel Mongkol Ampornpisit, Prem's adjutant (and future supreme commander); 2nd Army Region commander General Laksana Saligupta; 3rd Army Region commander General Sima Panigabutra; and Prem's unwavering follower, Lt. Col. Surayud Chulanond.[13] Another important officer who sided with Prem was General Pichit Kullanvanij, an able military strategist who had defeated the Communist Party of Thailand in the highland area of Khao Kor, which centres on a region abutting the provinces of Pitsanuloke, Petchabun and Loei. He was very close to the palace and was appointed commander of the 1st Infantry Division after the 1981 coup.[14] Moreover, there was General Sithi Jiraroj, a cadet school friend and peer of Prem who served as deputy army commander in 1978–79 and was also Prem's interior minister from 1981 to 1988. Sithi's loyal aide was the valedictorian of cadet school graduating class 5, Suchinda Kraprayoon.[15] But of all Prem's military allies, the one who proved most valuable in backing the prime minister—and, as a result, benefited in terms of promotions—was 2nd Army Region deputy commander Arthit, who also maintained close ties with Queen Sirikit. In 1980, as the Young Turks had sought to build their influence across the army, Arthit, General Yuthasak Krongtraujroke (then commander of Chulachomklao Military academy) and General Han had established a quasi-faction with class 5 and Chavalit to counter the Young Turks.

On 31 March, as soon as he discovered the coup plot, Arthit telephoned the queen to notify her of what was taking place. She immediately summoned Prem to the palace. The coup was already underway, however. But the plotters could do nothing but agree to the queen's request. Meanwhile, they quickly captured Bangkok and almost all state machinery in the capital. Still, they had to let Prem slip through their fingers to meet with the king and queen. By losing Prem, the coup group, ostensibly directed by General Sant but under the control of the Young Turks, lost their prime ministerial hostage. Prem thereupon fled to the base of the 2nd Army Region in Thailand's northeastern city of Khorat (Nakhon Ratchasima), where his military support was strongest. Most importantly, the entire royal family accompanied him. In Khorat, Prem established a counter-coup headquarters. He announced on radio that the 2nd and 3rd Region armies as well as the navy and the air force were with him, though this was only tentatively true. At the same time, Prem issued an ultimatum to the coup plotters to surrender, while a statement from the queen from Khorat implored both sides to restore unity. Moreover, the queen announced via radio that Prem was with the royal family in Khorat. By 2 April, following intense bargaining by Prem, several soldiers and politicians had defected to his side and began traveling to Khorat in droves.

The coup-borne "Revolutionary Party" made one final effort to retain power by appealing to the people. On 2 April, it organized a rally in which Young Turk Colonel Prachak Sawangchit promised that the group was under the monarchy, but anything helping the people must be the people's priority. Thus, his group only needed thirty days of control, during which a government would be formed, and the 1978 constitution would be changed so that the interim clauses,[16] which had slowed democratization, would be eliminated. This would be a gift to the people.[17] In the early morning hours of 3 April, however, Arthit's forces marched into Bangkok. Indeed, it was forces of the 21st Infantry Regiment, or Queen's Guard, that, against overwhelming odds, entered the city and began arresting key officers of the coup forces.[18] Led by Major Narongdej Nanda-Photidej, the Queen's Guardsmen that overpowered the rebellious troops on that day included the young officers Nipat Thonglek and Udomdej Sitabutr. Udomdej would later serve as army commander and Nipat as permanent minister of defence (2011–14).[19] Two officers later to become army commanders sided with the rebels: Prawit Wongsuwan of pre-cadet class 6, and Teerachai Nakwanich, pre-cadet 14 classmate of Nipat and Udomdej. Though they did not participate in the Bangkok operation, Queen's Guardsmen Anupong Paochinda and Prayut Chanocha received medals for helping quell the coup.[20]

Sant's forces were numerically stronger than those of Prem. Sant, as deputy army commander, held respect among Thai soldiers. As leader of the "Revolutionary Council", he was initially joined by navy commander Admiral Samut Sahanawin, air force commander ACM Paniang Kantat, police director Monchai Pankonchuen (all of whom later denied this), 1st Army Region commander General Wasin Itsarangkul na Ayutthaya, and fourteen battalions under the command of the Young Turks. Supreme commander General Serm na Nakorn was notably silent during the coup. Together, the force numbered well over eight thousand men; perhaps the greatest number of coup forces ever raised in Thai history.[21]

Whilst it seemed that Sant and the Young Turks had triumphed by taking the capital and forcing Prem to set up headquarters at the 2nd Army Region base, the rules of the game had changed since the pre-1957 situation when the king had much less political power. In 1981, palace influence trumped that of the factious military—and Prem's trump card was support from the palace. The king's endorsement or at least neutrality was now crucial for any coup to be successful.[22] As Chai-anan noted, the dictum for coup leaders after the 1981 coup attempt was, henceforth, "He who is with the King … emerges the winner in every coup."[23] Only three days after it had begun, the coup failed miserably without a shot being fired. In the aftermath, in what was likely part of the bargaining to end the revolt, coup participants received an amnesty. Only a month after the attempted putsch, the king pardoned all soldiers involved. Nevertheless, thirty-eight military officers, including General Sant, were discharged from the army in the aftermath of the coup (twenty-seven were reinstated in 1986). The light penalty partially helped to patch up the grievances of those soldiers who had resented the extension of Prem's term. At the same time, Prem was not given another extension. Though he may have supported the putsch, supreme commander Serm was retiring anyway in October 1981, so he was no longer a direct threat to Prem.

As a result of the April Fool's Day coup attempt, the restiveness in the armed forces became much more apparent. Following the failure of the coup, alternative cliques simply filled the void left by the ouster of the Young Turks. In particular, General Amnart Damrikarn (assistant army commander) emerged as a new patron for young officers. Many other army officers adopted much of the Young Turks' ideology. Those, such as Arthit, who supporting the ideology of the Democratic Soldiers' faction, however, were able to grow in influence (this faction formally dissolved in late 1981). The dismissals and/or demotions of the Young Turks led to the loss of important military expertise in the Thai military. Indeed, thirty-seven were expelled and twenty-one were transferred. The failed putsch was also detrimental to the military's self-esteem and corporate image.[24] But the defeat of the putsch demonstrated the power of the monarch. Finally, the failure of the coup decimated the Young Turks as a military faction, allowing other cliques to rise in its place. Indeed, factions centred on generals Arthit, Pichit, Chavalit and Suchinda's class 5 were ascending. The Young Turks remained to some extent, but in a much-weakened position.[25]

After quelling the Young Turks, Prem next had to contend with a retired military enemy in parliament: former prime minister General Kriangsak Chomanand. In summer 1981, in an attempt at a political comeback, Kriangsak began forming his own party (the National Democratic Party, NDP) in the lower house. Kriangsak's party was soon sucking numbers of MPs away from Social Action and other parties. But opposition parties were not the only ones affected. MPs from ruling coalition parties such as the United Parties and Mass Line were also switching to the NDP.[26] By autumn, the NDP claimed to have over seventy members. Kriangsak still enjoyed support in the Thai military—and growing support in parliament.

The growing parliamentary power of Kriangsak and continued reducing support for Prem in the lower house, upper house and military placed the prime minister in a precarious situation. By November 1981, Kriangsak was threatening to initiate a no confidence debate against Prem over economic issues. But Kriangsak's parliamentary power began to dwindle as various factions composed of members of the lower house migrated to parties in the governing coalition—where opportunities for making money and being appointed to government positions existed. Finally, in late 1981, Prem was able to manipulate the military-appointed Senate after the 1979–81 term of senators appointed by Kriangsak came to an end. If he could control the Senate, Prem's parliamentary strength seemed assured.

FIGURE 9.1
Thailand's Senate, 1981–85

Type of legislature	Years in office	Appointed or elected	Total number of members and military contingent
Bicameral (Fifth Senate)	1981–85 (served 6-year term)	Appointed	1981: 225, of which 176 (78.2%) military reserved domain 1983: 243, of which 145 (59.6%) military reserved domain

Source: Paul Chambers, "Superfluous, Irrelevant or Emancipating: Thailand's Evolving Senate Today", *Journal of Current Southeast Asian Affairs* 28, no. 3 (2009): 9, https://d-nb.info/999559311/34.

The October 1981 military reshuffle was one in which Prem purged and promoted officers he deemed assuredly loyal to him in the aftermath of the March 1981 coup attempt. First and foremost, Kriangsak ally General Tuangtong Suwannathat was promoted to the powerless post of permanent minister of defence, where he languished until his retirement in 1983. Prem's military saviour against that coup, Arthit, was appointed commander of the 1st Army Region. He then became, concurrently, assistant army chief. Prem's support in the military weakened in the post-coup period because he had succeeded in balancing the Young Turks against those opposed to them (particularly Arthit). Thus, following the failed coup, Prem now worried about the growing power of Arthit. In that year, he temporarily re-appointed General Amnart Damrikarn to command the 1st Army Region in order to arrest the meteoric rise of Arthit. But Amnart's close ties to Kriangsak and Kriangsak's continuing moves in parliament against Prem caused the prime minister to shelve any plan of appointing Amnart to the position vacated by Sant—deputy army commander. An ambitious Amnart could have been a problem, but this was ultimately resolved when Amnart died suddenly in June 1981. Prem thus easily appointed General Prayut Charumanee as army commander.[27] Prayut was a smart choice as he was a Prem loyalist who had very little in terms of a base of support in the military of his own. Prayut relied completely on Prem, and he was set to retire the following year (1982). He would thus temporarily keep Arthit's ambitions at bay.

The year 1982 was one of securing unity in the military and of girding against external enemies. As Arthit's role grew across Thailand, Prem seemed to fade into the periphery. Arthit became involved in politics and even acted as mediator between societal demand groups to arrive at settlements with unions and student groups. Reportedly, military factions were even involved in developing the tensions that Arthit could conveniently help to resolve.[28] During 1982, a period when the king was ill, the queen was accompanied in her trips by both Prem and Arthit. Meanwhile, the communist insurrection dwindled (with more and more insurgents surrendering and being granted amnesty). That year, Prem issued Prime Ministerial Order 65/2525, titled "Plan for Political Offensive to Win over the Communists". It was meant to promote faith and understanding among different Thai interest groups. The following year, Prem issued Order 83/2526, which placed all agencies involved in anti-communism efforts—whether civilian, police or military—under ISOC control.[29]

Meanwhile, the 1980 US election of conservative Ronald Reagan produced dividends for Prem and the Thai military in terms of more US military aid, joint exercises, and a more emphatic Cold War security alliance than under the Carter administration. In January 1982, Thai forces, under US pressure, flushed drug kingpin Khun Sa out of his hideout along the Thai-Burma border and across into Burma. The operation took four days and resulted in heavy casualties on both sides.[30] The army engaged in six more anti-narcotics operations against border traffickers during 1982. Also beginning in 1982, the US and Thailand began to hold the annual joint military exercise Cobra Gold, an event that would expand to include many more countries and which persists to this day. With Vietnam increasing its pressure on Thailand as it persisted in its occupation of Cambodia, The Thai-Cambodian border continued to be of major concern to Prem. In an effort to gain more international support against Vietnam, Prem pacified Washington by agreeing to support a "coalition" of the three rival Cambodian resistance groups. These included not only the China-supported, genocidal Khmer Rouge but also the KPNLF of Son Sann and the FUNCINPEC of Norodom Sihanouk.[31] The final agreement of the coalition marked not only a conciliation of the groups themselves but also a consensus between Bangkok, Beijing and Washington. Ultimately, on 9 July, Sihanouk announced the formation of the Coalition Government of Democratic Kampuchea (CGDK). But the CGDK masked the beginning of a Prem-backed CIA operation funding CGDK combat against Vietnamese occupying troops and soldiers of the proxy People's Republic of Kampuchea.[32]

Though political chaos in Thailand during 1982 continued (including anonymous coup threats and two assassination attempts on Prem), stability prevailed, with Thais preparing for an April 1983 election. Retired general Santi Chitpattima and former Young Turks colonels

Manoon and Prajak joined Kriangsak's National Democratic Party, while Colonel Narong Kittikachorn became a member of Praman Adireksan's Chart Thai.[33]

In 1982, Prem tried again to stymie the rise of Arthit by supporting the appointment of another weak officer, General Pramoj Thawornchan (then army chief of staff), to the post of army commander to replace the retiring General Prayut Charumanee. Prem's idea was to have army commanders holding the post for just a year each (with Prem ally General Han Leelanond then to step in after General Pramoj). But the palace vetoed Prem's preferences.[34] The October 1982 military reshuffle thus confirmed the ascendant power of Arthit. He was promoted to become army commander. Arthit allies Thianchai and Phak were also allocated top postings. Prem was influential with the remaining senior military officials. Prem also appointed Arthit to become commander of the Bangkok Peace-Keeping Force (or Capital Command), chief of ISOC, chair of the Telephone Organization of Thailand and chair of Thai Military Bank.

Arthit Kamlang-ek had suddenly become the shining light of the Thai military. But who was Arthit? He was a product of Bangkok. Born on 31 August 1925, he was usually dubbed by the media as "Big Sun". Arthit was the son of army lieutenant Phin Kamlang-ek and his wife Sakorn. Arthit had studied at what is now called Wat Benchamabophit High School before entering Chulachomklao Royal Military Academy and studying there between 1944 and 1948 (the same class as General Tienchai Sirisamphan and General Yuthasak Krongtraujroke). Nine years later, in March 1957, as a young battalion commander with the rank of captain, Arthit commanded his troops not to fire their weapons at people protesting against Prime Minister Phibun. For this he gained the nickname "Makkhawan Bridge Hero". He continued to be promoted. In 1976, Arthit was made deputy cohort commander of the 3rd Army Region. In 1977 he was appointed cohort commander of the 3rd Army Region simultaneous to being made a general. By 1979 he had become commander of the 1st Division of the 1st Army Region (the Royal Guards). But in October 1980 he was demoted to deputy commander of the 2nd Army Region. In terms of family, Arthit married two times; he had two sons, one daughter and one stepson.[35] By the time he died in 2015, his children had all entered and had successful careers in the security services. Arthit Kamlang-ek's family tree is depicted in Figure 9.2.

By early 1983, so great was Arthit's military power becoming that he overshadowed Prem. Open frictions between the two had become

FIGURE 9.2
Arthit Kamlang-ek Family Tree

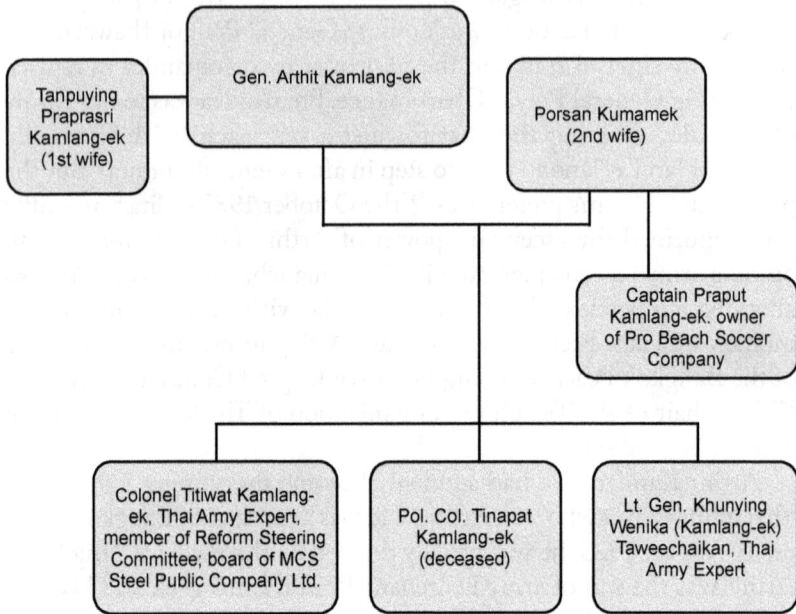

apparent by 1983. Indeed, without waiting for Prem's approval, Arthit increasingly involved himself in political activities. A case in point was the "interim clauses" of the 1978 constitution, which were approaching their expiry date (21 April 1983). If they were allowed to expire, active military officers would be unable to assume political positions. As such, a changing equilibrium would occur as greater parliamentary power would soon reside in political parties as opposed to the military. Army commander General Arthit, assisted by generals Chavalit, Pichit and a large segment of the military, thus began campaigning in parliament for a constitutional amendment for a continuation of the right for military officers to hold civilian positions, including sitting on an appointed Senate. General Pichit even insinuated that there might be a coup if the clauses were left to lapse.[36] In parliament, Arthit was assisted in his amendment efforts by rightist parliamentary leaders retired colonel Phol Ruengprasertvit (Siam Democratic Party) and Samak Sundaravej (Thai Citizen Party). Although the bill passed the first and second readings in parliament, it failed on the third (16 March 1983).[37] The failure of the vote owed partly to divisions within the military factions, as reflected in the appointed Senate. Supreme commander Saiyud Kerdpol, General Han Leelanond, the Young Turks and (finally) Prime Minister Prem all opposed Arthit's constitutional amendment, a fact that killed it in the upper house.

The failure of the amendments appeared to mean that the interim clauses had expired, giving civilians more control over the cabinet and parliament. Indeed, the armed forces looked set to soon lose important tools of domination as follows:

1. Senators (royal appointees, who mostly are either retired or active-duty military officers) could no longer vote on motions of no-confidence and the national budget.
2. Senate power to kill bills passed by the elected lower house was revoked.
3. Active-duty officers and government officials were no longer allowed to hold "political positions", defined as senatorial, judicial or cabinet-level posts.

Prem remained quiet during this time, allowing the military factions and political parties to quarrel amongst themselves while he appeared to stand above the banter.[38]

Arthit then convinced Prem to dissolve the lower house on 19 March, with snap elections to be held on 18 April 1983, just three days prior to the expiry of the "interim clauses". The new government formed would thus still exist under the transitory clauses, permitting Prem to continue as premier for four more years. Meanwhile, given that the transitory clauses were still in effect, the multi-member district (MMD) system used during the 1979 election was again utilized during the 1983 poll (it was expected by many that the use of MMD would harm larger parties such as the SAP, which was often against military interests).

But the armed forces (particularly Arthit) were dejected by the outcome of the 1983 election given that pro-army parties performed poorly. The army did, however, actively help put together a new coalition government. Retired general Pramarn Adireksan, leader of Chart Thai, had sought to establish a coalition with the National Democratic Party of retired general Kriangsak Chomanand. But the army vetoed this proposal, partly because both Pramarn and Kriangsak commanded loyalty in the armed forces that competed with that of Arthit and even of Prem. As a result, other parties formed a coalition under Prem.[39] Because Prem was acceptable to senior army officials as well as the SAP's Kukrit Pramoj, Prem was allowed to continue on in office. And he knew he was the only person that all sides would agree on (though

Arthit looked to be rapidly becoming a successor prime minister). Thus, Prem demanded—and received—the right to choose twenty-five per cent of his cabinet himself. Military leaders also compelled parliament to keep Chart Thai out of any ruling coalition and to include Samak Sundaravej's right-wing Prachakorn Thai.[40]

Meanwhile, military threats from Vietnam meant the armed forces could rationalize their dominant influence across Thai society. It also helped powerful army chief Arthit justify an expansion of his authority. Reflecting the balance of the power of the time, in the October 1983 annual reshuffle, Arthit became supreme commander concurrent with army chief. Five members of Arthit's cadet class also had top army posts. Even the new air force chief was an Arthit man. Only the 1st Army Region chief and 2nd Army Region chief were Prem men.

By January 1984, trouble along the Thai-Cambodian border was growing. Since 1979, the Thai military—led by the RTA's Tactical Operations Center (TOC) 315 and its units Taskforce 80 and Taskforce 838—had been working closely in support of Khmer Rouge insurgent forces against the Vietnamese occupation army in Cambodia as well as its proxy PRK government. Both taskforces were under Thailand's Supreme Command. Taskforce 80 ostensibly handled refugees along the Thai-border, but, starting in 1982, was coordinating attacks by the anti-Vietnamese CGDK from Thailand into Vietnam-occupied Cambodia. Since 1979, Taskforce 838 had trained, handled logistics for and helped arm Khmer Rouge forces and their leaders in Thailand. Soldiers assigned to this taskforce were drawn from Thailand's Special Forces division in Lopburi. By 1982, Taskforce 838 was assisting the broader CGDK, while TOC 315 planned Cambodian strategy in Bangkok.[41] Overall Cambodian policy was handled by the RTA's deputy chief of staff General Chavalit, foreign minister ACM Siddhi Savetsila and National Security Council secretary-general ACM Prasong Soonsiri. But Chavalit's policies had seemed to create more insecurity. In early 1984, a new colonel—Surayud Chulanond—was appointed to head Taskforce 838. But he was also under the new Special Warfare Command (SWC), which had been created in 1983. Surayud was commander of SWC Regiment 1 while also heading up Taskforce 838. His bosses at SWC were its commander, General Anek Bunyatee; Anek's deputy, General Sunthorn Kongsompong; and the SWC divisional commander, General Kajon Ramanwong. More so than Chavalit, Surayud answered to these men. Surayud's trusted subordinate was Lt. Col. Sonthi Boonyaratklin. Beginning in 1984, the SWC became much more involved in backing up the CGDK in terms of labour and expenses. The year 1984 thus saw the Thai military become much more overtly involved in supporting Cambodia's insurgency. Meanwhile, the CIA was giving at least US$12 million annually for Surayud's operations with the CGDK.[42]

With tensions growing between Thailand and Cambodia, Prem's government became embroiled in a brief border conflict with Laos. In June 1984, Thai forces entered three villages administered by the Lao government, claiming that they belonged to Thailand based upon an old US map. A series of shootings between the two sides followed. There were reports that a thousand Vietnamese troops were headed towards the region to reinforce Lao forces. Thus, Thai troops began to bolster those already at the boundary. Ultimately, though Thailand's foreign ministry made some threats, it found problems with the old map; following border talks, the Thai soldiers were quietly withdrawn.[43]

The year 1984 also witnessed an attempt in parliament by military leaders to amend the constitution to resurrect some political powers of the military: in this case, allowing active-duty military and police officials to concurrently hold political postings. But despite support from several conservative political parties, the move failed, further solidifying Prem's personalized control over politics since the military could not now enter politics on its own. Prem's allies in parliament and moderate voices in the military convinced Arthit to drop the matter, if only as a means of helping him to win an election following his eventual retirement.[44]

In September 1984, colonels Manoon Rupkachorn and Bolsak Polcharoen were arrested by police under pressure from the army's class 5 faction—the enemy of class 7, of which Manoon and Bolsak were members. The two were accused of the dubious charges of having plotted the assassinations of Prem, Arthit and Queen Sirikit. The two had visited Arthit the previous day to discuss the possible reinstatement of the previously discharged 1981 class 7 coup plotters. Arthit himself expressed support for their request. It was rumoured that class 5 had prevailed upon Prem not to support the reinstatements. After they had departed from the meeting with Arthit, Manoon and Bolsak were arrested by the police. In the end, generals Arthit, Pichit and Chavalit (as well as Thailand's crown prince) ensured that no charges were filed against the pair, who issued apologies to Arthit and Chavalit (with whom class 5 was closely associated) and the incident ended.[45]

By October 1984, a schism was beginning to develop between Arthit and Pichit on one side (supporting Arthit as a successor to Prem) and Chavalit and class 5 on the other. The remaining army factions were much less powerful.[46] Meanwhile, Prem, as prime minister, sought to offset these factions while deriving legitimacy from royal backing. But, as the most powerful military official at the time, the ambitious Arthit increasingly pressured Prem to give him more power. In a move to reward proven loyalists, Arthit started appointing members of the large class 5 faction to strategic positions. At the same time, he began mending fences with the officers of class 7 (Young Turks), increasingly supporting the return of them to active-duty military appointments. Though the Young Turks continued to be in conflict with class 5 and Chavalit, Arthit followed the example of Prem in balancing support from all of them to maintain his overall influence across the armed forces.

The October 1984 military reshuffle witnessed few changes to Arthit's dominance across the armed forces. His 1944 class predominated, though classes 1, 2 and 5 began receiving senior appointments. In 1984, the new 1st Army Region chief, General Pichit, and 1st Division chief General Issarapong—heading up key strategic commands—could be considered at the time of their appointments to be Arthit loyalists. Chavalit did not receive a promotion.

In November 1984, reacting to Thailand's continuing economic malaise, Prem devalued the Thai baht. Arthit reacted in consternation, publicly challenging the move. In a 7 November television address on Army TV, Arthit called for the removal of the finance minister and the reinstatement of the old exchange rate. Through manipulation by Arthit, and encouraged by senior army officers loyal to him, railway workers went on strike and opposition parliamentarians tried to reconvene parliament to debate the devaluation. But Prem refused to back down. The army commander had wrongly assumed that the prime minister's dismal popularity and his apparent weakness made this an appropriate time for Arthit to make demands. The next day, however, Prem made clear to the public that he was not going to be swayed by Arthit. In actuality, Prem had been notified that the king still supported him, as did many factions in the Thai military who were opposed to Arthit.[47] Prem met with Arthit and promised that the devaluation would not affect the defence budget. At the same time, the palace and the ruling coalition closely supported Prem, while there was disunity in the army. In the end, Arthit's campaign against the devaluation, though it demonstrated his capability as a national political leader, proved ineffective.[48]

Meanwhile, in early 1984, although Arthit was set for retirement in 1985, he had already begun requesting a two-year extension of duty.

Clearly, he saw himself as Prem's anointed successor. With the formation of the new government, General Pichit and others again began coming out strongly in favour of the amendment bill to extend the interim clauses. But, surprisingly, Arthit himself moved to cancel the motion. Apparently, Prem's approval of a military reshuffle favourable to the interests of Arthit—including Prem's support for a one-year extension of service for Arthit after 1985—led to the latter's move to postpone the bill.[49]

Problems between Prem and Arthit increasingly surfaced in mid-1984 when General Pichit publicly called for a further extension of Arthit's term. Such a move would have strengthened Arthit's power base at the expense of Prem. At the same time, Prem was ill in mid-1984, a situation that seemed to reinforce the need for Arthit's extension.

The year 1985 began as one of by-elections. Candidates included several recently retired senior military officials who had decided to enter politics. These included General Vitoon Yasawat (SAP), Admiral Somboon Chuapiboon (Democrat), General Pramoj Tavorachan (Prackakorn Thai), and General Han Leelanond (Democrat). All of them were close to Prem and they all won seats.

The most serious military-civilian clash in 1985 revolved around the extension of Arthit's tenure. The issue once and for all resolved itself in April when Prem stated he would support a one-year extension. But the single year, rather than Arthit's request for a two-year extension, effectively put the latter on probation—he would have to perform well enough to be acceptable for a second and final extension the following year. At the same time, Prem clearly communicated to Arthit that he wanted an end to the latter's political meddling. But, if anything, Arthit simply became less personally vocal in his interventions.

In the case of the 1985 Bangkok governor's election, it appears as though Arthit (and Prem) supported independent candidate and Young Turk Colonel Chamlong Srimuang despite Chamlong's public opposition to extending the interim clauses back in 1983. Indeed, the two had long been anything but close. But, given that Arthit in 1985 was trying to (1) build backing from the Young Turks, (2) support a candidate with a military background, and (3) keep any other candidate out of the governor's chair, he apparently (though reluctantly) supported Chamlong. Thus, Chamlong received the support of soldiers who belonged to most Bangkok-based military units, especially in the Bang Khen and Dusit districts, where there was heavy voting for him. In November, just before the polls opened, army radio voiced support for Chamlong. He went on to win in a landslide.[50]

Besides Chamlong, other Young Turks made news in more negative ways. On 9 September 1985, yet another coup attempt occurred
in Thailand. At the time, both Prem and Arthit were abroad, the king
and queen were in southern Thailand, and the crown prince was in
Italy. With these leaders away from Bangkok, the Young Turks faction attempted to finally carry out a putsch. During pre-dawn hours,
Colonel Manoon Rupkachorn, who had been dismissed in 1981, and
his brother Wing Commander Manas Rupkachorn, seized control of
parts of Bangkok with twenty-two tanks and five hundred soldiers,
mostly from the 4th Cavalry Regiment, which Manoon had earlier
commanded, but also from Manas's Air Force Security Unit.[51] Though
the likelihood of this coup's success was doubtful given that only a relatively few troops supported it, it was brought into action partly because
of a "green light" from the same royal family member who had backed
the 1981 coup attempt.[52] But the putsch failed thanks to quick action
taken by deputy army commander General Thienchai Sirisampan[53]
and deputy chief of staff General Chavalit Yongchaiyudh, who set up
a command centre at the 11th Infantry Regiment. Although by 3 p.m.
the army had regained control, gunfire from the tanks resulted in five
people being killed, including two NBC journalists: Neil Davis and
Bill Latch.[54] The attempted putsch collapsed when several expected
infantry divisions failed to appear to bolster it. A similar failure had
overtaken the attempted putsch by the Young Turks in 1981. For
their roles in quickly suppressing it, Thienchai, Chavalit and class 5
army officers were the big winners coming out of the crumbled coup
attempt.

Following the failed coup, most of the plotters who did not escape
abroad were subsequently imprisoned, but they were later freed on bail.
As is common in almost all coups in Thailand, they were eventually
all pardoned. Though led by Young Turk Manoon Rupkachorn, the
coup allegedly received support from former prime minister General
Kriangsak Chomanand, former supreme commander General Serm
na Nakorn, former deputy supreme commander ACM Krasae Intarat,
and former deputy army commander General Yot Thepasadin na
Ayuthaya. The official rationale for the coup was the deteriorating
economic situation and Prem's reaction to it; a contributing factor was
the continuing factiousness of the military.[55] Suchit argues that the
coup was actually the result of the build-up of conflict between Prem
and Arthit, that it was the last attempt by the Young Turks to obtain
power again by supporting Arthit against Prem, and finally that the
coup was thwarted because Suchinda's class 5 failed to support it.[56] In

addition, however, the coup group had failed to receive support from the palace, repeating the error of the 1981 coup instigators. The coup would have most clearly benefited General Arthit Kamlang-ek, and there were rumours that he staged the whole thing himself.[57] Still, there is no evidence of this. The fact that the coup occurred while Arthit was abroad reinforced the perception that Arthit was not aware of what was happening in his army. At the trial of the coup conspirators, one witness claimed to have observed Manoon in regular contact with Serm and Yot, receiving orders from them, and also in regular contact with General Pichit. Another beneficiary would have been the man who financed the coup—billionaire Ekkayudh Anchanbutr. And Ekkakudh's motive? Prem's financial policies had been harming his economic interests.[58]

In the aftermath of the 1985 coup, the Young Turks were forever destroyed as any viable military clique—though some of their members would subsequently emerge in politics. Meanwhile, Prem, who was seen to have intensified his favour with the palace, emerged much stronger. Arthit's clout seemed to be diminishing and his relationship with Prem increasingly tense. Finally, the power of Chavalit and class 5 grew by leaps and bounds. The coup also gave Prem a reason to remove Kriangsak's National Democratic Party from his cabinet.

In Spring 1985, Vietnamese and PRK forces succeeded in pushing all Cambodian resistance forces, and 230,000 accompanying civilians, into Thailand. The result was that, following consent from Thai officials, the United Nations built holding camps (with US, Chinese and some European support) for refugee families along the border inside of Thailand. As with all of Thailand's border areas, Thai terrain close to the Thai-Cambodian border was under martial law, which gave the army informal control over the refugee camps. The CIA, however, began to worry that Thailand's policy towards the Cambodian conflict was becoming mired in "military foot-dragging". In an internal report, the agency accused the armed forces of benefiting from the event by using it to justify purchases of sophisticated weaponry such as US F-16 aircraft. The report further accused Thai officers in the field of not "vigorously responding to Vietnamese action along the border", owing to fear, their concern about costs, assumptions that Vietnamese incursions will continue to be limited, taking US aid for granted, and a belief that the Cambodian resistance was simply a "nuisance" rather than a "foreign policy tool".[59] Perhaps more disturbingly, the advent of large numbers of Thai military officials along the Thai-Cambodian border (where martial law was enforced) meant that the Royal Thai

Army controlled, profited from and wanted to sustain the war-driven trade along that border.[60]

The October 1985 reshuffle (see Appendix 4) was important because it saw Arthit Kamlang-ek receive an extension of his term beyond his mandatory retirement.[61] In the aftermath of the 1985 coup attempt, Prem was ever more dependent on Arthit and his followers. Virtually all top postings were thus filled by Arthit loyalists except for incoming chief of staff General Chavalit Yongchaiyudh. The reshuffle was helpful to Chavalit and, at lower levels of the military, his factional ally class 5.

By the end of 1985, indirect military incisions across political parties were growing. Kukrit Pramoj resigned from leading the Social Action party, making way for Prem-loyalist ACM Siddhi Savetsila to succeed him. Thereupon, Prem replaced Social Action Party bigwig Bunteng with Siddhi as deputy prime minister in January 1986. In late December 1985, Arthit's army television and radio stations criticized the Democrat Party, which Arthit saw as too close to Prem. Then, in April 1986, General Arthit began forming alliances in the lower house with Social Action Party faction leaders Bunteng and Sawat Kamprakob as well as Chart Thai's Thawich Glinpratum and Phol Ruengprasertvit (Siam Democratic Party faction leader). Arthit's goal was to try and censure Prem when the House reopened in May 1986. Thus, Prem might resign as Kriangsak had done in 1980 and the parliament could then elect Arthit to finish the premier's term. When the House did reopen, the government was defeated over a diesel fuel tax decree. Bunteng's forty-one-member SAP faction defected from Prem during the vote, a move purportedly backed by Arthit.[62]

In danger of censure, Prem, rather than resigning (and paving the way for Arthit to assume the premiership), dissolved parliament and set new elections for July 1986. Thus ended the Prem II government. Military-backed factions belonging to Social Action and Chart Thai, grouped together, had indirectly forced the dissolution of parliament.[63] Yet, following the dissolution of parliament (and with senior officers pressuring the premier to extend Arthit's term a second time), there were rumours of an impending coup. In addition, Arthit reshuffled regimental and battalion commanders as well as declaring that he was setting up military control centres at various poll stations to "monitor" the election.[64] Prem thereupon, in a surprise move, announced on 27 May that he was immediately dismissing Arthit as army commander, replacing him with army chief of staff General Chavalit Yongchaiyudh, who had been associated with Arthit but had also been a member of the Democratic Soldiers faction, an informal part of Prem's Professional Soldiers clique, and was also close to the ascendant class 5. The king stood by Prem in this decision and, as such, Arthit could only accept Prem's order.[65] As Chavalit had publicly announced that he intended to retire early in two years in order to pursue a political career, most senior officers (other than Arthit) were not perturbed by his elevation. Under orders from Prem, Chavalit's first move was to dismantle Arthit's voting centres. Prem allowed Arthit to continue in the ceremonial post of supreme commander until the end of September 1986. The dismissal capped continuing antagonisms between the two men but came amidst rumours of another impending coup and perhaps owed to Prem's belief that Arthit would use the resources of the military to affect the upcoming election.[66] Arthit did manage to form the Puang Pon Chao Party in the election that followed, though it only gained a single seat. Among those running in the 27 July election were over sixty retired military officials, including thirty former generals.[67] These included ACM Sitthi, Han Leelanond, Kriangsak Chomanand, Narong Kittikachorn, Young Turk coup-maker Prajak Sawangkit, and the general who led the repression of that coup, Tienchai Sirisamphan. Clearly, party politics was emasculating military factional competition among retired officers.

In August 1986, Prem formed a coalition government for the third time, encompassing 232 MPs out of the 347 total. Included in his government were the Democrat, Social Action, Chart Thai and Rassadorn parties. Democrat leader Pichai Rattakul later claimed that army chief Chavalit had "requested" him to support Prem's reappointment.[68] Chart Thai still represented the interests of the former military faction Soi Rajachakru, and was now led by retired general Chatchai Chunhavan, son of the late General Phin. Chatchai enjoyed better relations with Prem and the king than did Chatchai's predecessor (and brother-in-law), General Pramarn Adireksan. The Rassadorn Party's leader was recently retired general Tienchai Sirisampan, who had gained fame for crushing the 1985 coup attempt.

During this period, the Senate continued to be a bastion of military influence. Prem was able to rely on this Senate to support his 1986 election as well as to make sure that no bills could be forwarded into law from the upper house that could threaten the standing of Thailand's arch-royalist ruling elite or the military leadership itself. As Figure 9.3 shows, the 61.9 per cent military reserved domain perpetuated armed forces control across the upper house.

FIGURE 9.3
Thailand's Senate, 1985–91

Type of legislature	Years in office	Appointed or elected	Total number of members and military contingent
Bicameral (Sixth Senate)	1985–91 (terminated by military coup)	Appointed	1985: 260, of which 161 (61.9%) military reserved domain 1987: 267, of which 156 (58.4%) military reserved domain 1989: 267, of which 161 (60.2%) military reserved domain

Source: Paul Chambers, "Superfluous, Irrelevant or Emancipating: Thailand's Evolving Senate Today", *Journal of Current Southeast Asian Affairs* 28, no. 3 (2009): 9, https://d-nb.info/999559311/34.

The October 1986 reshuffle reflected the power vacuum that appeared in the military following the departure of Arthit. Many of Arthit's followers already faced mandatory retirement in 1986, so a new generation of military leadership came to be ascendant. General Phisit, who had been a follower of Arthit, had in 1985–86 proven partial to Prem and Chavalit; he was promoted to be deputy army commander. Generals Sunthorn, Wanchai and Chaichana, friends of Chavalit from his class 1, were promoted to be an assistant army commander, chief of staff and 3rd Army Region commander, respectively. General Pichit, promoted to become an assistant army chief, and seeing how the king had endorsed Chavalit's appointment as army chief, fell in line to support him and Prem. Chavalit already had the backing of class 5, and the members of this clique were jubilant at his promotion. Two of their own, generals Issarapong and Wimol, were appointed as 2nd Army Region and Special Warfare Division commanders, respectively. Finally, Prem mollified the royal family by naming Admiral Supha Kojasenee as supreme commander. Supha was the son-in-law of Field Marsal Thanom Kittikachorn, who continued to be adored by the palace.

Prem's third government, elected in 1986, lasted only two years as factionalism engulfed most of the parties and many Thais were becoming tired of "Premocracy". During this time, General Chavalit Yongchaiyudh and class 5 came to dominate the armed forces. Admiral Supha Gajaseni proved to be a weak navy stop-gap replacement for General Arthit in the post of supreme commander. Thus, in April 1987 (after only six months), Chavalit replaced Supha, ensuring his personal control over the military's top two positions. Chavalit continued to try to grant the other four leading army positions (deputy, two assistants and chief of staff) to his class 1 peers, but Prem overruled him, granting only two of the top five postings to his factional colleagues, in 1986 and 1987.

On 24 January, army chief Chavalit publicly declared that soldiers had a political role to play, and if conditions in Thailand deteriorated below a certain level, the army would have to stage what he described, ambiguously, as a "revolution". Few ordinary people quite understood what Chavalit meant. The military, however, started modifying ISOC so that it would become the dominant institution spearheading democratic values, incorporating politicians, political parties, and farmers' and labour organizations. Some, such as Democrat Surin Pitsuwan, accused Chavalit of planning to lord over civilians and political parties. Kukrit Pramoj, who continuously attacked Chavalit's ideas, compared the new ISOC idea to a politburo, and questioned whether Chavalit was seeking to overthrow Thailand's political system in favour of communism.[69] Chavalit's "revolutionary" ideas led King Bhumipol to begin to despise him.

Seeking to turn the army into a patron of arch-royalist "modernization", Chavalit became a leading proponent of military-led development across Thailand's rural areas. His "Greening of the Northeast" (*Isaan Keaow*) promoted the construction of more irrigation projects and planting trees in the drought-stricken, impoverished region. The programme would, in addition to bringing development, increase the popularity of the military and Chavalit in particular, as he prepared to embark on a political career.[70]

Meanwhile, Thailand's armed forces came to Prem's rescue in a failed no confidence motion on 22 April 1987. Of eighty-four MPs who originally sponsored the motion in parliament, fifteen from five parties withdrew their names on the very day of the vote, leaving the opposition one vote shy of forcing a debate and thus perhaps able to censure Prem's government. To keep the Prem government in power, then army chief of staff (and Chavalit loyalist) General Sunthorn Kongsompong (who later headed the 1991 National Peace-Keeping Council) lobbied Charoen Pattanadamrongjit (Sia Leng), Sunthorn's close drinking companion. Sia Leng, known as the "Dragon of the Northeast", was the purported godfather of Khon Kaen province. He controlled a five-MP faction of the Community Action Party and had close ties to the Thai military.[71] Sia Leng compelled his five-MP group to withdraw support for the no confidence motion, thus allowing the survival of Prem.[72] This was clearly a case where the military had to beg support from a political party faction in order to achieve its goals: preventing a possible House dissolution.

The October 1987 reshuffle (Appendix 4) represented the consolidation of Chavalit's power over senior army posts. He was reappointed supreme commander as well as army commander, and as such became immensely powerful. Chavalit built his support by drawing from graduates of classes 1, 2, 4 and (the largest) 5. His friend and class 1 peer General Wanchai became deputy army chief, while another class 1 confidante, General Jaruai, was promoted to be chief of staff. Prem also gave one assistant army commander position to faction leader General Pichit, and another to class 5 faction leader Suchinda (Suchinda later moved up to deputy commander).[73] Ultimately, under the cliques of Chavalit, Pichit and class 5, Prem's palace-endorsed military remained united.

In December 1987, news emerged of a frontier skirmish between Thai and Lao forces on their shared border. The imbroglio was a resuscitation of the earlier 1984 conflict between the two countries. This time, Thai forces, under the command of then 3rd Army Region commander General Siri Tiwapan, occupied the disputed village of Ban Romklao and even raised the Thai flag over it.[74] Lao forces then drove Thai soldiers out of the village and raised their flag over it. Fighting continued for weeks, eventually ending on 19 February 1988. It later came out that Chavalit had led Thai forces in support of Thai logging companies that had been attacked by Lao forces for encroaching across an ill-defined portion of the Thai-Lao border. The fighting ended with a thousand deaths, a stalemate, and finally a negotiated settlement. But according to one account, the altercation was not about a border dispute. "Basically, a Thai company was harvesting timber in this area, having facilitated this by paying off both Thai and Laos army personnel. The fighting flared when the company, on Thai army advice, stopped paying the Laotians."[75] Many Thais were furious because it seemed as though Thailand had been the loser.

Also, in December 1987, marking the king's birthday, the government released thirty-three out of forty of the 1985 coup-makers. The move, perhaps implemented at the suggestion of the palace, increased unity within the armed forces.

In 1988, amidst allegations of corruption, a defeat against smaller Laotian forces in a border conflict, tension involving a dam proposal, and growing factionalism, especially in the Democrat Party, Prem seemed to suddenly face enemies on all sides. When the Democrats fractured over a copyright bill, the opposition used the opportunity to call for a vote of no confidence against Prem and his government in a move that purportedly received a green light from the military. Indeed, relations between Prem and Chavalit had reportedly become more distant. Amidst tensions with the army, and with the opposition threatening to make personal attacks against Prem's private life, Prem dissolved parliament and called new elections. At this point, the political landscape suddenly seemed to become more unstable. Anti-Prem sentiment had become intense among the public. When journalists suggested that the days of coups in Thailand were gone, Chavalit exploded: "I want to see what powers could keep in check on the Army if I want to do it (that is, launch a coup d'etat)".[76] But he added that he would never foment a putsch without first obtaining permission from the public. Thereupon, Kukrit Pramoj again began vociferously attacking Chavalit for implying he might stage a coup. Finally, parliamentarians and journalists criticized Prem when several military officers visited his home to show their loyalty to him. Thailand seemed to be becoming intensely divided between pro-Prem and anti-Prem groups.

In late July, a general election was held. Of the fifteen parties that won seats, ten were either led by retired military (or police) officers or were linked with Prem. These military-influenced parties included the Democrats (via General Han Leelanond), Social Action (via ACM Siddhi Savetsila), Chart Thai (via generals Chatchai Chunhavan and Pramarn Adireksan), Rassadorn (via General Tienchai Sirisamphan), Puang Chon Chao Thai party (via General Arthit Kamlang-ek and his Khorat friend's son Suwat Liptanpallop), the new Palang Dharma party (via General Chamlong Srimuang), Colonel Phol Rongprasertvit's Saha Prachathipathai party, the small Muanchon party of Captain Chalerm Yubamrong of the police, and the Liberal Party of Colonel Narong Kittikachorn. Prachakorn Thai, though not led by a former military officer (but rather by Samak Sundaravej) was considered pro-military. Chart Thai won the poll.

The election saw no party win a majority in the lower house. As such, it seemed that Prem would ready himself to again serve as prime minister. But, amidst unprecedented protests against his continuing rule, on 27 July he stepped down and allowed Chatchai Chunhavan, leader of Chart Thai, which had captured the most parliamentary seats, to become prime minister.[77] Had it wished, the military could have seated a non-elected prime minister in 1988 given that it controlled the majority of Senate seats and it could probably have found enough lower house MP allies to garner sufficient parliamentary votes. Moreover, the

1978 constitution remained ambiguous on this issue. Thus, the 1988 rise to office of elected PM Chatchai was more a matter of retiring PM General Prem Tinsulanond resigning and the armed forces reluctantly agreeing to it. Immediately thereafter, Prem was appointed by the king to the Privy Council, indicating palace cordiality with the ex-premier.

Prem's 1980–88 tenure as prime minister represented the period when a close yet asymmetrical affiliation between the monarchy and military (with the military as junior partner) came to stabilize its control over Thailand. As a result of the efforts of King Bhumipol and Prem, the armed forces became much more thoroughly connected with the monarchy: the armed forces became a "monarchized military", accruing legitimacy as a result of guarding the palace from any threats to the royal institution. The palace itself was a parallel state, nebulously situated above the law, above democracy, and answerable to no one. Throughout this period, for the apparent good of the monarchy, Prem saw to it that a frail, representative democracy persisted alongside an unelected, retired military premier; a military-dominated, unelected Senate; and a weak lower house. As such, the system was seen as a "semi-democracy", or even a "half-baked democracy".[78] When Prem retired from the premiership in 1988, he left no family relatives. His alleged homosexuality[79] precluded any marriages for Prem, which would have likely led to children and/or in-laws through which he might have expanded his personal, political and/or economic influence. In fact, Prem always liked to say that he was married to the army.[80] In 2023, he does have at least one relative, his great-nephew, the young musician Jaturawit Tinsulanonda.[81]

Notes

1. "'จิตตนาถ' ฝากบทกวีถึงทหารหาญ ตั้งคำถามกับ ผบ.ถึงเช่า สื่อผ่านคำพูด พล.อ.กฤษณ์ สีวะรา ที่ 'ป๋า' เอ่ยปาก" [Jittanat sends poem to the military, asking questions to the army commander through the words of General Krit Sivara that "Pa" speaks], *MGR Online*, 17 March 2014, https://mgronline.com/onlinesection/detail/9570000030018; Noranit Setabutr, หลวงวินิจทัณฑกรรม ต้นสกุล "ติณสูลานนท์" กับรักแรกพบ-ขายทรัพย์สินหมดแต่ส่งลูกเรียนได้ [Luang Winit Thanakam, the ancestor "Tinsulanon" and love at first sight—sold all his assets but was able to send his children to study], Silpa.mag.com, https://www.silpa-mag.com/history/article_33858; William Warren, *Prem Tinsulanonda: Soldier & Statesman* (Bangkok: M.L. Tridosyuth Devakul, 1997), pp. 25–68. See also ที่ระลึกงานพระราชทานเพลิงศพพลอากาศเอกสิทธิ เศวตศิลา [ณ เมรุหลวง หน้าพลับพลาอิศริยาภรณ์ วัดเทพศิรินทราวาส [Commemorative volume from the cremation ceremony of Air Chief Marshal Sitthi Savetsila (at the Royal Crematorium in front of the Issariyaporn Pavilion Wat Thepsirintrawat)], Bangkok, 26 June 2016.

2. Cable from secretary of state to US Embassy, Bangkok, "Anderson Alleges CIA Influence in Palace Guard", February 1975, declassified/released by US Department of State on 5 July 2005, https://thaipoliticalprisoners. files.wordpress.com/2009/01/palace-guards_1975.pdf.

3. See James Ockey, "Thailand's 'Professional Soldiers' and Coup-making: The Coup of 2006", *Crossroads: An Interdisciplinary Journal of Southeast Asian Studies* 19, no. 1 (2007): 95–127, https://www.jstor.org/stable/40860870.

4. Frederick A. Moritz, "Thailand's New Strongman is Also Nation's Mr. Clean", *Christian Science Monitor*, 4 March 1980, https://www.csmonitor.com/1980/0304/030438.html.

5. Larry Niksch, "Thailand in 1980: Confrontation with Vietnam and the Fall of Kriangsak", *Asian Survey* 21, no. 2 (February 1981): 223–26, https://doi.org/10.2307/2643767.

6. Paul Handley, *The King Never Smiles* (New Haven, CT: Yale University Press, 2005), p. 280.

7. Suchit Bunbongkarn, *The Military in Thai Politics, 1981–1986* (Singapore: Institute of Southeast Asian Studies, 1987), p. 13.

8. Chai-anan Samudavanija, *The Thai Young Turks* (Singapore: Institute of Southeast Asian Studies, 1982), p. 51.

9. Handley, *The King Never Smiles*, p. 181.

10. William Warren, *Prem Tinsulanonda: Soldier and Statesman* (Bangkok: M.L. Tridosyuth Devakul, 1997), pp. 134–38.

11. Supaluck Suwanajata, *The Thai Military Coup d'etat: Origins, Withdrawal/ Civilian Control and Perspectives* (PhD dissertation, Claremont Graduate School, Los Angeles, 1994), p. 139.

12. Personal interview with anonymous 21st Infantry Regiment (Queen's Guard) military officer who participated in putting down the coup, Bangkok, 17 November 2021.

13. Warren, *Prem Tinsulanonda*, p. 136.

14. Suchit, *The Military in Thai Politics*, pp. 18–22.

15. In 1981 (following his role in helping to suppress the abortive coup by the Young Turks), Suchinda rose from being a colonel and chief of Intelligence Division to being lieutenant general and assistant chief of staff of the army in 1985. "Obituary: Old Soldier Falls", *The Nation*, 11 February 2010, http://www.nationmultimedia.com.

16. Among the interim clauses, the most important was that the 1978 constitution would not take effect until four years after the 1979 election. Thus, the 1979 election allowed independents to compete, elected MPs could switch parties at will, and political parties remained weak, thus strengthening the power of the military and monarchy relative to them.

17. Rome Bunnag, "'กบฏเมษาฮาวาย' รัฐประหารเรื่องคอขาดบาดตาย! กลับกลายเป็นครึ่งเครง ได้ในเดือนเมษายน!!" ["April Hawaiian rebellion", a coup for the deadliest! It turned out to be joyful in April!!], *MGR Online*, 17 April 2020, https://

mgronline-com.translate.goog/onlinesection/detail/9630000040057?_x_
tr_sl=th&_x_tr_tl=en&_x_tr_hl=th&_x_tr_pto=nui,op,sc.

18. Yoshifumi Tamada, "Coups in Thailand, 1980–1991: Classmates, Internal
Conflicts and Relations with the Government of the Military", *Southeast
Asian Studies* 33, no. 3 (December 1995): 40, https://kyoto-seas.org/
pdf/33/3/330303.pdf.

19. Bunnag, "'กบฏเมษาฮาวาย'" ["April Hawaiian Rebellion"].

20. Personal interview with anonymous 21st Infantry Regiment (Queen's
Guard) military officer who participated in putting down the coup,
Bangkok, 17 November 2021.

21. Robert Kiener, *An Analysis of the 1981 Unsuccessful Thai Coup* (MA thesis,
University of Hong Kong, 1981), p. 64.

22. Kobkua Suwannathat-Pian, *Kings, Country, and Constitutions: Thailand's
Political Development, 1932–2000* (Richmond: Routledge Curzon, 2003),
p. 176.

23. Chai-anan, *The Thai Young Turks*, p. 66.

24. Kiener, *An Analysis of the 1981*, p. 64.

25. Tamada, "Coups in Thailand".

26. "Sixty MPs Join Kriangsak's Party", *Bangkok Post*, 19 June 1981, p. 1.

27. General Prayut Charumanee, 16 ปี ของสงครามยืดเยื้อ [16 years of protracted
war] (Bangkok: Thai Military Bank, 1994).

28. Suchitra Punyaratabandhu-Bhakdi, "Thailand in 1982: General Arthit
Takes Center Stage", *Asian Survey* 23, no. 2 (February 1983): 173, https://
doi.org/10.2307/2644349.

29. Puangthong Pawakapan, *The Central Role of Thailand's Internal Security
Operations Command in the Post-counterinsurgency Period*, Trends in
Southeast Asia, no. 17/2017 (Singapore: ISEAS – Yusof Ishak Institute,
2017), p. 17.

30. Bertil Lintner, *Burma in Revolt: Opium and Insurgency Since 1948*
(Silkworm Books, 1999), pp. 321–33.

31. Puangthong Rungswasdisab, "Thailand's Response to the Cambodian
Genocide", Yale Center for International and Area Studies, Genocide
Studies Working Paper (1999), p. 91, https://www.files.ethz.ch/
isn/46648/GS21.pdf.

32. Kenneth Conboy, *The Cambodian Wars: Clashing Armies and CIA Covert
Operations* (Lawrence: University Press of Kansas, 2013), p. 170.

33. Withaya Sucharithanarugse, "Thailand in 1982: The Year of Living in
Anxiety", in *Southeast Asian Affairs 1983*, edited by Huynh Kim Khanh
(Singapore: Institute of Southeast Asian Studies, 1983), pp. 280–82,
https://www.jstor.org/stable/27908486.

34. Niyom Rathamarit, *Military Governments in Thailand: Their Policies toward
Political Parties* (PhD dissertation, University of Pittsburgh, 1984), pp.
239–42.

35. อนุสรณ์พลเอกอาทิตย์ กำลังเอก «นายพลของแผ่นดิน [Memorial volume from the cremation ritual of General Arthit Kamlang-ek], Issriyaphon pavilion, Wat Thepsirintrawat Temple, Bangkok, 13 March 2016.

36. Tamada, "Coups in Thailand", p. 41.

37 Pisan Suriyamongkol, *Institutionalization of Democratic Political Processes in Thailand: A Three-Pronged Democratic Polity* (Bangkok: NIDA, 1988), pp. 65–68; Suchit, *The Military in Thai Politics*, pp. 46–56.

38. Niyom, *Military Governments*, pp. 249, 256.

39. Ibid., pp. 249, 256, 260–61.

40. Suchitra Punyaratabandhu-Bhakdi, "Thailand in 1983: Democracy, Thai Style", *Asian Survey* 24, no. 2 (February 1984): 190, https://doi.org/10.2307/2644437.

41. Tom Fawthrop and Helen Jarvis, *Getting Away with Genocide? Elusive Justice and the Khmer Rouge Tribunal* (Sydney: University of New South Wales Press, 2005), p. 59.

42. Conboy, *The Cambodian Wars*, pp. 181–82.

43. Christopher Wren, "Three Villages are Disputed on Thai-Laotian Border", *New York Times*, 28 June 1984, https://www.nytimes.com/1984/06/28/world/3-villages-are-disputed-on-thai-laotian-border.html.

44. CIA, "Thailand's Military: The Powerbrokers' Role in Transition: An Intelligence Assessment", October 1985, p. 5, https://www.cia.gov/readingroom/docs/CIA-RDP86T00590R000300510002-5.pdf.

45. Hong Lysa, "Thailand in 1984: Towards a Political Modus Vivendi", in *Southeast Asian Affairs 1985*, edited by Lim Joo-Jock (Singapore: Institute of Southeast Asian Studies, 1985), p. 323, https://www.jstor.org/stable/27908534; Handley, *The King Never Smiles*, p. 308.

46. Suchit, *The Military in Thai Politics*, p. 19.

47. Pisan, *Institutionalization of Democratic*, pp. 65–68; Suchit, *The Military in Thai Politics*, pp. 40–46.

48. CIA, "Thailand's Military: The Powerbrokers' Role in Transition: An Intelligence Assessment", October 1985, p. 5, https://www.cia.gov/readingroom/docs/CIA-RDP86T00590R000300510002-5.pdf.

49. Suchit, *The Military in Thai Politics*, p. 43

50. Duncan McCargo, *Chamlong Srimuang and the New Thai Politics* (London: Hurst, 1997), p. 54.

51. Sathien Chantimathorn, เส้นทางสู่อำนาจมนูญ รูปขจร อาทิตย์ กำลังเอก ใต้เงาเปรม ติณสูลานนท์ [The path to power: Manoon Rupkajorn, Arthit Kamlang-ek under the shadow of Prem Tinsulanonda] (Bangkok: Matichon, 2006).

52. Personal interview with anonymous 21st Infantry Regiment (Queen's Guard) military officer who participated in putting down the 1981 coup, Bangkok, 17 November 2021.

53. นายพล 5 แผ่นดิน บิดาแห่งทหารพลร่ม พลเอก เทียนชัย สิริสัมพันธ์ : อนุสรณ์งานพระราชทาน เพลิงศพ พลเอก เทียนชัย สิริสัมพันธ์ [General of the 5 Lands, Father of the Paratroopers, General Tianchai Sirisamphan: The royal cremation memorial ceremony of General Tianchai Sirisamphan], Bangkok, 2020.

54. Chulacheeb Chinwanno, "Thailand in 1985: Prem Continues to Survive", in *Southeast Asian Affairs 1986*, edited by Lim Joo-Jock (Singapore: Institute of Southeast Asian Studies, 1986), p. 318, https://www.jstor.org/stable/27908558.

55. Charles F. Keyes, *Thailand: Buddhist Kingdom as Modern Nation-State* (Boulder, CO: Westview, 1989), p. 106.

56. Suchit Bunbongkarn, *State of the Nation: Thailand* (Singapore: Institute of Southeast Asian Studies, 1996), pp. 49–50.

57. Joseph Wright, *The Balancing Act: A History of Modern Thailand* (Bangkok: Asia Books, 1991), pp. 293–94.

58. Ibid., p. 300.

59. CIA, "Thailand: Trouble ahead for Cambodian Policy?", 2 May 1985, https://www.cia.gov/readingroom/docs/CIA-RDP85T01058R000101410001-9.pdf.

60. Lindsay French, "From Politics to Economics at the Thai-Cambodian Border: *Plus, Ça Change*", *International Journal of Politics, Culture, and Society* 15, no. 3 (Spring 2002): 447, https://www.jstor.org/stable/20020126.

61. Pornsan Kamlang-ek, ที่ระลึกในงานพระราชทานเพลิงศพ พลเอกอาทิตย์ กำลังเอก ม.ป.ช., ม.ว.ม., ท.จ.ว. ณ เมรุหลวงหน้าพลับพลาอิศริยาภรณ์ วัดเทพศิรินทราวาส กรุงเทพมหานคร วันอาทิตย์ที่ 13 มีนาคม พ.ศ. 2559 [Commemorative volume from the cremation ceremony of General Athit Kamlang-ek, Wat Thepsirintrawat Bangkok, 13 March 2016] (Bangkok: Rungsil 2016).

62. Clark Neher, "Thailand in 1986: Prem, Parliament, and Political Pragmatism", *Asian Survey* 27, no. 2 (February 1987): 221–22, https://doi.org/10.2307/2644616.

63. Suchit Bunbongkorn, "The Military in the Participant Politics of Thailand", International Conference on Thai Studies, 6 July 1987, Canberra, Australia, pp. 5–6; Suchit, *The Military in Thai Politics*, 1987, pp. 44–46.

64. Ananda Rajah, "Thailand in 1986: Change and Continuity, Yet Again", in *Southeast Asian Affairs 1987*, edited by M. Ayoob (Singapore: Institute of Southeast Asian Studies, 1987), p. 315, https://www.jstor.org/stable/27908582.

65. Kobkua, *Kings, Country and Constitutions*, p. 176.

66. Suchit, *The Military in Thai Politics*, p. 45.

67. William Branigin, "Voters Set to Elect Parliament in Thailand", *Washington Post*, 27 July 1986, https://www.washingtonpost.com/archive/politics/1986/07/27/voters-set-to-elect-parliament-in-thailand/2ecc22d5-400e-4045-bf90-2cf2cdfcc40d/.

68. Ananda, 1987, p. 316.

69. Kusuma Snitwongse, "Thailand's Year of Stability: Illusion or Reality?", in *Southeast Asian Affairs 1988*, edited by M. Ayoob and Ng Chee Yuen (Singapore: Institute of Southeast Asian Studies, 1988), pp. 274–75, https://www.jstor.org/stable/27911960.

70. Neher, "Thailand in 1987, *Asian Survey* 28, no. 2 (February 1988): 196, https://doi.org/10.2307/2644820.

71. Sia Leng allegedly once said the following: "I don't know what political parties mean; I understand only factions [*puak*] … and I'd rather keep them." *Manager* [*MGR Online*] 5, no. 49 (October 1987); Somrudee Nicro, "Thailand's NIC Democracy", *Pacific Affairs* 66, no. 2 (1993): 178. In the article, Dr Nicro translates *puak* as "associates".

72. Sia Leng had been Boonchu Rojanasatien's financial backer ever since Boonchu had been with the Social Action Party. When Boonchu formed the Community Action Party, Sia Leng moved with him. But following Sia Leng's interference in the censure motion in 1987, Boonchu parted ways with him. Eventually, the CAP expelled the five rebel MPs. Sia Leng then simply withdrew his support from the CAP. In the 1988 election, he supported the Rassadorn Party. Sia Leng purportedly enriched himself though his association with General Chavalit Yongchaiyudh's *Isan Khieo* ("Green Northeast") development project. In the elections of March 1992, September 1992, 1995 and 1996, Sia Lang was a major financier and campaign coordinator in the Northeast for Chavalit's New Aspiration Party. Pasuk Pongpaichit and Sungsidh Piriyarangsan, *Corruption and Democracy in Thailand* (Bangkok: Chulalongkorn University, 1994).

73. Tamada, "Coups in Thailand", p. 330.

74. Personal interview with General Siri Tiwapan, 3 November 2022.

75. Robert Karniol, quoted in Isabelle Roughol, "Border Standoff Echoes 1980s Thai-Lao Conflict", *Cambodia Daily*, 28 October 2008, https://english.cambodiadaily.com/news/border-standoff-echoes-1980s-thai-lao-conflict-62276/.

76. Yos Santasombat, "The End of Premocracy in Thailand", in *Southeast Asian Affairs 1989*, edited by Ng Chee Yuen (Singapore: Institute of Southeast Asian Studies, 1989), p. 320, https://www.jstor.org/stable/27911983.

77. Handley, *The King Never Smiles*, p. 325; Niroj Khokongprasert, *Faction Politics: A Study of Factionalism in the Democrat Party* (in Thai) (MA dissertation, Chulalongkorn University, 1990), pp. 93–110.

78. See Yos, "The End of Premocracy", pp. 317, 325.

79. *The Independent*, "Prem Tinsulanonda" (obituary), 2 June 2019, https://www.independent.ie/life/prem-tinsulanonda-38171080.html.

80. Moritz, "Thailand's New Strong Man".

81. Switchaya Chompoophat, "My Relationship with Great Uncle is Music: Blood, Musician, Life 'Tinsulanonda'", *MGR Online*, 10 June 2019, https://mgronline.com/live/detail/9620000054477.

Chapter Ten

Sunthorn, Suchinda and "Black May" (1988–92)

The ascension to office of an elected civilian prime minister in 1988 suggested that democracy had finally arrived in Thailand in line with other democratization experiences throughout the world in the late 1980s. Though 1988 represented a watershed moment and even an opening or aperture for the advent of elected civilian rule, arch-royalist military praetorianism stood in the shadows. For this reason, political space was to have its constraints: Thailand's post-1988 democracy was to be a façade—even more limited than the guided democracy of post-1992.

On 4 August 1988, Chatchai Chunhavan took office, becoming the first elected civilian prime minister since 1976—despite being a retired general. But his electoral rise to office was slightly ironic. Had Field Marshal Sarit Thanarat failed in his 1957 coup against Phibun, Phao, Phin and Phin's Soi Rajakru clique, Chatchai might himself have risen to power by putsch-oriented means. Chatchai, as the son of 1948–54 army commander Field Marshal Phin Chunhavan, had as a child studied at the prestigious Dipsirin School (where Krit Sivara and Pramarn also studied) before entering Chulachomklao Royal Military Academy in 1939. With Thailand under Prime Minister Phibun Songkram, Chatchai graduated during World War II and served under his father, Field Marshal Phin Chunhavan, who commanded the Phayap Army (Army of the Northwest). During this period, Chatchai met several future military strongmen, including Sarit Thanarat, Thanom Kittikachorn, Praphas Charusatien and Krit Sivara. Chatchai saw action in Thailand's invasion of the Shan States of Burma. But after World War II, he studied at Fort Knox, Kentucky, USA. He was military attaché in Washington in 1949. But given his father's clout, Chatchai shot up the ranks to become a major-general that year (he was only 31). In fact, his father, Phin, became army commander in 1948, serving until 1954. That said, Phin had led the coup that overthrew Thailand's first democracy in 1947. Chatchai played a small supportive role in that putsch. In the 1951 "silent" or "radio" coup, Phin's Soi Rajakru faction consolidated its power over the country.[1] Meanwhile, Chatchai served in the Korean War (1950–53) as the commander of the 1st Cavalry Battalion.[2]

During this time, General Sarit Thanarat, who had led the principal unit that ensured the success of the 1947 coup, had been extending his power. In 1954 he succeeded Phin as army commander. At this point, Sarit's Sisao Thewes faction increasingly jousted with the Soi Rajakru clique for economic and political gain. Phin's Soi Rajakru had been grooming his son Chatchai as a future leader, while two of his daughters were married to powerful in-laws: Kunying Udomlak had married police director general Phao Sriyanond, and Tanpuying Jaroen Adireksan had married General Pramarn Adireksan. Indeed, Chatchai could, in his own right, eventually have become the military strongman of Thailand (linked with Phao and Pramarn).

This was not to be, however, because Phin's Soi Rajakru military faction was trumped by Field Marshal Sarit Thanarat's Sisao Thewes faction via Sarit's 1957 coup. Chatchai was forced to retire from the military. He was then compelled to enter Thailand's diplomatic service, where he served as ambassador in six postings. In 1972, Prime Minister Thanom Kittikachorn appointed Chatchai as deputy foreign minister. He continued in this post during the administration of appointed PM Sanya Dharmmasakdi. The year 1974 saw Chatchai, alongside his brothers-in-law General Pramarn and General Siri Siriyothin, organize and register Chart Thai (Thai Nation), a conservative, army-friendly political party. Chatchai was the foreign minister under Prime Minister M.R. Kukrit Pramoj's 1975–76 government, then was industry minister in M.R. Seni Pramoj's 1976 government. Chatchai served again as industry minister under the Prem Tinsulanonda government, was subsequently in the opposition, and took over from Pramarn as party leader in 1986[3] before ascending to the premiership in 1988.

But, of course, in 1988, Chatchai was not the young potential strongman-to-be of 1957, but rather the aging statesman. There had been a lot of water under the bridge in the three decades since Phibun,

Phao and Phin had dominated Thailand. Meanwhile, given Chart Thai's right-wing bent, the Soi Rajakru clan seemed to have proven its loyalty to the Crown. Besides this, Chatchai was even married to Boonruen Chunhavan, a step-sister of King Bhumipol (she died in 2021 at age 101). The two had two children, including son Kraisak Chunhavan, a future Thai senator. But Chatchai did not act as beholden to the king as Prem had, and that apparently grated on the palace.[4] Moreover, that Chatchai was a part of Soi Rajakru did not endear him to the king.

The Thai democracy over which Chatchai took charge in 1988 remained weak, with factions and fragile parties standing at the apex of governance. At the same time, the Senate remained an appointed body, mostly chosen from the military—as commanded by army chief Chavalit Yongchaiduh.[5] Meanwhile, Thailand's armed forces continued to be a key player, though army commander Chavalit publicly guaranteed that the military would not get involved in politics or stage a coup.[6] Reflecting his long civilian business career, Chatchai filled almost all cabinet seats with businessmen/politicians, which was a different approach than Prem's given the latter's propensity to often turn to retired soldiers or civilian bureaucrats. Where Prem had retired from the premiership embroiled in a tense relationship with Chavalit, Chatchai took office appeasing the army commander. He offered Chavalit the defence minister's portfolio and, when Chavalit refused (whereupon Chatchai formally took the post), he informally permitted the army chief to control military promotions, influence parts of the military budget, and even sit in on all cabinet meetings.[7] Moreover, Chatchai knew of Chavalit's dream of becoming a civilian prime minister through the "front door" of elections, succeeding Chatchai. As a result, Chatchai perceived that he could count on Chavalit to protect his government from any military coup attempts.

In foreign policy, Chatchai came to office as the Cold War neared its end. As such, upon taking office in July 1988, Chatchai declared his intention to turn Indochina "from a battlefield into a marketplace".[8] Chatchai increasingly sought to improve relations with Vietnam. Such a position was not shared by foreign minister (and Prem-favourite) ACM Siddhi Savetsila[9] or most of the military senior brass. Though Siddhi at least initially continued on as foreign minister (until August 1990), his voice began to lose influence amidst the preferences of Chatchai and Chavalit. Chatchai made attempts at starting peace talks with Vietnam in an effort to extricate its army from Cambodia. But this was made difficult by opposition from China and increased purchases of Chinese military hardware by the Chavalit-led Royal Thai Armed

Forces. Under the Chatchai government, direct Thai military relations with the China-subsidized Khmer Rouge continued. Continuing military repression in Burma in 1988 proved to be embarrassing to Chatchai, who had practised "constructive engagement". Though, under Prem, Thailand and Burma had been close, the Burmese military repression of September 1988 forced Chavalit to speak against the Burmese junta, claiming he would never visit that country until there was an election.[10]

The October 1988 military reshuffle represented a sweet victory for Chavalit Yongchaiyudh as he continued to consolidate his preferred military appointments with himself as army commander and supreme commander. Also victorious was his Chulachomklao Military Academy class 1 (the first Thai army class to use the United States West Point curriculum): deputy army commander General Wanchai and army chief of staff General Jaruai, class peers and friends of Chavalit, continued on in their postings. Chavalit also bolstered the standing of class 5, his erstwhile allies. Thus, three class 5 members continued on in leading army posts: class valedictorian General Suchinda serving as assistant army chief, his brother-in-law General Issarapong Noonpakdi serving in the post of 2nd Army Region commander, and General Wimol serving as Special Warfare Division commander. Chavalit gave a final one-year post in the slot of permanent minister of defence to his friend General Wichit Wichitsongkram.

Chavalit's reshuffle triumph would have been more golden had it not been immediately followed by international revelations about purported Thai military corruption pertaining to the CIA funds designated for supporting the non-communist Cambodian insurgent forces. In late October, a report appeared in the US newspaper the *Washington Post* alleging that Thai military officers had skimmed US$3.5 million from the 1988–89 US$12 million CIA covert assistance programme. From Chavalit on down, the Thai military hierarchy vehemently denied the charge. Chavalit even publicly told the *Washington Post* editor to "Go to Hell." Some thought the revelation was Washington's revenge for Chavalit's foreign policy gambit to move Thailand closer to China. The news story stated that the scandal had surfaced in 1987 following a report of auditors for the US Senate Intelligence Committee.[11] Actually, just prior to the 24 July 1988 election, the corruption became known to then prime minister Prem, his National Security Council secretary-general Prasong Soonsiri, United States ambassador William Brown and Bangkok CIA station chief Harry Slifer. The four met to discuss the ramifications of the final Senate report, issued at the beginning of July. As one of his last acts in office, Prem demanded that Chavalit initiate an investigation. But after Prem's sudden retirement that month, moves to investigate faded. Although Prem's successor Chatchai and Chavalit promised an investigation, one was never forthcoming. By October, allegations grew that senior army officials were involved in the skimming of both Chinese and US covert assistance to the Cambodian insurgents. In fact, according to a well-informed Western military official, at least with regard to the Chinese aid, Thai military officers had been skimming 10–15 per cent of that aid each year with no one complaining. The skimming could also have been happening to US aid since its inception. One friend of Chavalit, who was at the rank of general and who may have been involved in the corruption, was suddenly removed from the Thai military committee tasked with distributing the aid. Another officer involved, also a Chavalit loyalist, Colonel Supachai Rodpothong, had suddenly died in a helicopter accident only days prior to the July release of the US Senate report. Replacing the general, and also becoming chair of a new working group on Cambodia, was Prem-confidant General Surayud Chulanond.[12] Meanwhile, the Reagan administration succeeded in seeing to it that CIA assistance for the Cambodian war continued to be allocated through Congress. But there was now more CIA involvement in watching how the Thai military disbursed the money.

In 1989, foreign policy increasingly shifted towards a balancing among global powers. In January 1989, Chatchai invited Cambodian prime minister Hun Sen to Bangkok as his guest. With Thailand beginning to launch more economic agreements with its neighbours in mainland Southeast Asia, army chief Chavalit declared on 25 January that the military wanted to turn the region into a *Suwannaphum*, with Thailand as a financial and trade centre.

Thai relations with Burma (which its military masters renamed as Myanmar in 1989) improved markedly in 1989. Breaking an international boycott following the Burmese military massacre of September, Chavalit led a military delegation to Yangon in December 1988. Economic exchanges between the two countries followed. When General Than Shwe followed up with a visit to Bangkok in April 1989, the Thai army officially referred to it as "a visit by close friends and relatives".[13] Clearly, Thai-Myanmar relations were predicated upon comprehensive cordiality and brotherliness between the two countries' militaries.

Regarding the United States, relations with Washington continued to sour, with Chatchai demanding more US investment in Thailand.

Meanwhile, Chatchai and Siddhi did finally agree to approach the United Nations to convince the body to recognize Cambodian resistance forces, including the Khmer Rouge. As for China, Chatchai was silent on Beijing's Tiananmen Square massacre in 1989. This was no surprise as Chavalit was increasingly purchasing more Chinese military hardware and did not want to upset the Chinese.

Meanwhile, the army commander continued to publicly showcase his capacities to lead Thailand. In early November, following heavy flooding, he directed the army to offer immediate relief, while other state agencies seemed slow and incapable. Throughout the year, rumours grew about Chavalit deciding that he would soon retire and establish a political party. Such gossip coincided with the sudden creation of a new military-linked party called Pak Pracha Rat (National People's Party)—an interesting name given that a military proxy party with a similar name was later established in 2018. Chavalit now increasingly called for more democracy, a war on corruption and poverty, and grassroots development.[14] Chavalit's growing forays into public debates paralleled his moves to launch a party, though he could not decide when he would do so. What Chavalit wanted "was to become Prime Minister with the support of the military but without resorting to a coup d'etat".[15] In other words, Chavalit wanted to become an elected prime minister who was unquestionably backed by the military. A budding politician, Chavalit found less time for his military duties and thus increasingly considered an early military retirement. He cultivated the impression that he was a people's soldier, a politician, or even a "Confucius" for Thailand.[16]

Chatchai worked hard to cultivate support from Chavalit. He appointed the army chief's close friend and military classmate General Panya Singsakda as secretary-general of the Prime Minister's Office. Nevertheless, by mid-1989, Police Captain Chalerm Yubamrung, minister to the Office of the Prime Minister, had already made enemies with Chavalit by constantly attacking the pro-Chavalit newspaper *Thai Rath*. Chalerm had earlier attacked Chavalit's friend 1st Army Division commander General Mongkol Ampornpisit for apparently allowing the use of army radio to attack the government.[17] Also in 1989, the legislature made an unprecedented attempt to cut the military budget, while opposition leaders demanded that the armed forces demonstrate financial accountability. Several members of parliament called for a reduced military, and the Chatchai government began rejecting plans for more military facilities. Meanwhile, civilian legislators were able to turn back a military suggestion to change the electoral system.

At the same time, conservatives within the armed forces adamantly opposed Chatchai's policy to normalize relations with former Cold War enemies Vietnam, Cambodia and Laos. Moreover, military officers opposed Chatchai's incorporation of alleged "left-wing" intellectuals as governmental advisors. But Chatchai was a popular politician. In April 1989, the now retired General Han Leelanond, who had left the Democrat Party, led eight other Prachachon party MP defectors to join Chatchai's ruling coalition. Also in April, the prime minister appointed a new roster of senators. Since the 1978 constitution had taken effect, prime ministers Kriangsak and Prem had ensured that mostly military officials would become senators. Now, with a civilian helming the government, many in civil society considered that Chatchai should either amend the constitution to create elected senators or leave the Senate vacant. But, in the end, following enormous pressure from the armed forces, the premier appointed military-preferred candidates (see Figure 10.1).

Meanwhile, the new government seemed to be trying to make incisions across the interests of the military as Chatchai sought to have the president of the Senate (which was dominated by military officers) come directly from the lower house. The Royal Thai Air Force (RTAF) successfully fought back against Chatchai's efforts to have the RTAF's Thai Airways International publicly listed on the Stock Exchange of Thailand. Chatchai also earned the ire of the military's patron—the palace—when he allowed the TPI Group to compete with the monarch-owned Siam Cement Group in the building materials and petrochemicals market. To some extent, Chatchai's personal popularity helped him to succeed in such risky policy decisions. But other than the leader himself, most Thais did not find Chatchai's government to

FIGURE 10.1
Thailand's Senate, 1989–91

House type (Senate number)	Years	Method of selection	Third rotation of appointments
Bicameral (Sixth Senate)	1986–91 (terminated by military coup)	Appointed	1989: 267, of which 161 (60.2%) military reserved domain

Source: Paul Chambers, "Superfluous, Irrelevant or Emancipating: Thailand's Evolving Senate Today", *Journal of Current Southeast Asian Affairs* 28, 3 (2009): 9, https://d-nb.info/999559311/34.

be very redeeming. It was much more under the control of business politicians than Prem's had been, replacing a system of patronage that had depended upon entrenched bureaucrats. Yet, after Prem's apparent stable prosperity, there seemed now to be much more corruption than ever before.[18] The negative image of Chatchai's seemingly corrupt government played into the hands of his military enemies (for example, General Suchinda Kraprayoon) who had desperately been seeking an issue upon which to attack it. As the label of "corruption" increasingly festered around Chatchai, Chavalit started to join in the attacks. Both Suchinda and Chavalit began to criticize Chatchai—criticism that was supported by many Thais.

The October 1989 military reshuffle (see Appendix 4), as with that of 1988, saw Chavalit consolidate his power over the armed forces.[19] Though the army commander would reach mandatory retirement in 1992, he had pledged time and again to retire early as he wanted to enter politics. Initially he had planned to leave military service in 1988, but he had been convinced by Prem to stay on. In 1989, Chatchai refused to accept Chavalit's resignation, while Chavalit himself seemed to still be unsure as to when exactly his retirement would happen.[20] In fact, class 5 was pressuring Chavalit to leave the military. The 1989 reshuffle accomplished these goals by placing Suchinda Kraprayoon of class 5 in the post of deputy army commander, putting his brother-in-law Issarapong Noonpakdi in place as assistant army commander and their trusted class 5 comrade Sran Sripen in the strategic posting of 1st Army Region commander. Then, in December 1989, Chavalit announced he would soon be retiring and that deputy army chief General Suchinda Kraprayoon would be his successor. The move harked back to General Krit Sivara's October 1975 mandatory retirement and preparation for a political career (a path followed by generals Kriangsak and Arthit). To protect his government from what was perceived to be a much more rigid army chief, Chatchai invited Chavalit to become defence minister upon the latter's impending retirement in March 1990. Chavalit accepted.

Chatchai also quickly began to bolster his standing in security circles. On 2 January, he announced that he wanted Chavalit to succeed him as prime minister, but suggested that the army chief first retire, become prime minister, and then be elected as a member of parliament. Nevertheless, Chatchai's brother-in-law General Pramarn Adireksan was unhappy with this as he himself wanted to succeed Chatchai as premier. But Chatchai, like Kukrit Pramoj before him, an excellent coalition balancer, found ways to handle Pramarn, appointing him as minister of industry.[21] Despite his earlier castigations against the government, on 30 March 1990, Chavalit resigned from the military and was immediately appointed by Chatchai as both an independent (non-party) deputy prime minister and the defence minister.[22]

His retirement paved the way for a friend of Chavalit's to succeed him, while Chavalit's Chulachomklao Academy class 5 increasingly dominated the army. Thus, Chavalit's class 1 confidant General Sunthorn Kongpongsong replaced him as supreme commander, while class 5 valedictorian General Suchinda Kraprayoon became army chief.

Who was Sunthorn? He was a rough-and-tumble Thai army officer known for being sincere, perhaps quick-tempered, seemingly afraid of nothing, and someone you would want on your side in a fight. He always wore a tight-fitting uniform, smoked cigarettes, and he had a personal motto that was "ไม่ฆ่าน้อง ไม่ฟ้องนาย ไม่ขายเพื่อน" (Don't kill your brother, don't sue people, and don't sell out your friends). He was born on 31 August 1931 in what is today the Bang Khen district of Bangkok. He was the first child of Squadron Captain Supachai Kongsompong and Mrs Lamoon Kongsompong. (He had three other siblings; two male and one female.) He studied at Don Mueang High School (an air force institution). Later, during World War II, his father had to move to Saraburi Province. General Sunthorn Kongsompong therefore moved to study at Saraburi Boys' School (currently Saraburi Pittaya School). Following this, he studied at the prestigious Suankularb Wittayalai School in Bangok. In 1949, with help from his father, he was able to enter Chulachomklao Royal Military Academy, in class 1. Sunthorn's class peers included his close friend General Chavalit Yongchaiyudh. Sunthorn later studied at Fort Benning in the United States. He learned to fly aircraft, including helicopters, and instructed some members of Thailand's royal family in helicopter piloting. Sunthorn had begun his service as a 2nd lieutenant in 1953, participating in Thailand's contingent in the Korean War that year. By 1968 he was the head of the 1st Brigade Forces Division and he served with Thai forces in the Vietnam war in 1969. By 1974 he was the chief of staff of the Special Warfare Centre, where he commanded future army commanders Surayud Chulanond and Sonthi Boonyaratklin. Ten years later he was commander of the Special Warfare Command. In 1986 he became assistant commander of the army; in 1987, army chief of staff; and in 1990, supreme commander.[23] His son, Apirat Kongsompong, later became army commander. Sunthorn's family is notable for its numerous senior military officers (see Sunthorn's family tree in Figure 10.2).

FIGURE 10.2
Sunthorn's Family Tree

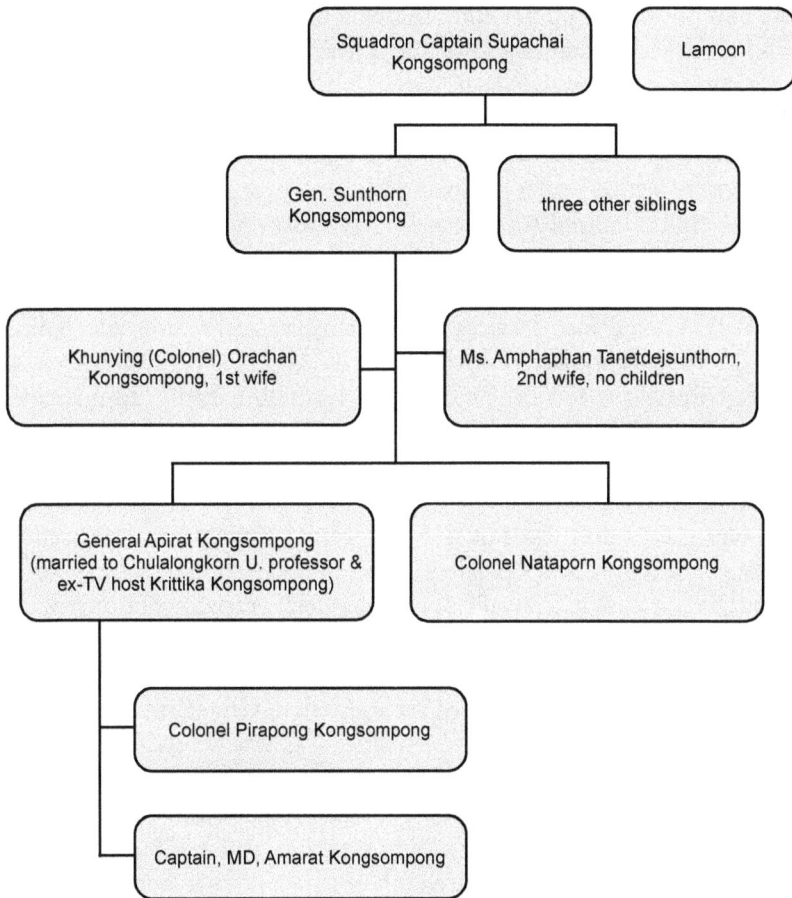

```
┌─────────────────────────┐   ┌──────────────┐
│ Squadron Captain Supachai│   │   Lamoon     │
│     Kongsompong          │   │              │
└─────────────────────────┘   └──────────────┘
           │
┌──────────────────┐   ┌──────────────────┐
│  Gen. Sunthorn   │   │ three other      │
│  Kongsompong     │   │ siblings         │
└──────────────────┘   └──────────────────┘

┌──────────────────────────┐   ┌────────────────────────────────┐
│ Khunying (Colonel) Orachan│   │ Ms. Amphaphan Tanetdejsunthorn,│
│ Kongsompong, 1st wife     │   │ 2nd wife, no children          │
└──────────────────────────┘   └────────────────────────────────┘

┌────────────────────────────────┐   ┌──────────────────────────┐
│ General Apirat Kongsompong      │   │ Colonel Nataporn         │
│ (married to Chulalongkorn U.    │   │ Kongsompong              │
│ professor & ex-TV host Krittika │   │                          │
│ Kongsompong)                    │   │                          │
└────────────────────────────────┘   └──────────────────────────┘

┌──────────────────────────────┐
│ Colonel Pirapong Kongsompong │
└──────────────────────────────┘

┌──────────────────────────────────┐
│ Captain, MD, Amarat Kongsompong  │
└──────────────────────────────────┘
```

Suchinda's accession to the army commander's slot was particularly significant given that he was a member of army class 5. The ideology of class 5 was ultra-conservative and arch-royalist, seeing the army as a necessary bulwark in national security but also deserving of political and economic privileges at the near pinnacle of Thai society.[24] The pre-announcement of Suchinda's succession ensured that the transition would be smooth. In April 1990, graduates from Chulachomklao class 5 (1958) were given almost every top position in Thailand's armed forces. As Tamada states, the domination by class 5 of "important posts in the Army was unprecedented".[25]

But the connections of class 5 went beyond the army. Non-army officers who had started military cadet school in 1953 (at the time that Chulachomklao Military Academy class 5 did) also became part of the new powerful military elite. These included ACM Kaset Rojananil, who became commander of the Royal Thai Air Force and later supreme commander; Admiral Prapas Kritanachan, who became navy commander and defence minister; and Police General Sawat Amornwiwat, who became head of the Royal Thai Police. Sawat's brother was an intra-party faction leader in Chiang Mai and became pro-Thaksin Pheu Thai party leader in 2019. Cross-service unity within class 5 was held together by code as well—Club 0143. The number 0143 comes from three numbers: 01 = the year that they graduated (2501 Buddhist Year [1958]); 4 = the four services of the army, air force, navy and police; and 3 = three schools.

Suchinda proved to be a more hard-line army commander than Chavalit.[26] As he fortified the military leadership with his minions, he menacingly emphasized that he would not allow civilian politicians to interfere in the armed forces, implied that any military corruption was not the business of civilians, and refused to renounce any future coup. Meanwhile, upon becoming a member of Chatchai's cabinet, Chavalit could not help persisting in criticizing other ministers. Indeed, he criticized Chalerm Yubamrung for being convicted by the Anti-Corruption Commission in May 1990. Thereupon, Chalerm publicly retorted that Chavalit's wife was a "walking jewellery box". In utter anger, Chavalit claimed he had lost dignity. Outraged by Chalerm, senior military officials stated that he had damaged the prestige of the armed forces. They were also critical of Chatchai for doing nothing about Chalerm's jibes. Thereupon, Suchinda met privately with Chatchai and also Privy Counsellor Prem. But though pressure was apparently placed on the prime minister to resign, he refused to leave office, and after visiting with the king, remained the head of government. At this point, on 11 June 1990, Chavalit resigned as defence minister. But Chatchai's strategy eventually unravelled. Following Chavalit's resignation, over ten thousand officers of the 1st Infantry division angrily demonstrated at the 11th Regiment headquarters in Ban Khen, and the two army-run television stations advertised the army's anger. The protest led to temporary jitters of a possible putsch. Nevertheless, supreme commander General Sunthorn Kongsompong dispelled these coup rumours. Days later, Chatchai offered to appoint Chavalit as his personal advisor, but Chavalit rejected this while also resigning as the government's whip in the appointed Senate. Thereupon, Chatchai resumed the post of defence minister.[27]

For his part, Chavalit began to work vigorously towards establishing his own political party—it was registered as New Aspiration Party (NAP) in September. NAP immediately began to prepare for the next general election, attracting numerous clients of Chavalit: ex-soldiers, civilian bureaucrats, business people, and godfathers of rural voting districts.[28]

Seeking to strengthen his government, Chatchai began seeking an alliance with Prem. Indeed, he appointed "three Prem and palace associates" in August 1990.[29] On 25 August, Chatchai brought into the coalition the small Puang Chao Chon Thai party in order to appoint its leader, General Arthit Kamlang-ek, to be deputy prime minister, the post Chavalit had turned down.

The October 1990 military reshuffle (see Appendix 4) marked a further consolidation of the power of class 5 over top security postings. The 3rd Army Region's commander, General Siri Tiwapan, retired early to join Chavalit Yongchaiyudh's New Aspiration Party and was replaced by yet another member of class 5—General Pairoj Jano-urai. At the same time, General Chainarong Noonpakdi, who had commanded the 2nd Infantry Division (Buraphapayak faction) and was the younger cousin of General Issarapong Noonpakdi (as well as an in-law of General Suchinda Kraprayoon), was appointed to become 1st Division commander. Class 5, backed up by class 11 and class 1, now predominated in the top military postings.

In November 1990, Chalerm Yubamrung, minister to the Office of the Prime Minister, became involved in another crisis when soldiers seized a truck attached to his ministry on the grounds of eavesdropping on military communications. An angry Suchinda, tired of civilian meddling, demanded Chalerm's resignation. But Chatchai, backed by Arthit, baulked at dismissing Chalerm. Thereupon, senior military officials began to seek Chatchai's own resignation. Chatchai was rumoured to be seeking the king's help in removing both Sunthorn and Suchinda. At that point, General Samphao Chusri, Anti-Aircraft Artillery Division commander and a Suchinda confidant, issued a veiled threat of a coup to Chatchai if any such purge was proposed.[30] Chatchai visited the king about the issue and resigned on 8 December. But the monarch immediately reappointed Chatchai and his cabinet on 9 December, though Chatchai ousted Chalerm from the new Council of Ministers.[31] With the king's tepid support, the rumours of a coup faded for the moment. Meanwhile, Chatchai refused to give in to an extraordinary military budget increase.[32] Sunthorn and Suchinda were infuriated, and the military next began to target former Young Turk coup leader Manoon Rupkachorn, who Chatchai had reinstated into the military, promoted to become a general and then given a top job in the permanent defence minister's office. Sunthorn ordered General Boonchu Wongkanont of the police (a class 5 peer) to re-open the criminal case against Manoon for his alleged 1982 murder attempts of Prem, Arthit and Queen Sirikit. Class 5 saw the resurrection of the case as a means of tarnishing class 7 and Chatchai himself.

Early January 1991 saw the ratcheting up of tensions between the elected government and the military. First, on 20 January, Chatchai had Boonchu Wongkanont transferred. The case against Manoon was thus stopped again—pursuing it would not only have embarrassed the government but also perhaps the palace as the incident purportedly involved a top royal. On 13 February, supreme commander General Sunthorn refused to approve handing over the legal papers. Rumours again circulated that Chatchai would soon purge the armed forces of officers he did not favour.[33] Meanwhile, Suchinda had been making "gutter" headlines because of revelations he had a secret mistress who was none other than a former Thai Miss Universe who previously had been married to the Queen's brother but was now married to a major Thai department store owner close to Chatchai. When a secret clip was publicly shared that allegedly showed Suchinda and the woman frolicking in a hotel, elements in the military became furious. What followed were unexplained fires at the woman's husband's department store.[34] To make matters worse, on 21 February 1991, Chatchai appointed retired general Arthit Kamlang-ek (no friend of Sunthorn or class 5) as deputy defence minister. At that point, a coup was in the works. One coup leader later admitted that had General Arthit not been appointed deputy defence minister, a coup would not have been staged.[35] On 22 February, field officers met with Chatchai and asked him to reconsider the appointment. The last straw came when Chatchai and Arthit sought to replace supreme commander Sunthorn with deputy supreme commander General Pichit.[36] As Chatchai and Arthit began to make their way to the king's palace in Chiang Mai to have the king endorse the appointments of Arthit and Pichit, the air force detained them at gunpoint at Don Muang airport. Thus, Thailand's armed forces, going in the opposite direction to the global trend towards democratization, staged a coup, bringing the country under authoritarian rule. But though the military seemed to be at odds with the king about the impending appointments, in actuality the palace was hardly on Chatchai's side. Indeed, the success of the putsch owed to royal support for it. Unlike the Young Turks, Suchinda and class 5 sought and obtained the endorsement of the palace.[37]

Though Suchinda and class 5 were clearly behind the coup, Chavalit Yongchaiyudh may initially have also supported it. According to Viroj Sangsanit, then army chief of staff, "Chavalit asked Suchinda and other military commanders to stage a coup after he left the government".[38] Suchinda later stated that there had been an informal plan to stage the coup as a means to formally install Chavalit as prime minister. Chavalit had been aggravated in January 1991 when interior minister Pramarn Adireksan transferred two appointed officials (governors of Mahasarakam and Udorn Thani provinces) because they were seen as too close to the former army and supreme commander.[39] Chavalit vehemently denied, however, any backing for a coup.[40] Indeed, he was clearly keeping his options open to enter electoral politics by registering and building up his New Aspiration Party. But perhaps being elected was simply his option "B", while a Suchinda-created instalment of Chavalit had all along been his option "A". Meanwhile, neither the king nor his Privy Council opposed the putsch. The monarch and Prem merely told the coup-leaders not to "let the people down".[41] In retrospect, it seemed that the military staged a coup in an attempt to re-impose a less "discreet" version of Prem's diluted form of democracy.[42]

On 23 February 1991, the king endorsed a newly established six-man National Peace-Keeping Council (NPKC), while Chatchai remained in exile. The NPKC leaders are detailed in Figure 10.3.

FIGURE 10.3
National Peace-Keeping Council (NPKC) Leaders

NPKC post	Name	Military post	Class
Chief	Gen. Sunthorn Kongsompong	Supreme Commander, RTAF	1
Deputy Chief	Gen. Suchinda Kraprayoon	Army Commander	5
Deputy Chief	Adm. Prapat Kishnachan	Navy Commander	5
Deputy Chief	ACM Kaset Rojananil	Air Force Commander	5
Deputy Chief	Pol. Gen. Sawat Amornwiwat	Police Commander	5
Secretary-General	Gen. Issarapong Noonpakdi	Deputy Army Commander	5

The coup led to the immediate dissolution of parliament and voiding of the 1978 constitution. NPKC leaders immediately placed the country under the Martial Law Act (1914).[43] The declared rationales for the coup were (1) enormous corruption in the Chatchai government; (2) harassment of honest civil servants by politicians; (3) tyranny of the lower house of parliament; (4) an attempt to destroy the military; and (5) an attempt to drop the legal case against Manoon Rupkachorn, who had allegedly sought to topple the monarchy.[44] Regarding this last point, the NPKC suddenly produced a video of class 7 MP Bansak Polcharoen—a suspect along with Manoon, who had become an MP in the dissolved lower house—now accusing Manoon of masterminding the assassination plot. As if to further justify the need for a military takeover, the NPKC, a day after the coup, announced the establishment of a committee to investigate "unusually wealthy" members of the previous cabinet. In 1992, the NPKC would join with "unusually wealthy" politicos to build a government.

Reacting to the coup on a radio broadcast, social critic Sulak Sivaraksa opined that it had been the fault of Chatchai: "They [the military] didn't want to intervene.... Unfortunately Chatchai thought that he was too smart."[45] According to academic Suchit Bunbongkarn, except for "some academicians and politicians who lost their jobs ... for the general public the coup seemed acceptable" to end the perceived corruption of the Chatchai government.[46] Suchit admitted that by the end of 1991 many "societal groups" had become frustrated by the military junta's "'undemocratic' [constitutional] clauses, implying that these groups would only accept 'perfect democracy'".[47]

Following the coup, class 5 was able to occupy all key postings in the military. After the 1991 mid-year reshuffle, each of the army's Five Tigers positions (army commander, deputy army commander, assistant army commander 1, assistant army commander 2, and army chief of staff) were henceforth taken by graduates of class 5. In addition, three out of four of the regional command posts in the army were assumed by class 5 graduates. Only General Kitti Ratanachaiya, who assumed command over the 4th Army Region, was not a class 5 officer—though he was considered a friend.

Class 11 and class 12 also greatly benefited from the coup—they each took the greatest number of valuable postings after class 5. This was logical as the leader of class 11 was Chainarong, who was connected to Suchinda given that his cousin Issarapong was Suchinda's brother-in-law. Meanwhile, class 12 was led by Suchinda-confidant General Samphao Chusri (as well as by General Surayud Chulanond).

Familial connections were important: Tamada has surmised that the NPKC was seeking to create a decade-long military dynasty led first by class 5's Suchinda (1990–92) then followed by Issarapong (1992–94), Viroj (1994–96), class 11's Chainarong (1996–99), and finally class 12's Samphao (1999–2001).[48] It would actually have been safer for the Kraprayoon-Noonpakdi alliance to keep power within the family by excluding Viroj, going directly to Chainarong and then allowing Chainarong's younger brother, former military intelligence commander General Taweesak Noonpakdi (Chulachomklao class 13, pre-cadet class 2) to succeed him during 1999–2001, though that would have produced angry calls of familial nepotism from the military establishment. The family tree depicted in Figure 10.4 represents the Kraprayoon-Noonpakdi power structure.

The reshuffle of 1 April 1991 dominated by class-5 is shown in Appendix 4. Notice that the class occupies 12 postings (out of 16), with class 1 (of Sunthorn and Chavalit) possessing two slots, class 11 a

FIGURE 10.4
Kraprayoon-Noonpakdi Power Structure

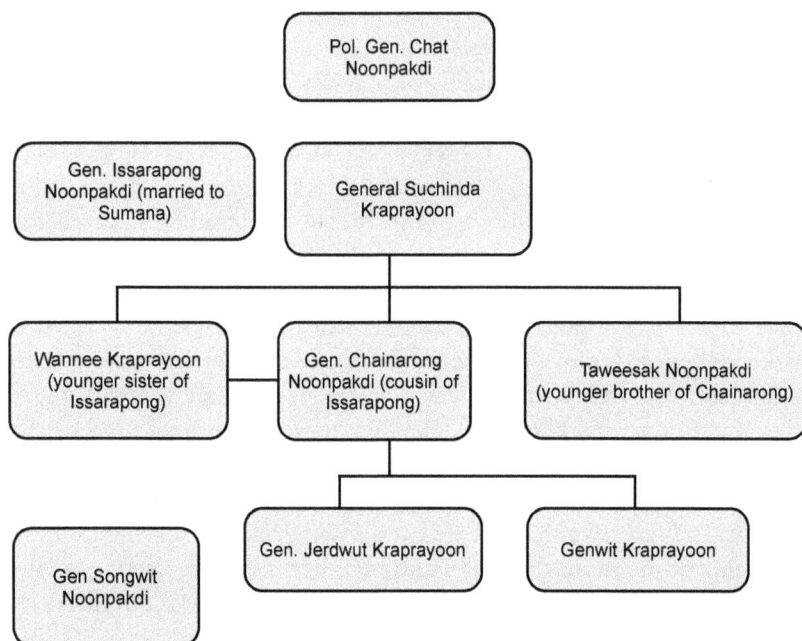

single posting (by a brother of a member of class 5), and only General
Kitti Ratanachaiya (class 8) commanding the rather significant (at the
time) 4th Army Region.

The coup group quickly chose the civilian statesman/entrepre-
neur Anand Panyarachun to administer the country. Suchinda had
known Anand from when he had been Thailand's defence attaché
in Washington during the early 1970s while Anand had been Thai
ambassador to the United Nations and then to the United States.
The appointment of Anand, together with an appointed Council of
Ministers and appointed unicameral National Legislative Assembly
(see Figure 10.5, row A) came under the aegis of the interim charter,
which entered into force on 1 March 1991, lasting until 9 December
of the same year. But this charter did not specifically enshrine military
supremacy into law, instead allowing for ambiguity, which facilitated
the establishment of a domain of military appointments within various
political posts. For example, 152 (52 per cent) of the 292 appointed
lawmakers in the unicameral assembly were soldiers (active or retired).[49]
The March 1991 charter also allowed the NPKC to forbid political
activities not sanctioned by the state.

Thereupon, the NPKC's 292-person legislative assembly, drawn
from junta appointees, drafted what became the December 1991 constitution. More enhanced military prerogatives were clearly enshrined
into this constitution, which gave inordinate powers to the chair of
the NPKC coup group as well as to interim PM Anand. Indeed, this
charter allowed for the possibility of non-elected MPs and ministers as
well as the continuation of the partially appointed, military dominated
Senate as part of a bicameral legislative structure.[50] As such, deputy
army commander General Issarapong Noonpakdee became interior
minister, navy commander Admiral Prapat Kishnachan became defence minister, and there were rumours that Suchinda or Admiral Kaset
would, while still serving in their military positions, simultaneously
have themselves appointed as prime minister. Military officials seemed
to be looking to create a Senate that would be empowered to work with
a medium-sized party in the lower house—presumably a proxy party
that the military could control. The Senate would be appointed by the
NPKC and be allowed to select or help select the prime minister—
similar to the provisions of the 1968, 1978 and 2017 constitutions. The
premier did not have to be elected and could even be a serving military
official. But the more that MPs and members of civil society read the
constitutional draft, the more they saw an attempt by the military to
usurp power

On 17 November, amidst growing popular protests against the new constitutional clauses, Suchinda and Kaset each denied that they were seeking a secret way to the premiership. A compromise in the clauses was eventually reached whereby unelected officers could become prime minister but only after they retired from their permanent posts. The constitutional assembly also voted down a clause harshly criticized by the protestors: making it possible for the appointed Senate to select a prime minister.

Not to be left out of the political picture, on 4 December, King Bhumipol made a birthday speech. Referring to democracy, the monarch stated that "procedures and principles that we have imported from abroad are sometimes not suitable to the conditions of Thailand or the character of Thai people".[51] The words of the beloved king carried the day. Despite opposition from many academics and parliamentarians, the constitution was approved. Nevertheless, the ability of the demonstrators to pressure the assembly to prevent approving a clause allowing for active-duty soldiers to simultaneously be sitting politicians indicated that the people could still place pressure on attempts by the military to expand its legal power.

Following passage of the December 1991 charter, the new military-dominated Senate was appointed in March 1992 (see Figure 10.5).

The political prowess of the armed forces was further accentuated by the establishment by class 5 of the Samakkhitham (or STP) political party. The creation of a proxy party to boost military interests was

FIGURE 10.5
Legislatures Deriving from the 1991 Coup

	Type of legislature	Years in office	Appointed or elected	Total number of members and military contingent
A.	Unicameral	1991–92	Appointed	292, of which 152 (52%) military reserved domain
B.	Bicameral (Seventh Senate)	1992–96 (served 4-year term)	Appointed	270, of which 154 (55.2%) military reserved domain

Source: Paul Chambers, "Superfluous, Irrelevant or Emancipating: Thailand's Evolving Senate Today", *Journal of Current Southeast Asian Affairs* 28, no. 3 (2009): 9, https://d-nb.info/999559311/34.

nothing novel in Thailand. Phibun, Sarit, Thanom and Praphas had all done the same when they ruled the country. The STP was established to act as a "'buffer' party between the old power group ... and the new power group of the then recently formed New Aspiration Party".[52] Benefiting from state resources and political connections and bringing together numerous parliamentary intra-party factions, STP was formed in April 1991 by Wing Commander Thiti Nakorntab, who would act as the NPKC's surrogate in the lower house. Thiti was a former air force officer, now businessman, who was close to ACM Kaset as well as generals Suchinda Isarapong and Wirot. By May, leadership of STP had passed from Thiti to the more experienced party hand of Narong Wongwan, former leader of the Solidarity Party from the northern Phrae province. Nevertheless, Thiti retained the job of STP secretary-general. Since everyone knew that STP was closely linked to the powerful military, many politicians were enthusiastic to defect from their own parties to join this new one. The STP appeared to be buying up MPs and their vote canvassing networks—and the tactic seemed to be working. By October, the party had attracted eighty MPs, including eleven former cabinet ministers, allegedly offering candidates 0.5 million Thai baht for their electoral campaigns, and with 3 million Thai baht to follow. Money was clearly no issue.

Ultimately, by creating STP, the class 5 military faction was able to compete from a financial advantage with civilian parties as well as other military factions in post-military political competition. Jumping into parliamentary politics in 1991, STP was doing quite well on the parliamentary stage, locking horns not only with the Democrats and Social Action but also with Chavalit's military faction (New Aspiration Party) as well as Chatchai and Pramarn's Soi Rajakru (Chart Thai).

Meanwhile, the foreign affairs situation of 1991 saw Prime Minister Anand try to keep Thailand's authoritarian regime at a low external profile. The February 1991 putsch had been followed by multiple condemnations from the West. Many reactions were rather muted. For example, Australia merely expressed its "regret".[53] The United States, under President George H.W. Bush, was tempered in its own criticisms of the military regime, especially given that Anand, Sunthorn and Suchinda allowed US aircraft to refuel in Thailand on route to the Persian Gulf War. In a sign of thawing relations between Thailand and Cambodia (Vietnamese troops had gone home in 1989), foreign minister Arsa Sarasin visited Phnom Penh in November, simultaneously reopening the Thai embassy in that country (closed since 1975). Suchinda's influence did influence the continuing Cambodian civil war:

under orders from Suchinda (who had close ties to the Khmer Rouge), the RTA's Task Force 838 had Pol Pot stashed in a Pattaya hotel room, where he participated in a meeting with leaders of other Cambodian insurgent groups as well as other Khmer Rouge representatives via headphones. As a result of his presence, the factions agreed to a cease-fire and a promise to end all external military assistance.[54] Suchinda had met Pol Pot previously and had told a visiting US senator back in April 1991 that Pol Pot "was a nice guy".[55]

With class 5 lording over so many of the leading military positions, the October 1991 reshuffle was one of examining which commanders did not belong to the faction. Wanchai, a classmate and confidant of Sunthorn, was given a final year in the post of permanent minister of defence. Wanchai was well-liked in the military and would do what he was told. Suchinda now took the supreme commander slot while retaining the post of army commander. Meanwhile, three new class 5 members were given commands: generals San, Phaiboon and Ariya. And General Kitti (class 8) held on to command Region 4. The important newcomer was General Chainarong Noonpakdi, cousin of General Issarapong Noonpakdi, the deputy army commander (and in-law of army chief Suchinda Kraprayoon). Chainarong in this reshuffle was appointed 1st Army Cohort commander—in line to become 1st Army Region commander and eventually army commander.

The year 1992 was a historical one for Thai civil-military relations. It began with an election campaign given that Suchinda's class 5, lording over the military, ironically was seeking to extend its power by electoral means. With an election date of 22 March 1992 established, all eyes were on Suchinda, whose political ambitions were well known. But he refused to be an electoral candidate. That would mean he would have to step down as a bureaucrat.

Nevertheless, prognosticators could not be blamed for predicting that the military's proxy party, STP, was likely to be victorious. The March 1992 election seemed clearly to involve competition among military factions: General Suchinda's class 5 (along with classes 11 and 12) as manifested in the STP, versus General Chavalit's class 1 (as manifested in his New Aspiration Party), versus General Chamlong Srimuang's class 7 (as manifested in his Palang Dharma party). Meanwhile, another military-linked party, Chart Thai (the leadership of which had devolved to General Pramarn Adireksan when Chatchai had been putsched), invited ACM Somboon Rahong to be its new party leader. Somboon was a close friend of ACM Kaset but had served Pramarn when the latter was defence minister back in 1975–76. With

Somboon leading Chart Thai, the NPKC could count on that party to be a supporting member of an STP-led coalition.[56] Concentrating on capturing the rural vote, but successfully using local factions and vote-canvassing networks, the military vehicle—STP—achieved victory.[57]

Within hours of STP's triumph, five pro-military parties met at armed forces headquarters and put together a ruling coalition of 195 out of 360 seats: STP, 79; Chart Thai, 74; Social Action, 31; Prachakorn Thai, 7; and Rassadorn, 4.[58] The new coalition first offered the premiership to Suchinda but he declined. Thus, the coalition offered the post to STP leader Narong Wongwan. But, following US allegations of narcotics trafficking by Narong (which later proved unfounded), on 7 April, the coalition persuaded Suchinda to accept. He thereupon resigned from the armed forces and bureaucracy in order to be duly endorsed as prime minister by the king.[59]

Like Phraya Phahon (1933, 1937), Phibun (1938, 1952, 1957), Sarit (December 1957) and Thanom (1969) before him, military strongman Suchinda used a political party to become leader of Thailand—though via military-manipulated parliamentary legitimacy. But who exactly was Suchinda? Born on 6 August 1933 in Thonburi Province next to Bangkok, he was the youngest son of Chuang and Sompong Kraprayoon. As his father worked for Siam's railway, he came from a family of bureaucrats. During the chaos of World War II, the child Suchinda lived in rural Nong Khai province. After the war, he completed his high school education in Bangkok at the prestigious Amnuay Silpa School. In 1953, Suchinda entered Chulachomklao Royal Military Academy as part of class 5. His class peers became important military and political personages: Issarapong Noonpakdee, Sai Sriphen, Viroj Pao-in, Wimol Wongwanich, Viroj Saengsanit, ACM Kaset Rojananil, Colonel Narong Kittikachorn and General Krit Sivara's younger brother Suthep. Upon graduation, Suchinda studied further at Fort Sill and Fort Leavenworth in the United States. Suchinda became a 2nd lieutenant in 1958 under army chief General Sarit Thanarat, a leader highly admired by army class 5. During 1969–79, Suchinda was part of the anti-communist Thai contingent in South Vietnam. He then became deputy assistant to the army attaché in Washington during 1971–74. By 1982 he had become a general, was a "royal guard" and was appointed as director-general of the Army Operations Department.[60] Married to Khunying Wannee (Noonpakdi) Kraprayoon, Suchinda has two children: General Jerdwut Kraprayoon, who became rector of Thailand's Military Staff College; and Janwit Kraprayoon, the general manager of True Internet Data Center Co., Ltd.

Simultaneous to Suchinda's election victory, the NPKC effected another military reshuffle. These appointments were necessary given that
Suchinda became prime minister and military loyalists were needed to
not only fill the slots he had vacated but also to fill the positions that
the officers filling his posts had left.

Prime Minister Suchinda formed a cabinet on 16 April. Seven out
of the fifty ministers had military backgrounds. The new military-dominated Senate assumed office contemporaneously. Moreover, at least
thirty-six senior armed forces personnel were allowed to either chair
or sit near the top of state enterprise boards.[61] It looked like class 5
had succeeded in enshrining itself in power for a long time to come.
With Suchinda's accession to the prime minister's seat, Suchinda's
brother-in-law Issarapong Noonpakdi became army commander. The
kinship-oriented power configuration bore an uncomfortable resem-
blance to that of Thanom and Praphas. Might this be merely a new
attempt to create something similar?

But many Thai political parties and civil society groups opposed the
military's new political monopoly. Demonstrations began on 23 March,
the day the election results became known, seeing protests by opposition parties, student groups and NGOs. On 20 April, a demonstration
of approximately fifty thousand people began protesting Suchinda's
ascendance to the premiership without first running for election. A
key leader in the resistance was retired general Chamlong Srimuang.
By this time, Chamlong—a former agent of ISOC, a member of the
military "Young Turks" and founder of the Palang Dharma party—had
been governor of Bangkok for six years (he retired in January 1992).
He had also remained on speaking terms with General Prem, having
previously served as Prem's personal secretary.[62] Chamlong's enmity
for Suchinda, however, reflected the travails of his own Young Turks
faction with Suchinda's class 5. A retired soldier, Chamlong's clout was
reborn through elections.

Joining Chamlong in opposition to Prime Minister Suchinda's new
government was Chavalit. The sudden creation of STP in 1991 by
Suchinda as well as his control over state resources and the regime's
manipulation of a new pro-military constitution to benefit STP had
been hindering Chavalit's chances of a future electoral victory. Also,
Suchinda and class 5 were suspicious that Chavalit held republican
sympathies, seeing his new political party riddled with leftists. But
Chamlong and Chavalit supported the rally against Suchinda until the
end. Suchinda, however, tried to maintain power at all costs.[63]

On 5 May, standing before seventy thousand people in front of
parliament, Chamlong began a hunger strike. At this point, ACM

Kaset Rojananil, supreme commander since April 1992 (and head of the Internal Peace Keeping Command[64]), and General Issarapong Noonpakdi, army chief since April 1992 (and head of the Bangkok Peacekeeping Command), demanded that protestors disperse. The rally persisted at the Sanam Luang park nearby. Chamlong's hunger strike ended when coalition parties agreed to amend the constitution to disqualify a non-elected person from holding the premiership—but the amendment never passed. On 17 May, with the prime minister feeling increasingly under siege, he had his new army commander, Issarapong (who also served as head of the Capital Command), prepare Operation Pairee Pinat. This was an army plan to combat urban terrorism.[65]

At 12:30 a.m., Suchinda declared a state of emergency in Bangkok and surrounding provinces.[66] Security forces purportedly started to beat demonstrators with truncheons and advanced onto the streets firing automatic weapons. At first they fired into the air, but at 4:15 a.m. they turned their M-16 rifles directly at the protestors. This resulted in at least five deaths and scores injured. According to Amnesty International, "there were widespread reports of military-backed agents provocateurs committing violence".[67] In the morning of 18 May, troops again fired their weapons into the air, which injured dozens of people. Chamlong, alongside several hundred demonstrators, was thereupon arrested and detained. At 10.30 p.m., soldiers wearing full combat gear fired their M-16s directly, deliberately and continuously into a crowd of demonstrators at head height. An audio tape later revealed a recorded "radio order to shoot with live ammunition at demonstrators given at approximately 10.30 p.m. from a major general to the 2nd Brigade, 19th regiment of the Kanchanaburi-based 9th Infantry Division". Officers affiliated with Task Force 90 allegedly participated in the killings.[68] At approximately 9 a.m. on 19 April, soldiers forced their way into the Royal Hotel, which was being used as a medical refuge for injured protestors. These troops were under the command of General Surayud Chulanond, then commander of Special Forces. Future coup leader Sonthi Boonyaratklin was a member of Surayud's Special Warfare Unit. The elite forces that Surayud and Sonthi led were seen kicking and pointing weapons at injured protestors in later video footage.[69] According to Police General Uthai Assavavilai, who was a witness to this behaviour, soldiers forced demonstrators to lie on the floor of the hotel lobby. Thereupon, troops trod on them with heavy boots and pointed loaded guns at them. On the evening of 20 April, a 9 p.m. to 4 a.m. curfew was announced. Meanwhile, there were unconfirmed reports that troops from the north were moving towards the capital to stage a coup.

Though Thailand's Special Forces were clearly involved in "mopping up" the protestors, leading the operations on the ground were class 11 peers General Thitipong, then 1st Division commander; and General Chainarong, then 1st Army Region commander. They were commanded by Chainarong's cousin army commander Issarapong Noonpakdi.

The unpopularity of the violence on television took its toll on the Suchinda government's relations with the king as well as with the international community. In the morning and afternoon of 20 May, Princess Sirinthorn appealed via television for an end to the violence. Her appeal was later joined by a similar broadcast from her brother Crown Prince Vajiralongkorn. At 9:30 p.m. on 20 May, Thai television broadcast an audience that King Bhumipol Adulyadej granted to Chamlong, Suchinda and privy councillor General Prem Tinsulanonda, who were shown kneeling before their liege. The king angrily demanded that Chamlong and Suchinda cooperate to end the crisis. The monarch's apparent frustration helped to remove any doubts about his own role in supporting the NPKC since its 1990 coup. Following the king's stern lecture, Suchinda immediately released Chamlong and most other detainees. He also announced that he would give his full support to an early amendment to the constitution requiring the prime minister to be an elected member of parliament, and Chamlong appealed for a halt to street demonstrations. On 21 May, the government lifted the curfew, but the state of emergency continued in effect until 26 May. According to state sources, there had been 52 deaths, 696 injuries, and 175 persons who simply "disappeared".[70] Unofficial sources put the number of missing as much higher. Thus ended "Black [or 'Dark'] May" 1992. On 23 May, the monarch issued a general amnesty to government leaders and military officers involved in the brutal suppression of the protests. The agreement granted "amnesty to everyone involved in the demonstrations and those who suppressed them, including 'commanders and those commanded'".[71] But the amnesty also involved a major military reshuffle in August. Indeed, only King Bhumipol could have successfully forced senior military leaders to carry out a change of leadership—effectively demoting most of themselves.

Anand was now reappointed as temporary PM, and key Club 0143 officers loyal to Suchinda were dismissed. In their place, a new cohort of senior officers more amenable to civilian control was installed. General Voranat Apichari, former air chief marshal (class A1), became supreme commander, replacing his classmate Kaset. Meanwhile, General Wimol Wongwanich, then deputy supreme commander of the armed forces, was promoted to army commander, replacing General Issarapong Noonpakdi. Wimol was known to be closely affiliated with Prem.

General San Siphen, assistant commander of the army, was elevated to become deputy army commander, replacing Suchinda ally General Wiroj Saengsanit. General Chetta Thanarajo edged out Chainarong Noonpakdi from command of the 1st Army Region.

It is important to emphasize, however, that these personnel changes, while almost entirely wiping out the future of class 11, only targeted part of class 5—the specific allies of Suchinda. For example, General San was also close to Suchinda and had held the strategically important position of 1st Army Region commander from 1989 (when Suchinda became army commander) until 1991, when San was moved to a Five Tigers position (assistant army commander). As such, he was actually rewarded after Black May with a move up to deputy army commander. Moreover, General Wirot Saengsanit would make a comeback later on. Still, one could argue that Prem's decision on the August 1992 senior military reshuffle merely followed the policy of "divide and conquer". The pro-Suchinda sub-clique of class 5 lost out, while class 5 soldiers more distant to Suchinda (e.g., Wimol) were victorious.

Meanwhile, the government abolished the Capital Security Command and the Internal Security Act, laws that the military had used to legally rationalize their orders to suppress protestors. On 9 July, Anand revoked an executive order making the supreme commander the head of the National Peacekeeping Force. Meanwhile, General Pichit Kullanamit, who had come to despise Suchinda as he had lost out in military promotions (as Suchinda's clique had ascended), was tasked to chair a report on the military's actions in May 1992. The report, though never released, apparently placed primary responsibility on the armed forces themselves. Pichit, a favourite of the palace, was appointed to the king's Privy Council in 1993. The government never did come up with a full accounting of how many people died during Black May, though combined numbers from non-government organizations were well over seven hundred. There were claims of soldiers "disappearing" large numbers of protestors.[72]

Following May 1992, the image of Thailand's armed forces was tarnished. The military, once viewed by many in a positive light as the protector of the kingdom, was now generally perceived as merely soldiers firing into crowds of unarmed protestors demonstrating for democracy. This image would prove hard to shake, and it gave civilian policymakers leverage over the next several years to formulate and implement policies without fear of soldiers breathing down their necks. It also helped Privy Councillor Prem Tinsulanond re-establish his own power over the military.

Anand proved to be a careful caretaker, picking up the pieces of a Thailand tainted by a military dictatorship and its massacre of peaceful civilians. In this light, he set the stage for a new general election to be held on 13 September 1992. Post-election, the Democrats were the winners, followed by New Aspiration and Palang Dharma. The STP, as a party, was dissolved and the military, anxious to at least superficially be trustworthy, did its best to cooperate in ensuring a stable election.

In the final analysis, 1988–92 was crucial for civil-military relations in Thailand because the period represented a rupture in the dominant path of military ascendancy and praetorianism across the country. The 1988 rise of Chatchai proved to be an intermediate point in time between military control. During this period, political space for elected civilians remained limited by the constraints of monarchy and military. Suchinda's 1991–92 junta was a slight retrograde step to the authoritarian past. The success of the September 1992 election in bringing to office a majority of MPs opposed to the military indicated that Thailand's move towards more political space was growing. Nevertheless, civilian governments in the post-1992 period would have to realize that their newfound freedom was to be tempered by the fact that post-1992 democracy was to be guided by the monarchy, as advised by Privy Councillor Prem.

Notes

1. Thak Chaloemtiarana, *Thailand: The Politics of Despotic Paternalism* (Ithaca: Cornell University Press, 2007), pp. 56–64.

2. อนุสรณ์งานพระราชทานเพลิงศพ ฯพณฯ พลเอกชาติชาย ชุณหะวัณ ณ เมรุหลวงหน้าพลับพลาอิศริยาภรณ์ วัดเทพศิรินทราวาส [Memorial volume from the cremation ritual of His Excellency General Chatchai Chunhavan at the royal crematorium in front of the Isariyaphon Pavilion Wat Thepsirintrawat], 8 November 1998, p. 352.

3. Ibid., p. 353.

4. Paul Handley, *The King Never Smiles* (New Haven, CT: Yale University Press), p. 327.

5. General Kantinan Sepu, พลเอกชวลิต ยงใจยุทธ: ทหารประชาธิปไตย [General Chavalit Yongchaiyudh: People's soldier] (Bangkok: King Prajadhipok Institute, 2007), https://kpi-lib.com/elib/cgi-bin/opacexe.exe?op=mmvw&db=Main&skin=s&mmid=571&bid=11200.

6. Yos Santasombot, "The End of Premocracy in Thailand", in *Southeast Asian Affairs 1989*, edited by Ng Chee Yuen (Singapore: Institute of Southeast Asian Affairs, 1989), p. 323, https://www.jstor.org/stable/27911983.

7. Pasuk Phongpaichit and Chris Baker, *Thailand: Economy and Politics* (Oxford: Oxford University Press, 2000), p. 354.

8. Steven Erlanger, "Thailand Seeks to Shape a 'Golden Peninsula'", *New York Times*, 30 April 1989, https://www.nytimes.com/1989/04/30/world/thailand-seeks-to-shape-a-golden-peninsula.html.

9. Siddhi, as National Security Council Chair (1974–80), had disagreed with Chatchai when he had been foreign minister, supporting closer relations with China rather than Vietnam.

10. Larry Niksch, "Thailand in 1988: The Economic Surge", *Asian Survey* 29, no. 2 (1989): 169–72, https://doi.org/10.2307/2644576.

11. Murray Hiebert, "Thais Deny Knowledge of Corruption", *Washington Post*, 5 November 1988, https://www.washingtonpost.com/archive/politics/1988/11/05/thais-deny-knowledge-of-corruption/e6a85188-e451-4220-a9e1-90aa99c8d5c4/.

12. Kenneth Conboy, *The Cambodian Wars: Clashing Armies and CIA Covert Operations* (Lawrence: University Press of Kansas, 2013), pp. 255–56.

13. Donald Weatherbee, "Thailand in 1989: Democracy Ascendant in the Golden Peninsula", in *Southeast Asian Affairs 1990*, edited by Ng Chee Yuen and Chandran Jeshurun (Singapore: Institute of Southeast Asian Studies, 1990), p. 354, https://www.jstor.org/stable/27912008.

14. Scott Christensen, "Thailand in 1989: Consensus at Bay", *Asian Survey* 30, no. 2 (1990): 184–86, https://doi.org/10.2307/2644896.

15. Yoshifumi Tamada, *Myths and Realities: The Democratization of Thai Politics* (Kyoto: Kyoto University Press, 2008), p. 82.

16. Boonkrom Dongbangsathan … and others, eds, ชีวิตและผลงาน พลเอกชวลิต ยงใจยุทธ ขงเบ้งแห่งกองทัพ [Life and works of General Chavalit Yongchaiyudh: The military "Confucius"] (Bangkok, 1996?).

17. Weatherbee, "Thailand in 1989", pp. 338–39, 342.

18. Handley, *The King Never Smiles*, pp. 329, 330.

19. His class 1 peer General Wanchai was moved up to be permanent minister of defence (traditionally a post that extracted lucrative rent), while General Jaruai continued on as army chief of staff. Otherwise, Chavalit increasingly bolstered class 5, giving its clique five top postings.

20. He still needed more money, an established political party of which he was in sole control, and an army hierarchy that assuredly left his ally class 5 in charge.

21. Tan Lian Choo, "Personality Politics in Thailand", in *Southeast Asian Affairs 1991*, edited by Sharon Siddique and Ng Chee Yuen (Singapore: Institute of Southeast Asian Studies, 1991), pp. 279–80, https://www.jstor.org/stable/27912031.

22. Handley, *The King Never Smiles*, p. 335.

23. ในงานพระราชทานเพลิงศพ พลเอก พลเอก สุนทร คงสมพงษ์ ม.ป.ช., ม.ว.ม., ท.จ.ว. ณ เมรุหลวงหน้าพลับพลาอิศริยาภรณ์ วัดเทพศิรินทราวาส [Memorial volume from the cremation ceremony of General Sunthorn Kongsompong, the royal crematorium in front of Issriyaphon Pavilion Wat Thepsirintrawat], Bangkok, 21 October 1999.

24. For more on the political thought of Suchinda Kraprayoon and class 5, see Wassana Nanuam, ความคิดทางการเมืองของพลเอกสุจินดา [Political thoughts of General Suchinda Kraprayoon] (Bangkok: Matichon, 2002).

25. Yoshifumi Tamada, "Coups in Thailand, 1980–1991: Classmates, Internal Conflicts and Relations with the Government of the Military", *Southeast Asian Studies* 33, no. 3 (1995): 49.

26. Wassana Nanuam, บันทึกคำให้การ สุจินดา คราประยูร กำเนิดและอวสาน รสช [The testimony of Suchinda Kraprayoon: The origin and end of the Royal Thai Army], 3rd ed. (Bangkok: Matichon, 2002).

27. Tan Lian Choo, "Personality Politics in Thailand", in *Southeast Asian Affairs 1991*, edited by Sharon Siddique and Ng Chee Yuen (Singapore: Institute of Southeast Asian Studies, 1991), p. 286, https://www.jstor.org/stable/27912031.

28. Scott Christenson, "Thailand in 1990: Political Tangles", *Asian Survey* 31, no. 2 (1991): 198, https://doi.org/10.2307/2644931.

29. Handley, *The King Never Smiles*, p. 336.

30. Tamada, "Coups in Thailand", p. 333.

31. "Military at Odds with Civilian Government in Thailand", *Los Angeles Times*, 6 January 1991, p. 2; Handley, *The King Never Smiles*, p. 336.

32. Pasuk and Baker, *Thailand: Economy*, p. 354.

33. Tamada, "Coups in Thailand", p. 334.

34. อากัสรา หงสกุล ประวัตินางงามจักรวาลของไทย สาวสวยคงกระพั [Apasara Hongsakul: The history of a beauty pageant winner of Thailand, still beautiful], *Kapook!*, 16 October 2007, https://women.kapook.com/view101650.html.

35. Interview with ACM Kaset Rojananil, in "Kaset's View on May Event", *Bangkok Post*, 28 January 1993.

36. Pasuk and Baker, *Thailand: Economy*, p. 354.

37. Kevin Hewison, "The Monarchy and Democratization", in *Political Change in Thailand*, edited by Kevin Hewison (New York: Routledge, 1997), p. 70.

38. "Bloody May: Former Strongman Admits Mistakes", *The Nation*, 23 February 2002, http://www.nationmultimedia.com.

39. Ananya Bhuchongkul, "Thailand 1991: The Return of the Military", in *Southeast Asian Affairs 1992*, edited by Sharon Siddique and Ng Chee Yuen (Singapore: Institute of Southeast Asian Affairs, 1992), p. 325, https://www.jstor.org/stable/27912055.

40. "Chavalit Denies he Called a Coup in '91", *The Nation*, 23 February 2002, http://www.nationmultimedia.com.

41. Handley, *The King Never Smiles*, p. 338.

42. Chris Baker and Pasuk Phongpaichit, *A History of Thailand* (Cambridge: Cambridge University Press, 2005).

43. Frank Frost, "The Coup in Thailand 23 February 1991: Background and Implications", Foreign Affairs Groups, Parliamentary Research Service,

Parliament of Australia, 15 March 1991, p. 15, https://www.aph.gov.au/binaries/library/pubs/bp/1991/91bp05.pdf.

44. Supaluck Suvarnajata, *The Thai Military Coup d'etat: Origins, Withdrawal/Civilian Control, and Perspectives* (PhD dissertation, Claremont Graduate School, California, 1994), p. 141.

45. Frost, "The Coup in Thailand", p. 16.

46 Suchit Bunbongkarn, "Thailand in 1991: Coping with Military Guardianship", *Asian Survey* 32, no. 2, (1992): 132, https://doi.org/10.2307/2645210.

47. Ibid., p. 137.

48. Tamada, *Myths and Realities*, pp. 86–87.

49. Author's own calculations, based upon Thailand Senate data.

50. David Murray, *Angels and Devils* (Bangkok: White Orchid Press, 1996), p. 13; Pasuk and Baker, *Thailand: Economy and Politics* (Oxford: Oxford University Press, 2000), pp. 357–58.

51. Handley, *The King Never Smiles*, p. 343.

52. Murray, *Angels and Devils*, p. 39.

53. Frost, "The Coup in Thailand", p. 23.

54. In 1987, Suchinda "elbowed his way into operational control of the RTA's Cambodia programs". He soon became aware of the massive overcharging by Thai military officers of both US and Chinese aid to the Cambodian opposition forces. But Suchinda's rise to power in 1991 directly affected Thai-Cambodian relations because Suchinda was considered very close to the Khmer Rouge. As a result, the Chinese immediately increased their supplies to the Khmer Rouge. Conboy, *The Cambodian Wars*, pp. 252, 310, 312.

55. Tom Fawthrop and Helen Jarvis, *Getting Away with Genocide? Cambodia's Long Struggle against the Khmer Rouge* (London: Pluto, 2005), p. 97.

56. Surin Maisrikrod, "Thailand's Two General Elections in 1992: Democracy Sustained", Research Notes and Discussion Paper no. 75 (Singapore: Institute of Southeast Asian Studies, 1992), p. 23.

57. Murray, *Angels and Devils*, p. 5.

58. Surin Maisrikrod, "Thailand 1992: Repression and Return of Democracy", in *Southeast Asian Affairs 1993*, edited by Daljit Singh (Singapore: Institute of Southeast Asian Studies, 1993), p. 329, https://www.jstor.org/stable/27912083.

59. Handley, *The King Never Smiles*, p. 347.

60. Wassana Nanuam, ความคิดทางการเมืองของพลเอก สุจินดา คราประยูร [Political thoughts of General Suchinda Kraprayoon] (Bangkok: Matichon, 2002).

61. Murray, *Angels and Devils*, p. 193.

62. "Biography of Chamlong Srimuang", the 1992 Ramon Magsaysay Award for Government Service, http://www.rmaf.org.ph/Awardees/Biography/BiographySrimuangCha.htm.

63. Tamada, *Myths and Realities*, p. 87.

64. The Internal Peace Keeping Act, rescinded by the second Anand government in 1992, allowed the supreme commander to suppress riots and rebellions.

65. Murray, *Angels and Devils*, p. 153.

66. The Martial Law Act of 1914, by which the NPKC had legally held power, had been revoked since Suchinda had taken office as elected premier on 6 April.

67. Amnesty International, "Thailand: The Massacre in Bangkok", October 1992, p. 4, https://www.amnesty.org/fr/wp-content/uploads/2021/06/asa390101992en.pdf.

68. Ibid., p. 4.

69. "พฤษภาทมิฬปี 35 คลิปบันทึกเหตุการณ์จริง [Black May clip of the real incident] Thai coup d'état 1992", YouTube video, 9:28, https://www.youtube.com/watch?v=vx4sM4zYNLE.

70. Amnesty International, "Thailand: The Massacre", pp. 1, 5.

71. "Amnesty Paves Way for Ouster of Thai Leader", *Baltimore Sun*, 24 May 1992, https://www.baltimoresun.com/news/bs-xpm-1992-05-24-1992145023-story.html.

72. Murray, *Angels and Devils*, pp. 196–99.

Chapter Eleven

Prem, Chavalit and Military-Guided Democracy (1992–2001)

The year 1992 was the beginning of a fourteen-year period that seemed to transition Thailand towards democracy and civilian control over the military. During the first part of this period (1992–2001), three principals (the palace, the king's Privy Council and key retired generals) dominated the country, given that Thailand possessed a defective democracy (defective because most power was centred upon the aforementioned principals). The only "civilian" who really could control the country was King Bhumipol, lording over the people and the armed forces. Thailand after 1992 thus became what Thongchai Winichakul calls a "royalist democracy":

> Royalist democracy is a form of "guided democracy"—an ostensibly democratic polity but one in which the electorate and elected authority do not have substantive power or have little impact on public policy because true power remains in the hands of the oligarchy or autocracy. Its formal name, "the Democratic Regime with the Monarchy as the Head of the State," is quite a revealing euphemism for a political system in which the formal parliamentary system is under the domination of the unelected, undemocratic power of the monarchy.[1]

A "guided democracy or 'managed democracy' is a formally democratic government that functions as a de facto authoritarian government.... Such governments are legitimized by elections that are free and fair, but do not change the state's policies, motives, and goals."[2] Merkel (2004) refers to this "guided" or "managed", defective variant of democracy as "tutelary democracy" because unelected entities exert veto power over democratically elected civilian governments.³ Thailand has experienced such democracies.

But at the post–Black May inception of this "royalist democracy", the 13 September 1992 election resulted in the centrist Democrats taking 79 seats, while the conservative Chart Thai received 77, indicating that a political divide was alive and well in Thailand's lower house. A Democrat-led ruling coalition formed on 29 September with General Chavalit Yongchaiyudh's New Aspiration Party and General Chamlong Srimuang's Palang Dharma.

Chuan's personal history meant he had never been close to the military.⁴ He was the leading parliamentary opponent to Suchinda and the NPKC. An excellent speaker and defender of democracy, he was distrusted by many traditional soldiers.

The king (and Prem) reluctantly accepted the accession to office of Chuan, if only to be seen as supportive of the popular push towards democratization.⁵ But for them and many in the military, Chuan was preferable to either Chamlong, Chavalit or former prime minister Chatchai Chunhavan. The first two were seen as potentially too radical, and Chatchai had worked against the military leadership when he headed the government; Chuan might be a greater stabilizer. They thus considered Chuan to be "the lesser of the four evils".⁶ Besides, whilst the military was still strong in 1992, it was in a weakened position after the events of Black May. Following the demise of Suchinda, class 5, class 11 and much of class 12, the retirement of Pichit and the disintegration of the Young Turks, military factions were now much weaker. Retired soldier Chamlong's political career was also rather damaged by the events of Black May when Thais saw him on television being scolded by the king for leading the demonstrations. Ultimately, the 1990s was a period of institutional frailty. Political parties were "weak and divided" and "no strong factions" existed in the military.⁷

Behind the veneer of Thailand's guided democracy, however, two powerful retired military officers continued to exercise influence across the armed forces: Prem (backed by the palace) and Chavalit (who sought to build his populist New Aspiration Party). Until the advent of Prime Minister Thaksin Shinawatra in 2001, these two men jousted for power.

Prem, of course, had much greater influence than Chavalit. Prem was a tried and tested loyalist to King Bhumipol, and as such had earned the favour of the monarch. When Sanya Dharmasakti, the aging chair of the King's Privy Council, became increasingly ill, Prem took over as de facto council head. Prem officially became Privy Council chair in 1998. As former army commander and prime minister, and perhaps the closest advisor to the monarch, Prem exerted enormous influence. McCargo paints a picture of the 1990s as an era when the king worked indirectly and mostly through Prem "to shape the direction of the country".[8] From 1992 until 2001, with strong active-duty military brass or factions absent from the potential coup-making and political equation, Prem became what Chai-anan has famously referred to as "a surrogate strongman".[9] And as a Thai newspaper commented at the time: "No one can deny that every military transfer and promotion has to be seen by Prem before it is publicly announced."[10]

Like Prem, Chavalit was also influential with the armed forces, despite having retired from the corps in 1990. Though Chavalit had been Prem's loyal subordinate in the military, he had enormous ambitions of his own. Moreover, as a former army and supreme commander—as well as being former defence minister and deputy prime minister—he maintained a vast network of connections with active-duty soldiers. In addition, Chavalit's leadership within the former army clique "Democratic Soldiers" and his formation and leadership of the New Aspiration Party made him a military/political force to be reckoned with. Many rural farmers in the populous Northeast (Isaan) looked favourably upon Chavalit partly because of his "Operation Green Isaan", in which the army had targeted the Northeast for much development. A similar programme in Thailand's Deep South had likewise garnered him popular support in that region. Minor differences between Chavalit and Prem perhaps began to arise in 1987 when Prem countermanded some of Chavalit's choices of senior military appointments. In 1987 and 1988, Chavalit started propagating the notion of "democratic revolution" and a "revolutionary council" that would take the reins of power from ineffective political parties in parliament and expeditiously resolve socioeconomic and political problems for the people. The notion came from Prasert Sabsunthorn, a former communist popular in some military circles. Though these ideas faded and Chavalit's interest in them seemed to wane, Chavalit's detractors saw it all as evidence that the general wanted a presidential form of government, republicanism, and perhaps even communism.[11] The palace never trusted Chavalit after this.[12]

As new prime minister Chuan Leekpai came to office, he was perhaps the first elected prime minister who did not have to deal with a military that may have wished to seize power for itself. With the image of the armed forces tarnished, and following the punitive military demotions of 1 August, the military sought to reinvent itself. Wimol immediately let it be known that he would work towards military reforms and not be party to any coup against a government. For example, he publicly stated in May 1993, "I have declared again and again that the army will not interfere in politics."[13] Meanwhile, ACM Gun Pamarnthip, who had been air force commander under Suchinda, stated that the air force would now be professional.[14]

So who exactly was Wimol? Was he really so different from his predecessors that he could institute enormous military changes?[15] Prime Minister Chuan immediately named eight retired military men to cabinet positions, including Prem-favourite retired general Vichit Sukmark (class 2) as defence minister.[16] At the same time, Wimol became deputy defence minister. In an effort to make good on his promises of military reform and thus win back public trust for the armed forces, Wimol announced modernizations plans in four areas: "command, control and communication; training and personnel development; weapons systems and logistics; and welfare". Moreover, Wimol, following the lead of Chavalit before him, sought to streamline the 200,000-member Thai army by reducing its manpower, shrinking the reserve corps, enhancing training, and being more careful in buying foreign weaponry. In general, General Wimol's apparent commitment to real reform of the military seemed to reflect his integrity as a symbol of change for the armed forces. Still, Wimol did not commit to putting a lid on the military's business activities. According to one Western military analyst, he seemed "to be treading a fine line" between professionalizing the military without interfering in their other activities.[17] Indeed, military officers continued to hold seats on state enterprise boards, while other perks included huge kickbacks for military contracts. Moreover, forty per cent of senior officers continued to have "no identifiable responsibilities". The ubiquitous corruption in the armed forces was, however, something that Wimol seemed unaware of in an interview with a journalist.[18] The October 1992 military reshuffle offered hope of opportunities for elected civilian control (see appendix 4).[19]

As Chuan's coalition government entered 1993, it was somewhat hindered by a powerful military as well as obstacles from Prem and the palace. The appointed Senate remained dominated by military officers. In March 1994, Chuan sought help from Prem for support in passing amendments in the Senate. But Prem was suspicious of his motives, as was the king. The two guaranteed that military senators showed up to vote down one of Chuan's amendments and propose a constitution very similar to the pro-military one of 1978.[20] At the same time, Chuan's government refused to work with civil society to support attempts to bring the perpetrators of Black May 1992 to justice given that Suchinda had negotiated an amnesty when he exited the premiership. In March 1993, the appointed Senate—under pressure because of the unpopular behaviour of the army—confirmed the lower house's abrogation of the Internal Peacekeeping Directorate Act, used specifically as the legal justification for the brutal suppression of the May 1992 demonstration. In June, the house tried to go further, approving a bill that would require the cabinet to give its permission before any troops could be deployed to put down any disturbances. Meanwhile, the NPKC's seizure of assets from the "unusually wealthy" was declared unconstitutional.[21]

Regarding Cambodia, the Chuan government pledged its support for the new 1993 elected government there but refused to cut its indirect connections with the Khmer Rouge. After China stopped its flow of aid to the Khmer Rouge in 1991, Thailand was the insurgent group's only remaining patron. RTA Task Force 838 had formally ended its activities with the 1991 Peace Accord in Cambodia. But when the forward forces of the peacekeeping United Nations Transitional Authority in Cambodia (UNTAC) entered the country to prepare for its administration in late 1991, they discovered continuing Thai military activity: Thai soldiers providing transportation, medical care and other support to insurgents, while Thai loggers and gem merchants were profiting with the Khmer Rouge in the export of gems and timber through Thailand in a multi-million-dollar business—violating international sanctions put in place against the Khmer Rouge. In response to charges that Thailand was contravening the sanctions, Thai military commanders claimed that their support of the Khmer Rouge had been tacitly backed by the United States. Indeed, as this study has made clear, from 1982 until 1989, Washington used the Thai army to funnel military assistance to two non-communist insurgent Cambodian groups that were allied with the Khmer Rouge to wage war against the Vietnamese occupation force in Cambodia and its proxy government there. But the Thai military began financially backing the Khmer Rouge in 1979, while the United States began providing money through the Thai military to non-communist Cambodian insurgent groups in 1982. By 1993, Thai army-funded Khmer Rouge activities were continuing. There were US intelligence reports of "continuing heavy flows of heavy weapons from Thailand into Khmer Rouge zones just before the [Cambodian 1993 elections]".[22] Moreover, despite Thai official denials, the Royal Thai Army's Task Force 838 continued its close ties with the Khmer

Rouge (which had begun in 1978) well after the 1993 election. In November, veteran Australian Indochina journalist Denis Warner published an article alleging that Thai troops had cooperated with the Khmer Rouge in attacking a United Nations checkpoint in Cambodia in July 1993—something that Bangkok denied.[23]

On 7 December 1993, Thai police stopped a truck in the border province of Chanthaburi carrying 1,500 tons of arms destined for the Khmer Rouge. Accompanying the truck and arrested at the scene was a Thai army special forces master sergeant. The police also discovered twelve large warehouses at the border full of Chinese-made weapons meant for the Khmer Rouge.[24] After discussions between the police and a Thai army general, however, the sergeant was released—as was the weapons cache. Meanwhile, in late summer 1993, on the Cambodian side of the same border, the Cambodian military overran a village controlled by the Khmer Rouge just inside Cambodia. Many modern homes were found in the village, including a "spacious house" allegedly used by Pol Pot and another "spacious house" utilized by RTA Unit 838 as an office.[25] Prime Minister Chuan and army commander General Wimol tried to officially distance Thailand from the Khmer Rouge. According to Chuan's spokesman and future prime minister Abhisit Vechachiwa, "The Prime Minister states clearly what the policy is—no interference in the internal affairs of Cambodia—and he expects the military and other Government agencies to carry out that order." Wimol huffed that "any movement of the arms [without authorization] is illegal".[26]

But why would there still be Thai support for the Khmer Rouge in 1993? First, Thailand's civilian government may not have been privy to the fact that certain elements of Thailand's military, police and business community continued to pursue close connections with the Khmer Rouge. Factions and units within Thailand's military were independent of civilian control and were receptive to border corruption—especially when it involved cross-border trade worth millions of US dollars. Thus, these units supported the Khmer Rouge for their own financial reasons.

Some Thai military commanders along the border reportedly earned kickbacks on shipments of lumber and gems. Border traders said in 1993 that loggers had to pay officers of RTA Task Force 838 $1.50 for every cubic metre of timber brought across the border from guerrilla-held areas of Cambodia. Gem trade profits were divided fifty-fifty between the Khmer Rouge and Thai businesspeople after paying ten per cent to the Thai military units that controlled the border.[27] According to a May 1993 United Nations report, the Thai military maintained a "Mafia-like control" over the border, and it suggested that some Thai soldiers and border-control officers were also involved in the smuggling of cars stolen in Thailand. Besides Unit 838, the other Thai military element charged with overseeing the border of eastern Thailand was the 2nd Infantry Division, which is the 12th Infantry Regiment. In addition, a Thai navy marine base is charged with security in Chanthaburi and Trat provinces. According to Global Witness, Thai marines at this base were "assigned to protect the interests of the timber companies" that felled timber in areas of Cambodia controlled by the Khmer Rouge. Thus, ultimately, senior Thai army officers, police and businesspeople received boundless profits by importing lumber, gems and other illicit goods from Cambodia with the help of the Khmer Rouge, while the Khmer Rouge received logistical support from the Thai military.[28]

A second explanation for continuing Thai military involvement with the Khmer Rouge goes beyond simple corruption. Cambodia had long been a useful barrier to Vietnam and its military. When the Vietnamese occupied Cambodia during 1979–89, that barrier disappeared. Thus, Thailand's support of insurgency in Cambodia kept the Vietnamese forces busy[29] and gave Bangkok a means of indirectly dominating Cambodia.

Thailand's October 1993 military reshuffle was, if anything, a reinforcement of army commander General Wimol Wongwanit's control of the armed forces.[30] Nevertheless, the Thai military remained superficially detached from interfering in domestic politics. The king and privy councillor General Prem continued to manage or guide Thai democracy. Chavalit Yongchaiyudh, still a powerful force in the Thai military, was solidly against any coup, as was army commander General Wimol Wongwanich. Besides, the military's image remained tarnished, the economy was growing and Prime Minister Chuan Leekpai, despite a reputation for hesitation, was respected for his non-corrupt character.

Three of the four coalition parties (Democrats, Palang Dharma and Seritham) brought forward amendments to the constitution to initiate decentralization and local-level elections. Army commander Wimol and the secretary-general of the National Security Council voted against the amendments. Only after the army ambiguously backed Chuan and the palace frontman, Senate Speaker Meechai Ruchupan, indicated his support for the measures were they able to pass—although barely—in parliament.[31] The failure of the opposition to fell Chuan's government led to coup rumours, though a putsch never materialized.[32] Eventually, in December 1994, Chavalit withdrew his New Aspiration Party from Chuan's coalition, hoping that Chuan's government would now fall and Chavalit might become prime minister. At this point, however, the palace—through Prem—again intervened. Prem convinced Chatchai Chunhavan and his new Chart Pattana Party to join Chuan's coalition in place of New Aspiration. Clearly, the palace despised Chavalit much more than it did Chuan or electoral decentralization.[33] Prem's influence gave Chuan's government another six months in office before it was finally felled by a corruption scandal in June 1995.

Meanwhile, during 1994, certain actions of the Chuan government displeased the military. First, the government made few major arms purchases. Indeed, in a move that frustrated the senior brass, Chuan attempted to limit the rate of growth of the military budget to only seven per cent per annum.[34] Second, Chuan tried to publicly establish Thailand as a beacon for democracy and human rights. Despite Chuan's platitudes, the Thai military persisted in supporting the Tatmadaw (Myanmar's military) as well as the Khmer Rouge in Cambodia.[35] Third, the Chuan government sought to issue a new policy for barter trade regarding arms imports. In this instance the military felt threatened by Chuan and fought his policy tooth-and-nail, and he was forced eventually to drop it.[36]

The thorniest problem for Thai foreign policy in 1994 remained Cambodia. As growing evidence revealed the Thai military's clear support for the Khmer Rouge, in March 1993, Cambodian prime minister Norodom Ranariddh accused Bangkok of offering refuge to Khmer Rouge forces after the latter had fled from the Cambodian military (and been welcomed) into Thailand. In early April, several Thai Rangers deployed in eastern Chantaburi province admitted in an interview with journalists that RTA Unit 838 was still operating along the Thai-Cambodian border with its principal purpose still being to coordinate with the Khmer Rouge. "'When senior Khmer Rouge officials travel via our checkpoint, 838 will inform us ahead of time', said one of the rangers."[37] The revelation came despite denials from army spokesman Colonel Palangkoon Kraharn, who said he was unaware of the existence of Unit 838. The rangers admitted that "at least 14 task forces of Unit 838—each with between 10 and 15 men—were still deployed on the border."[38] There is also evidence that in 1994 Khmer Rouge troops were still launching attacks on Cambodian forces from areas just inside Thailand. The 1st Army Region commander at the time, Lt. Gen. Chettha Thanacharo, stated in an interview that "we [the RTA] are trying not to interfere with the Khmer Rouge. We get along fine, but people want us to become enemies." Most Thai logistical support for the Khmer Rouge, however, seems finally to have come to an end in mid-1994, possibly because of Thai embarrassment about its continuing intervention in Cambodia, and also because of a massacre of Thai timber employees by the Khmer Rouge in November.[39]

Changes in policy, though, only took place after 2 July, when elements of the Thai army aligned with Thai businesspeople attempted to overthrow Cambodia's government. The latter immediately accused the Thai government or Thai nationals of fomenting the coup attempt against Cambodian prime ministers Norodom Ranariddh and Hun Sen. The formal coup leaders were former interior minister and Hun Sen rival Sin Song, as well as Ranariddh's brother and enemy, Prince Norodom Chakrapong. But when the coup failed, Sin Song was arrested at home and imprisoned. Miraculously, he escaped to Thailand, where Thais protected him. Nevertheless, following the coup attempt, as many as thirty-three members of Thailand's security forces were arrested in Phnom Penh.[40] They were later deported. The Cambodian government specifically alleged that Adul Boonsert, a member of Chavalit Yongchaiyudh's NAP party (who had fled Phnom Penh the day after the failed plot), had been a coup point man.[41] According to Adams, the coup attempt was supported by Thai military officials and businesspeople (including Thaksin Shinawatra) who were incensed that they had been deprived of profitable deals by the Cambodian government.[42]

Following the coup attempt, the Chuan government finally began to get serious about ending Thailand's links with the Khmer Rouge. In mid-July 1994, the Royal Thai Supreme Command sent an order to all border units emphasizing the policy of no direct links with the Khmer Rouge. In October 1994, the Thai National Security Council decided to cut off entry and exit through the border for the Khmer Rouge, although contracts between the Thai commercial sector and the Khmer Rouge continued. Then, on 21 November, a Khmer Rouge group massacred twenty-four Thai loggers. That was enough for the Thai government. In December, Chuan reiterated the policy of cutting all connections with the Khmer Rouge to Thai governors of all provinces bordering Cambodia. Still, in late 1994, Thai entrepreneurs continued to be involved in the gem and logging trade through some unofficial entry points into Thailand, with imports facilitated by Thai military officials.[43]

The October 1994 military reshuffle (see Appendix 4) represented another annual consolidation of power for officers aligned with army chief Wimol.[44] Thailand entered 1995 with a buoyant economy as the royalist guided democracy helmed by Prime Minister Chuan Leekpai continued. But Chuan's premiership did not last. Though military coups seemed to be a thing of the past, parliamentary changes that year affected the legislative balance of power. A land scandal in December 1994 had descended upon leading Democrat Party members. Then, on 19 May 1995, Chamlong's PDP left the coalition and Chuan was forced to dissolve the house.[45]

In the ensuing general election, Chart Thai Party, now led by provincial business tycoon Banharn Silpa-archa, was the winner. The new coalition totaled 232 MPs out of 391.[46] Once established as prime minister in July, Banharn, unlike Chuan, did not have Prem readily supporting him. In fact, the palace looked upon Banharn with utter disdain. To bolster the military's opinion of his government, Banharn chose General Chavalit Yongchaiyudh as defence minister (army chief Wimol's retirement was only months away).

The Banharn government in many respects was more amenable to the military top brass than Chuan had been. For example, his coalition government supported a conciliatory approach towards Thailand's neighbours (Myanmar, Cambodia and the Lao PDR), sharply downgrading Chuan's earlier policy emphasizing human rights. As to Cambodia, despite Prime Minister Chuan Leekpai's 1994 termination of official contacts between the Thai military and the Khmer Rouge, the Thai-Cambodian border remained open to the timber trade from timbering areas in Cambodia controlled by the Khmer Rouge. In Thailand's Chantaburi province, timber imports continued to pass by a Thai Marine base and a Thai military/police checkpoint. According to Global Witness, the Thai military in 1995 continued to be "assigned to protect the interests of timber companies [with] timber from known Khmer Rouge zones ... stored in Thai government yards and Thai concession holders ... paying off the Khmer Rouge."[47] By April 1996, Global Witness had obtained documents that authorized the export of 1.1 million logs from Cambodia to Thailand. This "Million Meter Deal" consisted of three letters to Thai prime minister Banharn Silpa-archa signed by Cambodia's co-prime ministers. Then, following a meeting between Cambodia's Ministry of Agriculture and Thailand's deputy prime minister (and defence minister) General Chavalit, the Cambodian government agreed to export the 1.1 million logs to Thailand. All the timber came from territory held by the Khmer Rouge and was intended for eleven Thai timber companies. According to an anonymous source cited in the *Phnom Penh Post*, "If you assume that much of the business was done on a local level, between the Khmer Rouge, the Thai military and the Royal Cambodian Armed Forces, it makes sense that senior levels of both [Thai and Cambodian] Governments would want to work out arrangements on how to control this themselves."[48]

Meanwhile, the coalition proved to be quite soft towards military appropriations and, as such, earned greater support from the armed forces. The government greenlit acquisition requests from the navy for new submarines and from the army for more fighter jets.[49] Moreover, Banharn cancelled Chuan's previous limit of seven per cent on defence procurement. At the same time, defence minister Chavalit worked hard to acquire even more weapons for the armed forces. These included support equipment for a new helicopter carrier, two submarines and a new military satellite. Deputy Prime Minister Thaksin Shinawatra strongly opposed the acquisition of the satellite, alleging that the military simply wanted it for commercial purposes. Army Radio countered that Thaksin opposed the satellite merely on the grounds it would interfere with his own commercial satellites.[50] In the end, the satellite project was shelved. Meanwhile, another scandal involving military purchases hit the Banharn government. In November, Swedish media reported that Swedish defence contractor Kockums had paid off Thailand's Chart Thai Party to support its bid for a Thai defence contract. The episode discredited the government and led to calls in parliament for military procurement to be placed under the closer scrutiny of parliamentary committees.[51]

The October 1995 military reshuffle (see Appendix 4) saw many new faces. Of the top sixteen postings, twelve underwent changes. The reshuffle was the last to be influenced by retiring army commander General Wimol Wongwanich. But the reshuffle was also influenced by the new defence minister, Chavalit, who sought to ensure that active-duty military leadership was weak if only to bolster his own sway over the armed forces.[52] Ultimately, the reshuffle was rather balanced in terms of class promotions. Chavalit's success in getting his favourites appointed to top military positions demonstrated that, like Prem, he could trump the influence of active-duty military officers. But the fact that a civilian defence minister could countermand the preferences of active-duty senior officers seemed to bode well for civilian control. On the other hand, Chavalit was also a powerful former army commander who seemed to be manipulating the reshuffle to benefit his New Aspiration Party. As he himself said: "From the outside I may seem 100 per cent a politician; but in my heart I'm still 70 per cent a soldier".[53]

By late 1996, it had become clear that the power of active-duty military officers was slipping. Evidence for this could be seen in the 1996 Senate, which underwent a rotation of appointments that year.

Since Banharn could nominate the new senators, he wanted to improve his image with civilians. As a result of his efforts, only 18.4 per cent of the new senators were soldiers, marking a decline of military influence in the Senate, down from the earlier percentage of 55.2 per cent (see Figure 11.1).

Indeed, the beginning of economic woes amidst growing tensions at the intra-party and inter-party level finally led to a no-confidence parliamentary debate in September against Banharn. Though he survived the censure vote, he was only able to secure enough votes by promising his coalition partners and Chart Thai factions that he would resign as prime minister to make way for another candidate. On 21 September, threatened by imminent defection not only from three coalition parties but also from the powerful factions of Therd Thai, Wang Nam Yen and Paknam (who were on the verge of throwing their support to either New Aspiration's Chavalit Yongchaiyudh, the Chart Pattana Party's Chatchai Chunhavan, or Montree Pongpanit's Social Action Party), Banharn announced his resignation.[54] He refused to agree to New Aspiration's Chavalit Yongchaiyudh succeeding him, considering the NAP leader a coalition traitor. Chavalit had already secured the support of the other coalition parties and both the Wang Nam Yen and Paknam factions of Chart Thai Party.[55] Yet Banharn still had the ultimate weapon: the premier's right to dissolve parliament and call new elections. This he did on 27 September, setting the election date for 17 November 1996.

Under Banharn and then Chavalit, the military budget and military procurement grew—even though the current accounts deficit was high. Banharn had relied on Chavalit's NAP party remaining in the coalition to keep his government in office, but Chavalit continuously lobbied for new weapons systems. Thus, Banharn backed him up. At the time,

FIGURE 11.1
Thailand's Senate, 1996–2000

Type of legislature	Years in office	Appointed or elected	Total number of members and military contingent
Bicameral (Eighth Senate)	1996–2000 (served 4-year term)	Appointed	260, of which 48 (18.4%) military reserved domain

Source: Paul Chambers, "Superfluous, Irrelevant or Emancipating: Thailand's Evolving Senate Today", *Journal of Current Southeast Asian Affairs* 28, no. 3 (2009): 9.

Chavalit exploded at journalists: "Arms acquisitions are an internal affair of the military. Civilians should stay away. It's not right for them to get involved."[56]

Meanwhile, the October 1996 military reshuffle saw the retirement of army commander Pramon Plasin, replaced by the pro-Chavalit General Chettha Thanajaro (Chulachomklao Academy class 9).[57] Banharn wanted to make sure that Chavalit's NAP was in the coalition. Thus, most of Chavalit's preferred military candidates were appointed.[58]

The 1996 reshuffle marked the beginning of the rise of generals Prawit Wongsuwan, Anupong Paochinda and Prayut Chanocha. The first became head of the 2nd Army Division, Queen's Guard; the second was appointed as commander of the 21st Regiment, 2nd Army Division; and the third was Anupong's deputy. One of Prawit's patrons was incoming army commander General Chettha—Prawit had previously been Chettha's close aide.[59] Finally, with Chavalit's support, General Pracha Promnok became police commander.

The 17 November 1996 election handed Chavalit's New Aspiration Party a two-seat victory over the Democrat Party. He became prime minister, heading a coalition of NAP, Chart Pattana, Social Action, Thai Citizens, Muanchon, and Seritham Party—221 seats of the 393 in the house.

Indeed, November 1996 saw Chavalit reach the pinnacle of his ambitions—becoming Thai prime minister. He had been born into a military family on 15 May 1932 in Nonthaburi Province, the son of Captain Chan Yongchaiyudh, ex-mayor of Nakhon Panom. The surname Yongchaiyudh had been bestowed by descendants of King Rama IV.[60] Chavalit has been married four times. He has three children (see Figure 11.2 for his family tree).

Under the new government, Chavalit acted as both prime minister and defence minister. The election of a recently retired powerful military officer as prime minister proved that soldiers did not have to come to office solely via a coup. Future retired military officers could follow the Chavalit model and use elections to achieve power, something that could give such winning candidates popular legitimacy. When Chavalit became prime minister and defence minister in November 1997, there was, as a result, no true civilian in the line of command; thus, the problem of civilian control remained unresolved.[61]

In foreign policy under Chavalit, relations between Thailand and other members of ASEAN, especially Thailand's mainland neighbours, were quite cordial, continuing the policy of Banharn. This owed to Chavalit's long career as a senior military man who was already well

FIGURE 11.2
Chavalit Yongchaiyudh Family Tree

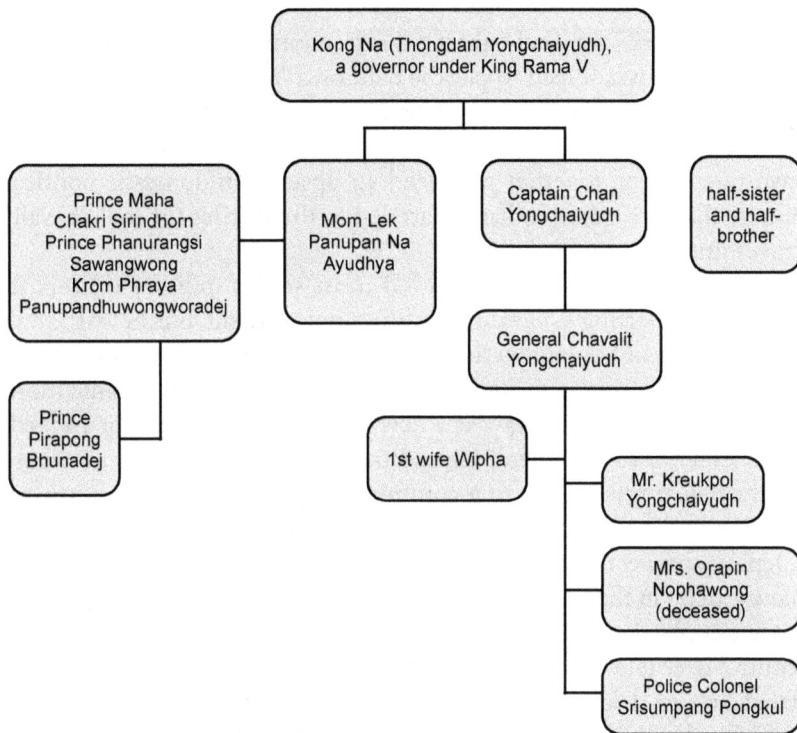

acquainted with leaders in the region as well as his prioritization of regional economic goals. Thus, relations with Vietnam, Laos and Cambodia generally improved.[62] Given Chavalit's close ties with Tatmadaw generals, Myanmar became a closer ally of Thailand. Chavalit was an avid proponent of "constructive engagement" with Myanmar and was an instrumental facilitator of that country's accession into ASEAN in 1997. Only border issues involving refugees or illegal immigrants created tense moments for Bangkok. Chavalit's warm linkages with Tatmadaw generals owed to his long and extensive business interests with them.[63] In Cambodia, though some senior members of the Khmer Rouge negotiated a peace settlement with the Cambodian government, others continued to collaborate with the Thai army. Evidence points to their strolling across the border to obtain supplies from Thai army border guards[64] as well as being allowed to escape across the border from pursuing Cambodian soldiers as late as October 1996.[65]

In 1997, Thailand experienced an immense financial crisis, but in the same year a progressive constitution was enacted. Both the economic shock and the new constitution contributed to limiting military power in the country.

In May 1997 the Thai baht was hit by enormous speculative attacks and Chavalit was forced to put the baht on a "managed float" on 2 July. Thereupon Thailand's economy began to plummet, a situation that paralleled a growing civilian drive for a more progressive constitution. The two phenomena together produced an upsurge in domestic political unrest that, according to Englehart, led to three crises for the Chavalit government.[66]

In the first crisis, Prem had led most senior military officers in initially supporting Chavalit's coalition government, but he withdrew this backing in September 1997. Meanwhile, popular pressure intensified for a new constitution. But senior military officers became more suspicious of what they saw as a new threat to military power. Indeed, army chief of staff General Chan Boonprasert claimed that members of the constitutional drafting committee were simply trying to stir up tension and he threatened that a coup might occur if this persisted. Deputy army commander General Preecha Rojanasen denounced the new articles in the draft constitution that legally forbade military coups, gave people the right to resist such coups, and transferred military control over television and radio stations to a civilian board.[67] Chavalit tried first to delay a vote on the charter and then to amend it. This decision brought angry crowds out onto the streets in opposition, and foreign investor confidence in Thailand's economy continued to plummet. Thereupon army commander General Chettha Thanajaro and supreme commander Mongkol Ampornpiset told Chavalit that he ought to support the draft constitution.[68] Chettha even publicly stated that the charter should be passed and that any amendments should take place only after new elections.[69] Given this support for the passage of the charter by the military, the prime minister reluctantly complied, changing the government's stand, and supported the charter's passage.

As a result, on 11 October 1997, a new constitution was ratified into law. One of the most prominent changes in the country's political system brought about by the charter was the method by which the Senate was chosen. Instead of an appointed Senate, it now became all-elected. This was unprecedented and it diminished the political influence of the armed forces, given that in previous Senates the military benefited from having its own appointees sit in the upper house. Still, the top brass were successful in preventing the adoption of a clause in the constitution making a military *coup d'etat* illegal (though Article 63 did forbid any extra-constitutional "overthrow" of "the democratic regime of government with the King as Head of the State").[70] A compromise was reached between civilian drafters and military leaders in the charter's final wording that any civilian resistance to a coup would have to be peaceful. Meanwhile, "the military's role in the suppression and curtailment of civil unrest and riots [was] left out, but its role in development remain[ed]".[71] Perhaps because of this compromise, army radio, under instructions from supreme commander Mongkol and army commander Chettha, urged the government to back the bill.[72]

In the second crisis, by October 1997, amidst intensifying demonstrations by crowds demanding Chavalit's resignation, Prem's name was floated as a possible alternative prime minister. Moreover, Prem appeared to advance the idea of him returning to office along with some of his advisors.[73] Reacting to the financial crisis and protests, Chavalit attempted to declare a state of emergency, asking army commander Chettha to move in and enforce a curfew, media censorship and more. But what amounted to Chavalit's attempted self-coup—with echoes of 1971—was not to be. The palace and Prem would have none of it. They pressured Chettha to resist the prime ministerial request. Realizing that the royal wind was blowing against Chavalit, senior officers refused to participate in a putsch, with army commander Chettha telling reporters following a meeting with the prime minister, "No leader with mental stability would opt for this choice."[74] Following the incident, Sukhum Nualskul, an academic at Ramkhamhaeng University, stated: "The military is now exerting a strong influence on Thai politics.... When the army commander says something, the prime minister listens."[75] Instead, the prime minister announced that a cabinet reshuffle would soon occur. The reshuffle was advocated in particular by Chart Pattana Party leader Chatchai Chunhavan to instil greater confidence in the government and the economy.[76] Yet, with the reshuffle pleasing few coalition members, Chavalit, under pressure from the palace, agreed to resign (though not dissolve the lower house) on 6 November 1997.

This led to the third crisis. On that day, a coalition bloc led by the Democrat Party managed to gather the support of 196 MPs. Another bloc led by Chatchai Chunhavan's Chart Pattana meanwhile commanded the support of 196 seats in the lower house, with one MP out of the country undergoing medical treatment.[77] Under these conditions, Prachakorn Thai (Thai Citizens') Party (TCP) leader Samak Sundaravej held a late-night party conference meeting and attempted to gavel through support for Chart Pattana. But the TCP factions of "Paknam", Nonthaburi Pitsanuloke and one member of the two-man Uttaradit team refused to go along; they instead announced their intention to defy Samak and back Chuan Leekpai. The support from these three factions and the Uttaradit member— "the Cobras", as party leader Samak angrily called them—was instrumental in pushing Chuan to the premiership.[78] But the TCP factional backing for Chuan came at the insistence of the palace and Privy Council—the factions could not refuse. Thus, what occurred was a "silent coup"—something that academic M.R. Sukhumphand Paribatra had predicted back in August that Prem would make happen.[79] And indeed it was Prem who had pressured and manipulated the exodus of the Cobras to the Democrat-led coalition.[80] Indeed, the surreptitious nature of Prem's manipulated ouster of Chavalit reflected the monarchy's preference for concealing involvement in the removal of a prime minister suspected of republican sympathies.[81]

With the fall of the Chavalit government, three things became immediately clear. First, ironically, by standing behind greater democratization efforts (and against any coup), the military was trying to regain the legitimacy it had lost during the events of Black May. Moreover, by standing up to Chavalit and refusing a putsch, senior brass demonstrated that they could and would refuse the will of a (retired military) civilian prime minister. Second, though Chettha may have increased his influence by standing up to Chavalit, he was hemmed in by mandatory retirement in 1998. Third, Prem, who had backed Chettha, was once again victorious over a potential (retired) military adversary. Chavalit's bumbling stand against the draft constitution and lacklustre attempts to shore up the economy in 1997 de-legitimized him as a stable, serving prime minister. As such, Chavalit's political standing weakened, allowing Prem to increasingly dominate the armed forces. As a result of Chavalit's frailty, "Prem secured more promotions for his loyalists to senior military positions, including the 1998 appointment of his confidant General Surayud Chulanond as army commander."[82]

Chavalit had been able to oversee and manipulate the October 1997 military reshuffle (see Appendix 4) a month before his forced resignation (given his simultaneous dual powers of being prime minister and defence minister). The reshuffle itself brought about few changes in appointments. Army commander General Chettha Thanajaro retained his post, while Chavalit specifically promoted class 11 (which had suffered an overall Prem-directed demotion after Black May). Chavalit had been grooming his loyalist general Chan Boonprasert (class 11) to succeed General Chettha in 1998 when the latter was to retire. But the prime minister did not last long enough in office to make the appointment. Another rising star close to Chavalit was General Sampao Chusri (class 12), who had also been close to Suchinda. Chavalit appointed Sampao as assistant army chief and shunted Sampao's rival, the pro-Prem Surayud Chulanond (also class 12), off to an inactive position (special advisor).[83]

Though the incoming Chuan Leekpai II government was non-elected, its quick endorsement by the palace—reflecting the preference of the king—was enough to legitimize its ascension to power. Chuan formed a coalition on 9 November comprising the Democrats, Chart Thai, Social Action, Seritham, Ekkapap, Palang Dharma, the Thai Party, and the 12 "Cobras" (the three and one-half factions) of the 18-MP Thai Citizens' Party for a total of 210 out of 393 seats. Besides being prime minister, Chuan also assumed the post of defence minister. This was significant because he was a "true civilian" defence minister—that is, not a retired military officer who assumed that post.

With Chuan as prime minister rather than Chavalit (but Chuan having no influence within the armed forces), Prem was able to better influence the 1998 military reshuffle, though some compromises were made with Chettha. Chettha, who was retiring, sought to have his friend General Chainarong Noonpakdi replace him as army commander. But Chainarong had played a major role in the 1992 Black May massacre as he was one of the officers in the chain of command who had ordered soldiers to fire at demonstrators. As such, the latter was unsuitable for the post. Besides, Chainarong was not close to the palace. After advice from Prem, Chuan thus selected Prem-loyalist General Surayud Chulanond (Chulachomklao Academy class 12, pre-cadet class 1), who thereupon moved back from a mere advisory position in the Supreme Command to become army commander-in-chief.[84] Surayud was a royalist and moderately reformist loyalist to Prem. He was only fifty-five and would not have to retire until 2003.[85] He represented a new professional military man for Thailand. Indeed, he was quoted in 1997 as stating that "as long as parliamentary democracy continues to provide the formal rules of the political game and conventional coup-making is therefore less feasible, military leaders and their cliques … have to be seen to be non-political".[86] In other words, the military might still play a significant low-key role on the political stage though it would do so only in the dark shadow of party politics.

Surayud's family history was unique to say the least. Born on 28 August 1943 in Chakrapongse army camp residence (Prachinburi province), Surayud ("Big Ed") was the second son of Lt. Col. Payom

Chulanond (the son of the noble "Chao Phraya" Wiset Singhanat) and Mrs Amphot (Tharap) Chulanont. Amphot was the daughter of Colonel Phraya Sri Sitthi Songkram (Din Tharap), who had been part of General Phraya Phahon's original government before joining the Bowaradej rebellion in 1933. As that rebellion ended, Sri Sitthi Songkram was shot dead by Praphas Charusathien (a lieutenant at the time). Surayud's familial identification with Sri Sitthi Songkram seemed to mark him as a royalist. But his father, Lt. Col. Payom—who had been an ally of Field Marshal Plaek Phibun Songkram and Phin Chunhavan in their 1947 military putsch and who later failed to oust them from power—became an elected MP in February 1957 (in Phetburi Province). Following Sarit's 1957 coup, however, Payom joined the Thai communist movement.[87]

His father gone, Surayud grew up in military camps and had a royalist upbringing.[88] In 1989, he headed the 1st Special Forces Division under General Sunthorn Kongsompong.

Throughout his life, Surayud faced suspicion from army circles because of his father's defection to the Thai communist insurgency. Surayud let it be known publicly that if he ever faced his father in combat he would have no hesitation but to kill him. Payom's defection to the communists had so affected Surayud that he once told his son Non that "we must help each other redeem the family name of Chulanont tarnished by [father Payom] so that Thais can look up to it".[89] During the events of Black May in 1992, Surayud commanded soldiers who shot at and rounded up protestors; these troops were seen by journalists kicking and stepping on demonstrators who had been arrested and were being held (some wounded) at the Royal (Ratanakosin) Hotel. Surayud later said that he never ordered his soldiers to fire upon anyone.[90] The Surayud-backed coup of 2006 suggested that Black May 1992 had not convinced him that the military should stay in the barracks. Surayud married twice and has three children. Figure 11.3 shows his family tree.

Surayud's appointment as army commander in 1998 came as a surprise to many senior military officials; first, because his father had been a communist, and second, because Surayud's promotion had been irregular—through the command of the Royal Thai Armed Forces rather than ascending through the army alone. Thus, rumours grew that elements in the army were preparing a coup.[91] Prem-ally supreme commander Mongkol would, meanwhile, not be retiring until 2000. This meant that Prem's influence across the senior brass positions was assured until the end of Chuan's term. Chuan himself owed his position since 1997 as prime minister to Prem's interventions.

FIGURE 11.3
Surayud Chulanont Family Tree

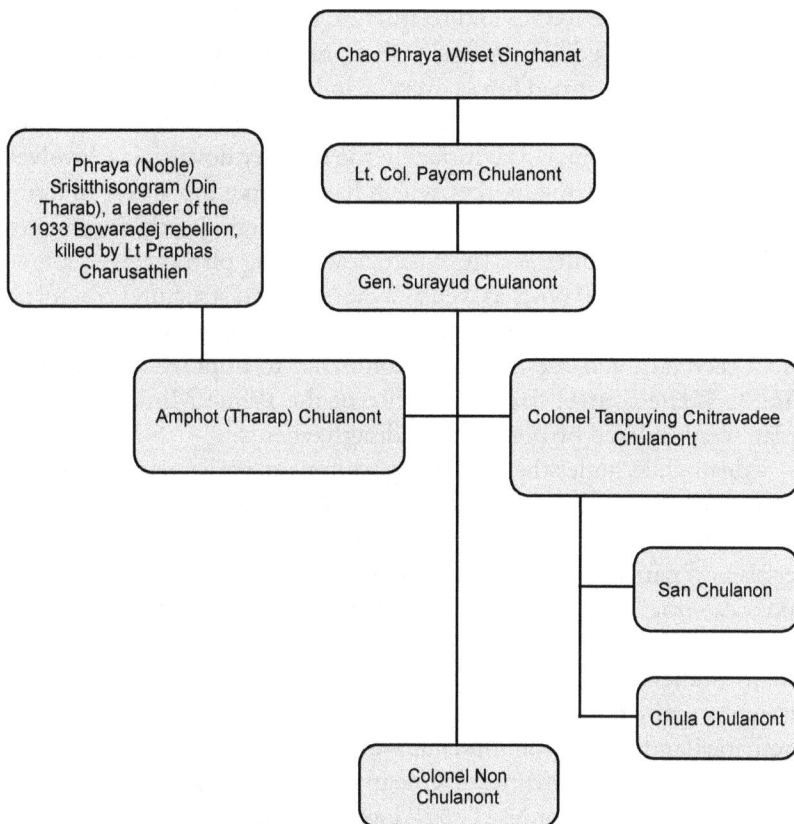

```
                        ┌─────────────────────────────┐
                        │ Chao Phraya Wiset Singhanat │
                        └─────────────────────────────┘
                                      │
┌──────────────────────┐   ┌─────────────────────────────┐
│ Phraya (Noble)       │   │ Lt. Col. Payom Chulanont    │
│ Srisitthisongram (Din│   └─────────────────────────────┘
│ Tharab), a leader of │                │
│ the 1933 Bowaradej   │   ┌─────────────────────────────┐
│ rebellion, killed by │   │ Gen. Surayud Chulanont      │
│ Lt Praphas           │   └─────────────────────────────┘
│ Charusathien         │
└──────────────────────┘
           │
┌──────────────────────┐      ┌──────────────────────────────┐
│ Amphot (Tharap)      │──────│ Colonel Tanpuying Chitravadee│
│ Chulanont            │      │ Chulanont                    │
└──────────────────────┘      └──────────────────────────────┘
                                            │
                                   ┌──────────────────┐
                                   │ San Chulanon     │
                                   └──────────────────┘
                                   ┌──────────────────┐
                                   │ Chula Chulanont  │
                                   └──────────────────┘
              ┌──────────────────┐
              │ Colonel Non      │
              │ Chulanont        │
              └──────────────────┘
```

Chettha also insisted that Chuan give an award to former dictator Field Marshal Thanom Kittikachorn. Meanwhile, Chettha appointed his crony General Teeradej Meepien (who maintained ties with Prem and Surayud) as permanent minister of defence.[92]

During 1999, efforts at reform of the Thai security sector that had previously begun under former army commander General Wimol after the 1992 Black May incident were prioritized owing to the need for a cheaper, more efficient military in the wake of the 1997 Asian financial crisis—which had severely affected Thailand's economy. Taking the cue from prime minister and defence minister Chuan Leekpai, army chief Surayud spearheaded the reform. Actually, the Chavalit Yongchaiyudh government had vetted proposals aimed at restructuring the armed forces and improving public oversight of the military. The incoming Chuan Leekpai government took up these recommendations (through the Ministry of Defence, or MOD) and, in October 1999, approved a plan to reform the MOD and restructure the military. The goal was to build a smaller, credible, professional, more efficient, more capable and more transparent armed forces over the following ten years.[93] There was also to be a "reallocation of military spending from personnel to procurement and training".[94] Ultimately, the military downsizing involved transforming the armed forces, which had become top-heavy in terms of an excess of high-ranking officers, by encouraging early retirements by many of these officials. The entire downsizing plan involved a total reduction of 72,000 posts as well as a more unified structural command among the three services (army, navy and air force), the defence permanent secretary, and the Supreme Command to improve coordination and facilitate control from the Office of the Prime Minister. Yet the plan was hindered by bureaucratic disagreements.

Meanwhile, under the Chuan II government, parliamentary scrutiny of military appropriations had grown. This owed partly to the post-1992 tainted image of the military, partly to the 1997 Asian financial crisis and partly to the growing supremacy of "civilianization" in Thai politics—the "people's" constitution was adopted in 1997.[95] The result was a reduction in the Thai defence budget. This loss in revenue led many soldiers to increasingly expand their commercial interests as well as rely on sometimes-shady business activities. To rein in illegal military activities and limit economic autonomy of the armed forces, beginning in 1999, Prime Minister Chuan Leekpai and army commander Surayud Chulanond ordered crackdowns on military-related "narcotics trafficking, extortion rackets, illegal bookmaking, unsecured loans from Thai Military Bank, and corruption in the conscription process".[96] The Chuan government also sought to centralize weapons procurement in order to establish greater government control over armed forces funding. But confronted with intense military resistance, this proposal was eventually shelved.[97]

In foreign affairs, the Thai military appeared to be attempting to appear as a more stabilized contributor to international order. One factor that helped this was the capture on 6 March 1999 of General Ta Mok, the last senior Khmer Rouge official who had not surrendered to the Cambodian government. Ta Mok was arrested by Thai law officials just inside Thai territory.[98] His capture and transfer to Phnom Penh finally ended years of both protection by the Royal Thai Army of the Khmer Rouge and participation in its commercial activities. With the

Khmer Rouge gone, the Thai military became a clear enforcer of Thai-Cambodian border security. But, as journalist Tom Fawthrop pointed out in April 1999, though Ta Mok had been captured, Thai military commercial dealings with the Khmer Rouge had continued up until that year. His assets in Thailand's Khukan district, Sisaket province, along the Thai-Cambodian border, included two petrol stations, a logging company, electrical and spare parts shops, and a sawmill; they were all closely tied to the Boonthot/Aroonsawat family, a Khukan business family with close connections to the Thai military in Sisaket.[99] The point is that as late as 1999 Thailand's military was still closely connected with the Khmer Rouge.

Meanwhile, 1999 saw Thailand's military begin to engage United Nations peacekeeping missions abroad. Indeed, in 1998, seven years after the end of the Cold War, a year after the 1997 financial crisis and amidst efforts to restructure the armed forces, Chuan and Surayud had attempted to reshape military objectives. As such, they added a new role for the military: participation in United Nations peacekeeping missions.[100]

In terms of border policy, upon his appointment as army chief in 1998, Surayud initiated a hawkish policy towards the military government in Myanmar. Indeed, he supported the Chuan II government's new approach of "flexible engagement", whereby "peers" could exert "pressure" on their neighbours.[101] The goal of Thailand was to staunch the inflow of narcotics and refugees from across the border. Surayud's tilt against Myanmar frustrated Myanmar "friends" such as General Chavalit Yongchaiyudh and Thaksin Shinawatra. Meanwhile, in December 1998 and January 1999, two armed clashes between an unidentified ocean vessel of Myanmar and a Thai navy boat resulted in the deaths of two Thai navy officials. Tensions grew between the two countries. But frictions grew even more following the temporary takeover of the Myanmar embassy in Bangkok on 1 October 1999 by a group of Myanma university students calling themselves the Vigorous Burmese Student Warriors.

The October 1999 military reshuffle saw a consolidation of Surayud's (and Prem's) control over the armed forces.[102] To handle Thailand's increasingly prickly border relations with Myanmar, Surayud appointed General Wattanachai Chaimuenwong, his close friend and fellow graduate of class 12, to command Region 3, the northern border.[103]

The 1997 charter had made Thailand's new Senate fully elected. Thaksin's Thai Rak Thai Party quickly gained influence over a majority of senators—the Senate took office on 22 July 2000. By law, the new

Senate contained no active-duty military officials. However, 2 per cent of senators were retired military or police (see Figure 11.4).

October 1999 saw the United Nations Security Council vote to replace INTERFET with the United Nations Transitional Administration in East Timor (UNTAET). Thai general Boonsrang Niumpradit, future Thai armed forces supreme commander, became commander of UNTAET forces until 31 August 2001.

In December 1999, four Thai soldiers were killed when they stepped on landmines planted by God's Army rebels on the Thai-Myanmar border. The guerrillas alleged that Thai forces were intentionally bombing Myanma refugees.[104] On 17–19 January 2000, the God's Army base was purportedly shelled with heavy artillery by Thailand's 9th Infantry Division. Soldiers of the Thai 9th Infantry Division later detained many of the rebels: fifty-five men from the group were arrested and disappeared. The Thai military later claimed that the fifty-five voluntarily returned to Myanmar, but there has been no evidence of this allegation.[105] Ultimately, on 16 January 2001, Thailand's 9th Infantry Division encircled the remnants of God's Army along the border, forcing it to surrender.

Meanwhile, a more serious border threat was brewing: the United Wa State Army (UWSA) and its marketing of highly addictive methamphetamine tablets—or *ya ba* (mad drug). UWSA troops were said to have acquired shoulder-launched anti-aircraft missiles, probably from Cambodian sources. This was plausible, since the Cambodian government had in 1999 won its war against the Khmer Rouge, which had been supported by the Thai army; some Thai military elements were now willing to sell military hardware (meant for Khmer Rouge insurgents) to the UWSA. Beijing had sent engineers and other "advisors" to assist the Wa—a fact that was worrisome to some Thai officials.[106]

FIGURE 11.4
Thailand's Senate, 2000–2006

Type of legislature	Years in office	Appointed or elected	Total number of members and military contingent
Bicameral (Ninth Senate)	2000–2006 (served 6-year term)	Directly elected	200 (2% ex-military)

Source: Paul Chambers, "Superfluous, Irrelevant or Emancipating: Thailand's Evolving Senate Today", *Journal of Current Southeast Asian Affairs* 28, no. 3 (2009): 9.

Amidst this heightened frontier violence close to Myanmar, in 1999–2000, army chief Surayud had begun to redeploy Thai forces stationed along the Thai-Cambodian border to the Thai-Myanmar border. At the same time, the Thai navy began to amass much of its forces close to the Thai-Myanmar maritime boundary. The Thai military began to strictly enforce a policy against cross-border intervention by Myanmar's forces. Army commander Surayud and supreme commander Mongkol vigorously supported Chuan's tough policy towards Myanmar's military. At the same time, Chuan, concerned that giving his military primary responsibility over Thai-Myanmar relations might lead to interstate violence, entrusted the Thai Foreign Ministry with authority over relations with Myanmar. In relation to this, following supreme commander General Mongkol's mandatory retirement in 2000, his replacement, General Sampao, a friend of Chavalit's, sought to improve military-to-military linkages with Myanmar—a position also supported by those military officers who were aligned with Thaksin Shinawatra's newly created Thai Rak Thai Party. While a return to such cosiness might have improved relations on a military level, there was a danger it could lead to the Thai military simply looking the other way when the Tatmadaw pursued insurgents across the border into Thailand. At the same time, the Thai military soon began cooperating with Myanmar's armed forces in importing raw materials into Thailand—a venture Chavalit had been involved with (both as an active-duty and retired military officer) since at least December 1988.[107]

The October 2000 military reshuffle (see Appendix 4) saw Surayud favour the promotion of pre-cadet military classes 1, 2, 3 and 7 to senior armed forces postings. At the same time, he appointed his Chulachomklao Academy class 12 competitor General Sampao Chusri to the largely ceremonial position of supreme commander (where Sampao served for one year until his 2001 mandatory retirement).[108]

Ultimately, in the aftermath of Black May 1992, the image of the military had been tarnished and euphoria had spread about a new paradigm of Thai leadership characterized by elected civilian rule—from the people—though loyal to the palace. What emerged was a guided royalist democracy, and it seemed to work. But by December 2000, although a general election was fast approaching (in which Chuan sought four more years), most of the Thai populace, which included many in the Thai military, were frustrated with the current state of affairs.

The bespectacled Chuan Leekpai seemed to have become a weak substitute for the strongmen who had previously led Thailand. For soldiers, Chuan hardly offered a military panacea. The military budget had diminished, the Surayud reforms were unwelcome to many officers, and the armed forces simply seemed to be underappreciated. Chuan's primary opponent, the telecommunications tycoon Thaksin Shinawatra, seemed to be a man who could get things done. Indeed, after Thaksin had formed his Thai Rak Thai Party in 1998, several active-duty and retired officers hopped aboard.[109] The majority of graduates in Chulachomklao classes 13 (Uthai Shinawatra) 14 (class of Rapin Shinawatra), 16 (class of Chaisit Shinawatra), 20 (class of Prawit Shinawatra) and 21 (Thaksin's own pre-cadet class 10) seemed to have gone over to Thaksin. There were still many military officers, however, such as army commander Surayud and his followers, who remained suspicious. Still other officers remained neutral. Nevertheless, with such divisions in the armed forces and Prime Minister Chuan extremely unpopular, a major change in politics looked soon to occur. This transformation—demonstrated in the total electoral defeat of the Democrats in the 2001 election—would represent a sea change for the Thai military.

Notes

1. Thongchai Winichakul, "Thailand's Royalist Democracy in Crisis", *CSEAS Newsletter*, no. 72 (Autumn 2015): 5, Center for Southeast Asian Studies, Kyoto University, https://repository.kulib.kyoto-u.ac.jp/dspace/bitstream/2433/202757/1/cseasnl72.pdf.

2. Sheldon Wolf, *Democracy Incorporated: Managed Democracy and the Specter of Inverted Totalitarianism* (Princeton: Princeton University Press, 2008), p. 47.

3. Wolfgang Merkel, "Embedded and Defective Democracies", *Democratization* 11, no. 5 (December 2004): 49.

4. He had been an elected Democrat in the lower house starting in 1969. The Democrats were then the parliamentary opposition to Prime Minister Thanom Kittikachorn and his party. Following the 1971 coup, Chuan had been seen by military leaders as a potential subversive: during the period 1971–73 he had sometimes been on the run from ISOC. Under Prime Minister Seni Pramoj in 1976, he had become minister of justice, and then, from 1980 to 1991, under party leaders Thanat Khoman and then Pichai Rattakul, he had held numerous cabinet postings. Chuan himself became party leader in 1991. Narong Pokket, ชวน หลีกภัย นายกรัฐมนตรีที่มาจาก เด็กวัด [Chuan Leekpai, prime minister who came from a temple boy], 2nd ed. (Chiang Mai: Sangsilp Printing House, 2001).

5. Paul Handley, *The King Never Smiles* (New Haven, CT: Yale University Press, 2005), pp. 365 and 372.

6. Surin Maisrikrod, *Thailand's Two General Elections in 1992: Democracy Sustained* (Singapore: Institute of Southeast Asian Studies, 1992), p. 43.

7. Chai-anan Samudavanija, "The Military, Bureaucracy, and Globalization", in *Political Change in Thailand*, edited by Kevin Hewison (London: Routledge, 1997), p. 56.

8. Duncan McCargo, "Network Monarchy and Legitimacy Crises in Thailand", *Pacific Review* 18, no. 4 (December 2005): 508.

9. Chai-anan, "The Military, Bureaucracy", p. 56.

10. *Raingan Naeo Na* (1993), as cited in McCargo, "Network Monarchy", pp. 508–9.

11. Michael Kelly Connors, *Democracy and National Identity in Thailand* (Copenhagen: NIAS, 2007), p. 110.

12. Handley, *The King Never Smiles*, p. 373.

13. Rodney Tasker, "Remodeled Army", *Far Eastern Economic Review*, 20 May 1993, p. 20.

14. David Murray, *Angels and Devils* (Bangkok: White Orchid Press, 1996), p. 192.

15. Wimol was a class 5 graduate of Chulachomklao Military Academy like Suchinda. And Like Suchinda, Wimol had had a hand in putting down the Young Turks' coup of 1981. He then served as commander of the 1st Division, His Majesty's Guard, before becoming (in 1986) commander of the Special Warfare Command. In this latter posting, he commanded Surayud Chulanond, who later headed the Special Warfare Unit himself. Finally, in 1989, Wimol was appointed as 2nd Army Region commander. In 1991 his career path took a turn downhill when he was suddenly appointed to the unappealing position of deputy supreme commander. This demotion may have distanced Wimol from Suchinda. Clearly Wimol was not considered close enough to the core of Suchinda's power base to ascend further in the army. But the demotion also preserved Wimol's distance from blame for the events of Black May. When Suchinda resigned as premier, he clearly did not want General Pichai Kullanamitr to succeed him, but nor would Suchinda be allowed a proven loyalist such as General Wirot Saengsanit. Thus, in August 1992, Wimol became the perfect compromise army commander to placate class 5 and those seeking completely new leadership in the army. Tamada Yoshifumi, *Myths and Realities: The Democratization of Thai Politics* (Kyoto: Kyoto University Press, 2008), pp. 90–91. See also General Wimol Wongwanich, พลเอก วิมล วงศ์วานิช ผู้บัญชาการทหารบก 2535–2538 [General Wimol Wongwanich, army commander 1992–1995] (Bangkok: 1995).

16. Surin Maisrikrod, *Thailand's Two General Elections in 1992* (Singapore: Institute of Southeast Asian Studies, 1992), p. 56.

17. Ken Stier, "Thai Military's Grip on Business is Still Strong", *Los Angeles Times*, 21 September 1992.

18. Ibid.

19. That was because General Prem, the de facto chair of the Privy Council, working with newly appointed (1992) councillor General Pichit Kullayanamitr and army chief General Wimol, ensured that military officers close to General Suchinda Kraprayoon as well as to Issarapong

and Chainarong Noonpakdi in Chulachomklao Academy classes 5 and 11 were all sidelined. Four top officers of class 5 close to Wimol were promoted to top postings, but they would all reach mandatory retirement by 1994. Members of classes 6, 9, 12 (pre-cadet class 1) and 14 (pre-cadet class 3) now joined the senior military leadership.

20. Handley, *The King Never Smiles*, p. 372.

21. John Girling, "Thailand: Twin Peaks, Disturbing Shadows", in *Southeast Asian Affairs 1994*, edited by Daljit Singh (Singapore: Institute of Southeast Asian Affairs, 1994), pp. 313–14, https://www.jstor.org/stable/27912108.

22. Ibid., p. 318.

23. Gary Brown, "Cambodia Catch 22: The Question of Australian Military Assistance to the Royal Government of Cambodia", Foreign Affairs, Defense and Trade Group, Parliamentary Research Service, Commonwealth of Australia, *Current Issues Brief*, no. 28 (1994): 4, https://www.aph.gov.au/binaries/library/pubs/cib/1994–95/95cib28.pdf.

24. Kenneth Stier, "Cambodian Peace Threatened by Arms Flow", *Christian Science Monitor*, 29 December 1993, https://www.csmonitor.com/1993/1229/29041.html.

25. Philip Shenon, "Pol Pot & Co.: The Thai Connection—A Special Report; In Big Threat to Cambodia, Thais Still Aid Khmer Rouge", *New York Times*, 19 December 1993, https://www.nytimes.com/1993/12/19/world/pol-pot-thai-connection-special-report-big-threat-cambodia-thais-still-aid-khmer.html.

26. Stier, "Cambodian Peace Threatened".

27. Puangthong Rungswasisab, *Thailand's Response to the Cambodian Genocide*, Yale University Working Paper no. 12 (2004): 106, https://www.files.ethz.ch/isn/46648/GS21.pdf.

28. Global Witness, *Forests, Famine and War: The Key to Cambodia's Future* (London, 1995), https://cdn.globalwitness.org/archive/files/pdfs/forests_famine_and_war_the_key_to_cambodias_future.htm.

29. Puangthong, *Thailand's Response*, p. 96.

30. Wimol's appointees from 1992 mostly stayed in place. Two of his class 5 friends, General Phaiboon Empan and Admiral Prachet Siridej, became army chief of staff and navy commander, respectively. Class 6, led by General Pramon Plasin, made gains in the sense that Pramon became assistant army commander, while General Prateep Santiprapop became police chief. Prateep got his job after Interior Minister General Chavalit fired his predecessor, Sawat Amornwiwat, partly because the latter had failed to resolve the infamous Saudi Arabian jewels case: jewels that had been stolen from the Saudi royal family with the connivance of Thais close to the highest institution.

31. Kusuma Snitwongse, "Thailand in 1994: The Trials of Transition", *Asian Survey* 35, no. 2 (February 1995): 194–97, https://doi.org/10.2307/2645030.

32. Chalidaporn Songsamphan, "Thailand: Slow Government, Sluggish Democratization", in *Southeast Asian Affairs 1995*, edited by Daljit Singh and Liak Teng Kiat (Singapore: Institute of Southeast Asian Affairs, 1995), p. 331, https://www.jstor.org/stable/27912134.

33. Handley, *The King Never Smiles*, p. 372; McCargo, "Network Monarchy", p. 509.

34. Surachart Bamrungsuk, *From Dominance to Power Sharing: The Military and Politics in Thailand, 1973–1992* (New York: Columbia University, 1999), pp. 157–58.

35. Handley, *The King Never Smiles*, p. 374.

36. Surachart, *From Dominance to Power Sharing*, pp. 152, 153 and 157.

37. Suvit Wannabovorn, "Covert Unit 838 Resurfaces", *Phnom Penh Post*, 8 April 1994, https://www.phnompenhpost.com/national/covert-thai-unit–838-resurfaces.

38. Suvit, "Covert Unit 838".

39. Human Rights Watch, *Cambodia at War*, 1-56432-150-9, 1 March 1995, https://www.refworld.org/docid/3ae6a7dd8.html.

40. Nate Thayer, "Cambodia: Asia's New Narco-State?", *Far Eastern Economic Review*, 23 November 1995, https://natethayer.typepad.com/blog/cambodia–19995/.

41. Chalidaporn, "Thailand: Slow Government", p. 339.

42. Brad Adams, "Marking the Anniversary of the Cambodian Coup Attempt", *Human Rights Watch*, 2 July 2014, https://www.hrw.org/node/254373/printable/print.

43. Human Rights Watch, *Cambodia at War*.

44. Wimol was able to provide five of his class 5 peers with new positions. Wimol also promoted his friends in class 6, class 8, class 9, class 10 and class 12. This included officers who had been discredited by the 1992 Black May incident. For example, he succeeded in having Chainarong reinstated in the army hierarchy in the position of deputy chief of staff. Technically, given that Chainarong retired in 1999, he could have reached the post of army commander in 1998—though that was not to be. The appointment of General Wattanachai Wootisiri as supreme commander was specifically endorsed by Prem and the king.

45. This is the opinion of a highly placed Democrat Party deputy leader. Author's interview with anonymous Democrat MP and deputy leader, 23 December 2001.

46. Suchitra Ghosh, *Thailand: Tryst with Modernity* (New Delhi: Vikas, 1997), p. 113.

47. Global Witness, *Forests, Famine and War*.

48. Matthew Grainger, "Chavalit Factor Mooted in Timber Politics", *Phnom Penh Post*, 20 September 1996, https://www.phnompenhpost.com/national/chavalit-factor-mooted-timber-politics.

49. Suchit Bunbongkarn, "Thailand in 1995: The More Things Change, The More They Remain the Same", in *Southeast Asian Affairs 1996*, edited by

Daljit Singh and Liak Teng Kiat (Singapore, Institute of Southeast Asian Affairs, 1996), p. 366, https://www.jstor.org/stable/27912161.

50. Surachart Bamrungsuk, *From Dominance*, pp. 157–58.

51. Suchit Bunbongkarn, "Thailand in 1995", p. 366.

52. Wimol moved to shunt aside General Pramon Phalasin (class 6) to the Supreme Command. However, Pramon was close with General Chavalit Yongchaiyudh, then defence minister. Thus, it was Phaibun who was shunted aside, while Chavalit's man, Pramon, took the slot as army commander. Pramon was a stopgap choice from the weak class 6 of Chulachomklao Academy, and he would only serve for one year as army chief since he would reach mandatory retirement in 1996. Chavalit could thus more easily influence the military (though so could Prem and the palace). Meanwhile, Chavalit placed two of his minions in the Supreme Command: General Watana Sanpanij became deputy commander, while General Mongkol Apornpisit became chief of staff of the armed forces. Rodney Tasker, "I'm in Charge Here: Politician Calls a Tune in Military Musical Chairs", *Far Eastern Economic Review*, vol. 158 (1995): 17–18.

53. Prem Tinsulanonda's confidant General Surayud Chulanond (Chulachomklao Academy class 12, pre-cadet class 1) took the slot of 2nd Army Region commander. The influence of Chavalit and Prem showed that retired senior officers now held an abundance of power in the 1990s, while the influence of active-duty senior officers seemed quite low. Daniel King, "Thailand in 1995: Open Society, Dynamic Economy, Troubled Politics", *Asian Survey* 36, no. 2 (February 1996): 138, https://doi.org/10.2307/2645810.

54. Somchai Meesane and Supawadee Susanpoolthong, *Bangkok Post*, 22 September 1996; see also Suvit-Swasdi, *Bangkok Post*, 6 October 1996.

55. "Banharn Agrees to Resign", *Bangkok Post*, 22 September 1996; "Chart Thai Split over Next PM", *Bangkok Post*, 27 September 1996.

56. James Ockey, "Thailand: The Crafting of Democracy", in *Southeast Asian Affairs 1997*, edited by Daljit Singh (Singapore: Institute of Southeast Asian Affairs, 1997), pp. 309–10, https://www.jstor.org/stable/27912184.

57. ชีวิตและผลงาน พลเอก เชษฐา ฐานะจาโร ผู้บังคับบัญชาทหารบก (1 ตุลาคม 2539–30 กันยายน 2541) [Life and works of General Chettha Thanajaro, army commander (1 October 1996 – 30 September 1998)] (Bangkok: 1998).

58. This included General Yuthasak as permanent defence minister.

59. Manop Thip-Osod, Nattaya Chetchotiros, and Wassana Nanuam, "New Police Chief Appointed", *Bangkok Post*, 6 February 2007, http://www.bangkokpost.com.

60. Chavalit had a half-sister named Sumon Somsarn and a half-brother named Thammanoon Yongchaiyudh. Being a military son (but also because he had princely connections), he was accepted into class 1 of the Chulachomklao Royal Military Academy in 1949 (the same class as his friend General Sunthorn Kongsompong). Here he gained the nickname "Jiw". Chavalit participated in the army's repression of a navy coup attempt (the "Manhattan Rebellion) on 29 June 1951. Appointed

second lieutenant in 1953 upon graduation, he went on to study at the Thai army Signal Corps School and at Fort Monmouth and Fort Leavenworth in the United States. In the 1960s, Chavalit was active in anti-communist suppression activities (with Colonel Saiyud Kerdphol). After 1973, Chavalit appeared to support military reform and was thought to be close to the "Democratic Soldiers" faction. Chavalit has a special connection to royalty because his aunt was Princess Peerapong Bhanudet, son of Princess Maha Chakri Sirindhorn Prince Phanurangsi Sawangwong Krom Phraya Panupandhuwongworadej, and Mom Lek Panupan Na Ayudhya (former surname Yongchaiyut), who was the sister of Chavalit's father. Chan Seesithong, เอาบ้านเมืองอยู่รอด แก้วิกฤตโดย พลเอก ชวลิต ยงใจยุทธ [Survive the country and solve the crisis by General Chavalit Yongchaiyudh] (Bangkok: Isan Federation, 2000).

61. James Ockey, "Thailand: The Crafting of Democracy", pp. 309–10.

62. Daniel King, "Thailand in 1996: Economic Slowdown Clouds Year", *Asian Survey* 37, no. 2 (1997): 165, https://doi:10.2307/2645483.

63. Tom Fawthrop, "Thai-Myanmar Ties: Drug Lord Cashes in", *Asia Times*, http://www.atimes.com/atimes/Southeast_Asia/EA17Ae02.html.

64. Seth Mydans, "Where Khmer Rouge Stroll in for a Can of Soda", *New York Times*, 13 September 1996, https://www.nytimes.com/1996/09/13/world/where-khmer-rouge-stroll-in-for-a-can-of-soda.html.

65. Associated Press, "Khmer Rouge Officers Said to Flee to Thailand", *New York Times*, 3 October 1996, https://www.nytimes.com/1996/10/03/world/khmer-rouge-officers-said-to-flee-to-thailand.html.

66. Neil Englehart, "Democracy & Thai Middle Class", *Asian Survey* 43, no. 2 (March/April 2003): 271.

67. Ibid., pp. 268–69.

68. Ibid., pp. 273–74.

69. Amy Freedman, "Thailand's Missed Opportunity for Democratic Consolidation", *Japanese Journal of Political Science* 7, no. 2 (2006): 179.

70. Kobkua Suwannathat-Pian, *Kings, Country, and Constitutions: Thailand's Political Development 1932–2000* (Richmond: Routledge Curzon, 2003), p. 19.

71. Prudhisan Jumbala, "Thailand: Constitutional Reform amidst Economic Crisis", in *Southeast Asian Affairs 1998*, edited by Derek da Cunha and John Funston (Singapore: Institute of Southeast Asian Studies, 1998), p. 274, https://www.jstor.org/stable/27912208.

72. Ibid., p. 282.

73. Handley, *The King Never Smiles*, p. 412.

74. Michael Vatikiotis, "Democracy First", *Far Eastern Economic Review*, 6 November 1997, p. 20.

75. Quoted in Thomas Crampton, "Military Gingerly Uses Influence on Leaders: Thai Crisis Puts Army in New Role", *New York Times*, 23 October 1997.

76. "Chatchai Calls for an Urgent Reshuffle", *Bangkok Post*, 2 October 1997.

77. "Political Stalemate: Prachakorn Thai Becomes Wild Card", *Bangkok Post*, 7 November 1997.

78. "Key Events in Fight to Form Government", *Bangkok Post*, 8 November 1997.

79. Prudhisan, "Thailand: Constitutional Reform, p. 282.

80. McCargo, "Network Monarchy", p. 510.

81. Handley, *The King Never Smiles*, p. 373.

82. Paul Chambers and Napisa Waitoolkiat, "The Resilience of Monarchised Military in Thailand", *Journal of Contemporary Asia* 46, no. 3 (2016): 432, https://doi.org/10.1080/00472336.2016.1161060.

83. Tamada Yoshifumi, *Myths and Realities: The Democratization of Thai Politics* (Kyoto: Kyoto University Press, 2008), pp. 93–95.

84. Ibid., p. 96.

85. Wassana Nanuam, เส้นทางเหล็ก พล.อ.สุรยุทธ์ จุลานนท์ นายกรัฐมนตรีคนที่ 24 [Steel Road, General Surayud Chulanont, the 24th prime minister] (Bangkok: Matichon, 2006).

86. Chai-anan, "The Military, Bureaucracy", p. 55.

87. "'สหายคำตัน' คนดีในหัวใจ พล.อ.สุรยุทธ์" ['Comrade Khamtan', a good man in the heart of General Surayud], *Nation Weekender*, 9 December 2005.

88. Surayud attended kindergarten at St. Francis Xavier Convent School in Bangkok before entering the highly prestigious Saint Gabriel's School for boys. He then entered the new Armed Forces Preparatory School, class 1, in 1958, before matriculating into Chulachomklao Military Academy in 1961 (class 12), graduating in 1965. He was then promoted to the rank of second lieutenant as an infantry soldier. He attended the Infantry Centre School in 1966 and then received advanced military training in the United States. In the late 1960s, Surayud began combat activities in rural Thailand as an infantry platoon leader. He soon became an adjutant to 2nd Army commander General Prem Tinsulanonda. He became a special warfare instructor at the Special Warfare Centre in 1972. In early 1981, Surayud was an aide to Prime Minister Prem Tinsulanonda. Indeed, Surayud guarded Prem during the coup of 1981; Surayud was a close loyalist of the arch-royalist Prem, and Prem was Surayud's patron. Surayud then became commander of the 1st Special Combat Regiment (as well as part of the Royal Guards) and the 1st Special Forces Brigade in 1983. In 1984, Surayud became the commander of Task Force 838 (with his deputy Sonthi Boonyaratklin), working with the US CIA along the Thai-Cambodian border. Kenneth Conboy, *The Cambodian Wars: Clashing Armies and CIA Covert Operations* (Lawrence: University of Kansas Press, 2013), p. 181.

89. "จาก 'ปู่พโยม' ถึง 'พี่อสุรยุทธ์' 'จุลานนท์' ในสายตา 'ร.อ.นนท์' 'นายกฯสุรยุทธ์' และการปฏิวัติ ในสายตาลูกทหาร" [From "Grandfather Phayom" to "Father Surayud", "Chulanont" in the eyes of "Captain Non", "Premier Surayud" and rebellion in the eyes of the son of a soldier], *Matichon Weekly*, 15–21 December 2006.

90. Surayud claimed that the events of Black May "convinced me that the army should never be involved in politics". Thomas Fuller, "Thai Junta Shores Up Role in Politics", *New York Times*, 1 October 2006, https:// www.nytimes.com/2006/10/01/world/asia/01iht-thai.2992962.html; Robert Horn, "Surayud Chulanont: A Soldier Who Answered to the People", *Time Magazine*, 28 April 2003, https://web.archive.org/ web/20030422123830/http://www.time.com/time/asia/2003/heroes/ surayud_chulanont.html.

91. Suchitra Punyaratabandhu, "Thailand in 1998: A False Sense of Recovery", *Asian Survey* 39, no. 1 (January–February): 85, https://doi. org/10.2307/2645597.

92. Surayud's rival, General Sampao, remained assistant army commander. Chavalit's favourite, General Chan Bunprasert, remained army chief of staff. General Prawit Wongsuwan was fast-tracked by Chettha to become deputy commander of the 1st Army Region, serving under the Prem-favoured 1st Army Region commander General Thawip Suwanasing. General Anupong became chief of staff and then deputy commander of the 2nd Infantry Division, Queen's Guard. General Prayut Chanocha became commander of the 21st Regiment within the 2nd Division. Pre-cadet academy class 2 garnered the most senior promotions, with four, though Chainarong's younger brother, General Tawisak Noonpakdi, did not receive one.

93. "Surayud Guns for Reforms", *Bangkok Post*, 19 February 1999, http:// www.bangkokpost.com.

94. Heiner Hänggi, "Democratization and Security Governance in Southeast Asia", paper presented at the international workshop-conference "Challenges and Prospects of Democratic Governance in Southeast Asia", Heidelberg, Germany, 15–17 January 2009, p. 11.

95. In 1997 the Thai defence budget was reduced by twenty-five per cent, the highest decline in years. See Thailand's Office of the Prime Minister for statistics.

96. James Ockey, "Thailand: The Struggle to Define Civil-Military Relations", in *Transition to Democratic Civilian Control*, edited by Multiah Alagappa (1999), p. 201.

97. Duncan McCargo and Ukrist Pathmanand, *The Thaksinization of Thailand* (Copenhagen: NIAS Press, 2005), p. 132.

98. BBC, "Obituary: Tak Mok", 21 July 2006, http://news.bbc.co.uk/2/hi/ asia-pacific/5128664.stm/.

99. Tom Fawthrop, "The Other Side of a Khmer Rouge 'Butcher'", *The Age* (Melbourne), 15 May 1999, p. 1.

100. The Thai army began to look for missions to help provide it with income. It donated peacekeeping troops to the International Force East Timor (INTERFET) from 1999 to 2000. Chieocharnpraphan Tossaporn, "Strategic Partnership between Australia and Thailand: A Case Study of East Timor", *IAFOR Journal of Politics, Economics & Law* 2, no. 1 (2015), https://doi.org/10.22492/ijpel.2.1.04.

101. Paul Chambers, "U.S.-Thai Relations after 9/11: A New Era in Cooperation?", *Contemporary Southeast Asia* 26, no. 3 (December 2004): 464.

102. Surayud's pre-cadet class 1 (and Chulachomklao Academy class 12) became the leading class.

103. Wattanachai initiated a tough, no-nonsense frontier policy that worsened relations between Chuan and the Burmese junta. To tackle narcotics threats, Wattanachai formed Force 399 and the 3rd Army's Pha Muang Task Force.

104. Richard Ehrlich, "Rebels with a Cause Make a Fatal Mistake", *Taipei Times*, 26 January 2000, https://www.taipeitimes.com/News/asia/archives/2000/01/26/0000021529.

105. Saw Takkaw, "The 55 That Disappeared", *Dictator Watch*, February 2003, http://www.dictatorwatch.org/articles/saw55.html.

106. *Asiaweek*, "The Enemy on the Border", 11 February 2000, http://edition.cnn.com/ASIANOW/asiaweek/magazine/2000/0211/nat.thailand.html.

107. *Global Witness*, "The Thai-Burma Border", 2003, p. 60, https://cdn2.globalwitness.org/archive/files/import/03sep3%20conflict%20of%20interests%2060–89.pdf.

108. Surayud promoted his friends: General Thawat Ketangkool (permanent secretary of defence), General Boonrawd Somthat (army chief of staff), General Narong Den-udom (4th Army Region commander), General Pathana Putatanon (army deputy chief), General Nipat Paranit (Army Assist CC), General Rewat Buntap (Army Assist CC), General Watanachai Chaimuengwong (3rd Army Region commander), General Pongthep Tesprateep (army chief of staff), and Special Forces confidant General Sonthi Boonyaratklin, who in 2000 became a deputy commander at the Special Warfare Command.

109. These included generals Yuthasak and Akaradej Sasiphrapha, Somthas Attanand, Thammarak Issarakul na Ayuthaya, Uthai Shinawatra, Chaisit Shinawatra, Chettha Thanajaro and Thawal Sawaengpan. See McCargo and Ukrist, *The Thaksinization of Thailand*.

Chapter Twelve

Thaksin, Sonthi and Surayud (2001–8)

The general election of 6 January 2001 produced a pro-business coalition led by a political face—telecommunications tycoon Thaksin Shinawatra—who was familiar to and trusted by Thailand's vested elite. Thaksin was helped by the 1997 constitution, which centralized power in political parties, making it near impossible for members of political parties to defect to other parties and which compelled party discipline. The 1997 charter made the Senate a fully elected body, and the Thai Rak Thai Party (TRT) quickly gained influence over a majority of senators. As for military influence in the upper house, very little could be found at all.

In the lower house, Thaksin merged several smaller parties into his own, enlarging TRT's share of the parliamentary pie. His popularity surged and he became a new pillar in the Thai political equilibrium— below the palace but above the military. He seemed to particularly threaten the influence of aging Privy Council chair General Prem Tinsulanonda. Across Thai society, Thaksin was a beacon for the rural masses, though urban elites were highly suspicious of him.

There was a repressive side to Thaksin, however. As a former police officer and corporate head, he advocated a top-down CEO management style of governance. To quell negative media coverage, Thaksin bought up the only independent television station, the others being government owned. They all soon towed the line of presenting only positive coverage of the government. Radio stations, meanwhile, were subject to greater censorship, while Thaksin and his associates

FIGURE 12.1
Thailand's Senates, 2000–2006

Type of legislature	Years in office	Appointed or elected	Total number of members and military contingent
Bicameral (Ninth Senate)	2000–2006 (served 6-year term)	Directly Elected	200 (2% ex-military)
Bicameral (Tenth Senate)	2006–2006 (terminated by military coup)	Directly Elected	200 (0% ex-military)

Source: Paul Chambers, "Superfluous, Irrelevant or Emancipating: Thailand's Evolving Senate Today", *Journal of Current Southeast Asian Affairs* 28, 3 (2009): 9.

intimidated newspapers that carped against him. He also managed to stack the courts with his own cronies while also dominating the Senate.

The king appeared satisfied, however. Moreover, the Thaksin government seemed to be a boon for the kingdom amidst the continuing economic morass that seemed to be undermining both national security and the Crown Property Bureau's finances. As such, the palace seemed intent on keeping Thaksin in office, if only to maintain some sense of administrative durability. Moreover, Thaksin, as a business tycoon, could help strengthen Thailand's economic health. Despite any misgivings he might have had about Thaksin, Prem was called upon to rescue the new prime minister when the latter encountered legal problems in 2001. After Prem apparently used his "enormous clout" to sway constitutional judges to acquit Thaksin during his 2001 assets concealment trial, Thaksin then agreed to keep Prem-loyalist General Surayud Chulanond as army chief for one more year.[1]

Nevertheless, Thailand's new prime minister intended to personalize control over the political landscape, and the military was to be no exception. Recognizing how Chavalit had previously thwarted the will of Prem in senior reshuffles, Thaksin concurrently appointed the discredited former prime minister as defence minister (2001–2) and deputy prime minister (2001–5). Chavalit's minion Yuthasak Sasiprapha returned to serve as deputy defence minister (2001–2). With Chavalit's blessing, Thaksin appointed up to fifty-three generals to advisory positions. Furthermore, he pleased the armed forces by initially increasing the military budget, which Chuan and Surayud had reined in since the 1997 financial crisis. Indeed, Surayud's military reforms were mostly cancelled.[2] Meanwhile, in April 2001, seeking to gain supremacy over the military's Internal Security Operations Command (ISOC), which had originally been created to thwart communism, Thaksin added the tasks of control over illegal migrants and refugees and other related border security responsibilities. But the military under Thaksin was specifically permitted to increase its business activities—the government approved a military-run irrigation project in September.[3] Thaksin did, however, weaken the legal rationale for ISOC and military interventions. Even though the Cold War had ended a decade earlier, the Anti-Communist Activities Act (1952) was still on the books. Thaksin repealed this act and all its provisions in June 2001.[4]

In foreign policy, upon taking office, Thaksin abandoned Chuan's contentious relationship with Myanmar, seeking to reinstate the pre-1997 cooperative arrangement that had mostly been led by the country's militaries. Some active-duty and retired Thai military personnel especially benefited from Thaksin's resumption of close ties with Myanmar. For example, according to Global Witness, retired army commander General Chettha Thanajaro, who had joined Thaksin's Thai Rak Thai Party, was an advisor to the Kanchanaburi Industrial Council, which had partnered with the Kanchanaburi-Tavoy Development Company to begin timbering and clearing forest in order to build a road to Tavoy, Myanmar, to be completed by March 2001. Tavoy was to be expanded into a deep sea port for Thai exports.[5]

But when Tatmadaw soldiers in February 2001 made an incursion into Thailand against Shan rebels, Thailand's 3rd Army—led by pro-Prem General Wattanachai Chaimueanwong—repelled them. Such incidents became common. Chavalit criticized Wattanachai for wasting Thai firepower in reaction to the Tatmadaw and Wa cross-border attacks and made plans to transfer the latter out of the 3rd Army altogether—to Bangkok. Thereupon, Chavalit visited Myanmar, Myanmar's General Khyin Nyunt visited Thailand, and even Thaksin made a trip to Myanmar, working to smooth over rough edges in relations between the two countries.[6] Following the 11 September 2001 attacks on the Twin Towers in New York City, Thaksin—under enormous pressure from Washington and the palace—pledged support for the United States, joined the latter's counter-terror coalition, and sent troops to Afghanistan in support of the US intervention there.[7]

Thaksin's interest in harnessing control over the military continued. With much-needed help from Chavalit and Yuthasak, as well as his own personal pre-cadet academy ties with officers from classes 13 (2),

14 (3), 16 (5), 20 (9) and 21 (10), the prime minister sought to harness control over senior military reshuffles. Demonstrating the sway of Chavalit and Thaksin together, in the October 2001 military appointments (the first over which Thaksin officially presided), the choices of Prem and Surayud mostly lost out.[8]

Friction between Thaksin and army commander Surayud continued to grow, partially because the latter was aligned with the prime minister's nemesis, Prem Tinsulanonda, and also because he refused to give in to the prime minister's attempt to dominate security policy in general. Surayud directed the army to secretly back minority ethnic armies in Myanmar that were fighting against the military government there. When in May the Tatmadaw launched an attack against the Shan State Army along the Thai-Myanmar border, the Thai Army worked with the Shan to repel it. Thereupon, the Myanmar junta, angry at Thailand, sealed the border. The result was a vociferous clash between Surayud (backed by Prem) and Thaksin (with Chavalit). Thereupon, Thaksin declared that Thailand would end its policy of utilizing the Shan State Army to help repel the United Wa State Army and the Tatmadaw.[9]

Meanwhile, violent attacks by armed groups against the government had been growing in Thailand's four Deep South provinces. By mid-2002, Thaksin's response was to dissolve the Southern Border Provinces Administrative Centre (SBPAC) and CPM-43—the two entities that had been created by Prem Tinsulanonda to help resolve the crisis when the latter had been prime minister in 1981.[10] But taking away military supremacy over Deep South policy clearly angered many in the armed forces while reinforcing police backing for Thaksin. The move clearly increased the prime minister's grip over security force policy—especially in the Deep South region.

The October 2002 reshuffle (see Appendix 4) proved to be another boon for Thaksin. This is because, by 2001, except for General Somthat Attanond (class 14) and General Pongthep Thesprateep (pre-cadet class 5; class 15), there were simply no senior army officers in high enough positions to succeed Surayud when he was supposed to retire in 2003.[11]

Catching Surayud (and Prem) by surprise, Thaksin fast-tracked the annual reshuffle from the usual 1 October date to August to gain tactical advantage over those officers opposed to him. Surayud was "kicked upstairs" to fill the powerless supreme commander post, and Somdhat Attanand, one year senior to Pongthep, succeeded him as army commander-in-chief. As chief of staff, Somdhat had disagreed with Surayud on taking a hardline policy towards Myanmar, reportedly stating that the army should follow the government line—a standpoint certainly agreeable to Thaksin.[12] Meanwhile, Thaksin's cousin General Chaisit Shinawatra (Armed Forces Preparatory School [AFAPS] class 5) (who only became a general when Thaksin became prime minister) was moved from a mere advisory posting in the Supreme Command to become assistant army commander.[13] Another cousin, General Uthai Shinawatra (AFAPS class 2), became deputy permanent secretary. General Jirasit Kesakomol and General Anupong Paochinda, both from Thaksin's pre-cadet class 10, were appointed to head the elite 1st Army Division and 2nd Infantry Division (Eastern Tigers), respectively.[14] The mercurial Prawit was now 1st Army Region chief. Prawit's patron, General Chettha (who had joined TRT), deepened his ties with Prawit and political strongman of Eastern Thailand Sanoh Tiengthong—all three had been close since Prawit led the Eastern Tigers division in eastern Thailand.[15]

By mid-2002, Chavalit increasingly was quarrelling with Thaksin about policy and the reshuffles. For example, in mid-August 2002, following attempts by the government to bring about greater reconciliation between Phnom Penh and Bangkok, Chavalit complained that Thaksin had "given in" to Myanmar's military regime.[16] Also, at times, Chavalit would seek to promote his favoured officers over those of the prime minister. Meanwhile, as far as Thaksin was concerned, Chavalit had already done what Thaksin had wanted the old general to do—jettison Surayud from the position of army commander. Following pressure from Thaksin, on 3 October 2002, Chavalit resigned as minister of defence (though he continuing as deputy prime minister) and was replaced by an ultra-loyalist (class 10) retired soldier, General Thammarak Issarangkul na Ayuthaya. Thammarak proved to be quite pliable, and with Chavalit gone, Thaksin was able to fill defence positions with more of his own choices. In fact, Thammarak, a highly partisan general, proved to be more than willing to try to transform the armed forces into a tool of Thaksin. The military seemed to be rapidly becoming simply one more lever in Thaksin's institutional power structure. By the end of 2002, Thaksin appeared to have achieved control over the military. In fact, as Yoshifumi Tamada has stated, its "shrinking political power" was "mainly due to the changes in military personnel shuffling".[17] By that point in time in Thailand, elections appeared to have become much more legitimate than coups. Moreover, elected prime ministers perhaps only needed to interfere with military appointments to prevent the possibility of putsches. Thaksin was a popular elected leader able to effect such changes.

The year 2003 began with a potential confrontation between Cambodian and Thai security forces. On 29 January, irate Cambodian mobs burned the Thai embassy and some Thai businesses in Phnom Penh following reports that a Thai soap opera actress had claimed Thai ownership of the ancient Angkor Wat temple. Thaksin sent five military planes to Phnom Penh to repatriate several trapped Thai citizens, and the government depicted the military aircrews as heroes for having helped to ferry stranded Thais out of Cambodia and back to Thailand.[18] Cambodia paid for damages to Thai property.[19]

Also, in early 2003, the prime minister initiated a month-long anti-narcotics campaign. This "drug war" began to take shape following three speeches in late November and early December 2002 by the king (including the monarch's 5 December birthday speech) where he said that the military must do something about Thailand's narcotics problem. As if taking the cue from the monarch's speeches, Prem urged all armed forces leaders to suppress those involved in the drug trade.[20] The palace, Prem and Surayud had earlier been annoyed at the government's efforts to de-prioritize the drug threat, especially along the Thailand-Myanmar border.[21] However, in late December, responding quickly to the king's call, realizing the potential popularity of a "drug war", and in an effort to satisfy Thailand's security sector, Thaksin and Deputy Prime Minister Chavalit unveiled a no-holds barred anti-narcotics strategy. Launched on 1 February, it focused principally on Thailand's north, but also covered other parts of the country. To achieve a quick victory, Thaksin authorized security personnel—spearheaded by the Royal Thai Police—to shoot to kill suspected, mostly small-scale, traffickers, though principal drug kingpins remained at large. In the North, the 3rd Army Region, then commanded by General Udomchai Ongkasing (Chaisit's class 5), led the military arm of the "drug war", but it also coordinated with police and other civilian agencies.[22]

On 1 May, Thaksin claimed "victory" in the drug war, with the government claiming ninety per cent "drug problem eradication" and 17,000 arrests. Most analysts, however, saw the operation more as a marketing exercise since it would only have a "passing impact" on narcotics commerce.[23] As a result of the "war", almost three thousand people were executed extrajudicially. Amnesty International harshly condemned the Thai police and military forces for carrying out these actions with legal impunity.[24]

To further appease the armed forces, Thaksin upped the budget for defence, rationalizing that since "The military budget has been drastically cut back since the 1997 financial crisis ... my government is considering increasing it to upgrade the armed forces." Moreover, he stated that in a post-9/11 world, the military should have more funds to gear up as a "precaution". At the same time, Thaksin praised the armed forces for quickly mobilizing to support the government stance during the 29 January anti-Thai riots in Phnom Penh.[25] Thus, the prime minister promised to increase the Defence Ministry budget by as much as 200 billion baht over nine years, with additional money to enhance its communications technology and upgrade its weapons systems for the period 2005–13.[26]

At the same time, though Thaksin paid lip service to the needs of reform, he did little about the bloated size of the armed forces. Indeed, in 2003, troop levels grew from 306,000 to 314,000 soldiers. Instead of seeking a genuine streamlining of the military, it seemed that Thaksin was more intent on gaining further backing and influence from an institution that might be able to challenge his sway.[27] Still, if one examines Thailand's military budget as a percentage of GDP, military funding actually decreased from 1.48 per cent in 2001 to 1.43 per cent in 2003. This is because in 2003 Thailand saw economic growth of 6.7 per cent, while military spending increased by 1.7 per cent from 2001 to 2003. This indicates that with a recovering Thai economy, Thaksin succeeded in increasing military spending without directing more of the national budget for the purposes of defence.[28]

Three developments further affected Thailand's security forces during 2003. First, a new intelligence coordinating centre was established (chaired by Chavalit), which integrated resources of the National Security Council, Police Special Branch, National Intelligence Agency, and the Armed Forces Security Centre. Second, Thailand became a major non-NATO ally (MNNA) of the United States. This designation allowed Thailand to purchase more weaponry from the United States at cheaper prices, while also increasing ties between Washington and Bangkok. Finally, in September, Thailand sent 443 military officers (including 250 technicians, 70 doctors, 26 frontline command officers, 50 security personnel, and a bomb-disposal team) to Iraq on a humanitarian mission for US forces in that country.[29]

The announcement by the prime minister that the government would be allocating more money to the military perhaps made the bitter pill of the 2003 military reshuffle easier for many soldiers to swallow—at least that was an apparent intention. Indeed, later that year, in October, Thaksin achieved the pinnacle of his hold over the armed forces. His cousin Chaisit was elevated to the coveted position of army commander, while loyalist Somthat Attanand (who had helped Chaisit obtain the army's top job) was appointed "upstairs" to succeed Surayud as supreme commander. The ascension of Chaisit reflected the growing confidence of Thaksin in his personal control over the armed forces. Thaksin's defence minister Chavalit had recommended his longtime aide and senior army advisor General Wichit Yathip for the post, while deputy defence minister Yuthasak Sasiprapha favoured his loyalist 2nd Army Region commander General Jirasak Prommoprakorn. But Thaksin instead supported his own under-experienced cousin, and the latter won out.[30]

Who then was Chaisit? Nicknamed "Big Tui", he was born on 25 June 1945, the son of Colonel Sak Shinawatra, in Ratchaburi, though the Shinawatra family is from Chiang Mai.[31] Chaisit is married to Veena Shinawatra and has two children: Ms Lakhawee Shinawatra and Mr Veerasit Shinawatra. Veerasit was in 2021 the Manager of Corporate Marketing, Thai Samsung Electronics Co., Ltd.[32]

Promotions of perceived Thaksin loyalists paralleled Chaisit's rise during 2003. In the mid-year military reshuffle on 1 April 2003, Thaksin ensured that seven of his class 10 peers were promoted. The seven included Thaksin's friend and AFAPS class 10 peer Songkitti Jaggabattara, who became commander of the 4th Army Region and could thus help Thaksin personalize the prime minister's control over Deep South policy.[33] Then, in the 1 October annual reshuffle, thirteen more members of AFAPS class 10 were promoted to important military positions.[34] Simultaneously, two fellow class 5 friends of Chaisit Shinawatra—General Chumaeng Sawadsongkram and General Peechanmet Muangmanee (who was also a crony of Thaksin's brother Payap)—were given the army commander posts of Region 2 and Region 3, respectively. Moreover, General Pornchai Kranlert, valedictorian of AFAPS class 10 and a very close confidant of Thaksin, became chief of staff of the Royal Thai Supreme Command's Armed Forces Development Command (AFDC), an organization responsible for overseeing military construction projects—and a post that affords many opportunities for graft. Meanwhile, though the pro-Thaksin General Lertrat Ratanavanich had anticipated promotion to become army chief of staff in 2003, Prem in this case managed to have his way, ensuring that his loyalist General Pongthep Thesprateep would get the slot. Another Prem disciple, General Pathompong Kesornsuk (class 7), had already been given the other deputy army chief of staff posting. Thus, Lertrat continued as deputy army chief of staff, though he was said to be in line to eventually succeed Chaisit when the latter was due to retire in October 2005 following Thaksin's anticipated re-election that year.[35]

Among other important promotions, General Oud Boungbon, a relative of Thaksin's wife, Pojaman, but who had also served as an aide to Prem, became permanent secretary of the Defence Ministry. Another interesting promotion was that of General Prawit Wongsuwan, who, as stated previously, was favoured specifically by Chettha and Sanoh. Moreover, the pro-Prem Admiral Chumpol Patchusanont was elevated to become navy commander. Two other notable appointments were those of General Anupong Paochinda (class 10), who became commander, 1st Army Region, 1st Division (Wonthewan, or King's Guard); and General Prayut Chanocha (class 12), who succeeded Anupong as commander, 1st Army Region, 2nd Division (Eastern Tigers). Surayud's acolyte General Sonthi Boonyaratklin soldiered on for one more year as head of the Special Warfare Division.

By the end of 2003, despite a smattering of opposition to Thaksin from some in the military, it only seemed a matter of time before he would completely dominate it. Besides, Prem and the king were elderly and ailing. Surayud, meanwhile, had retired in October 2003, and his power seemed to be at an end. Thaksin appeared unstoppable. Ultimately, in December, the palace and Prem appointed Surayud to the Privy Council as if to announce to Thaksin that though the prime minister may have opposed Surayud when the latter was leading the military, the royals viewed the general in highly positive terms. New privy councillor Surayud quickly became Prem's right-hand man (and potential successor) in opposing Thaksin at every turn. Prem and Surayud led a bevy of other privy councillors in resisting Thaksin: ACM Siddhi Savetsila, General Pichit Kullavanijaya, Palakorn Suwanrath and Kasem Watanachai.[36] But the Privy Council had no institutionalized powers of administration. Its influence depended upon the king alone. By the beginning of 2004, any resistance to Thaksin from the military seemed hopeless. But January would offer a chance.

On 4 January 2004, violence erupted in Thailand's Deep South. Militants launched a well-organized attack on an army camp in Narathiwat province. The militants seized close to 350 weapons and allegedly executed four soldiers. While the resistance to Thai rule over the Deep South has for decades presented the region with spectacles of violence, there was some reason to believe the raid had been hatched by soldiers for the benefit of the Thai military.[37] Thailand's army had in fact a lot to gain from the insurgent raid as it showed that the influence of Thaksin, Chaisit and the police over Thailand's Deep South was ineffective and the army's direct control over managing security in the Deep South should be restored.

Not long after this, Thaksin declared martial law in Narathiwat, Yala and Pattani. Fighting between insurgents and security forces intensified, and each was implicated in human rights abuses as increasing numbers of people were killed.[38] Southern security forces led by the police proved unable to quell the insurrection. Violence in the region escalated dramatically. On 28 April 2004, youthful militants resisting the Thai army retreated into the sacred Krue Se Mosque. Soldiers followed them in, leading to 30 militant deaths and, in total, 107 killings at the hands of the military that day. Then, on 25 October, where the military, police and paramilitaries were arresting Malay-Muslim protestors (who were calling for the release of villagers who themselves had been arrested for allegedly giving weapons to militants), some demonstrators were shot and over 1,000 were stacked on top of each other in trucks for transport to detention. Enroute to detention, 78 died of suffocation. Questions remain as to whether the stacking by security forces leading to the suffocations was intentional.

Increasingly, many in the military blamed the prime minister, especially given Thaksin's earlier decision to dismantle agencies for the Deep South erected by former PM Prem and place control over Deep South policy in the hands of the police, exacerbating tensions between the army and the police.[39] At the same time, Thaksin's rapid elevation of his cousin Chaisit to become army commander in 2003—despite Chaisit's apparent lack of army leadership experience—rankled many soldiers, who perceived that political connections and nepotism were outweighing professionalism in terms of senior military reshuffles.

In the 2004 mid-year reshuffle, Thaksin continued to have many of his military favourites appointed to coveted positions despite his government's failure to stem the southern insurgency. Soldiers promoted included General Pisan Wattanawongkiri, who was appointed the 4th Army Region chief, replacing Lt. Gen. Pongsak Ekbannasing. Pisan (AFAPS class 9) was "very close to Thaksin" and strongly supporting the prime minister's hardline policy in the South.[40] Meanwhile, four class 10 peers of Thaksin received military promotions: Maj. Gen. Pairote Rathprasert, Maj. Gen. Ruangsak Thongdee, General Piroon Paeowpongsong (becoming deputy army chief of staff) and Colonel Sophon Dityaem.[41] At the same time, Lt. Gen. Plat Phetsotsilp and Maj. Gen. Wisitthon Suksapha, both close friends of army commander General Chaisit, were also promoted. Plat became head of the Army Ordnance Division and Wisitthon was appointed as chief of the Military Intelligence Division.[42]

From March to October 2004, retired general Chettha Thanajaro, who had become an active member of the Thai Rak Thai Party, served as defence minister. This was highly significant because it involved both a punitive reshuffle (against officers deemed negligent for being unable to counter the far southern insurgency) and the elevation of General Prawit Wongsuwan to become army commander.

The far South insurgency proved to be the final straw as far as the palace's continued support for Thaksin's choices of promotions to senior military positions went. In the October annual 2004 reshuffle, a major sea-change in leadership of the armed forces again occurred. First, under pressure from the palace and Privy Council, General Chaisit was removed from his post as army commander and shifted to become supreme commander, as Thaksin had done to Surayud and Somthat. Meanwhile, another pro-Prem general, Sonthi Boonyaratklin—a loyalist of Surayud—was elevated to the position of assistant army commander. Prem loyalist General Pongthep remained army chief of staff. With Chaisit out of the picture, Thaksin was unwilling to promote Pongthep to be army commander. In fact, 2004–5 was to be Pongthep's final year of active-duty status. Still, given that Chettha was defence minister, the latter helped to persuade the prime minister to compromise and elevate Chettha's friend General Prawit Wongsuwan to take the army chief job. In fact, Prawit reportedly had often asked Thaksin if the latter might appoint him as army chief. According to one account, as Wednesdays were the days when military men would often participate in sports, Prawit used the occasion in early-mid 2004 to visit Thaksin, where he continuously asked the premier to make him army chief. Thaksin finally did just that.[43]

But who exactly was Prawit Wongsuwan? Born on 11 August 1945 into an elite Bangkok military family, Prawit (or "Big Pom") is the eldest son of Maj. Gen. Prasert Wongsuwan. His younger siblings are Admiral Sithiwat Wongsuwan, police general Patcharawat Wongsuwan, the late Pongphan Wongsuwan (former head coach of TOT Public Company Football Club), and Panpong Wongsuwan (a former advisor in the 2014–19 junta-era National Legislative Assembly). He attended the highly prestigious Saint Gabriel's grade school, graduating in 1962. He then went on to pre-cadet school class 6 (with Sonthi Boonyaratklin), continued to Chulachomklao Royal Military Academy class 17 (also with Sonthi) and graduated in 1969. Prawit never married or had children, concentrating on his career in the military. By 1970 he was an infantry platoon commander. In 1971 he entered the 21st Infantry Regiment Queen's Tiger Guard,

2nd Infantry Division (Buraphapayak [Eastern Tigers]). In 1977 he graduated from the Army Staff School (in the same class as then Crown Prince Vajiralongkorn), becoming a commissioned officer. In 1980 he was appointed deputy commander of the 1st Infantry Battalion, 21st Infantry Regiment, Queen's Tiger Guard. He was on his way to commanding the regiment itself. But in April 1981 he had supported the attempted coup against the prime minister General Prem Tinsulanonda.[44] The failure of the coup meant that Prawit was transferred close to the war-ravaged Thai-Cambodian border. By 1984 he was still stationed at the frontier: the 12th Infantry Regiment. It was here, in Sa Kaeow province, that Prawit befriended local political bigwig Sanoh Thienthong and, through Sanoh, met other politicians, including Newin Chidchob and future prime minister Banharn Silpa-archa. In 1989 Prawit became 12th infantry regiment commander in Sakaeo province, near the Aranyaprathet-Poipet border crossing. In Sakaeo, he oversaw trade along the frontier. By 1994 he was peripherally involved in General Chavalit Yongchaiyudh's New Aspiration Party, while his regiment was rumoured to be profiting from the export of blood diamonds from Cambodia. In 1996, under the government of Prime Minister Chavalit, Prawit was promoted to command the 2nd Infantry Division. In 1997, another of Prawit's mentors—then army commander General Chetta Thanajaro—appointed Prawit as deputy commander of the 1st Army Region. But in 2000, under army commander (and pro-Prem) General Surayud Chulanond, Prawit fell from grace. He was demoted to army advisor—allegedly because Surayud's patron, then privy council chair General Prem Tinsulanonda, was unhappy that Prawit had not sufficiently opposed the 1985 coup attempt against then prime minister Prem. Luckily for Prawit, following the 2001 election, his friend Chavalit became defence minister—appointing him first as 1st Army Region commander in 2002 and then as assistant army commander in 2003. Good fortune again assisted Prawit in 2004, when the escalating insurgency in Thailand's Deep South led Prime Minister Thaksin Shinawatra to appoint Prawit to the position of army commander. It helped that he had befriended Thaksin's wife, Potjaman Na Pombejra, and Thai Rak Thai Party deputies Sudarat Keyurapan and Wattana Muangsuk.[45] He had even developed a close business relationship with Thaksin.[46] These connections paid off. He was a shrewd, highly partisan general: a political opportunist, who was neither Thaksin's loyalist nor his enemy, having friends in both pro- and anti-Thaksin venues—rare for Thailand in 2005–6. At the same time, the fact that Prawit was due to retire in 2005 and would thus only spend one year as army commander contributed to both Thaksin and Prem not opposing him.

Meanwhile, Prime Minister Thaksin did manage to achieve some personal successes in the reshuffle. First, Lertlat was appointed to become another assistant army chief. At the same time, fifty-five AFAPS class 10 graduates received promotions. These included General Anupong Paochinda, who moved from being commander of the 1st Division (Royal Guards) to become deputy commander of the strategic 1st Army Area Command; General Prin Suwannatat, who was elevated from being commander of the 11th Army military circle to commander of the 1st Division (Royal Guards); and, in the navy, General Pornchai Kranlert, valedictorian of AFAPS class 10 and a confidant of Thaksin, moving up from being AFDC chief of staff to the position of AFDC deputy commander. A final notable appointment was that of Chavalit confidant Wichit Yathip, who was elevated to deputy permanent secretary in the Ministry of Defence.

In early February 2005, Thaksin was re-elected prime minister in a landslide win. Armed with a new popular mandate, the government continued to seek to dominate the military. In April, the cabinet approved the army's plan to create a new infantry division for the Deep South. Originally called the Development and Natural Resources Division, it was subsequently renamed the 15th Division. It comprised three regiments tasked to defeat Deep South Malay-Muslim insurgents. Nevertheless, the structure of Thai counterinsurgency forces in the Deep South was under the supervision of the Frontline Section of ISOC, Army Region 4, as officially led by the 4th Army Region commander, with assistance from a revised form of the Civilian-Police-Military (CPM) Joint Command, placing the army as the dominant institution in the state's struggle against the insurrection.[47] To legally assist the military in fighting Deep South militants and more easily cooperate as part of the US-led war on terror, the Thaksin government, in July 2005, enacted an Emergency Decree on Public Administration in a State of Emergency. Unlike the Martial Law Act and the Internal Security Act, the 2005 Emergency Decree Act is significant because it retains power in the hands of a prime minister (civilian or military), while granting the longest period of detention without trial for any threat to security: thirty days, with these thirty-day periods being renewable.[48] Not surprisingly, the act has been used and abused unsparingly by security forces in the Deep South. Moreover, the new Emergency Decree has been used by the government to conveniently quash political protests of any type and, beginning in 2020, has also been used to clear the streets in the face of the Covid-19 pandemic.

In the 2005 mid-year military reshuffle, thirty-three pro-Thaksin pre-cadet school class 10 graduates were elevated. Notable promotions included General Manas Paorik, commander of the 1st Calvary Division, who became deputy commander of the 3rd Army Region. Air marshal Sukampol Suwannathat (a relative of Thaksin's friend Phin) was promoted from assistant to RTAF chief of staff for operations to become deputy chief of staff of the Royal Thai Air Force. The annual reshuffle in October 2005 proved to once again be a mixed bag for Thaksin. On the bright side, supreme commander Chaisit succeeded in convincing Thaksin to have the former's AFAPS class 5 classmate General Ruangroj Mahasaront succeed him. And there was other good news.[49]

With three other positions, however, Thaksin was not so fortunate. He had sought to have General Songkitti Chakkrabat (class 10) become army chief of staff, replacing the pro-Prem General Pongthep Thepprateep who was retiring. At the same time, in place of the retiring army commander, General Prawit Wongsuwan, Thaksin tried to promote the then assistant army commander, General Lertrat Ratanavanich, a soldier who was very supportive of Thaksin. And in the air force, the prime minister attempted to have his close associate ACM Raden Puengpok (assistant air force commander), who was a class 5 peer of Chaisit Shinawatra, appointed as air force commander. But, after Thaksin had forwarded his proposed list to the palace, Prem intervened, kicking Songkitti, Lertrat and Raden out of the army and air force hierarchies and down to the impotent Supreme Command: Songkitti as deputy chief of staff, Lertrat as chief of staff and Raden as deputy supreme commander.[50] In their place, AFAPS class 6 officers emerged on top: General Sophon Silpiphat as army chief of staff, Surayud and Prawit protege Sonthi Boonyaratklin, a compromise choice, as the new army commander (Prem supported army chief of staff General Pongthep Theprateep), and anti-Thaksin ACM Chalit Phukpasuk as air force chief.[51]

But who was Sonthi? Sonthi was from Pathum Thani province and was the first Muslim to serve as army chief. (He was born into a Shia Muslim family but apparently later became Sunni. Most Muslims in Thailand's Deep South are Sunni.) He was also from a noble Persian family. An ancestor had held the post of *Chularajmontri* (head of Islamic affairs) in the Ayutthaya kingdom. Another ancestor was a senior navy officer, Luang Pinit Klueng, during the period of King

Rama VI.[52] Born on 2 October 1946, Sonthi was the son of Colonel Sanan Boonyaratkalin. While young he attended a school for Muslims at Assalafi College. Sonthi then moved to study at Wat Phra Si Mahathat School, Bang Khen, because his father came to serve in the 11th Infantry Regiment, King's Guard. Afterwards, Sonthi studied at pre-cadet academy class 6 and then Chulachomklao Military Academy class 17. In both military schools, his class peers included General Prawit Wongsuwan, Admiral Satiraphan Kayanon and ACM Chalit Pukphasuk. He later graduated from the Army Staff School Advanced Army Academy and the National Defence College (class 42). He began his military service in 1968 and became an infantry platoon leader. He saw combat in the Vietnam War during 1970–71. Following his return to Thailand, he engaged in anti-Communist activities in the 2nd Army Region, where General Prem Tinsulanonda became regional commander. In the early 1980s, Sonthi began to serve in the Special Warfare Command under General Surayud Chulanont.[53] By 1985, under the Surayud-led Task Force 838, Sonthi was tasked with liaising with CIA-funded Cambodian insurgents along the Thai-Cambodian border.[54] He became commander of the 1st Special Combat Regiment and commander of the Special Forces Brigade 1 until achieving the post of commander of the Special Warfare Command. In 2004 he caught the attention of Thaksin, partly because Sonthi was a class peer of General Prawit Wongsuwan and partly because he had worked in the Southern Border Provinces Peace Promotion Directorate, but also because Sonthi was a Muslim member of the Special Forces.[55]

Sonthi is known to have three wives simultaneously, which is illegal in Thailand, though that law is not enforced. He has six children, four of which have served in the military or police. In 2023, his son, retired lieutenant colonel Nithi Boonyaratklin, became a candidate for the general election under the banner of General Prawit Wongsuwan's Palang Pracharat party.[56] Sonthi's family tree is depicted in Figure 12.2.

Aside from Sonthi, the October 2005 reshuffle proved to be at least as much a boon for the more pro-Prem AFAPS class 6 as it was for Thaksin's AFAPS class 10. Indeed, though more class 10 graduates received positions, more higher-level postings went to class 6. For example, each of the chiefs of the army, navy and air force was now a class 6 grad.[57]

As Thaksin's power continued to grow, political parties, the military, civil society and the Thai populace in general were becoming increasingly polarized by the Thaksin "phenomenon". He was mostly perceived by urban Thais as a dictator. In late 2005, an anti-Thaksin movement

FIGURE 12.2
Sonthi Boonyaratklin's Family Tree

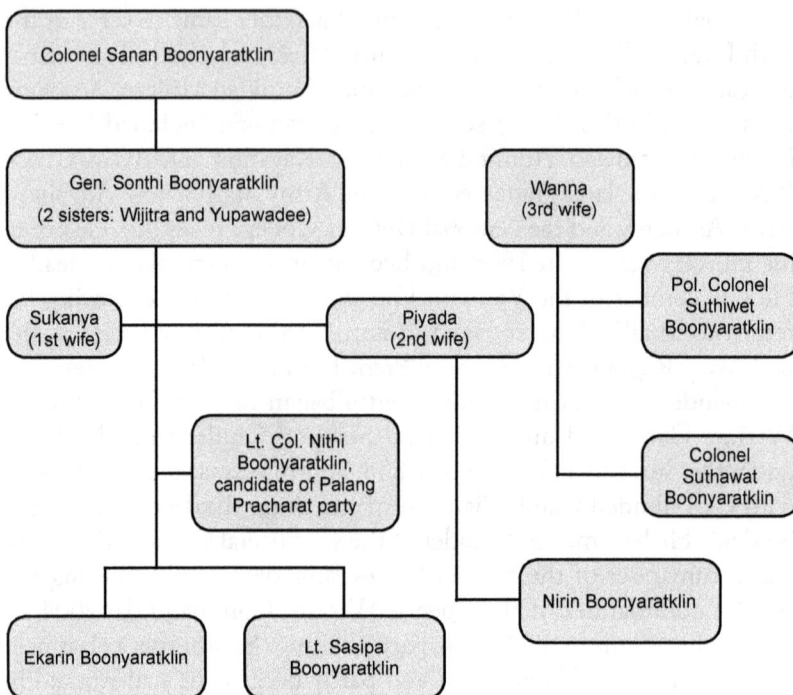

of "Yellow Shirt" rights activists and royalists (which later officially became known as the People's Alliance of Democracy, or PAD) began demonstrating against Thaksin.[58] On 4 February, as if in response to the demonstrations, Thaksin announced that only the king could make him resign, and if the monarch whispered in his ear that he should quit, "I'll go." That evening, approximately fifty thousand protestors in Bangkok listened to Yellow Shirt leader Sondhi Limthongkul castigate Thaksin on and on from a stage. Most ominously, Sondhi asked: "Where is the army? [Thaksin's] talk is enough to bring him to the execution post." Later that night, Sondhi took identical petitions to the Bureau of the Royal Household and the home of Privy Council president Prem. Sondhi also paid a visit to army chief Sonthi and later stated, "I asked [Sonthi], 'Are you going to stand by the people?' He nodded, 'I will stand by the people because I am a soldier of the King'."[59] Sonthi afterwards asserted that he only met with Sondhi in order to prevent political pandemonium.[60] The PAD later opined that

Sonthi's eventual coup against Thaksin occurred because the PAD had issued an invitation for the army to carry out the coup, and army chief Sonthi accepted the invitation.[61] But Sonthi refused to take part in any state of emergency, telling reporters after the meeting, "I believe [this] demonstration is the most peaceful in the world and should be recorded in the Guinness Book of World Records."[62]

Meanwhile there were many in the military who were not content with Thaksin. He had appeared to elevate the police over the armed forces. He practised nepotism and favouritism. And in the Deep South, soldiers were being killed in the counterinsurgency.[63]

On 1 April, the 2006 mid-year military reshuffle was carried out. The appointments under this appeared to be rather unremarkable as few key officers were moved. Perhaps the only exception was the anti-Thaksin General Jiradet Khocharat, who was elevated from being deputy commander of the 3rd Army Corps to become the commander. The most significant event of the reshuffle was that Thaksin was unable to promote many AFAPS class 10 grads to more key military positions.[64] Indeed, Thaksin and class 10 had sought to use the mid-year reshuffle to make some very major changes—but army commander Sonthi blocked them. First, the army chief sought to promote his proteges from the Special Warfare Division—the unit formerly under Sonthi's direct command—to balance the power of class 10. As such, Sonthi nominated Lt. Gen. Pamuk Uthaichai (class 6), commander of the Special Warfare Division, to the important post of chief of staff attached to the army chief. Moreover, Sonthi chose Maj. Gen. Chaiyaphat Thirathamrong (AFAPS class 8), deputy commander of the Special Warfare Division, to become the division's new commander. Sonthi furthermore nominated Colonel Arun Somton (class 14)—deputy commander of the Personnel Department, who used to serve in the Special Warfare Division—to the post of secretary to the Royal Thai Army. Second, Sonthi refused to promote former classmates of Prime Minister Thaksin Shinawatra to key commanding posts despite being asked by Thaksin to do so. Third, the army chief refused to transfer General Anupong Paochinda (AFAPS class 10), then commander of the 1st Army Region, to the inactive post of commander of the Army Reserve Division because of dissatisfaction that Anupong had not been loyal enough to the Thai Rak Thai government. Thaksin had wanted General Jirasit Kesakomon (AFAPS 10), commander of the 1st Brigade, to be promoted to replace Anupong, while Prin Suwannathat, commander of the 1st Infantry Division, King's Guard (Wongthewan), would be promoted as the 1st Brigade commander. Instead, Sonthi promoted Thaksin critic Maj. Gen. Montree Sangkhasap (leader of AFAPS class 9) from deputy commander of the Army Reserve Division to the post of commander of the division, given that the army commander refused to demote Lt. Gen. Anupong to the post as demanded by Thaksin.[65]

By late April, following a meeting of the king with the nation's top judges, the courts annulled the 2006 election results. And though Thaksin remained prime minister, his government remained only as a caretaker one. On 29 June, Thaksin declared publicly that the political chaos in Thai society then occurring was being stirred up by individuals "outside the Constitution" who were attempting to overthrow the government:

> Disorder arises from many things. One [such] thing is where there are normal organisation(s) being dominated by an organisation outside the system or by person(s) with greater influence than normal organisations.... [I]t would be said that today that [there are] organisation(s) outside the Constitution, not in the Constitution ... an individual who appears to have extra-constitutional influence/ charisma. He/she is causing disorder to organisations within the Constitution. There is no respect of the rules or in English this is called not observing [respecting] the rule of law. Many organisations are not following their duties as they should do so. Some people are not satisfied with the rules but want to change the rules [from] outside the democratic system [and] outside the Constitution. This is not possible.[66]

Chart Thai Party leader Banharn Silpa-archa dined with Thaksin at a shark's fin restaurant and inquired whether Thaksin had been referring to the king. Thaksin denied this. Yet, when Banharn asked whether Thaksin was referring to Prem, Thaksin was silent.[67] Following this, as if in response to Thaksin's 29 June speech, Prem gave a series of three talks at cadet academies accompanied by top brass, including army chief General Sonthi, privy councillor General Surayud, General Oud Boungbon, General Pongthep Thepprateep and even General Chavalit, who felt increasingly estranged from the prime minister. First, on 14 July, Prem delivered a lecture to 950 Chulachomklao Royal Military Academy cadets. He told the cadets to rally behind the monarch and the nation and that professional soldiers must support king and kingdom. "Soldiers are like horses, and governments are jockeys but not owners. You belong to the nation and His Majesty the King", Prem said.[68] Two weeks later, on 28 July at the Royal Navy Academy, Prem again appeared and declared: "In my lecture to army cadets two weeks ago, I told them about who owns the soldiers. This time I have to make it clear again that we soldiers belong to the country and to the King. A government supervises soldiers in compliance with the policy declared to parliament only."[69] Finally, on 31 August, in a speech at the Air Force Academy, Prem declared that it was the responsibility of all soldiers to make sure that bad people were not allowed to assume or stay in postings of power.[70]

Two days after Prem's first speech, on 16 July, army chief Sonthi, in a move probably approved by Prem,[71] ordered a military reshuffle of 129 mid-level officers (mostly battalion commanders) who belonged to or were led by AFAPS class 10 graduates or simply considered supportive of Thaksin. Of the 129 transfers, over fifty per cent had worked for class 10 officers. These were clearly key officials as they directly commanded troops and battalions on the ground in Bangkok. The transfer order, involving officers with the rank of colonel and lower, was legally valid because service commanders can make mid-level transfers without the approval of the prime minister.[72]

Meanwhile, the move paralleled Prem's arch-royalist speeches and came amidst speculation that Thaksin, in the upcoming October annual reshuffle, was on the verge of transferring Sonthi to the ceremonial position of supreme commander, replacing him with Thaksin-protege assistant army commander General Pornchai Kranlert, while also shifting AFAPS class 10's General Songkitti Chakkrabat back from the Supreme Command to become army chief of staff.[73] The timing of the mid-level transfers owed to two factors. First, acting defence minister Thammarak Isarankul na Ayuthaya had ordered a very early 27 July deadline for submission of the list of military personnel to be transferred. In this way, Sonthi's move was a reaction.[74] Second, back in 2003, Thaksin had surprised his opponents in the military with an early reshuffle in August (placing then army commander General Surayud Chulanond in the ceremonial post of supreme commander). Howevever, Sonthi's mid-level transfers, which were made in July 2006, countermanded Thaksin's preferences. Thus, key cavalry, infantry and artillery commanding officers—many loyal to Pornchai and the commander of the 1st Infantry Division of the King's Guard, General Pin Suwannatat—were transferred to remote or inactive positions. Indeed, Pin's mid-level subordinates were mostly replaced by troops loyal to 1st Army Region commander General Anupong Paochinda, who, though an AFAPS 10 classmate of Thaksin, had grown increasingly distant from the prime minister. Rumour had it that Thaksin would soon replace Anupong with a stauncher loyalist, 1st Army Corps commander Jirasit Kesakomol. Another rumour insisted that Anupong and Pin were embroiled in a personal dispute. In the end, however, following the transfer of Pin's men, most of the troops that Anupong brought in were veterans of the 2nd Infantry Division (specifically, the 21st Infantry Regiment—the Queen's Guard), which was based in Chonburi and commanded by General Kanit Sapitak.[75] The Queen's Guard was the direct rival faction of the 1st Infantry Division (King's Guard, or Wongthewan).

Aside from Prem, some senior active-duty soldiers were also beginning to vocalize their criticism of Thaksin. Admiral Bannawit Kengrien (AFAPS class 7), then deputy permanent secretary for defence and a staunch Prem (and sometimes Chavalit) protege, had called for Thaksin ally Samak Sundaravej to apologize for critical remarks Samak had made against Prem. When permanent secretary for defence General Sirichai Tanyasiri proposed Bannawit to succeed him in the October 2006 reshuffle, the government would have none of it. Instead, caretaker defence minister Thamarak Issarangkul na Ayuthaya overruled Sirichai, picking the pro-Thaksin General Lertrat Ratanavanich for the job.[76] Following news of this decision, Bannawit questioned whether, constitutionally, the military line-up could be submitted for royal approval by a caretaker government without the vetting of the Election Commission. He also accused the defence minister of placing political interests above the needs of normal military rotations.[77] "Thamarak is a turncoat who has abandoned … military professionalism to serve … political master Thaksin", he said.[78]

Meanwhile, Bannawit's friend and AFAPS class 7 peer General Saprang Kalayanamitr, who was also closely aligned with Prem, had, during supreme commander General Surayud's and deputy army commander Wattanachai's last month in office (2003), been promoted as 3rd Army Corps commander. Saprang reflected the interests of Surayud and Wattanachai to maintain a strong presence along the border with Myanmar. In 2005, Saprang was promoted to 3rd Army Region commander. Yet, at the same time, Thaksin promoted General Manas Paorik (AFAPS class 10) as his deputy, in part to keep a watch on Saprang. In July 2006, Manas publicly warned that Saprang was readying troops in preparation for a coup. Saprang retorted that Manas "smeared me just to flatter the prime minister and didn't take into account the damage it could cause to the army and to the country. He just wanted to climb to the top post in the 3rd Army."[79] Saprang had already begun making headlines in early July by staking out "a confrontational political position in opposition to caretaker Prime Minister Thaksin". Indeed, he stated that democracy in Thailand was "fake", and that he was a servant of the nation rather than any one individual (an apparent allusion to Thaksin). But Saprang did more than merely castigate Thaksin. In mid-July he ordered army radio stations in the seventeen northern provinces under 3rd Army jurisdiction to broadcast quotes from Saprang's earlier speeches expressing his aspirations for a better government and affirming the 3rd Army as "soldiers of the King who are prepared to stand by the people". On 18 July, Saprang assigned several army officers to northern provinces, especially Thaksin's home province of Chiang Mai, to discourage local TRT operatives from promoting Thaksin.[80]

Thaksin, increasingly infuriated by Saprang's insubordination, let it be known in August that Lt. Gen. Chartchai Boonyawatanakul, assistant army chief of staff for operations, perceived as a "neutral "officer, would succeed Saprang as 3rd Army Region chief in the October 2006 annual reshuffle, while Saprang himself would be transferred to an inactive posting.[81]

In early August, the monarch was discharged from hospital after having undergone surgery. Then, on 24 August, police, searching a Daewoo sedan that had been driving erratically near the prime minister's residence, uncovered a trunk load of explosives. The driver, an army lieutenant connected with ISOC, was arrested, and eventually five more arrests of army personnel (including one general) were made. Thaksin was deemed to have been fortunate to survive what was seen as an assassination plot against him. But the prime minister immediately dismissed ISOC chief General Pallop Pinmanee. As police continued their investigations, however, one of the accused alleged that three other generals had participated in planning the bomb plot, while a fourth, "General Por", was the mastermind. Two other sergeants were also implicated.[82] All were said to be connected with ISOC and General Pallop, though at least four of the accused had originally been part of the Special Operation Unit in Lopburi that Sonthi and Surayud had once commanded. The bomb was alleged to have been built in Lopburi.

Bombing suspect Sgt. Maj. Chakrit Jantana claimed that the masterminds were retired officers from Pallop's Chulachomklao class 7 (the Young Turks), retired soldiers close to retired general Chavalit Yongchaiyudh, and their allies who were still active-duty soldiers. These soldiers, who Thaksin had originally brought in to handle ISOC to help consolidate his hold on power among anti-Prem military cliques, had now become disillusioned with Thaksin following Chavalit's departure from the government.

Ultimately, however, the alleged assassination plot appeared to be a sort of proxy war between Thaksin and the military.[83] One theory held that Thaksin and his supporters planned the plot themselves as a way to rationalize the need for Thaksin to have his way in the upcoming military reshuffle. Indeed, prior to Pallop's removal as head of ISOC, Thaksin, on 3 August 2006, had already signed an order placing police general Chidchai Vanasatidya (class 10), the deputy prime minister, as head of ISOC. As such, Pallop's "firing" could merely have been a well-contrived performance. Yet another theory argued that military officers and other elements increasingly opposed to Thaksin saw the bombing as a way to get rid of the prime minister.[84] Perhaps, after the bomb attempt failed and as the police investigation homed in on the soldiers who masterminded it, a coup became necessary. Whatever may have been the situation, when the coup did occur, pertinent files related to the case disappeared and the investigation came to a virtual halt.[85]

By September 2006, the conflict over the impending military re-shuffle had become much more acrimonious. Besides Thaksin's AFAPS class 10 and Sonthi's AFAPS class 6, weaker cliques such as AFAPS class 7, led by General Paisal Katanyu, and AFAPS class 9, headed by Lt. Gen. Montree Sangkhasap, were also competing for promotions.[86] General Montree Suphaporn, military inspector-general and president of AFAPS class 5, announced on 19 August that the armed forces were in turmoil because of interference by ruling politicians and that in the past such interference had never been so severe.[87] This outburst was particularly surprising given that Montree was a class 5 peer and friend of Thaksin's cousin Chaisit. Montree's attack paralleled a refusal by permanent secretary of defence Sirichai Tanyasiri to push for the pro-motion of AFAPS class 10 officers.[88] At the beginning of September, Air Vice-Marshal Prasit Tananakin, AVM Surakit Jantasen, Lt. Gen. Witsanu Prayunsorn and Rear Adm. Itthichai Sripan—all anti-Thaksin allies of Bannawit and Saprang—petitioned Prem in his role as Privy Council chair about political meddling in the reshuffle.[89]

Meanwhile, citing the alleged assassination attempt against him, Thaksin, on 28 August, contended that more of his own AFAPS class 10 peers should be placed in key positions in the upcoming October annual reshuffle.[90] Specifically, though army chief Sonthi had attempted to elevate Thaksin loyalist and AFAPS class 10's General Pin Suwannatat, then 1st Infantry Brigade commander, as deputy com-mander of the 1st Army Region, Thaksin sought to promote Pin to the post of commander, 1st Army Corps, a much more strategic position charged with leading security in Bangkok. Thaksin was also seeking to have General Dapong Ratanasuwan—a King's Guard soldier (like Pin), and who seemed friendly with Thaksin—promoted to take Pin's place as head of the 1st Infantry Regiment.[91] The two generals would join General Sanit Phrommas (class 10), head of the 2nd Cavalry, 1st Army Region, as the commanders most loyal to Thaksin in Bangkok. Though Pin, Sanit and Dapong would be serving under 1st Army Region commander Anupong, they were commanding troops closer to the ground and could thus, if need be, take orders from assistant army commander General Pornchai Kranlert. At the same time, Thaksin was seeking to promote General Songkitti Chakkrabat (AFAPS class 10) to become army chief of staff. Moreover, though less likely, Thaksin had expended efforts in replacing Sonthi with Pornchai in the position of army commander. Finally, in the direct hierarchy above Pin Sanit and Dapong, Thaksin was manoeuvring to have General Anupong Paochinda, 1st Army Region commander, replaced by the more loyal General Jirasit Kesakomol (class 10). Furthermore, 3rd Army Region commander General Saprang Kalayanamitr was to be replaced by the more pliable General Chartchai Boonyawatanakul. Finally, Thaksin protege General Lertrat Ratanavanich was set to replace the pro-Prem Admiral Bannawit Kengkrien in the post of deputy permanent secretary. Crispin later commented, "the reshuffle, if accomplished, would have given Thaksin an unbroken chain of command over crack troops responsible for Bangkok's security".[92]

Many argued, however, that Thaksin would first have to surmount legal obstacles. Indeed, 1997 Charter writer Kanin Boonsuwan stated that Article 215 of the constitution required caretaker governments to seek prior approval of the Election Commission before appointing new state officials.[93] There seemed to be a crescendo of cries from many military officers that Thaksin was interfering in armed forces reshuffles in ways no one had ever done before and that he was seeking a "divide-and-conquer" strategy against the military. Growing rumours of an impending coup swept the country. Meanwhile, battalions of soldiers and tanks, apparently ordered to participate in military exercises south of Bangkok, were said to be part of an impending putsch. Yet it was a putsch that Thaksin had already expected for at least two months. Back in June 2006, Thaksin had asked Sonthi whether he would stage a coup. Thaksin was surprised when Sonthi replied "I will", and the prime minister was led to believe that Prem would fully back the army chief in any putsch.[94].

Planning for a coup reportedly had been going on since February 2006. Arch-royalist and former National Security Council head ACM

Prasong Soonsiri later stated that five people had been chiefly involved in planning the putsch: himself, army chief General Sonthi, 1st Army Region commander General Anupong, 3rd Army Region commander Saprang, and another unnamed person.[95] Those four names were confirmed to this author by an anonymous senior military official during that period. This same unnamed senior army officer named General Surayud Chulanond as the fifth 2006 coup plotter.[96] Other plotters likely included Prayut, ACM Chalit, and to some extent even Prem.[97] If coup preparations actually did begin six months prior to September 2006, this indicates that Sonthi, Anupong, Saprang and others began their putsch plans only four months after their promotions, one month after the PAD occupied Government House with little resistance from Sonthi, and alongside Thaksin's dissolution of the lower house on 24 February.

The coup finally did transpire, taking place on 19 September while Thaksin was in New York at a United Nations conference. The fact that the prime minister was away from the country and was at the time merely a caretaker prime minister made the putsch that much easier.[98] At the same time, with no functioning Election Commission and with opposition parties unwilling to participate in another election, the government and economy spiralled downhill. This was the recipe for a non-democratic force to usurp power. Civil-military antagonisms over the reshuffle list and the bomb plot investigation also served to push the coup forward. Yet the coup leaders later stated that the putsch had been necessary to avoid bloodshed given that, on 20 September, the PAD had planned to hold a major rally at the Royal Plaza and intelligence reports had reached the military that Thaksin supporters Yongyuth Tiyapairat and Newin Chidchob were planning to rally their supporters and instigate carnage.[99] Thaksin would then have used the excuse of the violence to step in, declare an emergency and place the country under martial law with his AFAPS class 10 loyalists in command positions.[100] These commanders could lead in the round-up of Thaksin's military opponents (e.g., Sonthi). Still, there is no evidence that this plot existed.

Whatever the case, coup plotters Sonthi, Anupong and Saprang—under the guidance of Prem and Surayud—agreed to act. But when it came to the day of the coup, 19 September, Sonthi was still apparently rather reluctant to lead the putsch. "Gen Saprang Kalyamanitr told him outright that morning: if he did not stage a coup, Saprang would do it himself."[101] Apparently the army chief changed his mind. Supreme commander General Ruangroj Mahajanon, navy commander Admiral

Sathiraphan Keyanont and police general Kowit Watana were all kept in the dark about the putsch—they were all considered to be too close to Thaksin.[102]

Because army commander Sonthi was reliant on the 1st Army Region command for the coup to be successful—and also owing to the intervention of his friend and class 6 peer (former army commander) General Prawit Wongsuwan—1st Army Region commander General Anupong Paochinda and his deputy, General Prayut Chanocha, were instrumental in leading the forces of the putsch. Anupong and Prayut both belonged to Prawit's Buraphapayak faction. They had been involved in planning the coup under Prem's and Surayud's direction. Thus, when it occurred on 19 September 2006, Anupong and Prayut commanded the soldiers that forced pro-Thaksin officers in Bangkok to surrender. Sonthi did not oversee the troops himself and he was a weak coup leader—he relied on Surayud, Anupong, Prayut and Prem.[103]

Numerology played a part in the coup's timing as Sonthi publicly announced it at 9:39 p.m. on 19 September, and the declaration of the coup was made on television and radio stations at 11:15 p.m. across the country. The televised announcement was read by retired general Praphas Sakuntanak, who had previously read the February 1991 coup announcement.[104] At 11:59 p.m., the coup leaders, led by army commander General Sonthi, visited Chitralada Palace, where they received royal endorsement for the coup. But after 9 p.m., military units—decorated with yellow ribbons—had already begun to enter Bangkok. These units were primarily derived from the 1st Army Region as commanded by Anupong and Prayut, but they also included troops of the Special Warfare Command (SWC) based in Lopburi, which were specifically loyal to Sonthi and Surayud (who had each commanded the SWC before). Other soldiers from the 9th Infantry Division (Kanchanaburi), 2nd Infantry Division (especially the 21st Infantry Regiment [Queen's Guard]) and the 11th Infantry Regiment descended across Bangkok to carry out the coup.[105] At the same time, 3rd Army Region commander General Saprang spearheaded the coup-leaders' drive to secure the North, capturing the pro-Thaksin hub of Chiang Mai before leading troops to Bangkok.[106] Many of Saprang's troops then moved on into Bangkok. The coup forces blocked the Bangkok army camps where key AFAPS class 10 commanders were positioned. In addition, troops surrounded the 1st Army Division, 4th Cavalry Command, in Bangkok and the 2nd Cavalry Command just north of Bangkok—units commanded by pro-Thaksin class 10 commanders. Tanks were also stationed at strategic locations around the capital such as at the parliament and Baan Phitsanuloke (Government House). Around 10:30 p.m., Thaksin attempted to declare a state of emergency. In a call from New York, the prime minister ordered the transfer of army chief Sonthi to an inactive posting and promoted supreme commander General Ruangroj Mahasaranon to manage the crisis. The prime minister apparently sought to hatch a counter-coup against Sonthi. But Thaksin's telephone message, which was broadcast on television, was suddenly cut as the coup leaders secured control over the country's state telecommunications.[107] Shortly thereafter, Ruangroj reluctantly defected to Sonthi's side. And at midnight, the commanders of the army, air force, navy, police and Supreme Command, as well as privy councillors Prem and Surayud, had an audience with the king and queen. Thereupon, the king endorsed the military regime.[108]

The coup-leaders, under General Sonthi Boonyaratklin, rationalized their move, stating that the Thaksin government was corrupt, nepotistic, had abused its power, had sown political polarization, did not sufficiently "protect His Majesty's dignity", and had committed human rights violations.[109] But such reasons did little to validate the six to seven months of coup planning. Perhaps a more important reason why the plotters and those handling them (Prem and Surayud) usurped power was that by removing Thaksin he would no longer present an obstacle to the traditionalist palace-centred forces—and their close advisors—who dominated the country. In this way, the demise of Thaksin would spell the resurrection of the arch-Royalist military/business order. The coup can also be explained in terms of internal army politics. It was, following Ockey, ultimately a clash between the Prem-led ambiguous "Democratic Soldiers" faction (which included Sonthi), who were seeking to maintain control over the military, and Thaksin's own pre-cadet class 10 (Chulachomklao class 21) officers. In fact, the reshuffle list had already been delivered to Thaksin and he was on the verge of replacing Sonthi when the coup occurred on 19 September. Thus, as Ockey has said, the "Professional Soldiers" resorted, ironically, to the "unprofessional" step of "couping" Thaksin from office.[110] As a result, Thailand's fourteen years of frail democratization was terminated and the prospects of future democracy considerably eroded. Meanwhile, Thaksin was still not out of the picture. Indeed, though the prime minister had been pushed into exile, he remained an implacable foe to Thailand's royalist-centred elite establishment for at least the next decade and a half.

Following the coup, the faction of the military that had been marginalized by Thaksin's rise was particularly elated. Seeking to rationalize his overthrow of democracy, coup-leader Sonthi praised the fact of Thailand being under authoritarian rule in a paradoxical statement: "Thailand is 100 percent democratic now; our reason for action is that we want real democracy in our country."[111] Realizing, however, that it needed popular support, the coup group immediately established a 12 million baht top-secret budget for a public relations campaign aimed at defaming Thaksin Shinawatra, headed by General Saprang Kalayamitr's brother.[112] But in a country that had experienced over a decade of vibrant civil society and where military authoritarianism had twice been overthrown—in 1973 and 1992—the post-2006 junta quickly became unpopular. Indeed, despite continuing deep divisions among civilians about Thaksin, a growing number of urban elements began to agree with rural Thais that a return to democracy was essential.[113] Ultimately, the government announced a general election for December 2007.

Nevertheless, with the ouster and exile of Thaksin, a new political structure without him commenced. The coup group immediately voided the 1997 constitution and set up a ruling junta, which referred to itself by various names, including the "Administrative Reform Group under the Democratic System with the King as the Head of

FIGURE 12.3
Council for National Security (CNS)
Initial Junta Leadership (2006)

No.	Name	Class	Role
1.	Army commander General Sonthi Boonyaratklin	pre-cadet class 6	Chief of Junta
2.	Navy commander Admiral Sathirapan Keyanon	pre-cadet class 6	1st deputy chief
3.	Air Force commander ACM Chalit Phukpasuk	pre-cadet class 6	2nd deputy chief
4.	Police commissioner General Kowit Wattana	pre-cadet class 6	3rd deputy chief
5.	National Security Council secretary-general General Winai Phattiyakul	pre-cadet class 6	Secretary-General
6.	Supreme commander General Ruangroj Mahasaranon	pre-cadet class 5	Chief Advisor

State", the "Council for Democratic Reform under Constitutional Monarchy" and the "Administrative Reform Council", until ultimately settling on the "Council for National Security", or CNS. Five of the CNS leaders (except Ruangroj and Sansern) were members of AFAPS class 6. Ruangroj (Chaisit's AFAPS class 5) only reluctantly joined the coup and junta because, with anti-Thaksin officers gaining the upper hand on 19 September, he had no other choice than to participate and, after all, he was anticipating retirement only eleven days after the coup. When Ruangroj did retire, his AFAPS class 6 peer, deputy supreme commander General Boonsrang Niempradit, succeeded him in the posting.

Each member of the CNS had an interesting background. Chalit was a Bangkokian who had married a professor of foreign languages at Chulalongkorn University—a centre of Yellow Shirt activity. He worked his way up the air force hierarchy to become chief of staff before his nomination as air force commander was cold-shouldered by Thaksin. Thaksin had sought to continue his domination of the air force in 2005 with the promotion of ACM Raden Peungpak (AFAPS class 5), a close ally of retiring air force chief ACM Kongsak Wattana and supreme commander General Chaisit Shinawatra back in 2005. But the palace refused to approve Raden's promotion and Chalit got the air force job instead. After 2005, Chalit demonstrated that he was an oasis of independence from Thaksin as he operated within an air force that had increasingly tilted away from the prime minister. In 2006 Chalit publicly voiced his displeasure with Thaksin's attempts to purchase Russian-made SU-30 jets as the air force commander preferred US-made ones.[114] It seemed only a matter of time before the prime minister would sideline Chalit to an inactive position. During the 2006 coup, no air force personnel participated in it and army troops were deployed to air force headquarters to make sure its senior officers joined the coup leaders.[115] Actually, Sonthi had little fear that Chalit would defect to Thaksin's side. Many other senior air force officers seemed to tilt towards the premier. These included Air Marshal Sukampol Suwannathat, air force chief of staff (AFAPS class 10); air vice marshal Sumet Pomanee, RTAF Security Force commander, (AFAPS class 10); ACM Akkarachai Sakulrattana, deputy air-commander-in-chief (Chaisit's AFAPS class 5); and ACM Napruet Mantajitr, assistant to air-commander-in-chief (AFAPS class 5).

Regarding navy commander Admiral Sathirapan Keyanon (AFAPS class 6), he rose through many naval positions before becoming navy chief of staff. Although a member of AFPAS class 6, Sathirapan was generally rather distant from other AFAPS "sixers". This perhaps derived from the tradition of the navy to be divorced from the army when it came to political issues. Yet it also owed to suspicions by some officers that Sathirapan was simply too close to Thaksin. Many privately griped that supreme commander General Chaisit Shinawatra had fast-tracked Admiral Sathirapan's promotion over the normal career paths of other naval officers simply because of Sathirapan's political connections—he was favoured by Thaksin's wife and brother.[116] As navy chief, Sathirapan came out to publicly deride the anti-Thaksin demonstrators. In November 2005, he joined the pro-Thaksin top brass generals Ruangroj Mahasarananon and Prin Suwannathat in castigating *Manager* editor Sondhi Limthongkul for invoking the monarchy when criticizing the government.[117] In May 2006, Sathirapan publicly announced that "The Navy is worried things have not fallen into place, even though military leaders have been trying to encourage relevant parties to sort out the political mess."[118] Ultimately, when the coup of 19 September 2006 took place, the plotters told him about it only at the last minute. Sathirapan was a reluctant co-conspirator and did not send any navy personnel to participate in the putsch.[119]

Meanwhile, General Winai Phatthiyakul (AFAPS class 6) had a rich history of connections with political luminaries. First, he was the son-in-law of 1976 coup leader Admiral Sagnad Chaloryu. Second, he served for some years as a close aide to General Arthit Kamlang-ek and was close to Suwat Liptanpanlop, a rising politician. In fact, he worked with both Arthit and Suwat when the two put together the Puang Chon Chao Thai Party back in 1988. In 1997 he worked under the pro-Prem supreme commander General Mongkol Ampornpiset as director for joint intelligence and was also close to General Boonsrang Niampradit. Indeed, he succeeded Boonsrang as commander of the United Nations Transitional Administration in East Timor (UNTAET) in 2001. Winai has also had a long relationship with General Chavalit Yongchaiyudh. And under Thaksin, with help from Chavalit, Winai became the secretary-general of Thaksin's National Security Council. Winai's relations with Sonthi owed to their shared AFAPS class 6 ties as well as the fact that as Thaksin became increasingly dissatisfied with both Sonthi and Winai, the two increasingly stuck together.[120] Winai today holds huge investments in Big C Supercenter and Thai Life Insurance.[121]

Turning to General Ruangroj Mahasaranon, he initially served in the 1st Infantry Battalion, King's Guard, partly under General Somthat Attanand, before starting his ascent up the military ladder.

He participated peripherally in the previous coup of 1991 when he worked in the office as chief of staff to 1991 coup leader General Sunthorn Kongsongpong.[122] As a member of AFAPS class 5, Ruangroj had close peer ties with Thaksin's cousin Chaisit. Indeed, in October 2005, Thaksin drew criticism from military quarters when he promoted Ruangroj ahead of others from a relatively inactive posting—chairman of the Advisory Board of the Supreme Command—to become supreme commander, replacing Ruangroj's friend Chaisit. After 2005, Ruangroj effectively became Thaksin's point man in the Supreme Command, while Pornchai Kranlert was, as assistant army chief, the most senior Thaksin loyalist in the army. When the coup transpired on 19 September 2006, Thaksin sacked Sonthi and appointed Ruangroj to enforce the state of emergency.[123] Ruangroj only grudgingly accepted, realizing that the palace was endorsing the putsch. A week later, he retired from the military. Like ACM Chalit, Ruangroj is married to a university professor, Dr Pornpimon Mahasaranon.

Ruangroj's successor as CNS advisor and supreme commander of the armed forces was Boonsrang Niumpradit, who assumed the positions on 29 and 30 September, respectively. Like other CNS leaders, Boonsrang was an AFAPS class 6 graduate and had served closely under Surayud Chulanond. Most of Boonsrang's career was spent in the Supreme Command, and he was the director of the National Defence College (1999–2000). In 2000, then army chief Surayud appointed Boonsrang as force commander of UNTAET.[124] He was succeeded in this position in 2001 by Winai. Reflecting the reformism of Surayud, Boonsrang engendered a view that the military should be streamlined, professionalized and "in the barracks". It was thus rather ironic that Boonsrang was chosen to help lead the CNS. This owed to his close ties to Sonthi, Winai and Surayud. Actually, his name had been proposed as a successor to Ruangroj even before the coup in August.[125] Yet, as CNS advisor, he quickly proved to be one of the most reticent junta members. After a year in his junta position, Boonsrang urged an end to the CNS itself and a return to quasi democracy. He even publicly urged that the CNS be dissolved, saying: "I feel the CNS is like a comedy show."[126] In 2007, the US Embassy in Bangkok considered Boonsrang to "be a moderating influence among the senior military leadership in Thailand since the coup".[127]

As for the CNS police representative, police general Kowit Watana, he was—like Sonthi, Chalit, Boonsrang and Sathirapan—a graduate of AFAPS class 6. But Kowit also attended the Royal Thai Army Command and General Staff College (class 56), the same class as

Crown Prince Vajiralongkorn. It is thus assumed that Kowit maintains close ties with the palace, including the prince. In the mid-1970s, at the height of the Thai military's fight against the Communist Party of Thailand, he was a rising member of Thailand's Border Patrol Police (BPP), which is ostensibly under the control of the Ministry of the Interior but is operationally under the army's Supreme Command. Kowit rose from being a BPP second lieutenant in 1970 to BPP commissioner in 1994.[128] From 2002 until 2004, when Thaksin transferred most security affairs from under the control of the army to that of the police, Kowit served as deputy police chief. In the midst of criticism of Thaksin's southern Thailand policy by Privy Council chair Prem, Thaksin appointed Kowit to serve as chief of police in 2004, though this selection apparently bypassed Thaksin's preference for the more junior police general Chidchai Wannasatit (AFAPS class 10), a Thaksin loyalist.[129] During the coup against Thaksin in September 2006, Kowit reportedly was reluctant to support it. He was likely kept on initially by coup-leaders because of his close ties to the crown prince. But his seemingly reluctant support for the putsch, his slowness in transferring to inactive positions those police officials seen to have been close to Thaksin, and his slow processing of *lèse-majesté* complaints together contributed to Kowit's fall from the CNS in 2007.[130] Another factor owed to the result of his investigation into multiple bombings that occurred in Bangkok on New Year's Eve 2006. He dared to focus on soldiers as the culprits (those he arrested were quickly released by the junta). In February 2007, Surayud and the CNS transferred Kowit, replacing him as police chief and deputy CNS head with the anti-Thaksin police general Seripisut Temiyavej (AFAPS class 8).[131] The junta's ouster of Kowit likewise owed to an attempt to fully rid the police of pro-Thaksin elements. But that effort proved ultimately to be unsuccessful.

Seripisut had a reputation as a macho and mercurial tough guy who had been a one-time close friend of serial coup-plotter General Manoon Rupkachorn. The new police chief had already earned a reputation for combating mafiosos and rooting out corruption. In this capacity, Thaksin appointed him as inspector general in the early 2000s. Under Thaksin, Seripisut continued to be active in going after suspected mobsters as well as attacking corruption and nepotism. In 2005 he even appealed to the palace against the promotion to deputy police chief of Priewpan Damapong, brother of the wife of Thaksin.[132] In June 2006, a dispute between Seripisut and Kowit Watana surfaced when the former accused Kowit of not following the rules in helping

Seripisut crack down on gambling dens.[133] In the same case, Seripisut accused General Kattiya Sawasdipol (Seh Daeng) of involvement in such illegal gambling dens. The police chief's actions against Seh Daeng continued until 2009, after Thai electoral governance had been restored.[134] Beginning as deputy CNS leader and new police chief in 2007, Seripisut immediately purged senior police officers deemed to be close to Kowit and Thaksin. He demonstrated his own nepotism. Indeed, an AFAPS class 8 peer and close friend of Seripisut became Bangkok's new metropolitan police chief. Meanwhile, an elder brother of Seripisut's wife was promoted as advisor to the national police office. Finally, perhaps to curry favour, Seripisut appointed a brother-in-law of Premier Surayud's wife as police commissioner to tackle southern violence.[135]

Differences among CNS members arose throughout its existence, with Anupong, Prayut, Sonthi and Chalit tending to keep the core together the most. Saprang and Prayut were generally the most reactionary members, while Sathirapan and Boonsrang proved to be the most moderate. Prem and Surayud succeeded in keeping the CNS together.

As with Suchinda's 1991–92 National Peace Keeping Council fifteen years previously, the CNS appointed a civilian prime minister to head an interim government that was affiliated with Sonthi's CNS. But, at Prem's insistence, the new civilian prime minister was an ex-army commander and a privy councillor (retiring from government service), General Surayud, who was greatly trusted by Prem.[136] Surayud in turn nominated twenty-six individuals to serve in his cabinet, with two ministers coming from the military: longtime Surayud confidants and retired military officers General Boonrawd Somtas (AFAPS class 1) in the defence ministry and Admiral Theera Haocharoen (AFAPS class 1) in transportation.

At the same time, a special force was deployed to put down any unrest related to anti-CNS activities. This "Special Operations Centre" was made up of 13,625 security personnel recruited from the armed forces and police. It had a budget of 556 million baht and operated officially from 1 December 2006 until 30 September 2007. It was headed at the national level by assistant army commander General Saprang Kalayanamitr.[137] Moreover, a special regional force would monitor "suspicious activities" in Bangkok and central Thailand to counter potential unrest, which utilised a budget of 319.1 million baht. This special force was commanded by 1st Army Region head and Anupong loyalist General Prayut Chanocha.[138]

Yet another development triggered by the coup was an expansion of the military budget. Financial allocations to the armed forces had been reduced following the 1997 Asian financial crisis. Though Thaksin had early on in his term approved some resumption in military funding, it had ultimately continued at lower levels—something not satisfactory to the military, especially following the beginning of the Deep South insurgency in 2004. Just after the 2006 coup, however, the military budget grew by 34 per cent,[139] and it generally continued to rise every year afterward. Rationalizing the enhanced budget, the state invoked the need for resources to protect the kingdom from Thaksin as well as the Deep South insurrection. Moreover, the legitimization for more military funding found its way into the new 2007 constitution, which mandated that the state arrange for the maintenance of necessary and adequate armed forces and ordnances as well as up-to-date technology for the protection and upholding of its independence, sovereignty, security of the state, the monarchy, national interests, national development, and the democratic regime of government with the king as head of state.[140]

Turning to the counter-insurgency in the Deep South, the CNS restored Prem's military and ISOC-dominated Southern Border Provinces Administrative Centre as a hub for interactions between the security forces and civilians in the Deep South. The junta also pursued limited dialogue while also carrying out increased repression and arrests. Most importantly, following Thaksin's downfall, the army once again led Thai state policy in the region.

Meanwhile, a 242-member National Legislative Assembly was appointed under a Royal Command. This assembly acted as the legislative branch during military rule.

FIGURE 12.4
Thailand's National Legislative Assembly, 2006–8

Type of legislature	Years in office	Appointed or elected	Total number of members and military contingent
Unicameral	2006–8 (served 2-year term	Appointed	242, of which 76 (31.4%) active-duty or retired military/police

Source: Anonymous, "Superfluous, Irrelevant, or Emancipating: Thailand's Evolving Senate Today", *Journal of Current Southeast Asian Affairs* 28, no. 3 (2009): 10.

With the 24 August 2007 endorsement of King Bhumipol, the junta-appointed National Legislative Assembly enacted a new constitution that, unlike its predecessor, weakened the power of elected civilian governments while strengthening the military and judiciary (with many new judges appointed under the 2006–7 dictatorship).[141] Furthermore, the 2000–2006 elected Senate was scrapped in favour of a half-appointed body (allowing for 9.3 per cent of appointed senators in 2008 to be ex-military officials). Power of judicial review of the constitutionality of the law was maintained with a new Constitutional Tribunal.[142] This tribunal declared Thaksin's Thai Rak Thai Party to have violated the constitution, and on 30 May 2007 the party was officially dissolved. All 111 members of its party executive committee were banned from holding political office for five years.

Moreover, the coup leaders established an Assets Scrutiny Committee to investigate corruption in the Thaksin government. Finally, the charter granted an amnesty to the coup instigators. Having been drafted by the CNS and endorsed by the military, the CNS next wanted to legitimize the draft constitution by having it approved through a popular referendum—a feat that would deceptively enhance the junta's democratic credentials. The referendum was set for 19 August 2007. Soldiers were said to be attempting to influence rural Thais to vote for it—soldiers had received instructions to urge voters to vote for it and had been ordered to vote for it themselves. Financial resources were also used to ensure the vote passed.[143] The CNS pressured local governments to mobilise the vote in favour of the constitution, and political parties were forbidden to advertise against it. To no one's surprise, the junta-ordered, organized and monitored referendum demonstrated that voters supported the junta-endorsed 2007 constitution. Still, the charter was ultimately approved by a much lower margin of voters than the CNS anticipated. Turnout was under sixty per cent.

Other than the constitution, the National Legislative Assembly approved a series of acts that gave the military more power. One new law required that reshuffles of high-ranking officers (the rank of brigadier general and up) be vetted by a committee, whose members included the army commander, navy commander, air force commander, supreme commander, and permanent defence secretary (himself/herself a military official) as well as the civilian defence minister and prime minister. Previously, the defence and prime minister had the ultimate say on appointments (though these were to be endorsed by the king). In future, if any dispute occurred as to an appointment, a simple committee vote would settle the dispute. Since the unelected military portion of the committee accounted for five votes whilst civilian members only held two, the new arrangement heightened military sway at the expense of civilian authority.[144]

A second law that enhanced the power of the military was the Internal Security Act (19 February 2008). This act establishes a structure of control whereby the premier is ISOC director, the army commander is deputy director, and the army chief of staff is secretary.

Throughout the 2006–8 period of military rule, political space was constrained. Political parties, demonstrations and related activities were banned by the junta until July 2007. Perhaps surprisingly, prior to the election campaign of late 2007, political competition was forbidden by the military except at the local level. Thus, though military authoritarianism existed at the national level under the junta, there continued to be elections and local democracy at the provincial, city and sub-district levels of governance. Even the elected governor of the Bangkok Metropolitan Area, Apirak Kosahodhin (of the Democrat Party), was allowed to continue in office (though he was an ally of the coup-makers).

After the coup, at least eleven army generals and two police generals became board members of approximately thirteen state enterprise agencies.[145] The trend of military involvement on the boards of state enterprise had gradually dissipated after 1992, but the 2006 coup saw new hope for soldiers to regain their status on these boards.

Finally, one could say with confidence that Thailand was under the military boot from 2006 until 2008. After all, the armed forces were ruling directly. As such, had Surayud fallen out of favour with Sonthi, one would think that Sonthi could simply replace him with a more trustworthy prime minister. But despite possessing such power, Sonthi could not simply have Surayud replaced. This is because Prem Tinsulanonda was Surayud's close patron and mentor. And Prem was influential throughout the coup government—including with Sonthi. Despite occasional disagreements, Sonthi's CNS coup group and the appointed government of Surayud managed to cooperate enough to maintain order, administer the economy, produce a new constitution, and carry out elections on 27 December 2008.

Under CNS control, army chief Sonthi worked to preserve order within the military, and particularly the army. But not every soldier was happy about the coup. Certainly, those military officers seen to have been too close to Thaksin and sidelined by the military junta (specifically in AFAPS class 10) were grumbling. Chavalit Yongchaiyudh—who was highly respected in the military—was also not happy. Only a little over a month after the coup, he publicly criticized the CNS for appointing officers to state enterprise boards.[146] Chavalit, who apparently had some role "in bringing down Thaksin", also criticized the CNS for failing to communicate with the people and for lacking transparency. Finally, Chavalit demanded that Thaksin be allowed to return home.[147] Chavalit's grumbling was generally brushed aside by Surayud and Sonthi. But the old general, according to an anonymous aide, now appeared to see himself in the role of mentor to the CNS as a means of establishing a new political party that would have a good chance of leading a coalition government once elections were held again.[148] By the end of 2006, however, Chavalit seemed to be edging towards an advisory or leadership position in the Thai Rak Thai Party, given that Thaksin was out of the picture.

Within the post-coup army, graduates of AFAPS class 6 and Army Cadet Academy class 17 controlled most of the top positions, reflecting the dominance of the classes of coup leader General Sonthi and his collaborators. Four days after the coup, Sonthi implemented a strategic reshuffle. Among key promotions, General Winai Phattiyakul (Sonthi's friend from class 6), secretary-general of the CNS, was elevated to become permanent secretary for defence. General Boonsrang Niampradit (class 6) was simultaneously promoted from the position of deputy supreme commander to that of supreme commander, replacing the pro-Thaksin General Ruangroj, who retired in 2006. At the same time, Lt. Gen. Anupong Paochinda, 1st Army Region commander, and General Saprang Kalayanamitr, 3rd Army Region commander, both became assistant army chiefs. This owed to their essential roles in the putsch. AFAPS classes 7 and 9 also benefited from the reshuffle given that they had generally not opposed the coup. General Paisan Katanyu (valedictorian of AFAPS class 7) was promoted from an army assistant commander position to the post of deputy army chief. The CNS was happy that General Wichit Yathip (class 9) was retiring in 2006 as he was seen as too close to Chavalit, "whose relationship with the CNS had soured".[149] As 2006–7 was to be Paisan's final year before retirement, this represented a terminal position for him. At the same time, General Montree Sangkhasap (president of AFAPS class 9) was elevated from his previous Army Reserve command post to that of army chief of staff. Other class 9 loyalist friends of Montree were also promoted, including General Jiradet Kotcharat, who succeeded Saprang as commander of the 3rd Army Region (after serving as commander of the 3rd Army Region Corps); and General Prayut Chanocha (who spearheaded the coup drive as deputy army commander of the 1st Army Region) to become commander of the 1st Army Region. Army chief of staff Sophon Silpapat (class 6), who had shown little compunction to lead during the coup, was transferred to the rather impotent posting of director of the Advisory Board of the Royal Thai Army.

As for those officers who had been on the side of Thaksin, Sonthi proved initially to be magnanimous in the punitive reshuffle. General Pornchai Kranlert, assistant army chief, became deputy chief of the joint chiefs of staff in the Supreme Command. General Lertrat Ratanavanich was made inspector general of the Defence Ministry. Songkitti Chakkrabat was promoted from deputy chief of staff to chief of staff in the Supreme Command. Thaksin's AFAPS class 10 allies that he had placed in key positions in the Bangkok area—generals Prin Suwanathat, Jirasit Kesakomol, Sanit Phrommas, Manas Paorik and Ruangsak Tongdee—were all transferred to inactive postings.

A couple of months after the annual reshuffle, however, and in the wake of Chavalit's complaints about CNS performance, Sonthi ordered a mid-level reshuffle involving 136 lieutenant colonels assigned to battalion-level positions. These rotations were "seen by critics as an attempt to foil a second coup".[150] Meanwhile, the bombing of 1 January 2007 triggered fear among Bangkokians about an imminent new coup. The culprits behind these explosions were never found. It is highly likely they stemmed from a growing fracture within the army between forces loyal to CNS assistant secretary General Saprang Kalayamitr and 1st Army Region commander Lt. Gen. Prayut Chanocha.[151] And it is for this reason that Anupong began to consolidate his control over the army—placing his most-trusted loyalists in all the highest positions of power, though his decision certainly annoyed senior officers who were not part of his Queen's Guard and Buraphapayak faction.

The 1 April 2007 mid-year reshuffle was immense. Including 452 appointments, it further purged the armed forces leadership of pro-Thaksin elements, consigning them to unimportant desk postings. General Pornchai Kranlert, already demoted to deputy chief of staff of the Supreme Command, now became a mere advisor in the office of the permanent secretary for defence. General Sujet Watanasuk (AFAPS class 7), commander of the 2nd Army Region—who was deemed to be too close to Thaksin's defence minister, Thammarak, and was also seen to have performed poorly in controlling pro-Thaksin activity in the Northeast—was transferred to the post of advisor to the office of the permanent secretary of defence. At the same time, General Chatchai Thavornbutr (class 10), deputy chief of staff of the army, who had previously been a close aide of Thaksin, was moved to become another advisor in the office of the permanent secretary.[152] General Pin Suwannatat was transferred from the posting of chief in the office of the permanent secretary to be a "special qualified general" in the Supreme Command. In the navy, Vice Admiral Sivichai Sirisalee (AFAPS class 10), chief of the Marine Corps, was similarly transferred to an advisory post. Moreover, ACM Sukampol Suwannathat (AFAPS class 10), assistant air force chief, was demoted to an inactive position. In total, except for four officers (including Anupong), all AFAPS class 10 officers were demoted to become advisors or "special qualified generals" in the 2007 mid-year reshuffle. AFAPS class 8 (of Lertrat but also Saprang) also mostly lost out in the reshuffle as few of its officers were promoted.

But the reshuffle was beneficial to AFAPS class 9—except for those members seen as having been close to the pro-Chavalit former deputy army commander General Wichit Yathip. Indeed, General Montree Sangkhasap was promoted to become deputy army commander, while General Jiradet Kocharat became assistant army commander. Simultaneously, General Samreng Seewadamrong and General Wiroj Buajaroen became commanders of the 3rd Army Region and 4th Army Region, respectively. Officers with personal ties to Sonthi also won out in the reshuffle. Indeed, the army chief appointed his aide General Sujit Sittiprapha (AFAPS class 8) as commander of the 2nd Army Region. Sujit was also known to be close to AFAPS class 9. At the same time, Sonthi promoted his friend General Sunai Sampattawanich (AFAPS class 11) as chief of the Special Warfare Command. General Phuchong Rattanawan (who was transferred to an inactive position) did not get the post, even though he was very close to Prime Minister Surayud Chulanont, perhaps because Puchong was a member of AFAPS class 10. Two more of Sonthi's friends, General Jittipong Suwaset (AFAPS class 9) and General Woradet Phumjit (AFAPS class 7), were promoted to, respectively, chief of the Air Defence Command and executive staff officer to the army chief. In another appointment, General Malai Kiewthieng, commander of the 1st Special Warfare Division and a close associate of General Prayut Chanocha, was elevated to become army assistant chief of staff for operations.[153] Finally, the Sitabutr brothers, considered close to the palace, were naturally promoted: ACM Paisan, who had been relegated to being a mere special qualified general under Thaksin during 2005–6, now rose to assistant air force commander in his final year of active duty. His younger brother, Udomdej, a member of the post-coup leading faction Queen's Guard

(21st Infantry Regiment) within the Eastern Tigers (2nd Infantry Division), became commander of the 11th Infantry Circle, though he was on a fast-track to eventually become army commander.

This mid-year reshuffle prepared the way for the struggle over who would succeed Sonthi as army commander in October 2007. There were only three candidates. First was assistant army chief General Saprang Kalanamitr, the vehemently anti-Thaksin officer who was favoured by Prem, Prasong Soonsiri and Admiral Bannawit Kengkrian.[154] Yet it was feared that Saprang might polarize Thai society with his anti-Thaksin vitriol, and, after all, he only had one more year of active-duty service. Second there was General Anupong Paochinda, though he might have been seen as a dark horse since he was a graduate of AFAPS class 10 and thus perhaps somewhat sympathetic to Thaksin. If Anupong had been chosen, there would have been uncertainty as to whether he could be trusted, especially given that he would probably remain army chief until retirement three years later in 2010. Third, there was deputy army chief Montree Sangkhasap, who was being groomed by Sonthi to fill the army chief post. But Montree had little real command experience. Moreover, he would have to retire in two years (2009), and he lacked backing in high places. Ultimately, Sonthi ensured that the 2007 mid-year reshuffle was not favourable to either Saprang's class 8 or Anupong's class 10. This deprived each of them a class-based support network to campaign for the top army slot, a decision that would be made only six months later.[155]

Who, then, was Anupong Paochinda? Born on 10 October 1949, he was the second son (out of five siblings) of Colonel Prachaow Paochinda. Anupong (nickname "Big Pok") grew up in military camps. He studied at the prestigious Amnuay Silpa School along with Admiral Kamthorn Phumviran and General Songkitti Chakkrabat. He then entered pre-cadet academy class 10 alongside General Songkitti and others, including police lieutenant colonel Thaksin Shinawatra. Anupong studied as a cadet at Chulachomklao Royal Military Academy, class 21 (Jor Por Ror. 21), and graduated in 1972, becoming an infantry platoon leader, 2nd Infantry Battalion, 21st Infantry Regiment (Queen's Tiger Guard), 2nd Infantry Division. He then advanced through the ranks in the Queen's Guard and by 1996 he had become its commander. In 2002 he became commander of the 2nd Infantry Division, in 2003 he was appointed commander of the 1st Infantry Division, and in 2005 he became commander of the 1st Infantry Region.[156]

General Anupong Paochinda's siblings (all younger) are retired general Thanadon Paochinda (CEO of Universal Utilities Group), Lt.

Gen. Arunwan Paochinda, Ms Chawawan Paochinda, and Lt. Col. Siriwan Phaochinda. Anupong is married to Mrs Kulaya Paochinda and they have a son and daughter—Mr Yutthapong Paochinda and Ms Wimalin Paochinda. Yutthapong has reportedly been involved in many entrepreneurial activities, including Montra Health and Solid Entertainment Company.[157] See the diagram of Anupong's family tree in Figure 12.5.

Aside from new army commander Anupong, General Montri Chompuchan (AFAPS class 6) became army chief of staff, not only because of his friendship with Sonthi, which would allow the latter to continue influencing the army after his retirement, but also because Montri was a stopgap decision given that he would retire the following year. Other notable changes included General Weerawit Kusamran (AFAPS class 7), who was promoted to be deputy army chief, and generals Jiradet Kotcharat (AFAPS class 9) and Theerawat Boonpradab (class 10), who were each promoted to assistant army commander posts.[158] Moreover, General Dulkrit Rakpao (AFAPS class 10) became 1st Army Region corps commander. Both Theerawat and Dulkrit were APAPS class 10 graduates who backed Anupong and Sonthi's coup against Thaksin.

In addition, General Dapong Rattanasuwan (AFAPS class 12) was switched out from commanding the 1st Division, King's Guard, to

FIGURE 12.5
Anupong Paochinda's Family Tree

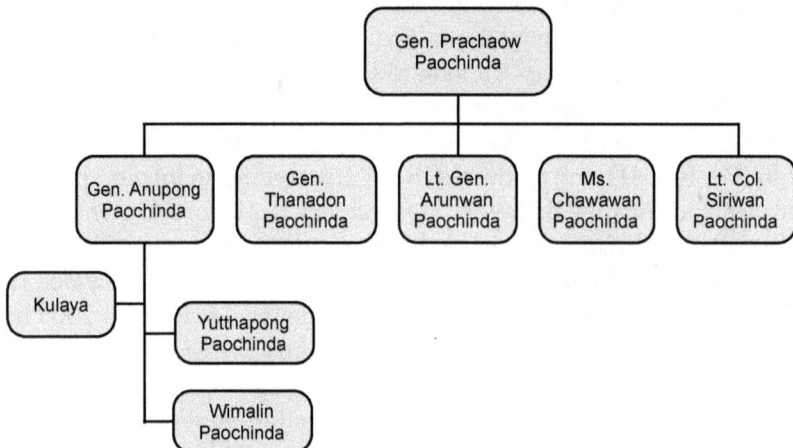

become deputy commander of the 1st Army Region serving under Prayut, who was 1st Army Region commander. Dapong was thought to be close to Prin Suwannathat since both had commanded the King's Guard. But since Dapong was a member of AFAPS class 12 and had a long friendship with Prayut, he was hardly a crony of Thaksin or Pin. To assist Prayut and Dapong, General Jiradet Mokkasamit (AFAPS class 13) was selected to command the 1st Army Support Command, 1st Army Area Corps slot. Prayut's protégé General Malai Kiutiang was promoted from assistant to RTA chief of staff for intelligence to become a deputy chief of staff, RTA.

Meanwhile, General Montree Sangkhasap was kicked upstairs to become deputy supreme commander. For his last year of military service before retirement, Saprang was ignominiously transferred to the post of deputy permanent secretary for defence.[159] Ultimately, only a few members of AFAPS class 10 were elevated with Anupong when he became army commander. Yet AFAPS class 12, of which Prayut was a member and which Anupong specifically relied upon (since he had little support in AFAPS class 10), proved to be the base for the new army commander. Classes 9 and 13 also managed to receive plum promotions. In sum, the October annual reshuffle was especially a boon for a particular military clique based around a unit. This was the 2nd Infantry Division of the 1st Army Region (Eastern Tigers). Its dynastic leaders—active-duty generals Anupong, Prayut, Thanasak Patimapakorn and Kanit Sapitak—appeared to be triumphing in the aftermath of Anupong's promotion. Retired general Prawit Wongsuwan, also formerly commander of the Eastern Tigers, acted as a sort of informal advisor to the faction.

With the promotion of class 10 graduate Anupong Paochinda to army commander in 2007, pro-Anupong class 10 graduates were allowed to return to active positions. Sonthi Boonyaratklin was given the position of deputy prime minister for security affairs as a sort of reward for his agreeing to Anupong over Montree. From this position, Sonthi began to stress the need to find peace in the far South, showing an interest in politics. (Later, in retirement, he started the small Mataphum Party.)

Only three days after succeeding Sonthi, army chief Anupong ordered a mid-ranking reshuffle similar to the one implemented by Sonthi back in July 2006. This reshuffle was meant to consolidate the power of Anupong and his Queen's Guard (and Eastern Tigers) loyalist General Prayut Chanocha over the army (especially in the 3rd Army Region, which had been commanded by Saprang). Only this time it involved 215 unit commanders. First, Colonel Preecha Chanocha, younger brother of 1st Army Region chief Prayut, was elevated to become deputy chief of staff of the 3rd Army Region. Second, Colonel Apirak Kongsompong, son of 1991 coup participant General Sunthorn Kongsompong, was named 11th Infantry Regiment commander. Third, Colonel Pachon Tampratheep was promoted as deputy chief of staff of the elite forces, the Special Warfare Division in Lopburi, which Surayud had once commanded. Prachon "is a younger brother of Vice-Adm Pachun, secretary to Privy Council president Gen Prem Tinsulanonda".[160]

Amidst October 2007 military reshuffles, preparations were already being made for the December 2007 election. Several parties had been formed earlier to compete in the polls, many with military encouragement and even money. General Sonthi's friend General Winai Pattiyakul was the CNS point man for assembling these parties.

In early 2007, Suwat, with Winai's blessing, had broken away from Thai Rak Thai to run under the banner of his new Ruam Jai Thai Chart Pattana Party. At the same time, the Matchima political faction, formerly the Wang Nam Yom clique in the Thai Rak Thai Party, was making preparations in mid-2007 to run in the December election. Wang Nam Yom leader Somsak Thepsuthin apparently met with General Winai to discuss the eventual formation of his political party. Matchima's political headquarters was owned by the daughter of Sonthi ally General Montri Supaporn.[161] Somsak was closely connected to political opportunist and longtime faction leader Newin Chidchob, himself an associate of several senior military officials, including General Prawit Wongsuwan.[162] Another political grouping with close ties to the military was Puea Paendin; a clique of military personnel was said to be supporting the party financially.[163] Another micro-party alleged to be the nominee of Winai was called Rak Chart, though he denied this. The CNS was also rumoured to be close to the Democrat Party: Winai's own son Sakolthee was a Democrat candidate in the December 2007 election.[164]

Martial law was lifted incrementally from provinces considered to be pro-Thaksin in time for the December 2007 pre-election campaign. Yet there were allegations of covert military involvement in seeking to influence the outcome of the election. The purported plan involved using state-run media to attack and discredit the pro-Thaksin Palang Prachachon (People's Power) Party PPP—in the name of national security.[165] The plan, likely hatched by ISOC, included public interviews with Thais claiming to be harmed by Thaksin's populist policies as well as cherry-picked accusations that a victory for PPP would increase national disunity. Further, the PPP schemes were advertised as directly contradicting the king's sufficiency economy theory—and hence opposing the king himself. Finally, a drawn-out campaign was waged to convince voters not to support PPP. But towards the end of November, army officials finally admitted that documents proving that it had concocted the smear campaign were in fact real. The scandal revealed that the army was continuing to involve itself directly in Thai politics, perhaps by trying to fix the election and thus engineering a second "quiet" coup to keep PPP from forming a government. Another alleged plot entailed military lobbying of political parties in a bid to prevent PPP from forming a government after the election.[166] Though these plots may have continued despite the revelations about them, Thailand's Election Commission in December 2007 dismissed a petition by supporters of Thaksin claiming that the CNS had plotted to stop the new pro-Thaksin party PPP from winning the 2007 general election. Rumours of military involvement in the 2007 election did, however, persist. In the countdown to the election, some army officers even ordered their subordinates to vote for the Democrat Party. One promised that in return they would be treated to chicken curry noodles.[167] On election day, ANFREL noted the presence of multiple police and army personnel at polling booths.[168]

In the end the micro-parties constructed with the help of the military fared poorly in the 2007 election. Moreover, despite the intervention of the military in the 2007 election, Thaksin's PPP won a landslide victory at the polls, securing 233 out of 480 seats. Though this showing certainly disappointed Prem, Surayud and the CNS generals, they accepted the results and allowed the new government to come to office. PPP formed a coalition government on 28 January 2008 under party leader and veteran politician Samak Sundaravej, who stood as Thaksin's nominee PM. Simultaneously, the CNS, now headed by air force chief Chalit, dissolved itself, though its members continued to act in senior military positions. As events would demonstrate, the military's magnanimity towards Thaksin and his proxies within PPP would prove highly deceptive. Though the events of Black May in 1992 had tarnished the image of the military, forcing it back to the barracks behind elected civilian rule, the 2006 coup had let the genie of Thai military intervention back out of the bottle, and the armed forces were not going to return to that bottle any time soon, especially given the apparent post-2006 endorsement by the palace of a politically proactive "couping" military in Thailand's political landscape.

Notes

1. The popularity and political assertiveness of this new prime minister was not lost on the king. Moreover, in 2001 Thaksin was still on good terms with the palace as he echoed the king's sufficiency economy philosophy, left some royalist bureaucrats in key positions, and consistently sought to ingratiate himself with the monarch. See Paul Handley, *The King Never Smiles* (New Haven, CT: Yale University Press, 2006), p. 425. See also Duncan McCargo, "Network Monarchy and Legitimacy Crises in Thailand", *Pacific Review* 18, no. 4 (December 2005): 513.

2. Pasuk Phongpaichit and Chris Baker, *Thaksin* (Chiang Mai: Silkworm Books, 2009), pp. 183–84.

3. John Funston, "Thailand: Thaksin Fever", in *Southeast Asian Affairs 2002*, edited by Daljit Singh and Anthony L. Smith (Singapore: Institute of Southeast Asian Studies, 2002), p. 311, https://www.jstor.org/stable/27913214.

4. Paul Chambers, "A Short History of Military Influence in Thailand", in *Knights of the Realm: Thailand's Military and Police, Then and Now*, edited by Paul Chambers (Bangkok: White Lotus, 2013), p. 250.

5. *Global Witness*, "The Thai-Burma Border", 2003, p. 68, https://cdn2.globalwitness.org/archive/files/import/03sep3%20conflict%20of%20interests%2060-89.pdf.

6. Michael Montesano, "Thailand in 2001: Learning to Live with Thaksin", *Asian Survey* 42, no. 1 (2002): 96–98, https://doi.org/10.1525/as.2002.42.1.90.

7. Paul Chambers, "U.S.-Thai Relations after 9/11: A New Era in Cooperation?", *Contemporary Southeast Asia* 26, no. 3 (December 2004): 460–79, https://doi.org/10.1355/CS26-3D.

8. The pro-Chavalit Somthat Attanand (who had been working for Thai Rak Thai) rose from 2nd Army Region commander to become army chief of staff. At the same time, two of Somthat's class 14 (AFAPS class 3) companions also took a couple of the Five Tigers slots. Beneath the Five Tigers posts, class 14 dominated the senior positions. The only pluses for Prem were that Surayud was allowed to soldier on in his job as army commander, Wattanachai was appointed to become assistant army commander, and Pongthep managed to take the somewhat insignificant post of deputy chief of staff. But these were small potatoes compared what Thaksin had reaped.

9. Thitinan Pongsudhirak, "Thailand: Democratic Authoritarianism", in *Southeast Asian Affairs 2003*, edited by Daljit Singh and Chin Kin Wah (Singapore: Institute of Southeast Asian Studies, 2003), p. 283, https://www.jstor.org/stable/27913239.

10. Srisompob Jitpiromsri, "The New Challenges of Thailand's Security Forces in Southern Frontiers", in *Knights of the Realm: Thailand's Military and Police, Then and Now*, edited by Paul Chambers (Bangkok: White Lotus, 2013), pp. 552–53.

11. Moreover, by 2001 it seemed as though Surayud might soon banish Yuthasak's brother-in-law Somthat Attanand to sit in the Supreme Command with Yuthasak's brother Akaradej. (Somthat was also an in-law of the then deputy defence minister, the pro-Thaksin General Thammarak Isarangkul na Ayuthaya.) With Somthat gone, Surayud would have stopped all officers competing with his favourite to take the top job of army commander—Pongthep. But when the populist Thaksin Shinawatra won the 2001 election by a landslide, it changed everything for Surayud and his military clique.

12. Alex Mutebi, "Thailand in 2002: Political Consolidation amid Economic Uncertainties", *Asian Survey* 43, no. 1 (January/February 2003): 109, https://doi.org/10.1525/as.2003.43.1.101.

13. Chaisit was placed in charge of overseeing the military budget, which helped Thaksin gain greater control over it. See "Forces' Favorite: Thaksin's Brothers in Arms", *The Nation*, 8 December 2002, http://www.nationmultimedia.com; Duncan McCargo and Ukrist Pathmanand, *The Thaksinization of Thailand* (Copenhagen: NIAS Press, 2005), pp. 140–41.

14. At the same time, ACM Kongsak Wattana (AFAPS class 5), a peer of Chaisit Shinawatra who had close relations with Thaksin's wife Pojaman and sister Yaowapha Wongsawat, became air force commander, serving until 2005. Finally, the pro-Thaksin Admiral Taweesak Somapa was appointed to command the navy. "Thailand: Sudarat Defends Interior Minister", *Bangkok Post*, 7 December 2005, http://www.bangkokpost.com; McCargo and Ukrist, *The Thaksinization*, p. 150. Moreover, Thaksin loyalist General Lertrat Rattanawanit became deputy chief of staff. "Military Reshuffle: Jobs for the Boys", *The Nation*, 29 September 2002, http://www.nationmultimedia.com.

15. Perhaps the only consolations for Prem and Surayud were the promotion of Wattanachai to become deputy army commander and the appointment of the pro-Prem General Sonthi Boonyaraklin to head the Special Operations Unit (which Surayud had previously commanded). But Wattanachai would retire the following year. With the TRT in the picture, it was difficult for Prem to be sure about Prawit's loyalty. Finally, General Sonthi Boonyaratklin was still far removed from the Five Tigers senior army positions. "Snoh Keeps Pushing the Line", *The Nation*, 14 May 2009, http://www.nationmultimedia.com.

16. "Chavalit Breaks Ranks: PM 'Giving In' to Rangoon", *The Nation*, 13 August 2002, http://www.nationmultimedia.com.

17. Yoshifumi Tamada, *Myths and Realities: The Democratization of Thai Politics* (Kyoto: Kyoto University Press, 2008), p. 109

18. "Survivors Tell of Escape from Mob", *The Nation*, 31 January 2003, http://www.nationmultimedia.com.

19. Alex Mutebi, "Thailand in 2003: Riding High Again", *Asian Survey* 44, no. 1 (2004): 79, https://doi.org/10.1525/as.2004.44.1.78.

20. Wassana Nanuam, "Identify Drug Foes, Says Prem", *Bangkok Post*, 28 December 2002, http://www.bangkokpost.com.

21. McCargo and Ukrist, *The Thaksinization*, p. 150.

22. Supatatt Dangkrueng, "War on Drugs Escalates 3rd Army Region Mobilizes Full Support", *Chiang Mai Mail*, 15–21 February 2003, http://www.chiangmai-mail.com/017/news.shtml#hd11.

23. Amy Kazmin and William Barnes, "Thailand Hails Victory in War on Dealers", *Financial Times*, 1 May 2003.

24. Amnesty International, "Thailand: Grave developments – Killings and Other Abuses", 5 November 2003.

25. "Defence Budget: Government to Spend More on Arms", *The Nation*, 15 March 2003, http://www.nationmultimedia.com.

26. "The Military Faces a Future of Reform", *The Nation*, 20 September 2003, http://www.nationmultimedia.com.

27. Warren Matthews, "Civil-Military Relations in Thailand: Military Autonomy or Civilian Control?" (Master's thesis, Naval Postgraduate School, Monterrey, California, 2005), p. 56.

28. Ibid., p. 57.

29. Chookiat Panaspornprasit, "Thailand: Politicized Thaksinization", in *Southeast Asian Affairs 2004*, edited by Daljit Singh and Chin Kin Wah (Singapore: Institute of Southeast Asian Studies, 2004), p. 265, https://www.jstor.org/stable/27913264.

30. "Military Reshuffle: Chaiyasit Transfer 'Not PM's Idea'", *The Nation*, 8 August 2002, http://www.nationmultimedia.com.

31. Chaisit entered pre-cadet school class 5 and Chulachomklao Military Academy class 16 (the same pre-cadet and cadet classes as his close friend General Ruangroj Mahasaranon). After graduating in 1968, Chaisit chose to become an army engineer and went on to command an engineer platoon. Chaisit is the older brother of Fleet Lieutenant Prawit Shinawatra (pre-cadet class 9), former deputy director-general of Thai Airways International Public Company Limited. Two other brothers were Lieutenant Surachit (pre-cadet 1), who was killed in 1970 when his helicopter crashed in Laos, and General Uthai (pre-cadet 2), who served under Thaksin as deputy permanent secretary of defence. Chaisit is also connected to senior police through his cousin (police colonel) Thaksin Shinawatra (pre-cadet class 10), Thaksin's wife Pojaman (Damapong), her father—police general Samoe Damapong—and her brothers: police general Priewpan Damapong (who became police chief in 2011–12), police general Priewpan Damapong and police lieutenant general Dr Peerapong Damapong. Finally, Chaisit is the cousin of former prime minister Yingluck Shinawatra. In 2023, Chaisit had retired as a military man and was despised by other officers for moving to the top through his linkages with Thaksin, but he is indeed part of Thaksin's political spotlight. McCargo and Ukrist, *The Thaksinization*, p. 162.

32. Siam Turakij, "The Launch of the Series "You're My Sky, the Destination Is the Sky" [เปิดตัวซีรีส์ส่วาย "You're My Sky จุดหมายคือท้องฟ้า"], *Siam Turakij News*, 27 December 2021.

33. Chookiat, "Thailand: Politicized", p. 259.

34. McCargo and Ukrist, *The Thaksinization*, pp. 141, 147.

35. "PM Amends Reshuffle List", *The Nation*, 21 August 2003, http://www.nationmultimedia.com.

36. Paul Handley, "Princes, Politicians, Bureaucrats, Generals: The Evolution of the Privy Council under the Constitutional Monarchy", paper presented at the 10th International Conference on Thai Studies, Thammasat University, Bangkok, Thailand, 9–11 January 2008, pp. 13–14.

37. Michael Connors, "The Facts and F(r)ictions of Ruling", in *Southeast Asian Affairs 2005*, edited by Chin Kin Wah and Daljit Singh (Singapore: Institute of Southeast Asian Studies, 2005), pp. 377–78, https://www.jstor.org/stable/27913291.

38. Srisompob Jitpiromsri and Panyasak Sophonvasu, "Unpacking Thailand's Southern Conflict: The Poverty of Structural Explanations", in *Rethinking Thailand's Southern Violence*, edited by Duncan McCargo (Singapore: NUS Press, 2007), pp. 89–111.

39. John Cole and Steve Sciaccitano, "Yingluck and the Generals", *Asia Times*, 18 August 2011, http://www.atimes.com/atimes/Southeast_Asia/MH18Ae02.html.

40. Ukrist Pathamanand, "Thaksin's Achilles Heel: The Failure of Hawkish Approaches in the Thai South", *Critical Asian Studies* 38, no. 1 (2006): 8.

41. "Class 10 Prominent, Pisan Rises to Region 4 Commander", *Thai Rath*, 30 March 2004, http://wbns.oas.psu.ac.th/shownews.php?news_id=5982.

42. "PM's Classmates Figure Prominently in Transfer List", *The Nation*, 30 March 2004, http://www.nationmultimedia.com

43. Personal interview with very senior general, former member of 21st Regiment, 2nd Army Infantry Division, 1st Army Region, Bangkok, Thailand, 30 December 2021.

44. Personal interview with anonymous retired senior military official, Bangkok, Thailand, 28 August 2022.

45. Paul Chambers, "Prawit Wongsuwan's Path to Power", *East Asia Forum*, 1 September 2022, https://www.eastasiaforum.org/2022/09/01/prawit-wongsuwans-path-to-power/.

46. Panuwat Panduprasert, *The Military and Democratic Backsliding in Thailand* (PhD dissertation, University of Leeds, 2019), p. 134, https://etheses.whiterose.ac.uk/23895/1/Panduprasert_P_POLIS_PhD_2019.pdf.

47. Srisompob, "The New Challenges", pp. 558–59.

48. Sections 5, 11 and 12, *Emergency Decree on Public Administration in a State of Emergency*, 16 July 2005, http://web.Kritdika.go.th/data/document/ext810/810259_0001.pdf.

49. Thaksin and Chaisit agreed to appoint Admiral Sathirapan Keyanon (AFAPS class 6), then deputy supreme commander, as navy chief. The choice of Sathirapan owed partly to the fact that, though he was from class 6 (deemed to be less supportive of Thaksin), Sathirapan had close connections to Thaksin's wife Pojaman and Thaksin's brother Payap.

Thaksin and Chaisit also nominated Chavalit loyalist General Wichit Yathip, deputy permanent secretary for defence, as deputy army chief, replacing the retiring General Thepthat Phrommopakorn. Meanwhile, at least fifty-eight AFAPS class 10 graduates received promotions. These included General Pornchai Kranlert, who made the unbelievable leap from a mere deputy commander of the Armed Forces Development Command to taking one of the Five Tigers positions—assistant to the army commander-in-chief. In addition, the prime minister looked to appoint class 10 graduates to command the strategic area in and around Bangkok. As such, General Anupong Paochinda was elevated to become commander of the 1st Army Region, and General Jirasit Kesakomol was promoted to the position of commander, 1st Army Corps. Finally, two pro-Thaksin class 10 grads transferred in. Wassana Nanuam and Yawadee Tanyasiri, "Politics Dominate Reshuffle: Hopes for Merit Promotions Dashed", *Bangkok Post*, 9 September 2005, http://www.bangkokpost.com;

50. Pasuk and Baker, *Thaksin*, p. 249.

51. "Race for Top Army Post Heats Up with Review Bid", *Bangkok Post*, 7 August 2005, http://www.bangkokpost.com; "PM's Military Pals Get Nod in Latest Reshuffle", *The Nation*, 9 September 2005, http://www. nationmultimedia.com.

52. เนชั่น สุดสัปดาห์, "ปูมชีวิตสายเลือด «เฉกอะหมัด»: จากประธาน «คมช.» สู่หัวหน้าพรรค «มาตุภูมิ" [Bloodline "Like Ahmad": From the chairman of the "CNS" to the leader of the "Motherland" Party], 14 June 2010, reproduced in blog, https://arin-article.blogspot.com/2010/06/blog-post_14.html.

53. Matichon Editorial Office, พล.อ. สนธิ บุญยรัตกลิน ผบ.ทบ. "ม้ามืด" ผู้นำรัฐประหาร [General Sonthi Bunyaratkalin, army commander, "Dark Horse" coup leader] (Bangkok: Matichon, 2007)

54. Kenneth Conboy, *The Cambodian Wars* (Lawrence: University of Kansas Press, 2013), p. 204.

55. Matichon Editorial Office, พล.อ. สนธิ บุญยรัตกลิน ผบ.ทบ.

56. *The Standard*, "'Palang Pracharath is the Party That Believes in Democracy' Exclaims the Open-Minded Maj. Gen. Sonthi's Son, Lieutenant Colonel Nithi as He Wears a Palang Pracharat Shirt to Enter Bangkok", 24 January 2023, https://thestandard.co/nithi-boonyaratglin-pprp-bangkok/.

57. At the same time, two of the deputy supreme commanders, General Boonsrang Niempradit and Admiral Surin Roengarom, were also members of class 6. Finally, in the office of the permanent secretary for defence, ACM Thares Punsri (class 6) and General Apichart Penkitti (class 8) were promoted to become deputy permanent secretaries. Other notable appointments included the promotion of pro-Prem senior officers General Saprang Kallayamitr (class 7) as commander of the 3rd Army Region, General Jiradet Kotcharat (AFAPS class 9) as deputy commander of the 3rd Army Corps, and General Prayut Chanocha (class 12) as commander, Region 1, 2nd Division (Eastern Tigers). Among other reshuffle appointments, Thaksin elevated General Paisan Katanyu to become assistant army commander-in-chief. Paisan, though, was unpopular with many because he had worked with General

Chainarong Noonpakdi during Black May 1992 in ordering the violent dispersal of protestors. "Long-Delayed Military Reshuffle Approved", *The Nation*, 8 September 2005, http://www.nationmultimedia.com.

58. "A Right Royal Mess", *The Economist*, 4 December 2008, http://www. economist.com/world/asia/displayStory.cfm?story_id=12724800.

59. Pasuk and Baker, *Thaksin*, p. 267.

60. Ukrist Pathmanand, "A Different Coup d'Etat?", *Journal of Democracy* 38, no. 1 (February 2008): 132.

61. Thanapol Eiswsakul, "People's Alliance for Democracy: The People Who Issued an Invitation to the Coup Group", *Fa Dieogan*, special issue, 2007.

62. "No State of Emergency: Army", *The Nation*, 23 March 2006, http://www.nationmultimedia.com.

63. James Ockey, "Thailand in 2006: Retreat to Military Rule", *Asian Survey* 47, no. 1 (January/February 2007): 136, https://www.jstor.org/stable/10.1525/as.2007.47.1.133.

64. "Mid-year Senior Reshuffles Announced", *The Nation*, 29 April 2006, http://www.nationmultimedia.com.

65. "Thai Army Chief Resists Political Pressure on Appointments", *Krungthep Turakit*, 27 March 2006, www.bangkokbiznews.com/.

66. "Thaksin Declares 'Do not Listen to Charismatic People outside the Constitution'", *MGR Online*, 29 June 2006, http://www.manager. co.th/Politics/ViewNews.aspx?NewsID=9490000084361. Translated by *Bangkok Pundit* in "Media Reporting on Thaksin's Speech", *Bangkok Pundit* (blog), 17 July 2006, http://asiancorrespondent.com/19951/media-reporting-on-thaksins-speech/.

67. *Matichon Daily*, 21 August 2006, p. 11, cited in Kasian Tejapira, *Coups and Thai Democracy* (Bangkok: The Foundation for the Promotion of Social Science and Humanities Texbooks Project, 2007), p. 16.

68. "Military Must Back King", *The Nation*, 15 August 2006, http://www.nationmultimedia.com.

69. Wassana Nanuam, "Prem Slams 'Unethical Leaders'", *Bangkok Post*, 26 July 2006, http://www.bangkokpost.com.

70. "Prem: Bad Leaders are Doomed to Failure", *The Nation*, 1 August 2006, http://www.nationmultimedia.com. See also Wassana Nanuam, อมตะแห่ง "ป่าเปรม": จากปฏิวัติ 19 กันยาฯ ถึงจุดจบ ทักษิณ [The immortality of "Father Prem": From 19 September to the end of Thaksin] (Bangkok: Post Books, 2008).

71. Wikileaks, Thai Cables, US Embassy Bangkok, "06BANGKOK4610 More on Military Reshuffle—Thai Army Puts Apolitical Officers in Charge of Key Units", http://thaicables.wordpress. com/2011/07/12/06bangkok4610-more-on-military-reshuffle-thai-army-puts-apolitical-officers-in-charge-of-key-units/.

72. "Sonthi Stuns by Shifting PM's Allies", *The Nation*, 20 July 2006, http://www.nationmultimedia.com.

73. Ibid.

74. Ukrist Pathmanand, "A Different Coup d'Etat?", *Journal of Democracy* 38, no. 1 (February 2008): 128.

75. Panananda Avudh, "PM Ouflanked at Annual Military Reshuffle", *The Nation*, 21 July 2006, http://www.nationmultimedia.com.

76. Avudh Panananda, "Military Reshuffle Rattles a Few Sabres", *The Nation*, 3 August 2006, http://www.nationmultimedia.com.

77. "Thamarak Reprimands Bannawit over Political Interference Remarks", *The Nation*, 11 September 2006, http://www.nationmultimedia.com.

78. "Reshuffle Row Escalates into Conflict", *The Nation*, 12 September 2006, http://www.nationmultimedia.com.

79. Wassana Nanuam, "Two Top Army Brass Launch War of Words", *Bangkok Post*, 21 July 2006, http://www.bangkokpost.com.

80. Wikileaks, US Embassy Bangkok, Consulate Chiang Mai, "Third Army Commander Challenges Thaksin's Northern Power", 27 July 2006, http://dazzlepod.com/cable/06CHIANGMAI120/.

81. Wassana Nanuam, "Neutral Officer Tipped to Succeed Saprang", *Bangkok Post*, 11 August 2006, http://www.bangkokpost.com.

82. "Police Raid Homes of Alleged Bomb Plotters", *The Nation*, 10 September 2006, http://www.nationmultimedia.com.

83. "This Is No Time to Call Out the Troops", *The Nation*, 18 September 2006, http://www.nationmultimedia.com.

84. "Reshuffle Row Escalates into Conflict", *The Nation*, 12 September 2006, http://www.nationmultimedia.com.

85. "Bomb Plot Comes to a Screeching Halt", *Bangkok Post*, 22 September 2006, http://www.bangkokpost.com.

86. "This Is No Time to Call Out the Troops", *The Nation*, 18 September 2006, http://www.nationmultimedia.com.

87. "Interference by Politicians Leaves Armed Forces in Turmoil: Inspector General", *The Nation*, 20 August 2008, http://www.nationmultimedia.com.

88. Wassana Nanuam, "General Says No to Premier", *Bangkok Post*, 17 August 2006, http://www.bangkokpost.com.

89. Wassana Nanuam, "Prem Given More 'Evidence of Interference' in Reshuffle", *Bangkok Post*, 2 September 2006, http://www.bangkokpost.com.

90. Wassana Nanuam, "PM 'Wants Chums in Key Army Posts", *Bangkok Post*, 29 August 2006, http://www.bangkokpost.com.

91. "Premier 'Made Changes to Army Reshuffle List'", *The Nation*, 29 August 2006, http://www.nationmultimedia.com.

92. Shawn Crispin, "Thailand: All the King's Men", *Asia Times*, 21 September 2006, http://www.atimes.com/atimes/Southeast_Asia/HI21Ae02.html.

93. Wassana Nanuam, "PM Delays Approving Reshuffle", *Bangkok Post*, 13 September 2006, http://www.bangkokpost.com.

94. "Sonthi Told Thaksin That He Would Stage Coup", *The Nation*, 27 October 2006, http://www.nationmultimedia.com.

95. Rodney Tasker, "Grumbles, Revelations of a Thai Coup Maker", *Asia Times*, 22 December 2006, http://www.atimes.com/atimes/Southeast_Asia/HL22Ae01.html.

96. Personal interview with an anonymous senior Thai army officer, 20 January 2022.

97. Tasker, "Grumbles, Revelations"; Wassana Nanuam, "Timing Could Not Have Been Better, Says Army Source", *Bangkok Post*, 21 September 2006, http://www.bangkokpost.com; "Prayut Issues Another Coup Denial", *The Nation*, 23 April 2011, http://www.nationmultimedia.com.

98. Wichai Bunlue, ปิดตำนานทักษิณ วิชัย บุญเหลือ [Ending the legend of Thaksin] (Bangkok: October 2549 [2006]).

99. Andrew C. O'Connor, *Why Thailand's Military Stepped In* (Master's thesis, Naval Postgraduate School, Monterrey, California, 2011), p. 65.

100. Thanong Kanthong, "Sonthi Outsmarted Thaksin at the Eleventh Hour", *The Nation*, 22 September 2006, http://www.nationmultimedia.com.

101. Thanong Kanthong, "Thailand Takes a Step Back to Square One", *The Nation*, 1 February 2008, http://www.nationmultimedia.com.

102. Wassana Nanuam, "Timing Could not have been Better, Says Army Source", *Bangkok Post*, 21 September 2006, http://www.bangkokpost.com.

103. Paul Chambers and Napisa Waitoolkiat, "The Resilience of Monarchised Military in Thailand", *Journal of Contemporary Asia* 46, no. 3 (2016): 432, https://doi.org/10.1080/00472336.2016.1161060.

104. Wassana Nanuam, ลับ ลวง พราง ปฏิวัติปราสาททราย [Secret, false, hidden: Sandcastle revolution] (Bangkok: Matichon, 2010).

105. Wassana Nanuam, "Timing Could Not Have Been Better, Says Army Source", *Bangkok Post*, 21 September 2006, http://www.bangkokpost.com.

106. "Straight-Talking General on the Rise", *Straits Times*, 21 February 2007.

107. Thanong Kanthong, "Sonthi Outsmarted Thaksin at the Eleventh Hour", *The Nation*, 22 September 2006, http://www.nationmultimedia.com.

108. "Thai King 'Endorses Coup Leader'", BBC News, 20 September 2006, http://news.bbc.co.uk/2/hi/asia-pacific/5365362.stm.

109. "CNS Coup White Paper", *The Nation*, 12 December 2006, http://www.nationmultimedia.com.

110. James Ockey, "Thailand's 'Professional Soldiers' and Coup-Making: The Coup of 2006", *Crossroads: An Interdisciplinary Journal of Southeast Asian Studies* 19, no. 1 (2007): 120–121, https://www.jstor.org/stable/40860870.

111. Wikileaks, "Thailand Military Coup Leader Briefs Foreign Envoys, Promises to Appoint Civilian Prime Minister within Two Weeks", US Embassy Bangkok, 20 September 2006, 06BANGKOK5814, http://thaicables.wordpress.com/2011/07/13/06bangkok5814-thailand-

military-coup-leader-briefs-foreign-envoys-promises-to-appoint-civilian-prime-minister-within-two-weeks/.

112. "CNS' Anti-Thaksin Campaign", *Bangkok Post*, 8 April 2007, http://www.bangkokpost.com.

113. Pasuk and Baker, *Thaksin*, pp. 290–93.

114. "Chalit About Face on Russian Jets", *Bangkok Post*, 6 January 2006, http://www.bangkokpost.com.

115. "Figures behind the Coup", *The Nation*, 20 September 2006, http://www.nationmultimedia.com.

116. "Political Crisis", *The Nation*, 30 August 2005, http://www.nationmultimedia.com.

117. "Military Warning: A Not So Veiled Threat for Sondhi", *The Nation*, 19 November 2005, http://www.nationmultimedia.com.

118. "Military Flags Concern over Political Mess", *The Nation*, 19 May 2006, http://www.nationmultimedia.com.

119. "Figures behind the Coup", *The Nation*, 20 September 2006, http://www.nationmultimedia.com.

120. "Winai's Moves Have Got People Talking", *The Nation*, 1 November 2007, http://www.nationmultimedia.com; "Thawil Firms as NSC Favorite", *Bangkok Post*, 2 July 2009, http://www.bangkokpost.com.

121. Ukrist Patthmanand, "A Different Coup d'Etat?", *Journal of Contemporary Asia* 38, no. 1 (February 2008): 126.

122. "Figures behind the Coup", *The Nation*, 20 September 2006, http://www.nationmultimedia.com.

123. "Developments of the Military Coup in Thailand during the First 24 hours", Xinhua, 20 September 2006, http://news.xinhuanet.com/english/2006-09/21/content_5117446.htm.

124. "Biography: Gen. Boonsrang Niumpradit", http://etmr.dstd.mi.th/boonsrang.html; "Interview with Boonsrang Niempradit", *Krungthep Turakij*, 11 February 2008, http://www.bangkokbiznews.com.

125. "AITAA President May be Named Supreme Commander of Thai Military", *Asian Institute of Technology News and Events*, Asian Institute of Technology, http://203.159.12.5:8082/AIT/news-and-events/archive/2006/News.2007-09-12.095356-4.

126. Boonsrang: Its Time CNS Called it a Day", *Bangkok Post*, 25 October 2007, http://www.bangkokpost.com.

127. Wikileaks, US Embassy Bangkok, "Mission Views on Two Top Generals' Proposed U.S. Visits", 20 July 2007 08:59, 07BANGKOK3979. From http://www.dazzlepod.com.

128. John Cole and Steve Sciaccitano, "Yingluck and the Generals", *Asia Times*, 18 August 2011, http://www.atimes.com/atimes/Southeast_Asia/MH18Ae02.html.

129. "PM 'Wants Junior Deputy' for Job", *Bangkok Post*, 6 August 2004, http://www.bangkokpost.com.

130. "National Police Chief: Surayud Denies Plans to Replace Kowit", *The Nation*, 3 November 2006, http://www.nationmultimedia.com.

131. James Ockey, "Thailand in 2007: The Struggle to Control Democracy", *Asian Survey* 48, no. 1 (January/February 2008): 20–21, https://www.jstor.org/stable/10.1525/as.2008.48.1.20.

132. "Thaksin's Brother-in-Law Still Holding Position despite Appeal to Palace", *The Nation*, 1 March 2004, http://www.nationmultimedia.com.

133. "Police Feud over Gambling Raid", *The Nation*, 29 June 2006, http://wwwnationmultimedia.com.

134. "Court Dismisses Lawsuit against Seh Daeng", *The Nation*, 20 November 2009, http://www.nationmultimedia.com.

135. Wassayos Ngamkham, "Officers Close to Government Promoted", *Bangkok Post*, 22 February 2007, http://www.bangkokpost.com.

136. Wassana Nanuam, เส้นทางเหล็ก พล.อ.สุรยุทธ์ จุลานนท์ นายกรัฐมนตรีคนที่ 24 [Steel Road, General Surayud Chulanont, the 24th prime minister] (Bangkok: Matichon, 2006).

137. "'Undercurrents': Secret Military Division Deployed", *The Nation*, 27 December 2006, http://www.nationmultimedia.com.

138. "CNS Accused of Secret Army Operations", *Bangkok Post*, 6 May 2007, http://www.bangkokpost.com.

139. Ockey, "Thailand in 2007", p. 26.

140. Section 77, Constitution of Thailand, promulgated 24 August 2007, http://www.asianlii.org/th/legis/const/2007/1.html.

141. Paul Chambers, "Thailand 2010", *Bertelsmann Transformation Index*, p. 7; Paul Chambers, "Superfluous, Mischievous, or Emancipating? Thailand's Evolving Senate Today", *Journal of Current Southeast Asian Affairs* (*Südostasien Aktuell*) 28, no. 3 (2009): 78; Interview with Lt. Gen. Peerapong Manakit, 16 February 2009.

142. "CNS Coup White Paper", *The Nation*, 12 December 2006, http://www.nationmultimedia.com.

143. Pasuk and Baker, *Thaksin*, pp. 303–4.

144. "PM Loses Army Reshuffle Powers", *Bangkok Post*, 2 February 2008, http://www.bangkokpost.com; see Defence Ministry Administration Act (2008), Article 25, published by Thailand Lawyer Center, http://www.thailandlawyercenter.com/index.php?lay=show&ac=article&Id=538974219&Ntype=19.

145. Ukrist Patthmanand, "A Different Coup d'Etat?", *Journal of Contemporary Asia* 38, no. 1 (February 2008): 137.

146. "Chavalit Attacks CNS, Saying Junta Needs to Restore Public Image", *The Nation*, 10 November 2006, http://www.nationmultimedia.com.

147. "Generals Meet Chavalit to Clear Air", *The Nation*, 14 November 2006, http://www.nationmultimedia.com.

148. "Chavalit 'To Form Party'", *The Nation*, 15 November 2006, http://www.nationmultimedia.com.

149. Wassana Nanuam Yuwadee Tunyasiri, "Sonthi Loyalists Placed in Key Military Positions", *Bangkok Post*, 22 March 2007, http://www. bangkokpost.com.

150. "Military Battalion Leaders Reshuffled in Perceived Bid to Foil Coup", *The Nation*, 18 November 2006, p. 1.

151. "Top Boot Politics, Sequel III", *The Nation*, 5 January 2007, https://web. archive.org/web/20070228061227/http://www.nationmultimedia.com/ webblog/view_blog.php?uid=321&bid=1422.

152. "Thai Military Reshuffle Announced", Xinhua, 22 March 2007, http:// en.ce.cn/World/Asia-Pacific/200703/22/t20070322_10782017.shtml.

153. Wassana Nanuam Yuwadee Tunyasiri, "Sonthi Loyalists Placed in Key Military Positions", *Bangkok Post*, 22 March 2007, http://www. bangkokpost.com.

154. Wassana Nanuam, "Prem Said to Prefer Saprang to Head Army", *Bangkok Post*, 27 August 2007, http://www.bangkokpost.com; Shawn Crispin, "Thai Reshuffle Exposes Cracks in Military", *Asia Times*, 7 September 2007, http://www.atimes.com/atimes/Southeast_Asia/II07Ae01.html.

155. The fierce competition between the three candidates led Sonthi to propose extending his own term for another year, but Prime Minister Surayud disagreed. In September 2007, deep divisions remained over who should take the helm. In the end, Anupong was chosen, with Saprang deemed too reactionary, while Montree appeared too weak. Anupong was also chosen because he had commanded the 21st Infantry Regiment (its honorary commander was the queen, a distinction shared by his deputy, Prayut).

156. Wattaya Wai. พล.อ.อนุพงษ์ เผ่าจินดา บูรพาพยัคฆ์ซ่อนคม [General Anupong Paochinda, Eastern Sword] (Bangkok: Green-Panyayan, 2010).

157. "'เสียอ้อ-ยุทธพงษ์ เผ่าจินดา' เจ้าของธุรกิจชื่อดัง" ["Sia O-Yutthapong Paochinda", a famous business owner"], *MGR Online*, 14 August 2018, https://m. mgronline.com/politics/detail/9610000080666.

158. "Army Faces a New Era", *The Nation*, 21 September 2007, http://www. nationmultimedia.com.

159. "Anupong to Lead Army", *The Nation*, 20 September 2007, http://www. nationmultimedia.com.

160. Wassana Nanuam, "Anupong Tightens his Grip", *Bangkok Post*, 4 October 2007, p. 1.

161. "Military's Matchima Link", *The Nation*, 27 January 2007, http:// wwwnationmultimedia.com.

162. Udonmap, "Sondhi's Interview: Reaching Out", May 2009, https:// webcache.googleusercontent.com/search?q=cache:liQ3N6w9UGUJ: https://www.udonmap.com/udonthaniforum/viewtopic.php %3Ft%3D13473%26p%3D166842+&cd=29&hl=en&ct=clnk&gl=th.

163. "The Mystery That Is Puea Paendin", *The Nation*, 16 November 2007, http://www.nationmultimedia.com.

164. "No Guns behind Him", *The Nation*, 31 October 2007, http://www. nationmultimedia.com.

165. "Junta's Media War a Big Mistake", *The Nation*, 26 October 2007, p. 1.

166. "People Power Party Uncovers Another Military Plot, *The Nation*, 3 November 2007, p. 1.

167. See Wassana Nanuam, "Anupong Rewards his Coup Allies", *Bangkok Post*, 19 June 2009, p. 1; Wassana Nanuam, "ISOC Ordered to Promoted Democracy", *Bangkok Post*, 20 December 2007, p. 1.

168. Asian Network for Free Elections (ANFREL) Thailand, "Restoring Democracy—Elections to the House of Representatives", March 2008, p. 42.

Chapter Thirteen

Enter Prawit, Anupong and Prayut (2008–14)

The period 2008–14 proved to be a resurrection of the 1988–91 period of Prime Minister Chatchai Chunhavan, to the extent that Thailand's highly defective democracy was overshadowed by the military, which itself was eclipsed by the monarchy. As such, though elected civilians appeared to be the ostensible leaders, the monarchy and military obscurely dictated to Thailand's government from the sidelines. In fact, these two authoritarian actors (and their allies) sought not to consolidate pluralism in Thailand but instead to dominate the eroded vestiges of it. Military power during this period was dominated by three military brothers-in-arms: retired general Prawit Wongsuwan (army commander 2004–5), army commander General Anupong Paochinda (army commander 2007–10), and General Prayut Chanocha (2010–14). Their names or nicknames all began with "P": Prawit, "Big Pom"; Anupong, "Big Pok"; and Prayut, "Big Thu". Each had commanded the 2nd Infantry Division and were thus members of the division's faction, "Buraphapayak"—in English, "Eastern Tigers". Anupong and Prayut had commanded the 21st Regiment (Sua Taharn Rachanee, or Queen's Tiger Guard) within the 2nd Division, of which Queen Sirikit was the honorary commandant. Prawit had also served in the 21st Regiment but was hustled away to the 12th Regiment in 1981, a parochial border unit, for participating in a coup attempt in April that year. Nevertheless, in 2004 Thaksin appointed Prawit to be army commander, where he served until his retirement in 2005. The October 2007 annual military reshuffle saw his two younger "brothers", Anupong and Prayut, ascend to the top of the army.

But following the December 2007 general election, Thaksin's new political party returned to office. Indeed, with 266 seats out of 480 total, the pro-Thaksin Palang Prachachon Party (PPP) formed a co-alition government on 28 January 2008. Firebrand politician Samak Sundaravej, an ultra-right-wing political fixture since the 1970s, became Thaksin's nominee prime minister—since Thaksin himself remained a fugitive outside of Thailand. Yet even though the new pro-Thaksin government appeared to threaten the three "brothers" and Thailand's arch-royalist elites, such was not the case. Unlike during 2006, a new 150-member Senate had been created (following the new 2007 constitution). Seventy-four senators of these 150 had been appointed in mid-January by a committee of judges and bureaucrats established by the then ruling junta and vetted by the junta-appointed Election Commission. Thailand's security sector was permitted a small quota of the appointed senators: fourteen ex-soldiers being elevated to serve in the upper house for a 9.3 per cent military-reserved domain.[1] All of the appointed senators were chosen by the junta because they seemed to tilt towards the military.[2] Only with the appointed senators in office were elections held for the remaining 76—in March 2008.

FIGURE 13.1
Thailand's Senate, 2008–14

Type	Term	Dividing the 150 members	Military/police quota
Bicameral (11th Senate) legislature	(2008–14) Senate served 6-year term	74 appointed/76 elected + any newly created province produces 1 additional senator	2008–11: 14 retired security sector personnel (9.3%) of the appointed senators; 2011–14: 16 retired security sector personnel (10.6%) of the appointed senators

Source: Paul Chambers, "Superfluous, Irrelevant or Emancipating: Thailand's Evolving Senate Today", *Journal of Current Southeast Asian Affairs* 28, no. 3 (2009): 26–28, https://d-nb.info/999559311/34; Attrayuth Butrispoom, Prapasri Othanon, and Praparn Chindalert-Udomdee, "Many Thai Senators Have Links to Coup", *The Nation*, ASEAN Now, 12 April 2011, https://aseannow.com/topic/460135-many-thai-senators-have-links-to-coup/.

Meanwhile, Samak tried to harness PM power to assist PPP, Thaksin and himself. Born and raised in Bangkok, his father had been a palace official. He was trained as a lawyer and graduated from Thammasat University. In the 1950s and early 1960s, before entering politics, Samak was a journalist for *Siam Rath* newspaper and then worked as a public relations officer at the Israeli Embassy in Bangkok. Samak became a member of Thailand's Democrat Party in the late 1960s but left it in 1976, founding the Thai Citizen Party (TCP), which remained his political vehicle until he resigned as party leader in 2001, placing it under the leadership of his younger brother, Sumit Sundaravej. Samak was elected as a Bangkok member of the House of Representatives ten times, from 1975 to 1996.

Samak gained fame for targeting for arrest people accused of being subversives or leftists. He reportedly maintained close ties with Queen Sirikit, and in August 1976 he travelled to Singapore to notify retired general Thanom Kittikachorn that the palace would support the former field marshal's return home.[3] When student protests took place on 6 October 1976, Samak accused the students of being "communists", statements that contributed to the massacre of many of them and a coup on that day. Following the 1976 coup, he was appointed interior minister under the rabidly anti-communist 1976–77 government of PM Thanin Kravichien. In May 1992, Samak defended the military's shooting of students in the Black May demonstrations.

But it was during the early 1990s that Samak began to have a personal falling out with Prime Minister Prem Tinsulanonda, who, according to Samak, only invited Prachakorn Thai to join a coalition over the telephone with Samak rather than in person.[4] Such perceived personal slights by Samak as well as Prem's alleged 1997 luring of Prachakorn Thai factions away from Samak to support Chuan Leekpai for prime minister effectively poisoned Samak's feelings towards Prem. His party became moribund in the late 1990s.

But by 2000, Samak had rebounded politically and was elected governor of Bangkok, where he served a term until 2004 and grew close to Thaksin. Following the May 2007 banning of Thai Rak Thai, Thaksin moved his politicians to PPP, making Samak its party leader in August. Samak advertised himself as Thaksin's "nominee".[5] Thaksin perhaps chose Samak to reassure the king and military of his own arch-royalist credentials.

Upon becoming prime minister in late January 2008, Samak sought to amend the 2007 constitution and delay or even stop court cases against Thaksin. But Samak knew that achieving such an objective would be no cakewalk whilst the military opposed Thaksin. Samak thus sought to cultivate an accommodating relationship with army chief Anupong and the military. Nevertheless, senior brass effectively vetoed several names put forward by Samak's administration for defence minister, such as Ruangroj and Chaisit. Anupong instead proposed retired army commander General Prawit Wongsuwan (AFAPS class 6) but Samak refused.[6] Instead, Samak became defence minister.[7] With the reluctant agreement of Anupong, Samak became both prime minister and defence minister. No deputy defence minister was appointed, but, to placate Thaksin loyalists, a team of retired generals and defence experts—including Chaisit Shinawatra and AFAPS class 10 school peers of Thaksin—served as unofficial advisors to Samak at the Ministry of Defence.[8] Samak sought to placate Anupong by agreeing to the promulgation of the 2008 Internal Security Act (ISA) and 2008 Defence Act, which took effect in early February and gave greatly increased autonomy to the armed forces when it came to military reshuffles. The first of these acts increased military power by reinvigorating the Internal Security Operations Command (ISOC). Though the prime minister was formally the director of ISOC and the army chief was the deputy director, the latter was effectively in charge. When the ISA is triggered during a crisis, the military has total power to do what it wants.[9] Meanwhile, the modified Defence Act of 2008 established a new senior military vetting committee to oversee high-level military reshuffles above the rank of major general. According to Section 25, any such promotion must be approved by a committee of seven, comprising the defence minister, deputy defence minister (optional), supreme commander, chiefs of the army, navy and air force, and the permanent minister of defence. Section 25 gave a veto for the military against elected governments.[10]

Samak vowed not to meddle with the military:

> They can do whatever they want. We don't plan to interfere with their affairs anyway so why do they have to prevent us from doing so. They don't need to close the doors as we don't plan to go into their house anyway.[11]

In March, Samak unofficially gave Anupong complete control over ISOC (even appointing the army chief as ISOC director) and counter-insurgency operations in the South, acquiescing to the post-2006 enhanced military prerogatives.[12] Meanwhile, rumours of an impending military coup began to grow despite army chief Anupong's statements to the contrary. Samak promised that the PPP would not attempt to interfere in manipulating military reshuffles.

In the mid-year military reshuffle of 1 April 2008 (see appendix 4), Samak did his best to make good on that pledge and to prove to the military that he was his own man rather than simply a vehicle for Thaksin. In fact, Samak tried to show that he could favour the military. Such a position even made some military officers happy that Samak had taken the defence portfolio for himself.[13] The appointments, which involved 383 personnel, saw no officers associated with the 2006 coup demoted. Samak even demonstrated favour for Anupong over Sonthi Boonyaratklin, as the two had become rivals. General Anupong generally got his way with very little interference from Samak, while officers more loyal to Sonthi Boonyaratklin were sent to inactive positions.[14] For example, Anupong's friend General Piroon Paewpolsong (AFAPS class 10) was promoted from being a mere special qualified general to being deputy chief of staff of the army. Likewise, General Puchong Rattanawan (AFAPS class 10) was elevated from inspector general to be commander of the Special Warfare Command (SWC). Puchong replaced the Sonthi loyalist General Sunai Sampattawanich (AFAPS class 11), who was transferred to an inactive advisory posting. Puchong was no friend of Sonthi, but he had a good relationship with Surayud Chulanond. Furthermore, General Somjet Boonthanom (AFAPS class 8), head of the Defence Ministry's Budget Office, was elevated to become chief advisor to the permanent secretary for defence despite Somjet having served as the chief of the Council for National Security (CNS) secretariat and had earlier given evidence against Yongyuth Tiyapairat for alleged vote-buying.[15] Perhaps the only concession to Thaksin was the promotion of General Prin Suwannathat from a mere adviser to become another aide to prime minister and defence minister Samak—and effectively the eyes and ears of Thaksin.[16] Meanwhile, in April, Anupong ordered a mid-level reshuffle of 104 regiment commanders in the Special Warfare Command considered close to former coup leader General Sonthi. Specifically targeted were colonels Phumiphat Chansawang and Chaichana Nakkerd. The move strengthened the control of Anupong over the SWC while helping to convince Samak and Thaksin that Anupong was not a proxy of Sonthi.[17] More fundamentally, however, the transition in control over the SWC helped to centralize power away from the unit to that of the Queen's Guard.

Aside from the SWC, Anupong effectively weakened another army faction that had traditionally lorded over the army—Wongthewan (Divine Progeny), also called the King's Guard, and Thailand's oldest faction, which had originated in 1870. Thaksin had managed to attract several up-and-coming members of this clique to his side such as former army and supreme commander General Somthas Attanand as well as senior brass generals Prin Suwannathat and Pornchai Kranlert. Under Anupong, Wongthewan officers were thus viewed with suspicion and could not expect to ascend to the top of the military.

Thus, the Queen's Guard became the dominant unit in the military. Ultimately, in acquiescing to most of what Anupong wanted in the 2008 mid-year reshuffle, it seemed that Samak was attempting to curry favour with the armed forces in order to intensify his personal hold—minus the influence of Thaksin—over the premiership.[18] But in so doing, Samak granted the Queen's Guard faction of Anupong greater power across the military while retreating from exercising civilian control over soldiers. It was thus partly because of Samak that the Queen's Guard encountered little army resistance to its ascent.

In March, Thaksin had returned to Thailand. By April, there commenced a re-awakening of the PAD, which initiated anti-PPP and anti-Thaksin rallies in Bangkok. Their demonstrations became a permanent day-to-day affair by the end of May. As the PAD protests dragged on into June, many viewed them "as an attempt to create conditions for the army to come out of its barracks and take action."[19] As such, this was a repeat of the PAD strategy during its demonstrations of 2006. Increasingly unruly PAD protests paralleled renewed gossip about a possible coup. Though Anupong and supreme commander General Boonsrang Niempradit denied that a putsch would occur, the sudden recall of 1st Army Region commander and Anupong confidant General Prayut Chanocha from a trip abroad testified to even military unease about the political environment.[20]

The new PAD, led once again by newspaper businessman Sondhi Limthongkul and retired general Chamlong Srimuang, was well prepared and well armed. First, it enjoyed brimming coffers thanks to financial support from the urban middle and upper class. There was also a great deal of royal financial assistance. Second, key elements in the Thai military (aligned with army chief Anupong Paochinda) were alleged to be assisting the PAD.[21]

Amidst growing PAD protests, the Samak government sought to reach an agreement to permit an ancient temple straddling the Thai-Cambodian border to be jointly inscribed by UNESCO. But the dispute offered a new rationale for a larger military role in border security.

On 20 June, the PAD declared that the Samak government had sold out to Cambodia regarding the Preah Vihear border temple. Demonstrators besieged Government House and eventually broke through police lines. Thereupon, PAD leaders Sondhi and Chamlong declared victory over the government. With the PAD at the gates of Government House, Anupong advised Samak to dissolve the lower house and hold fresh elections. Meanwhile, the army chief ordered all army units to remain on standby.[22] The prime minister, however, refused to step down. In the end, with the palace tepidly supporting the prime minister, the military stood behind Samak, as did his coalition parties, and the government remained in office. The PAD, however, continued its permanent protest in Bangkok.

During June and July 2008, a group of pro-Thaksin demonstrators began to develop in the north and northeast—the geographical areas where Thaksin was most popular. Wearing red shirts, the group (calling itself the United Front of Democracy against Dictatorship, or UDD) protested against the court rulings against Thaksin and showed its support for the Samak government. In August 2007, the PAD and UDD clashed violently in a pro-Thaksin province, foreshadowing future violence based around support for or hatred towards Thaksin.

Late August saw the PAD make a dramatic move to express its growing disapproval of the Samak government. Referring to 27 August as "Whistle Day", "Yellow Shirt" protestors began besieging and occupying Government House (the prime minister's compound), the National Broadcasting Television Office and some other government agencies. The timing of this strategy was significant because PAD leaders knew that many of their allies in the military would soon be retiring—in September that year.[23] Responding to the demonstrators, Samak demanded that the police and army expel the protestors and arrest them. Yet the response of security officials was lacklustre. The police dithered, while army commander Anupong refused to involve the military in politics. Still, Anupong did order 1st Army Region commander General Prayut to make ready a thousand soldiers trained in riot control to give support to the police if that became necessary. Interestingly, these thousand troops were to come from the 1st Division of the King's Guard (Wongthewan) in Bangkok as commanded by General Paiboon Khumchaya (AFAPS class 9).[24] The King's Guard is the factional rival of the Eastern Tigers of Anupong and Prayut. So, it would be King's Guard soldiers who might be blamed for attacking demonstrators instead of the Eastern Tigers. At the same time, if instability grew beyond the acceptable, these forces could be used for the "other mission"—a coup. But Anupong had decided to deal with Samak, and thus this option would remain unlikely.[25] Besides, as events later proved, Paiboon was a foe of Thaksin.

With the PAD occupying Government House, Samak set up a secure headquarters at Supreme Command, given the more moderate and supportive stance of supreme commander Boonsrang Niampradit towards Samak's government. This came amid rumours that a reactionary wing of the military led by General Prayut Chanocha was preparing to carry out a coup. At the same time, Samak proposed that Anupong take up the position of supreme commander (as Boonsrang prepared to retire) and hold this post concurrent to being army commander. While Anupong refused the offer, he did suggest that his friend Songkitti Chakkrabat (AFAPS class 10) be elevated to the position.[26]

On 1 September, clashes commenced between the PAD and UDD demonstrators, leaving one dead and forty injured. Samak declared a state of emergency, effectively thrusting the army chief into the command position of the crisis. Indeed, Samak made Anupong chairperson of an emergency committee to settle the crisis, with the assistance of police chief General Patcharawat Wongsuwan and 1st Army Region commander General Prayut Chanocha. Once again whispers echoed that a military putsch was approaching. General Somjet Boonthanom, one of the former CNS leaders, reportedly stated that "if the problems cannot be resolved by democratic means and the country is caught in a deadlock, a coup may be necessary".[27] Such tough words were backed by other soldiers such as Saprang, who was only days away from the end of his active-duty career and now in an inactive position. Anupong, however, declared that there would not be a coup, but also emphasized that he would not enforce the state of emergency. Instead, parliament needed to do more to achieve political reconciliation.[28] With Anupong refusing to enforce security against the PAD onslaught, Samak's tough words against the PAD lost their bite. What Samak did not know was that, on 2 September, Anupong telephoned Banharn Silpa-archa, at the time Chart Thai Party leader, in an effort to get Banharn to take Chart Thai out of the PPP-led coalition government. Banharn refused. An ex-Chart Thai minister told the US Embassy on 19 December 2008 that Chart Thai had prepared to break away from the ruling coalition "after the outbreak of violence on 7 October but was waiting for the independent commission report before doing so".[29]

Meanwhile, on 7 September, the army chief publicly called on Samak to lift the state of emergency and even expressed his backing for a government of national unity involving all parties.[30] By early September, Thailand was being torn asunder by violent demonstrations by the opposing PAD and UDD and a Samak government that seemed increasingly ineffectual. Only Anupong's army appeared to have any cohesive sway. Yet, with the protestors holding their ground, Samak refusing to resign, and the military opposing any new coup, it appeared as though pandemonium would continue to dominate.

At this point, a convenient court verdict resolved part of the crisis. On 9 September, the Constitutional Court found Samak guilty of violating the constitution for accepting a tiny payment after appearing on a television cooking show. As a result, he was forced to resign. Thereupon, Thaksin's brother-in-law Somchai Wongsawat became acting prime minister. When Samak, on 12 September, sought to be reinstated as prime minister through a vote in the lower house, Thaksin loyalists in PPP took the opportunity of Samak's judicial ouster to rally enough PPP votes to ensure he would not be re-nominated. Instead, on 17 September 2008, Somchai Wongsawat was nominated by PPP and voted in as prime minister. The following day, he was officially appointed by the king.

Somchai, a long-time judge, is married to Thaksin's younger sister and political firebrand Yaowapha. A US Embassy cable stated that because Somchai was "not seen as a strong-willed personality, [his] ability to … exert authority over the security forces … is unproven".[31] Upon becoming prime minister, Somchai, like Samak, doubled as defence minister. At the same time, he took Anupong's advice and discontinued the state of emergency (which security forces were scarcely enforcing anyway), while also opening talks with the PAD. The prime minister even visited Prem to seek reconciliation.[32]

But if the PPP was expecting renewed stability, they were totally mistaken. In fact the PPP was already on shaky ground. First, the Election Commission was poised to send to the Constitutional Court a malfeasance case against a PPP executive, which could lead to the dissolution of the PPP itself and thereupon force the government to resign. Second, the PAD continued to occupy Government House. Third, the military under Anupong was refusing to protect the government from PAD advances.[33] Meanwhile, the police seemed disorganized.

Eventually, PAD leaders sought to block Somchai from delivering his constitutionally mandated 7 October policy statement to the National Assembly. Somchai then did what Samak had avoided: he ordered police to clear the way to parliament. Police utilized tear gas in the early morning to achieve their objective, but protestors became ever more chaotic. The police engaged to clear the protestors, however, were Border Patrol Police (BPP), not the metropolitan police (who were better schooled in riot control). The BPP over the years had shown a greater willingness to use violence against urban Thai civilians.

When BPP personnel hurled tear gas canisters into the heart of the protestors, carnage erupted, and fighting began between the BPP and protestors. Ultimately, two protesters were killed (one by a defective Chinese-manufactured tear gas canister) and hundreds were injured. To escape the PAD siege, Somchai was forced to climb over a fence to safety. Soldiers finally arrived to help control the situation. At this point, the deputy prime minister (in charge of security)—Chavalit Yongchaidyudh—resigned his position to accept responsibility. Anupong reiterated that the military would not disperse protestors nor carry out a coup.

In the aftermath, Queen Sirikit, along with her daughter Princess Chulabhorn, attended a funeral ceremony for a young female PAD demonstrator named Anghana who had been killed in the fighting. The princess's personnel distributed assistance to the injured PAD.[34] At the funeral, the queen declared that the demonstrator had died in a noble cause. Such words suggested that the palace was clearly siding against the government.[35] Her response to the 6 October incident seemed to indicate support for anti-Thaksin demonstrators. At this point, PAD resistance to Somchai's government became even more pronounced. UDD protestors thereupon entered Bangkok and began demonstrating against the PAD. The two groups even came to blows intermittently.

Anupong's resistance to staging a coup likely owed to opposition from the king. According to Queen Sirikit's advisor Piya Malakul (who spoke to US ambassador Eric John on 4 November), King Bhumipol told the army commander explicitly not to launch a coup. Referring to the 2006 coup, the king stated that there should be no more putsches. Piya also asserted that Queen Sirikit had not meant to signal support for the PAD agenda when she presided over funeral ceremonies on 13 October. Finally, Piya said that the PAD demonstrations had "irritated" the monarch.[36]

But Anupong faced pressure from the palace and society to take some sort of decisive action to restore order—in a way that would jettison Somchai from office. On 8 October, Prem summoned Anupong to his home to express his concerns. Following the meeting, Anupong publicly stated: "I don't care who the government is, it is not related to us. This government will go, another one will replace it, but the military will remain neutral and protect the country."[37] But he added that the military was duty-bound to "save the country from seeing Thais killing each other".[38] Meanwhile, Chavalit Yongchaiyudh, having just retired from his post as Somchai's deputy prime minister and perhaps seeking to shift blame for the continuing chaos to the army chief, publicly implied that Anupong was indecisive and urged the army chief to stage a coup.[39] At the same time, the PAD accused the army leader of aligning with the government and deeply criticized new deputy police chief General Jongrak Juthanont and recently promoted Metropolitan police chief General Suchart Muenkaew for ordering police to use force against the protesters.[40] Anupong demanded that the Somchai government admit responsibility for the 6 October crackdown.

By mid-October, with the public perception that at least the queen supported the PAD, Somchai could no longer turn to the police to ensure a parliamentary session free from PAD interference. Indeed, following the 7 October incident, the police were now quite demoralized and would only agree to negotiate between the two sides. And besides, the PAD had by this point become so well-armed and organized that the police may not have been large enough to quell them. As such, it seemed that the only institution that could resolve the crisis was the army. Though Anupong refused to stage a coup, he stressed that Somchai must either resign or dissolve parliament. These suggestions were echoed by the supreme commander and heads of the navy, air force and police.[41] Indeed, on 18 October, Anupong and the other three service chiefs (plus the chief of police) appeared on national television to demand the prime minister's resignation. Somchai refused.[42] He instead appointed an investigative body to look into the 7 October incident. Navy chief Kamthorn Phumviharn, an AFAPS 10 classmate of Thaksin, later stated that he had opposed Anupong's public statement demanding that Somchai resign. Two days after the broadcast, Anupong appointed new commanders for three army regiments based in Bangkok—the 1st Infantry Division, 2nd Cavalry Division, and Anti-Aircraft Artillery Division. He placed his own loyalists or those of his friend new army chief of staff General Prayut Chanocha in full control of the three divisions. The reshuffle involved more than a hundred regiment commanders.[43]

By the end of October, the Supreme Court had convicted Thaksin of conflict of interest and sentenced him to two years imprisonment. Thereupon the self-exiled ex-PM spoke by phone to his supporters at a mass rally in which he requested a king's pardon. At that, military leaders accused Thaksin of involving the monarchy in politics.[44]

Nevertheless, the armed forces leadership now seemed torn between those supporting Thaksin and those opposing him. Among the former was General Khattiya Sawasdipol (AFAPS class 11), or "Seh Daeng". Khattiya had had a long and distinguished career fighting communists in Thailand's Northeast and Muslim insurgents in the South. Under Thaksin, Khattiya had been an aide to former ISOC head General Pallop Pinmanee and had fallen out with anti-Thaksin forces at least since 2007. At that time, then CNS police chief General Seripusit was investigating Khattiya's connections to gambling dens. Seh Daeng established his own website, wrote books about his adventures (many fictional) and even began to establish his own political party. By October 2008, Khattiya was a regular presence among UDD protestors, and he advised them and provided training for them in a self-appointed capacity. He was accused by many of being behind numerous bomb attacks against the PAD—a charge he denied. He declared that he would mobilise government supporters against any military attempt to seize political power.[45] In November, Anupong insultingly transferred Seh Daeng to become a military aerobics instructor. At this, the latter reportedly stated, "I have prepared one dance. It's called the 'throwing-a-hand-grenade' dance."[46]

Another UDD backer was Khattiya's former ISOC boss General Pallop Pinmanee (Chulachomklao class 7). A fiery member of the "Young Turks", he had participated in the 1976 and 1977 coups as well as the 1981 coup attempt against Prem. He retired from the military in 1996. Pallop had been the head of ISOC under the Thaksin government but had been accused of possessing knowledge about the assassination attempt against Thaksin back in 2006. In 2007 he was appointed as ISOC public relations officer. When PAD demonstrations swelled in 2008, Pallop was initially very supportive of his class 7 peer Chamlong Srimuang. But in November, Pallop suddenly visited Thaksin in Hong Kong and came away a sudden convert to supporting the former prime minister once again. In late November 2008, Pallop was on the verge of being appointed deputy director of ISOC.[47]

As for anti-Thaksin military supporters of the PAD, General Saprang Kallayamitr was foremost among them. Saprang publicly supported PAD street protests against the Samak government. Another avid PAD backer was former permanent defence secretary Admiral Bannawit Kenkrian.[48] There was also General Pathompong Kesornsuk. Pathompong is the husband of Democrat Party bigwig Supatra Masdit. In 2008, Pathompong became an active and conspicuous member of the PAD when he appeared on PAD stages in full military uniform. At the time, he was an active-duty soldier who was chief advisor of the Supreme Command. In late November, Pathompong publicly urged Anupong to stage a coup against the Somchai government.[49] Interestingly, all three PAD supporters—Saprang, Bannawit and

Pathompong—were from AFAPS class 7 and deemed to be close to Privy Council chair Prem Tinsulanonda.

By late November, PAD demonstrators decided to ramp up their chaos to higher decibels of anarchy. Demanding that Somchai immediately dissolve the lower house and call a new election, PAD demonstrators, on 25 November, occupied and shut down Thailand's two international airports—Don Muang and Suwannaphum.[50] Anupong stood idly by, refusing to intervene or hatch a coup. But Somchai still refused to submit to PAD demands even when army commander Anupong, surrounded by other soldiers and leading civil servants, again publicly called for him to step down. Like Samak before him, Somchai declared a state of emergency. At the same time, though Anupong had ruled out a coup, other elements in the military were not so sure. 1st Army Region commander General Kanit Sapitak refused to rule out a putsch and declared that the term "military" did not only mean "Army Chief".[51] While Anupong came up with a plan for the PAD to go home and the government to dissolve the lower house to allow for fresh elections, the PAD refused to agree to it. Meanwhile, Somchai ordered police chief General Patcharawat to clear thousands of PAD demonstrators from Don Muang and Suwannaphum airports. When Patcharawat balked at this, the prime minister demoted him.[52]

Once again, both army and police officials refused to enforce the decree. Only the PAD militia and a rapidly growing though fledgling UDD seemed to be willing and capable of using force to either forcibly affect a change in government or keep it in office. This was particularly the case given the king's earlier refusal to support a coup. In the end, the arch-royalist Constitutional Court, in what appeared to be a rapid manipulated process, issued a ruling on 2 December that dissolved the PPP citing apparent illegalities by MP Yongyuth Tiyapairat in the December 2007 election.[53] Two other parties (Chart Thai and Matchimathipathai) in the PPP-led coalition were also dissolved. The government was thus forced to resign. A similar case against the opposition Democrats never reached the court.[54]

The fall of the Somchai government and banning of PPP did not end pro-Thaksin parties. The phoenix of PPP now rose to form a new party called Pheu Thai (For Thais). It still accounted for the majority of MPs, especially with the smaller parties that had earlier worked with it in the governing coalition. Perhaps Thaksin and Pheu Thai assumed that they could form a new coalition. But times had changed. With the break-up of PPP and the other two parties, MPs in these parties were, under the constitution, free to switch parties. Indeed, they had sixty days to do so.[55] At this point some forces apparently encouraged most of these MPs to defect. Indeed, the senior-most members of Thailand's army brass—as well as, mostly likely, a senior Privy Councillor—were instrumental in cobbling together a new coalition led by the anti-Thaksin Democrat Party.[56]

The extent of military involvement remains unclear. But at the least, on 6 December, army chief Anupong opened his home to anti-Thaksin political parties who were seeking to form a new coalition government.[57]

> Many key members of the coalition parties and key factions within them were seen visiting Gen Anupong at his official residence in the compound of the First Infantry Regiment off Vibhavadi Rangsit Road, both in small and large groups. Among these special visitors were reportedly Newin Chidchob and Sora-at Klinprathum, two faction leaders in the now dissolved PPP. The two men were seen at Gen Anupong's residence on Dec 4 along with Gen Prayut Chanocha, the army's chief of staff. Later, Pradit Phataraprasit, secretary-general of Ruam Jai Thai Chart Pattana party reportedly called on Gen Prayut at his residence, also in the regiment compound. In the meantime, Democrat secretary-general Suthep Thaugsuban kept in touch with Gen Anupong by phone. Mr Suthep and Gen Anupong became acquaintances when the Council for National Security was in power. On Dec 6, shortly before the Democrat's plan to form a new coalition government was announced, Mr Suthep reportedly led a group of key members of the Democrats' prospective coalition partners to meet Gen Anupong at the residence of former army chief Gen Prawit Wongsuwan, who is well respected by Gen Anupong. Even though the meetings were supposed to be secret events, they ended up in the open because of the unusual manner of the visits. Suddenly, Gen Anupong was viewed by the media as the "coalition formation manager".[58]

Thaksin loyalist Jakrapob Penkair alleged to the US Embassy on 9 December that army commander Anupong Paochinda had financed the defections from the PPP coalition to one led by the Democrats, providing 25–30 million baht per head (over US$700,000).[59] The affair was not unlike the events of November 1997 when a faction in Samak's Prachakorn Thai Party had been drawn over by Prem to the Democrat Party.[60] Unsurprisingly, Anupong denied any involvement in forming the Abhisit government.[61]

The military "soft coup" efforts coalesced around a group of over thirty MPs led by banned ex-MP Newin Chidchob. Faction-leader Newin had joined and defected from several parties over the years. So moving over to the Democrats was not something that would be difficult for him—and persuasion by the military would make things even easier. Besides these "Friends of Newin", the Democrats also lobbied MPs in smaller parties of the ruling coalition to switch sides. This included Chart Thai Pattana, Ruamjai Thai Chart Pattana, the new Bhumjai Thai, Puea Paendin and Pracharas. Eventually, most MPs in these parties (except Puea Paendin and Pracharas) voiced their support for a Democrat-led coalition.[62] It seemed as if these politicians, once loyal to Thaksin, perceived that the time had come to abandon him as they could achieve greater payoffs if they moved to a new coalition so apparently favoured by powerful extra-constitutional forces.

Anupong's political powerplay had been guaranteed as a result of his 1 October 2008 military reshuffle. The new line-up represented the further consolidation of his power throughout the army. While his friend Songkitti was indeed promoted to be supreme commander, Anupong's close friend Prayut was elevated to the post of army chief of staff. At the same time, Admiral Kamthorn Pumviharn (AFAPS class 10), another friend of Anupong's, succeeded Admiral Sathirapan Keyanon as navy commander. Following the elevation of Prayut, the Queen's Guard continued to be buttressed with the promotion of Queen's Guard commander General Kanit Sapitak from deputy commander to commander, 1st Army Region. Furthermore, any remaining Sonthi Boonyaratklin loyalists were sidelined. In particular, many AFAPS class 9 officers seen as generally supportive of Sonthi were not given promotions. Most specifically, General Montree Sangkasap, who had been favoured by Sonthi to succeed him as army chief, was left in place as army chief of staff. Anupong and Winai also vetoed Boonsrang's efforts to have Montree succeed him as supreme commander.[63] Other class 9 officers, however, fared better. General Jiradet Kotcharat moved up from being assistant army commander to deputy army chief. At the same time, General Wiroj Buacharoen (AFAPS class 9), who had struggled to oversee Thai counter-insurgency as head of the 4th Army Region in the South, was elevated to become the other assistant army commander. The new reshuffle list also showed that the promotions of Thaksin's associates in the armed forces were being curtailed. Indeed, ACM Sukampol Suwannathat (AFAPS class 10) failed to become air force commander and was instead relegated to the post of inspector general in the Defence Ministry.[64] Instead, the anti-Thaksin Ittaphorn Subhawong (AFAPS class 11) was appointed to replace Chalit.

In mid-December, a new government was thus formed under the leadership of the anti-Thaksin Democrat Party. Its leader, the young and ambitious Abhisit Vechachiwa, was formally endorsed by the palace as premier on 17 December 2008. The price of the Democrats' newfound power was its legitimation of a military-brokered coalition and the bequeathing of several cabinet positions to Newin's military-influenced Bhumjai Thai Party.[65]

As Thailand ushered in 2009, the Democrat government faced a growing number of UDD (red-shirt) anti-government protests. At each of these, Thailand's armed forces applied the Internal Security Act to legally prohibit the protests or forcibly repress them. Thaksin started to step up his telephone call-ins to UDD rallies, egging them on and proclaiming a conspiracy against him by army commander Anupong, other elements of the military, and privy councillors Prem and Surayud.[66] None of these challenges augured well for the survival of stable tutelary democracy in Thailand.

The new ruling coalition allowed the military, dominated by the Queen's Guard, to have its way at every turn. With Anupong and Prayut—former Queen's Guard commanders—in the senior-most positions of the army, and with former Queen's Guard commander General Kanit Sapitak in the vital position of 1st Army Region commander, Anupong's former commander and fellow Eastern Tiger, retired general Prawit Wongsuwan, was also brought in as defence minister. While Prawit himself had previously served as the boss to both Anupong and Prayut in the Eastern Tigers (1st Army Region, 2nd Division), he was also close to Sonthi Boonyaratklin and other leaders of the CNS, especially having been valedictorian of AFAPS class 6. His close ties to Sonthi also paralleled a friendship with Privy Council members Surayud Chulanond and Prem Tinsulanonda. Prawit furthermore maintained close ties to Newin Chidchob and was said to have been instrumental in convincing the Chidchob faction to merge into the Abhisit-led coalition.[67]

By April 2009, the level of domestic polarization had soared. Thaksin's continued telephoning-in to UDD rallies was succeeding in perpetuating them. Privy councillors themselves were now entering the fray, defending Prem and accusing Thaksin of endangering the king with his criticisms. Former Thaksin-stalwart but now Abhisit-ally Newin Chidchob also called on Thaksin to be silent in order not to offend the monarchy.[68] At the same time, anti-Thaksin diehards put a bounty on Thaksin's head and criticized Abhisit for not taking a harder line against him. With Thai security forces remaining on the sidelines, it seemed that soon a UDD-PAD clash would occur.

April witnessed the 2009 mid-year military reshuffle. The armed forces rotations represented a further purge of Thaksin's loyalists and the further shoring up of Anupong over the military. The remaining members of Thaksin's closest military friends—ACM Sumet Phomanee, General Manas Paorik, General Prin Suwannathat and Air Marshal Pongsathorn Buasap—were all relegated to even more inactive positions. At the same time, General Pongsathat Sawetseranee, General Sophon Dityaem, General Dulkrit Rakpao and twelve other pro-Thaksin AFAPS class 10 peers were also given lesser positions. Sophon and Dulkrit were moved from being commanders of the 2nd and 1st Army Corps, respectively, to inactive positions.

Meanwhile, friends of Anupong, Prayut and defence minister Prawit found themselves promoted. These included General Weewalit Jorasamrit (AFAPS class 10), who was elevated from 2nd Army Region deputy commander to commander of the 2nd Army Corps. General Thongchai Theparak (AFAPS class 10) moved from the position of commander of the 33rd Military Circle to become 3rd Army Region deputy commander. At least three other Anupong loyalists in the army were appointed to top positions, including General Thanapol Paochinda (AFAPS class 11), younger brother of the army chief, who became deputy commander of the Department of Reserve Command, renamed the Territorial Defence Command. In the navy, Vice Admiral Nikhom Homcharoen (AFAPS class 10) was appointed deputy chief of staff of the navy from the lowly post of naval specialist.[69] In the air force, Prayut's army general friend ACM Khanit Suwannet (AFAPS class 12) was elevated from being chief of the Air Combat Command to the post of director of Air Operations Command. Finally, Colonel Nat Intharacharoen (AFAPS class 20), a close aide of defence minister Prawit, was promoted to become chief in the office of the defence minister.

Early April also saw a Red Shirt attack on the prime minister's motorcade, and he was lucky to escape from his car unscathed.[70] The new prime ministerial security set-up—Task Force 5221—placed the Eastern Tigers military faction, under Anupong and Prayut, as the direct guarantor of the physical survival of the prime minister and Privy Council chair.

In mid-April 2009, the armed forces—dominated by the Queen's Guard—illustrated its readiness to support the anti-Thaksin government of Abhisit (in conspicuous contrast to its abandonment of the Somchai government) when it dispersed Red Shirt demonstrators in Pattaya and Bangkok. The clash left over two hundred injured and some dead, though there were conflicting reports as to the exact number.[71] Further, the military, through ISOC, clamped down on Red Shirt activities, forbidding them to demonstrate at ASEAN summits (e.g., Phuket in July) and discouraging most Red Shirt protests in general. Indeed, after August 2009, the Internal Security Act was invoked on numerous occasions to coincide with planned Red Shirt demonstrations.[72]

On 17 April, an assassination attempt was made on the life of PAD leader Sondhi Limthongkul. Sondhi survived the attack with injuries and subsequently told reporters that he believed those responsible were Anupong, Prayut and Prawit, who he said were keen on seizing power from the Abhisit government.[73] Though Anupong denied any knowledge of such a plot, the bullets fired were traced back to the army.[74] In June 2009, Anupong and Prayut increasingly consolidated their hold on top positions in the armed forces—helping themselves and other military friends. On 17 June 2009, Anupong promoted seventy-five mid-level officers as a reward for their involvement in the 2006 coup.[75]

Under the Abhisit government, the prime minister began to try to gain more elected civilian control over Thailand's policy in the Deep South where the military had been prosecuting a counter-insurgency against Malay-Muslim insurgents since 2004. Abhisit's solution was to gain ultimate prime ministerial control over policies in the region through his "Politics leading the Military" agenda. But army commander Anupong opposed such reforms, declaring in August that there would be no discussions with insurgents.[76]

By September, to many among the police, Abhisit had gained a notorious reputation for interfering in what they considered "their" affairs. On 12 September, Abhisit removed the police chief, General Patcharawat Wongsuwan—brother of the defence minister, retired general Prawit Wongsuwan of the Bhumjaithai Party, who was seen as sometimes loyal to Thaksin—instead appointing the more arch-royalist police general Wichean Potephosree as acting police chief. Abhisit was likely frustrated with Patcharawat because of the lacklustre performance by the police in quelling UDD Red Shirt protestors. But the PM's actions towards Patcharawat pleased angry PAD leaders who saw Patcharawat at least partly responsible for the violent dispersal of PAD protestors on 7 October 2008. Six months earlier, in March 2009, the National Anti-Corruption Commission (NACC) had indicted former PM Somchai Wongsawat; retired general Chavalit Yongchaiyudh, former deputy PM in charge of security (and former prime minister); and Patcharawat, among others, for abuse of authority with regard to the bloody crackdown that day.[77] In September, the NACC had filed criminal charges against Somchai, Chavalit and Patcharawat for their roles.[78] In response, Patcharawat sought to resign, but Abhisit threatened to fire him first—a move that would have diminished the former's pension. However, amidst rumours of pressure from Patcharawat's brother Prawit (who threatened to resign from the government if Abhisit dismissed his brother), Abhisit allowed Patcharawat to retire.[79]

Meanwhile, in late September 2009, a story emerged that the armed forces had received another 10 billion baht while Abhisit attended the G-8 meeting in New York. Purportedly, this was to be a quid pro quo in exchange for the army's pledge not to oust Abhisit while he was outside of Thailand.[80]

In the annual October 2009 military reshuffle (see Appendix 4), Anupong's close friend Prayut was ultimately promoted to the position of deputy army commander, continuing his fast-track to the top army job. Prayut was already thought by the US Embassy as among the "closest to Queen Sirikit and the expected successor to Anupong" when the latter was to retire in 2010.[81]

In October, the NACC charges against Chavalit pushed him further to align with Abhisit's opponents. On 2 October, only two weeks after the NACC began filing its case against Chavalit, Thaksin successfully convinced the former army chief and prime minister Yongchaiyudh to become chairperson of Pheu Thai Party. But in doing so, Chavalit's decision was certainly not good news for the military's political ally the Bhumjaithai Party (and its leader Newin Chidchob) given that Chavalit possessed strong support among voters and vote canvassers in the northeast, where Newin was also seeking to expand his voting base. At the same time, Chavalit's decision created tensions within the military. At that point, Privy Council chair and former PM General Prem publicly warned Chavalit to "'think carefully', otherwise his move would risk being treated as 'an act of betrayal against the country.'"[82] Following Prem's admonition, however, several retired senior military and police officers close to Thaksin who were still influential crowded into Pheu Thai. These included General Pallop Pinmanee and fifty to sixty former AFAPS class 10 schoolmates of Thaksin.[83] Some of the retired officers, known as "G60", were rumoured to be assisting certain Red Shirts with military training. In addition, a former deputy army commander, retired general Jiradet Kotcharat (under Anupong), also prepared to sign up for Pheu Thai. Jiradet registered along with another AFAPS class 9 graduate, retired general Wichit Yathip, who was also a former deputy army commander who had close ties to Chavalit. Ultimately, it appeared that Chavalit's entry into Pheu Thai represented the growing influence of ex-soldiers in the Thaksin-influenced party.[84]

Only Prem's continued backing—along with that of Surayud, Anupong and Prayut—appeared to be guaranteeing the survival of the

Abhisit government. The sway of Anupong and Prayut derived from their leadership roles during their military careers. Despite being re-tired, Prem and Surayud continued to wield informal influence through their positions on the Privy Council as well as their long patron-client linkages with military officials. In late December 2009, a delegation of service commanders greeting Prem was met by the privy councillor dressed in military attire. The last time Prem had worn such apparel was just prior to the 2006 coup. This time he recommended that they read a Thai newspaper article suggesting that Thailand is now falling into civil war.[85]

As 2010 began, rumours of a military coup were again resonating. It was said that the supposed takeover would be instigated by generals Prawit, Anupong and Prayut as well as politician Newin Chidchob. Such rumours had last occurred when the Red Shirts had held a demonstration on 17 August 2009, when they sought to petition the king to pardon Thaksin Shinawatra. At the time it had been speculated that potential violence might provide the necessary pretext for military intervention.[86] But, at the beginning of 2010, the political situation was becoming increasingly fluid. Moreover, fractures appeared to be growing in the military. An undercurrent of soldiers who believed that the Queen's Guard leadership of Anupong, Prawit and Prayut were pushing politicized promotions while sidelining other "professional" officers—such as the Wongthewan military faction—was becoming increasingly prevalent. Wongthewan had led many past coups because many of its members have been senior military brass and because of its proximity to the centre of power in Bangkok.[87]

In early January, amidst continuing demonstrations by the Red Shirts, surreptitious manoeuvring by Thaksin from abroad, quarrels within the ruling coalition, and legal trouble for the Democrat Party, reports surfaced that a grenade had been launched (from an M79 grenade launcher) into the army commander's office.[88] The fiercely pro-Thaksin Maj. Gen. Khattiya ("Seh Daeng") was suspected of complicity in the attack, indicating at least some military dissidence towards Anupong.[89] General Pallop Pinmanee urged (unsuccessfully) Pheu Thai Party chairman Chavalit to lead a Red Shirt people's army crusade.

Amidst these pro-Thaksin efforts, pro-Anupong officers ral-lied at different military camps in a show of force against him. On 7 February, General Apirat Kongsompong, a close acolyte of Anupong (and future army commander), who the latter had hand-picked to command the strategic 11th Infantry Regiment in Bangkok, led a "boot-thumping" campaign of military officers in support of Anupong. Among Apirat's pre-cadet class 20 peers who supported the rally were the 1st Infantry Regiment's Colonel Natthawat Aknibutr; the 2nd Infantry Regiment's Colonel Kukiart Srinakha and the 1st Artillery Regiment's Colonel Kritdanai Itthimonthon, as well as Maj. Gen. Nat Intharacharoen and Maj. Gen. Atthaporn Bowsuwan (the latter two were close aides to Defence Minister Prawit Wongsuwan). In all, seventeen battalion and regimental commanders participated in Apirat's rally.[90]

Simultaneous to these events, rumours were spreading of an impending Prayut-sponsored military coup—which ultimately did not transpire. As a late February court verdict on Thaksin's assets was approaching, both sides seemed to be seeking leverage against the other. To prevent any possible chaos following the decision, up to 25,000 soldiers were deployed in thirty-eight provinces and at two hundred checkpoints just outside of Bangkok. This followed a late January cabinet resolution that henceforth the military could now help police (if requested) to quell domestic disorder without imposition of the Internal Security Act.[91]

By early February 2010, four generals were in contention to replace Anupong once he retired in October 2010: Prayut (class 12), Wit Thepadadin Na Ayutthaya (class 11), Theerawat Boonyapradap (AFAPS class 10) and Piroon Phaeopolsong (AFAPS class 10). Prayut, however, due to retire in 2014, remained the frontrunner. The other three would retire in 2011. Piroon was seen as a neutral candidate—acceptable to Anupong and Thaksin alike. At the same time, Piroon was liked by Privy Council chair Prem since, like Prem, Piroon was from Thailand's cavalry unit. Because of this it was rumoured that tensions had developed between Prayut and Piroon. Theerawat, meanwhile, hailed from the ordnance department, which, according to army tradition, kept him out of line to become army commander. Finally, there was Wit, who in 2009 had become assistant army commander. Wit was a loyalist of General Prawit Wongsuwan, a son of former deputy army commander General Yos Thepsadin na Ayuthaya (a perennial coup plotter), who had been a friend of Anupong since they were children. But Wit was in General Khattiya's (Seh Daeng) pre-cadet class 11 and was friendly with pro-Thaksin military elements, including former army chief Chaisit Shinawatra and General Pornchai Kranlert, who had almost become army commander in 2007 and who was Wit's brother-in-law.[92] Wit and Prayut allegedly became the two main choices of Anupong when he was choosing his successor. After Prayut beat out Wit, the two continued to have a tense relationship. Further down the line, in 2021, Wit became chairperson of the military-created Palang Pracharat Party when Prawit began to dispute with Prayut.

On 26 February 2010, Thailand's Supreme Court ruled in favour of seizing 46 billion of the 70 billion baht of Thaksin's money frozen by the state. Simultaneously, rumours circulated that Cambodia would no longer allow Thaksin to direct campaigns against Thailand from Cambodian soil.[93] The result was that Thaksin headed off to Dubai, while March 2010 saw thousands of Red Shirts arrive in Bangkok where they demanded the dissolution of the Abhisit government. They protested at Government House and other key state facilities.

To avoid encountering the UDD protestors, Abhisit set up a temporary home and workplace at the Apirat-commanded 11th Infantry Regiment headquarters in Bangkok's Bang Khen district. This venue had been established by Abhisit, Suthep and Anupong as a war room.[94] The air force headquarters at Don Muang emerged as a second refuge for Abhisit—as it had been for Samak and Somchai previously. Nevertheless, Red Shirt protestors demonstrated at the 11th Infantry headquarters, among other venues, and threatened to "invade" the compound. On 28 March, two grenades were fired into the compound injuring four soldiers. In response, the government threatened to declare martial law at the headquarters.[95] Continuing protests finally led to lacklustre negotiations between Abhisit and the UDD—the former urging Red Shirt restraint, while the latter continued to demand a dissolution. Though the government did not favour any immediate dissolution, the military and Privy Council chair sent out signals that Abhisit must completely rule out any dissolution. Indeed, the top brass realized that any return of a pro-Thaksin government at this stage of the game might upset the anticipated army chief succession: Anupong was to retire in October 2010 and Prayut was set to succeed him. At the same time, any pro-Thaksin government might allocate less funding to the military.[96]

Amidst the government's negotiations with the Red Shirts, the military's 2010 mid-year reshuffle of seventy-nine positions bolstered dominance over the armed forces of the Queen's Guard, particularly officers close to Anupong and Prayut.[97] General Thanin Ketthap (AFAPS class 10), seen as not necessarily a thorough-enough Anupong loyalist (he was in charge of fifty thousand troops deployed at the Red Shirt rallies) was demoted from his post as deputy chief of staff to an inactive posting. Still, he was promoted to a full general. Also, Prayut's friend and classmate deputy comptroller-general General Chatchai

Satrikaliya (AFAPS class 12) was elevated to become assistant chief of staff.[98] Four other associates of Anupong, including General Apichai Songsilp (AFAPS class 10), were promoted to become chief advisers to the defence minister.[99]

Abhisit now offered the armed forces a greater military budget "in a move seen to shore up its support".[100] More specifically, Abhisit announced his continuing support for a ten-year plan to enhance the military's capabilities in a move seen as solidifying Democrat Party relations with the armed forces. Among several big-ticket items were an airship costing 350 million baht, the new 7th Infantry Division in Chiang Mai costing 10 billion baht (which would monitor Red Shirts, the northern narcotics situation and the border), and the purchase of 121 armoured personnel carriers from the Ukraine at a cost of 5 billion baht.[101] The military's request for more money paralleled a trend since the 2006 coup of a skyrocketing defence budget.

Although powerful elements in Thai society remained stacked against the UDD, the demonstrations in April intensified. Abhisit thus imposed the Emergency Decree on Public Administration on 7 April 2010. This act permitted the state to hold suspects without charge for up to thirty days. Nevertheless, the security forces seemed unwilling to forcefully disperse the Red Shirts, partly given that some "watermelon" (khaki green outside, pro–Red Shirt inside) soldiers sympathized with the protestors and also because officers feared similar legal repercussions to those that had befallen the Somchai government after the latter's violent dispersal of PAD protestors in October 2008. There were also rumours that the palace was divided in terms of how to deal with the UDD demonstrators.

The events of 10 April 2010, in which twenty-six died and hundreds were injured, considerably amplified tensions between the Abhisit government and the UDD. At the same time though, the incident included an armed attack against Queen's Guard military faction leaders on the ground, resulting in the death of rising star Colonel Romklao Tuwatham[102] (AFAPS class 23)—who was favoured by the Queen—and the serious injury of Maj. Gen. Walit Rojanapakdi (AFAPS class 15) who was then nominally commanding the Queen's Guard 2nd Division.[103] The assault is believed to have been carried out by "well-trained army officers" acting as mercenaries who were aligned with a pro-Thaksin clique of junior/retired military officers embittered with the military leadership. These same "watermelon" soldiers were alleged to have fired grenades at sites identified as anti-Thaksin entities. Furthermore, the former ISOC head, retired general Panlop Pinmanee, and army special major general Khattiya Sawasdipol (nicknamed Sae Daeng) were seen by some as organizing UDD "troops" or "Ronin" "Black Shirts". Other alleged UDD military advisors included active duty military officers loyal to Thaksin: General Prin Suwannathat (AFAPS class 10), General Manas Paorik (AFAPS class 10) and General Pornchai Kranlert (AFAPS class 10).[104] If that is true, then other elements of the pro-Thaksin grouping of senior military officers could have been involved, including men such as General Wit Thepsasdin na Ayuthaya. Many police officers who had either been loyal to Thaksin, Patcharawat Wongsuwan or both could also have been involved. Indeed, on 27 April, police sergeant-major Prinya Maneekhot had been arrested for transporting sixty-three rounds of M79 grenades to Red Shirts.[105]

With the military and the police increasingly divided on to how to handle the demonstrators, cracks were also appearing between the more moderate Anupong on the one side and Abhisit and more hardline top military brass (such as Prayut) on the other about how to address the Red Shirt problem.[106]

For a short period after 10 April, the military suffered a negative image; it was accused of running rampage against the UDD and thus causing needless deaths. During this period, the military top brass appeared to become more divided and desperate about how to put down the Red Shirt protests. Abhisit appointed the army chief as chief officer of a new Centre for Resolution of the Emergency Situation (CRES), which seemed to be akin to the Capital Command military structure that had been in charge of security in Bangkok until 1992. Anupong, however, seemed to prefer a softer policy—as he had in his dealings with the previous Samak government. Indeed, Anupong was now increasingly buoyed by the idea of the lower house being dissolved, while hardliners were encouraging a more reactionary solution. But Anupong's longtime associate, deputy army commander Prayut Chanocha, reportedly either favoured a coup or even a half-coup, whereby only Anupong would be removed and the Abhisit government would be allowed to stay on. Of course, Prayut denied these designs. But by late April, as the Red Shirt demonstrations continued with no end in sight (and the economy suffering as a result), the opinions of Bangkokians mostly united in favour of some sort of dispersal.[107] Simultaneously, the appearance of a fractured UDD leadership in the face of a fig-leaf compromise offer by Abhisit finally helped to unite the military leadership to try again to forcefully quell the protests.

During this time it has been alleged that Prayut quietly began proposing a "half-coup" whereby Anupong and a few others would be removed.[108] Although this intervention never occurred, members of the royal establishment had long worried about Anupong's ability or commitment to stifle the UDD demonstrations. As early as 2010, members of the Privy Council had already informed the US ambassador that support for Anupong from Prem and the palace had dwindled, whilst the backing for Prayut, seen by privy councillors as a trusted ultra-royalist and the next army commander, was strong. Following a meeting with privy councillor Siddhi Savetsila, US ambassador Eric John wrote:

> Siddhi said he had higher hopes for deputy Commander Prayut, widely expected to replace Anupong in October [2010] and seen as particularly close to the Queen. Siddhi claimed Prem had sent a signal of his displeasure with Anupong by snubbing him during a group call at Prem's residence to pass birthday greetings, not stopping to talk to Anupong personally as he did with other key military commanders.[109]

By early May, Anupong's more cautious approach faded in favour of a more bellicose policy. A harbinger of the repressive turn came on 14 May with the sudden assassination of Khattiya Sawasdipol (in a coma, he died in hospital on 17 May). Then, on 19 May, soldiers suddenly swept forward in a brutal mopping-up operation that caused between 92 and 99 deaths and between one thousand and two thousand injuries.[110] The operation, which successfully led to the arrest of UDD leaders at the rally, exemplified Prayut's proclivity for violence and repression. Directing the assault was Prayut's eventual successor as army commander (and member of Taharn Sua Rachinee) General Udomdej Sitabutr; a key commander on the ground was army general Apirat Kongsompong.

Scores of Red Shirt leaders and alleged "core" members were arrested and imprisoned. The Emergency Decree remained in force in all fifty districts of Bangkok and certain other provinces (specifically those near Bangkok: Nonthaburi, Pathum Thani and Samut Prakan) until December 2010. Despite their use of repressive measures, Thailand's military emerged from the May operation relatively unscathed in terms of middle and upper class Bangkokian public opinion. The Abhisit government helped soldiers in this regard by appointing a committee to investigate the 19 May deaths and publicly pushing for reconciliation, moves that the opposition claimed was merely a whitewash aimed at swaying public opinion in Abhisit's (and hence the royalist military's) favour.[111]

The vanquishing of the Red Shirts paved the way for the arch-royalist Queen's Guard faction to further dominate the military. In the annual October military reshuffle, Prayut was rewarded by succeeding Anupong as army chief[112] and the Abhisit government remained in office for ten more months. As commander, Prayut purged the ranks of most officers perceived to be Thaksin loyalists and portrayed himself as an ultra-royalist.[113]

Indeed, in that year's annual military reshuffle, the Queen's Guard faction and Prayut's class 12 succeeded in monopolizing the top military positions. In the army, five of the top sixteen positions were held by pre-cadet class 12 graduates. Of the Five Tigers postings, two were bestowed upon class 12 (Prayut and Daowapong), with classes 10 and 11 taking the remaining three. Yet the new deputy commander, General Theerawat Bunyapradap (class 10), and army assistants, General Yuthasin Doicherngan and General Pichet Wisaijorn (class 11), were but stopgap appointments as Theerawat retired in 2011 and the other two in 2012. Noticeably absent from the promotions was Prayut-rival General Wit Thepsadin na Ayuthaya, who was shunted from his innocuous perch as chair of the Army Advisory Board to an even more inactive advisory posting. Supreme commander General Songkitti Chakkrapat (class 10) was also looking to retire in 2012. A crucial appointment was that of General Daowapong Rathonsuwan to the post of army chief of staff. Besides being a graduate of class 12, Daowapong helped to lead the successful army crackdown on the Red Shirts on 19 May 2010. He was also the nominal head of the Wongthewan military clique.[114]

Daowapong's promotion represented a possible attempt by the Queen's Guard to harmonize its relations with Wongthewan.[115] Indeed, the 2006 coup, which facilitated the trumping over Wongthewan by Queen's guardsmen, also exacerbated growing tensions between the two cliques. The apparent inability of the military to quickly respond to the Red Shirt demonstrations in March–May 2010 owed partly to fissures in the armed forces already ushered in by the rivalry between the Wongthewan and Queen's Guard. It is even rumoured that the assassination of Maj. Gen. Khattiya Sawasdipol came about following a May meeting in a hotel between the leaders (Prayut and Daowapong) of the two factions.[116] With Prayut now army commander and Daowapong ascendant, a careful balance was temporarily achieved between the two unit cliques. Meanwhile, class 12 generals Thawatchai Samutsakorn and Wannatip Wongwai were elevated to the posts of 2nd Army Region commander and 3rd Army Region commander, respectively. In the air force, ACM Srichao Janrueang (AFAPS class 12), commander of the Directorate of Air Operations Control, now became one of the two assistant air force chiefs. At the same time, at police headquarters, police general Wichean Potephosree assumed the position of police chief, while police lieutenant general Santhan Chayanon became Metropolitan Police Bureau commissioner. Both—like Prayut—were graduates of class 12.[117]

Prayut also had family ties to boost his influence. In October 2010, his younger brother Preecha (AFAPS class 15) was promoted from the post of chief of staff, 3rd Army Corps, to become deputy commander, 3rd Army Region (simultaneously acting as the commander of the Yala Task Force in the South). Preecha's AFAPS peer General Thana Wittayawiroj, chief of staff, Special Warfare Command, was at the same time promoted to become commander of the Special Warfare Command. Moreover, Prayut and deputy army commander Daowapong Ratanasuwan were close friends, and their amity included close ties between Prayut's younger brother Preecha and Daowapong's younger brother Karun (AFAPS class 16), who in 2010 had served with Preecha as the deputy chief of staff for the 3rd Army Region.

As for the Queen's Guard and Eastern Tigers factions, beyond Prayut, other members of this clique gained senior positions. In October 2010, General Kittipong Ketkowit (AFAPS class 8), an Eastern Tiger and a close friend of Prawit Wongsuwan, was promoted to become permanent defence secretary.[118] In addition, General Udomdet Sitabutr (AFAPS class 14) of the Eastern Tigers assumed the post of commander of the 1st Army Region. Another Eastern Tiger, General Tirachai Nakwanich (AFAPS class 14), was made commander of the 1st Army Corps. Meanwhile, Queen's Guard and Eastern Tiger General Walit Rojanapakdi (Preecha's AFAPS class 15) remained as commander of the 1st Army Region, 2nd Division (Queen's Guard)—though he was slated to become deputy commander of the 1st Army Region and then move up to 1st Army Region commander. His ascent was to begin as soon as he fully recovered.[119] In the Supreme Command headquarters, Lt. Gen. Thanasak Phatimapakorn (of class 12, the Queen's Guard and the Eastern Tigers) was promoted to be the chief of joint staff. Finally, under Abhisit, retired general Prawit Wongsawan, an Eastern Tiger, continued on as defence minister. The only Queen's Guard casualty in the transfers was General Kanit Sapitak. He was demoted from the post of 1st Army Region commander to become a mere special advisor—punishment for his perceived reluctance to disperse the Red

Shirts in the March–May 2010 protests.[120] But the demotion was meant to be only temporary.

Nevertheless, the Queen's Guard and class 12 were already facing potential challenges from inside the military. Within the Queen's Guard itself, the 2010 sidelining of former Queen's Guard commander and 1st Army Region head Khanit Sapitak (nominal leader of pre-cadet class 13)—occurring simultaneously with intensifying grip on power by class 12—had the potential to increase friction between class 12 and class 13. Perhaps to avoid such a scenario, the 2010 annual reshuffle granted three positions to class 13—amidst rumours that Khanit might be brought back to an advanced posting in 2012. Two of the class 13 posts became deputies to the army chief of staff. The last one—4th Army Region commander—is not a coveted position. Indeed, General Udomchai Thammasarororat, who assumed the post, became responsible for counter-insurgency operations against the Muslim rebels in the far south. Any policy errors he might commit there would damage his future promotion opportunities. Perhaps understandably, class 13 was not pleased with its new status in the army leadership.[121]

Aside from potential problems within the Queen's Guard, the dominant military clique was also confronted with challenges from soldiers outside of the clique. In terms of class allegiances, several members of Thaksin's class 10 had especially opposed the rise of the Queen's Guard given that many of them were demoted following the anti-Thaksin coup of 2006. Approximately fifty military retirees from class 10 joined the pro-Thaksin Pheu Thai Party in 2009, following the lead of retired general Chavalit Yongchaiyudh, who became Pheu Thai's chairman.[122] Moreover, some junior officers and certain high-ranking provincially based officers (perhaps with a rural background) had—along with various retired soldiers—become increasingly disenchanted with what they perceived as a biased promotions process in favour of soldiers who served in class 12 or were in some fashion connected with the Queen's Guard. Such disillusionment contributed to growing military disunity—most visibly illustrated by discord within the armed forces during the Red Shirt demonstrations.[123]

Prayut's appointment to the post of army commander had been expected since he was a trusted arch-royalist associate of Anupong Paochinda. But who exactly was Prayut Chanocha? Born on 21 March 1954 at Suranaree Camp in Nakhon Ratchasima Province at the gateway to Thailand's poor, rural Northeast, Prayut (nickname "Big Tu") was the eldest child of Colonel Praphas Chanocha. His family moved to south-central Prachuab Khiri Khan province because his father was transferred to that province for military reasons. Prayut's family subsequently had to move to Bangkok. He eventually entered and graduated from pre-cadet academy (class 12) in 1972 and Chulachomklao Royal Military Academy (class 23) in 1976. He was among the many young officers who supported and perhaps participated in the military coup of 6 October 1976. Prayut became a member of the 2nd Infantry Battalion, 21st Infantry Regiment (with Anupong Paochinda), commanded then by Colonel Narong-dej Nantaphodej.[124] By 1983, as part of the 21st Infantry Regiment, colonels Prayut and Udomdej Sitabutr led troops against Vietnamese forces along the Thai-Cambodian border at Khao Phanom Pra, Ta Phraya District, Prachin Buri Province. Meanwhile, their commander, Colonel Narong-dej, saw his career take off as he grew closer to Thailand's queen. When Narong-dej suddenly and mysteriously died in the United States in the mid-1980s, Prayut's own career began to improve.[125] In 1987, Prayut became a Royal Guard. In 1990 he was promoted to commander of the 2nd Infantry Battalion, 21st Army Regiment, 2nd Infantry Division. In 1998 he became commander of the 21st Infantry Regiment itself. Then, in 2003, he was promoted to commander of the 2nd Infantry Division. In 2005 he became deputy commander of the 1st Army Region, and the following year he helped lead the coup against Thaksin and became commander of the 1st Army Region.[126] Prayut was Anupong's right-hand man all the way up to the 2006 coup and Anupong's ascension to the post of army commander. Anupong then reciprocated, with the palace's blessing (and expectations), appointing Prayut as his successor in 2010.

Prayut is married to Mrs Naraporn Chanocha, formerly a lecturer at the Prem Purachatra Language Institute at Chulalongkorn University. They have twin daughters, Thanya and Nittha Chanocha. A diagram of the family tree of the Chanocha family is depicted in Figure 13.2.

Immediately following his appointment as army commander, Prayut instituted policies to keep a lid on any signs of political dissent, especially in areas in or close to Bangkok. Indeed, he advised Abhisit, who readily agreed, to extend the Emergency Decree for several more months, perhaps into 2011 (it was rescinded in December 2011). Moreover, on 18 October, the army deployed troops from the 1st Infantry Division, the 2nd Cavalry Division and the Air Defence Command to cover the areas still under the Emergency Decree.

> The soldiers' mission [was] to meet and form relationships with people in the community so that suspicious or subversive behavior [could] be reported more effectively; as a result, intelligence capabilities have improved. [An important reason for this

FIGURE 13.2
Chanocha Family Tree

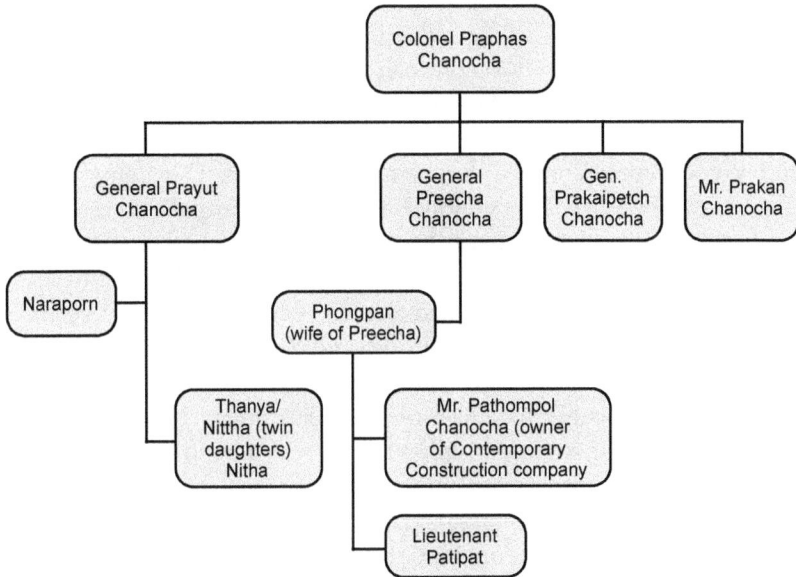

deployment was] the need for new army chief Prayut to consolidate power under his rule.... Like any new leader, Prayut faces opposition, and the Thai armed forces, like the Royal Police Force, contain internal divisions along the lines of the political split between rural and urban Thais. Moreover, corruption and a lack of discipline and competence have also caused problems. Prayut is attempting to firm up his control over the army and demonstrate his strength as chief early to maximize his effectiveness as a leader. Because the underlying causes of Thai political contests will become aggravated in the approach to national elections and the eventual death of the king, the army is preparing for potential instability while attempting to ensure a smooth succession and keep Thaksin and his supporters from acquiring governmental control. The army has strengthened its hand in political affairs in response to these destabilizing trends, and it will continue to do so. Since the 2006 coup it has preferred to exercise influence behind the scenes, but after the 2010 protests and Prayut's rise to the top post there is reason to believe the army's moves may become more overt.[127]

Also on 18 October, Prayut oversaw a further reshuffle, involving 229 intermediate level officers. Notable transfers included that of Colonel Natthawat Akkanibut, son of Chavalit-loyalist General Pat Akkanibut.

Natthawat had been commander of the 1st Infantry Division (King's Guard). He was now moved, however, to a much more minor posting. The reason for this and similar transfers was summed up in the words of an anonymous army source: "Gen Prayut is still concerned about soldiers who are close to the red shirts."[128] Meanwhile, Colonel Kiat Srinaka, who had served as commander of the 2nd Infantry Division (Eastern Tigers) and had shown leadership in fighting against the Red Shirts at the Khok Wua intersection on 10 April 2010, was elevated to become deputy commander of the 2nd Infantry Division (Eastern Tigers). At the same time, Colonel Apirat Kongsompong, commander of the 11th Infantry Regiment (King's Guard), who had demonstrated resolve in dealing with Red Shirt protestors, remained as the head of the regiment even though he had already been there for four years.[129] He was the son of the late coup leader and Suchinda-ally Sunthorn.

Meanwhile, to quell military dissent and shore up unity among the armed forces, Prayut initiated a four-pronged strategy. First, in October 2010, at least four hundred senior officers considered sympathetic to the Red Shirt movement were immediately moved to inactive military positions. Second, Prayut announced that the military would henceforth be proactive in seeking reconciliation among all Thais—both those opposed to and supporting Thaksin. Indeed, Prayut did grudgingly accept lifting the Emergency Decree in December 2010. But his sincerity regarding "accommodation" was called into question given his active role in overseeing the May 2010 repression of the Red Shirts. Third, he initiated a policy of shuffling out watermelons.[130] That is, there would be military reshuffles every six months to weed out any soldier deemed to be insufficiently loyal to Prayut.[131] This policy could be seen in the April 2011 army reshuffle (see below). In addition, just prior to the July 2011 election, Prayut initiated a mid-ranking reshuffle, dispatching hardline officers to take command of positions in the pro-Thaksin north.[132] Fourth, more than any of his recent predecessors (and in unison with defence minister Prawit and police chief Wichean), he trumpeted the need to quash anti-monarchism through legal methods, and he championed the monarchy as a sort of ideology connecting the armed forces together.[133] Fifth, he tried to appease military cliques other than his Queen's Guard faction as a way to keep unity within the armed forces. In particular, Prayut worked to give some higher promotions to the King's Guard Wongthewan faction, which numbered among its ranks his friend and AFAPS 12 classmate Daowapong Ratanasuwan.[134]

The April 2011 mid-year military reshuffle saw Prayut directing appointments for the first time. The exercise, which involved the promotions of 132 officers, was significant because it continued to entrench the power of Prayut's pre-cadet class 12 and the dominance of the Queen's Guard.[135] Perhaps the most important appointment was that of General Walit Rojanapakdee, who had been serving in the post of commander of the 1st Army Region, 2nd Infantry Division (Queen's Guard), to the position of deputy commander, 1st Army Region. Walit had been designated to rise to a more senior position paralleling the elevation of fellow Queen's guardsman Prayut to army chief back in October 2010. But Walit's rise had been delayed owing to his continuing recuperation from severe injuries after the violent clash of 10 April 2010 against Red Shirts. Walit's successor as head of the Queen's Guard was Colonel Pisit Sisithan (AFAPS class 17). Pisit was previously deputy commander of the 1st Infantry Division (Wongthewan). Pisit's promotion was apparently meant to end criticism that senior military officers only promoted Queen's Guard officers.[136] Meanwhile, Queen's guardsman General Kanit Sapitak was promoted from an inactive advisory posting to become chief advisor to the defence minister.[137] Other appointments included that of Prayut's friends General Danai Meechuwet (AFAPS class 12)—who rose from an inactive posting to become rector of Chulachomklao Army Academy (an institution in which Prem took special interest)—and General Chukiat Tiansunthorn (AFAPS class 12), who was promoted from deputy to commander of the Army Reserve Command.

The year 2011 would be the last that Abhisit could remain prime minister since the previous election had taken place in 2007. One of the PM's few accomplishments was to have approved the appointment of Prayut as army commander, which subsequently led to a stronger military hand across the country. But despite opposition from Anupong and Prayut alike, Abhisit had dug in his heels against attempts by the military to dominate security policy. One of the areas where Abhisit opposed army control was in the Deep South where the Malay-Muslim insurgency continued to be a problem. His policy "Politics Leading the Military", a name he had borrowed from the earlier Deep South policy of previous prime minister Prem Tinsulanonda, sought to reinvigorate the elected PM's control over Deep South policy, especially since the military had been unable to resolve the southern "problem". As part of this policy, Abhisit agreed to sit down for renewed peace talks, though these negotiations quickly petered out. The Democrat-led coalition government furthermore created a Special Development Zone for the three provinces, headed by Abhisit himself, and it sought to take the Southern Border Provinces

Administrative Centre (SBPAC) out from under the control of the military, instead making it directly answerable to the prime minister— ostensibly to produce unified policy delivery. The military was earlier criticized for using SBPAC funding for corrupt purposes. But despite enhanced control by civilians over SBPAC, the military still managed to retain supremacy over it, albeit indirectly.[138]

Yet, as the election approached, victory seemed assured for anyone not named Abhisit. The prime minister was identified by too many voters as the person who led the government during the bloody massacre of 19 May 2010. Abhisit's cordial relations with Prayut did not help him either. The image of Prayut, and indeed the military, had been thoroughly tarnished by those killings.

In the run-up to the July 2011 election, Prayut increased the deployment of soldiers throughout the country. ISOC Task Force 315 was formed in late April ostensibly to engage in drug suppression activities. But the pro-Thaksin Pheu Thai Party alleged that 315 was in fact seeking to monitor Red Shirts and sway votes against Pheu Thai— allegations that the military denied.[139] Meanwhile, ISOC officials travelled to the Northeast, heart of the Red Shirts, in the weeks prior to the election, championing the works of King Bhumipol, with the implication that northeastern voters should choose electoral candidates with proven loyalty to the crown—something that Thaksin was deemed not to possess.[140] This paralleled public calls by army chief Prayut that Thai people should elect "good people" rather than choose candidates living overseas who have broken the law and attacked the monarchy. His obvious insinuation was to the Pheu Thai Party. He added that, "If you allow the election [results] to be the same as before, you will not get anything new and you will not see any improvement from this election."[141] With such talk, it was easy to assume that Prayut meant that if the Pheu Thai Party won at the polls, then the armed forces might eventually carry out an overt or silent coup. But then again, throughout the election, the army chief constantly denied that there would be any putsch. Prayut also denied rumours that he had issued a standing order for all soldiers to vote for the anti-Thaksin Democrat Party.[142]

As the 3 July elections neared, Prayut quietened down. And the Pheu Thai prime ministerial candidate, Yingluck Shinawatra, who appeared on the verge of an easy victory over the Democrats, promised that, if elected, Pheu Thai would stay clear of the army's responsibilities. But the superficial cordiality was not to last, especially following an incident where a Pheu Thai candidate and his supporters in Bangkok allegedly waved pistols at a smaller group of soldiers who were part of Task Force 315. A furious Prayut responded to the situation publicly:

> Who do you think you are, threatening officials like that?... If sending two soldiers leads to problems like this, how about sending 50 next time? Let's see if they can lay siege to soldiers again. If 50 doesn't work, it will have to be 100. Will it have to come to that?... If nobody respects the law, what good is the election? How can the country survive if you have your election but outlawed measures are used to pressure [state officials doing their job]?[143]

After coming to office, new prime minister Yingluck placed security affairs and relations with the police and military squarely on the shoulders of two individuals: former CNS member General Kowit Wattana (AFAPS class 6) and former deputy defence chief General Yuthasak Sasiphrapa (Chulachomklao class 8).

Kowit was made deputy prime minister in charge of security. Kowit's amiable ties with the palace—particularly Crown Prince Vajiralongkorn—and the fact that the military was agreeable to his promotion ensured that he might, at least initially, prove successful in his job. Indeed, following pressure from Kowit and Deputy Prime Minister Chalerm Yubamrung, Priewpan Damapong, brother of Thaksin's former wife, Pojaman, was elevated to become police chief, replacing General Wichean Potephosree (Prayut's AFAPS class 12). Wichean was transferred to become secretary-general of Yingluck's National Security Council. Kowit also increased police authority in the far South vis-à-vis the army. In late September, the prime minister placed Kowit in charge of security in the Deep South. He was to head a committee for that purpose. Army chief Prayut would be the deputy chairperson. Under this committee, the civilian-led Southern Border Provinces Administrative Centre and the army-directed ISOC would collaborate in addressing problems of southern violence.[144]

At the same time, pro-Thaksin forces appeared to score a victory at the National Broadcasting and Telecommunications Commission (NBTC). In September 2011, a new NBTC board of eleven commissioners assumed office, six of whom were persons with a military or police background and aligned with Yingluck.[145]

Meanwhile, Yuthasak Sasiphrapa was appointed as defence minister. He was a former Wongthewan army officer and his father had served as commander of the 1st Army Region under generals Thanom and Prapas. Yuthasak was married to Praphas's daughter. Yuthasak was also a confidant of Chavalit Yongchaiyudh and had served as permanent secretary of defence under then prime minister Chavalit. Yuthasak had gone on to serve in the Thaksin administration and had been a member of Thaksin's Thai Rak Thai Party. Perhaps because of his high-level military connections, Yuthasak was never purged from the armed forces following the 2006 coup. Nevertheless, despite his apparent influence among senior military brass, it was apparently understood following Yingluck's election that he would not seek to reduce the military budget or control military reshuffles. The armed forces expected Yingluck to "tread lightly on these two aspects of military affairs and so maintain some equilibrium in civil-military relations".[146] Nevertheless, one major role that Yingluck gave to Yuthasak was to broadly resist the military's political power and prevent senior brass from finding a rationale for intervening in political matters. Yuthasak thus quickly moved to downplay the growing tension along the Thai-Cambodian border, especially where an ancient Khmer temple (Preah Vihear) straddled territory claimed by Thailand and Cambodia. Regarding this conflict, the Thai military had specifically taken a hardline position, while the previous Abhisit government had, at least initially, been more conciliatory. But Prayut and Abhisit were at loggerheads about any negotiations with Cambodia in a third country or any third country observers along the frontier.[147] The election of Yingluck, however, immediately reduced tensions between the two countries and Prayut's military ended its tough stance.

As for reshuffles, Yuthasak had previously proven his mettle with the military when he helped to bring pro-Thaksin officers into senior positions in the armed forces during Thaksin's first term of office. This time around, Yuthasak was assisted by a team of retired military officers from AFAPS classes 9 and 10. A test of his abilities was the 30 September reshuffle of military officers. Under Yingluck, however, times had changed. The new Pheu Thai government had to deal with the 2008 Defence Administration Act. Part of this new regulation stated that any reshuffle of an officer above the rank of general must be vetted by a committee of seven, including the four military service chiefs, the permanent secretary of defence (an active-duty military official), the defence minister, and another official (perhaps the prime minister or a deputy defence minister). So in cases of a united military against elected officials, the armed forces would always triumph because a vote of the seven officials would always end in the military's favour (5–2). But in August 2011 there was a possibility that things would not prove so smooth for Prayut. After all, the supreme commander, General Songkitti Jaggabatara, and navy leader Admiral Kamthorn Phumhiran were from AFAPS class 10. Their votes, along with those of Yuthasak and either the prime minister or an official selected by Yuthasak, could have changed the voting outcome to be 4–3 in their favour.[148]

The military chiefs remained united, however, and Yuthasak failed to make much headway in diminishing the favoured choices of Prayut and the Eastern Tigers. In the end, the military got almost all of its own way. Only the post of permanent secretary of defence went to an officer who was favoured by Pheu Thai. This was General Sathien Permthong-in, whose wife is an Ubon Ratchatani province politician who helped Pheu Thai candidates get elected.[149] Other than this exception, virtually every army, supreme command, air force and defence ministry promotion was unmarked by any preferences from the government, as lobbied by Yuthasak.

Indeed, promotions by the Prayut-led senior military brass centred on linkages based around the unit or class to which Prayut belonged. In terms of unit, the new supreme commander was General Tanasak Patimapakorn, while General Kanit Sapitak maintained his post as Defence Ministry advisor. Both Tanasak and Kanit were members of the Eastern Tigers faction. As for class, Prayut's pre-cadet class 12 faired quite well. Four new senior officials in the Supreme Command were class 12 peers of Prayut, whilst in the air force, the new deputy chief and assistant chief were alumni of class 12. In the army, of the three Five Tigers positions, one new appointment, General Podok Bunnag, became assistant army chief. With army chief Prayut and new deputy army commander Daowapong, this now positioned three alumni of class 12 at the forefront of the army. Another Five Tigers promotion was that of General Sirichai Dittakul (AFAPS class 13), appointed to take the place of Daowapong as new army chief of staff. Sirichai was rumoured to be close to former defence minister (and Eastern Tiger), the retired general Prawit Wongsuwan.[150] Working under Sirichai were two assistant chiefs of staff: General Chatchai Satrikaliya and General Surasak Kanjanarat. Both were AFAPS class 12 friends of Prayut. The final Five Tigers promotion was that of General Thanongsak Apirakyothin (AFAPS class 11), who was elevated from the post of special advisor to become assistant army commander. Thanongsak's promotion was a stopgap one; he was set to retire in 2012 and thus his seat was being kept warm for a more junior general.

Other significant appointments included General Supparat Pattanawisit, who was promoted from deputy to commander of the Special Warfare Division. Supparat is an alumnus of AFAPS class 12, and by placing a loyalist in this slot, Prayut could keep tabs on a unit that had been much more loyal to General Sonthi Boonyaratklin than to Anupong or himself. Meanwhile, General Utis Sunthorn (AFAPS class 14), who had shown distinction fighting the Red Shirts in 2010, was elevated to the post of 1st Army Region Corps commander. He replaced Teerachai Nakwanich (AFAPS class 14), who was promoted to become assistant chief of staff for logistics. General Kampnat Rudit (AFAPS class 16), another individual active in resisting the Red Shirts in 2010, was simultaneously appointed as deputy commander of the 1st Army Region. Furthermore, General Pisit Sisithan (AFAPS class 17) was transferred from commanding the 2nd Division, 1st Army Region (Eastern Tigers) to heading the 1st Division, 1st Army Region (Wongthewan). In his stead, Colonel Teppong Tippayajan (AFAPS class 18), formerly deputy commander of the 2nd Division, was promoted to command it.[151]

By October 2010, most members of AFAPS class 10 had reached the mandatory retirement age of sixty (though a few younger ones graduated in October 2012). Still, these positions were relatively powerless. And besides, by October 2012, all of them had retired. Of the late class 10 retirees, the most important was General Prin Suwannathat. Prin's son and Thaksin's daughter had been married in November 2011, bringing the Suwannathats even closer to the Shinawatras. Thaksin and Yingluck had sought unsuccessfully to have Prin—for his last year of service—be promoted to become army chief of staff, a position that would have given Prin direct control over ISOC. Instead, Prayut made sure that Prin remained sidelined, appointing him as chief of staff officers on defence matters to the prime minister.[152] Meanwhile, class 10 alumnus General Puchong Rattanawan (who was also close to Surayud), head of the National Defence College, was transferred to the lacklustre post of inspector general in the Ministry of Defence. Finally, General Apichart Timsuwan soldiered on as chief of research and development for the Ministry of Defence.[153]

Ultimately, those opposed to Thaksin remained in control of the military, though there were challenges for them. Regarding the army, the October 2011 reshuffle, while extending the power of Prayut's class 12, was also mostly good for class 14. Class 13 did not do so well; many class 13 alumni would be looking at the future of their peer General Kanit Sapitak as a reflection of their own prospects. Classes 15 and 16 were successful in obtaining important although more peripheral army slots.[154]

In her first cabinet reshuffle, which took place in January 2012, Yingluck replaced Yuthasak as defence minister with Thaksin loyalist and longtime friend retired ACM Sukampol Suwannathat, a relative of Prin Suwannathat, chief of staff of Yingluck's active-duty military advisors, who himself retired from the armed forces in October 2012. Like Thaksin, both Sukampol and Prin are from the pro-Thaksin wing of AFAPS class 10, a clique that was increasingly dominating Yingluck's defence policy. Moreover, Sukampol and Prin were Thaksin's chief advisors on military matters. Sukampol is close to Thaksin's ex-wife Pojaman.[155] No favourite of army chief Prayut, Sukampol would have been appointed air force chief if not for the 2006 coup. Instead, he was moved through a series of inactive positions before his retirement in 2011. Sukampol's transfer to head the Ministry of Defence (after having served for six months as minister of transport) represented more of a direct challenge to the armed forces than Sukampol's predecessor, Yuthasak Sasiphrapa, who had been a more acceptable candidate to Prayut. (Yingluck moved Yuthasak to the post of deputy prime minister, succeeding the more royalist-oriented Kowit Wattana, who was removed from the cabinet.) Few retired military officers other than those from the army have become defence ministers. Sukampol represents an exception since he came from the air force. As his role appeared to be to spearhead a harder line for Thaksin against the military, the new defence minister seemed to be looking to expedite amending Article 24 of the 2008 Defence Act so that the prime minister could gain greater control over senior military reshuffles.[156] In fact, in January 2012, Yingluck's government had already threatened to use its majority in the lower house of parliament to modify the Defence Act so that the government would gain more control over military reshuffles.[157] Meanwhile, army chief General Prayut denied any dissatisfaction from himself and the armed forces regarding Sukampol's appointment. He also denied rumours of a coup plan set for April 2012.[158] In the end, the government's threat to change the Defence Act faded away.

But gossip about a putsch had been more than idle chatter. Indeed, it came in response to calls for reform in the *lèse-majesté* law (enshrined under Article 112) of Thailand from a liberal law group—Nitirat. While the pro-Thaksin Pheu Thai Party stood with both the parliamentary opposition and the military in opposing Nitirat's proposals, many right-wing reactionaries and elements in the military were unsure of Pheu Thai's sincerity. On 21 January 2012, retired general Boonlert Kaewprasert, formerly rector of the Armed Forces Academy Preparatory School, publicly warned:

> Article 112 must not be touched, or amended, since it involves the monarchy. The military must take action and not only speak. The monarchy has been insulted a lot over the past seven to eight years.

If this continues too much, the military cannot tolerate it, they will stage a coup definitely.[159]

Almost simultaneously (20 January), *Putchagan* (*MGR Online*)—the newspaper of Sondhi Limthongkul, Yellow Shirt leader of the People's Alliance for Democracy—displayed the following headline: "Sondhi encourages military to cooperate with the people sector to stage a coup and protect the monarchy".[160] Meanwhile, an ABAC Assumption University poll conducted in January 2012 indicated that 81.7 per cent of respondents would not support a coup against Yingluck, while 18.3 per cent would favour a putsch. Only 21.1 per cent stated, however, that they would come out and actually support Yingluck if there was a coup, while 52.7 per cent would not. The remaining 26.2 per cent had no opinion.[161] The growing calls for coups and such polling results did not bode well for civil control in Thailand in 2012.

The 2012 mid-year armed forces reshuffle demonstrated the extent to which Thaksin's harder approach had proved successful. Mid-year appointments are almost always more low-key than annual rotations, and 2012 was no different. Five pre-cadet class 12 loyalists of Prayut were promoted to the position of full general for their final six months in office before mandatory retirement in October and elevated to ceremonial advisory positions. Replacing 3rd Army Region commander Wangthip Wongwai (class 12) was General Channarong Thanarun (class 13), while 2nd Army Region commander General Tawatchai Samutsakorn made way for new commander General Wibul Pongklansanoh (class 13). Ultimately, pre-cadet class 13 was perhaps the most successful in the reshuffle—though with the blessing of Prayut. The only position that appears to have reflected a defeat for Prayut was in the promotion of the 3rd Army Corps commander. Indeed, there had been speculation that Prayut's younger brother Preecha would be promoted to this slot. But because of Preecha's relatively junior status (pre-cadet class 15) a more senior military officer was given the post instead. This was Surachet Chaiyawong (pre-cadet class 14).[162] Surachet was rumoured to be favoured by the Red Shirts.[163] But leaving the 2nd and 3rd Army regions aside, no key changes were made in the much more strategic 1st Army Region. Queen's guardsman General Walit Rojanapakdee (like Preecha, pre-cadet class 15), as deputy commander of the 1st Army Region, was now well-positioned to move even higher. Ultimately, the 2012 mid-year reshuffle reflected continuing Eastern Tigers and Queen's Guard control over the military, as overseen by Prayut, but some small pro-Thaksin inroads had been made into the armed forces at lower levels.

April 2012 also saw the government-controlled Defence Ministry establish the Defence Ministry Operations Command, a new three-level operations centre designed to bring greater military efficiency in support of government security efforts. The first level, for normal conditions, was placed under the supervision of General Nipat Thonglek (pre-cadet class 14). Nipat also served as chief of the Defence Ministry's Office of Policy and Planning. A second level was concerned with natural disasters affecting the general public—supervised by permanent secretary for defence General Sathien Permthongin. Finally, should outbreaks of riots or clashes along the border occur, a third level would be triggered. This tier was supervised by Thaksin-loyalist Defence Minister Sukumpol Suwannatat.[164] While this structure under the Defence Ministry was designed ostensibly to increase military efficiency and improve coordination with the Internal Security Operations Command, it was rumoured to be a device to help discover and thwart any coup attempts.[165]

In 2011–12 there appeared to be an ironic transformation in alliances, with retired coup leader and now elected politician General Sonthi Boonyaratklin (leader of the miniscule Mataphum Party) taking the reins as chair of the lower house National Reconciliation Committee. In April 2012, Sonthi ushered a report through his committee that recommended a blanket amnesty in political cases dating back to 2005 relating to the Thaksin imbroglio. Yet, if such an amnesty was to be enacted, it could lead to a resumption of demonstrations by opponents of Thaksin and possible fighting between pro and anti-Thaksin groups.[166] Such anarchy could give the Prayut-led army an excuse to intervene. In fact, in 2013–14, this is exactly what happened. But in mid-2012, Prayut was trying to dampen any speculation that he would launch a coup. When in April the more sparsely grouped Yellow Shirts movement sought to protest in front of the Army Club, the army commander let it be known that the army would not allow demonstrations on its property. At the same time, Prayut and even Prem seemed to publicly display friendlier ties with Yingluck. Such apparent amity led to suspicions from the Yellow Shirts.[167]

Yet this was not a case of Prayut (or Prem) cowing to Thaksin or fearing dissent in the face of any coup from the ranks of the military. Instead, the army in 2012 appeared to be biding its time.

A crisis for the military soon arose when, in June 2012, it appeared that reconciliation bills and amendments to the 2007 constitution supported by Pheu Thai were on the cusp of being passed by the lower house of parliament. Thereupon, representatives from five anti-Thaksin groups separately petitioned the Constitutional Court for a judicial review of the government-sponsored draft amendments. On 1 June, the Charter Court accepted the petitions and advised parliament to suspend its consideration of the constitutional amendment bill pending the court's decision on its constitutionality.

Red Shirts later rallied in front of the parliament complex in support of the constitutional amendment readings. The country now seemed on the verge of violence, with the possibility either that pro-Thaksin police at parliament might scuffle with Yellow Shirts who might come to demonstrate there or that open fighting might erupt between the Yellow and Red Shirts. With people increasingly awaiting the military's reaction, army chief Prayut quickly ruled out the possibility of a putsch. In early June, however, Red Shirt leaders Jatuporn Prompan and Korkaew Pikulthong separately alleged that a military coup was in the offing. Jatuporn warned that if such a move was attempted, the Red Shirts would violently resist it in what he described as "the last war".[168] Another rumour alleged that the supreme commander, General Thanasak Patimapakorn, rather than Prayut, would lead a coup—a claim that Thanasak flatly denied. Still another rumour had it that Prime Minister Yingluck would be arrested and whisked off to the barracks of the 11th Infantry Regiment, King's Guard, in Bang Khen district of Bangkok, where she would be detained by its commander, Colonel Songwit Noonpakdee, son of retired general Issarapong Noonpakdee.

Although there is no evidence as yet to support these stories, what is known is that in the early morning hours of 1 June, Prayut called a meeting of all the army unit leaders (all generals), followed by another meeting in the afternoon with military colonels. On the same day, Prayut shifted the positions of sixty-seven army colonels. Yingluck and Deputy Prime Minister Yuthasak Sasiprapa telephoned Prayut to ask him what was happening. The army chief replied that the two meetings were nothing exceptional but rather prescheduled get-togethers that occurred every three months. In any case, Defence Minister Sukampol quickly returned to Bangkok from Singapore, where he had been attending a conference.[169] Suspicions among many in the Yingluck government that the military might lead a coup or repress any potentially disruptive Red Shirt demonstrations against the Constitutional Court were dispelled when the court, in early July, returned a verdict that allowed the lower house to proceed with its deliberations for constitutional amendment—although the court insisted on a popular constitutional referendum. Thereupon, Pheu

Thai legislators temporarily placed any lower house vetting of the amendments on the back burner.

But any assumptions that relations between the armed forces and Yingluck's government had somehow become smoother proved to be shortsighted. This owed to continuing investigations by the Department of Special Investigation (DSI) into the 2010 military crackdown that had resulted in at least ninety-two deaths. DSI chief Tharit Pengdit had earlier implied that soldiers had indeed been involved in the crackdown. This prompted army commander Prayut to complain personally to Prime Minister Yingluck that any DSI information about the investigation must remain confidential until the end of court proceedings. Pheu Thai and Red Shirt leaders privately assured Prayut that the military would be spared from prosecution as the Yingluck government's preferred targets would be Abhisit and Suthep Thaugsuban, the former having presided over the country during the 2010 military repression of the Red Shirts and the latter having served as director of the Centre for the Resolution of the Emergency Situation (CRES), which oversaw the quelling of the UDD protests. Pheu Thai's goal was to use the DSI investigations to force the Democrats to support Pheu Thai's proposed "reconciliation" bills.[170] Moreover, the Yingluck government had always been careful not to interfere with the armed forces.

Pheu Thai now stated that all it wanted was for military officials to testify solely against Abhisit and Suthep. But with the DSI continuing to make statements about military complicity in the 2010 repression, Prayut and other soldiers were becoming increasingly tense. The question as to whether the DSI was seeking to implicate military personnel refused to die. And, in reality, Prayut had been the actual leader of the 2010 anti–Red Shirt operation. As such, Pheu Thai might use any DSI investigation of Prayut or other senior army brass to unseat him as army chief and block the rise to high positions of any officers involved in the crackdown. It was rumoured that Prayut, in mid-2012, was seeking to have his confidant, deputy army chief Daowapong Rattanasuwan, become deputy minister for defence for his last year of military service (Daowapong retired on 1 October 2013). Pheu Thai and the UDD also sought to block the ascension of General Walit Rojanapakdi, the injured former commander of the Queen's Guard.[171] Ultimately, the 2012 attempts by Pheu Thai to use both carrots and sticks to cajole the military into throwing blame on the Democrats for the 2010 repression produced unintended negative effects for pro-Thaksin partisans. Whilst the objective had been to use DSI investigations to weaken the armed forces, soldiers became increasingly united against Pheu Thai. In the face of growing fractures between the two sides during mid-2012, Pheu Thai and Prayut's military soon came to a major clash over the 1 October annual military reshuffle.

Any vestige of smooth ties seem to have disappeared by 27 August 2012, when the pro-Thaksin permanent defence minister, General Sathien Permthongin; his deputy, General Chatree Thatti (AFAPS class 14); and the director general of the Secretariat Department of the Office of the Permanent Defence Minister, General Pinpas Sariwat, were temporarily transferred to inactive positions in the defence minister's office. Sukampol Suwannathat stated that he had been forced to issue the transfer order because the three officers had leaked information about the reshuffle. Sathien had only hours before complained aloud that Sukampol was trying to interfere in the annual military reshuffle.

Sathien and the armed forces service chiefs collectively agreed to nominate General Daowapong Rattanasuwan, the deputy army commander, to simultaneously fill this post instead of the army chief of staff, General Sirichai Dittakul, as Sukampol had preferred. Sirichai was a member of pre-cadet class 13, while Daowapong hailed from pre-cadet class 12, the same class as Prayut. Senior officers had never convened the Defence Council to vet appointments outside of the direct active-duty chain of command. Yet the message was clear: "The armed forces [were] ready to confront the government if necessary."[172] The Yingluck government responded by delaying the overall staffing for the centre and reviewing legal provisions related to its formation. Behind the scenes, Sukampol and Sathien were locked in a reshuffle disagreement as Sathien had sought to have permanent deputy defence minister Chatree Thatti succeed him as permanent defence minister upon his retirement on 1 October 2012, while Sukampol (and Thaksin) supported General Thanongsak Apirakyothin for the post.[173] Thanongsak, like Sathien, was a member of AFAPS class 11, while Chatree was a member of the much more junior AFAPS class 14. What is interesting about this case is that both Sathien and Sukampol enjoyed close links with the Pheu Thai Party. Indeed, Sathien is married to Natnicha Permthongin, the Pheu Thai–affiliated mayor of Ubon Ratchathani city, while Sukampol has also been a longtime Thaksin loyalist. At the same time, Sathien's nominee, Chatree, has had close ties to former army commander, prime minister and Pheu Thai bigwig Chavalit Yongchaiyudh. Finally, it has been claimed that Sukampol's preferred candidate, Thanongsak, was also being championed by Yaowapa Wongsawat, sister of Thaksin and wife of former prime minister Somchai Wongsawat. This owed to the fact that Thanongsak's elder sister was married to a member of parliament from Phayao province, an MP belonging to Yaowapha's parliamentary faction.[174] In the immediate aftermath of the transfers, Deputy Prime Minister Yuthasak Sasiprapa publicly stated that Sukampol should explain to the Defence Council about his action. He also advised Sukampol to check Article 25 of the Defence Act, which addressed the vetting of the annual reshuffle by the seven-member military committee.[175]

September saw the release of the final report of the Truth for Reconciliation Commission of Thailand (TRCT) on the deadly political violence of April–May 2010. It put most of the onus on Thaksin, since it declared that he should be the one to compromise.[176]

At this point, Sukampol temporarily appointed the permanent deputy defence minister, Viddhavat Rajatanun, a Yuthasak loyalist, to assume Sathien's post as acting permanent defence minister. Sukampol also ordered Viddhavat to sit in on the seven-member military committee vetting reshuffles. There was, however, a legal question as to whether Viddhavat, as only an acting permanent minister, had the right to attend these committee meetings. Yet, ultimately, no vote was taken on the senior military reshuffles. Rather, the selections were informally made following horse trading between Sukampol and Prayut. In the meantime, Sathien and Chatree appealed to the Administrative Court regarding Sukampol's order transferring them to inactive positions. They asked the court to enjoin the order and consider its legality.[177] If the court ruled in favour of Sathien and Chatree, or even refused to consider their complaint, the move could set a precedent such that a defence minister could transfer a general or even an army or supreme commander to an inactive post with legal impunity. Sukampol's case had been strengthened by the fact that the judge advocate general's office had already scrutinized and approved his decision beforehand. Moreover, as Wassana Nanuam points out, Sukampol's transfer of three top officials was not unprecedented, given that in 2006 the government of appointed prime minister Surayud Chulanont also interfered in military reshuffles.[178] In any case, Surayud was a retired army chief. But Sukampol, a former air force officer and civilian proxy of Thaksin, had less clout. Thus, his transfer of the three top soldiers—along with continuing investigations of the military by the DSI—produced the effect of deepening a rift between an increasingly united military on one side and the Yingluck government on the other. On 13 September, the Administrative Court returned a verdict that supported the transfer of Sathien but blocked that of Chatree. The defence minister immediately appealed this decision and set up a panel to more thoroughly investigate Chatree's alleged disciplinary violations.[179]

Yet Chatree's destiny was eventually meted out in the 1 October military reshuffle: he was transferred to the inactive post of inspector general. Meanwhile, concerns were growing in some quarters that Thaksin was seeking to influence the annual reshuffle list before its approval by his sister, Prime Minister Yingluck. Indeed, in early September 2012, despite denials from Thaksin aides, Defence Minister Sukampol reportedly met with the fugitive former prime minister in London, showing Thaksin a copy of the tentative list before submitting it to Yingluck.[180]

Ultimately, on 19 September, 811 new military appointments were announced for the annual 1 October 2012 military reshuffle. The news came coincidentally on the anniversary of the coup of six years earlier. The horse trading between Sukampol and Prayut produced more positive results for the army chief, although Sukampol had some reasons to be happy. For example, while Prayut had favoured Daowapong for the job of permanent defence minister, in the end, Thanongsak obtained the posting, which he would hold for just a single year until his retirement on 1 October 2013. Meanwhile, Prayut's favourite choice, air force general Prajin Jintong (AFAPS class 13), was appointed to succeed his friend, anti-Thaksin air force chief Ittaphorn Subhawong.[181] Finally, Sukampol ensured that the Defence Ministry was completely staffed with military loyalists. Indeed, he established 210 new senior postings in the ministry and promoted "an unprecedented 300 officers to the rank of general, taking the total number of generals to some 1,600".[182]

The year 2013 began with the Yingluck government seeking to initiate dialogue in Thailand's Deep South with the Barisan Revolusi Nasional (BRN) Malay-Muslim separatist group. Based upon contacts that Thaksin Shinawatra had made with the BRN beginning back in March 2012, on 28 February 2013, representatives of the Thai government and the BRN signed a "General Consensus on Peace Dialogue Process". Yingluck received little cooperation in support of the negotiations from four key actors: the Prayut-led army, the army-dominated ISOC, the National Intelligence Agency, and the Ministry of Foreign Affairs (which was a repository of conservative bureaucrats).[183] In fact, Prayut (and other senior brass) "threw cold water on" (or even tried to sabotage) the talks. However, by June 2013, an informal cessation of hostilities appeared to have finally arrived in the Deep South. The apparent peace was sabotaged with the killing of Muslim cleric Ahama Doroh.[184] Though the identity of the killer was never established, Doroh's death was beneficial in helping the military to begin re-establishing control over policy for Thailand's Deep South.

The 2013 mid-year reshuffle (decided by Prayut with acquiescence from the government) brought another expected boon to the army chief. The most important appointment was that of his own brother, Preecha, as 3rd Army Region commander (replacing General Chanchainarong Thanaroon). In addition, Prayut's loyal aide General Sakol Chuentrakul was appointed as 4th Army Region commander (replacing General Udomchai Thammasaroraj).

On 30 June 2013, Yingluck decided to become minister of defence in addition to being prime minister. Though she did have knowledgeable advisors assisting her,[185] the prime minister had no experience in defence issues, which may have made military officials hopeful that they could gain more control over the Defence Ministry. Nevertheless, army chief Prayut showed only slight elation at her assuming the additional post. He simply said: "The decision [to take on the defence portfolio] lies with the prime minister and the government. We subordinates must respect the decision made by our superiors.... I believe this decision will improve the southern situation because she can make decisions and issue orders immediately."[186] But, as Yingluck sought to achieve more control over the armed forces in her role as defence minister, she succeeded in angering senior brass and it was rumoured that some of them were plotting a coup against her. As a result, she became even more conciliatory towards Prayut. Indeed, she promised both the supreme and army commanders that she would not try to transfer them.

The problems between Yingluck and the senior brass likely related to an audio clip that suddenly surfaced in July 2013 which purportedly contained a conversation between Yingluck's deputy defence minister (former defence minister Yuthasak) and Thaksin Shinawatra. In the clip, Yuthasak promised to facilitate Thaksin's return to Thailand by using the National Security Council to implement an amnesty decree for him while also influencing the coming military reshuffle. According to the plan, Yuthasak would lobby supreme commander General Tanasak as well as the three military chiefs (army, navy and air force) to obtain their support for the amnesty as well as influence the impending military reshuffle. The Defence Council, as chaired by defence minister (and PM) Yingluck, would back the plan. National Security Council approval would represent a shortcut for the plan so it could avoid passing through parliamentary scrutiny, since the Democrat Party would surely oppose it. Two apparent accomplices named in the clip were Tanasak and army chief Prayut. Both vehemently denied their involvement. Prayut said: "I did not see Khun Thaksin.... What's the use of him seeing me? How can I help him? Please believe and trust me."[187] The Thaksin clip "affair" represented a worsening of relations between Yingluck and the military.

The October 2013 military reshuffle was almost entirely another victory for Prayut and Buraphapayak. With Yingluck as defence minister, the only concession to her government was General Nipat Tonglek (pre-cadet class 14), appointed as permanent defence minister. Prayut did not really like Nipat; they had known each other for years.

Meanwhile, anti-government demonstrations were intensifying. In August 2013, a small but evolving group of civilian demonstrators had begun to protest near Government House against purported Pheu Thai malfeasance and any attempts by the government to amnesty Thaksin or the Red Shirts. In parliament, the anti-Thaksin Democrat Party supported the protests. By mid-October 2013, with the National Security Council plan having been discarded, Yingluck's government and the Pheu Thai Party were intensifying efforts to obtain parliamentary approval for constitutional amendments and a "blanket amnesty" for those charged with or convicted of political crimes (including demonstrators, military personnel and politicians). Among those to be amnestied would be Thaksin, but also Abhisit and former deputy prime minister Suthep. On 1 November, the lower house passed the amnesty, though the Senate later rejected it. Anti-Thaksin hardliners in the military, both retired and active-duty, began to call for the ouster of Yingluck. At the same time, Red Shirts were not happy about any amnesty for Abhisit and Suthep. On 21 November, the Constitutional Court ruled that the amendments violated the constitution because they might harm the monarchy and national security. Nevertheless, the court refused to dissolve Pheu Thai, allowing the government to remain in office.

At this point, the People's Democratic Reform Council (PDRC), an ultra-royalist carry-over social organization that had originated with the Yellow Shirts, primarily led by politician Suthep Thugsaban, and formed on 29 November, began to organize demonstrations against the government.[188] Suthep managed to assemble close to 300,000 protestors in Bangkok, who began to occupy state facilities and engage in civil disobedience.[189] In response, the Yingluck government imposed the ISA in Bangkok and neighbouring Nonthaburi province (and parts of Pathum Thani province). A Centre for the Administration of Peace and Order (CAPO) was set up to re-establish order. The police, rather than the army, were assigned to maintain law and order. This is because the police had proven much more loyal to Yingluck than the army, which had ousted Yingluck's brother Thaksin. But Yingluck also began considering replacing the ISA with an Emergency Decree, since such would give more power to the prime minister rather than the army commander for matters of security.

In the meantime, the government had beefed up the police in Bangkok, but it issued orders to police and Red Shirts alike to avoid physical conflict with the protestors. Prayut Chanocha, speaking for the military as a whole, did not rule out a coup.[190] But he publicly stated that the armed forces would remain neutral, neither supporting Yingluck nor the protestors. In actuality, Prayut shared some common ground with Suthep: the former served as army deputy commander and commander when Suthep was deputy prime minister (2009–11). Also, Suthep and Prayut had long worked together against Thaksin. Because of such partisanship, Prayut's apparent "neutrality" in late 2013 amounted to a mere veneer for concealed hostility towards the Yingluck government.[191] Indeed, two powerful individuals surreptitiously working with Suthep against the government were Prayut's longtime allies General Prawit Wongsuwan and General Anupong Paochinda.[192] When the opposition Democrats resigned en masse (many joined the protestors), Yingluck sought to obtain a mandate from the people. She thus dissolved parliament on 9 December 2013 and called new elections, which were set for 2 February 2014. Meanwhile, Prayut publicly reassured her: "We never think about a coup. We have learnt the lessons.... [There] is no place for our country in this world if we have a coup."[193] Only sixteen days later, when Prayut was again asked about a coup, he stated that "the door was neither open nor closed ... anything can happen".[194] The same day, a leaked army document detailed how, if police lost control over the demonstrations, the army would impose a state of emergency or declare martial law and assume power "while acting in a neutral manner".[195]

The year 2013 ended in chaos. Mirroring February–May 2010, mayhem once again enveloped Bangkok and overflowed into provincial Thailand. The army refused to keep order, the police were unable to enforce the law, the Yingluck government remained legally in office, but Suthep's PDRC ran amok.

It was thus not surprising that Thailand entered 2014 with continuing rallies. These were dominated by the PDRC but also included other, smaller anti-government groups. The protests reached their apex across Bangkok in mid-January. Hundreds of thousands of people rampaged through central areas of the city. Several ministries were occupied, and the government seemed powerless to stop them. Demonstrators coalesced around the umbrella PDRC, but also included more specific right-wing groups, including members of the Democrat Party. Aware that a fair general election would likely return Pheu Thai to office to lead the country, the PDRC voiced its support for political reforms without an election. But the election came anyway. Bombings against both the Red Shirts (whose protestors remained on the outskirts of Bangkok) and the PDRC persisted, while the military maintained a publicly neutral posture, though on 29 January, with the election approaching, the army promised to deploy personnel in support of CAPO to ensure security for state officials, patrol anti-government rally sites, offer medical support and help negotiate.[196] But despite these deployments, the violence continued.

Meanwhile, police deployed over 200,000 personnel to secure the 2 February 2014 election. But police security proved insufficient in the districts where the PDRC attempted to disrupt the election.[197] On 21 March, the Constitutional Court, stacked with anti-Thaksin judges, annulled the 2 February election because of a technicality. Following the court decision, the caretaker Yingluck government refused to resign, and the Election Commission prepared to organize a new election.

In mid-February, reports surfaced of armed soldiers providing protection for PDRC rallies—two Navy SEALs arrested at the demonstrations admitted to their involvement.[198] Meanwhile, beginning back in late November 2013, unidentified gunmen—dubbed "popcorn warriors"—periodically exchanged gunfire with pro-Thaksin Red Shirts and police. These guards were reported to have included active-duty and retired navy and army men as well as individuals who had received training from professional soldiers.[199] This covert military involvement further destabilized the political situation, facilitating an environment conducive to a coup. By March 2014, Prayut hinted at resorting to "a special method" to resolve the situation: "I can't promise if there will be another coup or not ... but every coup is meant to end a crisis."[200] Meanwhile, a military reshuffle on 1 April placed royalist Wongthewan army faction officers in key positions of command in Bangkok. The most important appointment of that reshuffle was that of General Apirat Kongsompong, who became commander of the strategically placed 1st Division, King's Guard, 1st Army Region. In this posting, Apirat could work solidly with army commander Prayut and 1st Army Region commander Teerachai to either keep order in Bangkok or overthrow the Yingluck government that was based there.

For her part, Yingluck, attempting to keep her options open, asked Prem to help mediate the conflict. However, Privy Council president Prem (at an event at Prem's house at which neither Yingluck nor the permanent minister of defence, General Nipat Tonglek, were invited) expressed doubt that the clashing sides would listen to him,[201] thus indirectly lending support for a military solution to the political chaos. Yet, compared to the proactive Prayut, and perhaps given his advanced age, Prem's intervention seemed to have become weaker, ceding ground to the army commander.[202] In early May 2014, Yingluck was forced from office by Thailand's Constitutional Court, and a deputy prime minister officially replaced her. Then, in mid-May, with still no coup, Prem voiced to Prayut his preference for expediting a coup.[203] Privy councillors and royalist soldiers feared that the Shinawatra clan and its supporters might exploit the impending royal succession to further their interests. Officers from the Wongthewan faction stood ready to do Prem's bidding and oust the government.[204] When the Senate refused the PDRC's demand to immediately appoint an unelected prime minister, the stage was set for a military intervention. Prayut, for his part, was guided by Prawit to topple the government. Sources allege that the putsch on 22 May 2014 was expected by Thaksin following a prearranged plan led by Prawit and Prayut that did not directly involve Prem or Surayud—though the two privy councillors supported the government takeover.[205]

Those behind the 2 May coup had actually been preparing it since the election of Yingluck Shinawatra in 2011. Nevertheless, the actual planning of the coup apparently began shortly after the October 2013 military reshuffle—paralleling the rise of the chaotic PDRC protests in Bangkok. According to one well-placed and well-connected senior army officer, the plot to overthrow Thailand's democracy in 2013–14 was arranged by nine key individuals. Though Suthep was involved in the plot (to foment pandemonium through the PDRC), a grouping of retired and active-duty senior military officials formulated and implemented the blueprint for the actual putsch. The principal individuals leading this grouping were the "Three Musketeers" of the "Buraphapayak" 2nd Infantry Division army faction—retired former army commanders Prawit Wongsuwan and Anupong Paochinda along with active-duty army commander General Prayut. The three were supported by 1st Army Region commander Teerachai Nakwanich, 3rd Army Region commander General Preecha Chanocha and Special Forces commander General Chalermchai Sittisart. Since the "green light" for the coup was given by Prem and Surayud, the two privy councillors were directly involved in it.[206]

Ultimately, on 20 May, with demonstrations having persisted for half a year leading to scores of deaths and even more injuries, Prayut declared martial law under the authority of the 1914 Martial Law Act. Subsequently, he called the leaders of both sides to a negotiation table at the Army Club, placing himself in the role of mediator.[207] At the meeting, after five hours of talks, General Prayut eventually said to acting caretaker prime minister and minister of justice Chaikasem Nitisiri, "This talk is unending because you all [on the government side] only speak about the law.... The government is insisting that it won't resign, right?" Chaikasem replied: "Not at this moment." General Prayut then told the meeting that, "Sorry, I must seize power."[208] With those words, on the afternoon of 22 May, the army *coup d'etat* occurred, and all the negotiating leaders (on both sides) as well as several other pro-government politicians and demonstrators were detained by the military.

Thus ended Thailand's 2008–14 experience of limited, civilian-led democracy. One wonders why the army even gave a two-day window between the 20 May enactment of martial law and the coup. Analyst Kan Yuanyong of the Siam Intelligence Unit observed:

> Martial law may have been to test the waters, the army gave the opposing camps a chance to negotiate a way out, but I think the endgame was always the military taking over.... The possibility of conflict is now much higher ... Thaksin will fight back.[209]

Though the endgame proved to be the putsch, the question loomed as to how long the military would remain in power and when some sort of political space would again resurface. That question would only be partly answered five years later.

Notes

1. Author's calculations based on 2008 lists of senate members.
2. BBC News, 3 March 2008, "Low Turnout in Thai Senate Vote", http://news.bbc.co.uk/1/hi/world/asia-pacific/7273401.stm.
3. Paul Handley, *The King Never Smiles* (New Haven, CT: Yale University Press, 2006), p. 234.
4. Daniel Ten Kade, "Worries about Thailand's Invisible Hand, *Asia Sentinel*, http://konthaiuk.wordpress.com/2008/01/06/.
5. United States Cable from Ambassador Eric John to United States State Department, "Bio of Thai Prime Minister Samak Sundaravej",

28 January 2008, 08BANGKOK276_a, https://wikileaks.org/plusd/cables/08BANGKOK276_a.html.

6. "Surapong Widely Tipped", *The Nation*, 23 January 2008, http://www.nationmultimedia.com.

7. Saritdet Marukatat, "PM Keeps Armed Forces Happy on his Side", *Bangkok Post*, 22 March 2008, http://bangkokpost.com.

8. "Samak Backs Down", *The Nation*, 31 January 2008, http://www.nationmultimedia.com.

9. Kingdom of Thailand, Internal Security Act, 19 February 2008, http://web.Kritdika.go.th/data/document/ext809/809941_0001.pdf.

10. Kingdom of Thailand, Organization of Ministry of Defence Act, February 2008, Parliament, Library, Bangkok, Thailand.

11. "Defence Minister-Appointee Samak Vows Not to Interfere in Military Reshuffle", *The Nation*, 2 February 2008, http://www.nationmultimedia.com.

12. "Samak Appoints Anupong as ISOC Chief", *The Nation*, 25 March 2008, http://www.nationmultimedia.com.

13. Wassana Nanuam, "Reshuffle Spares Coup Officers", *Bangkok Post*, 21 March 2008, http://www.bangkokpost.com.

14. Saritdet Marukatat, "PM Keeps Armed Forces Happy on his Side", *Bangkok Post,* 22 March 2008, http://bangkokpost.com.

15. Wassana Nanuam, "Samak Unlikely to Upset Top Generals", *Bangkok Post*, 12 March 2008, http://www.bangkokpost.com.

16. "Thaksin Loyalists back in Fold", *The Nation*, 20 March 2008, http://www.nationmultimedia.com.

17. "Anupong Reshuffle 104 Regiment Commanders", *The Nation* 12 April 2008, http://www.nationmultimedia.com.

18. Wassana Nanuam, "Reshuffle Spares Coup Officers", *Bangkok Post*, 21 March 2008, http://www.bangkokpost.com.

19. Wassana Nanuam, "Army in the Middle", *Bangkok Post*, 12 June 2008, http://www.bangkokpost.com.

20. Wassana Nanuam, "First Army Chief Recalled", *Bangkok Post*, 29 May 2008, http://www.bangkokpost.com.

21. "Thailand's New Government Staggers Forward", *Asia Sentinel*, 4 February 2009, http://www.asiasentinel.com/index.php?Itemid=185&id=1703&option=com_content&task=view.

22. "Government House Seized", *Bangkok Post*, 21 June 2008, http://www.bangkokpost.com.

23. Kitti Prasirtsuk, "Thailand in 2008: Crisis Continued", *Asian Survey* 49, no. 1 (January/February 2009): 174–84, https://doi.org/10.1525/as.2009.49.1.174.

24. Wassana Nanuam, "1000 Riot Control Soldiers on Standby", *Bangkok Post*, 28 August 2008, http://www.bangkokpost.com.

25. Wassana Nanuam, "Army Chief Saves Nation from Another Military Coup", *Bangkok Post*, 25 September 2008, http://www.bangkokpost.com.

26. "PM Turns to Military Top Brass for Protection", *Bangkok Post*, 27 August 2008, http://www.bangkokpost.com.

27. "Another Coup is Possible, Says Close Aide to the CNS", *Bangkok Post*, 7 September 2008, http://www.bangkokpost.com.

28. "Army Chief a Reluctant Participant in PM's Ploy to End Crisis", *The Nation*, 2 September 2008, http://www.nationmultimedia.com.

29. US ambassador Eric John, "Thai Army Commanders Tells Ambassador Military Did Not Influence Formation of Government", 30 May 2008, Wikileaks, 08BANGKOK3778, https://wikileaks.org/plusd/cables/08BANGKOK3778_a.html.

30. "Anupong Backs the Idea of a National Government", *The Nation*, 11 September 2008, http://www.nationmultimedia.com; "Anupong Supports Lifting of State of Emergency", *The Nation*, 11 September 2008, http://www.nationmultimedia.com.

31. Ambassador Eric John to US State Department, "Somchai Wongsawat Elected as Thailand's Next Prime Minister, But for How Long?", 17 September 2008, Wikileaks, https://wikileaks.org/plusd/cables/08BANGKOK2810_a.html.

32. "PM Somchai Calls on Prem for Talks", *Bangkok Post*, 2 October 2008, http://www.bangkokpost.com.

33. "As Thai Army Refused to Cooperate with the Elected Thai Government, Unsettled Situation Prevails", *Asian Tribune*, 28 November 2008, http://www.asiantribune.com/?q=node/14442.

34. "Queen Gives Money for Medical Costs after Riot", *Bangkok Post*, 3 October 2008, http://www.bangkokpost.com.

35. "Chalathip Thirasoonthrakul, "Thai Queen Weighs in with Anti-government Protestors", Reuters, 13 October 2008, http://www.reuters.com/article/rbssInvestmentServices/idUSBKK40018720081013.

36. US ambassador Eric John to US State Department, "Palace Insider Tells Ambassador of the King's Opposition to a Coup and to PAD Protests", 6 November 2008, Wikileaks, 08BANGKOK3317_a, https://wikileaks.org/plusd/cables/08BANGKOK3317_a.html.

37. "Anupong, Prem and the Military", *Bangkok Pundit* (blog), 9 October 2008, http://asiancorrespondent.com/19273/anupong-prem-and-the-military/.

38. Ibid.

39. "Anupong-Chavalit Spat", *The Nation*, 11 October 2008, http://www.nationmultimedia.com.

40. Wassana Nanuam, Aekarach Sattaburuth, and Surasak Glahan, "Army Urges Chief to Do More", *Bangkok Post*, 9 October 2008, http://www.bangkokpost.com.

41. Wassana Nanuam, Pradit Ruangdit, and Nattaya Chetchotiros, "PM Must Resign, Says Anupong", *Bangkok Post*, 17 October 2008, http://www.bangkokpost.com.

42. "Coup by TV a Bad Mistake", *Bangkok Post*, 20 October 2008, http://www.bangkokpost.com.

43. Wassana Nanuam, "City Army Leaders Reshuffled", *Bangkok Post*, 20 October 2008, http://www.bangkokpost.com.

44. James Ockey, "Thailand in 2008: Democracy and Street Politics", in *Southeast Asian Affairs 2009*, edited by Daljit Singh (Singapore: Institute of Southeast Asian Studies, 2009), p. 325, https://www.jstor.org/stable/27913390.

45. "Salang Revives Threat", *The Nation*, 19 October 2008, http://www.nationmultimedia.com.

46. Ed Cropley, "Maverick Thai General Does the Hand-Grenade Waltz", Reuters, 21 November 2008.

47. Somroutai Sabsomboon, "Country Seems to be Racing to the Point of No Return", *The Nation*, 21 November 2008, http://www.nationmultimedia.com.

48. "Gen Saprang Back in the Picture, Sort of", *Bangkok Post*, 26 June 2008, http://www.bangkokpost.com.

49. "Pathompong Urges Army Chief to Stage Coup", *The Nation*, 27 November 2008, http://www.nationmultimedia.com.

50. Kitti Prasirtsuk, "Thailand in 2008: Crises Continued", *Asian Survey* 49, no. 1 (January/February 2009): 181.

51. Wassana Nanuam, "No Coup Says Anupong, But Kanit Equivocates", *Bangkok Post*, 26 November 2008, http://www.bangkokpost.com.

52. "Police Chief Ousted", *Bangkok Post*, 29 November 2008, http://www.bangkokpost.com.

53. US ambassador Eric John to US State Department, "Thailand's Democracy Continues to Face Challenges, One Year after Post-Coup Elections", 30 December 2008, Wikileaks, 08BANGKOK3780_a, https://wikileaks.org/plusd/cables/08BANGKOK3780_a.html.

54. "1 Democrat Acquitted, 2 Yellow-Carded", *The Nation*, 29 October 2008, http://www.nationmultimedia.com.

55. "Fortune Looks Favorably on Democrat Party", *Bangkok Post*, 13 December 2008, http://www.bangkokpost.com.

56. According to a party leader who attended these meetings, the formation of an anti-Thaksin coalition came about "due to a request by a senior military figure, who was conveying a message from a man who could not be refuted". That man was likely a senior member of the Privy Council. See "Democrat Govt a Shotgun Wedding?", *The Nation*, 10 December 2008. See also Pravit Rojanaphruk, "Army Comeback through Soft, Silent Coup", *The Nation*, 24 December 2008, http://www.nationmultimedia.com.

57. Pravit Rojanaphruk, "Army Comeback through Soft, Silent Coup", *The Nation*, 24 December 2008, http://www.nationmultimedia.com.

58. Wassana Nanuam, "Government Hopefuls Rendezvous with Anupong 'the Manager'", *Bangkok Post*, 11 December 2008, available at https://teakdoor.com/thailand-and-asia-news/41316-what-anupong-has-been-up.html?s=7d39d60061b6295d9473490f65c8b81d.

59. US ambassador Eric John to US State Department, US Embassy Bangkok, "Thai Political Maneuvering Continues as Vote for PM Approaches", 11 December 2008, Wikileaks, https://wikileaks.org/plusd/cables/08BANGKOK3618_a.html.

60. Pasuk Phongpaichit and Chris Baker, *Thaksin* (Chiang Mai: Silkworm Books, 2009), p. 343.

61. US Embassy, Bangkok, "Thai Army Commanders Tells Ambassador Military Did Not Influence Formation of Government", 30 May 2008, Wikileaks, 08BANGKOK3778, from http://www.dazzlepod.com.

62. "Opposition, Coalition Parties in Thailand to Form Government", Xinhua, 12 December 2008, http://www.chinadaily.com.cn/world/2008-12/07/content_7278895.htm.

63. Wassana Nanuam, "Vote Could Decide Armed Forces Top Jobs", *Bangkok Post*, 22 August 2008, http://www.bangkokpost.com.

64. "Anupong Shows that He's the Boss with Military Reshuffle", *The Nation*, 29 August 2008, http://www.nationmultimedia.com.

65. For indications of such influence, see "Chaovarat Welcomes Prawit with Open Arms", *Matichon*, 27 January 2009, http://www.matichon.co.th/news_detail.php?newsid=1232349203&grpid=03&catid=01.

66. "Prem, Surayud 'behind Coup'", *Bangkok Post*, 28 March 2009, http://www.bangkokpost.com.

67. Wassana Nanuam, "Top Brass Welcome Prawit's Assignment as Defense Minister", *Bangkok Post*, 23 December 2009, http://www.bangkokpost.com.

68. Kornchanok Raksaseri, "Stop Hurting the King: Newin", *The Nation*, 8 April 2009, http://www.nationmultimedia.com.

69. Wassana Nanuam, "Military Routs Last of Thaksin's Supporters", *Bangkok Post*, 28 April 2009, http://www.bangkokpost.com.

70. "PM Security Beefed Up after Riots", *Bangkok Post*, 23 April 2009, http://www.bangkokpost.com.

71. Official sources cited only two dead, killed by the Red Shirts. See *The Nation*, 14 April 2009. But the Red Shirts themselves stated that the military had killed up to eight demonstrators. See *Bangkok Pundit*, 13 April 2009.

72. The ISA law was invoked on 29–31 August, 18–22 September, 15–25 October and 15 November–1 December 2009. See *The Nation*, 25 August, 15 September and 1 December 2009.

73. Shawn Crispin, "My Friend is my Enemy in Thailand", *Asia Times Online*, 7 May 2009, http://www.atimes.com.

74. Ibid.

75. Wassana Nanuam, "Anupong Rewards his Coup Allies", *Bangkok Post*, 19 June 2009, http://www.bangkokpost.com.

76. US ambassador Eric John to US State Department, "Southern Thailand: Enduring Violence and the Way Forward", 12 August 2009, Wikileaks, 09BANGKOK1980_a, https://wikileaks.org/plusd/cables/09BANGKOK1980_a.html.

77. Hassaya Chartmontree, "NACC Indicts Somchai, Chavalit over Oct 7 Bloodshed", *The Nation*, 17 March 2009, http://www.nationmultimedia.com.

78. "Somchai, Chavalit and Patcharawat to Face Criminal Charges", *The Nation*, 7 September 2009, http://www.nationmultimedia.com.

79. Chairat Charoensin-o-larn, "Thailand in 2009: Unusual Politics Becomes Usual", in *Southeast Asian Affairs 2010*, edited by Daljit Singh (Singapore: Institute of Southeast Asian Affairs, 2010), p. 317, https://www.jstor.org/stable/41418572.

80. Ibid., p. 324.

81. Other key postings in this reshuffle were bestowed mostly upon generals deemed close to Anupong (those AFAPS 10 classmates close to him) or Prayut (his AFAPS 12 classmates), or to those with shared unit loyalties through the Queen's Guard. Notably, Queen's guardsman General Kanit Sapitak remained in the strategic post of 1st Army Region chief. See US ambassador Eric John to US State Department, "Thailand: Circles of Influence inside the Institution of the Monarchy in King Bhumipol's Twilight", 23 November 2009, Wikileaks, 09BANGKOK2967_a, https://wikileaks.org/plusd/cables/09BANGKOK2967_a.html.

82. Chairat, "Thailand in 2009", p. 323.

83. "Pheu Thai Welcomes New Members", *Bangkok Post*, 20 October 2010, http://www.bangkokpost.com

84. "Kalam: Bidtthaemailap" [Column: Closed but Not Out of Sight]: Special, *Matichon Daily*, 17 October 2009, http://www.matichon.co.th.

85. Chirmsak Pinthong, "เรากำลังอยู่ในยุค «สงครามกลางเมือง!»" [We are in the Period of Civil War!], *Naeowna*, 28 December 2009, http://www.naewna.com/news.asp?ID=193202.

86. "Pheu Thai Blows Whistle on Silent Coup Plot", *The Nation*, 17 August 2009, http://www.nationmultimedia.com.

87. "A Current of Displeasure Runs through Rank and File", *Bangkok Post*, 28 January 2010, http://www.bangkokpost.com.

88. There have, however, been doubts as to whether the attack actually occurred. See "Updated: Was There a Grenade Attack?", *Political Prisoners in Thailand* (blog), 23 January 2010, http://thaipoliticalprisoners.wordpress.com/2010/01/23/nwas-there-a-grenade-attack/.

89. Martin Petty, "Are Cracks Appearing in Thailand's Military?", Reuters, 27 January 2010, http://uk.reuters.com/article/idUKTRE60Q1SY20100127.

90. Avudh Panananda, "Anupong's Army: If There Is a Coup, It Can Only Go ahead with Army Chief Anupong's Blessing", *The Nation*, 8 February 2010, http://seasupply1.blogspot.com/2010/02/anupongs-army.html.

91. Somroutai Sapsomboon, "Another Leadership Test for Abhisit", *The Nation*, 10 February 2010.

92. Wassana Nanuam, "Anupong, Prayut, Piroon, Wit, Theerawat", *Bangkok Post*, 3 February 2010, http://www.bangkokpost.com.

93. Prateepchaikul, Veera, "Has Thaksin–Hun Sen Relationship Turned Sour?", *Bangkok Post*, 5 April 2010, http://www.bangkokpost.com.

94. The Abhisit government simultaneously authorized the Internal Security Act in Bangkok and several provinces beginning 12 March and promised to extend it if Abhisit-UDD negotiations proved fruitless. See "Army Base Targeted", *The Nation*, 15 March 2010, http://www.nationmultimedia.com; "Cabinet Likely to Extend ISA", *Bangkok Post*, 22 March 2010, http://www.bangkokpost.com.

95. "Grenades Fired into 11th Infantry Regiment", *Bangkok Post*, 28 March 2010, http://www.bangkokpost.com.

96. Wassayos Ngamkham, "Army Calls Shots on House Dissolution", *Bangkok Post*, 31 March 2010, http://www.bangkokpost.com.

97. "Mid-year Reshuffle Involves 79 Positions", *Daily News*, 2 April 2010, http://www.dailynews.co.th/newstartpage/index.cfm?page=content&categoryId=8&contentID=57673; "Yay Glang Pee PoTahan 79 Damnaeng" [Mid-year reshuffle involves 79 positions], *Daily News* (Bangkok), 2 April 2010.

98. Wassana Nanuam, "Anupong 'Steels the Troops'", Bangkok *Post*, 2 April 2010, http://www.bangkokpost.com.

99. "Low Key Reshuffle of 79 Military Positions", *The Nation*, 2 April 2010, http://www.nationmultimedia.com.

100. "Government Invites Forces Wish List", *Bangkok Post*, 23 March 2010, http://www.bangkokpost.com.

101. Wassana Nanuam, "Military Shopping List Grows", *Bangkok Post*, 24 July 2010, http://www.bangkokpost.com.

102. At the time, Colonel Romklao was the deputy chief of staff of the 2nd Battalion of the 21st Regiment, Queen's Guard.

103. Also severely wounded was Lt. Col. Kriangsak Nanda-photidej, half-brother of the late Colonel Narongdej Nanda-photidej, who had been close to the Queen.

104. John Cole and Steve Sciaccitano, "Machinations behind Thai Military Movements", *Asia Times*, 6 October 2011, http://www.atimes.com/atimes/Southeast_Asia/MJ06Ae01.html.

105. BBC Monitoring Asia Pacific, "Thai Police Officer Said Connected to Grenades Haul Arrested", 29 April 2010, http://seasupply1.blogspot.com/2010/04/ittiporn-suphawong.html.

106. Freelander (pseudonyum), "The Deep Political Crisis within the Royal Thai Army Officer Corps", *New Mandala* (blog), Australian

National University, 27 April 2010, http://asiapacific.anu.edu.au/newmandala/2010/04/27/the-deep-political-crisis-within-the-royal-thai-army-officer-corps/; Personal interview with anonymous mid-ranking naval officer, 7 June 2010; Shawn Crispin, "Abhisit's Democratic Choice", *Asia Times*, 12 June 2010, http://www.atimes.com/atimes/Southeast_Asia/LF12Ae01.html.

107. Denis Gray, "Anger Rises against Red Shirt Protests in Bangkok", *Seattle Times*, 21 April 2010, http://seattletimes.nwsource.com/html/nationworld/2011658676_apasthailandpolitics.html.

108. Shawn Crispin, "Abhisit's Democratic Choice", *Asia Times*, 12 June 2010, http://www.atimes.com/atimes/Southeast_Asia/LF12Ae01.html.

109. US ambassador Eric John to US State Department, "Thailand: Ambassador Engages Privy Council Chair Prem, Other 'Establishment' Figures on the Year Ahead", 25 January 2010, Wikileaks, "10BANGKOK192_a, https://wikileaks.org/plusd/cables/10BANGKOK192_a.html.

110. Hathaikan Treesuwan, "10 ปีสลายการชุมนุมคนเสื้อแดง : มองเมษา–พฤษภา 53 ผ่าน วาทกรรม 'จำไม่ลงม'" [10 years after dissolving the red shirt rally: Looking at April–May 2010 through the discourse of "I can't remember"], BBC Thailand, 11 May 2020. See also รำลึก 12 ปี ผู้เสียชีวิตจากเหตุสลายชุมนุมปี'53 และ ความยุติธรรมที่ยังดำมืด [12 years of commemoration of those who lost their lives in the '10 rally crackdown and the darkness of justice], *Prachatai*, 19 May 2022, https://prachatai.com/journal/2022/05/98676.

111. Nirmal Ghosh, "Abhisit Urges Thais to Join Hands 'to Rebuild Home'", *Straits Times*, 11 June 2010, http://www.asianewsnet.net/home/news.php?id=12456&sec=1.

112. Weekend Nation Editorial Office, เขาชื่อตู่ จากทหารเสือสู่ทำเนียบรัฐบาล [His Name is "Tu": From the musketeers to the Government House] (Bangkok: Nation Books, 2014), pp. 37–39.

113. Paul Chambers and Napisa Waitoolkiat, "The Resilience of Monarchised Military in Thailand", *Journal of Contemporary Asia* 46, no. 3 (2016): 436, https://doi.org/10.1080/00472336.2016.1161060.

114. Other key members include General Kampanat Ruddit, commander of the 1st Infantry Division, and General Paiboon Khumchaya, deputy commander of the 1st Army Region. See Avudh Panananda, "Is Prayut the Best Choice amid Signs of Army Rivalry?", *The Nation*, 8 June 2010, http://www.nationmultimedia.com.

115. Pracha Burapawiti, "2010 Military Reshuffle List Approved", *Krungtep Turakit* [Bangkok Biznews], 6 August 2010, http://www.bangkokbiznews.com.

116. Centre for Intelligence, "Thai Intel: Will the Last Ditch Effort Save the Thai Military", news study, http://tavivootuniverse.wordpress.com/2010/08/20/thai-intel-will-the-last-ditch-effort-save-the-thai-military/.

117. Wassana Nanuam, "Fortune Comes Knocking on Class 12 Door", *Bangkok Post*, 12 August 2010, http://www.bangkokpost.com.

118. Wassana Nanuam, "Two Key Units Tighten Grip on Armed Forces", *Bangkok Post*, 31 July 2010, http://www.bangkokpost.com.

119. Wassana Nanuam, "Red Shirts Remain Army's Priority, the South Can Wait", *Bangkok Post*, 21 October 2010, http://www.bangkokpost.com.

120. Wassana Nanuam, "Prayut Says Army Must Take Lead Role", *Bangkok Post*, 3 September 2010, http://www.bangkokpost.com.

121. Paul Chambers, "The Challenges for Thailand's Arch-Royalist Military", *New Mandala* (blog), 9 June 2010, http://asiapacific.anu.edu.au/newmandala/2010/06/09/the-challenges-for-thailand%E2%80%99s-arch-royalist-military/.

122. "The Militarization of Pheu Thai", *Asia Correspondent* (blog), 21 October 2009, http://asiancorrespondent.com/bangkok-pundit-blog/2009/10/militarization-of-puea-thai.html.

123. Personal interview with anonymous mid-ranking naval officer, 7 June 2010, Karlsrühe, Germany.

124. See Wassana Nanuam, เส้นทางพยัคฆ์ประยุทธ์ จันทร์โอชา จากทหารเสือสู่หลังเสือ [Phayak Prayut Chanocha's path from tiger soldier to tiger's back] (Bangkok: Matichon Publishing House, 2014).

125. Personal interview with anonymous senior military official, 30 December 2021.

126. Wassana Nanuam, "Prayut's Tactical Transfers Pave Way for Long Tenure", *Bangkok Post*, 11 September 2014, https://www.bangkokpost.com/opinion/opinion/431619/Prayut-tactical-transfers-pave-way-for-long-tenure.

127. Mike Marchio, Stratfor, "Military Deployment in the Thai Capital", 19 October 2010, Wikileaks (The Global Intelligence Files), https://wikileaks.org/gifiles/docs/12/1278172_re-fwd-military-deployment-in-the-thai-capital-.html.

128. Wassana Nanuam, "Army Chief Takes Aim at 'Red' Officers", *Bangkok Post*, 19 October 2010, http://www.bangkokpost.com.

129. Ibid.

130. Wassana Nanuam, "Chief of Hawks Starts Tenure as Reconciliatory Dove", *Bangkok Post*, 7 October 2010, http://www.bangkokpost.com.

131. Wassana Nanuam, "Red Shirts Remain Army's Priority, the South Can Wait", *Bangkok Post*, 21 October 2010, http://www.bangkokpost.com.

132. Marwaan Macan-Markar, "Thai Elections and Role of Powerful Military", *Brunei Times*, 18 May 2011, http://bruneitimes.com.

133. Pravit Rojanaphruk, "Burning Issue: Anti-monarchist Branding Simplistic", *The Nation*, 4 November 2010, http://www.nationmultimedia.com.

134. Centre for Intelligence, "Thai Intel: Will the Last Ditch".

135. Wassana Nanuam, "Mid-year Military Reshuffle Announced", *Bangkok Post*, 25 March 2011, http://www.bangkokpost.com.

136. "Second Infantry Dominates Limited Military Reshuffle", *Bangkok Post*, 26 March 2011, http://www.bangkokpost.com.

137. "Midyear Reshuffle", *The Nation*, 26 March 2011, http://www. bangkokpost.com.

138. Paul Chambers and Napisa Waitoolkiat, "The Role of Security Forces in Thailand's Deep South Counter-Insurgency", in "Conflict in the Deep South of Thailand: Never-ending Stalemate?", edited by Paul Chambers, Srisompob Jitpiromsri, and Napisa Waitoolkiat, special issue, *Asian International Studies Review* 20, no. 1 (2019): 59–60, http://www.asianisr.org/sub/archives_view.asp?mode=&restring=archives.asp%253Fxsearch%253D0%253D%253Dpage%253D1&idx=225&page=1&xyear=&xvol=&xno=&xsearch=1&cn_search=.

139. "Task Force 315 Not Linked to Politics: Army Spokesman", *The Nation*, 30 May 2011, http://www.nationmultimedia.com.

140. Rachel O'Brien, "Army Hovers over Tense Thai Election", Agence France-Presse, 25 June 2011.

141. "Gen Prayut Urges Voters to Back the 'Good People'", *Bangkok Post*, 15 July 2011, http://www.bangkokpost.com.

142. Panya Thiewsangan, "Politicians Warned Not to Involve Army to Sway Votes", *The Nation*, 4 June 2011, http://www.nationmultimedia.com.

143. "Prayut Warns Pheu Thai", *The Nation*, 10 June 2011, http://www. nationmultimedia.com.

144. "Yingluck Fine-Tunes Security Policies for Deep South", *The Nation*, 23 September 2011, http://www.nationmultimedia.com.

145. Nattaya Chetchotiros, "NBTC Line-Up Shows Clout of Yingluck Government", *Bangkok Post*, 8 September 2011, http://www.bangkokpost. com.

146. Catharin Dalpino, "Thailand in 2011: High Tides and Political Tensions", *Asian Survey* 52, no. 1 (January/February 2012): 198, https://www.jstor. org/stable/10.1525/as.2012.52.1.195.

147. Piyanart Srivalo and Nutida Puangthong, "Military Opposes Border Talks in Cambodia", 25 March 2011, http://www.bangkokpost.com.

148. Wassana Nanuam, "Reshuffle Tests Ties between Minister and Army Chief", *Bangkok Post*, 25 August 2011, http://www.bangkokpost.com.

149. John Cole and Sciaccitano Steve, "Machinations behind Thai Military Movements", *Asia Times*, 6 October 2011, http://www.atimes.com/atimes/Southeast_Asia/MJ06Ae01.html.

150. "584 Officer Reshuffle List", *Thai Post*, 15 October 2011, http://www. thaipost.net/news/011011/45889.

151. "Royal Endorsement of Military Reshuffle—Class 12 Favored", *Daily News*, 1 October 2011, http://www.dailynews.co.th/newstartpage/index. cfm?page=content&categoryID=8&contentID=166867.

152. Wassana Nanuam, "Big Changes Ahead", *Post Today*, 18 January 2012, http://www.posttoday.com.

153. John Cole and Sciaccitano Steve, "Machinations behind Thai Military Movements", *Asia Times*, 6 October 2011, http://www.atimes.com/atimes/Southeast_Asia/MJ06Ae01.html.

154. To keep stability and balance among military factions, Prayut would ultimately seek to create a hierarchy of army support with class 12 on top followed by class 14 then classes 15 and 16. Officers from classes 10 and 11 were close to retirement, whilst soldiers that graduated after class 16 were generally too junior to matter. If pro-Thaksin politicians such as Yingluck Shinawatra and Yuthasak Sasiphrapa were searching for new active-duty army friends in high places that might have been sympathetic to their cause, they might have searched out pre-cadet classes 11 or 13. Meanwhile, the air force looked set to be headed by class 12's Srichao in the 2012 annual reshuffle. As such, keeping the air corps intimate with the army seemed to be a reasonable possibility. Only in the navy were senior appointees not dominated by class 12. This reflected the navy's age-old antipathy with the army and also the fact that it might be more supportive of a pro-Thaksin government.

155. Wassana Nanuam, "Big Changes Ahead", *Post Today*, 18 January 2012, http://www.posttoday.com.

156. Saritdet Marukatat, "Thaksin's Stealth Fighter Ready to Hit Hard", *Bangkok Post*, 22 January 2012, http://www.bangkokpost.com.

157. Paul Chambers, "Thailand: Camouflaged Khakistocracy in Civil–Military Relations", Oxford Encyclopedia of Military in Politics, 28 June 2021, p. 15, https://doi.org/10.1093/acrefore/9780190228637.013.1859.

158. "Army Chief Denies Potential Conflict with New Defense Minister", *Bangkok Post*, 20 January 2012, http://www.bangkokpost.com.

159. "Worajet Pakeerat Reveals 'I Mobilized the Movement to Honor my Ananda Mahidol Scholarship'", *Matichon Subsabda*, vol. 32, 7 January – 2 February 2012, p. 13.

160. "Sondhi Encourages Military to Cooperate with the People Sector to Stage a Coup and Protect the Monarchy", *MGR Online* (ASTV), 20 January 2012, http://mgr.manager.co.th/Politics/ViewNews.aspx?NewsID=9550000009019.

161. "Coups Are Thus Not in the Past", *Matichon Subsabda*, vol. 32, 7 January – 2 February 2012, p. 21.

162. "The Reshuffle of 127 Positions", *Thairath*, 28 March 2012, m.thairath.co.th/content/pol/249012.

163. Wassana Nanuam, "Army Reshuffle is Left Unchanged by Premier", *Bangkok Post*, 17 March 2012, http://www.bangkokpost.com.

164. "Defence Operations Centre Launched", *Bangkok Post*, 20 April 2012, http://www.bangkokpost.com.

165. Wassana Nanuam, "Army Chief Cagey in Maintaining Neutrality", *Bangkok Post*, 22 April 2011, http://www.bangkokpost.com.

166. "Sonthi's Efforts to Do Right May Backfire", *Bangkok Post*, 2 April 2012, http://www.bangkokpost.com.

167. Chairat Charoensin-o-larn, "Thailand in 2012: A Year of Truth, Reconciliation, and Continued Divide", in *Southeast Asian Affairs 2013*, edited by Daljit Singh (Singapore: Institute of Southeast Asian Studies, 2013), p. 292, https://www.jstor.org/stable/23471150.

168. Wassana Nanuam, "Rumors of a Coup Are Greatly Exaggerated", *Bangkok Post*, 6 June 2012, http://bangkokpost.com.

169. Ibid.

170. Wassana Nanuam, "DSI Probe Frustrates Army Brass: Prayut Met Yingluck to Express Concerns", *Bangkok Post*, 21 August 2012, http://www.bangkokpost.com.

171. Ibid.

172. Avudh Panananda, "Thai Government Ties with Army Strained by Legal Ploy", *The Nation*, 27 August 2012, http://www.nationmultimedia.com.

173. "Sukampol Defends Actions", *Bangkok Post*, 28 August 2012, http://www.bangkokpost.com.

174. Wassana Nanuam, "Sukampol Seeks to End Sathien Row", *Bangkok Post*, 27 August 2012, http://www.bangokpost.com.

175. "Check the Facts First: Yutthasak", *The Nation*, 30 August 2012, http://www.nationmultimedia.com.

176. Chairat, "Thailand in 2012", p. 292.

177. "Reshuffle List on Way to Yingluck this Week", *Bangkok Post*, 7 September 2012, http://www.bangkokpost.com.

178. Wassana Nanuam, "Defense Rift Casts Army in Bad Light", *Bangkok Post*, 6 September 2012, http://www.bangkokpost.com.

179. Wassana Nanuam, "Sukampol Wants Leak Probe", *Bangkok Post*, 15 September 2012, http://www.bangkokpost.com.

180. Wassana Nanuam, "Sukampol Hits Back in Transfer Row", *Bangkok Post*, 10 September 2012, http://www.bangkokpost.com.

181. Pheu Thai had originally sought to prepare the groundwork for compelling Prayut, in 2013, to become supreme commander of the armed forces, a powerless position, replacing General Thanasak Patimapakorn, who was set to retire that year. To achieve this goal, Sukampol sought (unsuccessfully) to force Prayut to reveal his preferred lineup for the army's top echelons. The Yingluck government was seeking to have General Sirichai Dittakul, army chief of staff (AFAPS class 13), replace Prayut as army commander in 2013. Since his appointment in 2011, Sirichai had shown signs of cooperation with Sukampol and Pheu Thai. The latter thus favoured Sirichai's rise to replace Prayut. But Sukampol's row with Sathien and Chatree gave Prayut a chance to exploit the fissures between the defence minister and the permanent minister of defence. Moreover, Sukampol needed Prayut's support for his decision to transfer Sathien and Chatree to save face against the two officers. But Prayut's support came at a cost. Sirichai was demoted to the post of army assistant commander. At the same time, Prayut reluctantly accepted the promotion of the pro-Thaksin Jiradej Mokkasamit (AFAPS class 13) from the

post of deputy army chief of staff to become the other assistant army commander. The posting of Sirichai and Jiradej in "assistant" positions was insignificant, however, since the army commander and his allies had managed to keep control over the other three Tigers positions: Prayut and Daowapong remained in their posts as army commander and deputy army commander, respectively, while the army chief got his wish to have General Udomdej Sitabutr (AFAPS class 14)—a Queen's guardsman and commander of the strategic 1st Army Region—promoted to take Sirichai's place as army chief of staff. See Wassana Nanuam, "Defense Reshuffle Finalized", *Bangkok Post*, 5 September 2012, http://www.bangkokpost.com; Avudh Panananda, "Fight over Leadership of the Army Backfired", *The Nation*, 11 September 2012, http://www.nationmultimedia.com.

182. James Ockey, "Thailand in 2012: Reconciling a New Normal", *Asian Survey* 53, no. 1 (January/February 2013): 129, https://www.jstor.org/stable/10.1525/as.2013.53.1.126.

183. Paul Chambers and Napisa Waitoolkiat, "Thailand's Security Sector 'Deform' and 'Reform'", Peace Research Institute Frankfurt, working paper, February 2021, p. 9, https://www.ssoar.info/ssoar/bitstream/handle/document/73454/ssoar-2021-chambers_et_al-Thailands_Security_Sector_Deform_and.pdf?sequence=1&isAllowed=y&lnkname=ssoar-2021-chambers_et_al-Thailands_Security_Sector_Deform_and.pdf.

184. Chambers and Napisa, "The Role of Security", p. 60.

185. Former defence minister and retired general Yuthasak Sasiprapha began serving as deputy defence minister. Other advisors included Lt. Gen. Dithaporn Sasamit, former ISOC spokesman General Witawat Ratchatanan, and former deputy permanent secretary for defence and Thaksin loyalist General Prin Suwannathat.

186. "Prayut Backs Yingluck as Defence Minister", *Bangkok Post*, 3 July 2013, https://www.bangkokpost.com/thailand/politics/358152/army-endorses-pm-defence-role.

187. Wassana Nanuam, "Surviving the 'Curse' of the Defense Ministry", *Bangkok Post*, 18 July 2013, https://www.bangkokpost.com/opinion/opinion/360383/surviving-the-curse-of-the-defence-ministry.

188. Anchalee Phairirak, Pattharachai Phataraphon, and Sornsamon Buajampa, *The Power of Change*: กำนันสุเทพ เทือกส [Kamnan Suthep Thaugsuban] (Bangkok: Lips, 2014).

189. James Ockey, "Thailand in 2013: The Politics of Reconciliation", *Asian Survey* 54, no. 1 (January/February 2014): 45, https://www.jstor.org/stable/10.1525/as.2014.54.1.39.

190. Ibid. p. 46.

191. Paul Chambers, "Mediating the Mayhem: The Military and Thailand's Slide toward Pandemonium", *E-International Relations*, 27 February 2014, https://www.e-ir.info/2014/02/27/mediating-the-mayhem-the-military-and-thailands-slide-toward-pandemonium/.

192. Jason Szep and Amy Sawitta Lefevre, "Powerful Forces Revealed behind Thai Protest Movement", Reuters, 13 December 2013, https://www.reuters.com/article/us-thailand-protest-military-idUSBRE9BC0PB20131213.

193. Wassana Nanuam 2013, "'Silent' Military Coup Beats Having a Real One", *Bangkok Post*, 12 December 2013, https://www.bangkokpost.com/opinion/opinion/384364/silent-military-coup-beats-having-a-real-one.

194. Amy Sawitta Lefevre and Aubrey Belford, "Option B: The Blueprint for Thailand's Coup", 30 May 2014, https://www.reuters.com/article/us-thailand-politics-specialreport-idUSKBN0EA00B20140530.

195. Ibid.

196. Wassana Nanuam, "Army Boosts Support for CMPO, Cites Intensification of Violence", 30 January 2014, https://www.bangkokpost.com/thailand/politics/392276/army-boosts-support-for-cmpo-cites-intensification-of-violence.

197. Duncan McCargo, "The Trouble with Magic Swords: Thailand in 2014", in *Southeast Asian Affairs 2015*, edited by Daljit Singh (Singapore: Institute of Southeast Asian Affairs, 2015), pp. 342–43, https://www.jstor.org/stable/44112813.

198. Wassana Nanuam and online reporters, "Two PDRC Guard Seals Probed", *Bangkok Post*, 26 February 2014, https://www.bangkokpost.com/thailand/politics/397142/two-pdrc-guard-seals-to-be-investigated.

199. Jim Pollard, "Who Are Thailand's Popcorn Warriors?", Andalou Agency, 25 February 2014, https://www.aa.com.tr/en/world/who-are-thailands-popcorn-warriors/179679.

200. "City Shutdown to End as Army Chief Hints of Special Method", *Bangkok Post*, 1 March 2014, https://www.bangkokpost.com/learning/advanced/397649/ciy-shutdown-to-end-as-army-chief-hints-of-special-method.

201. Wassana Nanuam, "Prem Doubts Proposed Mediator Role", *Bangkok Post*, 10 April 2014, https://www.bangkokpost.com/thailand/politics/404363/prem-doubts-he-would-be-accepted-as-mediator.

202. Although Prem had long succeeded in connecting himself to the monarchized military, other linkages between the palace and the armed forces increasingly asserted themselves. The king and queen were both infirm, and Prem was aged ninety-three in late 2013. In addition, as succession approached, Crown Prince Vajiralongkorn took more interest in the military. In November 2013, the Defence Act was amended to add a Royal Administrative Security Unit (RASU) to the Defence Council (Royal Act 2013). The RASU was commanded by Crown Prince Vajiralongkorn. In April 2014, the Rachawallop Infantry Unit 904—also under the then-prince—was expanded.

203. Interview with anonymous source, 19 February 2015, Bangkok.

204. Chambers and Napisa, "The Resilience", p. 436.

205. Interviews conducted in Bangkok with an anonymous Chulalongkorn University professor, 19 February 2015, and with an anonymous army

general who was a member of the General State Commission, 18 February 2015.

206. Personal interview with anonymous senior army officer, 15 January 2023.

207. Wassana Nanuam, เส้นทางพยัคฆ์ประยุทธ์ จันทร์โอชา [Prayut Chanocha's path from tiger soldier to tiger's back] (Bangkok: Matichon Publishing House, 2014).

208. เผยเบื้องหลังระทึกยึดอำนาจ [Background of coup during the meeting], *Matichon*, 23 May 2014, https://web.archive.org/web/20140524022607/http://m. matichon.co.th/readnews.php?newsid=1400823069.

209. Quoted in Amy Sawitta Lefevre, "Thai Army Takes Power in Coup after Talks between Rivals Fail", Reuters, 22 May 2014, https://www.reuters. com/article/thailand-protest-coup-army-idINKBN0E20Y120140522.

Chapter Fourteen

From Prayut "Heavy" to Prayut "Light" (2014–23)

In 2014, praetorianism proved that it was no phenomenon of Thailand's past. During the evening of 22 May, Prayut, alongside all security service commanders (Supreme Command, navy, air force and police) appeared on television to announce the putsch. That same evening, the coup-created National Council for Peace and Order (NCPO), which Prayut headed, voided the 2007 constitution except for the articles dealing with the king, dissolved the civilian government, and two days later dissolved the Senate. The NCPO assumed control of all state agencies. The coup, though rumoured to have been planned months in advance, likely had its origins in late 2010, when anti-Thaksin senior officers and aristocrats were already understanding clearly that a pro-Thaksin government had a good chance to win the next general election. This assumption was confirmed by Democrat Party bigwig and PDRC leader Suthep Thaugsuban, who publicly stated in June 2014 (despite Prayut's denial) that he had regularly talked with then army commander Prayut about:

> strategies to root out the influence of former prime minister Thaksin Shinawatra and his allies since the 2010 political violence.... [Suthep and Prayut had] been actively plotting to bring down former prime minister Yingluck Shinwatra, including the period leading up to the coup when she was defense minister.[1]

Although Prayut and his new NCPO junta had come to power by force, and indeed he announced the accession of NCPO rule on televisions, Prayut refused to use the word "coup". The stated reasons for the putsch put forward by the junta were to safeguard the monarchy, help "the country ... return to normality quickly ... for society to love and be at peace again"; to "push through political reform", "stop violence" and seek "a way out of [the country's] crisis".[2] Nevertheless, there were several informal rationales that seemed more suited to the coup leaders' objectives. These included but were not limited to (1) ensuring arch-royalist order amidst an impending monarchical succession; (2) re-asserting monarchical-military domination over Thailand amidst perceived threats from civilians (especially Thaksin and Yingluck Shinawatra); (3) consolidating the domination over the armed forces and police by the junta leaders' military faction; and (4) enhancing military corporate interests, particularly those of the senior brass. On the day of the putsch, the NCPO claimed it had received a royal endorsement. But the king was not publicly seen with the junta leader until he received from a grovelling Prayut the 2014 interim constitution on 22 July 2014.[3]

The NCPO junta directorate was composed of the leaders of the army (Prayut), navy, air force, Supreme Command and police. A ten-member junta advisory team was headed by Prawit Wongsuwan and deputy Anupong Paochinda. By September, the junta numbered

FIGURE 14.1
NCPO Junta Leadership

1. Army chief General Prayut Chanocha (AFAPS class 12) as chief

2. Supreme commander General Tanasak Patimaprakorn
   (AFAPS class 12) as first deputy chief

3. Navy commander Admiral Narong Pipathanasai
   (AFAPS class 13) as second deputy chief

4. Air force commander ACM Prajin Chintong
   (AFAPS class 13) as third deputy chief

5. Police commissioner-general General Adul Saengsingkaew
   (Police Academy 29) as fourth deputy chief

6. 1st Army Region commander General Teerachai
   Nakwanich (AFAPS class 14) as secretary-general

7. General Chattudom Titthasiri (AFAPS
   class 15) as deputy secretary-general

8. Colonel Winthai Suvaree (AFAPS class 30) as NCPO spokesperson

fifteen individuals—only two (Meechai Ruchupan and Somkit Jatusripitak) were civilians.[4]

FIGURE 14.2
NCPO Board of Advisors

Position	Name and class (if military)	Background
Chairman	**General Prawit Wongsuwan** (AFAPS class 6)	Former army commander and minister of defence (in Abhisit Vechachiwa's cabinet)
Vice Chairman	**General Anupong Paochinda** (AFAPS class 10)	Former army commander
Vice Chairman	Pridiyathorn Devakula	Former governor of the Bank of Thailand
Consultant	Somkid Jatusripitak	Former deputy prime minister and minister of finance (Thaksin Shinawatra's cabinet)
Consultant	Narongchai Akrasanee	Member of Thai Monetary Policy Committee and former minister of trade (Chavalit Yongchaiyudh's cabinet)
Consultant	Wissanu Krea-ngam	Former deputy prime minister (Thaksin Shinawatra's cabinet)
Consultant	Yongyuth Yuthavong	Former minister of science and technology (Surayud Chulanond's cabinet)
Consultant	**ACM Itthaporn Subhawong** (AFAPS class 11)	Former commander-in-chief of the air force
Consultant	**General Noppadol Intapanya** (AFAPS class 6)	Former secretary to minister of defence (Prawit Wongsuwan)
Consultant and Secretary	General Daowapong Rattanasuwan (AFAPS class 12)	Former deputy commander-in-chief of the army

Note: Names in bold face indicates individuals who were retired military officials at the time.

Despite this sizeable group of individuals in the NCPO, the three that mattered most were Prayut, Prawit and Anupong. Indeed, the allocation of cabinet seats among them was as follows: Prayut as prime minister, Prawit as deputy prime minister and defence minister, and Anupong as interior minister. These postings guaranteed the most cabinet power in terms of administrative authority and access to graft. From the end of May until late July 2014, the NCPO directly ruled Thailand through over one hundred coup decrees and a temporary constitution. Bureaucrats considered sympathetic to the Shinawatras or hostile to the military were purged.

Shortly after the May 2014 coup, junta-leader Prayut began delivering weekly Friday evening addresses on television and radio called "Returning Happiness to the People". The addresses sought to connect the junta leader directly to Thais without interference from Prem or his proxies. Among discussion topics, Prayut emphasized loyalty to the king and reconciliation under the monarchy.[5] In addition—as part of a broader, psychological "Returning Happiness" campaign—the junta, through its National Reconciliation Centre for Reforms (NRCR), attempted to unite people under the monarchy while boosting the military's public image. The strategy included a bevy of shows, songs, movies, discounts, nationalistic rhetoric and twelve pseudo-fascist educational slogans that were required to be taught in schools. Third, the post-coup period saw the NCPO initiate heightened prosecutions of alleged violators of Section 112 (the *lèse-majesté* law). The NCPO issued eleven reform agendas relating to politics, administration, the economy and education, and it pledged to promote twelve national values that stressed protecting the nation, religions and the monarchy.[6]

Meanwhile, a Peace Maintaining Force (PMF) immediately became a principal mechanism for guaranteeing physical junta control. Specifically, the force would arrest and detain any person who defied the junta's orders to turn themselves in to the military. It would physically target anti-coup protest leaders perceived by the junta as insurgents, repress armed groups, and search out potential caches of weapons. In addition, suspected opponents of the junta were arrested for the intimidating purpose of "attitude adjustment". The force would also attempt to connect with rural people to convey to them the junta's policies and ideas. In sum, the PMF was the enforcer of junta decrees and the decisions of military courts. The PMF was composed of soldiers from across Thailand (the 1st, 2nd, 3rd and 4th Army Regions) as well as the Special Warfare Command and the Army Air Defence Command.

Its commander could also mobilize troops from the air force, navy and police.[7]

Finally, the NCPO placed military courts at the top of Thailand's judiciary. Post-coup Military Decree 37/2557 required that any criminal cases connected to national security must be tried in a military court. Procedures in these courts tended to be longer and mostly lacked transparency, with the judges all being military officers. Furthermore, a 2015 amendment to the Military Court Act of 1955 allowed military commanders to detain persons for up to eighty-four days without any charge even before the military trial began. This bypassed judicial oversight guarantees provided under Thailand's Criminal Procedure Code. There have been numerous allegations of torture by the Thai military of persons held incommunicado during detention. Only in May 2015 did military courts begin allowing lawyers for civilian defendants.[8]

With regard to the counterinsurgency in Thailand's Deep South, the 2014 coup immediately resurrected military control over policy towards that region. On 30 May 2014, the junta issued Announcement 34/2557, which declared that the Southern Border Provinces Administrative Centre (SBPAC) would be placed under the jurisdiction of the NCPO leader, voiding the 2010 law that had made the SBPAC into an independent agency. In other words, the SBPAC was placed back under the control of ISOC, as managed by the 4th Army Command. Then, on 30 July, the NCPO created an NCPO-controlled three-level organization to deal with the southern crisis, with junta leader Prime Minister Prayut spearheading policy formulation, deputy junta leader Prawit Wongsuwan in charge of a Steering Committee to Resolve the Protracted Southern Unrest, and the 4th Army Region commander in charge of implementation.[9]

On 22 July, the NCPO enacted a new constitution for Thailand, the country's nineteenth. Besides giving amnesty for any action the coup makers had taken during the 2014 coup (Section 48), the charter gave carte blanche power to Prayut as junta leader over the country while he retained that post. Section 44 specifically stated:

> Section 44. In the case where the Head of the National Council for Peace and Order deems necessary for the purpose of reforms in various fields, for the enhancement of unity and harmony among people in the country, or for the prevention, restraint, or suppression of any act which undermines public order or national security, the Monarchy, the national economy, or State affairs, irrespective of whether such act occurred inside or outside of the Kingdom, the Head of the National Council for Peace and Order, with the approval of the National Council for Peace and Order, *shall*

have power to order, restrain, or perform any act, whether such act has legislative, executive, or judicial force; the orders and the acts, including the performance in compliance with such orders, shall be deemed lawful and constitutional under this Constitution, and shall be final.[10] (italics added)

Initially, following the May 2014 putsch, the NCPO had administered Thailand through the Martial Law Act of 1914. The act placed Thailand under the direct control of the army commander and gave military courts veto power over civilian ones. But following the mandatory retirement of junta leader Prayut on 30 September 2014, the Martial Law Act would have placed power in the hands of Prayut's successor as army commander. The NCPO therefore found it necessary to begin utilizing its interim constitution. Thus, on 20 March 2015, the junta began to apply the charter's Section 44 in place of the Martial Law Act, since Section 44 gave ultimate power to the NCPO chief.

Meanwhile, Section 47 of the 2014 interim constitution stated that all junta acts would be "deemed to be legal, constitutional and conclusive". Furthermore, under Article 48, all junta members were completely amnestied from any future attempts to punish them for being coup makers. Finally, under sections 6, 10, 28, 30 and 32, the junta could indirectly appoint members of new institutions that would write a new constitution for a new Thai democracy.[11]

On 31 July 2014, with the endorsement of the king, the NCPO appointed a National Legislative Assembly (NLA) to rubber stamp junta decisions. The new body initially comprised 220 members but later expanded to 250. Throughout the entire term of the NLA, there were five rounds of appointments. The first round saw the appointment of 200 people, of which 105 were military (army, navy, air force) officials. The second round saw 28 people appointed (17 military officials). The third appointment involved 3 appointees (2 were soldiers). A fourth round saw the appointment of 33 people (26 military officials). The final fifth round saw 3 people appointed—all of which were military officials. In all, 155 military officials (104 army, 28 navy, 23 air force) served as members of the NLA. Of the remaining members, 12 of them were police officials. A great many of the military and police members of NLA were still active-duty officers. Of the civilian NLA members, at least 66 were civil servants, and 19 were businesspeople—all of whom were agreeable to the junta.[12] During the full tenure of the NLA, there were twelve resignations and two deaths.

Prayut formed his first cabinet on 31 August 2014. It existed in parallel to the NCPO, and the two overlapped considerably. Twelve of the cabinet's 36 members were active-duty or retired military officials. The NCPO appointed a committee to select 250 members of the National Reform Council (NRC). Appointed in October, the NRC was established to propose guidelines for national reform. The NRC included 44 security officials: 25 army officers, 7 navy officials, 6 air force personnel, and 6 police officials. Some of these were retired and some were active-duty officers.[13]

The first post-coup military reshuffle (1 October 2014) strengthened Prayut's hold over the armed forces leadership—especially since he simultaneously retired from being an active-duty security official. Sirichai Disakul, with close ties to the palace, was given the politically weak posting of permanent minister of defence. Prayut's friend and classmate Worapong Sangranetra got the supreme commander slot. The NCPO leader's trusted deputy Udomdej ("Big Dong") Sitabutr (a key member of the Buraphapayak faction) succeeded Prayut as army commander (but would reach mandatory retirement age in one year). Udomdej was a significant officer in his own right. The son of General Lertrob Sitabutr and younger brother of Air Chief Marshal Pairsarn Sitabutr, he had played a role in the April 1981 coup attempt, personally detaining Colonel Manoon Roopkachorn.[14] In addition, in 1983, he and Prayut had been colonels leading troops attempting to push back Vietnamese soldiers at the Battle of Phanom Pa in Sa Kaeow province along the Thai-Cambodian border. When Colonel Prayut became surrounded by Vietnamese soldiers, "it was the young Udomdej who came to his rescue amid fierce fighting".[15] Compared to the gruff and quick-tempered Prayut, Udomdej appeared to be more positive, transparent and friendly. Unfortunately, Udomdej was part of a junta, and he would only remain army commander for one year. As a reward for his role in the coup, Teerachai Nakwanich (another Buraphapayak) became assistant army chief, facilitating his path to later be appointed as army chief.[16]

By early 2015, the NRC had selected from among themselves a Constitutional Drafting Committee (CDC). Among the 36 CDC members in total, 25 were elected from the NRC, "while 6 and 5 members were appointed by the NCPO and the cabinet formed by the NCPO, respectively".[17] Ultimately, either directly or indirectly, the CDC was appointed by the military. The CDC then began to move towards writing a new constitution.

But after the CDC proposed establishing a National Strategic Committee (NSC) that could intervene in political matters in the event of a political crisis, the idea was criticised as being a mechanism to prolong military power. This was partly because the commission overseeing the NSC would be made up of military officials and conservative bureaucrats. Perhaps fearing criticism, and also seeking to extend the lifespan of the junta, the NRC, led by military members, rejected the draft. Thereafter, in September 2015, the junta scrapped both the NRC and the CDC it had created. It then set up a new CDC headed by aged arch-royalist Meechai Ruchupan. Following the scrapping of the NRC, a 200-person National Reform Steering Assembly (NRSA) was installed in its place. The NRSA comprised 87 security personnel, including both active-duty and retired officials. These included 49 army officers, 11 navy officials, 12 air force personnel and 15 police.[18]

Turning to the military appointments of 2015 (see appendix 4), on 1 October 2015, the annual military reshuffle was announced. Most significantly, Teerachai Nakwanich (or Big Moo) succeeded Udomdej Sitabutr as army commander, keeping this most coveted security post in the hands of Buraphapayak and also pre-cadet class 14.[19] Four of the new senior brass were members of pre-cadet class 15, including Prayut's brother Preecha (who took the post of permanent minister of defence). Udomdej had favoured Preecha to succeed him as army commander rather than Teerachai. Meanwhile, this would be the final year of service for the injured Walit, who became deputy army commander. Interestingly, none of the up-and-coming senior officers (who might have continued beyond 2016) were members of Buraphapayak, which showed that this faction's influence was beginning to ebb.

Following the reshuffles, a scandal hit the junta. In early November 2015, as a royally endorsed park (Rajabhakti Park) was nearing completion on army land in Hua Hin province, there were revelations about corruption in park funding and procurement. The park had been inaugurated by Crown Prince Vajiralongkorn in September. The alleged corruption angered the royal family and caused embarrassment for the junta, which had sought partly to legitimize its 2014 coup on ousting corrupt officials. General Udomdej Sitabutr, deputy defence minister and former army chief, admitted that some irregularities may have took place, and he supported a probe. Udomdej's successor, Teerachai, who had initiated the probe (but was not a friend of Udomdej's), emphasized that no military official was involved in corruption. Preecha Chanoocha also became involved in the probe. Ultimately, Udomdej's credibility was damaged by this crisis. The scandal exacerbated military divisions and distrust from the palace.[20]

In 2016, Thailand witnessed the growth of opposition to the junta in the form of protests by groups such as the New Democracy Movement and more subtle jibes by established Thai political parties. From 2014 to 2016, at least eighteen people alleged that they had been tortured or suffered periods of extended detention at the hands of the junta.[21]

On 7 August 2016, the junta arranged a referendum on its draft constitution. The regime soon after announced that 61.35 per cent of voters had approved it.[22] At least 180 people had been arrested for criticizing the draft. Many more were threatened with arrest for potential criticisms. The arrests were partly based upon Article 61 of the Referendum Act, which made it illegal to "promote confusion" about the referendum. One election station worker in Chiang Mai alleged that state officials had bused voters in to vote in favour of the referendum.[23] Meanwhile, the state used its Volunteer Defence Corps "to propagate the draft constitution, spreading video clips of the benefits of the draft, [and] various applications promoting the draft's benefits".[24]

In the October 2016 military reshuffle, the hand of Thailand's crown prince (and incoming king, Rama X) was perceptible. For the first time in nine years, no Buraphapayak faction member held the post of army commander. Instead, Chalermchai Sittisart ("Big Jeab") of the special forces faction, a favourite of privy councillor Surayud Chulanond, ascended to the post. In fact, the Five Tigers belonged to four different classes (15, 16, 17 and 18), representing a balance of those classes rather than domination by one class. This reshuffle furthermore represented the imminent growth in power of class 20, given that Wongthewan's Apirat Kongsompong was appointed as 1st Army Region commander. Another Wongthewan, and favourite of incoming king Maha Vajiralongkorn (Rama X), Narongphan Jitkaewthae, became the 1st Division commander of the 1st Army Region. Former army commander Teerachai was appointed as a member of the Privy Council, though he would be fired from that post for unspecified reasons not long thereafter.

On 13 October 2016, King Bhumipol Adulyadej passed away in Siriraj Hospital, Bangkok. Thereupon the junta began to lose a principal rationale for remaining in power: guarding an elderly and frail sovereign, a situation that occurred simultaneous to rising dissent against the junta and increasing economic problems for the country. Privy Council chair General Prem Tinsulanonda temporarily became regent while Crown Prince Vajiralongkorn made ready to become King Rama X (which he did officially on 1 December 2016). The coronation ceremony formally marking the regal accession of Vajiralongkorn from Crown Prince to becoming Rama X (Maha Vajiralongkorn) took place from 4 to 6 May 2019. The process of the royal succession gave the junta time to delay relinquishing power. In fact the NCPO's leaders—Prayut, Prawit and Anupong—argued that no election could take place until after the coronation. Moreover, the royal succession offered the NCPO some legitimacy given that its leaders participated in royal ceremonies in honour of the new monarch. In December, Rama X appointed ten new members of the seventeen-member Privy Council (while retiring others). Among its military members, he retained General Prem Tinsulanonda as chair, as well as General Surayud Chulanond (who succeeded Prem as Privy Council chair in July 2019) and ACM Chalit Pubhasuk, while appointing four new military members (generals Paiboon Kamchaya, Daowapong Ratanasuwan, Teerachai Nakwanich and Kampnat Ruddit), further militarizing the body.[25] In June 2017, the king appointed Admiral Pongthep Nuthep (pre-cadet class 16) as a new military member of the Privy Council. Altogether there were seven military members of the body. Although it was supposed to be made up of eighteen members, the king had not yet made appointments to reach that number. Moreover, although Rama X relied, as his father had, on the Privy Council for advice (especially the retired military members of that body), the new king would begin to make more use of the Office of the Royal Household as he reconstructed palace-military relations.

In January 2017, the king requested that the NCPO revise the constitutional draft with respect to sections involving royal prerogative. Some of the king's requests concerned the power of the regent. The constitution was thus immediately amended so that only the king could decide whether he would appoint a regent when he was not in the country or could not perform his duties. The junta also acquiesced to allow the palace more direct control over the Crown Property Bureau. In April 2017, the Royal Aide de Camp Department, the Office of His Majesty's Principal Private Secretary, the Bureau of the Royal Household (led by chair, ACM Satitpong Sukvimol), the Royal Security Command (effectively commanded by General Jakrapop Puridej) and the Royal Court Security Police were all brought under direct control of the palace.[26] Preparations were made to move more military units under the king's direction. The king signed the new constitution on 6 April 2017. In October 2017, the manner that the junta publicly dedicated efforts for carrying out the royal cremation for the late king Rama IX (Bhumipol) improved the public image of the junta.[27] The new king also seemed pleased to sustain the NCPO, since it was helping him to consolidate his own power.

With the king's endorsement of the charter, Thailand saw its twentieth constitution since 1932—a world record. The document extended semi-military power for years to come, albeit camouflaged by a façade democracy. Under this constitution, the Senate—in 2000 and 2006 fully elected, between 2007 and 2014 half-elected—now became a completely appointed body, with 244 senators selected by an NCPO-appointed committee, 6 of them being the military supreme commander; the army, navy, air force and police chiefs; and the permanent secretary of defence (Section 107).[28] If a majority of the lower house could not agree on who should be premier, the appointed senators could join lower house MPs in making the selection.[29] The constitution also allowed political parties to nominate unelected candidates as the premier, including ex-junta leaders or former military personnel. Meanwhile, an NCPO-appointed committee selected the commissioners on the Election Commission. The junta similarly approved the appointments of heads of the other "independent organizations", including the ombudsman, Constitutional Court, the State Audit Office, the National Human Rights Commission, and National Anti-Corruption Commission.[30] Moreover, junta as well as armed forces leaders retained influence across the country's future state structures by means of a newly created National Strategy Committee, which oversaw a new twenty-year national strategy for the period 2017–36 that aimed to resolve issues of reform, reconciliation and national security. Article 256 of the charter stated that any amendment to the constitution required both a lower house majority and agreement from one-third of the junta-appointed senators (84/250) for it to pass.

In August 2017, Thailand's Supreme Court convicted former prime minister Yingluck Shinawatra of negligence in a rice-pledging scheme. She fled the country and appeared in the United Kingdom, where she asked for political asylum. It is likely that the junta helped her to flee.[31]

The October 2017 reshuffle saw the growing clout of pre-cadet class 20: Apirat Kongsompong of the Wongthewan faction became assistant army commander and his comrade Kukiat Sinaka was appointed 1st Army Region commander. Kukiat, though close to Apirat, was also a member of Buraphapayak. Both had played major roles in the 2014 coup in terms of leading soldiers who swept through Bangkok. Thus, they both continued to rise. Because Buraphapayak's Theppong Tipyacharn (pre-cadet 18) only had one more year remaining as an active-duty officer (at a time when Chalermchai Sittisart [pre-cadet 16] still had one more year as army commander), the former was appointed to the post of permanent minister of defence. Another Buraphapayak, General Veerachai Intusophon (pre-cadet 18), became the second assistant army commander, but he would also need to retire the following year (2018). Meanwhile, another Wongthewan, General Nattapol Nakpanich (pre-cadet 16), became army chief of staff and looked destined to become a future option as the next army commander. It was within the 1st Army Region command, however, that more tense competition occurred—between two members of Wongthewan. General Narongphan Jitkaewthae (pre-cadet 22) and General Songwit Noonpakdi (pre-cadet 24), son of General Issarapong Noonpakdi, were each vying for the post of 1st Army Region commander. Narongphan, who was senior, was the 1st Division King's Guard commander, while Songwit took this posting on 1 April 2018 (when Narongphan became a deputy commander of the 1st Army Region). Finally, Admiral Luechai Ruddit, younger brother of privy councillor Kampnat Ruddit, became navy chief. Luechai's royal connections helped the navy to secure more money and military hardware (possibly including three Chinese submarines).

On 10 October 2017, Prime Minister Prayut announced that Thailand's next election would take place in November 2018. Such election announcements were nothing new as the NCPO had promised an election several times previously (these were then postponed). General Prawit, the deputy prime minister, when asked if the junta would establish a political party, answered that "when necessary, it [the party] needs to be set up".[32] Meanwhile, a pre-cadet classmate of Prayut, Colonel Suchart Chantarachotkul, stressed that he looked forward to establishing a party in support of the prime minister in the next election. These statements all suggested that the NCPO was preparing to create its own party. In 2018 the NCPO was making serious plans for the upcoming general election. The junta had delayed the polls for four years and now had only King Rama X's coronation in November to rationalize why Thailand could not yet hold elections.

In March 2018, Palang Pracharat was officially established by Prayut frontman and ISOC-connected Colonel Suchart Jantarachotikul[33] as well as businessman Chuan Chuchan and thirteen others. The timing was significant as the NCPO did not allow banned parties to resume their activities until August 2018 or permit them to begin campaigning until December that year.[34] By September 2018, the executive board of Palang Pracharat comprised a mixture of officials, including some who had previously helped administer the NCPO and others who had been Members of Parliament and were representatives of political factions which had previously belonged to other political parties.[35] This new party's name, emblem and policies mirrored the junta's Pracha Rat symbol and programme.

In 2018–19, ISOC teams raced around communities throughout the country reminding Thais to vote, but also advertising and delivering Pracha Rat populism—indirectly assisting the Palang Pracharat Party.[36] Indeed, Palang Pracharat had been rooted in the strategies of ISOC. Back in 2017, Prime Minister Prayut invoked his powers under Section 44 of the NCPO's 2014 interim constitution to establish an ISOC Internal Security Administrative "Superboard" with the ostensible objective of addressing broad domestic security threats. The superboard operated at three levels, with Prime Minister Prayut and Deputy Prime Minister Prawit responsible at the national level, the four regional army commanders directing the four regional committee levels, and provincial governors (who have always been influential in helping parties to elect candidates) heading up provincial committees. Governors were appointed by the minister of the interior, who had since 2014 been General Anupong Paochinda, a close friend of Prayut and Prawit and a powerful voice inside Palang Pracharat. The 2017 order also centralized police, interior officials and public prosecutors under army-dominated ISOC control. ISOC had access to between 5,000 and 6,000 staff as well as 500,000 to 600,000 internal security personnel to help implement the objectives of the order.[37] This superboard and ISOC "seed money" allowed the NCPO to achieve a major "security" objective—creating a junta party that would win the 2019 election.[38] This "Trojan Horse" party was soon ready for elections.

The 2018 reshuffle brought the monarch-favoured Wongthewan faction to the top of the army. Apirat Kongsompong (pre-cadet class 20) became army commander. Born 23 March 1960, Apirat, the son of former supreme commander and co-coup leader Sunthorn Kongsompong, had attended the highly prestigious Saint Gabriel's School in Bangkok. His younger brother is the retired major general Nattaporn Kongsompong. A trained military officer and trained pilot, Apirat was assigned to units within the 1st Division, King's Guard, eventually becoming the commander of that unit. He had played a major role in mopping up Red Shirt protestors in Bangkok in May 2010 as well as quelling resistance in Bangkok to the 2014 coup. Apirat has been an avid leader of the Young Turks, seeking a more efficient army, and the Wongthewan army faction. He also avidly supported the Red Rim (*Kaw Daeng*) faction created by King Maha Vajiralongkorn in 2018.[39]

Apirat's colleague and friend Kukiat Sinaka (pre-cadet class 20) was appointed as assistant army chief. Another friend of Apirat (also his classmate), Nat Intarajaroen (pre-cadet class 20), became permanent minister of defence. Nat was a member of the Buraphapayak faction and was close to deputy prime minister Prawit Wongsuwan. Wongthewan's Nattapol Nakpanich was elevated to become deputy army commander. Meanwhile, Narongphan Jitkaewthae was appointed 1st Army Region commander, while Songwit Noonpakdi succeeded the latter as 1st Division, 1st Army Region commander. The king appeared to be in control of the army. It was in 2018 that the palace established the Red Rim faction within the military. The intention was to replace the factionalism of the armed forces with unity based around the palace.

In November 2018, a rap song criticizing the junta shot across the internet. The song, "Prathet Ku Me", or "What My Country's Got", by Thai rap group Rap Against Dictatorship, received millions of plays on YouTube.[40] It denounced the repression and corruption of the NCPO, comparing it to the repression of 6 October 1976.

The year 2019 was supposed to be Thailand's year of moving to finally elected civilian rule and democracy. What happened, however, was a façade because the NCPO junta leaders became the "wolves in sheep's clothing"—perversely extending the junta by semi-democratic means. After numerous delays, a general election was held on 24 March 2019,[41] under the new 2017 constitution, which was essentially a charter designed by the junta to prolong its power. Four months before the election, constituencies had been gerrymandered to help the junta.[42] In addition, NCPO head Prayut had used Section 44 to divide constituencies where they could become most beneficial to Palang Pracharat during the election.[43] From January to March 2019, ISOC teams had raced around the country reminding Thais to vote, but also advertising and delivering Pracha Rat populism—indirectly assisting the Palang Pracharat Party. Meanwhile, Palang Pracharat used committees of province-level faction teams (with vote-canvassing networks) to contest Thailand's 2019 election, and to boost intra-party coordination after the election. Given that these committees and ISOC provincial committees were each striving for the same goal—sustaining military power—they overlapped (but few local politicians sat on ISOC committees).[44]

Following the election, to the consternation of the opposition parties, the Election Commission changed the electoral formula. The election results showed that the pro-Thaksin Pheu Thai won 136 constituency seats (though no party list seats), while the junta's Palang Pracharat won 97 constituency seats and 18 party list seats. Future Forward won 30 constituency seats and 50 party-list seats. Bhumjai Thai got 50 seats and the Democrats obtained 51. The new formula gave Future Forward

10 fewer seats, and its coalition with Pheu Thai had 245 seats, while the Palang Pracharat–led coalition was said to have the majority. But since Palang Pracharat had no clear majority, combined votes from the lower house and Senate would ensure that the Palang Pracharat candidate was appointed to the premiership.

The 2019–24 Senate was appointed on 19 May 2019. Comprising 250 members, it contained 105 officials from the security sector. These included 89 military officials and 15 police officers—some active-duty, some retired. Of the military senators, 69 were from the army, 11 from the navy and 5 from the air force. All were considered supportive of the Palang Pracharat government. Six of the appointed senators were the permanent minister of defence, the supreme commander, and the commanders of the army, navy, air force and police, who were rotated depending on when they retired.[45] This large number of reliable military senators ensured two results: first, Prayut would be selected as prime minister; and second, no amendments to the constitution would ever pass the Senate without the approval of whoever controlled the military at the time. With Senate backing, on 5 June, the 750-member National Assembly voted 500 to 244 to return Prayut to power as elected prime minister under the Palang Pracharat Party. Prayut himself was an unelected MP and was not a member of any party. Throughout June, as the ruling Palang Pracharat Party sought to put together a coalition, it was mired in factional bickering, and Prayut indirectly warned of another coup if this did not cease.[46] The coalition finally was formed on 10 July 2019.

In the midst of these political developments, the Prayut-led regime found another way to legitimize its power. On 1 May, there was a royal wedding between King Rama X and the former commander of his bodyguard, Tanpuying Suthida. Then, on 4–6 May, the coronation of the king took place. The televised ceremony—with Prayut, Prawit and Anupong in attendance—helped to bestow legitimacy upon the three as guardians of the kingship.

The king himself increasingly took an active role in military and social mobilization affairs. In mid-2019 he inaugurated a new pro-gramme called *Chit Arsa* (Volunteers of Spirit). This involved civil servants, teachers and police volunteers, who underwent training at military bases. By November, three thousand people had completed the course. The idea was to establish an organization to "develop and defend the country and create people who are loyal to the monarchy".[47] On 30 September 2019, the two infantry regiments within Bangkok (1st Infantry Regiment and 11th Infantry Regiment) were removed from the Royal Thai Army's chain of command and placed directly under palace control. The move was in line with the creation in May 2017 of the Royal Security Command by King Rama X as an agency independent of the Royal Thai Armed Forces. All other military units began to be moved outside of Bangkok as the king sought to directly control every security force in Thailand's capital.[48] Meanwhile, the palace established a police unit called the Ratchawallop Police Retainers, King's Guard 904, to be directly under its control.[49] Two prominent police commanders close to the king are police general Torsak Sukvimol, younger brother of ACM Satitpong Sukvimol, lord chamberlain to the king; and Jirapop Puridej, younger brother of General Jakrapop Puridej, the commander of the Royal Security Command.

The October 2019 military reshuffle continued to see the rise of the king's favourites. Wongthewan soldier Apirat Kongsompong (AFAPS 20) remained army chief, while Narongphan Jitkaewthae (AFAPS 22) ascended to become assistant army commander. Buraphapayak's Tamanoon Withi, a favourite of Prawit from the 12th Regiment, Second Infantry Division, was appointed as 1st Army Region commander. Another Wongthewan favourite of the king, General Sotapol Sadsaongern, was appointed to become 1st Division, 1st Army Region commander.

In February 2020, an incident at Suratham Phithak military camp starkly revealed the corruption within Thailand's military. The incident began on 8 February 2020 when a near-berserk soldier came to the house of his commander, Colonel Anantharot Krasae, to discuss a property dispute. The soldier shot and killed his superior and the man's mother-in-law. Afterwards, the gunman went to an army base, stole weapons and ammunition, and killed a soldier who was there. He then drove to the Terminal 21 Korat shopping mall and began shooting at shoppers there. During the gunman's shooting spree, he killed twenty-six people before being killed himself. The soldier was apparently upset because he felt cheated out of a property deal (his money was not returned by the commanding officer and the latter's mother-in-law).[50] The tragedy resulted in promises by then army commander Apirat Kongsompong to finally implement tangible security sector reforms. In mid-February, the army signed a memorandum of understanding that ostensibly paved the way for the transfer of state land and commercial businesses of the army to the Finance Ministry, allowing more army revenue to go to state coffers.[51] The air force and navy signed similar agreements. But despite these promises, little if any reform has taken place.

Meanwhile, in 2019–20, the military-dominated Palang Pracharat façade democracy had begun to experience much greater opposition to its hold on power—from the Pheu Thai and Future Forward parties. As a result, on 21 February, Future Forward—the new party that was extremely popular among the youth—was disbanded by order of the NCPO-appointed Constitutional Court. The party's executive board members, including charismatic politician Thanathorn, were banished from politics for ten years. Future Forward was immediately replaced by its clone party, Move Forward. Then, in June, young anti-monarchist Wanchalerm Satsaksit was forcibly disappeared in Phnom Penh, Cambodia, most obviously by Thai police/military officers assisted by Cambodian officials. The two incidents—the dissolution of Future Forward and the abduction of Wanchalerm—intensified youthful anger against both the junta and the king with the result that demonstrations led by young people (mostly students) began to take place in July 2020. These rallies crystalized into protestors' demands for Prayut's resignation, democracy, monarchical reform, and other constitutional changes during a rally on 3 August. The demonstrations centred upon Bangkok but began to proliferate beyond Bangkok during the year.

Nevertheless, the state found an excuse to repress the protests—exigences resulting from the Covid-19 pandemic. Covid-19, which had begun to rage across the country in February–March, was rapidly becoming a national crisis. Though tighter state controls were perhaps necessary to deal with the virus, the pandemic temporarily rationalized the government's 25 March 2020 declaration of a state of emergency through which the military could temporarily resurrect its pre-2019 autocracy. Applying the 2005 Emergency Decree on Public Administration in a State of Emergency, the regime forthwith banned "rallies ... or activities inciting unrest", forbade the dissemination of information that it considered "not true" or the "intentional distortion of information", and established long periods of daily curfew. Those violating these orders could be imprisoned for up to five years under the Computer Crimes Act or the Emergency Decree, following guidelines from the regime's newly created Anti-Fake News Centre. The decree also gave provincial governors total control over their provinces and permitted the military to support the police in enforcing emergency regulations.[52] The state of emergency was continuously extended. By the end of December it had still not been lifted. It conveniently justified the quelling of anti-government demonstrations. Army commander Apirat Kongsompong tried to convince cadets that criticism of one's nation was more dangerous than Covid-19. Meanwhile, right-wing elements claimed that the students were being organized by foreign agents, an argument that stirred up xenophobic nationalism against the students. But by late 2020, youthful demonstrators were continuing to thrive, structuring their protests via multiple flash mobs.[53]

Meanwhile, the leading party of the governing coalition, Palang Pracharat, began to change its leadership. As a party with as many as twenty factions, it had already become extremely divided by 2020. In June, General Prawit Wongsuwan took the helm of the party, ostensibly to stabilize it. But another possible reason for his assuming the post could be to gain leverage over Prime Minister Prayut, his Buraphapayak "brother". Following the 2019 election, Prawit, who had been ill, allowed Prayut to assume the post of prime minister as well as Prawit's slot of defence minister, while Prawit remained only deputy prime minister. It was rumoured that "Prayut [had] been maneuvering to become the sole supreme power through sidelining Prawit by not allotting him a cabinet seat" (the post of deputy prime minister is only an ad hoc cabinet posting).[54] But Prayut's premiership was unstable because, since he was not a member of a political party, he depended on Palang Pracharat to continue its support for him. Thus, Prawit's assumption of party leadership of Palang Pracharat meant that he potentially held life-or-death influence over Prayut's continuation as prime minister. For now, in 2020, Prawit chose not to test his power against Prayut; he was, however, working rapidly to expand his influence across the ruling coalition.

The October 2020 reshuffle (see appendix 4) represented another victory for King Rama X. This is because Narongphan Jitkaewthae (pre-cadet 22), nicknamed Big Bee—the monarch's trusted Wongthewan army officer who had been fast-tracked—was appointed army commander following pressure from the palace. Narongphan had been born on 1 January 1963 as Monthien Kaewthae, but changed his name. Natapol Nakwanich (pre-cadet 16), as the senior who had served two years in a row as deputy army chief and was also a member of Wongthewan, had more of a right to be appointed army commander. But Narongphan's closeness to the king and perhaps the fact that he would not retire until 2023 counted in his favour. Natapol became Prayut's national security advisor. Buraphapayak's Tammanoon Withi, though gaining the spot of assistant army commander, was barred by mandatory retirement in 2021 from moving any higher. Buraphapayak gained a slot, however, through the appointment of Chalermpol Srisawasdi as supreme commander, though Chalermpol's sub-faction was cavalry, not infantry. Meanwhile, the strategic post of commander of the 1st Army Region was given to Jaroenchai Hintao (pre-cadet 23), who was actually closer to Prayut and Prawit than the king. And the commanders of the air force, police and navy all retired in 2020. In their place, the king ensured the appointments of his favourites, ACM Airbull Sutsawan and police general Suwat Jaengyudsok. The former belonged to an air force faction that had served the king in Munich, Germany (and who was familiar to Queen Suthida). Suwat had previously served under the king in the police unit attached to the palace. Admiral Chatchai Srivorakan was a part of the Ruddit faction, which was headed by his predecessor, Luechai, and privy councillor Kampnat (Luechai's brother). These developments led to some disgruntlement, at least in the air force and police, as it was felt that Airbull and Suwat had leapfrogged other officers to obtain their positions.

With General Apirat Kongsompong no longer army commander, the king appointed him to be vice-chamberlain of the Royal Household Bureau and the deputy director of the Crown Property Bureau. At the Royal Household Bureau, Apirat joined police colonel Naras Savestanan as the other vice-chamberlain, working under head chamberlain ACM Satitpong Sukvimol. But Apirat's power (even in retirement) was overwhelming, given that he was the only chamberlain in the royal household with an army background. Since the ascension of King Rama X in 2016, the influence of the royal household has come to surpass that of the Privy Council, given that the king places more trust in the household (as led by his loyalist, Satitpong). This makes Apirat, despite his retirement, the most influential army strongman other than the army commander.

In 2021, demonstrations against the government and monarchy continued. But Prayut's government used two strategies to diminish the effectiveness of the protestors. First was to rationalize the Covid-19 pandemic as a reason to arrest demonstrators. Indeed, the Emergency Decree continued to be extended by the government. Arrests were also made under the authority of a 2021-amended Communicable Diseases Act.[55] Second, the government began to arrest leaders of the student movement. These tactics, combined with splits in the student movement itself, partially succeeded in weakening youth solidarity by late 2021.

Meanwhile, in mid-August, the opposition filed a no-confidence motion against the government for mishandling Covid-19 as well as mismanagement of vaccines and the economy. At this point, a plot allegedly began among senior members of Palang Pracharat to use the censure vote surreptitiously to unseat Prayut. Since becoming the party's secretary-general in June 2021, retired army captain Thammanat Prompao, a loyalist of Prawit, had coveted Anupong Paochinda's post of interior minister, while Prawit's choice for permanent secretary of the interior, a Thammanat loyalist, had been rejected by Anupong. At the same time, Prawit apparently began to see the censure motion as a chance to unseat Prayut, or at least to show the prime minister that the latter should not forget his friends or others in the cabinet.

Thammanat's idea was thus to have twenty members of the co-alition's small parties join the opposition in the vote against Prayut, arriving at approximately 212 votes, enough to unseat Prayut. With a successor unlikely to be chosen from the current list of prime ministerial candidates, an outsider could be selected. That outsider would have to be backed by both Palang Pracharat and Pheu Thai (with Thaksin's blessing)—and it would be Prawit.[56] Rumours of collusion emerged when Pheu Thai refused, strangely, to target Thammanat and Prawit in the no-confidence debate. Thaksin himself denied that he had paid Thammanat to secure Prayut's ouster.

In the end, in early September, the targeted ministers all survived, though Prayut had the second-fewest number of confidence votes. Prayut apparently discovered the plot at the last minute and may have bribed MPs to ensure they voted for him.[57] Afterwards, he immediately fired Thammanat and another minister who had been involved. But Prawit, who claimed ignorance of the plot, kept the two on as Palang Pracharat secretary-general and treasurer, respectively. He also told party factions to work towards party unity, and he appointed General Wit Thepasdin na Ayuttaya as chair of the party's strategic committee to party MPs. Wit, close to Prawit and Thammanat, had competed with Prayut to become army commander in 2010. On 30 September, Prawit ordered Palang Pracharat to nominate Prayut as its candidate in the next general election. Though thanking Prawit for this, Prayut took steps so that he would have less need to rely on him. Indeed, he began to meet more frequently with Palang Pracharat MPs, but also appears to have consented to a backup political party being established (should he need to jump ship to it), formed by Anupong-loyalist Chatchai Promlert.[58] Despite the partisan bickering, by 1 December 2021, Prayut, Prawit and Anupong were still working together inside of Palang Pracharat.

Turning now to weapons purchases, Prayut placed appropriations for the purchase of two Chinese submarines on hold following public pressure over their expensive procurement plan. A first submarine had already been bought from Beijing, but the economic impact of the Covid-19 pandemic had necessitated postponing the acquisition of the other two.[59] Despite the sale being "put on ice", it was highly likely that Prayut would reschedule the purchase for a future date—the pro-military character of the Palang Pracharat government naturally favoured any weapons procurement.

The October 2021 reshuffle saw Apirat's favourite, General Worakiat Ratanond, become permanent minister of defence (though he would need to retire in 2022). General Narongphan continued on as army commander. What was spectacular about this reshuffle was that several members of Buraphapayak took strategic slots at the helm of the army (see Appendix 4).[60] Meanwhile, in late 2021, as tensions grew between Prayut and Prawit, it became difficult to speculate which man had more sway over the Buraphapayak faction and its active-duty senior brass.

In February, rumours began to proliferate about growing divisions among prime minister General Prayut, deputy prime minister General Prawit Wongsuwan and interior minister General Anupong Paochinda. Thammanat Prompao and twenty of his factional followers were fired from Palang Pracharat. He and his group thereupon migrated to the Thai Economy Party, which was headed by Prawit-stalwart (and Prayut enemy) General Wit Thepsadin na Ayuthaya. Advisors for this party were none other than Prawit and Patcharawat Wongsuwan. Members of this party demanded that the government give Anupong's interior minister slot to Prawit, but Prawit denied that he was interested in it. Meanwhile, Anupong Paochinda and his former permanent minister of the interior, Chatchai Promlert, having established a political party for Prayut in October 2020, apparently were keeping it ready for Prayut as an option in case the prime minister wanted to join it. But in 2022 there were tales that Prayut and Anupong had experienced a falling out. Finally, in February 2022, Seksakol Atthawong, vice minister at the Prime Minister's Office, announced that he had set up a new party called Ruam Thai Sang Chart as a fall-back option in the event that Palang Pracharat nominated General Prayut as the next prime minister.[61] With the lower house plagued numerous times by an insufficient quorum to conduct votes (partly because of dissatisfaction among Palang Pracharat factions towards Prayut), it seemed that Prayut's government would lose a no-confidence motion soon or he himself would have to dissolve the government. Turbulence within Thai politics seemed to be growing precipitously.

By mid-2022, the unity that Prawit, Anupong and Prayut had seemed to enjoyed since their 2014 coup appeared finally to have broken. Distrust and bickering among them had replaced their cohesiveness when they had led the country as junior partners of kings Rama IX and X. Although the military-dominated Palang Pracharat government barely survived a July 2022 no-confidence motion, it looked set to complete its term in March 2023, while Prayut (and Prawit) made ready to contest the general election that would, according to the Election Commission, be held no later than 7 May 2023, given that this would be the final date of the parliamentary term.

The October 2022 military reshuffle mostly reflected continuity in terms of the faces among senior officers at the very top. But the reshuffle did produce some changes. Both Prayut and Prawit made gains in promotions for their Buraphapayak faction. At the same time, the traditionally arch-royalist Wongthewan faction made gains, and the king continued to seek unity across the army through his contrived Red Rim faction.[62]

By late 2022, Thais were gearing up for the general election. In September, the Constitutional Court had ruled that Prayut could only hold office until April 2025, given that the April 2017 charter held that a premier could only keep his post for eight years. This would mean that (barring a change in the constitution), if Prayut ran in the 2023 election, he could only be prime minister for two more years. But he stated he would run regardless.

In January 2023, a new political party called Ruam Thai Sang Chart (United Thai Nation Party) suddenly appeared, which was a mechanism for Prayut to run as prime minister. He joined the party and became its sole nominee for prime minister in the upcoming general election. Meanwhile, General Prawit Wongsuwan became the sole prime ministerial nominee of Palang Pracharat. Though Prayut and Prawit claimed to still be friends (and brothers-in-arms), their intensifying political clash made such claims seem unlikely.

Thailand in 2023 had thus taken a step further than in 2019 in terms of military involvement in parliamentary elections. Where in 2019 there was but one military-created party running in the poll (Palang Pracharat), 2023 saw two such parties—Prawit's Palang Pracharat and Prayut's Ruam Thai Sang Chart. Nevertheless, any popularity that Prayut and/or Prawit thought they enjoyed during the 2019 election had waned four years later amidst post-Covid-19 pandemic blues, intensifying civilian desires for more democracy, and persistent economic difficulties across the country. It thus increasingly

FIGURE 14.3
Thailand's National Legislative Assembly (2014–19) and Senate (2019–24)

Type	Term	Dividing the 250 members	Military/police quota
Unicameral	(2014–19)	250 appointed	167/250 (66.8%) of the appointed senators
Bicameral (12th Senate) legislature	(2019–24) Senate serves 5-year term	250 appointed	105/250 (42%) of the appointed senators

appeared as if a civilian such as moderate Bhumjai party leader Anutin Charnvirakul or even Paetongtarn Shinawatra of Pheu Thai might be elected as prime minister.

The negative perceptions of Prayut and Prawit (and their other brother, interior minister General Anupong) seemed to position both Palang Pracharat and Ruam Thai Sang Chart as increasingly weak mechanisms for the military to sustain its power in the lower house. Since 2014, the armed forces had dominated the legislature. Nevertheless, the military advertised its importance as the only institution able to resist the insurgency in Thailand's Deep South and the youthful, progressive demonstrators in Bangkok alike. As such, it was able to ensure continuing high degrees of budgeting for itself. Regardless of the results of the 2023 poll, the fact remains that a high level of military influence in Thai politics continues to be supported by the monarchy—one authoritarian institution supporting another and hindering democratization.

Despite popular exhaustion with Prayut and Prawit, two factors can be counted on to help either or both of their military-oriented parties. These are (1) the persistent frailties of Thai democracy; and (2) continuing divisions among Thais about the monarchy and the armed forces. In fact, these factors could extend military influence across Thai politics for the next decade. Moreover, in future, the election of a civilian seeking more democratic civilian control (e.g., Thaksin's Pheu Thai Party) might provoke another military coup. In that respect, Thailand in 2023 remains quite praetorian and has not moved beyond Thailand in 1991, 2006 or 2014. Ultimately, "coupism" in 2023 Thailand has remained alive and well. The post-1932 path of praetorianism in Thailand has persisted, although, since 1980, such praetorianism has become enmeshed with the monarchy. The introduction of this book discussed the notion of "monarchized military". Legitimizing itself as the protector of the crown, this "monarchized military" remains junior only to the palace, but it looks to remain highly active in ensuring the persistence of a praetorian kingdom.

Notes

1. Nauvarat Suksamran, "Suthep in Talks with Prayut since 2010", *Bangkok Post*, 23 June 2014, https://www.bangkokpost.com/thailand/politics/416810/suthep-in-talks-with-Prayut-since-2010. See also The Room 44 Channel, ย้อนสัมพันธ์ "กำนันสุเทพ-ประยุทธ์" จุดเริมต้นเก้าอี้ "นายกรัฐมนตรี 8 ปี" [Back to the relationship "Kamnan Suthep-Prayut', the beginning of the chair 'prime minister 8 years"], 22 August 2022, https://today.line.me/th/v2/article/9mZz5kE.

2. Witthaya Yuthakorn, "Be Careful What You Wish For: The Rhetoric and the Reality of the Thai Coup", *Prachathai*, 6 June 2014, http://www.prachatai.com/english/node/4095.

3. MCOT, "HM the King Endorses Provisional Constitution", *Pattaya Mail*, 23 July 2014, http://www.pattayamail.com/thailandnews/hm-the-king-endorses-provisional-constitution39743.

4. คสช.จัดทีมใหม่-รวมสมาชิก 15 คน "พล.อ.ประวิตร" ขึ้นรอง คสช [NCPO organizes a new team – including 15 members, "Gen. Prawit" becomes deputy NCPO], *Prachatai*, 22 September 2014, https://prachatai.com/journal/2014/09/55660.

5. Thanyarat Doksone (Associated Press), "Thailand's Coup Leader Outlines Policies", *WTOP News*, 12 September 2014, https://wtop.com/news/2014/09/thailands-coup-leader-outlines-policies/.

6. Paul Chambers and Napia Waitoolkiat, "The Resilience of Monarchised Military in Thailand", *Journal of Contemporary Asia* 46, no. 3 (2016): 338, https://doi.org/10.1080/00472336.2016.1161060.

7. Wassana Nanuam, "Army to Crack Down on Armed Groups", *Bangkok Post*, 28 May 2014, http://www.bangkokpost.com/print/412125/.

8. Lawyers Rights Watch Canada, "Thailand: Trials of Civilians in Military Courts Violate International Fair Trials (Judicial Harassment of Lawyers and Human Rights 28 Defenders' Statement, 25 May 2015)", http://www.lrwc.org/thailand-trials-ofcivilians-in-military-courts-violate-international-fair-trial-rights-statement/.

9. Paul Chambers and Napisa Waitoolkiat, "The Role of Security Forces in Thailand's Deep South Counter-Insurgency", special issue, *Asian International Studies Review*, vol. 20 (October 2019): 62, https://doi.org/10.1163/2667078X-02001003.

10. Section 44, Interim Constitution, 26 July 2014, http://web.Kritdika.go.th/data/outsitedata/outsite21/file/Constitution_of_the_Kingdom_of_Thailand_(Interim),B.E._2557_(2014).pdf.

11. Ibid.

12. iLaw, "ใครออกกฎหมาย? 1: สภาทหาร-สภาผลประโยชน์» เมื่อคนใกล้ชิดผู้นำ ประเทศ อยู่เต็ม สนช" [Who issued the law? 1: Assembly of soldiers–assembly of interests when the premier's close circle sits in the National Legislative Assembly], 5 February 2017, https://ilaw.or.th/node/4407.

13. Author's calculations based upon พระบรมราชโองการแต่งตั้งสมาชิกสภาปฏิรูปแห่งชาติ, ราชกิจจานุบกษา, 13 ตุลาคม 2557 [The appointment of members to the National Reform Council], *Royal Gazette*, vol. 131, special issue 199, 13 October 2014, http://www.ratchakitcha.soc.go.th/DATA/PDF/2557/E/199/1. PDF.

14. Personal interview with anonymous senior military official, 30 December 2021.

15. Wassana Nanuam, "Why the Military Regime Needs Udomdej", *Bangkok Post*, 9 October 2014, https://www.bangkokpost.com/opinion/opinion/436654/why-the-military-regime-needs-udomdej.

16. Two friends of Prayut and his brother Preecha (Chatchai Sarigalaya and Chatchalerm Chalermsuk) became deputy army chief and army chief of staff, respectively. Preecha himself ascended to become assistant army chief. Chatchai, Chatchalerm and Preecha were members of pre-cadet class 15. Wongthewan faction member Kampnat Ruddit became 1st Army Region chief. Finally, Chakthip Jaichinda, a crony of brothers Prawit and Patcharawat Wongsuwan, took up the position of police chief.

17. Kitti Prasirtsuk, "Thailand in 2015: Bill, Blast and Beyond", *Asian Survey* 56, no. 1, Asia in 2015: The Year in Review (January/February 2016): 170, https://www.jstor.org/stable/10.2307/26364357.

18. Author's calculations based upon ประกาศสำนักนายกรัฐมนตรี เรื่อง แต่งตั้งสมาชิกสภา ขับเคลื่อนการปฏิรูปประเทศ, เล่ม ๑๓๒ ตอนพิเศษ ๒๓๙ ง ราชกิจจานุเบกษา ๕ ตุลาคม ๒๕๕๘ [Prime ministerial announcement, the appointment of members to the National Reform Steering Assembly], *Royal Gazette*, vol. 132, special issue 239, 5 October 2015, http://www.ratchakitcha.soc.go.th/DATA/PDF/2558/E/239/3.PDF.

19. Born on 16 November 1955, he was the son of Maj. Gen. Thawatchai Nakwanich and Mom Rajawongse Phisawat Disakul Nakwanich. The former had been deputy to General Vitoon Yasawat beginning in 1964 for Thai clandestine military operations in Laos. His mother, Phisawat, was part of the royal family. Teerachai had three siblings: Maj. Gen. Manasawat Arnupap; Lt. Gen. Piyawat Nakwanich, who at one point became commander of the 4th Army Region; and General Wuttichai Nakwanich, a former commander of the 9th Infantry Division. Teerachai had been close to General Prawit Wongsuwan at least since 1981. In that year, he and Prawit had supported the coup against Prime Minister Prem. Teerachai became part of the 12th Infantry Regiment, where Prawit was his commander. Without his patron Prawit and the 2014 coup, Teerachai could not have become army commander. Teerachai is a member of pre-cadet class 14, the class of General Nipat Tonglek (the former permanent minister of defence under Prime Minister Yingluck Shinawatra) and former army commander Udomdej. Udomdej and Teerachai have had a

long-running feud. See Wassana Nanuam, "Long-Running Rift between Theerachai, Udomdej Flares", *Bangkok Post*, 6 October 2015, https://www.bangkokpost.com/thailand/general/719136/long-running-rift-between-theerachai-udomdej-flares.

20. Serhat Uenaldi, "Thailand in 2015: The Waiting Game", in *Southeast Asian Affairs 2016*, edited by Malcolm Cook and Daljit Singh (Singapore: Institute of Southeast Asian Studies, 2016), pp. 327–28, https://www.jstor.org/stable/10.2307/26466933; Kitti Prasirtsuk, "Thailand in 2015: Bill, Blast and Beyond", *Asian Survey* 56, no. 1, Asia in 2015: The Year in Review (January/ February 2016): 172–73, https://www.jstor.org/stable/10.2307/26364357.

21. Amnesty International, *Thailand: Lift Rights Restrictions during Political Transition*, July 2016, https://www.amnesty.or.th/files/8615/0648/9828/report_ol_-_referendum_eng.pdf; "Torture Allegation is a 'Distortion of Facts,' Thai Junta Says", *Khaosod English*, 19 March 2015, https://www.khaosodenglish.com/life/2015/03/19/1426764564/.

22. กกต.แถลงผลประชามติเป็นทางการคนเห็นชอบร่างรธน.61.35% [EC announces official results of referendum, 61.35% voters approve draft constitution], *Post Today*, 10 August 2016, https://www.youtube.com/watch? https://www.posttoday.com/politics/447841.

23. Interview with anonymous election station worker, 10 August 2016.

24. iLaw, "7 August Referendum Cannot Be Used to Claim Legitimacy of Power under New Constitution", 18 August 2016, https://ilaw.or.th/node/4243.

25. "King Appoints 10 Members to his Privy Council", *Bangkok Post*, 6 December 2016, https://www.bangkokpost.com/thailand/general/1152824/king-appoints-10-members-to-his-privy-council.

26. Paul Chambers "A Rebuke against a Sister", *New Mandala*, 19 February 2019, https://www.newmandala.org/a-rebuke-against-a-sister-and-the-personalising-of-monarchical-control/.

27. Pongphisoot Busbarat, "Thailand in 2017: Stability without Certainties", in *Southeast Asian Affairs 2018*, edited by Daljit Singh and Malcolm Cook (Singapore: ISEAS – Yusof Ishak Institute, 2018), p. 349, https://www.jstor.org/stable/10.2307/26492785.

28. Constitution of the Kingdom of Thailand, 6 April 2017, https://cdc.parliament.go.th/draftconstitution2/download/article/article_20180829093502.pdf.

29. Teeranai Charuvastra, "Suthep Endorses Constitutional Loophole to Keep Prayut in Power", *Khaosod*, 2 June 2017, https://www.khaosodenglish.com/politics/2017/06/02/suthep-endorses-constitutional-loophole-keep-Prayut-power/.

30. iLaw, "'The Prolongation of NCPO Power' Was Not Just a Discourse but Legally Concrete", 25 March 2019, https://www.ilaw.or.th/node/5301.

31. "Thai Junta Says Police Helped Yingluck Escape", *France 24*, 23 September 2017, https://www.france24.com/en/20170923-thai-junta-says-police-helped-yingluck-escape.

32. Ibid.

33. Suchart formerly commanded the 4th Infantry Battalion, 5th Infantry Regiment (Songkhla), and the 43rd Ranger Regiment (Narathiwat). He is an alumnus of Military Preparatory School class 12.

34. Wassana Nanuam, "NCPO to Allow Parties Limited Political Activities", *Bangkok Post*, 28 August 2018, https://www.bangkokpost.com/thailand/politics/1529894/ncpo-to-allow-parties-limited-political-activities.

35. "4 Ministers, 3 Ex-PDRC Leaders Join Palang Pracharath", *Bangkok Post*, 29 September 2018, https://www.bangkokpost.com/thailand/politics/1549002/4-ministers-3-pdrc-leaders-join-palang-pracharat.

36. See, for example, Internal Security Operations Command, "จังหวัด หนองบัวลำภู รณรงค์เชิญชวนให้พี่น้องประชาชนออกมาใช้สิทธิเลือกตั้ง ในวันอาทิตย์ที่ 24 มีนาคม 2562 โดยพร้อมเพรียงกัน" [Nong Bua Lamphu province campaign to invite people to vote on Sunday, 24 March 2019 in unison], 20 March 2019, https://www.isoc.go.th/?p=11294.

37. Wassana Nanuam, "ISOC Defends New Internal Security Move, *Bangkok Post*, 24 November 2017, https://www.bangkokpost.com/thailand/politics/1365787/isoc-defends-new-internal-security-move.

38. Interview with senior Thai military official, Bangkok, 26 December 2021.

39. Paul Chambers, "Red Rim Soldiers": The Changing Leadership of Thailand's Military in 2020, *New Mandala*, 21 September 2020, https://www.newmandala.org/the-changing-leadership-of-thailands-military-in-2020/.

40. Helen Regan, "How a Rap Video Could Become the Faultline of Thailand's Long-Awaited Elections", CNN, 5 November 2018, https://edition.cnn.com/2018/11/03/asia/thai-rap-junta-intl/index.html.

41. Hathaikan Trisuwan. เลือกตั้ง 2562: ทีสุดที่คุณอาจยัง ไม่รู้ก่อนเข้าคูหา [Election 2019: The best you may not know before entering the booth], BBC Thai Online, 18 February 2019, https://www.bbc.com/thai/thailand-46902175.

42. Kas Chanwanpen, "Parties Accuse EC of Bias in Constituency Mapping", *The Nation*, 30 November 2018, http://www.nationmultimedia.com/detail/politics/30359551.

43. See iLaw, "คสช. ใช้ ม.44 แบ่งเขตเลือกตั้งใหม่-เปิดทาง คสช. มีส่วนร่วม" [NCPO uses Section 44 to divide new constituencies – allow NCPO to participate], 25 November 2018, https://ilaw.or.th/node/5035.

44. Paul Chambers, "Thailand's Elected Junta: The Pluralistic Poverty of Phalang Pracharat", ISEAS Commentaries, 2021/29, 12 March 2021, https://www.iseas.edu.sg/articles-commentaries/iseas-perspective/2021-29-thailands-elected-junta-the-pluralistic-poverty-of-phalang-by-pracharat-paul-chambers/.

45. For that list, see ประกาศ แต่งตั้งสมาชิกวุฒิสภา พระบาทสมเด็จพระปรเมนทรรามาธิบดีศรี สินทรมหาวชิราลงกรณ พระวชิรเกล้าเจ้าอยู่หัว, เล่ม ๑๓๖ ตอนพิเศษ ๑๒๑ ง ราชกิจจานุเบกษา ๑๔ พฤษภาคม ๒๕๖๒ [Announcement, the appointment of senators, graciously endorsed by His Majesty King Bhumibol Adulyadej, Phra Wajira Klao Chao Yu Hua], *Royal Gazette*, book 136, special section 121, 14 May 2019,

http://www.ratchakitcha.soc.go.th/DATA/PDF/2562/E/121/T_0001. PDF.

46. Paul Chambers and Napisa Waitoolkiat, "Thailand's Thwarted Democratization", *Asian Affairs: An American Review* (2019) 22, https:// doi.org/10.1080/00927678.2019.1699226.

47. James Ockey, "Thailand in 2019: An Election, a Coronation, and Two Summits", *Asian Survey* 60, no. 1 (February 2020): 121, https://doi. org/10.1525/as.2020.60.1.117.

48. Teeranai Charuvastra, Teeranai, "'Emergency Order' Transfers Army Units to King's Command", *Khaosod English*, 1 October 2019, https:// www.khaosodenglish.com/politics/2019/10/01/emergency-order-transfers-army-units-to-kings-command/.

49. Teeranai Charuvastra, "Special Police Unit Rebranded as King's Guard", 29 January 2019, https://www.khaosodenglish.com/politics/2019/01/29/ special-police-unit-rebranded-as-kings-guard/.

50. Richard Paddock, Muktita Suhartono, and Ryn Jirenuwat, "Thai Soldier in Mass Shooting Had Business Clash with his Commander", *New York Times*, 10 February 2020, https://www.nytimes.com/2020/02/10/world/ asia/thai-shooting-gunman.html.

51. Wassana Nanuam, "Army Signs Deal to Let Finance Manage Welfare Assets", *Bangkok Post*, 17 February 2020, https://www.bangkokpost.com/ thailand/general/1859524/army-signs-deal-to-let-finance-manage-welfare-assets.

52. Royal Thai Government, "Requirements Issued According to Article 9 of the Emergency Decree on Public Administration in Emergency Situations" (2005), version 1, *Royal Gazette*, vol. 136, issue 69, p. 10 (in Thai), 25 March 2020. http://www.ratchakitcha.soc.go.th/DATA/ PDF/2563/E/069/T_0010.PDF.

53. James Ockey, "Thailand in 2020: Politics, Protests, and a Pandemic", *Asian Survey* 61, no. 1 (2021): 115–22, https://doi.org/10.1525/ as.2021.61.1.115.

54. Pithaya Pookaman, *Asia Sentinel,* 23 September 2021, https://www. asiasentinel.com/p/thailand-pprp-fissures-theaten-Prayut-Prayut-chan-ocha.

55. Maya Taylor, "Amended Communicable Disease Law Includes Powers to Retain Curfew, Order Lockdowns", *Thaiger (Bangkok Post)*, 23 September 2021, https://thethaiger.com/coronavirus/amended-communicable-disease-law-includes-powers-to-retain-curfew-order-lockdowns.

56. Termsuk Chalermpalanupap, "Thai PM Remains Vulnerable without a Party of His Own", *ISEAS Perspective*, no. 2017/127, 28 September 2021, https://www.iseas.edu.sg/articles-commentaries/iseas-perspective/2021-127-thai-pm-remains-vulnerable-without-a-party-of-his-own-by-termsak-chalermpalanupap/.

57. "Plot Aims to Oust Premier", *Bangkok Post*, 3 September 2021, https:// www.bangkokpost.com/thailand/politics/2175483/plot-aims-to-oust-premier.

58. "'ผู้การสุชาติ' เผย พรรคใหม่ 'ปลัดฉิ่ง' ขนาดใหญ่–หัวหน้า–ผู้บริหารขายได้ ยันไม่ใช่พรรคถ่วงดุล พปชร" ["Commander Suchart" reveals a new party, Plat Ching, large-scale, with executives, not a party to counterbalance Palang Pracharat], *Matichon*, 29 September 2021, https://www.matichon.co.th/politics/news_2965011.

59. Wassana Nanuam, "B22.5bn Subs Buy Put on Ice", *Bangkok Post*, 19 July 2021, https://www.bangkokpost.com/thailand/general/2150891/b22-5bn-subs-buy-put-on-ice.

60. For example, Jaroenchai Hintao became assistant army commander and looked set to succeed Narongphan upon the latter's retirement in 2023. Santipong Tampiya, another Buraphapayak member, took the post of army chief of staff. Suksawan Nongualang became 1st Army Region commander. In addition, Buraphapayak cavalryman Chalermpol continued on as supreme commander. All of these officers were members of Kaw Daeng (Red Rim), the faction created by the king. As a sub-faction, Buraphapayak remained cohesive.

61. Aekarach Sattaburuth, "New Party Ready to Welcome PM Prayut", *Bangkok Post*, 9 February 2022, https://www.bangkokpost.com/thailand/politics/2261455/new-party-ready-to-welcome-pm-prayut.

62 In 2022, Prawit ensured the appointment of his loyalists to the following posts: Buraphapayak faction members General Sanitchanok Sangkachan as permanent secretary of the Ministry of Defence; General Jaroenchai Hintao (also Red Rim) as deputy army chief; and General Damrongsak Kittiprapas as police chief. General Songwit Noonpadi (Red Rim and Wongthewan) moved from a peripheral armed forces posting to suddenly become deputy commander, which made it likely that he would succeed General Chalermpol as commander of the armed forces when the latter retired on 30 September 2023. The ascension of General Pana Plotthuk to command the 1st Army Region represented a boon for the king in terms of the Wongthewan/Red Rim faction. Paul Chambers, "Dissecting Thailand's 2022 Military and Police Reshuffles", *ISEAS Perspective*, no. 2022/95, 25, https://www.iseas.edu.sg/articles-commentaries/iseas-perspective/2022-95-dissecting-thailands-2022-military-and-police-reshuffles-palace-proactivity-by-paul-chambers/.

Chapter Fifteen

Conclusion

The evolution of military influence in contemporary Thailand represents a classic case of praetorianism. What is currently called Thailand has witnessed the evolution of multiple principalities into one kingdom through brute force under the supervision of managers of violence—the military. Though royalty has led this kingdom, the armed forces built it, consolidating it through coercion and making it a praetorian kingdom. The pyramid of the armed forces hierarchy revolves in entourages connected by kith and kin among military families as well as aristocracy, but ultimately achieving legitimacy via linkages to the royal family. It has been and remains a "khakistocracy", where military-buttressed royalty has been located—at least ceremonially, if not in actuality—at the macro-centre. Across time, military cohesion has functioned, at a macro level, through the martial role of guarding the monarchy, making the armed forces a "monarchized military". Yet, within the ranks and experiences of officers, the "glue" that has taken priority at the micro level in tying them together has not been the overarching ideology of "monarchization" but, rather, the camaraderie and brotherhood of the corps based upon the same military class, identical unit, or shared combat experience. At the lowest levels, such brotherhood has been based around the personal charisma of military "warlords". Informal hierarchies based upon fraternal codes or norms of trust have superseded a formal hierarchy of rules-based legitimacy. Ultimately, a political and bureaucratic culture permeates the armed forces to which officers have connected themselves through asymmetrical shared experiences. They see themselves as the guardians of the monarchy, intervene in politics to protect the palace as they see fit, and believe they deserve special privileges as coercive servants of the royalty. They are therefore a monarchized military that has sustained an arch-royalist praetorian status quo. Since 1980, the Thai armed forces have crucially undergirded a palace-led parallel state.

This study has argued that Thailand's military (as led by military strongmen) has been able to persevere as a leading societal actor primarily because it has managed to achieve and hold on to a monopoly of violence across the kingdom outside of any oversight by elected civilian actors, ousting those governments it deemed to impede its interests, and has retained its power over the years as a senior or junior associate of the monarchy in a partnership of power. The military has ensured that laws are in place that maximize its legal benefits, has continuously possessed an enormous and generally unmonitored budget, has remained beyond the scrutiny of the judiciary, and has rationalized its clout as essential for protecting that monarchy and guaranteeing national security. Persistent interventions by the military in Thai politics over time has led to the socially constructed belief among civilians that the military is either justified in protecting the king or cannot be stopped. And soldiers feel that they are privileged as royal protectors to intervene as they please. Thus, the praetorian character of the Thai polity is masked by the need to guard the monarchy, and the Thai armed forces are now a tool of the palace, functioning time and again as a "monarchized military".

The military achieved its monopoly over violence by defeating periodic insurgencies against the Thai kingdom while ensuring that enormous financial resources were consistently made available to the military to subsidize more and more armaments to be used by the largest number of security labourers of any bureaucracy. The armed forces have always promoted various forms of nationalist-authoritarianism as a means of safeguarding the kingdom. This has ensured that the state gives them access to enhanced resources of violence, while more laws have been enacted that allow the military to call out its forces as it pleases. The military has overthrown governments when it has been unified under a military personality to do so, it finds a rationale based around political pandemonium to usurp power, and is encouraged to act by the palace for all of these motives.

By 1980, incessant factionalism was weakening the armed forces. The military thus became a junior partner to the monarchy as a means of legitimizing its continuing pivotal role on the political stage. The military retained is influence under the monarchy, and this was reinforced by the coups of 1991, 2006 and 2014. Democratization remains lost in transition in Thailand because the monarchy and its agent, the military, remain unaccountable to the Thai people. Though many are willing to follow the preferences of the king, the palace would be unable to enforce its anti-pluralist control without the ready use of repression by the armed forces. Since the 2016 accession of King Rama X, the reciprocal relationship of monarchized military has tightened, diminishing the influence enjoyed by the Privy Council under King Rama IX and embedding the dyadism between the king and the military.

At the beginning of this book, this study applied the conceptual framework of praetorianism as a means of understanding military influence in Thailand. In that regard, three principal questions were asked. First, why did Thailand evolve to become a praetorian kingdom? Second, what is the detailed history of Thai praetorianism? And third, why has Thai military influence across politics never been curtailed?

In answer to the first question, Thailand has had a history not unlike other countries that are highly regionalized but have been plagued with insurgencies over several decades. Across fifty years, the Thai military used the threat of communism against the kingdom to legitimize its near dominance over the country. With the end of the Cold War, an active military involvement in politics continued by legitimizing the need to protect the monarchy from any sources. Today, Thailand is different from other countries in the sense that it is one of the few led by a powerful king alongside a frail democracy and growing, politically involved movements of demonstrators. Thus, a praetorian rationale exists in Thailand—a motive for the military to stay involved in politics and usurp power if necessary. That motive has been the same for all but two coups since 1947—protecting the palace.

In answer to the second question, the detailed history of Thai praetorianism is complicated, but it involves a chronology of the military and the monarchy, while elected Thai civilians have rarely played a lasting influence in politics outside of these two institutions.

In answer to the third question, regarding political power, Thai military influence has sometimes been curtailed—but only for short periods of time. It has always returned. This speaks to the endorsement of military coups by the monarch, insufficient democratic development whereby elected premiers can sanction military coup-makers, and a political culture whereby soldiers think they have the right to usurp power and enough Thai civilians agree to it.

The book also asked four secondary questions. Have there ever been security-sector reform efforts, and have they ever taken hold? Why does Thailand's military remain such an obstacle to democratization in 2023? What has been the history of military-monarchy relations in Thailand? And how have senior military officials intervened in Thai democratization efforts?

In answer to the first question, the only security sector reform efforts that have ever succeeded in Thailand have been those led by the military, which has sought to improve its fighting force capabilities. There have been reform efforts by civilian governments to establish greater control over the armed forces. These have included the periods 1946–47, 1973–76 and to some extent 1988–91, 1992–2001 and 2001–6. While the attempts beginning in 1992 succeeded to a degree in reining in direct military influence over corporate shares and board chairpersonships, the economic reforms also benefited the military because civilians proved better at managing military money, military shares became hidden behind civilian proxies, and more civilians representing military interests were appointed to corporate boards.

As for political reforms, none of these were successful because the military returned to power in 2006 and 2014 to resurrect their influence. Before and after the 2019 election, security sector reforms were front and centre of the agenda for many political parties. Many wanted to diminish the defence budget, while others sought to reduce the number of armed forces personnel. A third proposal was to abolish conscription altogether. A fourth reform sought to reduce the amount of military land, putting it to greater social use. A fifth was to improve social welfare, education and insurance for military officials. A sixth sought to improve transparency and accountability in defence procurement. A seventh was to increase elected civilians' control over the military, even seeking to further codify the ability of civilians to sanction military officers. Despite these calls for change, little has been done to reform the armed forces to bring them under civilian control. An example of such inaction was the 2020 promise by army commander General Apirat Kongsompong to transfer military property to be under the Finance Ministry. Two years later, Apirat had retired and nothing had been done. The post–2019 government of Prime Minister Prayut Chanocha concentrated on procuring more military hardware, including three highly priced Chinese submarines. There was little involvement of the legislature in this purchase. Ultimately, no security sector reforms led by elected civilians over the military's political influence have ever taken hold in Thailand. The reason is because no elected civilian government has ever lasted long enough to entrench its reforms. The military has such enormous bureaucratic pull over national security that it is difficult to control its clout without risking a coup.

In answer to the second question, the armed forces remain a clear obstacle to democratization because they have shown time and again that they are ready and willing to oust elected governments. Moreover, it is the very nature of the military as a hierarchical institution of ranked personnel to give and take orders rather than to be democratic. Indeed, with their monopoly on violence, the armed forces are a key part of the palace-led parallel state that has invariably resisted pluralistic advances in Thailand.

In answer to the third question, the history of military-monarchy relations in Thailand have been chaotic. From a period of direct monarchical control over the military until 1932, the armed forces enjoyed complete control over the kingdom until 1944 (the royal family possessed only ceremonial power from 1932 to 1947). During the period of 1947–51, the monarchy was the junior affiliate to the military in a power partnership, while 1951–57 saw the military dominate the country alone again. The period 1957–63 witnessed a return of the monarchy as the military's junior partner. From 1963 to 1976, the monarchy gradually enhanced its authority. During 1976–77, the palace attempted to lord over the senior brass of the armed forces, but the monarch-selected civilian prime minister was ousted in a coup. The period 1977–80 represented an attempt by the military to sustain power without necessarily having royal assent. It failed. From 1980 until 2016, the monarchy and the military dominated the kingdom, though the military was the junior partner. During this period, after 1988, the Privy Council became an important third element in the relationship, given that King Rama IX chose to rule in a rather decentralized manner. Under his successor since 2016, King Rama X, the monarchy has continued as the senior partner to the military, though the relationship has been much more centralized than during the period prior to 2016. In all, despite the ups and downs in power between the two, the armed forces have always been and will remain a monarchized military—seeking the legitimacy of the royal institution both when it has only been a ceremonial player and also when it has exerted enormous power.

In answer to the fourth question, senior military officials have been able to insert themselves into Thai democratization efforts in five ways. First, when faced with sitting civilian governments that they dislike, they have sought to intimidate them and/or ousted them, establishing a brief junta before returning to the barracks. This is what happened to the 1988–91 Chatchai Chunhavan and 2001–6 Thaksin Shinawatra governments. Second, the military has simply ousted civilian governments and established long-lasting juntas. Examples are the junta of General Sarit Thanarat, followed by General Thanom Kittikachorn and General Praphas Charusathien during 1958–69 (and 1971–73), as well as the junta of General Prayut Chanocha, General Prawit Wongsuwan and General Anupong Paochinda (2014–19). Third, where civilians have been united for change, the military has acquiesced to remain in the shadows of an elected government, perhaps biding their time for the opportunity to carry out a coup. This is what the military practised during 1973–76 and 2011–14. Fourth, the military has lorded over democratization efforts by instituting a "semi-democracy", where there is an elected lower house but the prime minister and Senate are selected by the military. Such was the status of the 1980–88 regime headed by General Prem Tinsulanonda. Fifth and finally, the military has sought to use elections and political parties to not only insert themselves into parliamentary politics but also to monopolize parliament altogether. Military leaders have used such practices during 1933, 1937, 1938, 1952, 1957, 1958, 1969, 1975 (attempted), 1976 (attempted), 1991 and 2019.

In 2023, the military's proxy Palang Pracharat party found itself nearing the end of a parliamentary term as the leader of the ruling coalition. The same military triumvirate that had led the 2014 putsch and ruled via authoritarian fiat for five years was still in power, heading a government through a façade democracy. September 2023 saw Srettha Thavisin of Pheu Thai become Thailand's newest elected prime minister and he formally headed up the country's latest 2023–27 cabinet. Then, on 1 October 2023, the pro-Prayuth General Jaroenchai Hintao (pre-cadet 23, retiring in 2024) became army commander alongside newly appointed commander of the Royal Armed Forces Headquarters, General Songwit Noonpakdee (class 24, retiring in 2025). Their retirements are likely to be followed by the appointments of new military commanders who will also safeguard the foremost clout of the monarchy.

What then is the future of the political clout of the Thai military? In terms of achieving lasting elected civilian control any time soon, the prospects appear to be dim. Though it is difficult to speculate about what is around the corner, there are four scenarios for the future. First, there is the South Korea/Taiwan model. In this scenario, countries led by a military dictatorship evolve to a military-dominated democracy until reaching a fuller, embedded, liberal democracy. In fact, this was where Thailand seemed to be headed after 1992, and especially following the election of Thaksin Shinawatra in 2001. But the arch-royalists were not ready to accept change. While Thailand may eventually reach entrenched civilian-led democracy, it does not look like this will happen any time soon since the monarchy and the military, the two authoritarian institutions guaranteeing that coups can easily happen again, remain quite powerful. Second, there is the Myanmar model. Thailand could revert to the military monopoly of the past, with a much more authoritarian regime akin to that of Sarit, Thanom and Praphas. This too is unlikely because both the Thai people and the international community are unlikely to tolerate an institutionalized lack of any form of democracy for long. A third scenario is that there will eventually be another military coup, with the military subsequently implementing a new constitution and rapidly returning to the barracks before new elections take place. This scenario is likely if we consider that the current monarch may endorse a putsch to reduce the power of Prayut, Prawit or both as a means of enhancing the direct clout of the palace. If there is another coup, it would follow the Thai political trend of one coup after another. A fourth and final scenario is that Thailand's military continues to enhance its political power by dominating the civilian sphere of politics—parliament. At this stage, in 2023, for the sake of sustaining popular legitimacy, it seems as though the armed forces will likely continue to play the parliamentary "game", building dominant political parties such as Palang Pracharat, which then form coalition governments, with the likely assistance of the Senate that was appointed by the previous junta. In this way the military can promote its interests without the use of coups. Such a strategy was originally employed by Field Marshal Phibun Songkram before he was overthrown in 1957. It remains perhaps the most successful means of sustaining military power—though the tactic might involve election rigging.

Scenario four is clearly the chosen strategy of Prime Minister Prayut (with Prawit and Anupong) as he seeks to maintain power. Yet there are both external and internal threats to his continued rule. External to the regime, by 2023, many Thai people had run out of patience with the military-dominated government, blaming Prayut for the kingdom's economic deterioration and less-than-satisfactory policies to combat the Covid-19 pandemic. Meanwhile, beginning in 2020, large demonstrations by young people against the government and the monarch did little to improve Prayut's popularity. To counter the demonstrators, Prayut's regime jailed demonstration leaders, used repression, and appealed to pro-palace sentiments among conservative Thais. Internal to the regime is another threat: factionalism. The growing division between Prayut and Anupong, on one side, and Prawit on the other, threatened to tear apart Palang Pracharat, or whichever grouping of pro-military parties won seats following the outcome of the 2023 general election. In the case that Palang Pracharat did dissolve, both Prayut and Prawit had their own individual backup parties already established—just in case. There were rumours that Prawit might even ally with Thaksin Shinawatra against Prayut.

While Thailand's former junta leaders remained divided and were embroiled in their political rivalry in the run-up to the 2023 general election, the active-duty senior brass in the armed forces were divided as well: most of the commanders of the strategic 1st Army Region were loyal to Prayut and Prawit, while army commander General Narongphan Jitgaewthae was extremely loyal to the king, who had personally selected him for the post. The point is that, in 2023, the Thai military leadership had become so fractious that there was room to speculate that a civilian—acceptable to the monarchy, military and most political parties—could perhaps become elected prime minister. The military would retain great power in the shadows.

How might Thailand break out of its path-dependence of continuing royally endorsed praetorianism? I have saved this question for the end because there are no easy answers. It goes without saying that the palace could compel the armed forces to diminish its leading role in society and make it more accountable and transparent. But the monarchy, which depends upon the military to protect its dominant political and economic clout, has no reason to reduce the power of the armed forces. Another answer might be to increase education in Thailand of both Thai soldiers and civilians to give more value to democracy as a means of reducing the Thai military's clout. But this strategy depends too heavily, and unrealistically, on cognitive adaptation to enhance civilian control. Finally, Thailand could adopt the Costa Rica model: simply dissolve the military altogether, replacing it with a strong police force. While there might be numerous financial savings by enacting this plan, the police, which would come to hold the monopoly on violence, could easily become the unaccountable military of Thailand's past. Thus, there are no ready methods for achieving civilian control in Thailand.

In sum, despite the appearance of moves towards expanding efforts at democratization and the civilianization of politics in Thailand, this has all happened before in the country (1946, 1957, 1969, 1974, 1979,

1988, 1992 and 2008) only to come crashing down under the weight of renewed military intrusions. Thailand is not moving in a linear direction towards civilian control over the armed forces, but rather remains in a cycle of continuing military activism. As the land of fourteen successful overt military coups since 1932 and twenty (mostly military-established) constitutions since 1932, Thailand finds itself as the classic example of a praetorian country—specifically, a praetorian kingdom. The insight here is that the lengthy path of royally endorsed military entrenchment across Thai politics has made such praetorianism highly sticky—and it will be difficult to dislodge. Given Thailand's military history, the prospects for civilian control unfettered by the restraints of the armed forces any time soon is doubtful.

In the end, this study has focused on Thailand's armed forces, striving to demonstrate through an examination of Thai military history that the country's armed forces have been and remain a leading force in Thai politics. The military became entrenched under the palace through the help of Prime Minister Prem Tinsulanonda in 1980 and thus second in power only to the monarchy, with the king depending upon the military to preserve the pivotal standing of the palace. Though adept at coup-making, since the 2019 election, the military has proven successful in seeing junta-created political parties come to office, although there were election irregularities. Judging by the ability of the military over time to persist in exerting enormous influence in politics, it is likely that it will continue being able to do so, through coups, political party proxies, intimidation of elected governments, and mostly via monarchical backing.

Thai politics continues to be influenced by a monarchized military, which guarantees that Thailand is a praetorian kingdom. Thai façade democracy represents a sideshow to this parallel state of monarchy-military cooperation. King Maha Vajiralongkorn has co-opted retired senior military officials into an increasingly militarized Privy Council, Office of the Royal Household, and Royal Security Command. Sadly, for those seeking fuller democracy, elected civilian control and political space in Thailand, there are few indications that—minus a dangerously courageous stand for change—the arch-royalist, praetorian nature of Thai politics is likely to change any time soon.

Appendices

Evidence of Praetorianism
in Thailand (1932–2023)

Appendix 1
18 Overt and Silent Coups in Thailand (1932–2023)

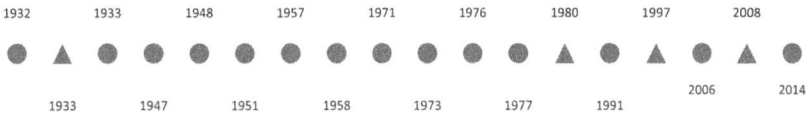

| 1932 | 1933 | 1948 | 1957 | 1971 | 1976 | 1980 | 1997 | 2008 |

●　▲　●　●　●　●　●　●　●　●　●　●　▲　●　▲　●　▲　●

| | 1933 | 1947 | 1951 | 1958 | 1973 | 1977 | 1991 | 2006 | 2014 |

Note: Circle = Overt coup; Triangle = "Silent" coup.

Appendix 2
Percentage of Active Duty/Retired Military/Police
in the Legislature (1932–2023)

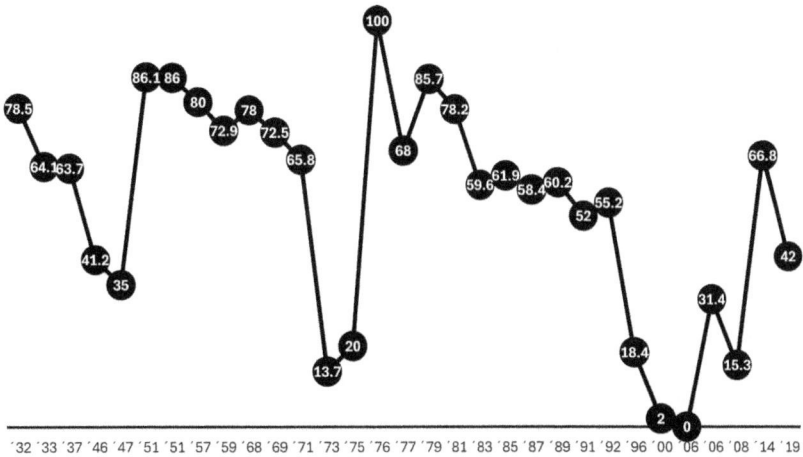

Data points: 78.5, 64.1, 63.7, 41.2, 35, 86.1, 86, 80, 72.9, 78, 72.5, 65.8, 13.7, 20, 100, 68, 85.7, 78.2, 59.6, 61.9, 58.4, 60.2, 52, 55.2, 18.4, 2, 0, 31.4, 15.3, 66.8, 42

'32 '33 '37 '46 '47 '51 '51 '57 '59 '68 '69 '71 '73 '75 '76 '77 '79 '81 '83 '85 '87 '89 '91 '92 '96 '00 '06 '06 '08 '14 '19

Source: Author's calculations based on data collected from the library at Thailand's National Parliament.

Appendix 3
Percentage of Active Duty or Retired Military/Police Cabinet Ministers (1932–2023)

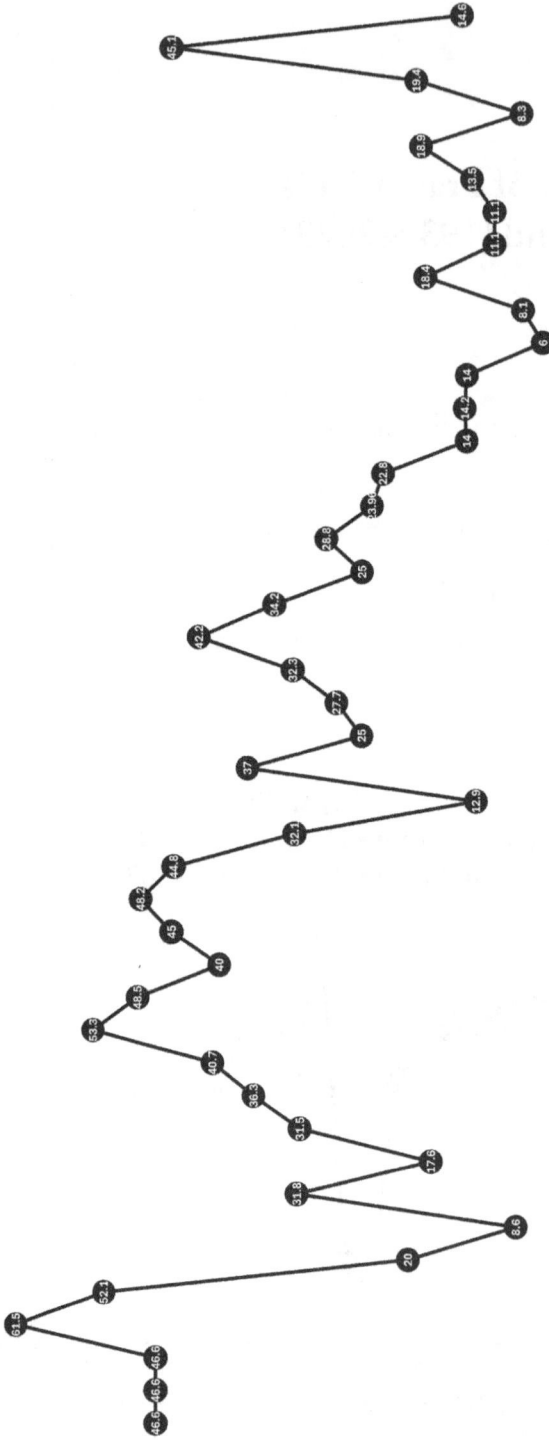

Note: Includes active/retired personnel of the army, air force, navy and police. *Royal Gazette,* พระบรมราชโองการ ประกาศ แต่งตั้งรัฐมนตรี (Announcements Cabinets), 1932–2023, https://ratchakitcha.soc.go.th/.

Appendix 4
Chronology of Key Military Reshuffles (1932–2022)

In the tables that follow, next to each name, the corresponding military school class has been placed in parentheses. Since military schools changed over time, different types of school numbers will be seen. Until and including 1939, simply the class year is placed next to the prospective military officer (e.g., Prem 1939/1981, or in some cases 39/1981). From 1940 until 1948, a preparatory class for all military officers existed. This has been denoted beginning with (P1)/1982, for example. Starting in 1949, the class of Chulachomklao Army Cadet Academy is used. Thus, the corresponding year is the class number, such as Chavalit (1)/1990. Finally, beginning in 1958, the Armed Forces Academy Preparatory School (AFAPS) was created, with almost all officers attending this school before attending the army, air force, navy or police academies. Officers after this date have their names and corresponding AFAPS class/Chulachomklao Army Cadet Academy denoted (e.g., Surayud 1/2003).

For each person in the tables that follow, the faction and end-of-service (retirement/ dismissal/death) dates (if known) are given.

The faction of the First Division is King's Guard, or Wongthewan (Heavenly Progeny; 1870), while the faction of the Second Division is Burapapayak (Tigers of the East; 1955).

Source: *Royal Gazette*, Library of the National Parliament.

Post	6 July 1932	1933	1934	1935	1936	1937	1938	1939
Defence Minister	Phraya Rajawangsan (palace/1933)	Phraya Rajawangsan (palace/1933)	Phraya Phahon 1901/1946	Plaek Phibun Songkram 1909/1948	Plaek Phibun Songkram 1909/1948	Plaek Phibun Songkram 1909/1948	Plaek Phibun Songkram 1909/1948	Plaek Phibun Songkram 1909/1948
Permanent Minister of Defence	Phraya Prasert-songkram 1896/1934	Phraya Ritthiaknay 1899/1849	Plaek Phibun Songkram 1909/1948	Phraya Sakda-dunyut 1895/1945	Phraya Sakda-dunyut 1895/1945	Phraya Sakda-dunyut 1895/1945	Phraya Sakda-dunyut 1895/1945	Phraya Sakda-dunyut 1895/1945
Navy CC	Phraya Prichachon layu 1909/1957	Phraya Prichachon layu 1909/1957	Luang Sinthu Songkram 1914/1951	Phraya Wichanach 1905/1938	Phraya Wichanach 1905/1938	Phraya Wichanach 1905/1938	Luang Sinthu Songkram 1914/1951	Luang Sinthu Songkram 1914/1951
Air Force CC	Phraya Vehasayan Silapasit ?/1935	Phraya Vehasayan Silapasit ?/1935	Phraya Vehasayan Silapasit ?/1935	Muni MahasantaVejayan-tarunsarit 1911/1953	Muni MahasantaVejayan-tarunsarit 1911/1953	Muni MahasantaVejayan-tarunsarit 1911/1953	Muni MahasantaVejayan-tarunsarit 1911/1953	Muni MahasantaVejayan-tarunsarit 1911/1953
Army CC	Phraya Phahon 1901/1946	Phraya Pichai Songkram (acting) (palace/1934)	Phraya Phahon 1901/1946	Phraya Phahon 1901/1946	Phraya Phahon 1901/1946	Phraya Phahon 1901/1946	Plaek Phibun Songkram 1909/1948	Plaek Phibun Songkram 1909/1948
Deputy C	Phraya Song Suradej 1904/1944	Plaek Phibun Songkram 1909/1948	Plaek Phibun Songkram 1909/1948	Plaek Phibun Songkram 1909/1948	Plaek Phibun Songkram 1909/1948	Plaek Phibun Songkram 1909/1948	Phraya Songkram Pakdi 1907/1957	Mangkorn Promyothi 1912/1957
Assistant C	Phraya Apaisongkram 1898/1948	Phraya Apaisongkram 1898/1948	Phraya Apaisongkram 1898/1948	Phraya Apaisongkram 1898/1948	Phraya Apaisongkram 1898/1948	Phraya Apaisongkram 1898/1948	n/a	n/a
Assistant C	Phraya Songkram Pakdi 1907/1957	Phraya Songkram Pakdi 1907/1957	Phraya Songkram Pakdi 1907/1957	Phraya Songkram Pakdi 1907/1957	Phraya Songkram Pakdi 1907/1957	Phraya Songkram Pakdi 1907/1957	Phraya Songkram Pakdi 1907/1957	Phraya Songkram Pakdi 1907/1957
Comm, Infantry	Phra Sitthi Ruangdechapol 1902/1938	Phra Sitthi Ruangdechapol 1902/1938	Phra Sitthi Ruangdechapol 1902/1938	n/a	n/a	n/a	n/a	n/a
Comm, Artillery	Col. Phraya Ritthiaknay 1899/1849	Dismissed (n/a)		n/a		n/a	n/a	n/a
Deputy C, Artillery	Plaek Phibun Songkram 1909/1948	Plaek Phibun Songkram 1909/1948	Plaek Phibun Songkram 1909/1948					
Police Comm.	Phraya Buret Padungkit 1901–1932	Phraya Anusorn Turakan 1901/1936	Phraya Anusorn Turakan 1901/1936	Phraya Anusorn Turakan 1901/1936	Luang Adul Aduldej Jaras 1909–1947	Luang Adul Aduldej Jaras 1909–1947	Luang Adul Aduldej Jaras 1909–1947	Luang Adul Aduldej Jaras 1909–1947

Post	1940	1941	1942	1943	1944	1945	1946	1947	1948
Defence Minister	Plaek Phibun Songkram 1909/1948	Mangkorn Promyothi 1912/1957	Plaek Phibun Songkram 1909/1948	Pichit Kriangsak-pichit 1909/1957	Luang Sinthu Songkram 1914/1951	Luang Chamnan Prasit Yutasilp 1909/1954	Gen. Jir Wichit songkram 1909/1954	Luang Chatnakrop ?/?	Luang Chatnakrop ?/?
Perma-nent Def. Min.	Phraya Sakda-dunyut 1895/1945	Sawasdi Sawasdi Narong ?/1943	Phra Prajana-paccanuek 1902/1952	Luang Yutasat Kosol 1911/1956	Phra Silapastrakom 1902/1948	Rueng Rueng-virayut 1916/1958	Rueng Rueng-virayut 1916/1958	Luang Senanarong 1909/1954	Luang Senanarong 1909/1954
Navy CC	Luang Sinthu Songkram 1914/1951	Luang Sinthu Songkram 1914/1951	Luang Sinthu Songkram 1914/1951	Luang Sinthu Songkram 1914/1951	Luang Sinthu Songkram 1914/1951	Luang Sinthu Songkram 1914/1951	Luang Sinthu Songkram 1914/1951	Luang Sinthu Songkram 1914/1951	Luang Sinthu Songkram 1914/1951
Air Force CC	Muni Mahasanta Vejayan-tarunsarit 1911/1953	Luang Atug-tevadej 1893/1943	Luang Atug-tevadej 1893/1943	Luang Tevarit-panleuk 1904/1954	Luang Tevarit-panleuk 1904/1954	Luang Tevarit-panleuk 1904/1954	Luang Tevarit-panleuk 1904/1954	Luang Tevarit-panleuk 1904/1954	Luang Tevarit-panleuk 1904/1954
Army CC	Plaek Phibun Songkram 1909/1948	Plaek Phibun Songkram 1909/1948	Plaek Phibun Songkram 1909/1948	Plaek Phibun Songkram 1909/1948	Phraya Phahon 1901/1946	Phraya Phahon 1901/1946	Luang Adul Aduldej Jaras 1909–1947	Plaek Phibun Songkram 1909/1948	Phin Chunhavan 1912/1954
Army Deputy CC	Mangkorn Promyothi 1912/1957	Mangkorn Promyothi 1912/1957	Pichit Kriangsak-pichit 1909/1944	Pichit Kriangsak-pichit 1909/1944	Manilp Sinat Yotarak 1908/1946	Manilp Sinat Yotarak 1908/1946	Luang Chatnakrop 1909/1954	Phin Chunhavan 1912/1954	Kat Katsongkram 1900/1950
Army Chief of Staff	Gen. Jir Wichit songkram 1909/1954	Gen. Jir Wichit songkram 1909/1954	Luang Prasit Yutthasin ?/?	Luang Chatnakrop 1909/1954	Luang Chatnakrop 1909/1954	Luang Chatnakrop 1909/1954	Luang Han Songkram ?/1956	n/a	Det Depradit-iyut 1912/1962
Army Ass. CC	n/a	n/a	n/a	n/a	Luang Senanarong 1909/1954	Luang Senanarong 1909/1954	none	n/a	Luang Safit Yutagan 1912/1961
Army Ass. CC	Phraya Songkram Pakdi 1907/1957	Phraya Songkram Pakdi 1907/1957	Phraya Songkram Pakdi 1907/1957	Phraya Songkram Pakdi 1907/1957	n/a	n/a	none	Kat Katsongkram 1900/1950	Luang Suthi Suthisan Ronakary 1911/1963
1st Army Region Commander	non-existing	non-existing	non-existing	non-existing	non-existing	non-existing	non-existing	Kat Katsongkram 1900/1950	Kat Katsongkram 1900/1950
2nd Army Region Commander	non-existing	non-existing	non-existing	non-existing	non-existing	non-existing	non-existing	non-existing	Wirawat Yothin 1917/1959
1st Division CC (Wongthewan)	n/a	n/a	Kunplotpornpaks 1912/1962	Kunplotpornpaks 1912/1962	Wirawat Yothin 1917/1959	Wirawat Yothin 1917/1959	Wirawat Yothin 1917/1959	Wirawat Yothin 1917/1959	Sarit Thanarat 19/1963
Police CC	Luang Adul Aduldej Jaras 1909–1947	Luang Adul Aduldej Jaras 1909–1947	Luang Adul Aduldej Jaras 1909–1947	Luang Adul Aduldej Jaras 1909–1947	Luang Adul Aduldej Jaras 1909–1947	Praram Inthra 1905/1946	Prapjian Polkit 1909/1952	Luang Chat Trakankoso 1917/1962	Luang Chat Trakankoso 1917/1962

Post	1949	1950	1951	1952	1953	1954	1955	1956
Defence Minister	Plaek Phibun Songkram 1909/1948	Plaek Phibun Songkram 1909/1948	Plaek Phibun Songkram 1909/1948	Plaek Phibun Songkram 1909/1948	Plaek Phibun Songkram 1909/1948	Plaek Phibun Songkram 1909/1948	Plaek Phibun Songkram 1909/1948	Plaek Phibun Songkram 1909/1948
Permanent Def. Min.	Luang Senanarong 1909/1954	Luang Senanarong 1909/1954	Luang Senanarong 1909/1954	Luang Senanarong 1909/1954	Luang Senanarong 1909/1954	Luang Sanit Yutagan 1912/1961	Luang Sanit Yutagan 1912/1961	Luang Sanit Yutagan 1912/1961
Navy CC	Luang Sinthu Songkram 1914/1951	Luang Sinthu Songkram 1914/1951	Prayoon Yuthasas-trakosol 1926/1957	Prayoon Yuthasas-trakosol 1926/1957	Prayoon Yuthasas-trakosol 1926/1957	Prayoon Yuthasas-trakosol 1926/1957	Prayoon Yuthasas-trakosol 1926/1957	Prayoon Yuthasas-trakosol 1926/1957
Air Force CC	Fuen Ronafagrad 1911/1957	Fuen Ronafagrad 1911/1957	Fuen Ronafagrad 1911/1957	Fuen Ronafagarad 1911/1957	Fuen Ronafagarad 1911/1957	Fuen Ronafagrad 1911/1957	Fuen Ronafagrad 1911/1957	Fuen Ronafagrad 1911/1957
Army CC	Phin Chunhavan 1912/1954	Phin Chunhavan 1912/1954	Phin Chunhavan 1912/1954	Phin Chunhavan 1912/1954	Phin Chunhavan 1912/1954	Sarit Thanarat 19/1963	Sarit Thanarat 19/1963	Sarit Thanarat 19/1963
Army Deputy CC	n/a	Luang Sanit Yutagan 1912/1961	Det Depradit-iyut 1912/1962	Sarit Thanarat 19/1963	Sarit Thanarat 19/1963	Luang Suthi Suthisan Ronakary 1911/1963	Luang Suthi Suthisan Ronakary 1911/1963	Luang Suthi Suthisan Ronakary 1911/1963
Army Chief of Staff	n/a	Luang Suthi Suthisan Ronakary 1911/1963	Luang Suthi Suthisan Ronakary 1911/1963	Luang Suthi Suthisan Ronakary 1911/1963	Luang Suthi Suthisan Ronakary 1911/1963	Luang Suthi Suthisan Ronakary 1911/1963	Luang Suthi Suthisan Ronakary 1911/1963	Luang Suthi Suthisan Ronakary 1911/1963
Army Assist CC	n/a	Det Depradit-iyut 1912/1962	Sarit Thanarat 19/1963	Luang Suthi Suthisan Ronakary 1911/1963	Luang Suthi Suthisan Ronakary 1911/1963	Sawai Saenyagorn 1914/1965	Sawai Saenyagorn 1914/1965	Sawai Saenyagorn 1914/1965
1st Army Region Commander	Sarit Thanarat 19/1963	Sarit Thanarat 19/1963	Sarit Thanarat 19/1963	Sarit Thanarat 19/1963	Sarit Thanarat 19/1963	Thanom Kittikachorn 1920/1971	Thanom Kittikachorn 1920/1971	Thanom Kittikachorn 1920/1971
2nd Army Region Commander	Wirawat Yothin 1917/1959	Dun Bunnag ?/1955	Sawai Saenyagorn 1914/1965	Sawai Saenyagorn 1914/1965	Sawai Saenyagorn 1914/1965	Kruan Sutaninot 1912/1960	Sanit Santityutagan 1912/1961	Sawasdi Kunpan 1907/1957
3rd Army Region Commander	non-existing	Wirawat Yothin 1917/1959	Dun Bunnag ?/1956	Tongiun Supcharas ?/1954	Tongiun Supcharas ?/1954	Kruan Sutaninot 1912/1960	Kruan Sutaninot 1912/1960	Pong Boonsom 1920/1965
1st Divisional Commander (Wongthewan)	Sarit Thanarat 19/1963	Thanom Kittikachorn 1920/1971	Thanom Kittikachorn 1920/1971	Praphas Charusathien 1929/1973	Praphas Charusathien 1929/1973	Praphas Charusathien 1929/1973	Praphas Charusathien 1929/1973	Praphas Charusathien 1929/1973
2nd Infantry Division CC (Burapapayak)	n/a	Pong Boonsom 1920/1965	Chalor Jarugala 1921/1966	Chalor Jarugala 1921/1966	Chalor Jarugala 1921/1966	Chalor Jarugala 1921/1966	Chalor Jarugala 1921/1966	Chalor Jarugala 1921/1966
Police Commander	Luang Chat Trakankoso 1917/1962	Luang Chat Trakankoso 1917/1962	Phao Sriyanond 1926/1957	Phao Sriyanond 1926/1957	Phao Sriyanond 1926/1957	Phao Sriyanond 1926/1957	Phao Sriyanond 1926/1957	Phao Sriyanond 1926/1957

Post	1957	1958	1959	1960	1961	1962	1963	1964
Defence Minister	Thanom Kittikachorn 1920/1971	Thanom Kittikachorn 1920/1971	Thanom Kittikachorn 1920/1971	Thanom Kittikachorn 1920/1971	Thanom Kittikachorn 1920/1971	Thanom Kittikachorn 1920/1971	Thanom Kittikachorn 1920/1971	Thanom Kittikachorn 1920/1971
Permanent Sec. Defence	Luang Sanit Yutagan 1912/1961	Luang Sanit Yutagan 1912/1961	Luang Sanit Yutagan 1912/1961	Luang Sanit Yutagan 1912/1961	Luang Sanit Yutagan 1912/1961	Luang Sanit Yutagan 1912/1961	Luang Sanit Yutagan 1912/1961	Pong Bunsom 1920/1965
Supreme Commander	Sarit Thanarat 19/1963	Sarit Thanarat 19/1963	Sarit Thanarat 19/1963	Sarit Thanarat 19/1963	Sarit Thanarat 19/1963	Sarit Thanarat 19/1963	Sarit Thanarat 19/1963	Sarit Thanarat 19/1963
Navy CC	Luang Chamnan-arthayutha 1921/1962	Luang Chamnan-arthayutha 1921/1962	Luang Chamnan-arthayutha 1921/1962	Luang Chamnan-arthayutha 1921/1962	Luang Chamnan-arthayutha 1921/1962	Sawat Puthianan 1924/1964	Sawat Puthianan 1924/1964	MC Kanchitpon Aphakorn 1926/1966
Air Force CC	Chalermkiat Wattanakul 1934/1960	Chalermkiat Wattanakul 1934/1960	Chalermkiat Wattanakul 1934/1960	Bunchu Chantharubeksa 1933/1974	Bunchu Chantharubeksa 1933/1974	Bunchu Chantharu-beksa 1933/1974	Bunchu Chantharubeksa 1933/1974	Bunchu Chantharubeksa 1933/1974
Army CC	Sarit Thanarat 19/1963	Sarit Thanarat 19/1963	Sarit Thanarat 19/1963	Sarit Thanarat 19/1963	Sarit Thanarat 19/1963	Sarit Thanarat 19/1963	Sarit Thanarat 19/1963	Sarit Thanarat 19/1963
Army Deputy CC	Luang Suthi Suthisan Ronakary 1911/1963	Luang Suthi Suthisan Ronakary 1911/1963	Luang Suthi Suthisan Ronakary 1911/1963	Luang Suthi Suthisan Ronakary 1911/1963	Luang Suthi Suthisan Ronakary 1911/1963	Luang Suthi Suthisan Ronakary 1911/1963	Chitti Navisatien 1929/1972	Sanit SanitYutagan 1925/1965
Army Chief of Staff	Kruan Sutanitot 1912/1960	Kruan Sutanitot 1912/1960	Kruan Sutanitot 1912/1960	Chitti Navisatien 1929/1972	Chitti Navisatien 1929/1972	Chitti Navisatien 1929/1972	Sanit SanitYutagan 1925/1965	Boribun Julajarit 1924/1966
Army Assist CC	Sawai Saenyagorn 1914/1965	Sawai Saenyagorn 1914/1965	Sawai Saenyagorn 1914/1965	Sawai Saenyagorn 1914/1965	Sawai Saenyagorn 1914/1965	Sawai Saenyagorn 1914/1965	Chalor Jarugala 1921/1966	Chalor Jarugala 1921/1966
Army Assist CC	Thanom Kittikachorn 1920/1971	Thanom Kittikachorn 1920/1971	Praphas Charusathien 1929/1973	Praphas Charusathien 1929/1973	Praphas Charusathien 1929/1973	Praphas Charusathien 1929/1973	Prapan Kunpichit 1918/1967	Prapan Kunpichit 1918/1967
1st Army Region Commander		Praphas Charusathien 1929/1973	Thanom Kittikachorn 1920/1971	Krit Sivara 1931/1975	Krit Sivara 1931/1975	Krit Sivara 1931/1975	Krit Sivara 1931/1975	Krit Sivara 1931/1975
2nd Army Region Commander	Chalor Jarugala 1921/1966	Chalor Jarugala 1921/1966	Chalor Jarugala 1921/1966	Chalor Jarugala 1921/1966	Chalor Jarugala 1921/1966	Chalor Jarugala 1921/1966	Jit Suntranon 1924/1965	Tongjim Sanwanit 1929/1972
3rd Army Region Commander	Prapan Kunpichit 1918/1967	Prapan Kunpichit 1918/1967	Prapan Kunpichit 1918/1967	Prapan Kunpichit 1918/1967	Prapan Kunpichit 1918/1967	Prapan Kunpichit 1918/1967	Aat Sasiprapha 1926/1968	Aat Sasiprapha 1926/1968
1st Divisional Commander (Wongthewan)	Krit Sivara 1931/1975	Krit Sivara 1931/1975	Krit Sivara 1931/1975	Krit Sivara 1931/1975	Prayoon Nunpakdi 1925/1964	Kriengkrai Attanand 1931/1973	Kriengkrai Attanand 1931/1973	Kriengkrai Attanand 1931/1973
Police Commander	Sawai Saenyagorn 1914/1965	Sawai Saenyagorn 1914/1965	Sarit Thanarat 19/1963	Sarit Thanarat 19/1963	Sarit Thanarat 19/1963	Sarit Thanarat 19/1963	Sarit Thanarat 19/1963	Sarit Thanarat 19/1963

Post	1965	1966	1967	1968	1969	1970	1971	1972
Defence Minister	Thanom Kittikachorn 1920/1971	Thanom Kittikachorn 1920/1971	Thanom Kittikachorn 1920/1971	Thanom Kittikachorn 1920/1971	Thanom Kittikachorn 1920/1971	Thanom Kittikachorn 1920/1971	Thanom Kittikachorn 1920/1971	Thanom Kittikachorn 1920/1971
Permanent Sec. Defence	Prapan Kunpichit 1918/1967	Chalor Jarugala 1921/1966	Uab Awsanarong 1929/1971	Uab Awsanarong 1929/1971	Thanom Kittikachorn 1920/1971	Thanom Kittikachorn 1920/1971	Thanom Kittikachorn 1920/1971	Thanom Kittikachorn 1920/1971
Supreme CC	Thanom Kittikachorn 1920/1971	Thanom Kittikachorn 1920/1971	Thanom Kittikachorn 1920/1971	Thanom Kittikachorn 1920/1971	Thanom Kittikachorn 1920/1971	Thanom Kittikachorn 1920/1971	Thanom Kittikachorn 1920/1971	Thanom Kittikachorn 1920/1971
Navy CC	Kanchitporn Apakorn 1926/1966	Jaroon Chalerm tiarana 1920/1971	Jaroon Chalerm tiarana 1920/1971	Jaroon Chalerm tiarana 1920/1971	Jaroon Chalerm tiarana 1920/1971	Jaroon Chalerm tiarana 1920/1971	Thawin Rayananda 1933/1972	Cherdchai Thomya 1933/1974
Air Force CC	Bunchu Chantharubeksa 1933/1974	Bunchu Chantharubeksa 1933/1974	Bunchu Chantharubeksa 1933/1974	Bunchu Chantharubeksa 1933/1974	Bunchu Chantharubeksa 1933/1974	Bunchu Chantharubeksa 1933/1974	Bunchu Chantharubeksa 1933/1974	Bunchu Chantharubeksa 1933/1974
Army CC	Praphas Charusathien 1929/1973	Praphas Charusathien 1929/1973	Praphas Charusathien 1929/1973	Praphas Charusathien 1929/1973	Praphas Charusathien 1929/1973	Praphas Charusathien 1929/1973	Praphas Charusathien 1929/1973	Praphas Charusathien 1929/1973
Army Deputy CC	Boribun Julajarit 1924/1966	Krit Sivara 1931/1975	Krit Sivara 1931/1975	Krit Sivara 1931/1975	Krit Sivara 1931/1975	Krit Sivara 1931/1975	Krit Sivara 1931/1975	Krit Sivara 1931/1975
Army Chief of Staff	Surakit Mayalarp 1933/1974	Surakit Mayalarp 1933/1974	Surakit Mayalarp 1933/1974	Surakit Mayalarp 1933/1974	Surakit Mayalarp 1933/1974	Surakit Mayalarp 1933/1974	Surakit Mayalarp 1933/1974	Surakit Mayalarp 1933/1974
Army Assist CC	Chalor Jarugala 1921/1966	Dem Homsethi 1929/1969	Dem Homsethi 1929/1969	Dem Homsethi 1929/1969	Tuanchai Kosinanon 1930/1974	Tuanchai Kosinanon 1930/1974	Tawich Seniwong na Ayuthaya 1929/1974	Samran Paetiyakul 1932/1975 Palace
Army Assist CC	Krit Sivara 1931/1975	Pisit Chaimuanwong 1930/1973	Pisit Chaimuanwong 1930/1973	Tuanchai Kosinanon 1930/1974	Tongjim Sanwanit 1929/1972	Tongjim Sanwanit 1929/1972	Tuanchai Kosinanon 1930/1974	Chote Hiranyatthi 1933/1976
1st Army Region CC	Krit Sivara 1931/1975	Aat Sasiprapha 1926/1968	Samran Paetiyakul 1932/1975 Palace	Samran Paetiyakul 1932/1975 palace	Kriengkrai Attanand 1931/1973	Kriengkrai Attanand 1931/1973	Prasert Thammasiri 1936/1977	Prasert Thammasiri 1936/1977
2nd Army Region CC	Tongjim Sanwanit 1929/1972	Tongjim Sanwanit 1929/1972	Tongjim Sanwanit 1929/1972	Tongjim Sanwanit 1929/1972	Jamlong Singha 1932/1970	Payom Pahonrat 1934/1973	Payom Pahonrat 1934/1973	Tomkam Pornapong 1933/1974
3rd Army Region CC	Aat Sasiprapha 1926/1968	Ong Potikanit 1930/1969	Ong Potikanit 1930/1969	Ong Potikanit 1930/1969	Samran Paetiyakul 1932/1975 palace	Samran Paetiyakul 1932/1975 palace	Samran Paetiyakul 1932/1975 palace	Prasan Raengla 1932/1974
1st Divisional Commander (Wongthewan)	Prasert Thammasiri 1936/1977	Prasert Thammasiri 1936/1977	Prasert Thammasiri 1936/1977	Prasert Thammasiri 1936/1977	Prasert Thammasiri 1936/1977	Prasert Thammasiri 1936/1977	Uem Jirapong King/1940/1981	Uem JirapongKing/ P1/1981
Police Commander	Prasert Ruchirawong 1926/1972	Prasert Ruchirawong 1926/1972	Prasert Ruchirawong 1926/1972	Prasert Ruchirawong 1926/1972	Prasert Ruchirawong 1926/1972	Prasert Ruchirawong 1926/1972	Praphas Charusathien 1929/1973	Praphas Charusathien 1929/1973

Post	1973	1974	1975	1976	1977	1978	1979	1980
Defence Minister	Tawee Chulasap 33/1974	Kruan Sutantot 1912/1960	Pramarn Adireksan 1931/1957	Seni Pramoj/Sanga Chaloryu 1932/1976	Lek Naeomali ?/1977	Kriangsak Chomanan 1937/1980	Prem Tinsulanonda 1939/1981	Prem Tinsulanonda 1939/1981
Permanent Secretary of Defence	Tuanchai Kosinanon 30/1974	Jitt Sankadul 33/1977	Jitt Sankadul 33/1977	Jitt Sankadul 33/1977	Pralong Wiraprea 35/1979	Pralong Wiraprea 35/1979	Sitthi Jiraroj 38/1980	Tep Kranlert (P1)
Supreme Commander	Thawee Chulasap 33/1974	Krit Sivara 31/1975	Sangad Chaloryu 1932/1976	Kamon Dechatung ?/1977	Kriangsak Chomanan 37/1978	Kriangsak Chomanan 37/1978	Serm na Nakom 35/1981	Serm na Nakom 35/1981
Air Force CC	Bunchu Chantharubeksa 33/1974	Kamon Dechatung ?/1977	Kamon Dechatung ?/1977	Kamon Dechatung ?/1977	Paniang Kanarat 41/1981	Paniang Kanarat 41/1981	Paniang Kanarat 41/1981	Paniang Kanarat 41/1981
Navy CC	Cherdchai Thomya 33/1974	Sangad Chaloryu 1932/1976	Sangad Chaloryu 1932/1976	Amom Sirikaya ?/1978	Amorn ?/1978	Kawee Singha ?/1980	Kawee Singha ?/1980	Samut Sanawin ?/1981
Army CC	Krit Sivara 31/1975	Krit Sivara 31/1975	Serm na Nakom 35/1981	Serm na Nakom 35/1981	Serm na Nakom 35/1981	Prem Tinsulanonda. 39/1981	Prem Tinsulanonda 39/1981	Prem Tinsulanonda 39/1981
Army Deputy CC	Tawich Seniwong n.A. 29/1974	Bunchai Bamrungpong 34/1976	Choti Hiranyathiti 33/1976	Prasert Thammasiri 36/1977	Yot Tepsadin n.Ayutaya 37/1978	Sant Chitpatima 39/1981	Sant Chitpatima 39/1981	Sant Chitpatima 39/1981
Army Chief of Staff	Bunchai Bamrungpong 34/1976	Serm na Nakom 35/1981	Serm na Nakom 35/1981	Pralong Wirapriya. 34/1977	Sitthi Jiraroj 38/1980	Sitthi Jiraroj 38/1980	Prayut Charumani P1/1982	Prayut Charumani P1/1982
Army Assistant CC	Samram Paetiyakul 32/1975	Samram Paetiyakul 32/1975	Chalard Hiransiri 39/1977	Sitthi Jiraroj 38/1980	Chao Swasdisongkram 39/1981	Chao Swasdisongkram 39/1981	Amnat Damrikam P1/1981	Amnat Damrikam P1/1981
Army Assistant Commander	Choti Hiranyathiti 33/1976	Choti Hiranyathiti 33/1976	Prasert Thammasiri 36/1977	Yot Tepsadin na Ayutaya 37/1978	Prem Tinsulanonda 1939/1981	Boonserm Ayuwatana P1/1982	Tep Kranlert P1/1982	Pin Tammasiri 39/1981
1st Army Region Commander	Prasert Thammasiri 36/1977	Prasert Thammasiri 36/1977	Yot Tepsadin na Ayutaya 37/1978	Amnat Damrikam P1/1981	Amnat Damrikam P1/1981	Tep Kranlert P1/1982	Pin Tammasiri 39/1981	Vasin Isarakul n.A P3/1984
2nd Army Region Commander	Tongkam Pornmapong 33/1974	Prem Tinsulanonda 39/1981	Prem Tinsulanonda 39/1981	Prem Tinsulanonda 39/1981	Sawaeng Jamonchan 38/1980	Laksana Salipupta 39/1981	Laksana Salipupta 39/1981	Laksana Salipupta 39/1981
3rd Army Region Commander	Prasan Raengla 32/1974	Prasan Raengla 32/1974	Somsak Pajamanond 38/1980	Somsak Pajamanond 38/1980	Somsak Pajamano38/1980	Sima Panigbutra P1/1982	Sima Panigbutra P1/1982	Sima Panigbutra P1/1982
4th Army Region Commander	non-existing	non-existing	Sant Chitpatima 39/1981	Pin Tammasiri 39/1981	Pin Tammasiri 39/1981	Pin Tammasiri 39/1981	Juan Vanarat P1/1982	Juan Vanarat P1/1982
1st Divisional Commander (Wongthewan)	Uem Jirapong King (P1)	Uem Jirapong King (P1)	Arun Twatsin (P1) 42/1977	Arun Twatsin (P1) 42/1977	Pat Urailert P7/1984	Pat Urailert P7/1984	Arthit KamlangekP5/1986	Suchin Arayakul P5/1986
2nd Infantry Division CC (Burapapayak)	Pat Urailert P6/1984	Pat Urailert P6/1984	Pat Urailert P6/1984	Pat Urailert P6/1984	Yongyut Ditsabunjong P7/1986	Yongyut DitsabunjP7/1986	Yongyut Ditsabunjong P7/1986	Aram Siauginot P7/?
Police Commander	Praphas Charusathien 1929/1973	Prachuab Suntornkul 1939/1980	Sisuk Mahntomtep 1937/1977	Monchai Pankonguen 1942/1981	Monchai Pankongue 1942/1981	Monchai Pankongi42/1981	Monchai Pankongue 1942/1981	Monchai Pankongue 1942/1981

Post	1981	1982	1983	1984	1985	1986	1987	1988
Defence Minister	Prem Tinsulanonda 1939/1981	Prem Tinsulanonda 1939/1981	Prem Tinsulanonda 1939/1981	Prem Tinsulanonda 1939/1981	Prem Tinsulanonda 1939/1981	Panieng Kantarat 41/1981	Panieng Kantarat 41/1981	Chatchai Chunhavan 1939/1980
Permanent Secretary of Defence	Tuantong Suwannatat P3/1983	Tuantong Suwannatat P3/1983	Channaan Nilwiset P5/1885	Channaan Nilwiset P5/1985	Prayun Bunnak P4/1986	Sansern Wanich P6/1987	Sansern Wanich P6/1988	Wichit WichitsongkraP7/1989
Supreme Commander	Saiyud K. 39/1983	Saiyud K. 39/1983	Arthit Kamlangek P5/1986	Arthit Kamlangek P5/1986	Arthit Kamlangek P5/1986	Supha Kojaseni King 1987	Chavalit Yongchaiyud (1)/1990	Chavalit Yongchaiyud (1)/1990
Air Force Commander-in-Chief	Thakiaeo Susiwon ?/1983	Thakiaeo Susiwon ?/1983	Prapan Dupatemeia P4/1987	Prapan Dupatemeia P4/1987	Prapan Dupatemeia P4/1987	Prapan Dupatemeia P4/1987	Voranat Apichari ?/1989	Voranat ?/1989
Navy Commander-in-Chief	Somboon Chuapibun ?/1983	Somboon Chuapibun ?/1983	Prapat Chantawirat ?/1984	Niphon Siritom ?/1986	Niphon Siritom ?/1986	Thada Ditabanchong ?/1987	Prapat Kishnachan?/1991	Prapat Kishnachan?/1991
Army Commander	Prayut Charumani P1/1982	Arthit Kamlangek P5/1986	Arthit Kamlangek P5/1986	Arthit Kamlangek P5/1986	Arthit Kamlangek P5/1986	Chavalit Yongchaiyud (1)/1990	Chavalit Yongchaiyud (1)/1990	Chavalit Yongchaiyud (1)/1990
Army Deputy Commander	Sak Buntrakul 39/1982	Suep Akaranukroh P3/1984	Suep Akaranukroh P3/1984	Thianchai Sirisampan P5/1985	Chutha Saengtwip P5/1986	Phisit Hemabutr P6/1987	Wanchai Jitjamnong (1)/1986	Wanchai Jitjamnong (1)/1986
Army Chief of Staff	Pamot Tavornchan P3/1983	Pamot Tavornchan P3/1983	Banchop Bunnag P6/1986	Banchop Bunnag P6/1986	Chavalit Yongchaiyud (1)/1990	Wanchai Jitjamnong (1)/1986	Jaruai Wongsayan (1)/1990	Jaruai Wongsayan (1)/1990
Army Assistant Commander	Arthit Kamlangek P5/1986	Thianchai Sirisampan P5/1985	Thianchai Sirisampan P5/1985	Mana Ratanakoset P5/1985	Surapon Sriutai P5/1986	Pichit Kullawanit (2)/1992	Pichit Kullawanit (2)/1992	Pichit Kullawanit (2)/1992
Army Assistant Commander	Paichit Somsuwan 39/1982	Pathom Sermsin P4/1984	Pathom Sermsin P4/1984	Ongat Supamat P5/1985	Akkaragon Somrup P5/1986	Sunthorn Kongsompon (1)/1991	Suchinda Kraprayoon (5)/1992	Suchinda Kraprayoon (5)/1992
1st Army Region Commander	Arthit Kamlangek P5/1986	Pat Ulailert P6/1984	Pat Ulailert P6/1984	Pichit Kullawanit (2)/1984	Pichit Kullawanit (2)/1992	Pichit Kullawanit (2)/1992	Watanachai Wutisiri (1)/1995	Watanachai Wutisiri (1)/1995
2nd Army Region Commander	Phak Minakanit P5/1985	Phak Minakanit P5/1985	Phak Minakanit P5/1985	Phisit Hemabutr P6/1985	Phisit Hemabutr P6/1987	Isarapong Noonpakdi (5)/1992	Isarapong Noonpakdi (5)/1992	Isarapong Noonpakdi (5)/1992
3rd Army Region Commander	Phrom Piew naun P1/1983	Phrom Piew naun P1/1983	Thiap Gromsurisak P5/1983	Thiap Gromsurisak P5/1983	Ruamsak Chaigominat P7/1996	Chaichana Tarichat (1)/1987	Siri Tiwapan (4)/1990	Siri (4)/1990
4th Army Region Commander	Han Leelanond P5/1984	Han Leelanond P5/1984	Wanchai Jitjamnong (1)/1986	Wanchai Jitjamnong (1)/1986	Wanchai Jitjamnong (1)/1986	Wisit Ajkumwon (2)/1989	Wisit Ajkumwon (2)/1989	Wisit Ajkumwon (2)/1989
Special Warfare CC	not existing	not existing	Anek Bunyatee (P1)/1984	Suntorn Kongsompon (1)/1991	Suntorn Kongsompon (1)/1991	Wimol Wongwanit (5)/1995	Wimol Wongwanit (5)/1995	Wimol Wongwanit (5)/1995
1st Divisional Commander (Wongthewan)	Pichit Kullawanit (2)/1992	Pichit Kullawanit (2)/1992	Pichit Kullawanit (2)/1992	Isarapong Noonpakdi (5)/1992	Wimol Wongwanit (5)/1995	San Sipen (5)/1994	San Sipen (5)/1994	Mongkol Ampornpisit (9)/2000
Police Commander	Surapol Pramon ?/1982	Narong Mahanon King/1987	Narong Mahanon King/1987	Narong Mahanon King/1987	Narong Mahanon King/1987	Narong Mahanon King/1987	Pao Sarasin 1954/1989	Pao Sarasin 1954/1989

Post	1989	1990	1991	1992	1993	1994	1995	1996
Permanent Secretary of Defence	Wanchai Ruangtrakul (1)/1992	Wanchai Ruangtrakul (1)/1992	Wanchai Ruangtrakul (1)/1992	Acm. Suwit Chanthapradit ?/1994	Suwit Chanthapradit/ ?/1994	Prasert Sararit (5)/1995	Paibul Empan (5)/1996	Yuthasak Sasiprapha (8)/1998
Supreme Commander	Chavalit Yongchaiyud (1)/1990	Sunthorn Kongsompon (1)/1991	Suchinda (5); Kaset (5); Voranat	Voranat Apichari King/1994	Voranat Apichari King/1994	Wattanachai Wutisiri (1)/1995	Wirot Saengsanit (5)/1996	Mongkol Ampornpisit (9)/2000
Air Force Commander-in-Chief	Kaset Rojananil (5)/1992	Kaset Rojananil (5)/1992	Kaset Rojananil (5)/1992	Kan Pimantip (6)/1993	Siripong King/1996	Siripong Tongyai King/1996	Siripong Tongyai King/1996	Amon Naewmalee/ King/1997
Navy Commander-in-Chief	Prapat Kishnachan ?/1991	Prapat Kishnachan ?/1991	Vichet Karunyavanij 5/1953	Vichet Karunyavanij 5/1953	Prachet Siridej 5/1996	Prachet Siridej 5/1996	Prachet Siridej 5/1996	Wichit Chanakan King/1997
Army Commander	Chavalit Yongchaiyud (1)/1990	Suchinda Kraprayoon (5)/1992	Suchinda (5); Issarapong (5)	Wimol Wongwanit (5)/1995	Wimol Wongwanit (5)/1995	Wimol Wongwanit (5)/1995	Pramon Plasin (6)/1996	Chettha Tanajaro (9)/1998
Army Deputy Commander	Suchinda Kraprayoon (5)/1992	Issarapong Noonpakdi (5)/1992	Issarapong Noonpakdi (5)/1992	San Sipen (5)/1994	San Sipen (5)/1994	Phaibun Empan (5)/1994	Chettha Tanajaro (9)/1998	Thawan Sawaengpal (7)/1997
Army Chief of Staff	Jaruai Wongsayan (1)/1990	Wirot Saengsanit (5)/1996	Chatchom Ganlong (5)/1992	Pramon Plasin (6)/1996	Phaibun Empan (5)/1994	Suthep Sivara (5)/1996	Suthep Sivara (5)/1996	Chan Bunprasert (11)/1999
Army Assistant Commander	Issarapong Noonpakdi (5)/1992	Arun Pariyatitam (3)/1991	Wirot Saengsanit (5)/1996	Yuthana Yaempan (4)/1993	Pramon Plasin (6)/1996	Anuphap Songsunton (5)/1994	Thawan Sawaengpal (7)/1997	Bandit Malaiarisun (8)/1998
Army Assistant Commander	Arun Pariyatitam (3)/1991	Wimol Wongwanit (5)/1995	San Sipen (5)/1994	Choetchai Tiratanon (5)/1994	Choetchai Tiratanon (5)/1994	Chettha Tanajaro (9)/1998	Bandit Malaiarisun (8)/1998	Samphao Chusri 1/2001
1st Army Region Commander	San Sipen (5)/1994	San Sipen (5)/1994	Paiboon Hongsinlak (5)/1992	Chettha Tanajaro (9)/1998	Chettha Tanajaro (9)/1998	Bandit Malaiarisun (8)/1998	Winit Grajangson (9)/1997	Winit Grajangson (9)/1997
2nd Army Region Commander	Wimol Wongwanit (5)/1995	Paiboon Hongsinlak (5)/1992	Ariya Ukosakit (5)/1992	Anuphap Songsunton (5)/1994	Anuphap Songsunton (5)/1994	Surayud Chulanond 1/2003	Surayud Chulanond 1/2003	Surayud Chulanond 1/2003
3rd Army Region Commander	Siri Tiwapan (4)/1990	Phairoj Jano-urai (5)/1992	Phairoj Jano-urai (5)/1992	Yingyot Jotipimai (6)/1995	Yingyot Jotipimai (6)/1995	Surachet (8)Dejadi n.A.8/1995	Thanom Wajputom (9)/1998	Thanom Wajputom (9)/1998
4th Army Region Commander	Yuthana Yaempan (4)/1993	Yuthana Yaempan (4)/1993	Kitti Rattanachaiya (8)/1996	Kitti Rattanachaiya (8)/1996	Kitti Rattanachaiya (8)/1996	Panthep Puanarok (9)/1996	Panthep Puanarok (9)/1998	Preecha S uwanasiri (11)/1999
Special Warfare Unit Commander	Kachon Ramanwong (5)/1992	Kachon Ramanwong (5)/1992	Kachon Ramanwong (5)/1992	Surayud Chulanond 1/2003	Surayud Chulanond 1/2003	Chalong-chai (10)/1996	Chalongcha Yaemsaso (10)/1996	Hom (11) Holamyang (11)/1999
1st Divisional Commander (Wongthewan)	Watthana S. (8)	Chainarong Noonpakdi (11)/2000	Thitipong Jenuwat (11)/?	Somthat Attanand 3/2004	Somthat Attanand 3/2004	Somthat Attanand 3/2004	Somthat Attanand 3/2004	Atchawin Saodejani 4/2005
2nd Infantry Division CC (Burapapayak)	Chainarong Noonpakdi (11)/2000	Thitipong Jenuwat (11)/?	Phanom Jenawitjarana (11)/?	Nipon P. 3/2002	Nipon Paranit 3/2002	Nipon P. 3/2002	Atchawin Saodejani 4/?	Prawit Wongsuwan 6/2005
Police Commander	Sawaeng Teerasawat 1951/1991	Sawaeng Teerasawat 1951/1991	Sawat Amornwiwat (5)/1993	Sawat Amornwiwat (5)/1993	Pratin Santiprapob ?/1994	Poj BunyajindaKing/1996	Poj BunyajindaKing/1996	Pracha Promnok 3/2002

Post	1997	1998	1999	2000	2001	2002	2003	2004
Permanent Secretary of Defence	Yuthasak Sasiprapha (8)/1998	Teeradej Meepien (9)/2000	Teeradej Meepien (9)/2000	Thawat Ketangkon 1/2001	Thawat Ketangkon 1/2001	Sampan Boonyanan 4/2003	Sampan Boonyanan 4/2003	Oud Buangbon 6/2005
Supreme Commander	Mongkol Ampornpisit (9)/2000	Mongkol Ampornpisit (9)/2000	Mongkol Ampornpisit (9)/2000	Samphao Chusri 1/2001	Adm. Narong Yuthavong 1/2001	Surayud Chulanond 1/2003	Somthat Atthanand 3/2004	Chaisit Shinawatra 5/2005
Air Force CC	Thananit Niemtadi 2/1999	Thananit Niemtadi 2/1999	Sanan Tuatip King/2000	Pong Maneesil 2/2002	Pong Maneesil 2/2002	Kongsak Watana 5/2005	Kongsak Watana 5/2005	Kongsak Watana 5/2005
Navy Commander	Suvatchai Kasemsuk King/1998	Thira Haocharoen King/2000	Thira Haocharoen King/2000	Prasert Bunsong 7/2002	Prasert Bunsong 7/2002	Taweesak Somapa 1/2003	Chumpol Pajusanon. 3/2005	Samphop Amprapan 4/2005
Army CC	Chettha Tanajaro (9)/1998	Surayud Chulanond 1/2003	Surayud Chulanond 1/2003	Surayud Chulanond 1/2003	Surayud Chulanond 1/2003	Somthat Atthanand 3/2004	Chaisit Shinawatra 5/2005	Prawit Wongsuwan 6/2005
Army Deputy Commander	Thawan Sawaengpal (7)/1997	Samphao Chusri 1/2001	Patana Putatanon (11)/2001	Patana Putatanon (11)/2001	Niphon Paranit. 3/2002	Watanachai Wutisiri (1)/1995	Sirichai Tanyasiri 4/2006	Chirasak Pornhompok 2/2005
Army Chief of Staff	Chan Bunprasert (11)/1999	Chan Bunprasert (11)/1999	Montrisak Bunwong 1/2000	Boonrawd Somtat 1/2002	Somthat Atthanand 3/2004	Wirachai Pligyajiwa 2/2003	Pongthep Tesprateep 4/2005	Pongthep Tesprateep 4/2005
Army Assistant Commander	Samphao Chusri 1/2001	Niphon Paranit. 3/2002	Niphon Paranit. 3/2002	Niphon Paranit. 3/2002	Sanan Marengsit 2/2002	Chaisit Shinawatra 5/2005	Prawit Wongsuwan 6/2005	Lertiat Ratanawich 7/2008
Army Assistant Commander	Bandit Malairisun (8)/1998	Rewat Buntap 2/2001	Rewat Buntap 2/2001	Rewat Buntap 2/2001	Watanachai Wutisiri (1)/1995	Sirichai Tanyasiri 4/2006	Chirasak Pornhompok 2/2005	Sonthi Bunyaratkin 6/2007
1st Army Region Commander	Niphon Paranit. 3/2002	Thawip Suwanasing 2/2000	Thawip Suwanasing 2/2000	Somthat Atthanand 3/2004	Phoncha Dechatiwong 3/2002	Prawit Wongsuwan 6/2005	Phaisan Kananon 7/2007	Phaisan Kananon 7/2007
2nd Army Region Commander	Rewat Buntap 2/2001	Sanan Marengsit 2/2002	Sanan Marengsit 2/2002	Sanan Marengsit 2/2002	Chirasak Pornhompok 2/2005	Chirasak Pornhompok 2/2005	Chumsaeng Sawasdisongkr 5/2004	Han Wanprasert 6/2005
3rd Army Region Commander	Thanom Wajputorn (9)/1998	Sommai Wichaworn (11)/1999	Watanachai Wutisiri (1)/1995	Watanachai Wutisiri (1)/1995	Udomchai Ongkasing 2/2003	Udomchai Ongkasing 2/2003	Peechanmet Muangmani 5/2005	Peechanmet Muangmani 5/2005
4th Army Region Commander	Preecha Suwanasiri (11)/1999	Preecha Suwanasiri (11)/1999	Narong Denudom 1/2001	Narong Denudom 1/2001	Wichai Buarod 3/2003	Wichai Buarod 3/2003	Pongsak E. (7-18); Pisan W. (9-20)	Pisan Watanawongsiri 9/2009
Special Warfare Unit Commander	Hom Holamyang (11)/1999	Hom Holamyang (11)/1999	Sathon Suansri 1/2000	Tharin Lutapana 2/2002	Tharin Lutapana 2/2002	Sonthi Bunyaratkin 6/2007	Sonthi Bunyaratkin 6/2007	Pamuk Utaichai 6/2006
1st Divisional Commander (Wongthewan)	Achawin Sewotsini 4/2005	Noppadon Inapanya 6/2005	Wanchai Tongsukum 6/2005	Phaisan Kananon 7/2007	Phaisan Kananon 7/2007	Jirasit Kesakomol 10/2010	Anupong Paochinda 10/2010	Prin Suwannatat 10/2010
2nd Infantry Division CC (Burapapayak)	Wanchai Tongsukum 6/2005	Wanchai Tongsukum 6/2005	Udom Promyothin 7/2006	Udom Promyothin 7/2006	Udom Promyothin 7/2006	Anupong Paochinda 10/2010	Prayut Chanocha 12/2014	Kanit Sapitak 13/2015
Police Commander	Pracha Promnok 2/2002	Pracha Promnok 2/2002	Pracha Promnok 2/2002	Pornsak Durongkibun 18/2001	San Sarutanon 1965/2004	San Sarutanon 1965/2004	San Sarutanon 1965/2004	Kowit Wattana 6/2007

Post	2005	2006	2007	2008	2009	2010	2011	2012	2013
Permanent Sec. of Defence	S Sirichai Tanyasiri 4/2006	Winai Pattiyakul 6/2008	Winai Pattiyakul 6/2008	Apichart Penkitti 8/2010	Apichart Penkitti 8/2010	Kittipong Keskowit 8/2011	Satien Permtonginot 11/2012	Tanongsak Apirayothin 11/2013	Nipat Tonglek 14/2016
Supreme CC	Rueangroj Mahasanon. 5/2006	Boonsang Niempradit 6/2008	Boonsang Niempradit 6/2008	Songkitti Jaggabattara 10/2011	Songkitti Jaggabattara 10/2011	Songkitti Jaggabattara 10/2011	Thanasak Patimakorn 12/2014	Thanasak Patimakorn 12/2014	Thanasak Patimakorn 12/2014
Air Force CC	Chalit Phubasak 6/2008	Chalit Phubasak 6/2008	Chalit Phubasak 6/2008	Itthaporn Subawong 11/2012	Itthaporn Subawong 11/2012	Itthaporn Subawong 11/2012	Itthaporn Subawong 11/2012	Prajin Jintong 13/2014	Prajin Jintong 13/2014
Navy CC	Satirapan Keyanon 6/2009	Satirapan Keyanon 6/2009	Satirapan Keyanon 6/2009	Kamthorn Phumiran 10/2010	Kamthorn Phumiran 10/2010	Kamthorn Phumiran 10/2010	Surasak Runregrom King/2013	Surasak Runregrom King/2013	Narong Pipatanasai 13/2014
Army CC	Sonthi Bunyaratklin6/2007	Sonthi Bunyaratklin6/2007	Anupong Paochinda 10/2010	Anupong Paochinda 10/2010	Anupong Paochinda 10/2010	Prayut Chanocha 12/2014	Prayut Chanoch12/2014	Prayut Chanoch12/2014	Prayut Chanoch 12/2014
Army Deputy CC	Wichit Yathip 9/2009	Phaisan Kananon 7/2007	Wirawit Kumsamran 7/2008	Jiradet Kocharat 9/2009	Thirawat Bunyapradab 10/2010	Thirawat Bunyapradab 10/2010	Daowapong Ratanasuwan 12/2013	Daowapong Ratanasuwan 12/2013	Udomdejt Sitabutr 14/2014
Army Chief of Staff	Sophon Silpipat 6/2006	Montree Sangkasap 9/2009	Montree Chumpujan 9/2009	Prayut Chanocha 12/2014	Piroon Paewponsong 10/2010	Daowapong Ratanasuwan 12/2013	Sirichai Disakul 13/2015	Sirichai Disakul 13/2015	Aksara Kerdpol 14/2015
Army Assistant CC	Phaisan Kananon 7/2007	Anupong Paochinda 10/2010	Thirawat Bunyapradab 10/2010	Thirawat Bunyapradab 10/2010	Thirawat Bunyapradab 10/2010	Pichet Wisaijorn 11/2010	Tanongsak Apirakyothi 11/2013	Wangtip Wongyai 12/2012	Chatchai Sarigulya 12/2015
Army Assistant CC	Pornchai Kranlert 10/2010	Saprang Kallayamitr 7/2007	Jiradet Kocharat 9/2009	Viroj Buarun 9/2009	Wit Tepsad n Ayuthaya. 11/2011	Yuttasilp Doijungam 11/2013	Podpk Bunnag 12/2012	Podok Bunnag 12/2012	Paiboon Kumchaya 15/2015
1st Army Region CC	Anupong Paochinda 10/2010	Prayut Chanocha 12/2014	Prayut Chanocha 12/2014	Kanit Sapitak 13/2015	Kanit Sapitak 13/2015	Udomdejt Sitabutr 14/2015	Udomdejt Sitabutr 14/2015	Paiboon Kumchaya 15/2015	Teerachai Nakwani114/2016
2nd Army Region CC	Sujet Watanasuk 7/2007	Sujet Watanasuk 7/2007	Sujitom Sitiprapa 8/2008	Viboonsak Nipan 9/2009	Wiwalit Jarasamlit 10/2010	Thawatchai Samutsakom 12/2012	Thawatchai Samutsakom 12/2012	Thawatchai Samutsakom 12/2012	Chanchai Putong 13/2013
3rd Army Region CC	Saprang Kallayamitr 7/2007	Jiradet Kocharat 9/2009	Samrerng Swadamrong 9/2008	Tanongsak Apirakyothi 11/2013	Tanongsak Apirakyothi 11/2013	Wangtip Wongwai 12/2012	Wangtip Wongwai 12/2012	Chanchai Tanarun 13/2013	Preecha Chanocha15/2016
4th Army Region CC	Kwanchat Glaharm 8/2008	Viroj Buarun 9/2009	Viroj Buarun 9/2009	Pichet Wisaijorn 11/2010	Pichet Wisaijorn 11/2010	Udomchai Tamasarot 13/2013	Udomchai T.amasarot 13/2013	Udomchai Tamasarot 13/2013	Sakol Chuentralu 13/2013
Special Warfare Command	Chaiyapat Thirathamron8/2008	Chaiyapat Thirathamron8/2008	Sunai Sampatawanit 11/2014	Punchong Ratananasuwan 10/2009	Podok Bunnag 12/2012	Tana Withyawirot 15/2012	Supparat Patanaweesut 12/2013	Supparat Patanaweesut 12/2013	Chalermchai Sittisart 16/2018
1st Divisional Commander (Wongthewan)	Prin Suwanatat 10/2010	Daowapong Ratanasuwan 12/2013	Paibun Kumchaya 15/2015	Kampnat Ruddit 16/2016	Kampnat Ruddit 16/2016	Kampnat Ruddit 16/2016	Pisit Sitisan 17/2017	Pisit Sitisan 17/2017	Apirat Kongsompong 20/2020
2nd Infantry Division CC (Burapapayak)	Kanit Sapitak 13/2015	Kanit Sapitak 13/2015	Walit Rojanapakdi 15/2015	Walit Rojanapakdi 15/2015	Pisit Sitisan 17/2017	Pisit Sitisan 17/2017	Theppong Tipyacharoen 18/2018	Theppong Tipyacharoen 18/2018	Kukiat Srinaka 20/2020
Police CC	Kowit Wattana 6/2007	Kowit Wattana 6/2007	Seripisut Temiwet 8/2008	Patcharawat Wongsuwan 9/2009	Pateep Tansprasert 9/2010	Wichien Pojphosri ?/2013	Priewpan Damapong ?/2012	Adul Sangsing14/2014	Adul Sangsing 14/2014

Post	2014	2015	2016	2017	2018	2019	2020	2021	2022
Defence Minister	Prawit Wongsuwan 6/2005	Prawit Wongsuwan 6/2005	Prawit Wongsuwan 6/2005	Prawit Wongsuwan 6/2005	Prawit Wongsuwan 6/2005	Prayut Chanocha 12/2014	Prayut Chanocha 12/2014	Prayut Chanocha 12/2014	Prayut Chanocha 12/2014
Permanent Def. Min.	Sirichai Disakul 13/2015	Preecha Chanocha 15/2016	Chaichan Changmonkol 16/2017	Teppong Tipyachan 18/2018	Nat Intarajaroen 20/2021	Nat Intarajaroen 20/2021	Nat Intarajaroen 20/2021	Worakiat Ratanon 20/2021	Sanitchanok Sangkachan 24/2023
Supreme CC	Worapong Sangranetra 12/2015	Sommai Kaotira 15/2016	Surapong Suwanna-at 15/2018	Tanchaiyan Srisawan 17/2018	Pornpipat Benyasiri 18/2020	Pornpipat Benyasiri 18/2020	Chalermpol Srisawasdi 21/2023	ChalermpolSrisawasdi 21/2023	Chalermpol Srisawasdi 21/2023
Navy CC	Kraison Chansuwanit 13/2015	Na Areenit 15/2015	Na Areenit 15/2015	Luechai Ruddit 18/2020	Luechai Ruddit 18/2020	Luechai Ruddit 18/20	Chatchai Srivorakan 20/2021	Somprasong Nilsamai 20/2022	Cherngchai Chomchengu 22/2023
Air Force CC	Treetod Sonjang 14/2016	Treetod Sonjang 14/2016	Jarum Rumsuwan 16/20 19	Jaum Rumsuwan 16/20 19	Chaiyapluk Didyasarin 18/2019	Manat Wongwat, 20/2020	Airbull Sutsawan 21/2021	Napadej Dupatemiya 21/2022	Alongkorn Wanarat 22/2023
Army CC	Udomdej Sitabutr 14/2015	Teerachai Nakwanich 14/2016	Chalermchai Sittisart 16/2018	Chalermchai Sittisart 16/2018	Apirat Kongsompong 20/2020	Apirat Kongsompong 20/2020	Narongpan Jitkaewtae 22/2023	Narong-pan Jitkaewtae 22/2023	Narongpan Jitkaewtae 22/2023
Army Deputy CC	Chatchai Sarigalaya 15/2015	Walit Rojanapakdi 15/2016	Pisit Sitisam 17/2017	Sasin Tongpakdi 17/2018	Nattapol Nakpanic 16/2021	Nattapol Nakpanic 16/2021	Teerawat Bunyawat 19/2021	Apinan Kampheo 22/2022	Jaroenchai Hintao 23/2024
Army Chief of Staff	Chatchalerm Chalermsuk 15/2015	Pisit Sitisam 17/2017	Sasin Tongpakdi 17/2018	Nattapol Nakpanich 16/2021	Teerawat Bunyawat 19/2021	Teerawat Bunyawat 19/2021	Worakiat Ratanon 20/2021	Santipong Tampiya 22/2022	UKrit Buntanon 24/2025
Army Assist CC	Teerachai Nakwanich 14/2016	Kampnat Ruddit 16/2018	Teppong Tipyachan 18/2018	Veerachai Intusopon 18/2018	Kukiat Srinaka 20/2020	Narongpan Jitkaewtae 22/2023	Tamanoon Withi 22/2021	Phumipat Jansawang 24/2023	Kriangkrai Srirak 22/2023
Army Assist CC	Preecha Chanocha 15/2016	Chalermchai Sittisart 16/2018	Somsak Nilbonjedgul 16/2017	Apirat Kongsompong 20/2020	Wijak Siripansop 18/2019	Sunai Prapuchanei 21/2021	Pomsawat Putsawan 20/2021	Jaroenchai Hintao 23/2024	Suksawan Nongbualang 23/2025
1st Army Region Commander	Kampnat Ruddit 16/2018	Teppong Tipyachan 18/2018	Somsak Nilbonjedgul 16/2017	Apirat Kongsompong 20/2020	Narong-pan Jitkaewtae 22/2023	Narongpan Jitkaewtae 22/2023	Pomsawat Putsawan 20/2021	Suksawan Nongbualang 23/2025	Pana Plotuk 26/2027
2nd Army Region Commander	Tawach Sukplang 16/2016	Tawach Sukplang 16/2016	Wichai Chaejawhaw 17/2018	Tarakom Tama-win 18/2018	Tarakom Tama-win 18/2018	Tanya Griedsan 21/2021	Tanet Wongchaum 21/2021	Sawarat Saengpol 23/2024	Sawarat Saengpol 23/2024
3rd Army Region Commander	Satit Pitarat 15/2016	Somsak Nilbonjedgul 16/2017	Wijak Siripansop 18/2019	Wijak Siripansop 18/2019	Chalong Jai Chaiyakam 20/2021	Chalong Jai Chaiyakam 20/2021	Apichet Suasa-ad 21/2022	Apichet Suasa-ad 21/2022	Sueriya Uemsuro 22/2023
Special Warfare Command	Chalermchai Sittisart 16/2018	Tanasak Gengtanonma 16/2018	Tanasak Gengtanonma 16/2018	Tanasak Gengtanonma 16/2018	Sunai Prapuchanei 21/2021	Phumipat Jansawang 24/2023	Pomsawat Putsawan 20/2021	Natawut Nakanakorn 24/2025	Isara Damrongsak 27/2028
4th Army Region Commander	Prakom Choruyt 15/2016	Wiworoj Pakompak 16/2017	Piyawit Nakwanich 18/2018	Piyawit Nakwanich 18/2018	Pomsawat Putsawan 20/2021	Pomsawat Putsawan 20/2021	Phumipat Jansawang 24/2023	Kriangkrai Srirak 22/2023	Santi Sakuntanak 25/2026
1st Divisional Commander (Wongthewan)	Apirat Kongsompong 20/2020	Narongpan Jitkaewtae 22/2023	Narongpan Jitkaewtae 22/2023	Narongpan Jitkaewtae 22/2023	Songwit Noonpadi 24/2025	Sotapol Sadsaongerm 27/2028	Sotapol Sadsaongerm 27/2028	Worayot Luangsuwan 28/2029	Natadej Jantharangsu 28/2029
2nd Infantry Division CC (Burapapayak)	Kukiat Srinaka 20/2020	Santipong Tampiya 22/2022	Jaroenchai Hintao 23/2024	Suksawan Nongbualang 23/2025	Piyapong Glinpan 23/2024	Tarapong Malakam 24/2025	Amrit Bunsuya 27/2029	Amrit Bunsuya 27/2029	Sarawat Chaiyasit 28/2030
Police CC	Chaktip Chaijinda Pol 36/2020	Chaktip Chaijinda Pol 36/2020	Chaktip Chaijinda 36/2020	Chaktip Chaijinda 36/2020	Chaktip Chaijinda 36/2020	Chaktip Chaijinda 36/2020	Suwat Jaengyadsuk 20/2022	Suwat Jaengyadsuk, 20/2022	Damrongsak Kittiprapas 22/2030

Index

Note: Numbers prefixed by "n" refer to notes.

About the Author

Paul Chambers is Lecturer and Special Advisor on International Affairs at the Center of ASEAN Community Studies, Faculty of Social Sciences, Naresuan University (Thailand). He is a Fellow at the Peace Research Institute Frankfurt, the German-Southeast Asian Center of Excellence for Public Policy and Good Governance, and the Cambodian Institute for Cooperation and Peace. He is also the executive editor of the Taylor & Francis (Scopus) journal *Asian Affairs: An American Review*. Paul has been a Visiting Fellow at Heidelberg University, the German Institute of Global and Area Studies (GIGA) in Hamburg, Kyoto University, De La Salle University in Manila, and the ISEAS – Yusof Ishak Institute in Singapore. He has authored or co-authored over a hundred publications, including journal articles, book chapters and six books. Recent publications include his co-edited book *Khaki Capital: The Political Economy of the Military in Southeast Asia* (NIAS, 2017). His research centres upon civil-military relations and international affairs in Southeast Asia with a particular focus on Thailand, and he has lectured before both the European Parliament and the US State Department.